INSIGHT GUIDES

GReece

Discovery
CHANNEL

APA PUBLICATIONS

Part of the Langenscheidt Publishing Group

ABOUT THIS BOOK

Editorial

Project Editor
Maria Lord
Editorial Director
Brian Bell

Distribution

UK & Ireland
GeoCenter International Ltd
The Viables Centre, Harrow Way
Basingstoke, Hants RG22 4BJ
Fax: (44) 1256-817988

United States
Langenscheidt Publishers, Inc.
46–35 54th Road, Maspeth, NY 11378
Fax: (1) 718 784-0640

Canada
Thomas Allen & Son Ltd
390 Steelcase Road East
Markham, Ontario L3R 1G2
Fax: (1) 905 475 6747

Australia
Universal Publishers
1 Waterloo Road
Macquarie Park, NSW 2113
Fax: (61) 2 9888 9074

New Zealand
Hema Maps New Zealand Ltd (HNZ)
Unit D, 24 Ra ORA Drive
East Tamaki, Auckland
Fax: (64) 9 273 6479

Worldwide
Apa Publications GmbH & Co.
Verlag KG (Singapore branch)
38 Joo Koon Road, Singapore 628990
Tel: (65) 6865-1600. Fax: (65) 6861-6438

Printing

Insight Print Services (Pte) Ltd
38 Joo Koon Road, Singapore 628990
Tel: (65) 6865-1600. Fax: (65) 6861-6438

This guidebook combines the interests and enthusiasms of two of the world's best-known information providers: Insight Guides, whose titles have set the standard for visual travel guides since 1970, and Discovery Channel, the world's premier source of non-fiction television programming.

The editors of Insight Guides provide both practical advice and general understanding about a destination's history, culture, institutions and people. Discovery Channel and its website, www.discovery.com, help millions of viewers explore their world from the comfort of their own home and also encourage them to explore it first-hand.

How to use this book

Insight Guide: Greece is structured to convey an understanding of Greece, its people and its culture, as well as to guide readers through its sights and everyday activities:

◆ To understand Greece, you need to know something about its past. The **Features** section covers the history and culture of the country.

◆ The main **Places** section ia a complete guide to

all the sights and areas worth visiting. Places of interest are coordinated by number with the maps.
♦ The **Travel Tips** listings section provides a handy point of reference for information on travel, hotels, restaurants, shops and more.

The contributors

This new edition was put together by **Maria Lord**, an Insight Guides editor. She updated the chapters on Athens, Itháki, Kefalloniá and Zákynthos, and also wrote the feature on the Cycladic Bronze Age.

The Ancient, Byzantine and Ottoman history chapters were revised by **Jeffrey Pike**, who also did much editing work on the rest of the text. The Independent Greece chapter was revised by eminent historian **Professor Richard Clogg**.

Anthropologist **Dr David Sutton**, Assistant Professor at Southern Illinois University, wrote the sections on Modern Greece and Peoples and Identities. **Professor Gail Holst-Warhaft** of Cornell University contributed the chapters on Literature and Music and Dance.

The section on Food and Drink was written by **Aglaia Kremezi**, a highly respected food writer and consultant. Art historian and sculptor **Dr John Lord** wrote the wide-ranging chapter on Art and Architecture. **Danny Aeberhard**, a long-standing Insight travel writer, contributed the Flora and Fauna chapter.

Marc Dubin, a well-travelled Londoner and part-time resident of Sámos, updated the chapters on Rhodes, the Dodecanese, Northeast Aegean, Corfu, Paxí and Levkáda, as well as central Greece and Epirus. He also overhauled the Travel Tips, and contributed the Geography essay. The feature on Italian Architecture was written by **John Chapple**.

Crete and the Peloponnese were covered by writer, tour leader and botanist **Lance Chilton**. **Paul Hellander**, writer and historian, updated the chapters on Thessaloníki, Macedonia and Thrace, as well as the Argo-Saronic Islands, the Sporádes and Évia, and Samothráki. **Jeffrey Carson**, a long-time resident of Páros, wrote and updated the chapter on the Cyclades.

Photographers included **Gregory Wrona**, **Phil Wood**, **Terry Harris** and **Blaine Harrington**. The book was proofread by **Emma Sangster** and indexed by **Elizabeth Cook**.

Map Legend

—··—	International Boundary
————	Province
⊖	Border Crossing
—•—	National Park/Reserve
————	Ferry Route
Ⓜ	Metro
✈ ✈	Airport International / Regional
🚍	Bus Station
🅿	Parking
❶	Tourist Information
✉	Post Office
✝ ✝	Church / Ruins
✝	Monastery
☾	Mosque
✡	Synagogue
🏰	Castle / Ruins
∴	Archaeological Site
∩	Cave
⚊	Statue / Monument
★	Place of Interest

The main places of interest in the Places section are coordinated by number with a full-colour map (e.g. ❶), and a symbol at the top of every right-hand page tells you where to find the map.

INSIGHT GUIDE
Greece

CONTENTS

Maps

Greece **120**

Athens **124**

Acropolis **128**

Peloponnese **148**

Central Greece **166**

Epirus and Northwest Macedonia **178**

Thessaloníki **194**

Macedonia and Thrace **202**

Argo-Saronic Islands **218**

Cyclades **226**

Rhodes City **247**

Rhodes **248**

Dodecanese **254**

Thásos, Samothráki and Límnos **268**

Lésvos, Híos, Sámos and Ikaría **274**

Sporádes **286**

Évia (Euboea) **290**

Corfu Town **294**

Corfu **296**

Southern Ionian Islands **300**

Crete **308**

Iráklio **310**

A map of Greece is also on the front inside cover, and a map of the main ferry routes is on the back inside cover.

Introduction

Welcome to Greece **13**

Geography **15**

History

Decisive Dates **20**

Ancient Greece **23**

Byzantine Greece....................**33**

Ottoman Greece **39**

Modern Greece **45**

Contemporary Greece **54**

Features

People and Identities **61**

Literature **71**

Music and Dance....................**79**

Food and Drink **88**

Art and Architecture...............**95**

Flora and Fauna....................**105**

The Acropolis towers
above the market
place of Athens on a
white rocky platform

Insight on ...

Religious Festivals **86**
The National Archaeological
    Museum **144**
Wild Flowers **242**
The Palace of Knossos **318**

Information panels

The Cycladic Bronze Age **230**
Ancient Delos **241**
Italian Architecture in
    the Dodecanese **251**

Places

Introduction **119**
The Mainland **123**
Athens **127**
The Peloponnese **147**
Central Greece **165**
Epirus..................................**177**
Thessaloníki **193**
Macedonia and Thrace **201**

The Islands **215**
Islands of the Saronic Gulf **217**
The Cyclades........................**225**
Rhodes................................**245**
The Dodecanese **253**
The Northeast Aegean **267**
The Sporádes and Évia.........**285**
Corfu **293**
The Ionian Islands **299**
Crete **307**

Travel Tips

Getting Acquainted **322**
Planning the Trip **323**
Practical Tips **326**
Getting Around **329**
Where to Stay **333**
Where to Eat **356**
Culture **374**
Nightlife **375**
Sport **375**
Language **371**
Further Reading **380**

◆ **Full Travel Tips index**
   is on page 321

AN ANCIENT STORY

A heady mix of sun, sea and ancient sites bathed in brilliant Aegean light, Greece has enchanted travellers for centuries

Modern Greece, which emerged in the 19th century from 500 years of Ottoman rule, lies in a rocky pile of peninsulas and islands at the bottom of the Balkans in the eastern Mediterranean, with a language and landscape redolent of its pre-eminent place in the development of the western world. History, drama, politics, philosophy: the words as well as the concepts have their roots here. Around its rugged terrain are the names of the city states which vied for supremacy in this region 2,000 years ago: Corinth, Sparta, Mycenae, Thrace, Athens. And here too are Delphi, the Parthenon and Mount Olympos, forever associated with the ancient gods.

Whether you arrive in Greece by boat, train or plane, your first impression as you stretch your legs is likely to be of the sun. Glimmering on the water, reflecting off metal and glass, casting shadows, the Mediterranean sun is omnipresent. Like the flash of a hidden camera, the brilliant light catches you unawares and transfixes you.

From that minute, you seem effortlessly to become a part of the Greek landscape – blue sky above, white sand below, ancient ruins, olive groves, a wine festival... It is easy to fall in love with this radiant country, not least because so many of its 11 million people are emotionally open, unafraid of shedding a tear, either in sorrow or in joy. Many travellers first experience this passion in the warmth of the welcome they receive, and they may even feel a little uneasy at the exuberance of their hosts. Yet those travellers tend to return time after time – for the mirror-smooth Aegean Sea shimmering in the still of the morning, for the *kafenia* with their wooden stools and rickety tables offering some shade from the blistering afternoon heat, and for the silvery green olive groves where the cicadas drone at evening time.

The country's membership of the European Union and its capital's hosting of the 2004 Olympic Games have done much to accelerate modernisation. But modern is less a synonym for homogeneous than it is in many other rapidly changing countries. A sense of history and a respect for tradition remain powerful, and most Greeks are proud to share their culture with visitors. The Greek word *xénos* means not only "stranger" but also "guest", and a fortunate *xénos* will be invited into a Greek family's house to be lavishly supplied with food and drink and questioned with genuine curiosity. The aim of this book is both to guide visitors around Greece and its islands and to preview what is likely to be an entirely captivating experience. ❑

PRECEDING PAGES: a back street on Ýdra; classic Cycladic architecture; a view on Santoríni. **LEFT:** a quiet morning on Mýkonos.

A DIVERSE LAND

Mountains and caves, salt marshes and rainforest, blazing summers
and snow in winter – few countries have such varied landscape and climate

People perceive Greece as a land where people eat oranges and the sun shines all the time, but it is equally accurate (if not more so) to describe it as a place where it rains a lot and apples figure largely in the diet. Greece is actually the most varied country in the Mediterranean, with habitats ranging from near-deserts to temperate rainforests, from salt marshes to alpine peaks.

The splintered outline of the southeastern Balkan peninsula is the result of the flooding of the Mediterranean basin, which occurred when a debris dam at the future Strait of Gibraltar gave way. Waters from the Atlantic surged in and gradually submerged the mountain ranges, which segmented the deep, hot depression – a process completed only after the last Ice Age, and probably the basis of the Biblical flood account. Isolated, exposed summits became the Greek islands, Crete being the highest and largest. If the Mediterranean could be re-drained, the coastal ranges of former Yugoslavia, the Albano-Greek Píndos, the Peloponnesian mountains, Crete and the Turkish Toros would form one unbroken system: the so-called Dinaric Arc. The arc has a core of karstic limestone, extremely porous and peppered with caves, sinkholes and subterranean rivers. Glaciers of the last Ice Age also had a role in shaping the mountains as far south as the present-day Gulf of Corinth.

Earthquake zone

Greece remains an active subduction zone, where the African tectonic plate burrows under the European plate. This means numerous faults, frequent – often destructive – earthquakes and a significant level of geothermal activity. Over 100 thermal spas are scattered across both the mainland and the islands. The geothermalism is predictably accompanied by vulcanism: you can trace the boundary of the plate collision zone by "joining up" the extinct

---

LEFT: dramatic arches at Cape Skinári, Zákynthos.
RIGHT: the west coast cliffs, Zákynthos.

or dormant volcanic islands of Méthana (now a peninsula), Póros, the submerged calderas of Mílos and Thíra, and Nísyros, which has erupted within historical memory. In the northeast Aegean, Lésvos, Límnos and Aí Strátis islands are also of volcanic origin.

Only about one quarter of Greece's surface

area is cultivable, the greater part of this in Thessaly and Macedonia. Much of the farmland occupies low-lying plains or upland plateaux, often the beds of former lakes long since drained to reclaim the land for agriculture or eliminate malarial mosquitoes. Only a few perennial freshwater lakes survive on the mainland north of the Gulf of Corinth: they tend to be shallow and murky, more suited to irrigation, fishing and wildlife conservation than recreation. The largest and most scenic is Lake Trihonída in Étolo-Akarnanía; runners-up include Vegoritída, Mikrá Préspa and Kastoriá in western Macedonia, plus Pamvótida in Epirus. The Epirote Píndos

Mountains have a few glacial tarns, but lakes are almost entirely absent from the large islands owing to overly porous rock strata. Koúrnas, near Haniá on Crete, is the largest and most famous.

Stony or partly forested mountains make up three-quarters of the country – and as Henry Miller put it, nowhere has God been so lavish with rocks as in Greece. The hills are often bonily naked; the country's forests have been under steady attack since ancient times, and the rate of deforestation has

MINERAL RESOURCES

Greece once made a modest profit from its minerals – bauxite and chromite on the central mainland, assorted substances of volcanic origin on Mílos and Nísyros – but today mining is in sharp decline.

precipitation is highest in the Ionian Islands (particularly Corfu and Zákynthos) and the western mainland, where the Píndos mountain range forces moisture-laden air from the Ionian Sea to disgorge its load as rain or snow.

The rest of the country lies effectively in a "rain shadow", although the directional pattern is reversed at Mt Olympos near Thessaloníki, rising nearly 3,000 metres (9,800 ft) in the space of a few kilometres inland from the moist Thermaic Gulf, which duly sends wet air masses west to be

accelerated alarmingly since World War I. Fires, usually deliberately started, are the main cause: under current climatic conditions, it takes a Greek pine wood more than 50 years to recover from a blaze.

Hot summers, cold winters

Greece's stereotypical "Mediterranean" climate and vegetation is in fact limited to the coastal areas; "modified continental" is a more accurate tag for the weather elsewhere, with hot, muggy summers and cold winters. Although there are numerous microclimates – such as the northeast coast of the Pílio peninsula with its temperate rainforest – in general

trapped on the summit of the ancient gods. Olympos is the highest of a score of peaks over 2,300 metres (7,500 ft), home to about a dozen ski resorts. While nobody is likely to fly in from northern Europe specially to ski – snowfall patterns are too unreliable – the resorts are increasingly popular with the Greeks themselves.

Greece's fabled, convoluted coast is claimed to cover a distance equal to that of France, a country four times larger. But, despite figuring prominently on tourist posters, beaches are the exception rather than the rule. Much of the shoreline is inhospitable cliff, providing neither satisfaction for sand-seekers, nor anchorage for mariners. In fact, the most likely visitors are birds, as Greece lies under major migratory paths linking north-central Europe and Africa. When it is not cliff or beach, the Greek littoral is peppered with lagoons, estuaries and salt marshes that serve as important wildlife refuges. Some of the most important of these are at Kalógria near Pátra, Kalloní on Lésvos, the delta of the Évros river in Thrace, the Korissíon lagoon on Corfu, the Alykí marsh on Kós and the vast lagoon complex at Mesolóngi.

Controversial dams

No point in Greece is more than 100 km (60 miles) from the sea, so the numerous rivers

for irrigation and flood control rather than for hydroelectric power. Such projects, evidence of a nonaccountable, central-planning mentality which has waned almost everywhere else in Europe, remain highly controversial – none more so than the Mesohára dam on the Ahelóos, which has been declared illegal by the Greek Council of State, and had its funding revoked by the European Union. If ever completed, this massive project – intended to water the thirsty Thessalian plain – would finish off already threatened fisheries and wetlands at the Ahelóos delta.

Greece's rugged terrain, and its high pro-

are not only short but swift as they lose altitude quickly, to the delight of the local kayaking and rafting fraternity. The only major rivers to flow lazily along as in northern Europe, in their lower reaches anyway, are the Aliákmonas, the Pínios, the Ahelóos and the Árahthos; the Áxios and Strymónas and Évros in Macedonia and Thrace also conform to most people's idea of a continental river, but have their sources in other Balkan states. Since World War II most rivers north of the Gulf of Corinth have been dammed, usually

portion of territory in island groups, have since the time of the ancient city-states encouraged separate regional development. For such a small country there are numerous dialects, in contrast to, say, the far vaster Russia, which has little variation in its speech. Land communications were late in coming; well into the 20th century, it was easier to sail from Athens to the eastern Peloponnesian coast, or from Haniá to Crete's southern shore, than to go overland. Geographical determinism is an easy trap to fall into, but the mutual isolation of the provinces has undoubtedly been a dominant factor in shaping Greek identity, for better or worse. ❑

LEFT: Aráhova, a mountain town near Delphi.
ABOVE: the bridge at Árta, on coastal Epirus.

THRACIÆ PARS oggi ROMANIA

CONSTANTINOPOLI

Bistones

MARE DI MARMARA
olim
PROPONTIS

Bebryces

Mysia Minor

Mysia Maior

Stretto di Gallipoli
Dardanelli

Tasso I. et Thassus et Eria

ARCIPELAGO

oggi

MAR BIANCO

anticamente

ÆGÆVM MARE

Metelino I.
olim Lesbos

Scio I. et Chius et Chios

Stalimene I. et Lemnos

Lembro I. et Imbrus

Pelagnesi I. et Alonesus

Sciro I. et Syrus

ICARIVM MARE

Andro I. et Andros

Tino I. et Tenos

Nicaria I.
ol. Icaria

Samo I. et Samos

Sarcan ol Lydia

Caras ol Lydia

NATOLIA PROPRIA

CARIA MINOR

Rocho I.

Delos grande et Rhenea

Macolo I. et Miconus

Nicsia I. et Naxus

Palmosa et Patino
et Patmos

Lero I. et Leria

MARE MIRTOVM

Cariar

Insulæ Cyclades

Parol et Paros

Morgo I. et Amorgus

Capra I. et Claros

Lango et Cos

Doris

Spora des Insulæ

MARE MIRTOVM

Nio I. et Ios

Zinara I.

Leuita I. et Levinthus

Nicsia I. et Nisyrus

Milo I.

Namfio I. et Anaphe

Gierra I.
et Hiera

Serpe I.

Stampalia I. et Astypalæa

Isola di Rodi et Rhodus

Santorini o S. Erini
et Thera Insula

Plana I.

MARE DI CANDIA ol. CRETICVM Mare

Standia I. et Dia

Candia

Scarpanto I. et Carpathus

MARE DI SCARPANTO olim Carpathium Mare

Cassio I. et Cassus

CANDIA olim CRETA

Scala
Miglia d'Italia
Leghe comuni di Francia
Leghe comuni di Germania
Leghe d'un hora di comuni

Decisive Dates

MINOAN PERIOD: *CIRCA* 3000–1400 BC

3000 BC The Minoan civilisation arises on Crete; outposts are established and contact is made with the Egyptians.

2100–1500 BC Minoan culture, noted for its great cities and palaces, and sophisticated art, reaches its zenith.

CIRCA **1400 BC** The settlement at Akrotiri on Santoríni is annihilated by a volcanic eruption. Most other centres of Minoan power are destroyed by fire and abandoned.

THE BIRTH OF EUROPE

Greece – or to be more precise, Crete – was present at the birth of Europe. A myth, now thousands of years old, recounts how Zeus, the father of the gods, abducted a beautiful, shy princess from her palace in Phoenicia. He fell in love with her and gained her trust by posing as a white bull.

However, as soon as the princess sat on the bull's back she was carried away against her will to the shores of a distant continent, which from then on bore her name: Europa. The rest, as they say, is history...

MYCENAEAN AND DORIAN PERIOD: 1400–700 BC

1400 BC A Peloponnesian tribe, the Myceneans, rise to prominence, building grand fortifications to defend their citadels at Mycenae and Tiryns.

1200 BC The Dorian tribe conquer large areas of the Peloponnese.

776 BC The Dorians hold the first Olympic games, in honour of Zeus and Hera.

ARCHAIC PERIOD: 700–500 BC

700 BC onwards Dorian invasions create city-states, including Athens, Sparta, Thebes and Corinth, which compete for supremacy.

550 BC Sparta forms Peloponnesian League with neighbouring states. Rivalry with Athens increases.

500 BC The Greek city-states control large parts of the Mediterranean coast.

CLASSICAL PERIOD: 500–338 BC

490 BC The Persian king, Darius, attempts to invade and conquer Greece but is convincingly defeated by the Athenian army at Marathon.

480 BC Xerxes, Darius's son, invades. The Spartan king, Leonidas, fails to hold back the Persian army at the Battle of Thermopylae. Athens is captured, but then in a surprise attack, Greek boats sink the Persian fleet off Salamis.

431–404 BC The Peloponnesian Wars, with Sparta and Athens the main protagonists. Athens capitulates; Sparta takes control of much of Greece.

338 BC Philip II of Macedonia defeats Athens and Thebes at the Battle of Chaeronea and unites all Greek cities except Sparta.

HELLENISTIC AND ROMAN PERIOD: 338 BC–AD 395

336 BC Philip II assassinated. His son, Alexander the Great, develops Greece into an imperial power with Macedonia at the centre of government.

323 BC Alexander's huge empire is divided on his death amongst his successors, the Diadochi; the centres of political power consequently shift from Greece to the Middle East and Egypt.

320–275 BC The Diadochi war among themselves; Macedonia struggles to maintain its position. Rome emerges as a major power.

146 BC Rome annexes Greece as a province of the Roman Empire.

BYZANTINE PERIOD: AD 395–1453

395 The Roman Empire is divided into East and West, with the Greeks dominant in the East.

1204 The Crusaders, assisted by the Venetians, attack and plunder Constantinople. The Franks and

Venetians divide Greek territory among themselves. Fortified harbours and fortresses are built in the Peloponnese and on Rhodes and Crete against the Turkish threat.

1453 The Byzantine Empire is defeated by the Ottomans.

OTTOMAN PERIOD: 1453–1821

1453 The sultan hands over the civil administration of Greece to the Greek Orthodox Church. Initially, life for the Greeks is tolerable.

1500s High per capita and land taxes prove to be a heavy burden for the Greek population.

1600s The burden of taxation now becomes unbearable, and the Greek struggle for independence starts to take shape. The Church takes the side of the rebels.

1821 After a number of failed attempts, Archbishop Germanos in the Peloponnese calls for an armed struggle against the Turks. Troops succeed in liberating Athens at the first attempt.

MODERN TIMES: FROM 1821

1820s The major European powers intervene in the Greek War of Independence. Their military assistance helps expel the Turks from southern and central Greece.

1832 Russia, France and Great Britain install Prince Otto of Bavaria as the new king of Greece.

1863 King George I succeeds the ousted Otto.

1909 The Liberal Party under Elevtherios Venizelos comes to power and governs until 1920.

1912 The Balkan Wars erupt. Greece wrests southern Macedonia, Epirus, Crete and the east Aegean Islands from the Turks.

1917 Greece enters World War I after bitter wrangles between republicans and monarchists.

1922 Encouraged by the Allies, Greek troops attempt to annex Smyrna from Turkey but fail. King Constantine goes into exile; a parliamentary republic is established.

1923 The borders between Greece and Turkey are finally settled and in a traumatic population transfer, 1.1 million Orthodox Greeks leave Asia Minor and 380,000 Muslims leave Greece for Turkey.

1928–32 Venizelos is restored to power.

1933 The royalist Populist Party is voted in.

1935 The monarchy is restored.

PRECEDING PAGES: a 17th-century map of Greece.
LEFT: ancient myth revived in a bust of Poseidon.
RIGHT: Count Ioannis Kapodistrias, Greek president from 1827 until his assassination in 1831.

1936–41 Military (and fascist) dictatorship under General Metaxas. When World War II is declared, Greece is initially neutral.

1940 Mussolini sends troops into Greece.

1941–4 Hitler's forces occupy Greece. Resistance groups base themselves in the mountains.

1944–9 The Germans retreat, and the Allies attempt to reintroduce civilian rule. Rebel forces defy the right-wing government the Allies install.

1950s The conservatives rule and an uneasy peace reigns. The Communist Party is outlawed.

1967 A group of army colonels under Georgios Papadopoulos seize control of the country.

1974 The junta attempts to take over Cyprus but

fails and is forced to resign. The monarchy is abolished and Greece declares itself a republic.

1981–98 The Greek Socialist Party, PASOK, gains power and, apart from a brief interruption (1989–93), Papandreou remains the prime minister.

1993 A breakaway republic of the former Yugoslavia calling itself (to Greece's anger) Macedonia gains recognition from the European Union and the UN as the Former Yugoslav Republic of Macedonia.

1996 Andreas Papandreou dies; Kostas Simitis succeeds him and wins re-election (and again in 2000).

2002 Greece adopts the euro as its currency.

2004 The right-wing Néa Dimokratía wins the general election under Kostas Karamanlis. Athens plays host to the Olympic Games. ❑

ANCIENT GREECE

The rich civilisations that rose and fell in the Aegean
have left a precious inheritance that is still relevant today

The basis for the modern way of life in Greece was laid around 3000 BC, when settlers moved down from the northeast plains on to rockier land in the Peloponnese (Pelopónnisos) and the islands, and began to cultivate olives and vines, as well as the cereals they had originally grown. At about the same time a prosperous Bronze Age civilisation arose on Crete (Kríti), and spread its influence throughout the Aegean.

The Minoans, whose rituals have filtered down to us through the legend of Theseus and his labyrinthine struggle with the Minotaur, left proof of their architectural genius in the ruined palaces of Knossos and Phaistos (Festós). Adventurous sailors, they appear to have preferred commerce to agriculture. The 5th-century BC historian Thucydides reports that King Minos of Crete established his sons as governors in the Cyclades and cleared the Aegean of pirates. The Minoans also established a number of outposts in the Peloponnese and made contact with the Egyptians.

By 1500 BC their civilisation had reached its zenith. Yet barely a century later, for reasons that remain unexplained, most centres of their power were destroyed by fire and abandoned. The settlement on Santoríni (Thíra), at Akrotiri, was annihilated by a volcanic eruption. But the causes of the wider disintegration of Minoan control remain a mystery. Only Knossos continued to be inhabited as Cretan dominance in the Aegean came to an end.

The Minoans' place was taken by Myceneans, inhabitants of Mycenae (Mykínes), the bleak citadel in the Peloponnese. We do not know whether the rulers of Mycenae exerted direct power over the remainder of the mainland. But in the *Iliad* Homer portrays their king, Agamemnon, as the most powerful figure in the Greek forces, which suggests that Mycenae had achieved some sort of overall authority.

LEFT: a Bronze Age Cycladic figure.
RIGHT: an ancient inscription at Olympia.

In its heyday the Mycenean world contained men rich enough to commission massive stone tombs and delicate gold work. Rulers were served by a complex array of palace scribes and administrators who controlled the economic life of the state, exacting tribute, collecting taxes and allocating rations of scarce metals.

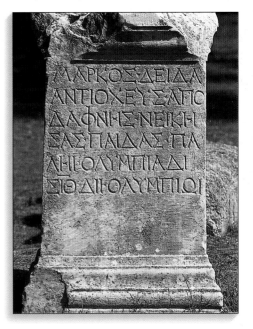

The Geometric Period

In the 13th century BC this society, like the Cretan one before it, came to an end. Classical myth connects the decline of the Mycenean age with the arrival of Dorian tribes. In fact, there was no clear connection between the two events. Mycenean power had broken down irreversibly by the time the Dorians entered Greece. These invaders, like later ones, entered Greece from the northwest, down over the Píndos Mountains into the Peloponnese. They were probably nomads, which would explain their willingness to travel and account for their lower level of culture.

They also brought their own form of the Greek language. In areas where they settled heavily we find West Greek dialects, while Attica, the Aegean Islands and the Ionian colonies continued to use East Greek forms. The hostility, at a later date, between Athens and Sparta (Spárti) was based in part on this division between Ionian and Dorian peoples.

The Dorian invasion coincided with the onset of the Geometric period (named after its pottery). Historical evidence for the period between the 11th and 8th centuries BC is patchy, but it is clear that civilised life suffered. Trade

A CULTURAL DECLINE

By the 13th century BC the Myceneans had adapted Minoan script into the first written Greek, but the art of writing was all but forgotten until around 700 BC.

the east was increasingly evident in metalwork and pottery. With the adoption of the Phoenician alphabet, writing revived among a much larger circle than before.

Another, equally important Greek concept was borrowed from the Phoenicians; the notion of the *polis* (city-state). In the Geometric small, isolated settlements were loosely grouped into large kingdoms. This system survived in both western and northern Greece into classical times when Thucydides described how "the Aetolian nation, although

dwindled and communities became isolated from one another. Building in stone seems to have been too great an effort for the small pastoral settlements that had replaced the centres of Mycenean power. Homer's *Odyssey* is set in a simple society where even the rulers busy themselves with menial tasks; where wealth is measured in flocks and herds.

Writing revives

In the 8th century BC there were signs of revival: trade spread further afield. There were contacts with civilised peoples such as the Etruscans in the west, and the Phoenicians and Egyptians in the east. Artistic influence from

numerous and warlike, yet dwell in unwalled villages scattered far apart".

Elsewhere, however, a network of small independent states grew up. At first, these were based around clusters of villages rather than one large urban centre. But with the population explosion of the 8th century, large conurbations evolved and expanded as surplus population moved from the country to the town. Land became more intensively cultivated and highly priced. In the Geometric the slump in population had caused arable land to fall into disuse. Farmers turned from sowing cereals to stockbreeding; now the process was thrown into reverse. The available land could not support such a rapidly growing population. (There is a clear parallel with the Peloponnese in the 19th century, and in both cases the outcome was the same: emigration on a massive scale.)

Together with the division between the new *polis* and the older *ethnos* (kingdom), there was now a further distinction. Some states, mostly in the Dorian-speaking parts of the country, were reliant on a population of slaves who were excluded from power, such as Sparta, a major *polis*, and Thessaly, an *ethnos*. Other states, such as Athens, although not unfamiliar with slaves, had a more broadly based citizen body that included Greeks from outside the city.

states began to increase in size, and infantry forces acquired a greater degree of strength, more persons were admitted to the enjoyment of political rights". Just as the shift from monarchy to aristocracy had been reflected in the move from chariots to horseback fighting, the emphasis now switched from cavalry to infantry; aristocracy lost ground to democratic pressure. Men would only fight in the new larger armies if the aristocrats granted them political rights.

Military power swung away from the traditional horse-breeding aristocracies of Chalkis, Eretria and Thessaly to new powers: Corinth (Kórinthos), Argos and, above all, Sparta,

From kings to aristocrats

In general, Homer's kings must have surrendered power towards the end of the Geometric, giving way to an aristocratic form of rule. But they too became entrenched in power and increasingly resistant to change. As commoners settled on land and amassed wealth, pressure grew for constitutional reform. Aristotle seems to have been right in identifying the connection between the demand for reform and changes in military technique. He said "when

LEFT: entrance to a beehive tomb, Mycenae.
ABOVE: Theseus and Procrustes portrayed on a vase painting from around 470 BC.

where the state was protected by an army of heavily-armed foot-soldiers known as hoplites, whose core was a body of citizens who were trained as infantrymen from birth.

Often the demand for radical reform met with resistance from the upper classes, but some individuals, more far-sighted, recognised the need for change. One such was Solon, nicknamed "the Law-Giver", who was elected in early 6th-century Athens to introduce sweeping constitutional changes. Realising that the city's strength would depend upon the organisation of the citizen body, he opened up the Assembly to the poorest citizens and in other ways loosened the grip of the aristocracy.

Inevitably these changes were attacked from both sides, as Solon himself complains in a number of his poems. But they did lay the foundations for the tremendous expansion of Athenian power throughout the next century.

Another symptom of these political tensions was tyranny. To the ancient Greeks the word "tyrant" was not pejorative; it simply referred to a ruler who had usurped power instead of inheriting it. In the 6th century, tyrants seized power in a number of states. Usually they were dissident aristocrats, who gained the support of the lower classes with promises of radical change – promises which were often kept, as it was in

factor. While the popular religious festivals and games earned revenues – enormous in some cases – for the city that staged them, temples, sacrifices and other rituals were very costly. Apart from waging wars, temple-building was probably the greatest drain on a city-state's resources. Thus it was the scale of its religious activities that provided some measure of the wealth of a community.

Greeks and outsiders

Now, alongside the rise of an artistic culture shared across state boundaries, a process of political unification began to grow. People in

the new ruler's interest to weaken the power of his peers. In the mid-7th century, for example, Kipselis of Corinth was supposed to have redistributed land belonging to his fellow-aristocrats.

But it would be wrong to regard the tyrants as great innovators. They were symptoms of social change rather than causes of it. Conscious of their own vulnerability, they resorted to various propaganda expedients to stay in power. The most potent of these was the religious cult, and it is from the time of the tyrants that religion came directly to serve the purposes of the state.

Religion was not only important to the state as propaganda; it was also a major economic

different cities started to become aware of a common Hellenic culture. The historian Herodotus was a keen promoter of the idea of one Greece, and asserted that the Greeks were "a single race because of common blood, common customs, common language and common religion". This common cultural identity was reinforced by increasing numbers of religious festivals and athletic competitions that attracted participants from numerous Greek states.

But the sharpest spur to unity was a threat from outside: the rise of the Persian Empire. Midway through the 6th century, King Cyrus had conquered the Greek cities on the Asia Minor coast, and Persian aspirations were further encouraged by his son Darius (521–486 BC) who conquered Thrace, subdued Macedonia and, after quashing an Ionian revolt in Asia Minor, sent a massive expeditionary force westwards into Greece. Athens appealed for help from Sparta, militarily the strongest Greek city, but succeeded in defeating the Persians at Marathon before the Spartan forces managed to arrive.

This victory did more than save Attica; it also confirmed Athens as the standard-bearer for the Greek military effort against the Persians. This explains why a frieze displaying the warriors killed at Marathon (situated just

Athens and Sparta

Ten years after the battle of Marathon, when Darius's son Xerxes organised a second attack on Greece, the city-states rallied around Sparta. For while Athens had the largest navy, the Spartans controlled the Peloponnesian League, with its considerable combined land forces. Both the crucial naval victory at Salamis in 480 BC and the military victory at Plataea the following year, were won under Spartan leadership.

But no sooner had the Persian menace been banished than the Greek alliance broke up. There was intense suspicion among the rival city-states, especially between Sparta and

over 23 km/20 miles from Athens) was placed in a prominent and highly unusual position around the Parthenon in the 440s BC. Only then was Athens becoming a power to be reckoned with. The silver mines at Laurion (modern Lávrion) in Attica began producing enough ore to finance a major shipbuilding programme from early in the 5th century. Even so, for two generations after that, Aegina (Égina) remained superior to Athens as a Saronic Gulf trading force.

LEFT: the theatre at Epidauros.
ABOVE: the Caryatids of the Erechtheion, built on the Acropolis at the peak of Athens' glory.

THE RISE OF ATHENS

The Athenian Empire owed much to the Confederation of Delos, a naval alliance formed in 478 BC to liberate the East Greeks and continue the struggle against the Persians. It was also underlaid by much anti-Spartan sentiment. Sparta's own version of the alliance, the Peloponnesian League, consisted of land forces, requiring minimum financing. But the creation of a navy called for long-term planning and central coordination – a crucial difference. Athens' smaller allies found it increasingly difficult to equip their own ships, and instead sent money to the Athenians. Thus Athens grew in strength as its allies became impoverished.

Athens. Thucydides described how, as soon as the Persians withdrew, the Athenians rebuilt their city walls for fear that the Spartans would try to stop them.

The development of a classical "cold war" became obvious as Athens extended its control over the Aegean with the help of the Confederation of Delos. Significantly, the Persian threat had receded long before peace was officially declared in 449 BC. Next, between 460 and 446 BC, Athens fought a series of wars with its neighbours in an effort to assert

HOW TO BUILD EMPIRES

One reason the Greek city-states failed as imperial powers, the Roman Emperor Claudius observed, was because they "treated their subjects as foreigners".

a Spartan ally, Thebes, attacked an Athenian ally, Plataea, and open war broke out between the two superpowers.

The Second Peloponnesian War dragged on for years since neither side was able to deal the deathblow to the other. The Peace of Nikias in 421 BC gave both sides a breathing space, but lasted just six years.

The uncertain peace was finally shattered when the Athenians launched a massive assault against Sicily. Aided by a force of Spartans, Syracuse was able to break

its supremacy. Naval rivals such as Aegina were singled out for attack. There was even small-scale fighting between Athens and Sparta (the First Peloponnesian War), until the so-called "Thirty Years' Treaty" brought an uneasy truce in 445.

In 433 BC Athens allied itself with Corcyra, a strategically important colony of Corinth. Fighting ensued, and the Athenians took steps that explicitly violated the Thirty Years' Treaty. Sparta and its allies accused Athens of aggression and threatened war. On the advice of Pericles, its most influential leader, Athens refused to back down. Diplomatic efforts to resolve the dispute failed. Finally, in the spring of 431 BC,

an Athenian blockade. Even after gaining reinforcements in 413 BC, the Athenian army was defeated again. Soon afterward the navy was also beaten, and the Athenians were utterly destroyed as they tried to retreat.

But even the Sicilian disaster did not put a stop to hostilities – although it had a huge impact on Athenian domestic politics. By 411 BC Athens was in political turmoil: democracy was overthrown by the oligarchical party, which was in turn replaced by the more moderate regime of the Five Thousand. At the end of 411 the rebuilt Athenian navy, fresh from several victories, acted to restore democratic rule. But the democratic leaders refused Spartan peace offerings, and the war continued at sea, with the Spartan and Athenian fleets exchanging costly victories. The end came in 405 when the Athenian navy was destroyed at Aegospotami by the Spartan fleet under Lysander, who had received much aid from the Persians. The next year, starved by an impenetrable blockade, Athens capitulated. Athens' defeat was perhaps the worst casualty in a war that crippled Greek military strength. The most culturally advanced Greek state had been brought into final eclipse.

Civic breakdown

Literature and art both flourished even during these incessant periods of fighting, but economic activity did not. A world where each tiny *polis* was determined to safeguard its independence at any cost carried within it the seeds of its own destruction.

The paradox was that city-states with imperial pretensions chose not to take the steps that might have brought success. Unlike Rome, Greek city-states did not extend citizenship to their subject territories. Nor could the military strength of Athens keep pace with its imperial commitments, which explains the permanent cycle of conquest and revolt. The Spartans had the additional headache of a large slave population, the helots, often prone to revolt in their own province.

The first half of the 4th century continued the pattern. On the one hand, there were long wars between cities; on the other, evidence of prolonged economic difficulties as Corinth fell into irreversible decline, and Athens struggled in vain to recapture its previous prominence. Spartan power remained supreme until 371 BC when Thebes defeated the Spartan army at Leuctra.

The city-state system was gradually starting to fall apart. The old form of citizen army was superseded by a more professional force, which relied upon trained mercenaries. Aristotle noted that "when the Spartans were alone in their strenuous military discipline they were superior to everybody, but now they are beaten by everybody; the reason is that in former times they trained and others did not". Things had certainly changed.

LEFT: a Corinthian column at ancient Corinth.
RIGHT: Alexander the Great's campaigns dramatically extended the boundaries of the Greek world.

The spread of mercenaries, in fact, reflects the economic problems of the 4th century. Mercenary service, like emigration or piracy, was a demographic safety valve, and whereas in archaic Greece mercenaries had come from just a few backward areas, in the 4th century they were increasingly drawn from the major cities as well. This points to economic difficulties over an increasingly wide area.

As in earlier times, military changes were connected with political ones. The decline of the citizen armies coincided with a trend away from democracy in favour of more autocratic government. Power shifted from the city-states

towards Thessaly, an *ethnos* state, and later still, towards Macedonia, which had been another old-fashioned kingdom.

Both regions had the advantage over Attica in that they were fertile and not short of land. More rural than the city-states to their south, they managed to avoid the domestic political turmoil that periodically erupted in the latter. The military successes of the Thessalian tyrant, Jason of Pherae, in the early 4th century, indicated the confidence of these newcomers.

A little later King Philip II of Macedonia moved southwards, secured the vital Thermopylae (Thermopýles) Pass and, after gaining control of Thessaly, defeated an alliance of

Thebes and Athens at Chaeronea in 338 BC. Banded together in the League of Corinth, the Greek city-states were compelled to recognise a new centre of power, Macedonia.

Alexander's Empire

In the *Republic*, Plato writes: "We shall speak of war when Greeks fight with barbarians, whom we may call their natural enemies. But Greeks are by nature friends of Greeks, and when they fight, it means that Hellas is afflicted by dissension which ought to be called civil strife."

This passage reflects three sentiments that were becoming widespread in the 4th century:

first, that the Greeks were all of one race; second, that warfare between city-states was undesirable; third, that it was natural for the Greeks to fight their enemies in the east. It is ironic in this regard that a successful concerted effort against the Persians was made only under the leadership of Macedonia, traditionally a border power in the Greek world.

Philip's son Alexander mopped up any remaining resistance in Greece, then led a Greek-Macedonian army on a brilliant rampaging campaign to the east and south. In a little over 10 years, he systematically swallowed up the ancient Persian Empire, reaching as far as the Indus Valley (in modern Pakistan). He even found time to conquer Egypt, where he founded Alexandria.

Alexander the Great's overseas empire drastically altered the boundaries of the Greek world. The city-states of mainland Greece no longer occupied centre stage. The mainland was drained of manpower as soldiers, settlers and administrators moved eastwards to consolidate Greek rule. At the same time, the intellectual and religious world of the Greeks was opened up to new influences.

The Greek-speaking world was not only expanding, it was also coming together: "common" Greek replaced local dialects in most areas. In 3rd-century Macedonia, for example, local culture was "Hellenised", and the native gods were replaced by Olympian deities. For the first time coinage became widely used in trade – something which had been impossible so long as each city had its own currency. Now the Attic drachma became acceptable in an area ranging from Athens to the Black Sea, from Cappadocia to Italy.

But there were limits to this process, for although the city-states gave up their political freedom, they clung to self-determination in other spheres such as local taxation and customs duties. Likewise the calendar: in Athens the year began in July, in Sparta in October, on the island of Delos, January.

Philosophers were debating ideas of communal loyalties that transcended the old civic boundaries. Perhaps this reflected the way in which these were being absorbed within larger units, such as the Hellenistic kingdoms, the Greek federal leagues and, eventually, the Roman Empire. Whatever the cause, the most influential philosophical school, Stoicism, emphasised the concept of universal brotherhood and talked of a world state ruled by one supreme power.

Roman expansion

Gradually but inexorably, the expansion of Macedonia curtailed the political autonomy of the city-states. In the 3rd century they formed federations, and tried to exploit disputes between the generals who had inherited Alexander's empire. The policy had only limited success, mainly because of the paltry military resources available to the Greek leagues.

Early in the 2nd century, disputes among the city-states brought about Roman intervention for the first time in Greek history. Within 20 years Rome had defeated first Macedonia, and then the Achaean League which had organised a desperate Greek resistance to Roman rule. The Roman consul Memmius marked his victory over the League by devastating Corinth, killing the entire male population, and selling its women and children into slavery. As a deterrent to further resistance this was brutal but effective. Conservative factions were confirmed in power in the cities and Greece became a Roman protectorate. In 27 BC, when the Roman Empire was proclaimed, the protectorate became the province of Achaea.

permitted a degree of political self-rule. Philhellenic emperors such as Hadrian even encouraged groups of cities to federate in an effort to encourage a panhellenic spirit.

But the *polis* was no longer a political force. Hellenistic rulers had feared the Greek cities' power; the Roman and later the Byzantine emperors feared their weakness and did what they could to keep them alive. After all, they were vital administrative cogs in the imperial machine. If they failed, the machine would not function.

Two centuries of relative tranquillity were shattered by the invasions of the Goths in the

Greece – a Roman backwater?

By the 1st century AD, Greece was no longer the centre of the civilised world. Athens and Corinth could not rival Alexandria or Antioch, let alone Rome. The main routes to the east went overland through Macedonia; to the south, by sea to Egypt. But while Greece was certainly a commercial backwater, its decline was only relative: along the coast, cities flourished. The *polis* remained much as it had been in Hellenistic times, and the Roman authorities

3rd century AD. The invasions were successfully repelled, but the shock led to a loss of confidence and economic deterioration. Civic building programmes continued on a much reduced scale. The wealthy classes became increasingly reluctant benefactors, and two centuries passed before imperial authorities and the church revived the demand for architectural skills.

By that time much had changed. In AD 330, Emperor Constantine had moved his capital from Rome to Constantinople. Christianity had been made the official religion of the empire. The transition from Rome to Byzantium had begun. ❑

LEFT: the temple of Olympian Zeus in Athens was completed by the Roman emperor Hadrian.
ABOVE: the Arch of Galerius, Thessaloníki, built in AD 305.

BYZANTINE GREECE

*The legendary wealth of Rome's eastern empire attracted many potential
invaders, from the Franks and Venetians to the Ottomans*

The Byzantine Empire was established with the foundation of Constantinople, but the final separation of the eastern and western empires was not complete until the late 5th century. With its political structure anchored in Greek tradition and a new religion stimulated by Greek philosophy, the Byzantine Empire survived a millennium of triumphs and declines until Constantinople fell to the Ottoman Turks in 1453.

A revealing incident occurred in the capital Constantinople in AD 968. Legates from the Holy Roman Empire in the west brought a letter for Nicephorus, the Byzantine Emperor, in which Nicephorus was simply styled "Emperor of the Greeks" while the Holy Roman Emperor, Otto, was termed "august Emperor of the Romans". The Byzantine courtiers were scandalised. The audacity of it – to call the universal emperor of the Romans, the one and only Nicephorus, the great, the august, "Emperor of the Greeks" and to style a poor barbaric creature "Emperor of the Romans"!

Cultural mixture

Behind this reaction lies the curious fusion of cultures which made up the Byzantine tradition. From the Hellenistic world came the belief in the superiority of the Greek world, and the summary dismissal of outsiders as barbarians. From Rome came a strong sense of loyalty to empire and emperor. And in the fervour that marked their belief in the moral superiority of *their* empire – which they regarded not as the "Eastern Roman Empire" but as the only true empire – is the stamp of evangelical Christianity.

The inhabitants of this empire did not call themselves Greeks or Byzantines: they were Romans, "Roméï". But the mark of a *Romaiós* was that he spoke Greek and followed the rite of the Orthodox Church. Thus three elements of identity – Greek culture and language, Roman

LEFT: a Byzantine icon depicting the baptism of Christ.
RIGHT: the 14th-century Anafonítria
monastery on Zákynthos

laws and regulations, and Christian morality – became intermingled.

Two crises between AD 330 and 518 helped shape the Greek part of the empire. The first was the invasion by barbarian Huns, Visigoths and Ostrogoths in the 5th century. Constantinople avoided the fate of Rome, which fell to

similar onslaughts, by a combination of skilful bribery and a strong army. So it was that, as the West was carved into minor kingdoms, the East remained largely intact, and the balance of power in the former Roman Empire moved conclusively to the East.

The Emperor Justinian (AD 527–65) laid the foundation on which the Byzantine Empire would rest for nearly a century. An ambitious and dynamic leader, he greatly expanded the empire's territory by conquering the southern Levant, northern Africa and Italy, in an effort to re-create the domain of the old Roman Empire. Justinian's administrative reforms created a centralised bureaucracy, a new fiscal system, and a provincial administration. The codes of Roman law were revised and unified in the Justinianic Code, which remains to this day a cornerstone of European jurisprudence. These reforms greatly advanced the unification of the diverse peoples of the empire in a Hellenic context. In the end, Justinian's institutional reforms proved far more lasting than his military conquests.

The end of antiquity

Justinian's wars brought the empire to the verge of bankruptcy and left it in a vulnerable military position. Threats from both East and West

The real break with Greek antiquity came late in the 6th century when Greece was first attacked and then settled by Slavic-speaking tribes from the north. Major cities such as Athens, Thebes and Thessaloníki were safe behind defensible walls. But much of the indigenous population of the Balkans, Greeks included, fled, especially to Calabria on the southern tip of Italy, or relocated their settlements to higher, more secure regions of the Balkans. The invasions marked the end of the classical tradition in Greece, destroying the urban civilisation of the *polis*, and with it Roman and Greek culture.

plunged the empire into a spiral of decline that lasted for nearly 300 years. The first menace to the Empire from the East came from the Persian Sassanid Empire. Sassanid forces took control of Palestine, Syria and Egypt, and even threatened the capital, Constantinople, at one point. A more serious threat soon developed with the advent of Islamic expansionism. Exploding out of the Arabian Peninsula, Muslim forces swept northward and westward, taking Egypt, Syria, Iraq, Iran and Afghanistan. Portions of Asia Minor were wrested from the Byzantine Empire, and twice between AD 668 and 725 Constantinople was nearly overrun by Muslim forces.

But the Slavic arrivals were unable to preserve their own distinct cultural identities; very soon their Hellenisation process began. Greek remained the mother tongue of the region, and Christianity remained the dominant faith. Although the Slavic invasions and Islamic conquests of the 7th and 8th centuries reduced the extent of the Byzantine state, it survived as a recognisable entity grounded more firmly than ever in the Balkans and Asia Minor.

The Greek language may have survived, but the old urban culture did not. The disappearance of the city-states is shown by the way in which the word *"pólis"* came to refer exclusively to Constantinople as though there were no other cities. A small urban elite studied and wrote in Ancient Greek but had little impact on the mass of the population; their books were probably read by less than 300 people at any one time. Ancient monuments were left untouched because peasants thought that they were inhabited by demons.

Byzantine revival

When a new dynasty, which came to be called Macedonian, took the throne of the Byzantine Empire in 867, its forces began to roll back the tide of Islamic expansion. Antioch, Syria, Geor-

TEMPLE TO CHURCH

In AD 841 Greece's most famous ancient temple, the Parthenon, became the Orthodox cathedral church of Our Lady of Athens.

reward military service, the area under cultivation expanded. The prosperity of improved agricultural conditions and the export of woven silk and other craft articles allowed the population to grow. Expanding commercial opportunities increased the influence of the nearby Italian maritime republics of Venice, Genoa and Amalfi, which eventually gained control of the Mediterranean trade routes into Greece.

But Byzantium's period of glory was short-lived, lasting from the mid-9th to mid-11th

gia and Armenia were reconquered. The Byzantine fleet regained Crete and drove Muslim pirates from the Aegean Sea, reopening it to commercial traffic. Consolidation of the Balkans was completed with the defeat of the Bulgarian Empire by Basil II in 1018.

The military conquests of the Macedonian Dynasty initiated a period of economic growth and prosperity and a cultural renaissance. Agriculture flourished as conditions stabilised and, as emperors increasingly used land grants to

LEFT: the spectacular location of Agíou Ioánnou Prodrómou on the Peloponnese.
ABOVE: mosaic from the Kapnikaréa church, Athens.

centuries. The empire lacked the resources to maintain tight control over its territories. It was beset on all sides – by the Italian city-states to the west, the Slav kingdoms to the north, the Persians and Turks in the east. The Greek provinces, being less vital than Anatolia, which supplied Constantinople with corn, were ceded more readily to other powers.

The prosperity of the Macedonian Dynasty was followed by a period of decline. In 1071 a new enemy, Seljuk Turks from central Asia, cut the Byzantine army to pieces at Manzikert in Anatolia. The threat from the west was soon felt, too. In the late 11th century, a Norman army, allied with the Pope and commanded by

Robert Guiscard, ravaged parts of Greece, including Thebes and Corinth. Civil war among rival military factions impaired the empire's ability to respond to such incursions, so Byzantium gave Venice trading rights in Greece in return for protection against the Normans. But before long the Byzantines needed to counter Venetian power by encouraging the Genoese.

Crusaders and Venetians

When the Turks seized Jerusalem, some European kings, claiming Christian ideology as their motive, but in fact seeing political and commercial advantages too, sailed east to

la Roche, the west coast and various islands by Italians – particularly the Venetians.

Venice was a powerful naval power, with boundless ambition for trade and territory. As a pay-off for the assistance given to the Crusaders, after the sack of Constantinople Venetians were allowed to take control of many of the Greek islands that had been part of the Byzantine Empire. The Ionian Islands were divided into fiefdoms among noble Venetian families (and remained under Venetian control for nearly 600 years); other Venetian aristocrats helped themselves to islands in the Aegean – notably Marco Sanudo, a nephew of the Doge,

recover the Christian holy places from Muslim control. In the process. they established power bases in territories that had been part of the Byzantine Empire – Cyprus, for example, taken by Richard I of England during the Third Crusade.

This was only a foretaste of still worse misfortune. In 1204 Constantinople itself was sacked by the Crusader forces en route to the Holy Land for the Fourth Crusade – and transported there by the Venetians. The empire was fragmented. Successor states arose in Epirus, Nicaea and Trebizond. Greece itself was divided into small kingdoms ruled by Western princes – the Duchy of Athens under the Burgundian de

who claimed Náxos, founded a duchy and effectively ruled the whole of the Cyclades from there. Even Crete, "the Great Island", became a Venetian territory, sold to Venice for a nominal sum by Prince Boniface of Montferrat, the leader of the Fourth Crusade, in return for its assistance in the conquest of Constantinople. Thus by the mid-13th century, Venice had control of the shipping routes to the Black Sea and Asian Minor, Egypt and North Africa.

Byzantium fights back

Only the resolute resistance of the Palaeologos Dynasty (1261–1453) prevented the Byzantine Empire from collapsing completely. The

Palaeologi fought back into mainland Greece, recaptured Constantinople and most of the southern Balkans. But there was considerable confusion in western Greece, which briefly came under Serbian control, and in Thessaly, where the Vlachs established a separate principality.

Southern Greece and the islands remained under the control of the Venetians, the Genoese, various other Italian adventurers and, in the case of Rhodes and Cyprus, the Knights of St John, a military order which had arisen during the

> **A FIERCE RESISTANCE**
>
> The Aegean Islands held out longest against the Turks. Tínos resisted until 1715 – over 250 years after the mainland fell.

at Bursa, Nicomedia (Izmit) and Nicea. Leadership subsequently passed to his son, Osman I, the eponymous founder of a dynasty – the Osmanli, better known in the West as the Ottomans – that was to endure for 600 years.

Towards the end of the 14th century, Asia Minor and the Balkans had fallen to the Ottoman Turks, and by 1400 the Byzantine Empire had shrunk to just Constantinople, Thessaloníki and the Peloponnese. In April 1453 Mehmet II ("the Conqueror") besieged Constantinople and took it

Crusades – although in the 14th century the Palaeologi re-established a Byzantine presence at Mystrás. One of the results of this political confusion was ethnically mixed populations.

A threat from the east

According to semi-legendary accounts, Estugrul, khan of the Kayi tribe of the Oguz Turks, fled from Persia in the mid-13th century to escape Genghis Khan's Mongol hordes. He was granted territory – if he could seize and hold it – in Bithynia, facing the Byzantine strongholds

within two months. Eight years later, the rest of the mainland had succumbed, too.

The fall of "The City" reverberated throughout Europe: with it had fallen the last descendants of the Roman Empire itself. Before long, Constantinople would again be the centre of a Mediterranean empire stretching from Vienna to the Caspian Sea and from the Persian Gulf to the Strait of Gibraltar – but now it would be as a Muslim city in the empire of the Ottomans. The great Greek Byzantine Empire had come to an end. Although in the West this seemed the inevitable result of Byzantine decline, to the Greeks it was a much more traumatic moment. They had passed from freedom into slavery. ❑

LEFT: 17th century iconostasis, Zákynthos Museum.
ABOVE: Mystrás on the Peloponnese.

OTTOMAN GREECE

Greek nationalism grew slowly as the Turkish Empire declined – until
in the 17th century a bloody struggle for independence was launched

The Ottoman Turks who now controlled the Balkans were the latest in a stream of nomadic tribes who had moved westwards from central Asia. They were highly mobile, and their determination to pursue military conquests made up for their lack of numbers.

News of the fall of Constantinople was heard with horror in Europe, but as an isolated military action it did not have a critical effect on European security. To the Ottoman Empire, however, the capture of the imperial capital was of supreme symbolic importance. The sultan Mehmet II, a man of culture and learning as well as a superb warrior, regarded himself as the successor of the Byzantine emperors without a break in continuity. He made Constantinople the capital of the Ottoman Empire as it had been of the Byzantine Empire, and he set about rebuilding the city. The basilica of Agía Sófia was converted to a mosque, and Constantinople – which the Turks called Istanbul (from the Greek phrase *eis tin pólin*, "to the city") – replaced Baghdad as the centre of Sunni Islam.

But Constantinople also remained the ecclesiastical centre of the Greek church. The Ottomans' religious tolerance was reflected in the "millet" system of imperial government. The sultan recognised minority religions, and permitted each "millet", or religious community, a measure of self-government. Thus Mehmet II proclaimed himself the protector of the Greek Orthodox Church, and appointed a new patriarch after the custom of the Byzantine emperors. Patriarch Gennadius II Scholarius guaranteed loyalty and taxes to the Turks, in return for a degree of self-government for the Greeks. The church came to exert both religious and civil powers over Ottoman Greeks.

Under their new masters the Greeks lived in much the same way as they had done earlier. Their houses, like those of the Turks, tended to

be miniature fortresses, built on two floors around a central courtyard. The restored merchant's house in Kastoriá gives a good idea of the effect. Most elements of contemporary Greek cuisine were common then – from the *resináto* wine so distasteful to foreign travellers to the strong coffee which Ali Pasha, the "Lion

of Ioánnina", found helpful in poisoning his rival, the Pasha of Vallona.

Restricted rights

Although the Orthodox Greeks were allowed to conduct their religious affairs without too much interference from the Ottoman hierarchy, they nevertheless had to bear several impositions that did not apply to Muslims. Christians were not allowed to bear arms and were disqualified from military service. But in return they had to pay a special tax, the *haradj*.

In a court of law, a Muslim's word was always taken over that of a Christian, although disputes between Greeks were usually settled in

LEFT: Ali Pasha, tyrant of Ioánnina.
RIGHT: Ottoman inscription on a Muslim tomb in Ioánnina.

Greek-run courts. A Christian could not marry a Muslim, and Christians who adopted Islam then reverted to Christianity were invariably punished by death. These "neo-martyrs", however, helped to sustain the faith of the Ortho-dox populations under the Ottoman rule.

The most feared and loathed imposition on the Greeks was the janissary levy or *pedoma-zoma*: Christian families were required, at irregular intervals, to surrender a quota of their fittest and most intelligent male children to the

Ionian Islands, with the Venetians well entrenched, never succumbed to the Ottomans).

Lésvos, for example, fell to the Turks in 1462, but it was not until the conquest of Híos in 1566 that all the islands of the northeast Aegean were under Ottoman control. Similarly, the Dode-canese, with its motley popula-tion of Greeks, pirates and Italian adventurers, held out until 1521, when the Knights of St John on Rhodes finally yielded to a Turkish force num-bering over 100,000, after a siege lasting five

Ottomans. These were forcibly converted to Islam and trained to serve as imperial troops (janissaries) or civil servants. Some of those conscripted rose to high office and were some-times able to help their relatives or home vil-lages, but the levy was deeply resented by Greeks. It was abandoned in the 17th century – largely because families deprived of their young men found it difficult to pay taxes.

A long-drawn-out conquest

Although the Turks had an undisputed hold on Constantinople/Istanbul after 1453, it took more than two centuries for them to establish control over all of Greece and its islands (indeed, the

months. With the fall of Rhodes, the security of the neighbouring islands was undermined, and by 1537 they had all been incorporated into the Ottoman Empire.

Crete took even longer to subdue. Since the early 13th century, the "Great Island" had been Venice's stronghold in the eastern Mediter-ranean, and its strategic value encouraged the Venetians to reinforce the major cities – Iráklio, Haniá and Réthymno – with solid fortresses that can still be seen today. An attack on an Ottoman convoy in 1645 provided the excuse for a Turkish assault on Crete. The Turks took Haniá after a bloody battle, then Réthymno, and soon had control over the whole island except the capital, Iráklio. It was not until 1669, after a gruelling 22-year siege, that the Turks took the city and finally ruled all of Crete.

Attempts at revolt

Powerful enemies continually threatened the Ottoman grip on Greece. The Venetians (and later the French) were thorns in the Ottoman flesh. Within the empire the Albanians, backbone of the Ottoman armies, often threatened to break loose. The resulting conflicts left Greece much weaker. In 1537, for instance, an Ottoman army carried off half the population of Corfu after an attack on the Venetian colony

similar fate befell the short-lived revolt launched by Dionysios Skylosofos in Epirus in 1611.

The Peloponnese was also caught in a bloody tug-of-war between Turks and their enemies. During the Russo-Turkish war of 1768–74, Greeks in the Máni region attempted to revolt against the Ottomans, with devastating results. Their uprising was initially supported by Alexis and Theodor Grigorievitch, members of the aristocratic Russian Orlof family, who brought their fleet to Greece in 1770, freed the cities of Kaláma, Mystrás and Kyparíssia and burned the Turkish fleet. But they soon abandoned the Greeks to the mercy of the Turks, whose

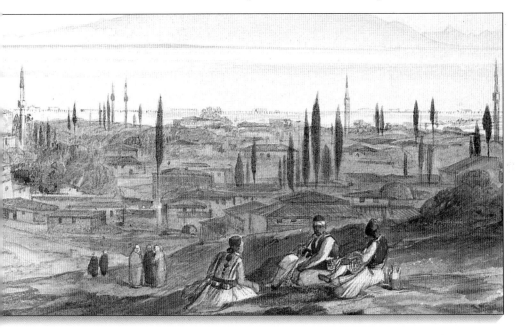

there, leaving the island with barely one-sixth of the numbers it had had in antiquity.

The expansionist ambitions of the Ottomans brought them into conflict with other European powers – which provided opportunities for Greeks to stage optimistic but vain uprisings against the empire. In the aftermath of the defeat inflicted on the Turkish navy by Don John of Austria in 1571, revolts broke out on the Greek mainland and the Aegean Islands, but were promptly crushed by the Ottomans. A

ABOVE: a water colour of Thessaloníki by the great traveller and artist Edward Lear, clearly showing the city's minarets.

reprisals took the form of terrible massacres. Many Greek families fled from the mainland to the nearby island of Kýthira.

Unruly bands

In truth, the Ottomans had never established total control over the Peloponnese. In the mountains, where the Ottoman grip had never been as firm as elsewhere, groups of brigands known as *klefts* had formed. They were bandits, equally likely to plunder a Greek village as a Muslim estate but, thanks to their attacks on Ottoman officials such as tax collectors, in folklore they came to symbolise the spirit of Greek resistance to the Ottoman authorities. They are certainly viewed in this light in the klefitic ballads that emerged, extolling the bravery and military prowess of the *klefts* and their heroic resistance to the Turkish oppressors.

In an effort to counter the depradations of the *klefts* and to control the mountain passes, the Ottomans etsablished a militia of *armatoli*. Like the *klefts*, these were Christians – and the distinction between *kleft* and *armatolos* was sometimes hard to define. However, the existence of these armed forces meant that, when the struggle for Greek independence broke out in the early 19th century, there was a reserve of military experience on hand.

trines that emanated from the French Revolution – and also discovered the reverence in which the language and culture of Ancient Greece were held throughout Europe. By the end of the 18th century, two ideas in particular, philhellenism and nationalism, had found a fertile ground among young educated Greeks.

The struggle for independence

In 1814 three Greek merchants in Odessa formed a secret organisation called "The Friendly Society" (*Filikí Etería*) devoted to "the betterment of the nation", which rapidly acquired a network of sympathisers throughout

Perhaps more important for the development of Greek nationalism was the growth of a Greek merchant community. Commercial links with Europe introduced wealthy Greeks to European lifestyles, and also to European cultural and political ideas. It was this mercantile middle class that supplied the material resources for the intellectual revival which characterised the late 18th century in Greece. They endowed schools and libraries, and sponsored higher education. Large numbers of schoolteachers, with the backing of merchant benefactors, studied in the universities of Europe, notably in Italy and Germany. There they encountered the heady nationalist doc-

the Ottoman lands. A number of vain attempts to secure themselves powerful backing were finally rewarded when their members organised an uprising against Ottoman rule in 1821.

Scattered violent incidents merged into a major revolt in the Peloponnese. With atrocities committed on both sides, the Turks found themselves outnumbered and were forced to retreat to their coastal fortresses. Further destruction came in the wake of the uprising. Greeks slaughtered Turks in Trípoli; Turks slaughtered the Greek inhabitants of Híos. Finally Egyptian troops, under Ibrahim Ali, laid waste most of the area.

The struggle for Greek independence, which lasted from 1821 to 1832, was not a straightforward affair. Opposing the Ottomans was a motley crew of *klefts*, *armatoli*, merchants, landowners and aristocratic families known as Phanariots – all as keen to further their own interests as to advance the cause of Greek nationalism. When they were not fighting the Turks they turned on each other.

Soon after the 1821 uprising, no fewer than three provisional Greek governments proclaimed themselves, each poised to take control of the liberated territories. A democratic constitution was drawn up in 1822, then revised in 1823, by which time the three local governments were unified in a central authority. But the

Russia, all initially unsympathetic to the Hellenic dream, came to put military and diplomatic pressure on the Turks to acknowledge Greek independence – a policy of "peaceful interference", as the British Prime Minister Lord Canning described it. The turning point came with the almost accidental destruction of the Ottoman fleet by an allied force at Navarino in 1827.

This intervention by the Great Powers ensured that some form of independent Greece came into being, although its precise borders took some years to negotiate.

Count Ioannis Kapodistrias, a Greek diplomat formerly in the service of the Russian tsar, was

following year feuding between rival groups culminated in outright civil war (prompting one chieftain, Makrygiannis, to protest that he had not taken up arms against the Turks to end up fighting Greeks).

Ironically, the belief that this was a national struggle was held with greatest conviction by the foreign philhellenes – Lord Byron among them – who came to help the Greeks. These men were influential in getting Western public opinion behind Greece. Thus Britain, France and

elected the first president of independent Greece by a National Assembly in 1827. He encouraged Greek forces to push north of the Peloponnese, and his efforts were rewarded when the 1829 Conference of London fixed the new state's northern boundary on the Árta-Vólos line. But numerous Greeks were dissatisfied with his administration and suspected him of aiming at one-man rule.

In 1831 he was shot by two chieftains of the Máni as he went into a church at Návplio. While Britain, France and Russia tried to find a suitable candidate to lead the new country, Greece tumbled into a period of bloody anarchy and civil war. ❏

LEFT: Ermoúpoli on Sýros.
ABOVE: Ioannis Kapodistrias, who some feared was aiming for dictatorship, was assassinated.

INDEPENDENT GREECE

Independence did not guarantee peace and stability: civil war, enemy occupation and a military junta have all marked the path to today's democracy

The new state was desperately poor, over-run by armed bands of brigands and beset by quarrelling political factions. In 1834 a rebellion in the Máni resulted in government troops being defeated and sent home without their equipment. There were few good harbours or roads. Athens remained a poor, dusty, provincial town. Internally, conditions were worse than they had been under Ottoman rule.

Bavarian absolutism was partly to blame. On Kapodistrias's death the crown of the new king-dom was given to Otto, the son of Ludwig I of Bavaria, who arrived at Návplio in 1833 on a British man-of-war. Since he was under age, a regency was established.

Widespread calls for a constitution were ignored until, in 1843, a bloodless coup in Athens forced Otto to dismiss the last of his Bavarian advisers and accept the idea of con-stitutional rule and parliamentary government for Greece. Despite a poor economy, the 1844 and later the 1864 constitutions endowed the country with the trappings of a democratic state.

The "Great Idea"

The new kingdom contained less than one-third of the Greeks in the Near East. The prospect of "liberating" the Greeks still under Ottoman rule, of creating a new Byzantium by recaptur-ing Constantinople and avenging the humilia-tion of 1453 was known as the "Great Idea" and aroused enormous enthusiasm. This had roots embedded in the soil of a fervent nation-alism. When King George I succeeded the ousted King Otto in 1863 he characteristically assumed the title of "King of the Hellenes" rather than simply "King of Greece". But the Great Idea was never a realistic policy since, without allies, the Greek army was no match for the Ottomans; yet it survived repeated humiliations such as the defeat of 1897. Only after the catastrophic defeat of 1922 at the

hands of the Turkish nationalists did the vision of the "Great Idea" collapse.

The most prominent populist of the late 19th century, Theodoros Deligiannis, encouraged foolhardy irredentist expeditions to Thessaly and Crete. His more far-sighted rival, Harilaos Trikoupis, realised that such a policy was

unwise so long as Greece was dependent on foreign loans, which gave its creditors the whip hand over any foreign policy initiatives. Trik-oupis set out to reduce this dependency by boosting economic activity. Roads were improved, railways constructed and the Corinth Canal dug. Piraeus expanded to become one of the Mediterranean's busiest ports.

But despite the appearance of a few textile and food-processing factories, industrial activ-ity remained minimal right up to World War I. Greece was a rural nation, a country of peasant smallholders. The lack of large estates may have ironed out social inequalities but it also meant that most farmers remained miserably

---

LEFT: a former partisan with a photograph of himself when he was 18.

RIGHT: a naive depiction of Elevtherios Venizelos.

too poor to adopt modern farming methods. The export of currants brought prosperity for a while, but a world slump in 1893 hit the entire economy. Greece became bankrupt, and hunger drove many peasants to emigrate.

A new government

Such domestic problems only increased Greek enthusiasm for the Great Idea. Further territory had been acquired in 1881, without any fighting, as a by-product of the Congress of Berlin. When troubles on Ottoman Crete in 1897

OVERSEAS AID

In the early 20th century, many Greek villages depended heavily on money sent home by young men who had emigrated, particularly to the United States.

provoked a wave of sympathy on the mainland, Greek naval forces were sent to the island while the army marched northwards – only to be checked by Ottoman forces in what turned into a humiliating defeat.

On Crete and in Macedonia, Ottoman rule was crumbling. But the emergence of the new Balkan nations – Bulgaria and Serbia – added a new complication for Greek foreign policy, for both countries shared Greece's aspiration for territory in Macedonia.

A precedent for military intervention in politics had been set with the army's support for the adoption of a constitution in 1843. In 1909 junior army officers staged a revolt against the political establishment and invited a new politician with a radical reputation, Elevtherios Venizelos, to come over to the mainland from Crete and form a government. A consummate diplomat, Venizelos channelled the untapped energies of the Greek middle class into his own Liberal Party, which was to remain a dominant force in politics for the next 25 years.

A decade of wars

When the Balkan Wars erupted in 1912, Greece was strong enough to wrest southern Macedonia from the Ottoman forces and then to defend its gains, in alliance with Serbia, from a hostile Bulgaria. The full gains from the fighting included – in addition to Macedonia – Epirus, Crete and the east Aegean Islands. Greece's area and population were nearly doubled at a stroke.

There was barely time to consider what burdens the new territories would impose before the country was embroiled in World War I. Venizelos and the new king, Constantine, quarrelled over whether to bring Greece into the conflict. The prime minister wanted Greece to give the Entente active support, while Constantine insisted on keeping the country neutral. The quarrel raised a number of vital issues: who had the final say over foreign policy – the king or parliament? The dispute reached the point of open civil war, ending only in 1917 with Constantine being forced to leave the country and Greece entering the war on the side of the Entente.

Venizelos had hoped that the Entente powers would reward Greece for its support with new territories. The annexation by Greece of Smyrna (Izmir), with its rich hinterland and large ethnic Greek population, had long been a basic tenet of the Great Idea. When in May 1919 the British, French and Americans sanctioned the landing of Greek troops in Smyrna, it began to look as though the dream might at last be realised. It was not to be.

The Asia Minor Disaster

In 1920 the pendulum of Greek political sentiment swung back, removing Venizelos from office and returning King Constantine from exile. Army morale was damaged by politically-motivated changes in command, but the revival of Turkish national fervour sparked by the Greek advance and galvanised by the emerging Turkish leader, Mustafa Kemal (subsequently Atatürk), was even more dangerous to Greek interests. The Greek military forces advanced to within 80 km (50 miles) of Ankara in June 1921, but were hampered by the European allies changing to a "neutralist" position and refusing to sell the Greeks arms. Kemal stopped the Greek advance and gradually forced the Greek army back behind long defensive lines ever closer to the coast. After a year-long stalemate, Kemal broke through the Greek

tion, a massive population transfer was agreed upon: 380,000 Muslim inhabitants of Greece moved to Turkey in exchange for 1.1 million Orthodox Greeks. But for a dwindling population in Istanbul and in the islands of Imbros and Tenedos, this exchange ended a 2,500-year Greek presence in Asia Minor. The Greeks refer to these events as "the Asia Minor Disaster", and they remain a defining factor in the Greek perception of both themselves and of the Turks.

The interwar years

Buffeted and impoverished by 10 years of war, the Greek nation now faced the huge problem

lines in late August 1922; the Greek army abandoned Smyrna a few days later. The Turkish army entered the city on 9 September and ran amok, burning both the Armenian and Greek quarters and killing an estimated 30,000 of the Christian inhabitants in the process.

The 1923 treaty of Lausanne, which finally ended the war between the two countries, fixed the boundaries which hold today (with the exception of the Dodecanese islands, held by the Italians until after World War II). In addi-

of absorbing these indigent newcomers into a country that had difficulty in sustaining its existing population. The economy benefited from the cheap labour, and it was in the interwar period that Greece began to become industrialised. But the refugees also increased social tensions. Over half a million of them settled in urban areas – often in squalid shanty towns outside the large cities – to search for jobs.

After the disaster of 1922, King Constantine was forced to leave Greece a second time, and a parliamentary republic was established. It lasted only 12 years and was characterised by political instability and military intervention, including two attempted coups d'état. Governments

LEFT: the notorious Dillesi gang who terrorised northern Greece.
ABOVE: victorious troops returning from Bulgaria.

routinely altered the electoral system in an attempt to keep themselves in power. The only period of stability – Venizelos's years in power from 1928 to 1932 – was terminated by the shock of international economic depression. In 1933 the Liberals were succeeded by the royalist People's Party, whose leaders only half-heartedly supported the republic. Apart from the constitutional issue, little separated the parties.

Return of the monarchy

The feuding of the politicians rendered parliamentary government vulnerable to military pressure. In 1935 this led to the restoration of the king, now George II, Constantine's son. In 1936 the king offered the premiership to an extreme right-wing politician, Ioannis Metaxas, a former senior army officer and a fervent royalist. Soon afterwards, Metaxas responded to a wave of strikes by declaring martial law and abolishing parliament. But the "First Peasant" (as Metaxas styled himself) never managed to establish firm foundations for his so-called "Third Hellenic Civilisation". Despite imitating some of the characteristics of fascist regimes, he remained attached to Britain as Greece's traditional patron in foreign affairs. Germany's increasing dominance in the Balkans

DICTATORSHIP IN ACTION

Italy occupied Rhodes and the Dodecanese from 1912 to 1943. During the years of Mussolini's rule, the islanders lived under the farcical prohibitions of a totalitarian regime intent on "Italianising" the islands. An extensive secret police network guarded against nationalist activity; the practice of orthodox religion was outlawed; the blue and white colours of the Greek flag were prohibited in public; all shop signs had to be painted in Italian, and slogans such as "*Viva il Duce, viva la nuova Italia imperiale!*" were daubed on the walls of recalcitrant shopkeepers. In the 1930s many islanders emigrated to the Greek mainland, to Egypt and to Australia.

had to be balanced against Britain's naval strength in the Mediterranean.

But Germany was not the only power with designs on the Balkans. In April 1939 Mussolini invaded Albania and in 1940 he tried to emulate Hitler's record of conquest by crossing the Albanian border into Greece. Metaxas could no longer hope to keep Greece neutral. Receiving the Italian ambassador in his dressing gown in the early hours of 28 October, he listened to a recital of trumped-up charges and responded to the ultimatum with a curt "This means war". *Óhi* or "No" Day is now a national holiday.

Fighting on their own in the mountains of Epirus, the Greek forces were remarkably successful and pushed the Makaronádes ("Spaghetti Eaters", as the Italians became known in later folk songs) back deep into Albania. But in the spring of 1941 Hitler sent German troops south to pacify the Balkans in preparation for his invasion of the Soviet Union.

Victory was swift: the German troops' invasion of Greece began on 6 April, and by the end of the month they had appointed General Tsolakoglou as a quisling prime minister.

Greece was occupied by German, Italian and Bulgarian forces. While the occupiers' hold over the countryside was often tenuous, it was firm in the towns, which suffered most from

Party but commanding a broad base of support. Other groups, drawing on the *kleft* tradition of mountain resistance, were also established, making forays down into the plains. Clashes between rival resistance groups were common.

The dominance of EAM meant that when the British first began to establish contact with resistance groups in 1942, they found that military considerations collided with political ones. EAM, with over 1 million supporters, was well placed to pin down the German troops. The British, suspecting that EAM intended to set up a communist state in Greece after the war, armed other groups to act as a counterweight.

the shortage of food, notably in the terrible famine of the winter of 1941–2. It was also from the towns that the Germans deported and exterminated Greece's long-established Jewish communities. King George and the legal government had left the country in 1941 and passed the war under British protection.

Yet in the hills, organised resistance began to emerge. One of the earliest, and certainly much the largest, of these groups was known as the National Liberation Front (the Greek initials of which are EAM), organised by the Communist

EAM, for its part, was concerned that Churchill wished to restore the monarchy without consulting the Greek people. In fact, Churchill had little sympathy for the guerrillas, whom he described as "miserable banditti".

In the autumn of 1944, the German forces retreated, to be replaced by Greek and British troops. In December 1944 bitter fighting erupted in Athens between communist-led resistance fighters and British troops. Inflation continued to soar, the black market flourished and violence spread through the country as old wartime scores were settled.

The fighting in December 1944 marked a decisive turning point in the slide towards the

LEFT: German officers on top of the Acropolis, Athens.
ABOVE: British troops liberate Athens in 1944.

civil war that subsequently broke out between the national government and communist insurgents and that raged from the autumn of 1946 into the summer of 1949. It was in these troubled circumstances that King George returned to Greece in September 1946 following a bitterly disputed plebiscite.

Into the Cold War

Greece in the late 1940s was a key battleground in the developing Cold War. In March 1947 the United States took over from Britain the role of Greece's principal external patron. American propaganda in the form of military

Greece looks West

Democracy had weathered the civil war – but only just. In the following decade a certain stability seemed to have been achieved, with only two prime ministers, both conservatives, in power between 1952 and 1963. Yet this stability was precarious, relying as it did on the restriction of civil liberties.

Greece had joined NATO in 1951, and the pro-Western orientation of its foreign policy secured financial support from the United States. However, the relationship was not straightforward: when the Cyprus dispute flared up in 1954 Greece refused to take part in NATO

and economic aid flooded in, and this was instrumental in enabling the national government, which at times had been very hard-pressed, to defeat the rebel communist army in the mountains of northwest Greece in October 1949. But the victory involved considerable human rights abuses, the rounding up of suspected left-wing sympathisers and the forcible evacuation of entire villages.

The violation of civil rights and the emergence of a powerful security apparatus did not come to an end in 1950. Politics continued to be polarised, although the old pre-war split between royalists and republicans had given way to one between the far Left and the royalist Right.

manoeuvres. This foreshadowed the problems later governments would have in defining Greece's role in Europe. Nonetheless, the Cyprus issue was resolved – for a time – when the island was established as an independent republic in 1960.

A troublesome "miracle"

In the 1950s and 1960s, Greece, like Italy and Spain, experienced an "economic miracle" which transformed the country. Electric power became widespread and communications improved. Athens mushroomed, becoming a chaotic concrete sprawl, until it contained more than one-third of the country's entire population.

Old forms of political control, which had operated best in the small rural communities, began to erode. A new urban middle class arose which regarded the conservative political elite as rooted in the rhetoric of the Cold War and lacking a vision of Greece as a modern state.

The 1961 elections saw the resurgence of the political centre under the leadership of a former Liberal, Georgios Papandreou. It was a bitter contest. When the results were announced in Konstantinos Karamanlis's favour, Papandreou alleged that they were fraudulent.

Public disquiet at possible links between the ruling party and extreme right-wing violence increased in May 1963 when a left-wing deputy, Georgios Lambrakis, was assassinated at a peace rally in Thessaloníki. Shortly afterwards Karamanlis resigned and in the elections that followed Papandreou's Centre Union Party won power, the first centrist ruling party in Greece for over a decade. However, with conservative politicians prepared to surrender power, an extended period of centrist rule now seemed possible, although extreme right-wingers in the military saw the new government as a threat.

Royal interference

When Papandreou demanded a reshuffle of senior army officers he found himself opposed by his defence minister and the young king, Constantine II. The king tried clumsily to bring down the Centre Union Government, but when Papandreou agreed with the main conservative opposition to hold elections in May 1967, Constantine was faced with the prospect of a further Centre Union victory.

However, schemes hatched between the king and senior army officers for military intervention were dramatically pre-empted when a group of junior army officers, working according to a NATO contingency plan, executed a swift coup d'état early on the morning of 21 April 1967. Martial law was proclaimed; all political parties were dissolved. The Colonels were in power.

The rule of the Colonels

The junta was motivated by a mixture of self-interest, anti-communism and ultra-nationalism.

LEFT: women fought with the Resistance during the civil war.
RIGHT: an anti-dictatorship poster.

This combination was certainly not new: on a number of occasions in the inter-war period army officers had used the rhetoric of national salvation to head off a possible purge in which they feared they might lose their jobs. In their policies and attitudes, too, the Colonels drew on earlier traditions. They claimed that they wanted the country to "radiate civilisation in all directions" by establishing a "Greece of the Christian Greeks" which would make it once again "a pole of ideological and spiritual attraction". This was the old dream: an escape from the modern world into a fantastic fusion of classical Athens and Byzantium.

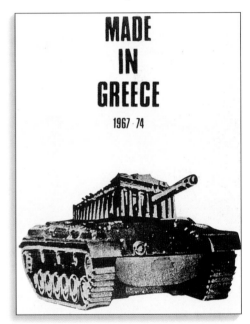

MADE
IN
GREECE
1967-74

A TOTALITARIAN APPROACH

With their peasant or lower-middle-class backgrounds, the Colonels symbolised a provincial reaction to the new world of urban consumers brought about by Greece's so-called economic "miracle" of the 1950s and 1960s. They constantly stressed the need for a return to traditional morality and religion, and set about this with a fanatical attention to detail. Not only did they close the frontiers to bearded, long-haired or mini-skirted foreigners (or at least they did until the tourist trade was hit), they also prevented Greeks from reading "subversive" literature – Greco-Bulgarian dictionaries included. This grim period of Greek history was marked by torture and deportations.

The first signs of widespread discontent coincided with the economic downturn of 1973. The leaders of the protest were students, whose occupations of university buildings in March and November were brutally broken up. Increasingly the regime was proving incapable of dealing with the ordinary problems of government. In the bloody aftermath of the November student sit-in at Athens Polytechnic, Colonel Papadopoulos, the regime's figurehead, was replaced by an even more sinister figure, Dimitrios Ioannides, who had previously been the commander of the military police.

In the end, it was the Cyprus problem that toppled the junta. A foolhardy Greek nationalist coup, prompted by Athens, against the Cypriot president Archbishop Makarios, led the Turks to invade northern Cyprus. Ioannides ordered Greek forces to retaliate, but the mobilisation had been so chaotic that local commanders refused to obey his orders. On 24 July 1974 the former premier, Karamanlis, made a triumphant return from exile in Paris to Athens to supervise the restoration of parliamentary democracy.

Karamanlis's "New Democracy"

The transition to democracy proceeded remarkably smoothly considering the enormous prob-

lems that Karamanlis faced. Aware of his own vulnerability, he moved slowly in dismissing collaborators of the regime. At the elections held in November 1974, Karamanlis's New Democracy (Néa Dimokratía or ND) party won an overwhelming victory, though many people seemed to have voted for Karamanlis simply as a guarantor of stability.

Karamanlis himself was well placed to make any necessary political reforms, since a referendum the month after the elections produced a decisive vote for the abolition of the monarchy, compromised by the king's actions before and during the junta. In its place Karamanlis created a presidency with sweeping powers. It was widely believed that in the event of a swing to the Left, Karamanlis would resign his parliamentary seat and become president.

A move to the Left

Signs of such a swing were evident after the 1977 elections in which Andreas Papandreou's Panhellenic Socialist Movement (PASOK) made large gains. The younger Papandreou, Georgios's son, represented a new post-war generation – at home with the "miracle" and its fruits. With his background as a professor of economics in the US, he was well placed to lead a party of technocrats. At this time he still had a reputation as a radical and he vehemently attacked Karamanlis's policies, taking a more belligerent stand over relations with Turkey, and threatening that a PASOK government would take Greece out of both NATO and the EEC, subject to a referendum. Support for PASOK grew, until in 1980 Karamanlis resigned as prime minister and was voted in as president by parliament.

Papandréou and PASOK

After PASOK's victory in the October 1981 elections, based on a simple campaign slogan of *Allagí* ("Change"), Papandreou took office, forming Greece's first socialist government. His significance lies not in his socialism, which was mainly at the level of rhetoric, but in his remarkable success in articulating populist leftist views.

PASOK rhetoric carried the party until the elections of 1989, when accumulated financial and domestic scandals returned the New Democracy party to power. This proved to be only a short interruption, for PASOK won the next elections, in October 1993, returning Andreas Papandreou to power until ill health forced him to leave office two years later. PASOK chose as his successor an uncharismatic pragmatist, Kostas Simitis.

There was a marked contrast with the flamboyant style of his predecessor. As prime minister, his task was been to oblige a population long accustomed to government largesse to accept economic reality. Particularly after Andreas Papandreou's death in June 1996, the government followed a tight economic policy to keep inflation down so as to allow Greece to meet the conditions for joining the European Monetary Union (EMU). This was not easy, since many PASOK deputies, not to mention labour unions, were unhappy with the apparent abandonment of their avowed socialist ideals.

Macedonia and Turkey

In foreign affairs, by the end of the 1990s Greece was reconciled to the existence of an independent Macedonian state on her northern border, although agreement had still to be reached on the name of the new state. Traditionally poor relations with Turkey took a marked turn for the better in 1999 when there was an upsurge of public sympathy in each country for the other when both were afflicted by earthquakes. But although "earthquake diplomacy" proved strong on the rhetoric of friendship, there was little sign of a resolution of the major problems dividing the two countries.

On the domestic front, the election of 2000 was closely fought, with Simitis securing a very narrow victory over Kostas Karamanlis's ND party. Simitis continued with the austerity measures aimed at controlling public expenditure and curbing inflation. These enabled Greece to join the euro-zone in 2001 and it adopted the euro on 1 January 2002 – a move that entailed the abandonment of Europe's oldest currency, the drachma.

The visit of Pope John Paul II to Athens in May 2002 demonstrated how long historical memories were in Greece when the Pope formally apologised for the wrong doings of Western Christendom and notably for the sack of Constantinople following the diversion of the Fourth Crusade in 1204.

LEFT AND RIGHT: "Mimi" and Andreas Papandreou: his second marriage in 1989 to the flamboyant former Olympic Airways hostess caused much controversy and amusement in Greece.

Simitis called snap elections in early 2004, and then promptly resigned, leaving his urbane foreign minister, George Papandreou (son of Andreas), as the PASOK candidate for prime minister. The elections were won by ND under Kostas Karamanlis (the nephew of Konstantinos). He appointed himself culture minister as well as premier in an attempt to push forward the overdue Olympic infrastructure projects.

The 17 November group

In the summer of 2002 there was a major breakthrough in the effort to split up the "17 November" left-wing terrorist group that for almost 30

years had operated with seeming impunity (killing 23 people in all). The apparent liquidation of "17 November" lifted the threat of domestic terrorist violence during the 2004 Olympic Games in Athens.

In connection with the Olympics a number of major projects began to change the face of the city, notably the construction of a metro system and of a new international airport. Another such project was the building of a new museum facing the Acropolis. This includes a gallery that will remain empty until the marble sculptures taken from the Parthenon in the early 19th century and presently housed in the British Museum in London, are returned to Greece. ❏

MODERN GREECE

In many ways, Greece has become a modern European country. But there
are other facets of the national character that have not changed in centuries

I
s the phrase "modern Greece" an oxymoron?
A Greek might well pose this question to
Western visitors, given the history of the past
200 years: to claim a place among the Western
European family of nations, Greeks have been
obliged to prove themselves more like their
2,500-year-old forebears than their peasant
anxious young women. The former stigma of
appearing underfed has been so eradicated that
some Greek-American women now dread summer holidays in Greece because they are perceived as "fat" by their Greek cousins. And
Westernisation has crept into everyday practices, such as the replacement of traditional

grandparents. Which is perhaps to say that
notions of "modernity" are always in the eye
of the beholder, and that contemporary Greece,
like the rest of the world, is shot through with
contradictions.

The spread of Westernisation

Anyone who has been a regular visitor to
Greece over the past 30 years cannot help but
be aware of the rampant Westernisation of consumption patterns – not just in Athens but also
in the small villages. In a country that until
recently associated thinness with meanness, one
can now find ubiquitous beauty salons hawking
the latest dietary and depilation secrets to

Orthodox name-day celebrations with birthdays
(on name-days you don't receive gifts, you feed
your guests).

Striking changes are also manifest in national
politics, as political campaigns – the subject of
tremendous passion throughout the 1970s and
1980s – have taken on a much more ho-hum
tenor. As Greeks say, politics have moved from
the "balconies" of the political rallies and rous-
ing speeches of charismatic leaders such as
Andreas Papandreou and Kostas Mitsotakis, to
the "couches" of peoples' living rooms, where
politics now take place on television.

This is reflected in the leadership shift of
the socialist party PASOK (which ruled from

1981 through to 2004, discounting the short hiatus of 1989–93): from the populist and familiar Papandreou, known to all simply as "Andreas", to the technocratic and seemingly distant Kostas Simitis, whom one rarely hears referred to simply as "Kostas". Simitis's claim to fame was not any great socialist vision, but rather his successful navigation of the Greek economy into the European Monetary Union and the consumers' paradise that it initially promised.

HOME AND AWAY

The population of Greece is currently around 11 million, of whom over 3 million live in Athens. Thanks to a century of emigration, there are also around 6 million Greeks living overseas.

It is reflected similarly in popular reactions to the new currency, the euro – from everyday confessions ("I can understand using the euro to buy a toaster, but a sack of tomatoes?") to the public strike over the perceived price-fiddling connected with the transition to the euro in 2002 (a phenomenon not confined to Greece). This resulted in many people refusing to use the currency for several weeks, including bus drivers who reportedly let their passengers ride for free.

A strong national identity

Yet there is another side to contemporary Greece that stands firm against the tide of Westernisation and homogenisation. It is reflected in such events as the public protest over a proposed law in the mid-1990s which would have forced tavernas and bars to close at 2am rather than 4am. This was supposedly to increase worker efficiency. The widespread and continued outcry over this proposal eventually led to it being shelved.

LEFT: priests attending the Óhi Day celebrations (28 October) on Skópelos.
ABOVE: a bar at Vromólimnos on Skiáthos.

What's your village?

Another facet of contemporary Greece that stresses the local can also be found in the unusual relationship that exists between villages and the large urban centres of Athens and Thessaloníki. While certainly not free of the snobbery that urban dwellers commonly express for the "backwardness" of their rural cousins, most of Greece is somewhat unusual in having a comparatively short urban memory. There are few Athenians whose grandparents were born in the city. Thus, a Greek who answers the question "Where are you from?" with "Athens" will invariably be asked "Yes, but where is your village?"

What seems an unusual query for anyone from a city such as London, Paris or New York makes perfect sense to the Athenian. These rural loyalties are manifested in the enormous flows of people out of the cities for Easter, the Feast of the Assumption (August 15) and at election time, when many who have grown up in Athens still retain voting privileges in their family's village of birth. Many city-dwellers – a rapidly increasing proportion of the population – will wax lyrical about the virtues of the food, the air and the water in their village "homeland"; about an uncle's freshly-pressed olive oil, a grandmother's cheese, an aunt's fig or prickly pear tree.

into pensions, providing women with a source of economic control as well. This meant that despite a rhetoric of male power, women have often been able to control things from behind the scenes.

As one woman from the island of Kálymnos put it: "Women would make the pretence of consulting their husbands, but more often they would simply make decisions for the family in their husbands' absence. My mother sold the family house while my father was away fishing and then found ways to sugar-coat the news to him when he returned." This notion of female power is perhaps best captured by Lainie

The women's sphere

Perhaps nowhere are the paradoxes of contemporary Greece more evident than in shifting gender relations. Gender in Greece has always been more complicated than the stereotype of Mediterranean male dominance. Men have certainly dominated the public sphere of politics, but women have always dominated in their own public sphere of the church and religious life (this in spite of the all-male church leadership).

In many parts of Greece, particularly the Aegean Islands, dowry and house ownership have given women a source of control not available to their husbands. With the tourist boom, many of these houses have been turned

Kazan *My Big, Fat Greek Wedding* (filmed by Hollywood in 2002): "Yes the man is the head of the family, but the woman is the neck – she can turn him in any direction she wants."

Thus the many recent changes in Greek society have been nothing if not ambiguous in terms of gender relations. The early 1980s and the coming to power of the socialist government brought legal changes to improve women's position in relation to property ownership. And women have moved into national politics in increasing numbers. The two Greek communist parties have been led by women in recent years (Aleka Papariga and Maria Damanaki) and the two largest parties include women who are likely to contend for the leadership in the near future – Vaso Papandreo (no relation to Andreas), a leading PASOK politician, and the ND's Dora Bakogianni (daughter of Kostas Mitsotakis), who was elected Athens' first woman mayor in 2002. Women, however, remain under-represented in the Greek Parliament as a whole.

Loosened family bonds

While these changes in the public sphere have been substantial, in everyday life it might be more accurate to think of the most striking changes less in terms of a shift in power from

Women in the men's world

Indeed, the traditional Greek coffee shop, the *kafenĺon*, serving Greek coffee and ouzo to an all-male clientele, must now compete for space with the growing numbers of café-bars, serving cappuccino and other exotic drinks to a young, mixed-sex crowd. Ironically, recent times have seen the simultaneous growth of "traditional coffee shops", establishments that pride themselves on making Greek coffee the old-fashioned way, heated ever-so-slowly over a bed of hot sand.

In late-night bars it is no longer uncommon to see women engaged in dances that were once

men to women than as a shift from the older to the younger generation. As Greece has moved away from agriculture and other "traditional" occupations into a fully consumer-driven society, parents and other relatives no longer have the crucial technical knowledge that will determine their children's future work lives. Thus the control over the lives and future marriages of the younger generation has largely withered away. No longer can parents "keep their daughters locked up in their houses", as many claimed to do in the old days.

LEFT: a café on Mýkonos.
ABOVE: young Athenian women.

the sole preserve of the man, like *zeibékiko*, the swaying, eagle-like solo dance which had long been a particular expression of Greek male passion and pain. And the dowry, a source of economic security to an older generation of women, is shunned by the daughters of these women – who indeed do have increased economic opportunities – as an insult to ideas about romantic love.

While older Greeks tend to see a struggle for power between the sexes, many younger people embrace at least a discourse of "equality". What this will mean for the actual practice of sexual equality or inequality in Greece only time will tell.　　❑

PEOPLES AND IDENTITIES

The population of Greece is more diverse today than it has been for
centuries, but Greek character is still defined by ancient traditions

U ntil the early 1990s Greece could be considered unusual in the remarkable homogeneity of the ethnic and religious identifications of its population. This apparent homogeneity was itself a historically recent development – the preceeding Byzantine and Ottoman empires were remarkably multicultural by today's standards – and was due in large part to events such as the exchange of populations between Greece and Turkey in 1922 and the extermination of Greek Jews by the Nazis during World War II. This relative homogeneity has meant that Greek citizenship and "Greek" ethnicity have been seen as almost synonymous.

Post-war populations

In the post-war period, then, upwards of 97 percent of the population identified themselves by ethnicity as Greek and by religion as members of the Greek Orthodox Church. This still left room for some different identifications, including a sizeable Muslim minority in Thrace; a Slav/Macedonian identified minority in Greek Macedonia; small Vlach villages throughout mainland Greece; the Pomaks, a separate Muslim group which claims ancestry from the army of Alexander the Great; a small remainder of the Jewish population in Thessaloníki and Rhodes; Greek Catholics largely on the island of Tínos; Roma and Jehovah's Witnesses throughout the country.

There are also ethnically identified Greeks who distinguish themselves in terms of language or origins, including the Greeks from the Pontic region around the Black Sea, Asia Minor Greeks who were expelled in 1922, and Arvanites, those Greeks whose ancestors migrated to Greece in the Middle Ages and who speak a dialect of Albanian.

PRECEDING PAGES: a priest hawks his wares, Skýros.
LEFT: a quiet transaction on a Skyriot backstreet.
RIGHT: a young boy with a bunch of parsley
on Rhodes.

Asia Minor Greeks

An interesting case of borderline "ethnic" difference is the Greek refugees from Asia Minor who came to Greece in the Greek-Turkish population exchange of 1922. Although relatively indistinguishable from mainland Greeks in physical features, language and religion, the refugees,

most of whom settled around Piraeus, Athens and Thessaloníki, held on to a separate identity several generations after their uprooting.

So what set this group apart from mainland Greeks? They brought with them a shared heritage and historical experience distinctive from that of the rest of Greece, a cosmopolitan outlook, a strong political identity (many of the refugees joined the Greek Communist Party in the 1930s), and a distinctive tradition in food and music – indeed, the once underground, now popular musical form called *rebétika* traces its roots to the Asia Minor refugees.

Being under the Ottoman Empire for a century longer than the rest of Greece, they felt a particular tie to Byzantium and the legacy of Constantinople. Their experience of major cosmopolitan cities, particularly Smyrna and Istanbul (or Constantinople as they still refer to it), gave them a sense of multiculturalism and high culture which didn't exist to the same degree on the Greek mainland. Indeed, most Asia Minor refugees have largely positive memories of Greek-Turkish intercommunal relations, claiming that it was the machinations of politicians and the "Great Powers" which caused problems between them.

They also brought with them a sense of class superiority: many of the refugees from Asia Minor had been merchants, and felt themselves superior to, what they saw as, the "peasants" of mainland Greece, even if they no longer enjoyed such financial advantages. As refugees, most were not able to bring many material possessions with them to remind them of home, although religious icons were sewn into clothing and carried with them. These icons were henceforth closely guarded, and passed down to children and grandchildren.

New immigrants

Since the 1990s over a million people, nearly one-tenth of the population of the Greek state,

HOME FROM HOME

The refugees were not able to bring many possessions to Greece, but they did carry their memories with them, and often preserved their spatial maps of life in Asia Minor by renaming parts of their new Greek neighbourhoods or even whole towns (Néos Mamarmás, for example) after the places that they had known for so long. One man now in his twenties whose grandparents were refugees notes: "It's hard to forget about Asia Minor, they are always reminding us. My grandmother has made me promise to go back to her home village just to see it, and to bring back some water and some soil. Even if she is no longer alive she wants me to pour it on her grave."

have migrated to Greece, the vast majority from Albania and other former Eastern Block countries. Most of these people have come as economic migrants, and now work in the lowest-paid jobs in Greek society, as manual labourers or as domestic servants.

It has taken some considerable time for Greek society to adjust to this influx of new people, and stereotypes of Albanians as criminals have been prevalent. In 2001 a student of Albanian parents had the highest Grade Point Average out of the high schools in the town of Halkidikí, but was denied the honour, customary in these circumstances, of carrying the Greek flag during celebrations of

Greek Independence Day, thus provoking a minor political scandal.

However, things are beginning to change as many of these immigrants (those who can show that they have some remote Greek ancestry) have been given green cards and now pay taxes, receive at least the minimum wage and are integrated into the Greek education and healthcare system.

Food for thought

What does it mean to be Greek? The Greeks say: "Eat, in order to remember!" In this simple, Proustian injunction lies a whole social

world, can be such a focus of everyday life, conversation and memory.

So what makes Greek food Greek? No doubt a cookbook writer will speak of ingredients and preparations. But equally key is the context of eating, that food be shared among friends, neighbours, even strangers and fortunate tourists, that people dip their forks into collective bowls, with one man spearing a particularly juicy tomato or nicely done bit of fish and force-feeding it to his friend; that there be music and boisterous conversation. That one should always have a full plate: there is no clearer symbol of the good life in Greece.

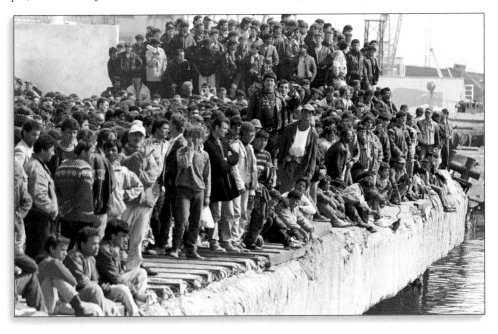

and moral philosophy. Indeed, if there is something that unites all the diverse regions, classes, rural and urban dwellers, ethnic groups and genders that make up modern Greece, it is perhaps best found in an attitude towards food as an embodiment of the good life, in which friends, family and community are all mixed in. It is striking to the outsider that Greek food, which has a certain simplicity of ingredients and combinations that does not rank it among the haute cuisines of the

LEFT: refugees in Thessaloníki after the exchange of populations in 1923.
ABOVE: recent Albanian refugees.

A cheese called *Féta*

Féta as a national symbol? The word *féta* means "slice", and it is certainly true that this pungent, delicately textured cheese has been embraced by tourists ever since they discovered slices of it sprinkled with olive oil complementing the motley flavours and colours of a Greek salad. *Féta's* origins in goat's and ewe's milk, advertised through its distinct odour, has often led it into the realm of stereotype of rural life. But in the mid-1990s, in the wake of challenges by Denmark to the EU calling for the right to produce a cheese called "Feta", this humble staple took on new national significance in Greece. In this case it was the whiteness of *féta* produced from ewe's milk, compared to what Greeks claimed was the yellower Danish Feta produced predominantly from cow's milk, which seemed to stand for the purity of Greek *féta* – a tasty reflection of the whiteness of those eternal symbols of Greekness themselves, the Parthenon Marbles!

But if *féta* seems simple from the outside, that is not the experience of the Greeks themselves who find endless fodder for conversational elaboration in the fine distinctions of taste, smell, texture and provenance between different types of tomato, olive oil, fig, even salt. In talking about food Greeks are not

wallowing in the mundane, but rather recognising the key role that it plays in creating social/family relations.

Eating with the dead

Kóllivo (plural: *kólliva*), made from boiled, sugared winter wheat kernels, is the food that the living offer in memory of the dead, or that the dead offer as part of their ongoing participation in the community of the Greek Orthodox faithful.

Kóllivo features as the food prepared for All Souls' Day, when the dead are collectively remembered. Women prepare wheat berries with a variety of other ingredients, which may

include pomegranate seeds, sesame seeds, almonds, walnuts, Jordan Almonds, parsley, breadcrumbs, currants and raisins.

Angeliki (the Greek form of Angela), a woman in her sixties from the island of Kálymnos, prefers almonds, currants and pistachios, formed into the shape of a carnation. She covers the dish with powdered sugar and silver-coloured decorative sweets, laid out in the form of a cross, or sometimes in the shape of flowers.

When preparing the wheat, the entire family must gather and sprinkle a handful of wheat into a plate in the shape of a cross, asking God to forgive the deceased. Once the *kóllivo* is prepared, the female head-of-house takes it to the church to be blessed. After the service, the priest reads each family's list of the names of dead relatives who they wish to be remembered. "It does good for our souls to remember them," says Angeliki. With the church service finished, Angeliki and her neighbours and friends retrieve their lists and decorated plates and, on the steps of the church, feed spoonfuls of *kóllivo* to each other, in a true moment of reciprocity and shared memory.

Any *kólliva* left over from this communal, commensal act is offered by Angeliki to passers-by, even tourists, as she makes her way home. But the obligation to share the food extends even beyond the community of family, neighbours and other visitors to Kálymnos, as Angeliki leaves out a plate of *kóllivo* that evening, with the door open, so that the dead can also come and partake. *Kóllivo* is community.

Honouring the departed

Kóllivo plays a key role not just in these collective rituals of eating with/remembering the dead, but in the regular memorial ceremonies that must be held for each dead person three, nine and 40 days after death, and then three, six and nine months after, and finally every year on the anniversary of the person's death. These memorials begin in church with a liturgy in honour of the dead, and are followed by a reception, sometimes in the church courtyard, sometimes in a nearby reception hall, or, more intimately, in people's homes. Coffee and a variety of baked goods are served, but *kóllivo* is the centrepiece of these memorials. A photograph of the deceased is often placed near the plate of *kóllivo*, as if he or she were offering it to the assembled mourners. This reflects the fact that the living are not only offering *kóllivo* to the dead, but on behalf of the dead; in other words, the soul of the dead person will be lightened of its sins by these acts of generosity on their behalf.

The custom of preparing *kóllivo* is no recently invented tradition, but has a long history, resembling practices carried out in Ancient Athens of *panspermies* – offerings of boiled grains to the dead or to Hermes, the god who guided the dead down to the underworld. The use of pomegranate is another link to the Ancient Greek symbolism of death.

sonal rhythms of life for many a Greek rural and urban dweller. As in many aspects of Greek religion, women are the caretakers of the observance, coaxing husbands, children and other family members to stick with the fast. If they prove unable to keep it up, the women will at least fast in their place during the 40 days of Lent that culminate in the Easter feast and other fasts throughout the year.

If you attend a Greek liturgy you will notice the predominance of women and children inside the church. Men, when they come to church, tend to sit outside and talk with their friends. It is not that Greek men are not reli-

In the Christian tradition (the practice was canonised by the patriarch of Alexandria in the 17th century) the symbolism is clearly one of death and rebirth, as the grain or seed which falls to the ground must rot before it gives forth new life.

Food and faith

Food plays an important role in another key aspect of Greek identity, the Orthodox religion, most notably in the cycle of fasting and feasting throughout the year that sets the daily and sea-

gious, but they do tend to have a long-standing distrust of priests and of women's spaces – some even refer to the church as the woman's coffee shop. Absence from church is further mitigated for men by the fact that women bring blessed bread, incense, basil and other items associated with the church, back to the home with them.

Women also prepare the appropriate foods for the different saints' days celebrations, which function like birthdays in Greece. This religious devotion gives women a particular power within the family. As one woman noted when her husband half-jokingly threatened to leave her and move back to his village for some

LEFT: Kyria Labroula from Fársa, Kefalloniá.
ABOVE: a name-day celebration.

peace and quiet, "If you leave, you won't have anyone to light a candle for you in church. If you leave, who will tend to your soul then?"

Name days

The great majority of Greeks are named after Orthodox saints, according to a system in which parents name children typically after the children's grandparents. A special bond tends to exist between a child and their eponymous grandparent, and in some cases that child will be favoured in property inheritance from that grandparent. Exceptions to this pattern include naming a child after a

throwing a party, but rather opening one's house to family and neighbours who wish to come by and give you their good wishes, while you provide them with sweets and coffee. Name days thus have a collective aspect absent in birthdays, tying individual Greeks to their community, to grandparents and ancestors who have shared that name, and to the history of Greek Orthodoxy.

A relatively common act of religious devotion in Greece is to build a chapel for one's saint (or for a miracle-working saint) and to hold liturgies in the saint's honour. Saints are protectors and intercessors between humans

recently deceased relative, after a protector saint (especially if the pregnancy or birth is difficult) or after an Ancient Greek name. But this basic pattern ensures that there are relatively few names circulating through the system at any one time.

Traditionally, Greeks did not celebrate on their birthdays (birthdays for children is a recent Western importation), but rather on a day associated with the saint after whom they are named. Thus everyone named Katerina will celebrate on the name day of Agía Katerína, a day associated with her life or martyrdom (25 November). Name-day celebrations do not involve receiving presents or

and God and are seen as responding to people's prayers if they show proper devotion.

Ritual as sensory experience

Orthodox ritual stimulates the senses. Entering a church or chapel in Greece can often be an overpowering sensory experience. From the scents of myrrh and frankincense which are spread by priests, swinging censers rhythmically back and forth, to the flicker of candles which each person lights and places in front of the icon when entering the church, or again to the reverberating nasal pitch of the liturgy being sung by the cantors (often projected via loudspeaker throughout the town or village). And of course there is the multicoloured sight of the icons, illustrating key stories from the Bible, and the taste of communion bread and wine mixed to the consistency of gruel and presented by the priest on a spoon. This sensory aspect of Greek Orthodoxy is part of official doctrine as well, an expression of the notion of the "deification of matter", the idea that humans manifest the spiritual not in opposition to the material but in and through the material world.

Localism and homeland

What Greece may have, until recently, lacked in ethnic diversity, it made up for in the multitude

become topics of lengthy discussion. Such localism should not be surprising given that in Greek the word "homeland" (*patrída*) is used to refer equally to one's country as to one's village of birth. Hence the condition of *xenitiá*, or "longing for homeland", experienced by many in the far-flung Greek diaspora is inherently ambiguous: is one primarily nostalgic for the sight of the Parthenon or for the view across the sheepfold?

Explosive Easter

Local differences come in many colours, from the typical colours used for housepainting, to

of claims to regional diversity. Local loyalties run high in Greece, as residents of villages, towns and cities are eager to discuss the myriad differences in manners and customs of their nearby neighbours. Often this may lead to hyperbole: "The Kalymniots are all crazy!" insisted a taxi driver on the neighbouring island of Kós. "The Koans are all lazy", a Kalymniot shoots back. But often it is a matter of more friendly rivalries, as differences in traditional costumes, wedding rituals, or whether Easter lamb is prepared on a spit or in a clay oven

LEFT: a clerical gathering on the holy island of Pátmos.
ABOVE: the *epitávios*, or Easter bier of Christ.

the different dialects – such as Cretan, where the sound "k" is replaced by an Italianesque "ch" – to the matrilineal inheritance patterns that characterise many of the Aegean Islands. On the island of Kálymnos difference takes the form of a sonic assault every Easter.

In most of Greece, Easter is celebrated with the setting off of fireworks, an index and an icon of the heavenly activity that Easter commemorates. On Kálymnos fireworks are replaced by dynamite – several thousand euros' worth, formed into projectiles and hurled from the courtyards of churches, from the two mountains that surround the harbour town, or in a "friendly" exchange across neighbouring back yards. No mere firecracker display can quite compare to the sound of dynamite going off around you, and Kálymnos's Easter celebrations have been known to both attract some stouthearted tourists and to send others scurrying for the next boat out.

The practice of dynamite-throwing from the island's mountains can be traced back to the Italian occupation of the Dodecanese in the early 20th century. Legend has it that one Easter, Kalymniots set off dynamite from one mountain and, while the Italian authorities were hurrying to investigate, then set off charges on the opposite mountain. As one

man put it, it was a way of saying "We're alive" to the colonisers. Why has this "tradition" persisted, with the Italian Occupation now a distant memory? Perhaps as a reminder, not only to neighbouring Turks but to Athenians and other Greeks, that Kálymnos is not to be trifled with.

Hospitality and "the Gift"

One aspect of localism that tourists may find themselves on the receiving end of is local claims to being more "hospitable" (*filóxeni*) than their neighbours. "Neighbours" is a relative term: people will claim that Southern Europeans are more *filóxeni* than Northern Europeans, Greeks more than Italians, their town or village more than Athenians, and they themselves more than the person across the street. Greeks often buy in bulk – 20 kg of cheese, 150 kg of watermelon – in order to always have food on hand to offer guests, invited and uninvited alike.

Generosity and honour

If you think you detect a competitive nature to hospitality in Greece you are not far off the mark, as generosity is closely tied to Greek notions of honour. Acts of generosity are part of building one's reputation. They also, in typical fashion noted by anthropologists, make claims to the higher status of the giver than the receiver.

This often has a faint feel of role reversal in cases where the receiver of hospitality comes from a Northern European country or the United States: Greeks are well aware that their country's voice is in danger of being ignored in international contexts, and so by being generous they are in a sense also subtly communicating the message: "You may be from a powerful country, but for the moment you are dependent on me."

All this is in no way to deny the genuineness of generous offers, nor the curiosity they may express about life in other countries over a proffered cup of coffee. A generous appreciation of your host's hospitality and, in some cases, a postcard from abroad is all that is usually expected in return. ❑

A SONG OF THE MOUNTAINS

Throughout the centuries the Greeks have used their landscape – rugged mountains, rolling plains – as a metaphor to describe the different natures of the people living there, a device this old Cretan folk song (composed by hill-dwellers, one presumes) cunningly exploits:

Fie on the young men down on the plains
Who taste the good things in life,
The choicest foods,
And are base to look at, like creeping lizards.
Joy to the young men up in the hills
Who eat the snow and the dew-fresh air
And are fine to look at, like the orange-tree.

LEFT: bread for the festival of Agía Marína (17 June).
RIGHT: a monk at the Evangelístria monastery on Skiáthos.

LITERATURE

Greece was the cradle of European poetry and drama; modern writers
keep the tradition alive with outstanding novels, drama and especially poetry

When someone asked Greece's most famous composer, Mikis Theodorakis, where he got his inspiration for the hundreds of songs he had written in his lifetime, he said: "It's perfectly simple. I never thought of my music as anything but a way of clothing Greek poetry".

Perhaps only a Greek would have given such an answer. Relative to the size of its population, more poetry is published in Greece than in any other country in Europe, and it is still common for Greeks to present their friends with slim volumes of verse they have written and published at their own expense. Poetry is something people still revere and read for pleasure, and the marriage of poetry and music, familiar from the folk-song tradition, still endures.

Folk songs and the oral tradition

Both Greeks and non-Greeks have sought traces of continuity between ancient and modern Greece, and found it – if only in their imagination – in the folk songs and dances of the Greek countryside. In the 19th century, philhellenes and early Greek nationalists looked to the folk tradition as a way of establishing Greece's unique claim to liberation from the Turks. Certainly the country's folk songs are remarkable in their rich variety of imagery and metaphor, and it is not surprising that the first poets of modern Greece turned to them as a source of inspiration.

Although the tradition is dying fast, it is still possible, in a village in the mountains of Epirus or the Peloponnese, to come upon a festival or a wedding where the night is filled with songs like this:

Now the birds, now the swallows,
now, now the partridges,
now the partridges chatter and speak:

Left: Constantine Cavafy (1863–1933).
Right: Dionysios Solomos, writer of the Greek national anthem.

– Wake, my lord, wake my good lord
wake, embrace a body like a cypress,
a white throat, breasts like lemons...

Some of the most memorable folk lyrics of Greece are the laments for the dead. In these powerful songs, usually performed by women,

Death is addressed in the person of Charos, a sinister figure on a black horse:

Why are the mountains black, why so heavy
* with clouds*
is the wind fighting them, is rain lashing them?
The wind doesn't fight, nor the rain lash.
Only Death crosses them, carrying off the dead.
He drags the young in front of him, the old
* behind*
and the tender children are lined up on his
* saddle.*

You will have to search hard to find the texts of these songs if your Greek neighbour does not translate for you. This is particularly true of the tourist-laden landscape of the Aegean Islands, once the source of an astonishing variety of music, song and dance. The island of Crete is exceptional in preserving a lively traditional music scene where song lyrics are still improvised by local performers, but do not expect to hear the old island songs of Mýkonos, Santoríni or Rhodes when you visit. Fortunately there is an exceptionally active recording industry in Greece, and among the best sources of folk-song texts are the booklets accompanying these recordings, some with translations supplied. Recording notes will also provide the serious

to the 17th centuries that mark the beginning of modern Greek literature. The most famous of these works is the *Erotókritos*, a long romance in verse by Vitsentzos Kornaros. Remarkably, this written text became part of the oral tradition of the island, all 10,000 lines of it being sung as if it were a folk song until the 20th century. It is rare to hear more than a small section of the poem sung today, but it is an exhilarating experience to listen to even a handful of these verses, preserved since the Renaissance in the folk memory, performed in a Cretan nightclub.

Another contender for the source of modern Greek poetry is the Ionian island of Zákynthos.

Greek music fan with lyrics to the popular urban songs of Greece, the *rebétika*. Risqué and laced with slang referring to hashish smoking, they open an interesting window onto the shady life of Piraeus in the early to mid-20th century.

What is modern Greek literature?

The question of where Ancient Greek literature ends and modern Greek literature begins has no clear answer. Most of Greece was untouched by the Renaissance, but a notable exception was the island of Crete, which had been under Venetian rule until its conquest by the Ottomans in the mid-17th century. Some argue that it is the plays and poems produced on that island from the 15th

Like Crete, the Ionian Islands had been part of the Venetian Empire from the 13th century. The aristocracy were Italians, often married to local women, and the poet who is often referred to as Greece's "national" poet was the child of just such a union. Born on the island of Zákynthos in 1798, Dionysios Solomos was educated in Italian but, fired by the spirit of the Greek revolution, he began to write in Greek. His most famous poem is the *Hymn to Liberty*, which became the text of the new nation's anthem. Solomos's compatriot Andreas Kalvos, who spent most of his life in Italy, also achieved national recognition as a poet. Between them, the two poets inspired the national school of Romantic poets.

The 19th century

Emmanuel Roidis's wickedly satiric novel *Pope Joan* has achieved a deservedly wide readership in several languages, but with this exception, it is difficult for the non-Greek reader to discover the prose of 19th-century Greece. This is a pity, especially because of two remarkable prose writers whose complete works are only now appearing in English: Alexandros Papadiamandis and Georgios Vizyenos. Papadiamandis (1851–1911) was the son of a village priest from the island of Skiáthos and most of his fiction is set on that small Aegean island. The 200 stories he

guilt punished by divine rather than human justice; but Papadiamandis's sympathetic treatment of her character brings many assumptions of traditional Greek behaviour into question.

Translations of the half-dozen stories of Georgios Vizyenos (1849–96) have only recently become available in English. Enigmatic and sophisticated, his short stories are, like Papadiamandis's, preoccupied with questions of guilt and traditional Greek mores.

The early 20th century

Poetry flourished during the 20th century in Greece, a period dominated by three tragedies:

produced in his lifetime, including the novella *The Murderess*, offer a vivid, unsentimental portrait of Greek island life. They are written in a combination of high style and village dialect reminiscent of Dickens or Hardy.

The Murderess may well be one of the most daring stories of its day in any language. It tells the story of an old woman who, having witnessed the misery of the local women's lives, begins to murder infant girls rather than let them grow up. At the end of the story she drowns while being pursued by the police, her

the Greco-Turkish War of 1920–2 that resulted in the loss of Greece's presence in Asia Minor; World War II, when Italian, and then German troops occupied the country; and the military dictatorship of 1967–74, which put a temporary end to the Greeks' struggle for democracy and freedom of expression. Poetry, often sung poetry, gave a voice to the suffering of the population during these periods. The banning of poetry and song during these crises was a reflection of how powerful such expression was.

With the restoration of democracy in 1974, Greece's entrance into the European Community and the galloping urbanisation of the

LEFT: a plaque commemorating Nikos Kazantzakis.
ABOVE: a statue of early writer Adamantios Korais.

post-dictatorship era, tastes in literature changed. Songs and poems no longer talked about the heroism of the people or the beauty of Greek nature, but about the disillusionment of urban life or the private concerns of individuals. Prose, which had occupied a secondary position to poetry, proliferated in the last quarter of the 20th century. With few exceptions, the best of modern Greek prose writers had favoured the short story over the novel; but in the aftermath of the Asia Minor defeat, a group of novelists emerged who chronicled the events of the period and became known as the Aeolian School. Two were

Prizewinning poets

It is the poets who matured in the early to mid-20th century who are best known outside of Greece. In 1963 and 1979 two Greek poets, George Seferis (pseudonym of Georgios Seferiadis) and Odysseus Elytis (Odysseas Alepoudelis), won the Nobel Prize for Literature, drawing attention to the extraordinary flourishing of poetry in a country that was considered a cultural backwater by many western Europeans. A third poet, Constantine Cavafy (Konstantinos Kavafis), was admired by E.M. Forster and W.H. Auden and became one of the most influential poets of the 20th century.

refugees from Asia Minor (Stratos Doukas and Ilias Venezis), and the third (Stratis Myrivilis) from the island of Lésvos, a few miles off the Turkish coast. All three began their literary careers on Lésvos; their prose was realistic and the Greece they depicted was rural.

Meanwhile, in Athens and Thessaloníki, a number of young writers began writing about the new urban reality of a country whose population had increased by almost a quarter as a result of the Asia Minor war. More daring than their rural contemporaries, they experimented with Modernist techniques. The most original of these writers were Nikos Pentzikis, Giannis Skaribas and Giannis Beratis.

Living and writing his whole life outside the borders of modern Greece, in Alexandria, Cavafy removed himself still further from his contemporaries by setting most of his poems in the past. Like Cavafy, the characters that inhabit his elegant, ironic poems are Greeks of the eastern Mediterranean whose Hellenism is based on language and a common respect for Greek culture. His poem *Ithaka* may be the most often quoted modern Greek poem of all:

Ithaka has given you your lovely voyage
Without Ithaka you would not have set out.
Ithaka has no more to give you now.

Two other poets who received international attention and whose works were translated into many languages were Nikos Kazantzakis and Giannis Ritsos. Kazantzakis's modern sequel to *The Odyssey* (1938), in Kimon Friar's fine translation, was probably read by more English-speakers than Greeks, despite the fact that it is twice as long as Homer's original. These figures tower over modern Greek literature like a formidable Dead Poets' Society, their works overshadowing those of their contemporaries and followers. Kazantzakis, of course, was also a novelist, and if English-speakers have read any modern Greek

they saw as the enduring virtues of the Greek spirit as a way to confront the evils and privations of the war years. For Seferis, Ritsos, Kazantzakis, Empirikos, Elytis, Gatsos, Kavadias and many others, the war was a devastating experience that initially united Greeks against a common enemy and then tore them into two bitterly-opposed camps who fought one another in a civil war lasting until 1949. During this period many writers and intellectuals were persecuted by right-wing forces and imprisoned on Aegean Islands. Giannis Ritsos was among those who spent years in prison and exile. Others, like Seferis, spent the war years outside Greece. But

novels, they are probably his *Zorba*, *Christ Recrucified* or *Freedom or Death*.

Poetry out of conflict

Scarcely known outside Greece are the Greek poets who were Cavafy's contemporaries – Kostas Karyotakis, Kostis Palamas, Angelos Sikelianos and Kostas Varnalis. It was left to the somewhat younger poets who came of age in the 1930s to bring modern Greek poetry into the mainstream of European writing. Despite their political differences, these poets drew on what

LEFT: Odysseus Elytis, Nobel Prize winner in 1979.
ABOVE: George Seferis, Nobel Prize winner in 1963.

A NON-CONFORMIST LIFE

Thanks to his unorthodox views and writings, Nikos Kazantzakis was to court controversy not only throughout his life, but even after his death in 1957. When his book *The Last Temptation of Christ* was first published, the Orthodox Church sought to prosecute him. When it was made into a film in 1958, Athenian priests marched on the cinemas, and projection screens were slashed in anger. Today, admirers can make for the Kazantzakis Museum in the village of Myrtiá, 24 km/15 miles due south of Iráklio, where well-arranged displays illustrate what can be regarded as an extraordinary literary and political life.

no Greek writer was left unscathed, and it was these dark years that inspired some of the greatest works of modern Greek poetry.

Elytis, whose long poem *To Áxion Estí* (*Worthy it is*), memorably set to music by Mikis Theodorakis, earned him the Nobel Prize, drew on all the traditional resources of the Greek language – ancient, Byzantine, folk song – to create a modern secular liturgy. Beginning with the poet's childhood in Crete, *To Áxion Estí* spares the reader none of the horrors of the war but ends in a redeeming Gloria, praising the beauty of the Greek landscape and its lovely women:

Sífnos, Amorgós, Alónissos
Thásos, Itháki, Santoríni
Kós, Íos, Síkinos.

Praised be Myrto standing
on the stone wall facing the sea
like a beautiful eight or a jug
with a straw hat in her hand.

The post-war writers

The problem of Greek literature is that so few people read Greek. To become known outside the borders of Greece you have to be translated; and even then the chances of being recognised are small unless you are discovered, like

Cavafy, by an E.M. Forster, or recognised by a Nobel Prize. Tourism, which began to expand in the 1950s and continues to grow, has helped create a market for Greek literature, especially if it fits the traveller's ideas of what Greece is all about. Writers who ignore the Hellenic past, and concentrate on the less attractive themes of modern urban life, are less likely to appeal to the non-Greek reader.

Greek writers who began publishing in the 1950s and 1960s were mostly born in Athens or Thessaloníki. These writers, many of whom were women, matured in a period of tentative democracy that was rudely interrupted by seven years of stultifying dictatorship (1967–74). Reluctant to adopt the themes of an earlier generation, they wrote about personal relationships, disillusionment and Athenian life. Among the contemporary women Greek poets whose works are available in English translation are Katerina Angelaki-Rooke, Kiki Dimoula, Dzeni Mastoraki, Maria Laina and Rea Galanaki. This is necessarily a shortlist, and not intended to diminish the brilliance of their male contemporaries, among whom Manolis Anagnostakis, Titos Patrikios, Nasos Vagenas, Tassos Denegriis and Mihailis Ganas stand out.

Katerina Angelaki-Rooke

Of her generation, Katerina Angelaki-Rooke is probably the poet who has been most widely translated. She has also had a broad influence on the reception of Greek poetry abroad. Angelaki-Rooke is brilliantly articulate in French, English and Russian and has translated the works of many of the most "untranslatable" writers from those languages into Greek – including Dylan Thomas and Pushkin. Her old red house on Égina has long been a mecca for foreign writers and scholars of Greek literature, many of whom have relied on Angelaki's sharp insights into her country's literature as their guide to reading and translation. Her own poems are characterised by a combination of frank, lyrical sexuality and ironic self-criticism. As she writes in *Penelope Says*:

The body keeps remaking itself
getting up and falling into bed
as if it had been chopped down,
sometimes sick and sometimes in love hoping
that what it loses in touch it gains in essence.

In prose as in poetry, women writers have emerged, in the post-war period, to rival their male counterparts. Novels about Greek society may be the traveller's best guide to the changing mores and manners of Greek life. And since many Greek writers have chosen their own recent history as a subject for their fiction, novels and short stories may also be a good introduction to the vicissitudes of the period. Alki Zei's *Achilles' Fiancée*, for example, is a gripping *roman-à-clef* about the period of the civil war and its aftermath, when guerrilla fighters on the side of the Left took refuge in the Soviet Union. Among the other outstanding contem-

to satisfy the tastes of a large local audience, only a handful of Greek plays have been translated. Surprisingly, women dramatists were among the first to compose original plays, notably Evanthia Kairi, whose *Nikiratos* was produced in 1826.

Many writers better known in other fields turned their hand to writing plays, among them Kazantzakis, Palamas and Sikelianos; but in the post-war period, the theatre has been dominated by a group of writers whose primary concern is the theatre. The most outstanding of these is the prolific Iakovos Kambanellis.

porary Greek novelists whose works have been translated into English are Kostas Tahtsis, Thanasis Valtinos, Margarita Liberaki, Maro Douka, Eleni Fakinou, Menis Koumandereas and Ziranna Zateli.

Drama

Modern Greek dramatists have not, as yet, achieved the international recognition of their poetry- and fiction-writing colleagues. Despite a lively national theatrical scene that began promisingly in the 19th century and continues

Another delight for those who have some knowledge of Greek is the shadow puppet theatre. The hero of these charming, ribald, satiric performances, Karagiózis, is an anti-hero with whom Greeks have always identified. Set in the Ottoman period, the comic puppet plays, once watched by open-mouthed children and their guffawing parents in the village square, have always been tailored to fit each new political crisis and allowed Greeks to laugh at themselves, even in the harshest periods of their history. As the songwriter, Dionysios Savvopoulos, puts it:

LEFT: Rea Galanaki.
ABOVE: A Karagiózis shadow puppet show..

What consumes me, what saves me
Is that I dream like Karagiózis...   ❏

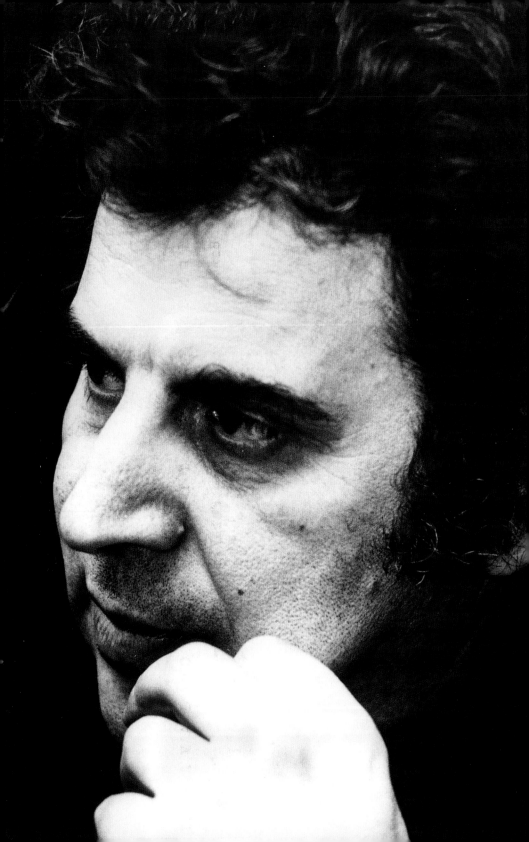

MUSIC AND DANCE

Music in Greece goes far beyond Zorba's Dance played on a bouzoúki
and reflects the country's complex political and cultural history

The sounds of Greece: the whine of motor-bikes; the deep roar of hydrofoils; men, women and taxi-drivers shouting at one another; the clang of church bells; sheep and goats bleating and tinkling, donkeys braying, and music – loud music blaring from radios, nightclubs, cars, cafés. The Greeks do not seem to need or desire quiet; they fill any silence with noise. They also love music, and even if it has to compete with the deafening roar of Athens' traffic or the engine of a ferry boat, they listen to it constantly.

What is surprising to the visitor is that nearly all of the music they play is distinctively Greek music. It may be influenced by American, Spanish or Brazilian music, but more often than not it is Greek in instrumentation or rhythm. Anyone who came to Greece 30 years ago must lament the steady erosion of Greece's trad-itional folk music; however, despite globalisa-tion and modernisation, Greek music is still flourishing and full of surprises.

A continuous tradition?

Anyone who has attended the famous Dora Stratou folk-dance performances in Athens, or any other performance of Greek music for tourists, will have been told that modern Greek music and dance preserve some of the features of their Ancient Greek origin. These claims are hard to substantiate, since we have almost no idea what Ancient Greek music sounded like. We know its instruments and its famous system of modes (such as Dorian, Lydian, Aeolian) but only a few tantalising fragments of notation have survived. Greek vases show dancing fig-ures, accompanied by lyre, flute and tam-bourine, who might be dancing at a modern Greek wedding, but neither these line-dancers nor their instruments are unique to Greece.

What was unique about Greece was the desire of 19th-century western philhellenes and

early Greek nationalists to see, in modern Greece, traces of continuity with the mythical world of antiquity. The claims that early folk-lorists made for a continuous tradition were not only slim, but they were based almost entirely on the poetry of Greek songs, ignoring both the astonishing variety and richness of the music, and also the ritual context in which it was per-formed. Like all folk music, Greek songs and dances were not originally performed for enter-tainment but were associated with religious fes-tivals, weddings, funerals or seasonal work.

Music of the mainland

While there is some overlap between these categories, Greeks usually make a distinction between regional folk music (*dimotikí mousikí*) and popular or city music (*laïkí*). In the case of regional folk music, they also dis-tinguish between music from the mainland (*ste-rianí*) and music from the islands and coastline (*nisiotiká, paralía*). Mainland Greece is further

---

LEFT: Mikis Theodorakis, who won international fame.
RIGHT: a busker in Athens plays a Pontian *lýra* from the Black Sea coast of Turkey.

divided into regions that have their own musical traditions: Epirus, in the northwest, Macedonia, Roúmeli, Thrace and the Peloponnese.

The most common rhythms of the mainland are the threes of the *tsamikós*, the sevens of the *kalamatianós* (named after the town of Kalamáta in the Peloponnese but common throughout central and southern Greece) and the slow duple and triple time of the *syrtós* and *sta tría*. Once, it was common to hear music performed outdoors by the classic pairs of instruments, either the large drum *(daoúli)* and folk oboe *(zourná)*, or the bagpipe *(gáïda)* and tambourine *(daïrés, défi)*; nowadays it is more common at festivals or wed-

Greece where the traveller may still be lucky enough to find live music at a summer *panigýri* (religious festival) are Thrace and Macedonia, both of which have a wide variety of local songs and dances. In central Greece and the Peloponnese you are these days more likely to find recorded music at such events.

The islands and Asia Minor

The islands of Greece once boasted an amazing variety of musical traditions. To the west of the Greek mainland in the Ionian Islands, which had for centuries been under Venetian control, people sang songs in four-part harmony. Called

dings to hear an ensemble that includes the clarinet, violin, drum and perhaps an accordion or a hammered dulcimer *(sandoúri)*.

A well-known Greek singer from the Aegean once said to me, "When I die I want to be born again as a Epirot." The music of Epirus is certainly among the most beautiful of any region in Greece. Epirus is famed for the skill of its clarinet players, who improvise like jazz masters on the folk clarinet (actually a B-flat Albert clarinet, still played by many musicians in Central Europe). It is also one of the regions of Greece where you are still likely to encounter live music at a festival or wedding, especially in the mountain villages. Other areas of mainland

kandádes, these songs, usually accompanied by a guitar, were clearly influenced by Neapolitan folk song. Partly because of their western European character and partly because they were songs that could be sung in a restaurant or tavern, *kandádes* became very popular in Athens where they continued to be sung by groups of men and women until the 1960s. The island of Zákynthos is still famous for its *kandádes* and, although the genre is slowly dying out, it is not uncommon to hear the islanders perform these light and charming songs. The Ionian Islands were also, in the 19th century, a regional centre for Italian opera, which was performed in small opera houses on both Corfu and Kefalloniá.

In the Aegean, music is usually somewhat arbitrarily divided into groups conforming to the grouping of islands. Here, the dance rhythms are mostly duple, with the most common dance being some variety of *syrtós*. The exceptions are the nine-beat rhythms of the *zeibekikó* and *karsilámas* found in the islands of the eastern Aegean, off the coast of Asia Minor, particularly Lésvos, the Dodecanese and Cyprus. The traditional instruments of these islands were the *lýra* (not to be confused with the Ancient Greek lyre) or bowed viol, and the *tsaboúna*, or island bagpipe. As with the mainland instruments, there has been a shift in

ing to discover more about Greek folk music might well begin his or her journey in Crete. Still performed on the classic combination of the Cretan *lýra* and *laoúto*, Cretan music continues to flourish and is being performed by young as well as older players. Not only is the tradition of improvised poetic couplets still preserved, but sections of the long poem *Erotókritos*, a 17th-century verse play, are still performed as part of many singers' repertoires. Cretan dancing is spectacular, and the combination of music and dance, whether it is performed in a noisy nightclub or on a mountainside, at a wedding, is still awe-inspiring.

instrumentation, with the violin replacing the *lýra* on most islands, accompanied by the *laoúto*, or folk lute, often with the addition of accordion, hand-drum or clarinet. Improvised rhymed couplets in 15-syllable metre *(mandinádes)* are a common feature of Aegean island music and persist to this day, especially on the island of Crete.

Whereas live music has all but disappeared from many of the Aegean Islands, Crete is something of an exception. Any traveller wanting to discover more about Greek folk music

---

LEFT: the closest most tourists get to traditional dance is in mediated displays.
ABOVE: a group singing *kandádes*.

The islands of the central Aegean, including the Cyclades, have become so overwhelmed by tourists that these days it is difficult, on most of them, to hear live music. Those who are lucky enough to encounter it at some special occasion like a wedding will discover the vanishing beauty of the *nisiotiká*, songs and dances performed by an ensemble that nearly always includes a violin. The islands near the Turkish mainland, especially the large island of Lésvos, once had a very different musical tradition, one strongly influenced by the cosmopolitan cities of Smyrna (modern Izmir) and Aivali (Ayvaluk), both of which had large Greek populations until the 1920s. On Lésvos, there were many local varieties of the Asia Minor songs and dances, some only found in a particular village, and it was through its principal town, Mytilíni, that many of the features of Asia Minor music found their way into the popular music of Greece.

One type of music that the tourist is not likely to encounter, but which is rich in its lyrics and striking in its emotional style of performance, is the music of funeral laments. It is becoming increasingly rare for women to perform these songs at funerals in urban centres, but in the countryside, especially in more remote areas, no funeral is complete without

women have been permitted to continue improvising these laments as part of the funeral service, with priest and female chorus taking turns to articulate conflicting messages about the afterlife.

Religious music

Greeks often refer to the music of the Orthodox Church simply as Byzantine music. This is only partly true. While some of the music heard in the Orthodox services dates to the Byzantine period, much of it was composed later. Early Byzantine music was influenced by the chant of Syria and Palestine rather than

its chorus of women lament-singers. In most regions of Greece laments are distinguished from songs. They are a genre apart, and yet they have melodies that may be performed as separate instrumental pieces in other contexts – even at weddings, strangely enough. It is through these songs that women communicate with the other world, addressing the dead directly and often berating them for leaving the living behind.

While these laments are performed in the context of a Christian ritual, they are remarkable in their lack of Christian references and in their striking pagan imagery. Despite repeated clashes with the Orthodox Church, village

Greece or Rome, and was probably based on melodies already familiar to the congregation from the local folk tradition. The *okotéhos* which forms the basis of all Byzantine chant was not a system of modes like those of ancient Greece, but based on such a collection of songs. What was important was the association of a set of melodic formulas with their liturgical function: certain tunes came to have a symbolic function in the Church and were incorporated into the hymns.

By far the greatest composer of Byzantine hymns was Romanos the Melodist, born in Syria in the late 5th century and probably active at the height of the Emperor Justinian's reign.

His combination of dramatic poetry with melody has never been surpassed in the Eastern Christian tradition and his hymns are still performed as part of the Orthodox liturgy.

There is now a considerable variety of music performed in Greek churches, some of it accompanied by an organ, and some including polyphonic arrangements, although many churches still retain the earlier style of monophonic singing (without harmonies) with a chorus supplying a drone. The richest music of the Church calendar can be heard at the Easter-festival, particularly at the Epitávios, or Easter Friday service.

most famous modern composer, Mikis Theodorakis. It is music and dancing derived from a particular style of Greek music called the *rebétika*, a style that still forms the basis of much of modern Greece's popular music and is played by revival groups all over Greece.

Rebétika is a music associated with certain ports of Asia Minor and Greece from the beginning of the 20th century onwards, though it probably existed around the east Aegean coast and the Black Sea for decades before that. On one occasion, an expatriate Soviet novelist, on exposure to the music, delightedly exclaimed that a nearly identical style, played on the bal-

The sound of the city

For many visitors to Greece, one of the attractions is the "Zorba factor". It is that dance of Anthony Quinn and Alan Bates on a Greek beach in the 1964 movie *Zorba the Greek*, accompanied by the rapid twanging of the *bouzoúki* that spells a particular exuberance and excitement regarded as quintessentially Greek. Granted, the two men are dancing on a Cretan beach, but they are not dancing a Cretan dance. They are dancing city music to a city instrument, music composed by Greece's

LEFT: a *tsaboúna*, the island bagpipe.
ABOVE: *laoúto* and violin played in the Cyclades.

alaika, had flourished in the harbour dives of Odessa before the 1917 Revolution.

Rebétika is often, but not always, divided into two types: the Piraeus-style *rebétika*, and the Asia Minor music brought into Greece through the islands and by the flood of refugees who arrived in the mainland following the Turko-Greek War of 1920–22.

The Asia Minor style was generally performed in cafés known as *cafés-aman*, where the ensembles were made up of a violin, guitar, *oud*, *sandoúri* or *kanun* (zither) and perhaps an accordion. Women and men both performed in these venues and their repertoire of songs often included rather daring and humorous songs of the underworld, songs about hashish, drinking, prison and prostitutes.

With the arrival of the refugees, many more cafés-aman sprang up in Piraeus and Athens, and the taste for this music in the Greek communities of the US led to a burgeoning recording industry. Refugees, many of them poor and unemployed, also joined local musicians in the back streets of Piraeus, where a new sort of music began to grow in popularity, This was performed not by the traditional instruments of the café ensemble, but on the *bouzoúki*, a long-necked, lute-like instrument that was common on some islands.

The heyday of the *rebétika* lasted from the 1930s to the 1950s, but the songs were revived in the 1970s, beginning in the years of the dictatorship (1967–74) when the music of Theodorakis was banned by the colonels and other composers either refused to compose or found their lyrics censored. References to smoking hashish also appealed to a generation of young Greeks who identified with the streetwise, social outcasts of the *rebétika*.

Popular music of the 1960s–1970s

Mikis Theodorakis and his fellow-composer Manos Hazidakis were the leaders of an extra-

By the 1930s the *bouzoúki* and the songs it accompanied were all the rage in Greece. Rather like the urban blues of the US, or the tango of Argentina, the songs of the pre-war *rebétika* were daring in their lyrics and appealed to an audience that revelled in hearing about the shady milieu they depicted.

Markos Vamvakaris, the central member of the "Piraeus Quartet", is often regarded as the "father" of the *rebétika*. Other outstanding figures were Stratos Pagioumtsis, Giannis Papaioannou, the prolific songwriter Vassilis Tsitanis, and the singer Sotiria Bellou, whose recordings are as fine an introduction as one could wish to the *rebétika*.

ordinary experiment in Greek popular music. After the terrible years of World War II, the German occupation and civil war, Greeks were demoralised and emotionally exhausted. The two composers deliberately set out to provide the public with a new sort of popular music that would elevate and inspire the population at large. They both recognised the *rebétika* as the only musical form that could reach a broad public, but as classically trained musicians, they wanted to extend the boundaries of popular song and combine it with the poetry of the country's leading poets. Beginning in the late 1950s the two composers transformed Greek music and produced some of the most exciting popular music in Europe by joining the rhythms of the *rebétika* (particularly the dramatic 9/8 of the solo male dance, the *zeibekikó*) with the poetry of Seferis, Ritsos, Gatsos and Elytis. In the case of Mikis Theodorakis, this music acquired a strong political dimension because of his commitment to the freedom of the persecuted Greek Left. During the dictatorship his music was banned and he was imprisoned for years, making his music still more popular among the population at large.

Theodorakis and Hadzidakis's music has had a lasting effect on Greek music. Not only are their songs still popular, but they inspired a

Dalaras), Mariza Koch, Haris Alexiou, Nena Venetsanou, Glykeria, Eleftheria Arvanitaki, Dimitra Galani and most recently Savina Giannatou have all become internationally popular. The phenomenon of World Music has created a demand for certain types of Greek music, both folk and urban, and these singers have represented Greek music to a broad audience.

Composers who came of age in the 1980s, like Stamatis Kraounakis and Nikos Xydakis, are less widely known. There is still a very lively musical scene in Athens, with an increasingly divergent instrumentation. The hottest music these days has a distinctly ori-

younger group of composers to follow in their footsteps. Among the best known of these composers, who belong to what is loosely termed the New Wave, are Dionysios Savvopoulos, Giannis Markopoulos, Manos Loizos and Stavros Xarhakos.

The contemporary music scene

Some of the best-known figures of the Greek musical scene are singers rather than composers: Maria Farandouri, George Dalaras (Giorgos

LEFT: a *bouzoúki* and guitar orchestra in a Pláka club around 1960.
ABOVE: *rebétes* in Piraeus in 1928.

ental flavour, and is often performed by a mixture of Greeks and musicians from Asia Minor or North Africa. The *boîtes* or musical clubs of the Pláka are not the place most Athenians now go to hear music, but there are many alternatives spread around the centre of Athens and the outer suburbs. Athens by night is still full of music that lifts the spirits and lasts till morning. And for those fortunate enough to catch a concert of Theodorakis, discover a good *rebétika* group performing in a small club, or stumble on a wedding in the mountains of Epirus, the splendid, haunting music that once filled the air of Greece may still set the night on fire. ❑

MIXING PIETY WITH PLEASURE

Greek religious festivals – and there are many –
celebrate saints' days and other events in the
religious calendar with devotion and high spirits

Greek island life is punctuated throughout the year by saints' days and religious festivals or *panigýria*. As there are around 300 saints in the Orthodox calendar, there is an excuse for a party most days of the year.

Easter is the most important festival (often preceded by a pre-Lenten carnival known as "Clean Monday"). It's a great time to visit, with traditional services marking the Resurrection everywhere from humble chapels to mighty monasteries. Colourful, noisy and potentially dangerous – on Kálymnos they throw dynamite to ensure Christ has truly risen *(see page 67)* – it's like Firework Night and Christmas rolled into one.

During Holy Week, or *Megáli Evdomáda*, churches are festooned in black. On Maundy Thursday monks on Pátmos re-enact the washing of Christ's feet at the Last Supper. On Good Friday the *Epitávios*, or bier of Christ, is decorated by the women and paraded through the streets *(see above and right)* as they sing hymns.

On Easter Saturday the churches are decked in white. At midnight everything is plunged in darkness as the priest lights the first candle from the holy flame, to represent the light of the world, and intones: *"Hristós anésti"* (Christ has risen). This is the signal for the congregation to light their candles. Families then break the Lenten fast with Easter soup made from the lamb's viscera and later play conkers with red-dyed eggs.

On Easter Sunday there is great rejoicing as a lamb or kid is barbecued outdoors over charcoal, with the usual music and dancing. There are often parties on Easter Monday, and on some islands an effigy of Judas is filled with fireworks and burned.

▽ **PARADING THE BIER**
Here the symbolic coffin of Christ *(Epitávios)* is seen parading though the streets of the town, attended to by the priest. The parade is accompanied by the singing of religious songs.

▷ **SCARLET SHELLS**
Hard-boiled eggs, dyed red to symbolise the blood of Christ, are cracked in a game like conkers on Easter Day.

◁ **EASTER TWISTS**
A sweet, twisted bread called *koulourákia* is made for Easter in various shapes, often with a red egg in the centre.

◁ **MONDAY MAYHEM**
"Clean Monday" is the end of the pre-Lenten carnival, with exuberant celebrations on some islands, including kite-flying and flour fights.

▽ **STEPS TO SALVATION**
Devout women crawl in penance to the church of the Panagía Evangelístria on Tínos at the feast of the Assumption in August.

◁ **MOUNTAINTOP MASS**
Saints' days are celebrated by *panigýria* (festivals) at hundreds of small chapels throughout the islands. Here Cycladic islanders honour Agía Marína, the protector of crops, on 17 July.

△ **ALL DRESSED UP**
In Ólympos, the remote mountain village on Kárpathos, the eldest daughter or *kanakará* wears her traditional costume and dowry of gold coins for major festivals.

◁ **EASTER PARADE**
Priest and villagers join in traditional chants in an Easter procession on Páros.

CELEBRATING ALL YEAR ROUND

Greeks mix piety and pleasure with gusto for all their festivals, from the most important to the smallest fair. The biggest religious festival after Easter, the Assumption of the Virgin (*Panagía*) on 15 August, draws Greeks home from all over the world.

Following the long liturgy on the night of the 14th, the icon of the Madonna is paraded and kissed. Then there's a communal feast – and the party can go on for days. The celebrations are spectacular in Kárpathos, with dazzling costumes, special dances and traditional songs.

Every month there are festivals on the islands for everything from sponges to snakes, and national holidays like *Óhi* or "No Day" (28 October), with patriotic parades to mark the Greeks' emphatic refusal of Mussolini's surrender ultimatum.

Celebrations begin the night before feast days and everyone in the community takes part, from babies to grannies. Patron saints are honoured with services followed by barbecues, music and dance. The picture above shows the feast of Ágios Dimítris on Síkinos in October, which is conveniently when the first wine is ready to drink.

FOOD AND DRINK

Simple cooking using seasonal, local ingredients is the key to Greek cuisine – but food for the Greeks is about more than just cooking and eating

The cook sets before you a large tray on which are five small plates. One of these holds garlic, another a pair of sea-urchins, another a sweet wine sop, another ten cockles, the last a small piece of sturgeon. While I'm eating this, another is eating that; and while he is eating that, I have made away with this. What I want, good sir, is both the one and the other, but my wish is impossible. For I have neither five mouths nor five hands...

– Athenaeus: The Deipnosophists

This scene describes the frustration Greeks, as well as tourists, often feel when they fail to taste all the dishes that are part of a meze spread. It is obviously an age-old problem, as the passage comes from a semi-ficitious Greek work of the 3rd century BC. Although pizza, hamburgers, *gýro* and the ubiquitous Greek salad tend to render modern Greek food banal, the age-old tradition of sharing many small dishes – the prelude to a meal or the meal itself – lives on.

Greeks were essentially vegetarian until about the mid-20th century, not by choice but because in their mountainous country it was not possible to pasture large herds and provide meat for everybody. The traditional Greek diet, frugal yet delicious, was mainly based on the agricultural produce of each region: vegetables, weeds and leafy greens – foraged from the hills and fields, or cultivated – and grains, mainly in the form of home-made bread. Fruity olive oil was the principal fat used, while olives, beans and other legumes, local cheeses and yogurt were everyday staples.

Only occasionally was the everyday diet enriched with some fresh or cured fish, or with meat. Meat was a rare, festive dish, consumed on Sundays, at the major festivals of Easter and Christmas, as well as on important family feasts. But after the mid-1960s, as the country became more affluent, imported meat gradually took a significant role at the Greek table. It was around that time that the Greek demographic structure changed.

At least four out of 10 middle-aged Greeks now living in big cities originally came from agricultural areas. They relocated in the last 50 years, bringing with them the cooking and culinary habits of their mothers and grandmothers. Although well settled in the urban environment, most of them have kept their ancestors' village

homes and visit them on long weekends, during the summer holidays, as well as at Christmas and Easter. Many have also kept much of their land, so it is common for Greek families to produce the olive oil they consume; about 18 kg (40 lb) per person each year. Olive oil is the core of the Greek diet, its most important element. People who do not produce it themselves buy it from friends who have a surplus.

Along with olive oil, *psomí* (bread) was the basic staple food up until the mid-1960s, as it used to be in ancient and Byzantine times. Although Greeks can now afford a great variety of foods, they still consume enormous quantities of bread. Traditional breads are often made with a combination of wheat, barley and sometimes maize flour, using sour old-dough starter as leavening. Barley grows easily in dry and mountainous southern Greece and on the islands, so it has been a staple for many centuries. Today in Crete and other islands *paximádia* (rusks) – slices of twice-baked and completely dry barley bread which need to be briefly soaked in water to soften – are still very popular. *Paximádia* are perfectly suited to traditional lifestyles: they keep well for many months, they are easy to carry in the field and are the ideal food for sailors. Moreover, baked every two or three months, they made good use of the oven heat, as wood is scarce on most islands.

FAST FOOD

An indication that Greeks still take their religious fasts seriously can be found in the branches of McDonald's in Greece, where special Lenten menus are served during these periods.

Greek cooking. But by far the most important element that has shaped people's eating habits was the rules of the Greek Orthodox Church. Even nonreligious Greeks sometimes abstain from foods deriving from animals – meat, dairy products and eggs – during the Lenten days that precede Easter, Christmas and other religious occasions. This is the reason why many traditional dishes such as *gemistá* (stuffed vegetables), *dolmádes* (stuffed grape or cabbage leaves), *pítes* (filo-wrapped pies) come in two versions: one with meat and/or cheese, and one without, often called *laderá* (with just olive oil) for the days of fast.

Outside influences

In its long history Greece has been subjected to many culinary influences. The Venetians and Genoans, who ruled much of the country during the Middle Ages, and later the Ottoman Turks, who ruled northern Greece and Crete up until the early 1900s, have all left their marks on

LEFT: a diet of greens, beans and olives.
ABOVE: cooks preparing favourite dishes on Rhodes.

Festival food

Numerous religious holidays are scattered throughout the year. Many of them have evolved from ancient celebrations and are often closely related to the seasons and the lunar calendar. Easter, Greece's most important feast, seems to have its roots in the agricultural spring festivals of antiquity. Celebrated in the open country, amid fragrant herbs and multicoloured flowers, the Easter table features succulent spit-roasted baby lamb or kid – at the right age for slaughter at that time of the year – and salads of wild greens, tender raw artichokes and fresh fava beans. *Magirítsa*, a delicious soup made with chopped lamb's innards, spring onions and dill, with a tart egg-and-lemon sauce, is eaten on Easter Saturday, after the midnight Resurrection Mass. The traditional Easter sweets are made with *myzíthra*, a generic name for the various regional creamy fresh cheeses of the season, usually made with a combination of goat's and sheep's milk.

SEASONAL FARE

Greek food traditionally follows the seasons. Cooks do not make *gemistá* (stuffed tomatoes and peppers) or *melitzanosaláta* (aubergine dip) in the winter, even though these vegetables are now available all year round.

Pork is associated with Christmas and New Year, as pig slaughtering and curing is done in the heart of the winter. Fish is consumed on 25 March, and always at the meals that follow funerals. Despite its many islands, fish and seafood has never been plentiful enough to become an everyday food in Greece, not even for those who live by the sea. The fish and seafood of the Aegean is delicious but scarce, and the best fish islanders manage to catch is sold to the big cities for much-needed cash.

Dining out

Despite its rich culinary heritage, Greece has no great restaurant tradition and the finest *magirevtá* (cooked dishes) are best savoured in the home. People eat lunch at around 2pm and dinner at around 8.30pm – in the summer at around 10pm at night or even later. Breakfast is usually just a cup of coffee and a biscuit. Wine accompanies the meals, especially dinner, and a salad of fresh, raw or blanched seasonal vegetables or greens is always part of the everyday menu. Seasonal fruits are the most common dessert. Sweets were originally part of the festive table but now tend to be eaten at all times of the day, while meat has become an almost everyday staple.

Traditionally there are two kinds of restaurants that attract the Greeks when they want to entertain their families and friends: *hasapotavérna* (butcher's tavern) offers charcoal-grilled meat (baby lamb, kid, pork, veal and occasionally chicken) by weight. Here meat-lovers have a feast at reasonable prices. Tourists are probably more familiar with the other Greek favourite restaurant, *psarotavérna* (fish tavern), as these are scattered all over the shoreline, on the islands and the mainland. Fresh fish and seafood, the catch of the day, is grilled or fried according to the customer's choice. Both meat and fish taverns offer a few appetisers and seasonal salads.

The frugal Greek cooks have learned to combine a few simple items of produce to create an incredible variety of foods. With remarkable ingenuity, they compliment them with rice, bulgur wheat, some cheese and a few pieces of meat to create dishes that dieticians now hold up as models of the famously healthy Mediterranean Diet. The irony is that modern Greeks, in their quest to distance themselves from their poverty-stricken past, have enthusiastically left behind this traditional fare and adopted the unhealthy eating habits of the wealthy Europeans and Americans.

Local foods

The traditional foods of Greece's poor past had nearly disappeared when, only recently, a trend towards grandmother's cooking began to emerge in Athens and gradually all over the country. Visitors need to ask for regional specialities – for example, *pítes* (pies wrapped in fylo) in Epirus; *trahaná* soup (the Greek pasta made with yogurt and cracked wheat) on the mainland and Crete; *dolmádes* (meat-stuffed vine leaves) in the Dodecanese; *loukánika* (sausages) and *loúza* or *lóza* (pork loin macerated in wine and air-dried or smoked) in the Cyclades. Look out, too, for thyme honey and *pastéli* (a sesame seed and honey sweet), home-cured capers, and wonderful local shepherd's cheeses, often just called *tyráki* (small cheese). In the Cyclades and the Dodecanese goat's and sheep's milk cheeses are a real treat, but visitors need to seek them out, because they seldom travel further than their village of origin. Greece, unlike Italy, has not yet managed to capitalise on its delicious artisanal foods.

The Byzantines continued to add resin to some wines. A more refined remnant of this is the modern *retsína*, a white wine mildly scented with pine resin. *Retsína* was widely consumed up until the mid-1970s. But as the new generation of quality Greek wines gradually spread, its consumption declined sharply. Today many medium and small wineries, employing modern techniques and talented oenologists, experiment combining indigenous and imported grape varieties and produce wines of excellent quality.

The Greek vineyards are diverse, following the contours of the country's morphology.

Greek wines

Some of the most admired wines in antiquity were produced in Greece. Manpowered cargo ships carried clay amphoras filled with the precious liquid to ports and markets all over the Mediterranean. Yet if we were to try these wines today, we would probably find them undrinkable. They were mainly sweet, and contained flavourings and herbs such as thyme, mint and even cinnamon. Seawater and pieces of pine bark were also added as preservatives, to keep the wine from turning sour.

LEFT: stuffed tomatoes and potatoes.
ABOVE: bread being baked in a traditional oven.

Omnipresent hills and mountains divide the land into small regions, each with its own microclimate. Several indigenous grape varieties – many of which existed also in antiquity – are grown, which acquire different characteristics in each region. According to EU regulations and the Greek law, the system of appellations of origin (AOC) matches the Greek varieties to the areas where the best of their kind is traditionally produced. Note, however, that you will also find exceptional regional wines outside of these AOC classifications. A description of the most important wines and grape varieties of each of the country's regions follows.

Northern Greece

Starting with Macedonia, the land of the *Xinó-mavro* grape which produces the most well-loved Greek *brusco* wine (a robust red). *Naoússa* is the best-known example, while *Amýndeon*, made from the same grape, is a light red and can also be a pleasant still or sparkling rosé. *Xinómavro* combined with the *Negóska* variety – another Macedonian native – makes *Gouménissa*, a meaty red. By itself, *Negóska* produces a soft red. Extended, relatively new vineyards on the central peninsula of Halkidikí produce the *Côtes de Meliton* wines, both white and red, from a combination of French (Caber-

Thessaly, where most of the Greek grain is cultivated, produces two distinguished wines: *Rapsáni* makes a red with a fine bouquet, from *Xinómavro*, *Stavrotó* and *Krasáto* varieties which grow on the northeastern slopes of Mount Olympos. *Anhíalos*, on the shores of Pagasitikos, produces a fresh white wine, made mostly from *Rodítis* grapes.

Central Greece and Peloponnese

Attica, the region around Athens (not an AOC region), produces very interesting wines. The main variety here is *Savatianó*, traditionally used for the production of *retsína*, the resinated wine.

net Sauvignon and Franc) and Greek varieties. On the eastern peninsula, in the secluded monastic community of Mount Athos, the monks, who have been producing wines since Byzantine times, still cultivate both white and red wine-producing grapes. Macedonia is a wonderful and lesser-known area for wine (for maps and details of its Wine Roads, visit www.wineroads.gr).

In Epirus, the most isolated, mountainous region of northwestern Greece, *Zítsa*, a lively, fresh, fruity sparkling white is produced from the *Debína* variety. In the same region, *Katói*, a fine, rich red, is made from imported Cabernet Sauvignon vines.

Château Matsa in Kantzá is one of the finest Greek whites, produced from grapes of an old family vineyard. Additionally, various Greek and foreign varieties produce a new range of wines, such as *Villítsa* and *Attica*.

In the Peloponnese, *Nemea*, made from *Aigiorgítiko* grapes grown in the northeastern part of the region, is one of the most versatile Greek reds. *Mandinía*, a delicate aromatic white wine, is produced on the vineyards east of Trípoli, from *Mavrodáfni* and *Asproúdes* grapes. The *Pátra* area yields dry and sweet white and red wines. *Muscat of Patras* and *Muscat of Rio* as well as *Mavrodáfni* are three well-loved sweet wines.

Some scholars believe that the medieval city of Monemvasía used to be the place where malmsey wine was made (called also malvesian or malvoisie, from the old name of the city). Others claim that the wine mentioned by Shakespeare was produced in Crete, and the boats that transported it stopped to Monemvasía on their way to Europe. That magnificent sweet white is no longer made in Greece but in Madeira.

The Islands

On the island of Límnos a lovely Muscat wine is produced from Alexandrian Muscat grapes, while the *Limnió* variety, mentioned by Aristotle, produces light, fragrant red wines. Vineyards on Sámos, a mountainous island, are planted on terraced hills, rising to 800 metres (2,625 ft). The Sámos sweet and muscat wines are well known and much praised by the French. Rhodes produces dry white wines mainly from *Athíri* grapes, as well as sparkling wines of good quality. The red dry wines of the region are made chiefly from *Mandilariá* grapes.

Crete produces 20 percent of Greek wines. Although far to the south, the cool etesian winds never let the temperature rise much, and the tall mountain of Mt Psilorítis keeps the hot winds of Africa from reaching the northern part where most of the grapes are cultivated. *Arhánes* is a dry red made from *Kotsifáli* and *Mandilariá* grapes. Another red, *Dafnés*, is made from *Liátiko*, probably an ancient variety. From this variety, a sweet red *vin de liqueur* is also produced. Sitía produces a dry and a sweet red. A dry red made from *Kotsifáli* and *Mandilariá*, and a very popular fruity white from *Vilána* grapes, are the Sitía AOC.

Santoríni, the spectacular volcanic island, produces a lovely white wine made from *Asýrtiko* grapes. To guard their vines from the strong etesian winds, local growers shape their branches like baskets in which the grapes grow. *Visánto* is a marvellous sweet wine made from partly sun-dried grapes. Similar sweet wines, often called *Liastó*, are produced throughout the Cyclades. In the very picturesque island of Páros, the low-pruned vines produce a red with dark colour and a characteristic bouquet, made from *Mandilariá* and *Monemvasía* grapes.

LEFT: wine-making on Síkinos.
RIGHT: a glass of *retsína*.

Corfu, Zákynthos and Levkáda produce interesting wines, but only *Robóla* from Kefalloniá, a dry white from the eponymous grapes, is an AOC, together with the local variety of *Mavrodáfni*, the sweet, rich red *vin de liqueur*.

Oúzo and other spirits

The most popular Greek drink, traditionally served with *mezédes*, is undoubtedly *oúzo*, which is produced in many parts of the country. Only *oúzo* made in Greece can bear that name according to EU regulations. *Oúzo* is made from distilled alcohol, and takes its flavour from anise, fennel seeds and other aromatics.

In the north of Greece, *oúzo* is dry, while in the south and the islands it is somewhat sweeter.

Some people say the best *oúzo* is from Lésvos. Others will insist that the *oúzo* of Tyrnávos, Thessaly, or that of Híos is superior. It's a matter of taste, often affected by a person's place of origin. In Híos, there is also *mastíha*, a sweeter version of *oúzo* flavoured exclusively with mastic, the aromatic sap of the mastic bushes that grow on the island. Another popular strong alcoholic drink, akin to the Italian *grappa*, is made from the distillation of grapeskins and stems. It is called *tsípouro* in central and northern Greece and *rakí* or *tsikoudiá* in Crete, where it is recommended as a universal panacea. ❏

ART AND ARCHITECTURE

The Classical, Hellenistic, Roman and Byzantine eras left Greece
with an artistic heritage that has inspired later artists and architects

Few countries have influenced Western art more than ancient Greece. But because of its geographical position, Greece itself has been subjected to many influences, from Europe, Asia and, through Crete, Africa. The origins of Greek art lay in neolithic Anatolia, the Middle East and Egypt. Greece in turn influenced Rome, and thus Western Europe and the Byzantine world. Absorbed into the Turkish Ottoman Empire for 500 years, on liberation Greece was on the receiving end of Western influences, often mixed with its Byzantine heritage. The region's fine marbles, good clays and early exploitation of Cypriot copper ensured an enduring artistic gift.

The Bronze Age

The earliest art is that of the Cyclades. Neolithic and Bronze Age cultures developed complex housing schemes, but the most characteristic artefacts are the Cycladic dolls, placed as protective amulets with early burials. Here the Greek love of idealised, perfect forms is already apparent. The facial details may have been added in paint.

By 2000 BC the Minoan civilisation had emerged in Crete and on neighbouring Santoríni, characterised by palace complexes such as Knossos and Phaestos. The architecture was labyrinthine, of stone with plastered and frescoed walls, and looked inwards on to courtyards which were the scene of elaborate games, including bull-leaping as represented in paint and ivory figures.

The sacred bull – suggested by the twin horn symbol – was represented in terracotta, and as rhytons (drinking vessels) of gold or soapstone. The frescoed composite plants and chariots pulled by winged beasts, and the sculpted flounced dress of the snake goddess, a protective deity, demonstrated Mesopotamian influence. Sea and land creatures – shells, octopuses, hornets – inspired vase decoration and jew-

ellery. The double-headed axe, used as a motif, was a sacred symbol.

The peaceable, sophisticated Minoan culture declined around 1400 BC. The Myceneans of the mainland were now a major power. Warlike and great sea traders, they adopted Minoan motifs such as wasp-waisted costumes and the

downward tapering column seen on the Lion Gate at Mycenae (*circa* 1600 BC). This entry to the citadel/palace is the first large-scale European sculpture. Set within a corbelled arch, this constructive technique was used for the Cyclopean-scale vaulted chambers at Tiryns, and more adventurously for the tholos ("beehive") tombs, the most impressive of which is the Treasury of Atreus (*circa* 1375 BC) at Mycenae, a 15-metre (49-ft) span dome with side chamber. Earlier shaft graves have revealed elaborate niello-inlaid bronze daggers, lion and bull head rhytons, and the remarkable, haunting and somewhat heraldic gold masks placed over the faces of the dead.

LEFT: *The Artist's Family*, by Nikolaos Kounelakis, 1864.
RIGHT: The Lion Gate, Mycenae.

The Geometric

Iron Age peoples entered Greece *circa* 1100 BC: Mycenean society collapsed and the so-called Dark Ages, more properly the Geometric period, began. Few artefacts except pottery vessels survive. Decorated with geometric horizontal banding, including spirals and diapers akin to Minoan and Mycenean work, and also the Greek key, these were often associated with burials: some depict funerary processions with geometrised figures. Others assumed anthropomorphic shapes. From *circa* 750 BC small figurines of seated goddesses, charioteers, animals and warriors appeared in bronze, ivory and ceramic.

came closer to reality, but the sense of idealisation was never lost.

Central to this concept was harmonic proportion. In the evolution of the temple a perfectly balanced system of horizontals and verticals developed. Archaic temples followed the Doric form: it was sturdy (it was likened to a man), with sharply fluted columns that had simple capitals and no base. These carried an entablature featuring square metope panels between vertical triglyph mouldings. The form of a colonnaded, box-like structure as a "home" for the deity, often sited on a hilltop, created a perfect backdrop for the open-air ceremonies.

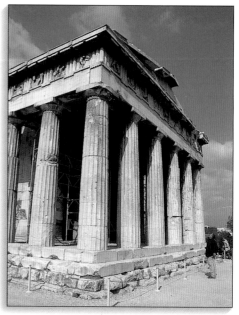

Archaic art

The Archaic period, *circa* 650–490 BC, was one of rapid development. In sculpture, large *kouros* (male youth) and *korai* (clothed female) standing figures were carved, perhaps as personifications of gods, as grave markers, or as worshipper figures. Early *kouroi* demonstrated Egyptian influence in their stance and braided hair. Over time the males become less anatomically stylised and the girls' draperies become more flowing; smiles were depicted, and the feel was for naturalism.

Herein lies a clue to Ancient Greek art. These statues represented ideal figures shown in the prime of life: in time the concept of the ideal

Classical art

The subsequent Classical period, 490–336 BC, saw further rapid developments. Although known by report, scarcely any early Greek painting survives: ceramic decoration gives some clues to its qualities. Archaic vase-painting had been dominated initially by a Corinthian "orientalising" style of fabulous beasts, and then by a vigorous Athenian style of figurative ware in which black figures were placed against the red of the pot (black figure ware). Around 500 BC, this gave way to a reversal of the process giving red figure ware, in which a finer linearism captured greater detail and movement, enhanced by the development of foreshortening and eventually a rudimentary perspective. Early writers tell of panel paintings of exact mimicry of nature by the masters Zeuxis and Apelles. In sculpture, too, much has been lost, and many works are now known only through Roman marble copies of lost bronzes. The greater structural strength of bronze when cast hollow led to more adventurous poses of movement, as with the *Poseidon* (Zeus?) recovered from the sea in 1928. The sculptor Polykleitos's *Doryphoros* (Javelin thrower) was originally in bronze. In this he realised *controposto* – the establishment of convincing weight distribution in a figure.

ing her sandal (Temple of Nike Apteros, Athens Acropolis). The narrative interest was paralled in dramas and the creation of semicircular theatres moulded from the contours of the land.

Late Classical sculpture saw the emergence of a more private attitude to the figure, particularly in portraiture and the self-involved statues of Praxiteles; notably his *Cnidian Aphrodite* and the *Hermes with the infant Dionysios*. The former introduced the nude figure, previously rare. A feminine architectural theme was provided by the more slender and elegant Ionic style of temple where the spiral volutes of the capitals were equated to a girl's curling hair. In

From 447 to 432 BC his contemporary, Pheidias, mastered the depiction of narrative schemes and vigorous action in his reliefs and statues for the Temple of Zeus at Olympia and the Parthenon in Athens. The Parthenon reliefs, like much Ancient Greek sculpture and architecture, were brightly painted, probably making them less "pure" to modern eyes. For both temples Pheidias created gigantic deities of ivory and gold, now lost. A perfect blend of naturalism with idealism had been achieved, well seen in the *Nike adjust-*

these temples the entablature rejects the Doric metopes and triglyphs, but might include a continuously sculpted frieze section. After 350 BC a more forceful sculptural manner emerged with Scopas. His active military reliefs foreshadowed the dynamic work of Alexander the Great's favoured sculptor Lycippos, whose *Apoxyomenos* (Sweat scraper) was given a tight muscularity and the smaller proportioned head of an aggressive figure.

Hellenistic art

Alexander's accession in 336 BC, marking the beginning of the Hellenistic phase, was followed by the rapid expansion of the Greek

FAR LEFT: the Cretan 'Lady of Auxerre', 640–630 BC.
LEFT: the Doric Hephaeiston, Athens' Agora.
ABOVE: a red figure vase, 5th century BC.

Empire: his capital was established at Babylon, and the centre of artistic production tended to move eastwards, particularly to Anatolia. Pergamon was especially important sculpturally during 250–160 BC. The adoption of the Babylonian cult of Tyche (Fortune), with its associated astrology, led to a breakdown of free thought. In sculpture emphasis was put on movement, as in the *Nike of Samothrace* (now in the Louvre in Paris), realism, the display of emotion and more complex poses. From this period survive many mass-produced ceramic figures of gods, dancing figures and satyrs, often known as Tanagra figures after the town

The absorption of Greece into the Roman Empire by 146 BC reaffirmed Roman admiration and development of Greek forms of art and architecture. Indeed, apart from sculptures a few larger paintings such as the mosaic *Battle of Issus* (Pompeii, *circa* 50 BC) are known by their Roman copies. Roman pillaging of sanctuaries and cities was matched by the employment of Greek artists. The practical bent of the Romans emphasised physically truthful portraiture and its use as propaganda (see the *Augustus* from Athens's Roman agora), and hero worship as with the bust of *Antinoos* from Pátra. Roman forms of arched architecture were

in Boeotia. During this luxury-loving age the continuance of refined goldwork for jewellery, and filigree and leaf diadems was matched by the remarkable Derveni krater, a copper alloy *repoussée* wine vase used as a cinerary urn despite its Dionysiac scenes.

In architecture a new, complex quality was introduced with the foliate Corinthian column capital, first used at the Choragic monument to Lysicrates, Athens, in 336 BC. It was often used on a gigantic scale as for the Olympeion, Athens, *circa* 170 BC. Houses appear to have been simple structures to judge from the painted Thracian tomb chests preserved in Thessaloníki museum.

adopted and also the preference for sumptuous palaces. The surviving Galerius Gateway, AD 298–303, at Thessaloníki conveys something of their splendour: its reliefs reflect the Roman-Hellenic interest in illusionism and narrative.

Christianity and Byzantium

That Christian communities were quickly established in Greece is demonstrated by St Paul's letters to the Corinthians and Thessalonians. Constantine the Great's assumption of Christianity as the offical Roman religion in 330, coupled with making Byzantium (modern Istanbul) his capital, determined the future direction of Greek religion and what is known as Byzantine art. Christianity led to an art of symbolism, and because of a fear of idolatry, sculpture in the round became rare, as did the mainstay of antiquity, the nude; figures thus became described by their drapery. Many artefacts of this mystic art were produced in Byzantium and exported to the Balkans. Levantine motifs, particularly from silks, were mixed with Roman ones in an art that emphasised richness and sophistication, religiously and secularly, although little survives of the latter.

Architecturally, two forms of church emerged alongside the Roman basilica form of nave, aisle and apse: one, the central domed space, some-

was challenged. However, Néa Móni on Híos has good mosaics from *circa* 1050, and Mystrás has fine 14th-century paintings. Other devotional works were relief-carved ivory codex (book) covers, boxes and pyxes; but most characteristic were icons (tempera- or occasionally encaustic-painted panels of saints). These were initially domestic and often for women at home, but were later placed on pillars flanking the space to the altar. In turn more icons were added to the *témplon* or barrier before the altar, and in time they multiplied to create an iconostasis or screen separating nave from chancel and congregation from clergy (as with the fine example found in the

times over an octagon (as in Ósios Loukás), and the other a cruciform domed space (such as Holy Apostles, Athens). In these the dome was often emphasised by the image of Christ giving his blessing (the Pandokrátor), a fitting symbol as one took communion below. Surviving paintings are often mosaics of glass, sometimes gilded, that were set at slight angles so that in the flickering candlelight the images shimmered. Many paintings were destroyed during the Iconoclastic crisis of 726–843 when the whole validity of imagery

Megálou Meteórou monastery). An arrangement of a central Christ flanked by Mary and St John the Baptist, Saints Peter and Paul and other apostles and saints in order of importance became known as the Great Deesis. Such screens greatly enhanced the mysticism of the Orthodox religion, which formally dates from the Great Schism of 1054.

Byzantine culture was increasingly under threat, first from Islam but also from the West, particularly its former allies Venice and Genoa. However, it did experience an artistic revival in manuscripts and the paintings at Mystrás, which show a greater interest in plasticity, under the Palaeologue dynasty (1261–1453).

LEFT: Corinthian columns on the Temple of the Olympian Zeus, Athens.
ABOVE: Byzantine mosaics, Ósios Loukás.

The capture of Byzantium by the Ottoman Turks in 1453 meant Greece became nominally part of the Islamic world, although from as early as 1204 the Ionian and some of the Aegean Islands, the Dodecanese, Crete and several mainland cities were ruled by Venice and other Western powers *(see page 40)*. In consequence, Venetian and Frankish influence was felt in architecture, notably at Haniá, Crete, and other fortresses. After 1453 many refugee painters emigrated to the Venet-

> ### "THE GREEK"
>
> Crete's most famous painter is Domeniko Theotokopoulos, whose *Adoration of the Magi* (Benáki Museum, Athens) shows his work as an icon painter before his move to Venice and later to Spain – where he was known as El Greco.

other domestic utensils). Often distinct, lively regional and island vernacular styles are apparent, particularly in embroidery.

Domestic architecture favoured timber-panelled rooms which stylistically linked traditions from Istanbul with European precedents. The emigration of many Greeks, both east and west and known as the diaspora, helped fuse many influences into the Greek arts. One notable example is that of Greek craftsmen working at Iznik on ceramic ware with Grecian subject

ian-held Ionian Islands and Crete, where Venetian influence tempered icon painting of the 15th to 17th centuries, as in the work of Ioannis Permeniatis and Michael Damaskinos.

Art under the Ottomans

Ottoman rule in Greece allowed religious tolerance, but the Islamic scepticism of figurative imagery was nevertheless felt, particularly in larger public works. Although icon painting persisted – often small-scale and domestic – more emphasis was put on the decorative arts in which Eastern and Western influences are found, especially in textiles, including kilims, jewellery and metalwork (lamps, platters and

matter. Much of the characteristically domed Ottoman buildings have been destroyed, including the mosque built in the Athens Parthenon. However, in Thessaloníki the baths, including the Yahudi Hamam, the market (Bezesténi) and Greece's largest mosque, the Hamza Bey, survive, at least in part. And Lésvos, which did not become part of the modern state until 1912, has a Turkish quarter in Mytilíni, numerous Turkish villages and a castle at Sígri (1757).

Neoclassicism

Roman Pompeii, discovered in 1763, provoked a renewed interest in antiquity, and the writings of the German scholar Winckelmann suggested that Greek art was superior to Roman. Consequently, a pro-Hellenic movement arose in western Europe which, allied to growing nationalist aspirations, led to a resurgence of interest in Classical Greece (often known as neoclassicism) which dominated the arts during and after the Wars of Independence of 1821–8 and full independence in 1830. A German, Otto of Wittelsbach, was appointed king and it is therefore Germanic influence, particularly from Schinkel, that dominates neoclassical architecture – especially in Athens, the capital from 1834. Monumental, largely Ionic structures that reflect mainstream European neoclassicism are Von

with the vernacular in his own house. This eclectic attitude gained pace and unsurprisingly the Byzantine style found favour, as with Kaftantzoglou's Athens Eye Clinic, and as late as 1933 with the church of Ágios Konstantínos, by Aristotelis Zahos, at Vólos. Scores of houses composed as assemblages of geometric forms with classical detailing and an overall symmetry show the popularity of the neoclassical style.

Just as architecture paralleled the mainstream European patterns, so too did painting and sculpture. Sculpture which had been marginalised during the Byzantine and Ottoman years revived, initially in the Classical taste, especially

Gartner's Royal Palace (1835–41), and the work of two Danish architects, Christian Hansen's National Capodistrian University (1837) and Theophilus Hansen's National Library (1859–91) and Academy (1859–87). Native architects adopted the style, notably Lysandros Kaftantzoglou (Athens Technical University) and Stamatis Kleanthis, Schinkel's student. The latter built the neoclassical Wortheim house (Athens, 1843) and also the revived Renaissance-style Byzantine Museum (Athens, 1840–8), as well as toying

at Tínos where a school of decorative carving had flourished. Examples are Prosalentis's *Plato*, 1815, or Drosis's *Penelope*, 1873 (both in the National Gallery in Athens). Given the dominance of German tutors at the Royal School of Fine Arts, Teutonic concepts affected students like Fytalis whose *Shepherd* (1856, National Gallery) owes something to Schadow. Vitsaris's Pavlópoulos Tomb (1890, Athens Próto Nekrotafío) demonstrated interest in western Baroque, while Demetriades's *Male Figure* (1910, National Gallery) or Philippolis's *Reaper* (1870, Athens Záppio) picked up contemporary naturalist tendencies. In painting, portraiture – at first somewhat naïve – and subject painting took

LEFT: The Mosque of the Janssaries, Haniá, Crete.
ABOVE: Hansen's neoclassical Academy, Athens.

off following independence, thus supplementing the Venetian-influenced religious works that had been popular in the Ionian Islands in the 18th century, such as Doraxas's *Birth of the Virgin* (Zákynthos Museum).

The 1821–8 wars provoked many dramatic paintings with a romantic flavour and occasional religious overtones, such as Vryzakis's *Exodus from Mesolóngi* (1853, National Gallery). Greek life was also celebrated, as in the German-influenced Gysis's *Children's Betrothal* (1877, National Gallery) or Lystras's *The Dirge on the Isle of Psara* (pre-1888). Both artists, perhaps surprisingly, were also attracted to Orientalist

terms much appears derivative. Elements of Cubism appear in the paintings of Parthenis, and Gika, whose *Athenian Houses* is of 1927–8; in *Sky* in 1966 Gika touches on futurism (both pictures are in the National Gallery). Surrealist imagery akin to de Chirico surfaced with Engonopoulos (*Poet and Muse*, 1938, National Gallery), and persisted in later artists such as Caras (*Three Graces*, 1974, National Gallery). Perhaps more successful was Tsarouhis's interpretation of Matisse's linearism, such as in *Youth in an Overcoat* (1937, National Gallery), which has a strong design also seen in Moralis's figurative work of the 1940s and 1950s (as in

subjects. By the late 19th century other artists were picking up on new subjects, landscape (Lampesis) and still life (Pantazis), while others became attracted to Impressionism and its offshoots – for example, Sabbides's *Lady in an Evening Dress* (1889, National Gallery).

The 20th century

Greek artists of the 20th century broadly followed the major European trends and readily accepted modernism, not least because many studied in Paris. However, where most progressive Western developments occurred before 1930, Greek modernist artists were latecomers of the 1920s; consequently, in international

Figure, 1951, National Gallery). Moralis's classicist realism was typical of much painting produced during the dictatorship; sometimes painterly as with Tetsis, or linear with Mavroidis, or reflective of Byzantine patterning as with Nikolaou. Such work can often feel more truly Greek than the experiments with abstraction and recent conceptual and post-modernist art.

Sculptors of the early 20th century were likewise often trained in Paris. Consequently the impact of Maillol is felt in Tombros's *Fat Woman* (1926, National Gallery), and Despiau in Raftopoulou's *Sculpture* (1932, National Gallery). These matched an interwar concern for the figure while embracing some abstraction, a trend that lingered into the 1950s and 1960s with Kastriotes's enchanting *Dance* (1953, National Gallery), and Pappas's *Male Figure* (1965, artist's collection). But generally, from 1949 abstraction and the international style tended to prevail. Koulentianos's *Tree* (1988, Athens, Portalakes collection) reflected the spirit of Chadwick; Takis's *Light Signals* (1985, Paris, private collection) revealed a dull post-modernist wit; and Hrysa's *New York Landscape* (1971–4, Athens, Mihalarias collection) used light intriguingly but in a formally predicable presentation.

In architecture the eclecticism that persisted into the 1930s extended to vernacular forms. Not

worked in Perret's studio. The latter worked on the ambitious ministry-led programme of new school building in the 1930s. Many Athenian blocks of flats were in the modernist manner, examples being those by Panagiotakos on Themistokléous Street, or those by Mihailidis and Valentis on Zémi and Stounára streets. Post-civil war (1944–9) rebuilding of the rapidly expanding cities saw, as in most countries, much shoddy and uninspired concrete building of official and private offices, apartment blocks, and vast numbers of "industrial vernacular" houses. Nevertheless, certain structures, essentially to internationalist patterns, are particularly distin-

just with Zahos, who drew inspiration from Macedonian and Aegean traditional building, but also Pikonis who, with a greater eye for unctionalism, came closer to modernism in his Pevkákia School (1933, Athens). Zahos was also in part responsible for the rebuilding of Thessaloníki following the fire of 1917, giving Byzantine overtones to the manner of Hausman in Paris. True modernism was introduced by the Bauhaus-trained Despotopoulo; Mihailidis, who worked with Le Corbusier; and Karantinos who

guished, especially around Athens: the Mégaro Mousikís (1975); the Athens School of Music (1976); the Museum of Cycladic Art by J. Vikelas (1985) with its serene interior; the solar-powered Mytaras house by Sauvatzidis (1985); the Agios Dimitrios School by Zenetos (1976); and the sculptural E. Benaki Street apartments by Atelier 66 (1972). These and others parallel the best architecture in any modern city. But perhaps one of the most satisfying and relatively modest structures to combine modernist with vernacular elements is Konstantiniidis's Hotel Xenia at Mýkonos, 1960. The confidence of the best recent architecture bodes well for the future cultural progression of Greek art as a whole. ❑

LEFT: War Scene, Theodoros Vryzakis, 1849.
ABOVE: Carmeni, Santoríni, Konstantinos Maleas, 1918–28.

FLORA AND FAUNA

As befits its wide variety of habitat, Greece contains a great diversity of wildlife – including some of Europe's last bears, wolves and jackals

Greece is a land of tremendous ecological diversity, second in Europe, in this respect, only to the Iberian Peninsula. From the temperate forests of the Píndos and Rodópi mountains in the north to the arid semi-desert of eastern Crete; and from the rocky Alpine vegetation on the bald upper slopes of mountains like Smólikas and Olympos to the delta marshlands of Évros or again the dunes of islands such as Kós. The current mosaic of landscapes and habitats is due to a combination of geography and the hand of man. Sited in the region where Europe butts up against Asia Minor, and only a short hop from Africa, Greece lies at a kind of ecological crossroads.

Since Neolithic times (12,000 to 3,000 BC) man has wrought enormous changes on the landscape, clearing the primeval forests that once covered much of the country for fuel, pasture and agriculture.

Typical trees

Somewhat less than a quarter of Greece is now forested, with the largest tracts being in the north of the country, in the Rodópi Mountains and the Píndos ranges. Here you have a range of oak, chestnut, beech and other broadleaf woodlands, with tracts of cedar and pine forest that are more related to the Scandinavian north than to the Mediterranean south of Europe. Drive inland, north from Amfípolis in Central Macedonia, and you will pass through three of Europe's major vegetation zones in the space of 150 km (90 miles): Mediterranean, Central European and Northern conifer, typified by trees like birch, Scots pine and Norway spruce.

Pastureland covers some 40 percent of the country, while some 30 percent is cultivated land. Areas where traditional agriculture is still practised are often rich in wildlife but, as elsewhere in Europe, labour-intensive traditional practices are declining. Lands that are unsuited

to modern agriculture are being abandoned to scrub, which means a decline in the diversity of habitat; and where intensive modern agriculture is practised, the use of herbicides, insecticides and fertilisers degrades the land from a wildlife perspective. There are, however, still plenty of mature olive groves which provide a

good habitat for birds and insects.

One of Greece's most emblematic habitats is Mediterranean *maquis* – the scrubby, drought-resistant vegetation that covers much of the mainland and islands. This consists of low trees like the glossy-leaved Kermes oak (*Quercus coccifera*) and the Holm oak (*Quercus suber*), with its thinner, tapering leaves; hardy shrubs like myrtles, arbutus, strawberry tree and bay; and the fragrant underlayer of phrygana – plants like wild rosemary, oregano, lavender and thyme.

On the banks of rivers, you will notice trees like willows, plane trees and poplars; species such as Australian eucalyptus have also been widely introduced. Eucalyptus thrives in the

LEFT: wolves roam the mountains of northern Greece.
RIGHT: a native plant known as "spikey bear's breeches".

dry climate, but ecologists view the species with circumspection or downright hostility due to the amount of water these trees suck out from the soil and the damaging effects that has on the soil's pH value.

Wetlands are one of the most threatened habitats in Greece – three-quarters of the country's original wetlands have been lost, and many others are under extreme pressure, what with the heavy demands for water for agriculture and tourist usage as well as targeted drainage for construction. Nevertheless, Greece still possesses several wetlands of great international importance, including 10 that are

listed as being of international importance under the Ramsar Convention: Pórto Lágos and lakes Vistonís and Ismáris; Néstos Delta; Lake Mikrá Préspa; Mesolóngi lagoons; Amvrakikós Gulf; Vólvi and Korónia lakes; Lake Kerkíni; Aliákmon Delta, Axiós and Loudías; Évros Delta; and the Kotýhi lagoons. These encompass a variety of habitats from river deltas, shallow lagoons, saltmarsh, swamps, reedbeds and lakes.

Elusive mammals

Man's impact on the wildlife of Greece has been as significant as his impact on the land's habitats. The Barbary lions and Anatolian

leopards known to the Ancient Greeks are long-since gone, hunted to extinction. And many of the most famous species that have survived are scarce and elusive – only the luckiest or most patient visitors will catch a glimpse of them in the wild.

In the mountains of northern Greece you can still find areas of real wilderness, and it is here that some of the country's rarest land mammals are to be found. First among these are the continent's most southerly population of European brown bears *(Ursos arctos)*, found in the North Píndos range along the border with Albania and FYROM, and also in the Rodópi Mountains of Eastern Macedonia and Thrace, close to the border with Bulgaria.

The conservation body Arcturos (www.arcturos.gr) – which has information centres in the prefecture of Flórina – sets out to protect both the 150-odd animals that survive and the habitat they live in. Bears have been protected by law since 1969, but still suffer from illegal hunting and habitat destruction.

Arcturos also works to protect Greece's population of wolves *(Canis lupus)* and has a sanctuary at Agrapidía, Flórina prefecture. It is only fairly recently that the wolf has enjoyed protected status – official bounties were paid until 1980 and, until 1991, it was still considered "vermin", which allowed hunting to protect livestock. Although wolves do take sheep from time to time, other ungulates form the preferred diet: mainly red deer *(Cervus elaphus)*, fallow deer *(Dama dama)* and roe deer *(Capreolus capreolus)*.

The wolf is officially listed as "vulnerable": population estimates range from a few hundred to low thousands, mainly in the Rodópi Mountains along the border with Bulgaria, but also along the borders with FYROM and Turkey, the high mountains of central Greece, Kerkíni, Falakró and the Évros region. Wolves died out in the Peloponnese some time between 1940 and 1970, and their survival elsewhere is by no means secure: they are threatened principally by habitat loss through logging, illegal hunting, road kills, hybridisation with dogs, and habitat disturbance through recreational tourism.

Other woodland mammals include the wild boar *(Sus scrofa)* and the common Eurasian badger *(Meles meles)*. Driving at night in northern Greece you may spot a crested porcupine *(Hys-*

trix cristata), an animal that may well have been introduced from Africa in ancient times as a food source. However, the most common nocturnal mammals you are likely to see are the country's numerous species of bat. In conifer forests, look out for the red squirrel *(Sciurus vulgaris)* with its bushy tail, white underbelly and ear tufts; and the pine marten *(Martes martes)*, distinguished from its cousin, the beech or stone marten *(Martes foina)*, by its creamy, yellowish throat patch, as compared with the latter's which is pure white. In

> **PYGMY PONY**
>
> A type of very small wild horse has lived on the island of Skýros since ancient times. There are a few hundred surviving members of this unique breed.

smaller wild cat *(Felix sylvestris)*, resembling a large grey domestic cat, with black stripes and a bushy tail – which are found in a variety of habitats on the mainland and as part of a small, threatened population on Crete.

The red fox *(Vulpes vulpes)* is common and widespread, unlike a similar-looking animal more commonly associated with Africa: the golden jackal *(Canis aureus)*. Greece is the northernmost limit of the jackal's range, but populations have collapsed even in the last 20 years. Now only a

addition to these two types of martens, you might see other members of the mustelid family, including the weasel *(Mustela nivalis)* and the polecat *(Mustela putorius)*.

Otters *(Lutra lutra)* can still be found but are scarce, and your best chance of seeing them is in national parks like Préspa or Víkos-Aóös in Epirus. Similarly elusive are members of the cat family – the endangered lynx *(Lynx lynx)*, with its characteristic ear tufts, which survives in the southern Dinaric Alps; and the much

LEFT: the Australian bottle brush shrub grows wild in the Ionian Islands and elsewhere.
ABOVE: brown bears in the Rodópi Mountains.

few hundred remain, mainly in wetlands and *maquis* regions of Fókis, the Peloponnese, Halkidikí and the island of Sámos. The World Wide Fund for Nature (WWFN) has recently instigated a project to study the country's jackal population and draw up an action plan to protect them (www.panda.org/about_wwf/where_we_work/europe/where/greece/jackals/index.cfm). Hunting jackals was forbidden in 1990, but they are still persecuted for stealing sheep and chickens, frequently taking the blame for kills by stray dogs. In fact, 50 percent of their diet is vegetarian, and the rest comes from carrion and hunting small animals such as reptiles, frogs, insects, small rodents and the ubiquitous rabbits.

Other notable mountain mammals include three species of wild sheep: the nimble chamois *(Rupicapra rupicapra)*, the European mouflon *(Ovis musimon)* and the Cretan wild goat/ibex (also known as the agrími or krí-krí; *Capra aegagrus cretica)*, with its bearded chin and curved horns, most dramatic on the large males. This latter species, worshipped in antiquity, is now endangered, largely due to hunting. It is mainly found in the Gorge of Samariá national park in Western Crete, but in the 1960s breeding colonies were established on nearby islands like Día and Ágii Pándes in an effort to save it from extinction.

Cold-blooded creatures

Not all of Greece's wildlife is elusive, and nor does tracking it down always demand hours of strenuous exercise. Some species actually visit you, in what you might call the wildlife equivalent of room service. Perhaps the most enchanting of these are the country's many species of geckos – the most keen-sighted of all lizards, whose large eyes are perfect for hunting insects at night or in darkened rooms. Most astonishing is their ability to run up and down vertical surfaces due to the adhesive pads on their feet.

Other curious lizards of Greece to look out for include the Mediterranean chameleon *(Chamaeleo chamaeleo)*, growing up to 30 cm (1 ft) long, and unmistakeable with its prehensile tail and bulbous eyes; and the large, rough-scaled agama lizard *(Laudakia* or *Agama stellio)*, found on Salamína, the Cyclades and islands of the eastern Aegean. The Aegean Islands have a high number of reptilian endemics: six species of lizards and three types of snake are not found anywhere else in Europe.

Greece's snake species include Europe's most venomous, the nose-horned viper *(Vipera ammodytes)*, with distinctive zigzags on its back; but most – like the grass snake *(Natrix natrix)* or the fast-moving Dahl's whip snake *(Columber najadum)* – are harmless.

One of Greece's most famous reptiles is the yellowish Hermann's tortoise *(Testudo hermanni)*, once heavily exploited for the pet trade, but now protected. It is found in scrubby land in coastal regions of the country; keep an eye out for it when looking around ruins. A more localised cousin found in northern Greece is the spur-thighed tortoise *(Testudo graeca)*.

Marine life

Many visitors to Greece will have more opportunity to familiarise themselves with the country's marine wildlife than that which is to be found inland. Greece has more coastline than any other Mediterranean country – some 15,000 km (9,300 miles) of it. The benign temperature of the Aegean and its relatively small tides make it good snorkelling territory. Look out for octopuses, of which there are two types – the common *(Octopus vulgaris)* and the musky *(Eledore moscata)* – cuttlefish, sea urchins, starfish, sea cucumbers and anemones. You may also see pipefish *(Sygnathus spp.)* and seahorses *(Hippocampus ramulosus)*.

Visit the local harbour and you might see conger eels, ocean fish, parrot fish, dolphin fish and even sharks – both blue *(Prionace glauca)* and mako *(Isurus oxyrinchus)* – among the fishermen's catch. The Mediterranean is heavily overfished, with industrial fleets being particularly to blame; one of the species that bears the brunt of this is the tuna *(Thunnus thynnus)*.

Resist the temptation to buy or collect other sea products, such as threatened red coral *(Coralium rubrum)* or bath sponges *(Spongia officinalis)*.

Loggerhead turtles

Another vulnerable marine species is the loggerhead turtle *(Caretta caretta)*. Many die each year, entangled and drowned by fishing nets, but the real threat to their continued survival is the status of their ancestral nesting sites. Many of the beaches turtles once chose to nest on in areas such as the Peloponnese and Crete have lost out over the years to tourism developments (the only large nesting sites are on Zákynthos). Natural hazards have always meant that only a tiny proportion of eggs laid make it to full turtlehood: animals like foxes predate on the eggs (which are laid between the end of May

If you are keen on turtle protection, stay away from nesting beaches and think of joining Archelon, the Sea Turtle Protection Society of Greece (Solomoú 57, GR-104 32 Athens, Greece, tel: 00 30-210-523-1342; www.archelon. gr). Things are not as bleak as they once were, and ecologists have scored a notable victory at Zákynthos in the Ionian Islands where a National Marine Park for turtles was established in 1999.

Marine mammals

On boat trips, keep your eyes peeled for one of the cetaceans that can be found in Greek waters:

and August), and birds eat hatchlings (which emerge from July to the end of October) as they make their way to the sea. But human disturbance can have an even more devastating effect. Noise and curious tourists can cause adult turtles to abandon nests, and light pollution can disorientate hatchlings, causing them to head inland, where they die, rather than out to sea. Similar problems afflict the green turtle *(Chelonia mydas)*, which can also be found in Greek waters and still breeds in Cyprus.

the common dolphin *(Delphinus delphis)*, which is frequently to be seen playing in schools in the bow wave of boats; its larger, darker cousin, the bottlenose dolphin *(Tursiops truncatus)*, which is the type of dolphin most commonly seen in aquariums; the striped dolphin *(Stenella coeruleoalba)*; a long-finned pilot whale *(Globicephala caretta)*; a sperm whale *(Physeter catadon)*; or a fin whale *(Balaenoptera physalus)*.

The monk seal

Perhaps Greece's most important marine mammal, however, is the Mediterranean monk seal *(Monachus monachus)*. This animal, predominantly brown or grey in colour, is unusual

LEFT: the endangered loggerhead turtle is a protected species.
ABOVE: Mediterranean monk seals are also protected.

among seals because it lives in warm waters. It eats mainly fish and octopus, and can grow over two metres (6 ft) in length and weigh more than 300 kg (660 lb). In ancient times, monk seals were common – they figured on Greek coins from as far back as 500 BC and featured in the writings of Homer, Plutarch and Aristotle. Now, however, they are one of the most endangered mammals in the world. Only 300 to 500 individuals survive, with Greece and Western Sahara having the only significant populations, and it is a battle to save them.

Whereas in Ancient Greek times they were trusting, they are now shy of man and are

confined to the most isolated coasts. In Roman times and in the Middle Ages they were hunted heavily for their pelts, meat and oil, but they have also been hard-hit in the last hundred years by pollution and a steep decline in fish stocks. Until very recently, they were persecuted by fishermen who viewed them as competition for fish stocks and who resented them for damaging fishing nets. Now one of the reasons for their continued vulnerability is disturbance through tourism – often unwittingly, such as when yachts seek out the type of deserted coves where the caves in which the seals live and breed are located.

One of their last remaining strongholds is the Alónisos National Marine Park in the Northern Sporades, created in 1992, but poorly managed by the Greek government. The main society fighting for their protection is the Hellenic Society for the Study and Protection of the Monk Seal (www.mom.gr/eng_version/eng_version.htm). It is based in Alónisos, where it runs an exhibition centre in Patitíri and the Seal Treatment and Rehabilitation Centre for sick and orphaned seal pups at Stení Vála. Its work has helped bring about some small encouraging signs: local attitudes towards the animals have shifted, and they are no longer intentionally killed; and scientists believe that seal birth rates may be rising. More information on this fascinating creature and the world's other monk seal species can be found at www.monachus.org

Birds

Sited on important avian migration routes, Greece is an excellent destination for birdwatchers, especially in spring and autumn, but also in winter, when many northern European birds come to avoid the cold. Enthusiasts should contact the Hellenic Ornithological Society (www.ornithologiki.gr/en/enmain.htm).

One of the best wetland sites in the country is Lake Mikrá Préspa National Park, on a mountainous plateau in western Macedonia, on the borders of Albania and FYROM. Here you can find breeding colonies of both white pelican (*Pelecanus onocrotalus*) and Dalmatian pelicans (*Pelecanus crispus*), as well as the threatened pygmy cormorant (*Phalacrocorax pygmaeus*), which also breeds on lakes Kerkíni and Petrón.

Another majorly important site is the Évros Delta, where you can see wetland and pastureland birds like the lesser white-fronted goose (*Anser erythropus*), the crane (*Grus grus*), the spoonbill (*Platalea leucorodia*), the glossy ibis (*Plegadis falcinellus*), the purple heron (*Ardea purpurea*) and the white stork (*Ciconia ciconia*). Greater flamingos (*Phoenicopterus ruber*) overwinter on the islands of Kós, Sámos, Lésvos and Límnos. As for seabirds, one of the most important is the Audouin's gull (*Larus audouinii*), which is endangered and pretty much endemic to the Mediterranean.

Short-toed larks (*Calandrella brachydactyla*) and calandra larks (*Melanocorypha calandra*) are common on open agricultural land. Your eye might also be caught by the vivid hues of the turquoise-coloured roller *(Coracias garrulus)*, not to mention the smaller bee-eater *(Merops apiaster)*, both of which you may see perched on fence or telegraph wires.

The most glamorously coloured birds of all are the golden oriole *(Oriolus oriolus)*, which is frequently found in woodland and orchards; and the kingfisher *(Alcedo atthis)*, found near streams and waterways. In olive groves and open country, watch out for the ground-feeding hoopoe *(Upupa epops)*, with its unmistakeable pinkish head and crest and its long curved bill. The *maquis* scrub is excellent

most birds of prey, they are vulnerable to hunting and bait laced with strychnine, often put down to kill foxes or – illegally – wolves. In Crete you can still find a few lammergeiers *(Gypaetus barbatus)*, a type of vulture that is famous for its habit of dropping bones from a great height to smash them so that it can extract the bone marrow from within. Three other types of vulture are also to be found in Greece – the griffon vulture *(Gyps fulvus)*, the black vulture *(Aegypius monachus)* and the white-and-black Egyptian vulture *(Neophron percnopterus)*. Other major birds of prey include the fish-eating osprey *(Pandion haliaetus)* and

territory to find songbirds such as warblers, linnets and buntings.

Birds of prey

The Dadiá Forest in Évros is one of the best places in Europe to see birds of prey, including two highly endangered birds: the imperial eagle *(Aquila heliaca)* and the white-tailed or sea eagle *(Haliaetus albicilla)*. Perhaps as many as 200 pairs of golden eagles exist in remote mountainous regions of the country, but, like

---

LEFT: the dramatically-marked hoopoe is often found in olive groves.

ABOVE: a white-tailed sea eagle.

numerous types of kites, harriers, hawks, buzzards and falcons.

Perhaps the most famous of Greece's falcons is the Eleonora's falcon *(Falco eleonorae)*. Similar to a peregrine but with a longer tail and more slender wings, it is often seen in groups hunting off coastal cliffs in the Aegean. Over two-thirds of the entire world population of this threatened bird spend their summer months in Greece, hunting insects during spring and early summer, and delaying their breeding season so that they can raise their fledglings on migrant birds heading to Africa in the autumn, before they too head off on their long annual migration to overwinter in Madagascar. ❏

PLACES

A detailed guide to the entire country, with principal sites clearly cross-referenced by number to the maps

As Henry Miller wrote in *The Colossus of Maroussi*, "marvellous things happen to one in Greece – marvellous *good* things which can happen to one nowhere else on earth. Somehow, almost as if He were nodding, Greece still remains under the protection of the Creator. Men may go about their puny, ineffectual bedevilment, even in Greece, but God's magic is still at work and, no matter what the race of men may do or try to do, Greece is still a sacred precinct – and my belief is it will remain so until the end of time."

Another quotation, this time from a dictionary, defines the Greek word "chaos" as "disordered, formless matter said to have existed before the ordered universe." Chaotic is certainly one way of describing the physical geography of a country characterised by heaps of rocks, furrowed mountain ranges and a jagged coastline. Green, fertile areas such as the Thessalian plain are the exception.

The extensive Pindos mountain range in the west forms the country's backbone, while in the east the peaks of Mount Olympos, at nearly 3,000 metres (10,000 ft), are the highest in Greece. The coast is a series of so many coves and inlets that it runs to a length of 15,000 km (9,300 miles). The hundreds of islands that spill out into the seas surrounding Greece are divided into distinct groups: the Ionian islands to the west, the Sporádes to the east, and the Cyclades and Dodecanese running out southeast from Athens. The two largest islands are Crete and Rhodes, the latter famous for its flowers, though the flora of all Greece is remarkable.

In this section, our expert writers will take you on 15 individual journeys, each author to the part of Greece he or she knows best. Starting with the capital, Athens, we travel from south to northeast through the mainland and then set sail for the many islands, finishing in the "Great Island" of Crete. En route, you will find the history, geography and local culture of each area covered in detail. All the sites of particular interest are numbered on specially drawn maps to help you find your way around. The opening hours given for sites and museums are for summer only (May–September), unless otherwise stated; different hours usually apply from October to April. Tourist facilities on the islands in particular tend to close abruptly once the summer season has finished.

The chapters have been loosely designed as two-week itineraries, but of course the longer you stay, the better. Perhaps, like Lord Byron, you will one day be able to declare: "It is the only place I ever was contented in." ❑

PRECEDING PAGES: Metéora; Ía on Santoríni; the view over Athens from the Acropolis.
LEFT: Fiskárdo harbour, Kefalloniá.

Greece

0 | 50 km
0 | 50 miles

N

ITALY

Brindisi

Lecce

Durrës
Tiranë
Cermenica
Elbasan
Ohridsko
Izero
Prespansko
Izero
Bitola
Nidže
Mavrovoúni 1179
Sér
Flórina
Édessa
Langadás
Berat Partizanit 2417
Vérnon Óros
L. Vegorítidas
Véria
Thessalon
Vlorë **ALBANIA**
Kozáni
Kateríni
Halkidí
Grevená
Tymfi Pindos
Tymfi 2204
Óros 2917
Olympos
Kassándra
Zagori
Elasóna
Thermaikós Kólpos
Kérkyra (Corfu)
Kérkyra
Ioánnina
Kalabáka
Larísa
Piniós
Igoumenítsa
Arahthos
G R E E C E
Tríkala
Pilio Óros
Párga
Notía Pindos
Kardítsa
Vólos
Paxí (Paxos)
Antípaxi
Árta
Tehnití Límni Kremastón
Fársala
Skíath
Tymfristós 2315
Skóp
Prevéza
Lamía
Levkáda
Levkáda (Lévkas)
Eláti 1158
Óri Vardoúsia
Ág. Konstandínos
Meganísi
Agrínio
Astakós
Ámfissa
Halkída
Itháki
Návpaktos
Livadiá
Palovoúna 1748
Argostóli
Póros
Kefalloniá (Cephallonia)
Korinthiakós Kólpos
Pátra
Athín (Ather
Körinthos
Pireás
Salamína
Zákynthos Kyllíni
2224
Árgos
Égi (Aegi
Zákynthos (Zante)
Kerí
Pýrgos
Pelopónnisos (Peloponnese)
Návplio
Argolikós Kólpos
P
Trípoli
Yé (Hy
I O N I A N
Pláka
Spêtses
I o n i a n   I s l a n d s
Kalamáta
Spárti
Taÿgetos
Páno
Argo-Saro
S E A
Gýthio
Lakonikós Kólpos
Neápoli
Kýthira
Kýthira
Andikýthir
Kaste
Kissám

MACEDONIA | **BULGARIA** | **TURKEY**

ALBANIA
Flórina Pela Kilkis
Dhrama
Xanthi Rodhopi
Evros
Kastoria
Serres Kavala
Kozani Imathia Thessaloniki
Grevena Pieria Halkidhiki Óros
Ágio
Ioannina Larisa
Thes-
protia Trikala Magnisía
Kérkyra
Prevéza Arta Kardhitsa Évri-
tania Fthiotida
Lésvos
Lefkáda Etolia Fokídha
Akarnania
G R E E C E
Évia
Viotia
Híos
Kefallonía
Ahaïa Korinthia Atikí
Pireas
TURKEY
Ilía Argolída
Sámos
Zákynthos Arkadía
Messinia Lakonia
Kykládes
Dodekánisa
Hanía
Réthymno
Iráklio Lasíthi

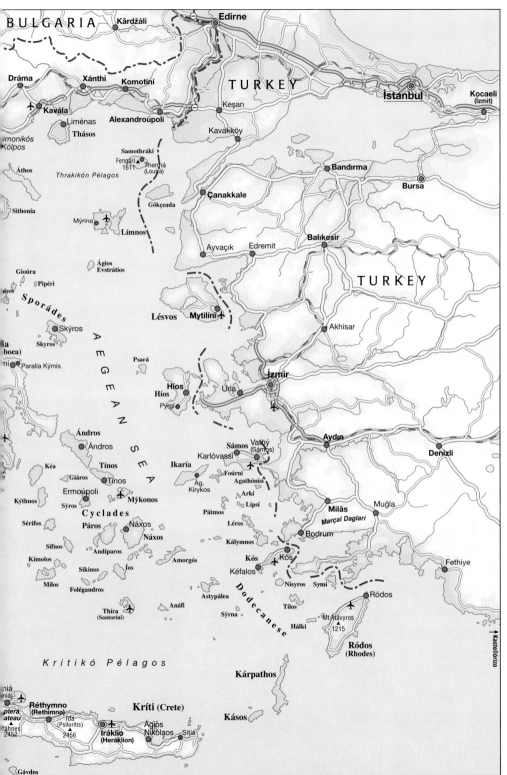

BULGARIA
Kárdžàli
Edirne
Dráma
Xánthi
Komotiní
TURKEY
Keşan
İstanbul
Kocaeli
(İzmit)
Kavála
Liménas
Alexandroúpoli
Kavakköy
Thásos
imonikós
Kólpos
Samothráki
Fengári
1611
Thermá
(Loutrá)
Bandırma
Bursa
Áthos
Thrakikón Pélagos
Çanakkale
Sithonía
Gökçeada
Balıkesir
Mýrina
Límnos
Ayvacık
Edremit
Ágios
Evstrátios
TURKEY
Gioúra
Pipéri
isos
Sporádes
Lésvos
Mytilíni
Akhisar
Skýros
A
E
G
Skyros
boea)
E
Psará
ni
Paralía Kýmis
A
İzmir
N
Híos
Úrla
Híos
Pýrgi
S
Ándros
E
Ándros
A
Aydın
Denizli
Sámos
Vathý
(Sámos)
Kéa
Tínos
Ikaría
Karlóvassí
Giáros
Foúrni
Agathónísi
Ermoúpoli
Tínos
Ág.
Kirykos
Arkí
Milás
Muğla
Kýthnos
Sýros
Mýkonos
Lipsí
Marçal Daglari
Sérifos
Cyclades
Pátmos
Léros
Páros
Náxos
Kálymnos
Bodrum
Sífnos
Andíparos
Náxos
Kímolos
Síkinos
Íos
Amorgós
Kós
Kós
Fethiye
Síkinos
Kéfalos
Mílos
Folégandros
Nísyros
Symi
Astypálea
Dodecanese
Ródos
Thíra
(Santoríni)
Anáfi
Tílos
Síryna
Sýrna
Hálki
Mt Atávyros
1215
Kritikó Pélagos
Kárpathos
Ródos
(Rhodes)
Kastellórizo
niá
niá
ptera
ateau
áhnes
2452
Réthymno
(Rethimno)
Kríti (Crete)
Kásos
Ida
(Psiloritis)
2456
Iráklio
(Heráklion)
Ágios
Nikólaos
Sitía
Gávdos

THE MAINLAND

The mainland of Greece contains a wealth of historical monuments, in landscapes that are often breathtaking

Many visitors to Greece head straight for the islands – and of course there are hundreds of them to choose from, offering everything from sybaritic nightlife to serene tranquillity, from historical marvels to stunning natural beauty. And naturally this book explores Greece's offshore assets in great detail later (*see page 215*). But to bypass the Greek mainland is to overlook the heart of the country, to miss its range of dramatic scenery, and to neglect some spectacular ruins that recall the grandeur of ancient civilisations.

The six chapters that follow explore this rich and varied land, starting in Athens, the birthplace of democracy and home to the most impressive remains from the Classical period anywhere. But there are relics of ancient civilisations to be seen throughout the mainland – the ancient strongholds of Mycenae and Tiryns, predating the Trojan War; the holy site of Delphi, regarded by the ancients as the centre of the world; the stadium and temples of Olympia, where the Olympic Games began; and wonderfully preserved theatres at Epidauros, Argos, Dodona and elsewhere.

Monuments from the Byzantine period include elegant churches and monasteries decorated with glorious mosaics. Thessaloníki, the second city of the Byzantine Empire, has a rich heritage of these stylish churches, and the monasteries of Dafní and Ósios Loukás are world famous for their art treasures. Venetian and Frankish occupation enriched Greece's coastline with picturesque castles and walled cities such as Monemvasía and Koróni. Throughout the country, archeological museums are treasure-houses of beautiful and intriguing relics of Greece's complex past.

But the Greek mainland is not just about history. The timeless landscapes are often breathtaking. The rugged mountain ranges of central and southern Greece descend through craggy ridges to sea-girt peninsulas and promontories. Deep gulfs and inlets penetrate the land, and the narrow coastal plain meets the sea in a fretwork of bays, some of them inaccessible from the land. Elsewhere, gulfs are bounded by mountains cradling tiny harbours and fishing villages, or bordered by pine slopes. ❑

LEFT: the roofs of Monemvasía, Peloponnese.

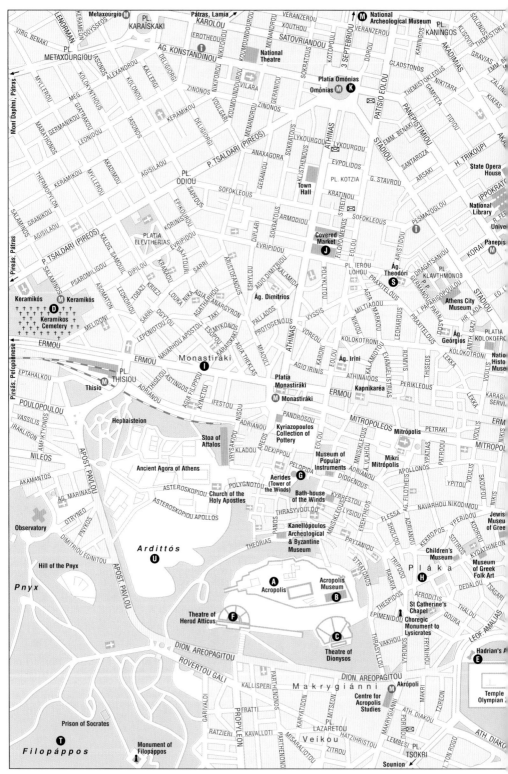

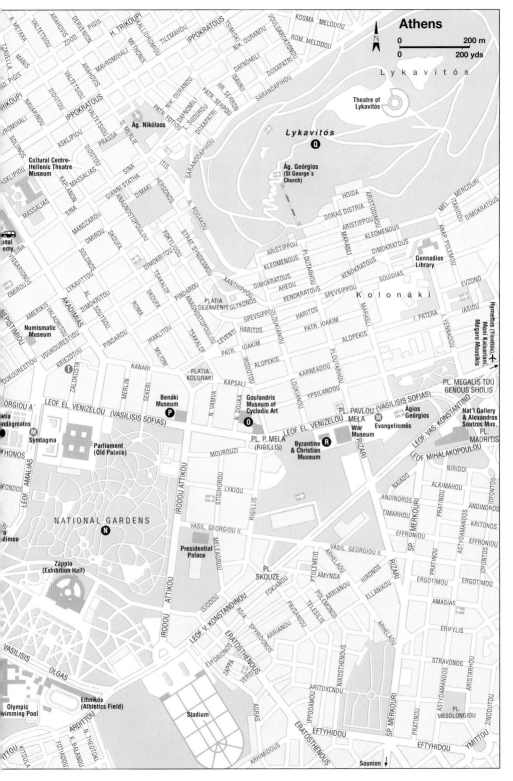

Athens

N

0   200 m
0   200 yds

L y k a v i t ó s

Theatre of
Lykavitós

Lykavitós Q

Ág. Geórgios
(St George's
Church)

K o l o n á k i

Gennadios
Library

Cultural Centre-
Hellenic Theatre
Museum

Ág. Nikólaos

Numismatic
Museum

Benáki
Museum P

Goulandris
Museum of
Cycladic Art O

PLATIA
KOLONÁKI

PLATIA
DEXAMENIS GLYKONOS

Agios
Geórgios

PL. PAVLOU (VASILISIS SOFIAS)

Evangelismós M

War
Museum

LEOF. EL. VENIZELOU (VASILISIS SOFIAS) MELA

PL. MEGALIS TOU
GENOUS SHOLIS

Nat'l Gallery
& Alexandros
Soutzos Mus.

PL.
MADRITIS

Syndagma M

Parliament
(Old Palace)

PL. P. MELA
(RIGILLIS)

Byzantine R
& Christian
Museum

Presidential
Palace

NATIONAL GARDENS N

Záppio
(Exhibition Hall)

PL.
SKOUZE

Olympic
Swimming Pool

Ethnikós
(Athletics Field)

Stadium

Sounion ↓

ATHENS

Both East and West converge in this vibrant metropolis, lively and brimming over, just like its inhabitants. The city is also home to some of the country's most important historical sites

Map, pages 124–5

If there is one quality for which Athens (Athína in Greek) should be credited, it is elasticity. Throughout its long history the city has been obscure, triumphant, forgotten and, now, the capital of the modern Greek state. Athens is barely mentioned in Homer. It emerged as a growing power in the 6th century BC. Then came the Periclean "golden age", when Athens became a great centre of art and literature, commerce and industry. With Macedonian expansion came the first shrinkage, though Athens remained a prestigious intellectual centre with particular emphasis on philosophy and oratory.

In the Hellenistic age, Athens was overshadowed by the great monarchies founded by Alexander's successors – but not obliterated. The rulers of Egypt, Syria and Pergamum courted the old city with gifts of buildings and works of art. Yet it was already beginning to rest on its laurels, to turn into a museum-city, a "cultural commodity" rather than an active, living organism. Besieged and sacked by Sulla in 86 BC, restored and pampered under two philathenian Roman emperors, Augustus and Hadrian, sacked again by the Herulians in AD 267 and Alaric the Goth in AD 395, Athens entered the Byzantine era shorn of all its glory – a small provincial town, a mere backwater. The edict of the Byzantine emperor Justinian forbidding the study of philosophy there (AD 529) dealt a deathblow to the ancient city.

LEFT: *Évzone* guards outside the Parliament.
BELOW: a café on Milióni in Kolonáki.

A sudden elevation

Under Latin rule (1204–1456), invaded, occupied and fought over by the French, Catalans, Florentines and Venetians, Athens shrank even further. It was only after the Ottoman conquest in the 15th century that it began to expand again, but still falling far short of its ancient limits. There were more setbacks, including a devastating Venetian incursion in 1687. Athens finally rose from its ruins after the War of Independence, an "exhausted city", as Christopher Wordsworth noted in 1832, and was suddenly raised, unprepared, to the status of capital of the new Greek state.

Athens is thus a city that has grown haphazardly, and too fast. It never had a chance to mellow into venerable old age. Old and new have not blended too well; you can still sense the small prewar city pushing through the huge sprawl of today's modern capital, like the proverbial thin man struggling to get out of every fat man. Occasionally, you come across what must have been a country villa, ensconced between tall office buildings, its owner still fighting against the tide, its windows hermetically closed against dust, pollution, the roar of the traffic.

Traffic in Athens can be unbelievable, particularly when there is some protest demonstration going on and traffic is forced off the main streets. The new

metro, however, has worked wonders. From the day it opened, huge numbers of Athenians have been using it, making journeys of just a few minutes through the heart of the city that once took well over an hour by car. Suddenly, central Athens has become accessible.

In addition, branching off from the frenzied central arteries are the minor veins of the city, relatively free from congestion. Most apartment blocks have balconies and verandas, and there you can see the Athenians in summer emerging from their afternoon siesta in underpants and nighties, reading the paper, watching the neighbours, watering their plants, eating their evening meal.

The previously traffic-clogged road of Dionysíou Areopagítou around the base of the Acropolis has been pedestrianised. With the Parthenon towering overhead, it quickly established itself as a popular place for the evening vólta, or stroll.

Ancient Athens

Seen from the right angle driving up the **Ierá Odós** (the Sacred Way) or looking up at its rocky bulk from high in Pláka, the **Acropolis ❶** still has a presence that makes the grimy concrete of modern Athens fade into insignificance. Climb up in early morning in summer or early afternoon in winter, when the crowds are thinnest, and a strip of blue sea edged with grey hills marks the horizon. On a wet or windy day, walking across its uneven limestone surface feels like being on a ship's deck in a gale (open daily 8am–7.30pm; the ticket for the Acropolis is also valid for the Ancient Greek Agora, *page 130*, the Theatre of Dionysos, *page 131*, the Roman Agora, *page 133*, the Keramikós Cemetery, *page 131*, and the Temple of Olympian Zeus, *page 132*).

The Acropolis nowadays looks like a stonemason's workshop, much as it must have done in the 440s BC when the **Parthenon** was under construction as the crowning glory of Pericles' giant public works programme. Some of his contemporaries thought it extravagant: Pericles was accused of dressing his

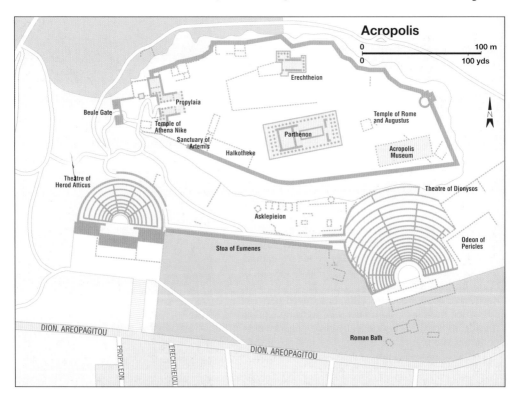

Acropolis

0   100 m
0   100 yds

Erechtheion

Beule Gate

Propylaia

Temple of Athena Nike

Sanctuary of Artemis

Halkotheke

Parthenon

Temple of Rome and Augustus

Acropolis Museum

Theatre of Herod Atticus

Theatre of Dionysos

Asklepieion

Odeon of Pericles

Stoa of Eumenes

N

DION. AREOPAGITOU

PROPYLEON

ERECHTHEIOU

Roman Bath

DION. AREOPAGITOU

city up like a harlot. In fact, the Parthenon celebrates Athena as a virgin goddess and the city's protector. Her statue, 12 metres (39 ft) tall and constructed of ivory and gold plate to Pheidias's design, once gleamed in its dim interior; in late antiquity it was taken to Constantinople, where it disappeared.

Conservators have lifted down hundreds of blocks of marble masonry from the Parthenon to replace the rusting iron clamps inserted in the 1920s with noncorrosive titanium (rust made the clamps expand, cracking the stone, while acid rain turned carved marble surfaces into soft plaster). The restorers also succeeded in identifying and collecting about 1,600 chunks of Parthenon marble scattered over the hilltop, many blown off in the 1687 explosion caused by a Venetian mortar igniting Ottoman munitions stored inside the temple. When they are replaced, about 15 percent more building will be on view. New blocks cut from near the ancient quarries on Mount Pendéli (14 km/ 9 miles north of Athens), which supplied the 5th-century BC constructors, will fill the gaps.

The **Erechtheion**, an elegant architecturally complex repository of ancient cults going back to the Bronze Age, is already restored. The Caryatids now supporting a porch over the tomb of King Kekrops, a mythical founder of the ancient Athenian royal family, are modern copies. The surviving originals were moved to the Acropolis Museum to prevent further damage from the *néfos*, the ochre blanket of pollution, now thankfully less frequent, that hangs over Athens.

Completed in 395 BC, a generation later than the Parthenon, the Erechtheion also housed an early wooden statue of Athena, along with the legendary olive tree that she conjured out of the rock to defeat Poseidon the sea god in their contest for sovereignty over Attica.

Map, pages 124–5

In Ottoman times the Turkish military commander housed his harem in the Erechtheion.

BELOW: recording the Parthenon remains.

THE PARTHENON FRIEZE

The Parthenon Marbles are a 76m² (500 ft²) stretch of sculpted figures – mostly from the frieze – carved under the direction of the master-sculptor and architect Pheidias. By 1799, when Lord Elgin was appointed British ambassador to Turkish-occupied Greece, the Parthenon was in a sorry state, having been practically destroyed and then plundered by the invading Venetians in 1687. Elgin negotiated a permit from the sultan to remove "some blocks of stone with inscriptions and figures", shipped the marbles back to Britain, and in 1816 sold them to the British Museum, where they remain today.

Below the Acropolis near the metro station, a new museum has been built in the **Centre for Acropolis Studies** (Makrygiánni 2–4; open 9–2.30 daily) in which all the sculptures can be housed together. The marbles are an integral part of one of the most beautiful buildings that still survives from antiquity, say the Greeks, and can be better appreciated in the city that made them. The world's major museums claim that to return the marbles would set a disastrous precedent. Recently, however, new proposals have been put forward by the Greeks whereby the marbles would still "belong" to the British Museum but would be put on display in Athens.

The Acropolis Museum houses a collection of sculptures and reliefs from the site.

BELOW: Lycavitós seen from the Acropolis.

The **Propylaia**, the battered official entrance to the Acropolis built by Mnesikles in the 430s BC, was cleverly designed with imposing outside columns to awe people coming up the hill. Parts of its coffered stone ceiling, once painted and gilded, are still visible as you walk through. Currently dismantled, the exquisite square temple of **Athena Nike** (finished in 421 BC) stood on what was once the citadel's southern bastion. It supposedly occupied one of the spots – the other is at Cape Sounion – where Theseus's father, King Aegeus, is said to have thrown himself to his death on seeing a black-sailed ship approaching the harbour. Theseus had promised to hoist a white sail for the return voyage if he had succeeded in killing the Minotaur on Crete, but carelessly forgot.

The sculptures that Lord Elgin left behind are in the **Acropolis Museum B**. The four surviving Caryatids that are in Greece (one was taken by the Ottomans and lost, another is in the British Museum in London) stare out from a nitrogen-filled case, scarred but still impressively female. The coquettish *korai* reveal a pre-classical ideal: if you look closely, you can make out their make-up and earrings, and the patterns of their crinkled, close-fitting dresses (open Tue–Sun 8am–7pm, Mon 11am–7pm; entrance fee included in Acropolis entrance fee).

Just to the north of the Acropolis is the **Ancient Greek Agora** (open daily 8am–7.15pm; entrance fee included in Acropolis entrance fee). The main entrance to this site is on Adrianoú Street, but there is an alternative way in behind the Church of the Holy Apostles. While the Acropolis was mainly a religious site, the Agora was used for all public purposes: commercial, religious, political, civic, educational, theatrical, athletic. Today it looks like a cluttered field of ruins. The reconstructed **Stoa of Attalos**, a 2nd-century BC line of shops,

contains a wonderful, small archeological museum (open Tue–Sun 8am–7pm, Mon 11am–7pm; entrance fee included in site fee). The **Hephaisteion** (also known as the "Theseion"), the temple opposite, is the most complete surviving Doric order temple and gives some idea of what the Parthenon looked like.

Across from the Agora, on the far side of the Piraeus metro line, one corner of the **Painted Stoa** has been exposed in Adrianoú Street. This building gave its name to Stoicism, the stiff-upper-lip brand of philosophy that Zeno the Cypriot taught there in the 3rd century BC.

On the south side of the Acropolis lies the **Theatre of Dionysos ◉**. The marble seating tiers date from around 320 BC and later, but scholars generally agree that plays by playwrights such as Aeschylus, Sophocles, Euripides and Aristophanes were first staged here at religious festivals during the 5th century BC. A state subsidy for theatre-goers meant that every Athenian citizen could take time off to attend (entrance on Leofóros Dionysíou Areopagítou; open daily 8am–7pm; entrance fee included in Acropolis entrance fee).

Past Monastiráki, the **Keramikós Cemetery ◉** in the potters' district of the city was a burial place for prominent ancient Athenians. An extraordinary variety of sculptured monuments – tall stone urns, a prancing bull, winged sphinxes and melancholy scenes of farewell – overlooked the paved Sacred Way leading to the Dipylon Gate from Eleusis, where the mysteries were held. The site museum's collection of grave goods is an excellent guide to Greek vase-painting, from a squat geometric urn with a rusting iron sword twisted around its neck to the white *lekythoi* of classical Athens and self-consciously sophisticated Hellenistic pottery (open daily 8am–7pm; entrance fee included in Acropolis entrance fee).

The Theatre of Dionysos had 64 tiers of seats and held 17,000.

LEFT: the Herod Atticus Theatre.
BELOW: monument to Lysicrates.

The kombolí – a small chain of stone or wooden "worry-beads" – is good for relieving tension.

BELOW: preparing for the festival in the Herod Atticus Theatre.

At the southern end of Pláka, on Platía Lysikrátous, is the **Choregic Monument to Lysicrates**. This is important as it is the earliest example of the use of external Corinthian columns (the latest and most ornate order of Ancient Greek architecture). The inscription commemorates the victory of Lysicrates in 334 BC in a drama contest; the elegant monument was originally crowned by a tripod.

Roman Athens

A few Roman monuments recall a time when Athens was a city to be revered, but stripped of its movable artworks. The 2nd-century **Emperor Hadrian**, a fervent admirer of classical Greek culture, erected an ornate **arch** ❺ marking the spot where the classical city ended and the provincial Roman university town began. On the side facing the Acropolis is the inscription "This is Athens, the ancient city of Theseus", on the side facing the Olympieion it reads "This is the city of Hadrian and not of Theseus". Little of this Roman city can be seen beneath the green of the **Záppio Park** and the archeological area behind the towering columns of the **Temple of Olympian Zeus** (the Olympieion), but recent excavations in the corner of the Záppio indicate that many Roman buildings were in this area, stretching at least to the stadium built by Herod Atticus. Work on the Temple of Olympian Zeus had been abandoned in around 520 BC when funds ran out, but Hadrian finished the construction and dedicated the temple to himself (open daily 8am–7pm; entrance fee).

Later in the century, Herod Atticus, a wealthy Greek landowner who served in the Roman senate, built the steeply raked theatre on the south slope of the Acropolis (the **Herod Atticus Theatre** ❻, now used for Athens Festival

performances) as a memorial to his wife. And a 1st-century BC Syrian was responsible for the picturesque **Tower of the Winds G**, in the **Roman Agora**, a well-preserved marble octagon overlooking the scanty remains of the Roman Agora. It is decorated with eight relief figures, each depicting a different wind direction, and once contained a water-clock (open daily 8am–7pm; entrance fee). In a later incarnation it served as a *tekke* (hall) for the Ottoman dervishes.

Map, pages 124–5

Pláka

Pláka H, the old quarter clustering at the foot of the Acropolis, has been refurbished and restored to its former condition (or rather to a fairly good reproduction of it), the more garish establishments have been closed down, cars prohibited (for the most part), houses repainted and streets tidied up. It has become a delightful, sheltered place to meander in; you might almost imagine yourself in a village, particularly in the winding narrow streets of the Anafiótika district that nestles below the Acropolis.

Pláka is also the best place to track down Athens' Ottoman past. The 15th-century **Fethiye Mosque** in the Roman Agora is one of the finest, and oldest, examples of Muslim architecture in the city; it is unfortunately closed to visitors. However, nearby on Platía Monastiráki is the Tsizdaráki Mosque (1759), now home to the **Kyriazopoulos Collection of Pottery** (open Tue–Sun 9am–2.30pm; entrance fee). The mosque's interior has been sensitively conserved and is well worth a look, especially the brightly painted *mihrab*. Perhaps the most fascinating remnant of Turkish life, however, is the 16th-century **Bath-House of the Winds** on Kyrrestoú (open Wed only, 10am–2pm; entrance fee). This *hamam* (Turkish bath) has been beautifully restored and its warren of rooms are

Pláka is full of tourist souvenirs.

BELOW: the Tower of the Winds.

very atmospheric to explore. A well-produced guide gives background on the building and the place of bathing in Greek and Turkish culture.

As well as those mentioned above, Pláka has a number of other excellent museums. Chief among these is the **Museum of Greek Folk Art** on Kydathinéon (open Tue–Sun 10am–2pm; entrance fee). Among the many exhibits is an excellent collection of regional Greek costume, including carnival costumes from the *dodekímero* (12 days of Christmas) and the faintly disturbing *géros* disguise from Skýros. Among the silverwork look for the *támata* (votive offerings) still seen attached to icons in Orthodox churches.

Opposite is the **Children's Museum** (open Tue–Sat 10am–2pm, Sun 10am–6pm; entrance fee; www.hcm.gr). Geared towards play, this is a good place to visit for people with young children. There is plenty to build, paint and deconstruct; in an inspired piece of foresight, overalls are provided. At the end of Kydathinéon, on Níkis (No. 39), is the **Jewish Museum of Greece** (open Mon–Fri 9am–2.30pm, Sun 10am–2pm; entrance fee; www.jewishmuseum.gr). After you have rung the doorbell to be admitted you find yourself in a cool, modern interior (based on a spiral) full of exemplary displays. The museum is particularly effective in demonstrating the long history of Jewish settlement, and tolerance towards it, in this part of the world.

The **Paul and Alexandra Kanellopoulos Archeological and Byzantine Museum** (open Tue–Sun 8.30am–3pm, Wed until 11pm; entrance fee) is housed in a 19th-century mansion in Anafiótika. It is a smaller treasure-trove of objects from many periods of Greek art, acquired by erudite, obsessive collectors. Also in Pláka and housed in a neoclassical mansion, is the excellent **Museum of Popular Instruments–Research Centre for Ethnomusicology** (open Tue, Thu–Sun 10am–2pm, Wed noon–6pm; free), based around the collection of Fivos Anoyanakis. The museum divides the exhibits into aerophones (blown instruments, such as the *flogéra* reed flute), chordophones (stringed instruments, like the *bouzoúki*), idiophones (instruments where the sound is produced by its body, like cymbals) and membranophones ("drums"); each can be heard at the adjacent listening posts. There is also a good shop where you can find rare recordings of Greek traditional music.

The history of Greek Jewry, celebrated in the Jewish Museum of Greece (right), stretches back unbroken to before the 3rd century BC, but 87 percent of local Jews were wiped out in World War II. Today only about 7,000 Jews live in the country.

BELOW: busy Pláka.

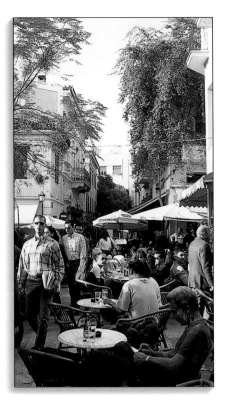

Monastiráki

This entire area, essentially Athens' bazaar, is a huge sprawl of shops, which get more upmarket towards Platía Syndágmatos. **Monastiráki ❶** brings to mind the market described in a 4th-century BC comedy by Euboulos: "Everything will be for sale together in the same place at Athens, figs, summoners, bunches of grapes, turnips, pears, apples, witnesses, roses, medlars, honeycombs, chickpeas, lawsuits, beestings-puddings, myrtle-berries, allotment machines, irises, lambs, waterclocks, laws, indictments." Beestings-puddings and allotment machines sound mysterious enough, but the weird assortment of objects to be found in the market today is just as intriguing. Kitsch-collectors will find much to interest them; Greek kitsch is perhaps the most orgiastically hideous in the world.

Retaining a traditional pattern, the whole area still falls into rough zones, as can be seen from the shops around the **Mitrópolis** (Athens' cathedral), specialising in ecclesiastical articles. The cathedral itself dates from the mid-19th century and is large if undistinguished. However, next door is the small **"old cathedral"** (formally known as Panagía Gorgoepikoös or Ágios Elevtheríos). This church dates from the 12th century but is a hotchpotch of materials reused from earlier churches of the 6th to 7th centuries. Above the door arch is a 2nd-century relief showing the calendar of Attic festivals.

Away from the robust vulgarity of **Pandrósou Street** to the narrow side streets off the **Flea Market**, you step back into time into an almost pre-industrial era. This is the district of traditional crafts (crafts minus "arts"), wholesale shops selling refreshingly nondecorative, down-to-earth stuff like screws, chains of varying thickness, nails, boxes and crates, brushes and brooms, mousetraps and herbs (the mountains of Greece are a botanist's paradise), shops selling resin in big amber-coloured chunks alongside incense and bright blue chunks of copper sulphate used for plants (and catching octopus) – truly a serendipitous accumulation.

As are the goods in the old **covered market ❶**, a 19th-century gem roughly halfway between Monastiráki and Omónia squares on the north side of Athinás Street (you can also enter far more dramatically from the passageway at 80 Eólou Street). This is the city's main meat and fish market, crowded with shoppers milling between open stands displaying fish, seafood and any variety and part of animal you can imagine. Fruit and vegetables are available in the far less successful open area directly across Athinás Street to the south, but the milling scene there is just as vibrant.

Map, pages 124–5

Guarding the Mitrópolis.

BELOW: the Bath-House of the Winds.

Relief in the National Archeological Museum.

BELOW: the pediment of the Academy building.

Omónia to Sýndagma

The city's heart lies within an almost equilateral triangle defined by **Platía Omónias Ⓚ** in the north, Monastiráki in the south and **Platía Syndágmatos Ⓛ** to the southeast. Except for three small cross streets, no cars are permitted in this area, which means it has taken on a new lease of life.

North of Omónia (close to Viktória metro station) and crammed with treasures from every period of antiquity is the **National Archeological Museum Ⓜ**. At present this, one of the city's most important sights, is closed for a complete renovation. Some hints of what the restructured museum might look like could be had from the beautifully displayed Egyptian galleries which were redesigned a few years ago. (Previously open Tue–Sun 8am–7pm, Mon 12.30–7pm; entrance fee; closed until at least June 2004; *see also pages 144–5*.)

Omónia itself has now shed the hoardings that surrounded the metro excavations and been given a new look. However, the rather bleak concrete piazza that now covers the centre of the busy square has been widely criticised, at best it can be said to be unimaginative. The parallel streets of Stadíou and E. Venizélou (also known as Panepistimíou) run southeast from Omónia to Platía Syndágmatos. Halfway down Venizélou is Christian and Theophilius Hansen's neoclassical trilogy of the **National Library**, **University** and **Academy**. Erected between 1839 and 1891, they are built of Pentelic marble and draw heavily on Ancient Greek architectural forms. The startlingly bright painting and gilding gives some idea of how the now stark marble of ancient monuments may have first appeared. Behind the university is the small **Hellenic Theatre Museum** (open Mon–Fri 9am–2pm), which has a charming series of re-created changing rooms of famous Greek actors, including Maria Callas.

Map, pages 124–5

Further on is the house of Heinrich Schliemann, designed in an Italianate style by Ziller (1878). It now houses the **Numismatic Museum** (open Tue–Sun 8.30am–3pm; entrance fee). Of greater interest is the **National Historical Museum** which occupies the prominent Old Parliament Building on Stádiou (open Tue–Sun 9am–2pm; entrance fee). This recounts the history of Greece from the fall of Constantinople (Istanbul) in 1453 to World War II.

Sýndagma Square (Platía Syndágmatos, or Constitution Square) is the centre of the city. Dominated by the **Parliament Building**, it has been pleasantly landscaped following the metro works. The Parliament meets in what was the old Royal Palace, built in 1836–42 for King Otto. The changing of the *Évzone* Guard, a favourite tourist spectacle, takes place in front of the Parliament.

Ermoú, running west from the square, was once a traffic-clogged mess, but is now a long pedestrian walkway with reinvigorated shops, and is enlivened by pavement buskers and pushcarts. Many buildings have been refurbished, while improved lighting makes this an attractive area to wander in the evening in search of a bar or café. Also on Ermoú is the attractive Byzantine church of **Kapnikaréa**, thought to date from the 11th century.

The **National Gardens** ⓝ (open sunrise to sunset; free) are just behind the parliament building. Full of tangled bowers, romantic arbours and quiet fish-ponds, there are thin but constant trickles of water running along secret leafy troughs, ducks and a large population of cats. It was laid out by Queen Amalia as the palace gardens in the 19th century. She used the new Greek navy to bring back botanical specimens from their voyages around the world. Here you can observe the Athenians at rest; lovers meet, old men meditate and businessmen hastily wolf sandwiches.

BELOW: an organ-grinder on Ermoú.

Kolonáki

Chic and expensive, Kolonáki is the city's upmarket shopping district, as well as being the location of many diplomatic missions and some highly desirable apartments. The haunt of Athenian ladies who lunch and shop, if you are looking for designer clothes, shoes and accessories Kolonáki is where you should head for. It is not, however, devoid of culture; Kolonáki has some of the finest museums in the city.

Going back to 3000 BC, the **Goulandris Museum of Cycladic Art** ⓞ (open Mon, Wed–Fri 10am–4pm, Sat 10am–3pm; entrance fee; www.cycladic-m.gr) displays a unique collection of slim, stylised Cycladic statuettes in white marble, beautifully mounted. These figures were scorned by 19th-century art critics as hopelessly primitive, but their smooth, simple lines attracted both Picasso and Modigliani. Mostly female and pregnant, the figures derive from robbed graves scattered throughout the Cyclades islands; to this day, scholars are still uncertain of their true purpose.

The **Benáki Museum** ⓟ can lay claim to being the best museum in Athens. Its wonderfully eclectic collection of treasures from all periods of Greek history, including jewellery, costumes and two icons attributed to El Greco. Among the most impressive displays are the collection of traditional costume, mostly bridal and festival dresses, and the reconstructed

The Benáki Museum contains treasures from all periods of Athens' history.

BELOW: the Museum of Cycladic Art.

reception rooms of a mid-18th-century Kozáni mansion. Also of great interest are the displays of gold on the ground floor, and the collections relating to the Greek struggle for independence. The museum has an excellent gift shop and a pleasant terrace restaurant (open Mon, Wed, Fri, Sat 9am–5pm, Thu 9am–midnight, Sun 9am–3pm; entrance fee; www.benaki.gr). (In Pláka the museum is opening the first separate museum of Greek Ottoman Art, which will put on display some superb artefacts, adding to that district's collection of Ottoman sights, *see page 133.*)

Mount Lycabettus (Lykavitós; 227 metres/744 ft) **❾** rises above Kolonáki, crowned by the tiny chapel of Ágios Geórgios. The easiest way to get to the summit is by the funicular railway that starts from Ploutárhou Street, near Platía Kolonáki (runs every 20 minutes, in summer 8am–10pm, in winter 9.30am–4.40pm). The views from the top over the city are spectacular.

While not strictly in Kolonáki (they are on the wrong side of Vasilísis Sofías), there are two other museums close by that are worth a visit. The **Byzantine and Christian Museum ❿** (open Tue–Sun 8.30am–3pm; entrance free at present) is housed in a mock-Tuscan villa, commssioned by the French 19th-century Duchesse de Plaisance. It contains a brilliant array of icons and church relics from the 13th to the 18th centuries. A long-running project to construct new underground galleries and restore the original buildings is still in progress; until the new galleries are open, only limited sections of the permanent collection are on display. When the stylish new areas do finally open, much more of the museum's huge collection will be on permanent display.

Near the Hilton hotel is the **National Gallery and Alexandros Soutzos Museum** (open Mon, Wed 9am–3pm, 6–9pm, Thu–Sat 9am–3pm, Sun

10am–2pm; entrance fee). This, the national collection of painting and sculpture, is housed in a cool, modern building. It is the Greek paintings here that are best. Particularly interesting are the works from the Ionian School, the late-19th-century realist works, and those which move towards a more Greek sensibility of the early 20th century (see those by Parthenis and Lystras).

Further along Vasilísis Sofías, beside the wonderful **Mégaro Mousikís** concert hall (www.megaron.gr), is **Elevtherías Park**. During the military dictatorship (1967–74) this was the location of the HQ of the military police, where dissidents were detained and tortured. After the fall of the junta the site was turned into a park and cultural centre; it is currently closed as the park receives a face-lift.

Byzantine Athens

Of the city's Byzantine past little remains, but a dozen or so churches, many dating from the 11th century, can be tracked down in Pláka. One of the best is **Ágii Theodóri ❺**, just off Platía Klavthmónos. It was built in the 11th century in characteristic cruciform shape with a tiled dome. The masonry is picked out with slabs of brick and decorated with a terracotta frieze of animals and plants. The church of **Sotíra Lykodímou** on Filellínon Street dates from the same era but was bought by the Tsar of Russia in 1845 and redecorated. It now serves the city's small Russian Orthodox community; the singing is renowned.

On Athens's eastern and western limits there lie two famous monasteries: Kaisarianí and Dafní. **Kaisarianí** on Mount Hymettus, surrounded by high stone walls, is named after a spring which fed an aqueduct constructed on Hadrian's orders. Its waters, once sacred to Aphrodite, the goddess of love, are still credited with healing powers (and encouraging child-bearing). The monastery

Athens is a treasury of Byzantine art.

BELOW: evening in Athens by Iakovos Ritsos, 1897.

church goes back to AD 1000 but the frescoed figures who gaze out of a blue-black ground date from the 17th century. The monks' wealth came from olive groves, beehives, vineyards and various medicines made from mountain herbs (open Tue–Sun 8.30am–3pm; entrance fee).

Dafní is out of town on the road to Corinth (take a bus from Platía Elevtherías, close to Omónia, and get off at the stop for the psychiatric hospital). This small monastery is a curious architectural combination of Gothic and Byzantine, decorated inside with magnificent 11th-century mosaics, and occupies the site of an ancient sanctuary of Apollo. A fierce-looking Christ Pandokrátor, set in gold and surrounded by Old Testament prophets, stares down from the vault of the dome. The building dates from 1080 and the Gothic porch was added in the 13th century when Dafní belonged to Cistercian monks from Burgundy and was used as the burial place of the Frankish Dukes of Athens (closed until further notice for restoration).

Christ Pandokrátor is surrounded by gold on the dome of Dafní monastery.

Piraeus

Athens' port is a city in its own right and is where most people pass through on their way to the islands. It is most easily reached by metro (line 1; allow around 45 minutes for the journey from the centre of town), alternatively, a bus leaves from Sýndagma, but this can be very slow. An express bus runs direct to Piraeus (Pireás) from Athens' new airport (the E96), and stops outside the Port Authority (OLP) passenger building on Aktí Miaoúli street.

Finding your boat can be confusing, but the ticket agent will be able to tell you which quay your ferry departs from. As a general guide: boats to the Cyclades depart from the quays opposite the metro station; boats to the Cycladic islands also go from the other side of Platía Karaiskáki (south of the metro); boats to Crete leave from Aktí Kondýli on the northern side of the port; large catamarans to most island groups, and Flying Dolphins to the Argo-Saronic islands, depart from the quays close by Platía Karaiskáki; and the Dodecanese are served by boats leaving from Aktí Miaoúli.

BELOW: serving in a Piraeus bar.

Piraeus Archeological Museum (open Tue–Sun 8.30am–3pm; entrance fee) has a number of wonderful bronzes. On the first floor is the graceful, archaic Apollo *kouros*, pulled from the sea in 1959, which was made in 530–20 BC and is the earliest life-sized bronze statue. Two other bronze statues, of Athena and Artemis and both dating to the 5th century BC, were found at about the same time in Piraeus when new sewers were being dug. There is a further superb bronze of Artemis, this one dating from the mid-4th century BC. Also impressive, on the ground floor, is the restored mausoleum of an Istrian merchant.

The **Hellenic Maritime Museum**, full of models of ships from all ages, is close by on Zéa Marina (Aktí Themistokléous; open Tue–Sat 9am–2pm; entrance fee). **Zéa Marina** is crowded with medium-sized yachts – a floating campsite in summer – and you may see huge, old-fashioned two- and three-masters as well as sleek motor-yachts moored. Further round the headland are cafés and fish restaurants overlooking the Saronic Gulf.

Map, pages 124–5

The hills

Athens is said to have eight hills. As well as Lykavitós and the equally conspicuous rock of the Acropolis, flanked by the **Pnyx** on one side, and the hill of **Philopappus** (Filopáppos) ❶ on the other, where Athenians fly kites on the first day of Lent, there are: the hill of **Ardittós** ⓤ, next to the marble horseshoe **stadium**, built by Herod Atticus in AD 143 and totally reconstructed in 1896 (the first modern Olympic Games were held there); the **Hill of the Nymphs**, capped by the grey dome of the **Observatory**; the barren, windblown **Tourkovoúnia**; and the hill of **Lófos Stréfi**, far less touristy than Lykavitós, and more built up.

Along with the small hidden cafés there is more than a measure of coolness on some of these hills. For a real escape, however, you have to go further afield, up one of the three mountains that encircle Athens. **Mount Hymettus** (Ymettós), 5 km (3 miles) east of Athens, beloved of honey-bees, glowing violet at sunset, is perhaps the most beautiful. Driving up the winding road past the monastery of **Kesarianí** you reach a tranquil vantage point from which to contemplate the whole of Attica. The city is panoramically visible, yet totally, eerily inaudible. On **Mount Párnitha** (Párnis), just over an hour northwest, there is a forest of fir trees, and you can also ski in winter. **Mount Pendéli**, to the north, is crowded, lively and popular.

Below Mount Pendéli is Athens' most exclusive suburb, **Kifisiá**. Populated, like Kolonáki, with the city's great and sometimes not so good, who reside in its neoclassical villas, Kifisiá is a pleasant place to hang out in one of its expensive cafés. Also here is the **Goulandris Museum of Natural History and Gaia Centre** (open Tue–Sun 9am–2.30pm; entrance fee) which has very informative collections devoted to the flora, fauna and geology of Greece.

BELOW: Zéa Marina.

A villa in leafy Kifisiá, Athens' most exclusive suburb.

Olympic sites

The 2004 Olympic Games have bequeathed the city and its environs a number of new buildings. While these have mostly been of a sporting nature, spin-offs include the renovation of many of the city's hotels and museums, and the completion of, or continuing work on, a number of major infrastructure projects (such as extensions to the Attiki Metro and the building of the new airport at Spáta). The new **Olympic Stadium** in Amaroúsi, to the north of the city centre, was built as the main centre for the games, holding the athletics and football competitions; the old Olympic Stadium *(see page 141)* has been called into service again as the end point of the marathon.

The old Ellinikón airport site at Glyfáda has now become the **Helleniko Olympic Complex**, with a large indoor arena surrounded by small outdoor stadiums and, bizarrely, a kayak slalom course. However, the main rowing and canoeing venue is out at Marathon *(see opposite)*. The new artificial lake provoked controversy as it is built on both an iconic archeological site and an important natural habitat. The huge **Olympic Village**, built to house the atheletes, press and administration, is sited well out of town near Dekélia.

Attica

Outside Athens, a 69-km (43-mile) drive to **Cape Sounion** on the windy tip of the Attica peninsula takes you to the Doric **Temple of Poseidon**. Completed in 440 BC, its slender, salt-white columns are still a landmark for ships headed toward Piraeus. Lord Byron carved his name on a column on the north side. The marble came from nearby Agríleza (open daily 10am–sunset; entrance fee). Down the hillside, you can see the remains of ancient ship sheds in the bay

BELOW: the Temple of Poseidon.

Map, pages 124–5

below: the Athenians once organised warship races off Sounion and it later became a pirates' lair.

The battle of **Marathon** in 490 BC was fought on a plain by the sea 42 km (26 miles) northeast of Athens, between the villages of Néa Mákri and Marathónas. What can be seen today associated with the battle are the burial mound of the Athenians, the burial mound identified by the excavator as that of the Plataeans, and the Archeological Museum (open Tue–Sun 8.30am–3pm; admission fee).

The burial mound of the Athenians, simply a circular mound of earth 9 metres (30 ft) high, 50 metres (164 ft) in diameter, and 185 metres (600 ft) in circumference, has a modern copy of the ancient stele on the top (the original is in the National Archeological Museum). The mound is impressive, but nothing compared to the victory it symbolises. The mighty Persian Empire, the largest on earth, had sent its army against Athens, and approximately 9,000 Athenian soldiers were joined before the battle by 1,000 soldiers from Plataea, a town in Boeotia. A runner was sent to ask the Spartans for help, but the Spartans did not arrive until after the battle. The Athenians won against overwhelming odds, with the Persians losing 6,400 men and the Athenians 192. The Athenians were cremated and buried together in the mound. The mound of the Plataeans is near the archeological museum, about 3 km (2 miles) to the west. There is nothing to mark the Persian graves, but they seem to have been buried to the northeast, in the area around the small church of the Panagía Mesosporítisa.

Rhamnous (open daily 8am–6pm; admission fee), the site of an ancient fortress town on the northern borders of Attica with a sanctuary of Nemesis, is 53 km (33 miles) from Athens. The sanctuary contains two temples. The older, built right after 490 BC, was dedicated to Nemesis and also to Themis, the god of justice. The slightly larger Doric temple of Nemesis, built in 436–32 BC, almost touches the older temple. The garrison town, roughly 800 metres (½ mile) down from the sanctuary on the shore, flourished in the 5th and 4th centuries BC.

The city-state that built the **Sanctuary of Amphiareion** (Tue–Sun 8.30am–3pm; admission fee) late in the 5th century BC was ancient Oropos, now buried beneath the modern town of Skála Oropós, where the ferry leaves for Évia. The sanctuary was particularly well known in the Hellenistic period, visited by people from all over the Greek world in search of advice or medical help. The supplicant sacrificed a ram to Amphiaraos, after which a dream would either cure the illness or answer a question.

More out of the way is the **Sanctuary of Artemis** at **Brauron** (now called Vravróna) on the east coast of Attica, 35 km (22 miles) from Athens. A 5th-century BC colonnade visited by owls at twilight is flanked by a 16th-century Byzantine chapel, built on the site of an altar to Artemis. In classical times, well-born girl children aged five to ten ("little bears") performed a ritual dance at a festival honouring Artemis as the goddess of childbirth. Their statues – plump, with solemn expressions, and dressed like miniature adults – are now in the site museum (both the site and the museum open Tue–Sun 8.30am–3pm; entrance fee). ❑

BELOW: an ancient exhibit.

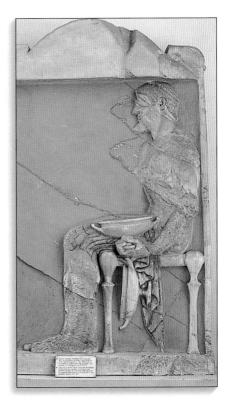

A NATIONAL TREASURE TROVE

The National Archeological Museum in Athens, closed for renovations until mid-2004, houses a fabulous collection of ancient art and artefacts.

Although it is not yet clear what the new layout of the museum will be, certain key collections will definitely be on display. A clue to how the museum will look was provided by the new pre-renovation rooms housing the Egyptian and Strathos collections. These were modern, light and displayed in an exemplary manner, boding well for the future of the museum.

A walk through the rooms of the National Archeological Museum will provide a survey of Greek art available nowhere else in the world. When it reopens, don't be intimidated by the apparent size of the collection but, at first, concentrate on certain key rooms.

The museum will certainly have rooms dedicated to its prehistoric artefacts, and finds from the Cycladic period, most of them dating between 3000 and 2000 BC.

There will also be a Mycenaean Room (1600–1100 BC) and rooms containing examples of Ancient Greek sculpture, in marble and bronze, from the Archaic period (700–480 BC) to the Classical (480–338 BC) and Hellenistic (338–146 BC) periods, and to the Roman Period (146 BC–AD 330).

There is also a vast array of Ancient Greek pottery from 900 BC to 300 BC held by the museum, and this will be on display, possibly as before on the first floor, along with the famous Thíra frescoes.

The picture at the top of this column is of the bronze Horse and Jockey of Artemesium (2nd century BC).

▷ AGAMEMNON

This gold mask found by Heinrich Schliemann at Mycenae and dating to the 16th century BC has become famous as the "Mask of Agamemnon". In fact, the Trojan Wars occurred much later.

▽ GRAVE STELAE

The range of exhibits in the museum is huge; it has one of the world's largest collections of carved reliefs.

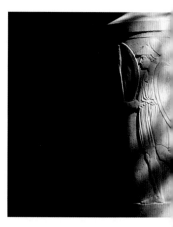

▷ ARCHAIC YOUTH

This *kouros* (statue of a young man) was found in the Sanctuary of Poseidon at Sounion, the tip of Attica. In the Archaic style, it was carved in the 7th century BC.

▷ **ANCIENT HARPIST**
This seated figure in marble playing the harp dates from the 3rd millennium BC and was found on the Cycladic island of Kéros, near Náxos.

FABULOUS FRESCOES

▽ **MOVEMENT IN STONE**
The museum gives an excellent overview of the development of Greek statuary, from early works to the classical ideal.

In the middle of the 2nd millennium BC the Cycladic island of Thíra, or Santoríni, was much influenced, perhaps even ruled, by the Minoan civilisation of Crete. A Minoan settlement at Akrotiri on Thíra, dating to approximately 1600 BC, was excavated by Spyridon Marinatos between 1967 and 1974. The most beautiful finds from Akrotiri are the frescoes. Most of these are kept in the National Archeological Museum but a few can be seen in Santoríni. Sometime around 1500 BC Thíra's volcano erupted in a tremendous explosion. The entire settlement of Akrotiri, including buildings up to three storeys high, was beautifully preserved beneath volcanic ash. Excavations began in 1967. The frescoes decorated the interior walls of houses in the ancient city. Most of them show everyday scenes, such as a naked fisherman carrying home a bountiful catch, the elegant ladies, the graceful antelopes, and the two boxing boys shown at the top of this column, but there is also a 6-metre (19-ft) long detailed fresco of a naval campaign.

▽ **TAKING AIM**
This bronze statue of Poseidon poised to throw his trident, a rare survivor from antiquity, dates from around 450 BC. It was found in the sea off Évia.

△ **IMPERIAL LIKENESS**
This wonderfully lifelike equestrian bronze statue of the Roman emperor Augustus dates from the late 1st century AD.

THE PELOPONNESE

Steeped in ancient history – from Agamemnon's Mycenae to the first Olympic stadium – the southern provinces also offer fine beaches, turquoise-coloured bays, and the wild and unspoilt Máni

Map, page 148

The Peloponnese (Pelopónnisos) takes its name from the legendary hero Pelops, plus the Greek for island, *nísos*, although it is seldom thought of as an island. Driving over from Attica (Attikí), it's easy to miss the little isthmus – riven by the Corinth Canal, lending some credence to the "island" tag – that joins the Peloponnese to the mainland. The area's medieval name was the Moreás, now rarely used; it derives either from an abundance of mulberry trees (*mouriá*) or more probably from the mulberry-leaf shape of the peninsula.

Korinthía: key to the Moreás

By an administrative quirk, Korinthía province in the northeast includes a bit of the geographical mainland northeast of the canal; 13 km (8 miles) beyond the spa resort of Loutráki lies the **Perahora Heraion**, with an archaic **Hera temple** and a *stoa*. Another important ancient sanctuary, the venue for the quadrennial Isthmian games, can be found at **Isthmía** on the southwest side of the canal; the Roman baths here retain extensive floor mosaics of sea creatures real and imaginary, while the site **museum** (open Tue–Sun 8.30am–3pm; entrance fee) features vivid *opus sectile* panels portraying harbour scenes, Nile bird life and revered ancient personalities. The canal itself, dug between 1882 and 1893, is obsolete in our era of mega-container ships, but a few freighters and tour ships still squeeze through its 23-metre (75-ft) channel, to the delight of spectators up on the bridge gangway.

Ancient **Corinth**, 4 km (2½ miles) southwest of modern **Kórinthos** ❶, could not help but prosper through domination of trans-Isthmian haulage in pre-canal days. The Hellenistic city was razed by the Romans in 146 BC in reprisal for resistance, but refounded a century later as capital of Greece. What remains, despite devastating earthquakes in AD 375 and 521, is the most complete imperial Roman town plan in Greece. Corinth's well-deserved reputation for vice and luxury predictably exercised Saint Paul when he arrived in AD 52 for an 18-month sojourn.

A typically Roman obsession with plumbing is evident: there are the graphically obvious latrines off the marble-paved **Lehaion Way**, the still-functioning **Lower Peirene Fountain** at its end, and the ingenious **Glauke Fountain**, its four cisterns hewn from a monolith and filled by an aqueduct (site open summer 8am–7pm; winter 8am–5pm; entrance fee).

Of the earlier Greek city, only seven columns from a Doric **Apollo Temple** still stand, though the site museum – despite a selective 1990 burglary – retains a generous collection of late archaic pottery and some intricate Roman-villa mosaics from Corinth's glory years (open Tue–Fri 8am–7pm, Sat–Sun 8.30am–3pm).

LEFT: parts of columns at Olympia. **BELOW:** stormy weather over the Máni.

Peloponnese

0   30 km

0   30 miles

Map, page 148

Rather more evocative, however, is the nearly impregnable hilltop fortress of **Acrocorinth** (open daily 8am–7pm; free), long the military key to the peninsula and necessarily held by every occupying power. Enter via the gentler west slope through a set of **triple fortifications** to find yourself amid weedy desolation; little is left of the Ottoman town here, evacuated after Greek rebels took it in 1822. Most sieges, however, were successfully resisted thanks to the **Upper Peirene Fountain**, a subterranean structure near the southeast corner of the ramparts. At the very summit stand foundations of an **Aphrodite Temple**, reputedly once attended by 1,000 sacred prostitutes; the view all around is quite marvellous, stretching up to 60 km (40 miles) in every direction.

The wide tollway to Trípoli forges southwest from modern Kórinthos. Near **Dersenákia**, exits lead west 8 km (5 miles) to ancient **Nemea**, yet another shrine with its own biennial games. You can see the stadium where these events – supposedly inaugurated by Hercules, slayer of the Nemean lion – were held, but the most enduring landmarks are three surviving Doric columns of a 4th-century BC **Zeus Temple**; its fellows, toppled by Byzantine vandals, lie all about like many giant sausage slices. The site (open daily 8am–7pm; entrance fee) occupies the floor of a bucolic valley; surrounding vineyards produce the grapes for the full-bodied Nemea red wines, some of Greece's best.

The word "currant" derives from the word "Corinth" – a reference to the city's long-established trade in dried grapes, still one of Greece's most successful exports.

Argolída: Mycenaean cradle

The old highway enters the Argolid plain at modern **Mykínes**, a village devoted to citrus and tourism; nearby stands ancient **Mycenae ❷**, a fortified palace complex covering an easily defendable, ravine-flanked ridge. Mycenae gave its name to an entire late Bronze-Age era – and made the reputation of a German

BELOW: the Corinth Canal was completed in 1893.

Mycenae's treasures were uncovered by the archeologist Heinrich Schliemann.

self-taught Classical scholar (and self-made millionaire), Heinrich Schliemann. From 1874 to 1876 he excavated here, relying on little other than intuition and a belief in the literal accuracy of Homer's epics. Greek archeologists had already revealed the imposing **Lion Gate** of the citadel, but the rich tomb finds Schliemann made, now in the National Museum of Athens, amply corroborate Mycenae's Homeric epithet "rich in gold". These days, revisionists point to Schliemann's sloppy excavating techniques and economy with the truth – the gold death mask which prompted his boast "I have gazed upon the face of Agamemnon" is now dated to 300 years earlier – but the dedicated amateur did beat the experts to the greatest archeological trove of that century.

At the site itself, little remains above waist height inside the perimeter walls of the palace, though a rather alarming secret stairway descends to a siege-proof cistern in the northeast corner. Outside, however, are two burial chambers of unsurpassed ingenuity: the *tholos* tombs dubbed, very speculatively, the **Treasury of Atreus** and the **Tomb of Clytemnestra**, also known as "beehives" after the manner of their construction (open daily 8am–7pm; entrance fee).

Ancient Argos

The road across the Argolid plain divides at **Árgos ❸**, capital of Argolída province and a major agricultural centre. Tomatoes and citrus – the latter introduced by American advisers after World War II – are grown extensively; the modern town itself is of little interest apart from its **Archeological Museum** (open daily 8.30am–3pm; entrance fee). But just south, beside the Trípoli-bound road, sprawl the ruins of **ancient Argos**, one of the oldest Greek settlements; most notable is the huge, steeply raked theatre. From here, walk up to the Frankish castle atop Lárissa hill, site of the ancient **acropolis**, for a view nearly on a par with Acrocorinth's. To the northwest is **Mount Kyllíni**, snowcapped in season. Ahead, beyond a foreground of orchards and the occasional cannery, you can make out Mycenae and the low hillock of ancient Tiryns en route to the town of Návplio (Nauplion), stacked up against the promontory on the far side of the Argolid Gulf.

BELOW: the first grave circle at Mycenae.

Just over halfway to Návplio from Árgos loom the 13th-century BC ruins of Homer's "wall-girt" **Tiryns** (open summer daily 8am–7pm; winter daily 8.30am–3pm; entrance fee), another royal palace complex. The site, an 18-metre (60-ft) bluff rising from an ancient marsh, was not as naturally defensible as its neighbour, Mycenae, so the man-made fortifications – originally twice their present height – were necessarily more involved. Massive masonry blocks reaching 3 cubic metres (100 cu. ft) each were joined in mortarless walls termed "Cyclopean", after the only beings thought capable of manoeuvring them. No heraldic lions over the entry-gate here, and no beehive tombs; but Tiryns satisfies enough with a **secret stairway** to the westerly postern gate and, near the southeast corner, a corbel-ceilinged **gallery**, its walls polished smooth by the millennial rubbings of sheltering sheep.

Návplio ❹, rising in tiers at the southeast corner of the valley, is more than a little mirage-like, for the well-preserved old town retains an elegance a world away from scruffy, utilitarian Árgos just 12 km (7 miles) to the northwest. The neoclassical architecture, pedestrian-friendly marble streets and interlocking fortresses date mostly from the second Venetian occupation of 1686–1715, and subsequent Ottoman reconquest; the fortified rock here had been a pivotal point in their struggles for control of the Aegean from the 15th century onward. Between 1829 and 1834 Návplio served as the country's first capital, but today it's a laid-back place, despite playing a role as an upmarket resort; it even stays busy in winter, thanks to Athenian weekenders.

Návplio is overawed by **Akronavpliá**, four separate fortresses of various ages just overhead, plus, on an easterly hill, the sprawling, early 18th-century castle of **Palamídi**, whose meandering curtain wall encloses seven self-contained bastions designed to withstand the strongest artillery of the era. Yet its Venetian garrison capitulated with barely a fight in 1715 to the Ottomans, who in turn surrendered to the Greek rebels after a more protracted siege in 1822. Just under 900 steps lead up from the Old Town to the summit – and to more eyefuls of the Argolid (open daily 8am–7pm; entrance fee).

Some 27 km (17 miles) east of Návplio, **Epidauros (Epídavros) ❺** is visited for the sake of its magnificent 4th-century BC **theatre**, whose perfect acoustics tour guides perpetually demonstrate with coins dropped on the orchestra floor. Because it lay buried until the late 19th century, the theatre masonry survived the ages relatively unscathed, and restoration has been minimal.

The theatre is just one part of a vast sanctuary to the healing demi-god Asklepios; its ruins, being re-excavated, extend to the northwest. The most accessible bits are the classical **stadium**, its stone benches and starting line still visible; the monumental gateway and stretch of buckled pavement, part of the sacred way to

Map, page 148

The fortress-island of Boúrtzi, off Návplio.

BELOW:
Návplio waterfront.

The shady grottoes of Arcadia were where Pan played his pipes and frolicked with nymphs.

the port (today's beach resort of **Paleá Epídavros**), and the *tholos*, a circular, originally domed structure with a concentric maze in the foundations thought to contain serpents (sacred to Asklepios) or to be the venue for a priestly initiation rite (open daily 8am–7pm; entrance fee).

The closest village to the site is **Lygoúrio**, which formerly lived mainly from its extensive olive groves but which now hosts most of the tourist traffic which comes for the summer festival of ancient drama. Performances by both Greek and international theatre companies take place by night in the ancient theatre, with special buses from Athens laid on for ticket-holders.

Heading west from Návplio, you can avoid re-entering Árgos by using the beachfront road along the gulf, joining the highway to Trípoli at **Lerna** (modern **Mýli**), where Hercules slew the many-headed Hydra.

Arkadía: Arcadian idylls

The modern 1970s highway – though not the 1990s toll expressway – leaves the flatlands of fragrant citrus at Mýli to enter gorges culminating in the high, pear- and apple-planted upland plateaux around **Trípoli** ❻, capital of Arkadía province. The name Trípoli recalls the three ancient towns of **Tegea**, **Mantineia** and **Palladium**, the latter an undistinguished Roman-imperial foundation. Mantineia, north of modern Trípoli, retains much of its ancient walls, and a reputation for excellent modern wine, while Tegea to the south offers the tumbled ruins of the **Temple to Athena Alea** in the middle of modern Aléa village.

Trípoli (then Tripolítza) was the Moreán capital in Ottoman times, but was burned during the War of Independence. Aside from a few fine neoclassical buildings, restaurants and a lively market, there's little here to interest casual tourists.

BELOW: the classical theatre at Epidauros.

The northbound, toll-free road skirts the base of forested, blade-like **Mount Ménalo** via the handsome villages of **Levídi** and **Vytína** ❼, the latter a popular "hill station" and ski resort for Greeks. Beyond Vytína, towards Ilía, the most logical and compelling halt is **Langádia** ❽, its famous masons responsible for sturdy stone houses teetering on a slope above the gorge of the same name. But the main attraction of montane Arkadía lies due west of Trípoli, accessible either from the Megalópoli road or a turning south between Vytína and Langádia. **Megalópoli** ❾ itself, saddled with steam-belching power plants, is a shabby modern successor to **ancient Megalopolis**, a vast artificial classical township abandoned within two centuries of inauguration, leaving only the largest amphitheatre in Greece to mark its passing.

Hyperbolically dubbed the "Toledo of Greece", thanks to its evocative castle and houses overlooking a kink in the **Alfiós River**, the sleepy demeanour of **Karýtena** ❿ belies a tumultuous history. Established as the seat of a Frankish barony during the 13th century, it was later retaken by the Byzantines, who endowed Karýtena with three churches and an arched bridge over the Alfiós. Both bridge and town figured on one side of the old 5,000-drachma note; the beturbanned Independence War chieftain Kolokotrónis glared out from the other, for he successfully resisted a long Ottoman siege here in 1826.

Shepherds' crooks in Langádia village.

Heading north along the paved road towards Dimitsána, you'll travel roughly parallel to the east flank of the **Loúsios Gorge**: a short route, but in terms of concentrated interest one equalled by few other parts of the Peloponnese. At **Ellinikó** village, a dirt track descends into the canyon, emerging at the medieval Kokkorás bridge and the Byzantine chapel of **Ágios Andréas**. Nearby are the excavations of ancient **Gortys**, an *asklipeion* or therapeutic

BELOW: three generations of Arcadian women.

Taking it easy in the mountain village of Vytína, a popular "hill station" for Greek tourists.

BELOW: Ioánnou Prodrómou is one of Greece's most spectacular monateries.

centre; the architectural highlight here is a peculiar round structure, thought to be a bath-house.

Stemnítsa ❶, further along the paved road, has been officially renamed **Ipsoúnda** but the Slavic name remains more popular; it's an atmospheric, introverted place in a hidden cirque, with imposing mansions looking only at each other. A single jewellery shop recalls the former silver-smithing industry. Near the head of the Loúsios valley, **Dimitsána** sprawls engagingly over a saddle demarcated by the river, its skyline graced by four belfries. The mansions here, like Stemnítsa's, date from its mercantile golden age, the 1700s.

Dimitsána also marks one end of the hiking route threading the gorge; the path proper begins in **Paleohóri** hamlet, following red-and-white blazes and diamonds with the legend "32". The first significant stop is the **Néa Filosófou monastery** on the west bank, with late 17th-century frescoes including Jesus walking on the Sea of Galilee; shortly beyond, the 10th-century **Paleá Filosófou** monastery is largely ruined and almost indistinguishable from its cliff-side surroundings. Finally, where the path divides (the west-bank option leads to Gortys), you should recross the river for the most spectacular monastery of all: 11th-century **Agíou Ioánnou Prodrómou** (St John the Baptist) is one of those martin's-nest-type monasteries which the Orthodox Church loves to tuck into cliff faces. It has limited accommodation (for male pilgrims only), so try to budget enough daylight time to hike onwards by trail to Stemnítsa.

From Karítena a westerly road follows the Alfiós, past its co-mingling with the Loúsios, to **Andrítsena** ❷, roughly halfway between Megalópoli and the sea. Resolutely traditional shops and a morning produce market in the central square recall the village's historical status as a major entrepôt. Today, however, it seems

Map, page 148

scarcely touched by the steady trickle of tourist traffic passing through to the 5th-century temple of **Apollo Epikourios** at **Bassae** (Vásses), 14 km (9 miles) south. Although the most intact ancient shrine in Greece and a UNESCO World Heritage site, it's unlikely to enchant in its present condition – concealed by a colossal, guy-wired tent to protect it from winter frosts, it is currently closed for major renovation. More rewarding for many is the **gorge of the River Nédas** a few kilometres south, just below the modern village and ancient ruins of **Figalia**, whose citizens originally built the temple in gratitude for Apollo having lifted a plague.

Lakonía: ancient Spartan heartland

As you descend the 60-km (37-mile) road from Trípoli to modern Spárti, the long ridge of **Mount Taýgetos** with its striated limestone bands looms into sight on the right. Ahead stretches the olive-and-citrus-rich floodplain of the Evrótas River, belying the stereotypical image of ancient Sparta as a harsh, "spartan" place (the province's name, Lakonía, also lives abroad as "laconic" – supposedly the distinguishing characteristic of the classical natives).

Spárti ⓭, the modern successor to ancient Sparta, is an unexciting place redeemed only by some attractive squares and neoclassical facades, vestiges of a bout of Bavarian town planning in 1834. Stop, if you do at all, for the excellent **museum** and traces of an **ancient acropolis**. The museum (open Tue–Sun 8.30am–3pm; entrance fee) is particularly rich in late Roman floor-mosaics from local villas, and eerie votive offerings from the **sanctuaries of Apollo** at Amýkles and **Artemis Orthia** on the acropolis – where youths were flogged until bloody to honour the goddess. At the acropolis itself, however, 700 metres (½ mile) northwest of town, not much remains aside

In 1821 Germanos, the local Archbishop of Dimitsána, called for an uprising against the Turks, which led to the liberation of all Arkadía.

BELOW: café life on the Peloponnese.

The Mitrópolis cathedral in Mystrás stands in a courtyard surrounded by stoas and balconies.

BELOW: Mystrás's Perívleptos church has some superb frescoes.

from a badly eroded theatre and the sparse remains of the Byzantine church of **Ágios Níkon**.

What little the Spartans built was appropriated for the construction of Byzantine **Mystrás** ⓮, 6 km (4 miles) west (open daily summer 8am–7pm; winter 8.30am–3pm; entrance fee). A romantically ruined walled town, clinging to a conical crag and topped by a castle, Mystrás's name is a corruption of *mezythrás*, the Greek for "cream-cheese maker" – thought to be a reference to this cheese's traditional conical shape.

Originally founded by the Franks in 1249, Mystrás grew to a city of 20,000 souls under the Byzantines, becoming the capital of the Morean despots after 1348. Until the Ottomans took over in 1460, it flourished as a major cultural centre, attracting scholars and artists from Serbia, Constantinople and Italy to its court. The latter's influence is evident in the brilliantly coloured (and remarkably well-preserved) frescoes which adorn Mystrás's churches – uniquely in Greece, these are as crammed with extraneous figures, buildings and landscapes as any Italian painting of the time. Architecturally, the churches are a composite of three-aisled-basilica ground plan and domed cross-in-square gallery, making them airily well lit by Byzantine standards. Proto-Renaissance sensibilities (and the Frankish wives of most of the despots) inspired belfries and colonnaded porticoes. It is easy to see why Mystrás is regarded as the last great Byzantine architectural outpouring before the onset of the Ottoman era.

The church of **Perívleptos monastery** contains a complete cycle of frescoes depicting the *Dodekaeorton* or 12 major feasts of the year, with such light touches as children playing in the Entry to Jerusalem. Nearby **Pandánassa**, the newest church built in 1428, has a typically Gothic exterior as well as vivid

frescoes within, the best of these neck-craningly high. By contrast, the oldest of the churches, the **Mitrópolis** or cathedral of Ágios Dimítrios, is resolutely conservative in structure, notwithstanding awkward domes added later; here frescoes include a complete cycle of Christ's Miracles. The **Vrondóhion** monastic complex harbours yet another 14th-century church, the more daring **Afendikó**, the weight of its six domes borne by a system of piers below and colonnaded gallery above. Sea monsters bob in the Baptism fresco, while above the altar, apostles marvel at a mandorla of ascending Christ.

Mystrás has a miniature "echo" in **Geráki** (25 km/16 miles east of Spárti), of which few have heard and fewer still bother to visit. Although an ancient town (Geronthrai) existed here, its masonry has been liberally recycled into the half-dozen churches scattered about. Geráki's fortified **acropolis** is less spectacular than that at Mystrás, and closes earlier (open daily 8.30am–3pm; entrance fee); if time is limited, find the key-keeper by the post office (8am–2pm) who will open up four frescoed churches in and around the modern village.

Completing the trio of Lakonian Byzantine towns is **Monemvasía** ⑮, 94 km (58 miles) southeast of Spárti. Like Mystrás, it's a fortified double town, clinging to a limestone plug rising 350 metres (1,150 ft) from the sea and inevitably nicknamed the "Gibraltar of Greece" – although the "Dubrovnik of Greece" would be an equally apt term for the tile-roofed, wall-encased lower town on the south slope. Supporting 50,000 souls in its heyday as a semi-autonomous city-state, Monemvasía prospered by virtue of its fleets and handy location, halfway between Italy and the Black Sea. Never taken by force, it did surrender, if necessary, to prolonged siege – no food could grow on the rock, though enormous cisterns provided water. Nearby vineyards produced the

Map, page 148

Monemvasía's fortifications cling to a crag by the sea.

BELOW: a view over Monemvasía.

Cherries for sale, in Monemvasía lower town. In medieval times, food supplies were the rock-city's weak point; everything had to be imported from the mainland.

famous Malvasia sweet wine – similar to Madeira, and known as Malmsey or Malvoisie in the west – but local production ceased by the 15th century. Following the opening of the Corinth Canal, Monemvasía lost all commercial and military significance.

The lower town, within its 900-metre (½-mile) circuit of Venetian walls on three sides, is invisible as you cross the causeway until the massive west gate (closed to vehicles) suddenly appears. Immediately above the gate perches the house in which prominent poet Giannis Ritsos was born in 1909; one wonders what the conservative locals made of his forthright Marxism and bisexuality. On his death in 1990 he was buried in the nearby cemetery, with one of his poems chiselled on the gravestone in lieu of religious sentiment.

Linked by a maze of tunnels, arcades and cul-de-sacs at the end of steep, cobbled lanes, many of the lower-town houses have been bought up and restored by wealthy Athenians and foreigners. Masoned steps zigzag up the cliff face overhead to the older, upper town, first settled and fortified in the 6th century AD but abandoned since the early 1900s and now utterly ruined. The sole exception to the desolation is the 14th-century **Agía Sofía** church with its 16-sided dome, poised at the edge of the northerly cliff and the first point in Monemvasía to catch the sunrise.

Gýthio ⓰, 47 km (29 miles) southeast of Spárti, is a port town on the ferry routes to Kýthira and Crete, a holiday resort in its own right, and a deceptively congenial gateway to the austere Máni. The quay is lined by tiled vernacular houses and pricey fish tavernas; across the Lakonian Gulf the sun rises over **Cape Maléa**, and Mount Taÿgetos is glimpsed one last time on the north. In ancient times Gýthio served as Sparta's port, and until recently it exported

acorns used in leather tanning. There are few sights, apart from a Roman the-atre and the historical museum (open Tue–Sun 9.30am–3pm, but often closed; entrance fee) on **Marathonísi** islet (ancient Kranae) tied to the mainland by a causeway. It was here that Paris and Helen legendarily spent their first night together, and so launched a thousand ships.

Map, page 148

The Máni – home of Greece's hard men

An arid, isolated region protected by Taÿgetos' southern spur, the **Máni** was the last part of Greece to espouse Christianity (in the 9th century), but made up for lost time by erecting dozens of small country chapels. Little grows except stunted olive trees, though in late summer an extra dash of colour is lent by hedges of fruiting prickly pears. "Outer" or **Éxo Máni** (Ítylo northwest to Kalamáta) is more tourist-friendly, fertile and better watered; "Inner" or **Mésa Máni**, south of a line connecting Ítylo with Gýthio, has the more noteworthy churches on the west shore, and tower-studded villages sprouting from the east-coast settlements. But extreme conditions have prompted wholesale depopula-tion, and the villages here only fill during the autumn hunting season.

In Roman times Gýthio supplied the nobility with murex, a purple dye extracted from a species of mollusc, which was used to give togas their aristocratic colour.

From Gýthio, the main road into the Máni passes by the castles of **Passavá** and **Kelefá**. These were the sole Ottoman attempts at imposing order locally. The road takes you to **Areópoli ⓱**, main market town and tourist base of the Inner Máni. Formerly Tsímova, stronghold of the Mavromihális clan, it was renamed after Ares the god of war after independence, in recognition of its con-tribution to the independence struggle. Two churches, both 18th-century, dis-tinguish it: **Taxiárhis** with its campanile and zodiacal apse reliefs, and frescoed **Ágios Ioánnis**.

BELOW: Pýrgos Diroú beach.

Some 8 km (5 miles) south, just off the west-coast road towards **Cape Mátapan** (Ténaro), the caverns at **Pýrgos Diroú** are the sole organised tourist attraction in the Máni; visits are partly by boat along a subterranean river, and queues can be long. Between here and Gerolimẻnas lie more than half-a-dozen frescoed Byzantine churches; unfortunately, most are permanently locked, and hunting for the warden can be time-consuming. Two of the best, at Áno Boularí, are also the easiest to access. Apply in the Gerolimẻnas post office for the key to **Ágios Stratigós**; nearby **Ágios Pandelímon** – scandalously doorless and unroofed – has the earliest (10th-century) frescoes around, with figures of saints Pandelímon and Nikítas in the apse. **Gerolimẻnas** ⑱ itself, 20 km (12 miles) from Areópoli, can offer tavernas and accommodation, but not much else – it dates only from 1870. The 35 ridgetop tower-houses of dramatic **Váthia** ⑲, 10 km (6 miles) further east, have become photogenic synonyms for the Máni.

The main tarred road out of Gerolimẻnas loops along the eastern shore via **Lágia** (famed for its broad-based, tapering towers and purple-marble quarries) and **Flomohóri** ⑳ (with the highest towers and pebbly **Kótronas** beach below) before re-emerging at Areópoli. Just across the ravine dividing Inner Máni and Areópoli from Outer is bluff-top **Ítylo** ㉑, lushly set and – unlike so many of its neighbours – relatively prosperous; below the village lie the frescoed monastery of **Dekoúlou** and the beach resort of **Néa Ítylo**.

The pride of **Langáda** village ㉒, 14 km (9 miles) north, is the central 11th-century church of **Ágios Sótiros**, whose frescoes still await uncovering and restoration; contiguous **Plátsa** and **Nomitsís** between them have four more Byzantine chapels. Tourism takes over at the picturesque fishing port of **Ágios**

FEUDS IN THE MÁNI

While there may be some truth to Maniot claims that they are descended from the ancient Spartans, more cruicial to the region's medieval history was the arrival, during the 13th to the 15th centuries, of refugee Byzantine nobility. These established a local aristocracy – the Nyklians – which formed competing clans, as in Scotland; only they had the right to erect tower-mansions.

Poor farmland and a fast-growing population spurred not just piracy and banditry, but complex vendettas between clans. Blood feuds could last for years, with sporadic truces to tend crops; women, who delivered supplies, were inviolate, as were doctors, who treated the wounded impartially. Combatants fired at each other from neighbouring towers, raising them as high as five storeys so as to lob rocks onto their opponents' flat roofs. The vendettas generally ended either with the annihilation or utter submission of the losing clan. Rather than rule the Máni directly, the Ottomans encouraged the feuding in the hopes of weakening any concerted rebellions, appointing a Nyklian chieftain as *bey* to represent the sultan.

The office passed between rival clans, but under the last *bey*, Petros Mavromihalis, the clans united, instigating the Greek independence uprising on 17 March 1821.

Map,
page
148

Nikólaos (Selenítsa); nearby **Stoúpa** ❷ has two sandy bays and plenty of facilities as well. **Kardamýli** ❷ ranks as the premier resort before Kalamáta, offering among its charms a long pebble beach, a late-medieval citadel and some good walking just inland.

Messinía: the Peloponnesian banana belt

Kalamáta can also be approached directly from Spárti via the spectacular 60-km (37-mile) road which crosses Mount Taýgetos. On the Lakonian side, near **Trýpi** village, is the **Keiádas**, an abyss where the ancient Spartans supposedly hurled their sickly or malformed babies. **Kalamáta** ❷ itself suffered a devastating 1986 earthquake which left half the population homeless; despite subsequent emigration it's still the biggest town hereabouts (40,000 people), with an attractive seafront, some lively untouristed tavernas and its famous shiny-black olives to recommend it.

Most visitors to Messinía province have their sights set on the low south-westerly promontory ending in **Cape Akrítas**, with its fine beaches and balmy climate. Prime target is **Koróni** ❷, founded by Venice in 1206 to guard the sea lanes between the Adriatic and Crete. The castle here still shelters a few houses, orchards and pine groves, but a convent occupies most of it. The town outside the walls (built since 1830) has weathered tourism well, its vernacular houses with their wooden balconies still lining the steep stair-streets. **Zánga beach**, one of the best in the Peloponnese, extends for 3 km (2 miles) west.

Methóni ❷, another "eye of Venice" lying 35 km (22 miles) west, grew wealthy after 1209 from the pilgrim trade to Palestine. Its sprawling castle, lapped on three sides by the sea, combines military architecture of various eras:

The caves at Pýrgos Diroú get very busy in high season; to preserve the magic, try to get there early.

BELOW:
a ruined church
in Kardamýli.

Kalamáta is best known for its prosperous export trade in large, shiny black olives. They are excellent eaten with oúzo.

beyond the Venetian sea-gate, a Turkish octagonal tower overlooks two islets, while a French arched bridge of 1828 spans the Venetian moat. Little remains of the medieval town inside, however, and the modern village outside the walls is not nearly as attractive as Koróni's, nor is the beach.

Pýlos ❷⓭, 12 km (7 miles) north, is another somewhat lacklustre town; despite its pleasant setting on huge, landlocked **Navaríno Bay**, what life there is seems confined to the immediate environs of **Platía Tríon Navárhon**, the main square. The bay has seen two momentous naval battles: in 425 BC, when the Athenians bested the Spartans off **Sfaktiría island**, and in October 1827, when a combined French, Russian and English armada sank Ibrahim Pasha's Ottoman fleet, thus guaranteeing Greek independence. The three allied admirals are honoured by an obelisk in their namesake square. For beaches you'll have to head for the north end of the bay, to Giálova just off the main road to the Bronze Age **Palace of Nestor**, discovered in 1939 and now protected by a synthetic roof.

Ilía: Olympia and the Cape

From pretty **Kyparissía**, north of Nestor's Palace, it's a pleasant coastal drive to the site of ancient **Olympia** ❷⓮, where the Kládeos River meets the Alfiós. The sanctuary here was in use for two millennia as a religious and athletic centre; of all the Hellenic competitions associated with shrines, the Olympic Games, held every four years at the late-summer full moon, were the most prestigious, and the Panhellenic truce declared for their duration was honoured by the various city-states on pain of stiff fines. Although the first verified games were held in 776 BC, the **Áltis**, a sacred forest at the base of Krónio hill, was consecrated to pre-Olympian deities as early as the second millennium BC.

BELOW: the bay of Voïdokiliá near Pýlos.

Map, page 148

The most salient monuments are the **Palaestra** training centre, whose courtyard colonnade has been re-erected; the **workshop of Pheidias**, the celebrated sculptor (identified by a cup found with his name inscribed); the archaic **Hera temple** with its dissimilar columns; the enormous **Zeus temple**, now reduced to column sections; and the **stadium** with its 192-metre (630-ft) running course and surviving vaulted entrance (open summer daily 8am–7pm; winter Mon–Fri 8am–5pm, Sat 8.30–3pm; entrance fee).

In the **site museum**, pride of place goes to the relief pediments recovered from the Zeus temple debris, now on display in the central hall (open summer Mon noon–7pm, Tue–Sun 8am–7pm; winter Mon 10.30am–5pm, Tue–Sun 8.30am–3pm; entrance fee).

Aháïa: Pátra and its hinterland

Entering Aháïa province along the coast north of **Kyllíni**, sample the enormous, 7-km (4-mile) beach of **Kalógria** and the swamps (plus umbrella-pine dune forest) just behind. This, one of the largest wetlands in the Balkans, has yet to gain significant protection as a wildlife reserve; go now before the developers scare off the incredibly rich birdlife.

Pátra ㉚, 38 km (24 miles) further, is Greece's third-largest city, and the principal port for ferries to Italy and some of the Ionian Islands. With its fearsome traffic, anonymous post-war architecture and lack of beaches, it's hardly the ideal spot for a quiet holiday retreat; only the ancient **acropolis** (with an originally Byzantine castle) seems peaceful. But linger at Carnival time to witness Greece's best observance, with parades, floats and conspicuous attendance by students and the gay community. ❏

Greece was the setting for the first Olympic Games, held in 776 BC, and the latest in 2004.

BELOW:
Pýlos harbour.

CENTRAL GREECE

A region rich in temples and monasteries, from Delphi – mythical centre of the ancient world – to the Monastery of Ósios Loukás and the dramatic Metéora peaks

Map, page 166

Roúmeli, the poetic medieval term for south-central Greece, encompasses the present-day provinces of Étolo-Akarnanía, Evrytanía, Fokída, Viotía and Fthiótida – even more ancient place-names revived by the modern Greek state. Few contemporary visitors concern themselves much with these tongue-twisting toponyms as they rush headlong towards the main attraction of the region, the Classical site at Delphi. Their single-mindedness is forgiveable, since Delphi uniquely combines a wealth of monuments with a breathtaking setting.

The drive from Athens takes anywhere from 2½ to 3½ hours depending on your route; the most historic, scenic one follows a steep but well-paved road over the pine-covered mountains from dreary **Elevsína** – perhaps detouring for a fish lunch at **Pórto Germenó** ❶ on the Gulf of Corinth – to **Thíva** (**Thebes**) ❷. The modern city has been built on top of the ancient one, so little is visible of the ancient Thebes so prominent in Greek myth and history. A small ancient palace has, however, been excavated and the excellent archeological museum (open at minimum Tue–Sun 8.30am–3pm, Mon 10.30am–5pm; later hours July-Aug; entrance fee) contains tomb and sanctuary finds from Bronze Age to Classical Boeotia, especially the painted sarcophagi from Tanagra. The next main town, **Livadiá** ❸, was a major power base for the Frankish Crusader fiefdoms during the 13th and 14th centuries. In the gorge of the River Érkyna yawns the entrance to the ancient Oracle of Trophonios, near a graceful Ottoman bridge and below the Catalan-built castle. The river's springs nurture a dense colony of plane trees, a pleasing backdrop to the handful of tavernas on the pedestrianised banks.

Beyond **Livadiá**, the road west begins to climb into the foothills of **Mt Parnassós**. The left turn for Dístomo village and the **Monastery of Ósios Loukás** ❹, dedicated to a local 10th-century ascetic named Luke, is clearly marked. The monastery (open May–mid-Sep 8am–2pm, 4–7pm; otherwise 8am– 5pm; entrance fee) commands a wonderful view over a secluded valley in the shadow of Mt Elikónas. The smaller chapel of the Virgin (on the left) dates from the 10th century; the 11th-century *katholikón* or main church contains superb mosaics, survivors of a 1659 earthquake. The best and easiest to view, including a *Resurrection* and *Washing of the Apostles' Feet*, are in the narthex.

The village of **Aráhova** ❺ clings to the toes of Parnassós; formerly a bastion of pastoral culture, it has now woken up to a new life as a ski resort, with Athenian-weekender chalets sprouting rapidly on the outskirts. Tourist souvenirs, including various types of noodles and the almost-purple wine particular to the area, are pitched more at Greeks than foreigners.

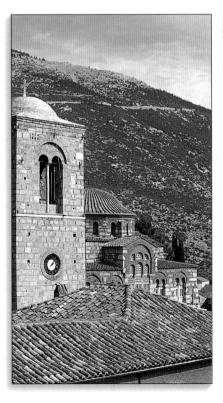

LEFT: Agías Triádos monastery, Metéora.
BELOW: Ósios Loukás monastery.

Central Greece

0 ——— 20 km
0 ——— 20 miles

↑ Bitola

Thessaloníki ↑

Sérvia
Potidéa ✈
Kassándra

Dytikí Makedonía

Ag. Dimítrios
Díon
Litóhoro
Limáni Litohórou
Leptokariá

Thermekós
Kólpos

Rýmnion
Dólihi
Óros Olympos
2917 ▲
Litóhoro

Ag. Theódori
Aliákmon
Moní Ág. Nikánoros †
Kalithéa
Karyá

Paljoúria
Deskáti
Kamvoúnia Óri
Kraniá
Elasóna
Káto Olympos
Pyrgetós
N. Mesángala

Agiófyllo
Hásia Óri
15
Verdikoúsa
1424
Elasóna
Góni
Stómio
Kókino Néro

Korydallós
Antihásia Óri
26
Doméniko
Óssa Óros
1978 ▲
Velíka

Trygóna
6
22 Metéora
Oxyá
Mesohóri
Tírnavos
Ambelónas
Melívia

1972 ▲
Kalabáka
1416
Plátanos
Damási
Eleuthério
Agiá
Agiókambos

Ráxa
Farkadóna
Larisa
Kastrí
Melía
1054 ▲
Sklíthro

-2204 ▲
Ag. Nikólaos
Megalohóri
6
Nikea
Melía
Ahílou
6
Kanália
Pourí
Zagorá

Tríkala
Piniós
Vlohós
Mavrovoúni
Kipséli
Rizómylos
Makrinítsa
19 ❤ Agios Ioánnis

Gorgogýri
Eláti
Lygariá
Agnanteró
Palamás
Doxarás
3
Velestíno
Pílio Óros
20 Tsangaráda

Avgó 2148 ▲
Moní Doussikoú †
Fanári
Thessalía
Orfaná
1
Óros
Vólos
17 ❤ 16
Agriá
18 Vyzítsa

Mouzáki
Karáva 2184 ▲
Kar_ditsa
Mitrópolis
30
Sofádes
Gefyría
Halkiádes
Ambeliá
Erétria
30
Pagasá ✈
39
Kalá Nerá

Neohóri
Tehnití Limní Tavropoú
Kallifónio
Fársala
Néa Aghíalos
Hersónisos Magnisía

Ptéri Óros 2128 ▲
2042 ▲
Kaslaniá
Kédros
1490
Néo Monastíri
1011 ▲
Almyrós
1
Pagasitikós Kólpos
Argalastí

Néráda
Voulgára 1654 ▲
Domokós
Skopiá
Vouná Goúras
Diávlos Tríkeri

Ágrafa
Mavromáta
1763 ▲
Vráha
Rendína
888 ▲
Melitéa
1694 ▲
Óros Óthrys
Gerakovoúni 1726
Pteleós
895 ▲
21 Tríkeri
Plataniá

Émbesós
1520 ▲
Anatolikí Fragísta
Agía Triás
Makrakómi
Trilofo
Moní Andinítsis †
Pelasgía
Glyfá
Óros
Akra Artemísio
Ellinikí ✈

Tehnití Limní Kremastón
Malesiáda
Tymfristós 2315 ▲
38
Sperhiás
Lamía
14
Malikós Kólpos
Dávlos Oreón
Orei
77
Artemísio
Istiéa

Hoúni
13
Karpenísi
Tymfristós
Kobotádes
Anthíli
1
Mólos
Loutrá Edipsoú
Ag. Geórgios
Évia (Euboea)

38
1974 ▲
Méga Horió
1467 ▲
Óros Íti 2152
Moshohóri
15 Thermopylae
Ag. Konstantínos
Roviés
Óros Teléthrio 991 ▲

Potamoúla
12
Kaliakoúda 2101 ▲
Gardíki 1926
Pávliani
Káto Brálos
Kaelídromo
Regínio
Arkítsa
Límni
Moní Galatáki ❤

Dytikí Ellás
Proúsos
Domnísta
Kaliakoúda
Óri Vardoúsia
2495 ▲
Graviá
2510 ▲
Elátia
Livanátes
Skála
Alaí

Strátos
1924 ▲
Astópetra
1734 ▲
Óros Gióna
48
Lílea
Tithoréa
Kalapódi
Atalándi
Málesina

Agrínio
1818 ▲
Pendagií
Eptálofos
Fthiótida
Hiomón 1080 ▲
Martíno

Angelókastro
L. Trihonída
Thérmo
Ámfissa
Óros Parnassós 2457 ▲
Heróna
Orhomenós
1
Akréfnion

5
Matarága
984
Káto Makrinoú
Mórnos
Trikorfá 1545
Lidoríki
Delphi
6
Aráhova
5
Livadiá
3
Kástro

Etolikó
10
Thermos
11
Pitsináíka
Kábos
Itéa
Desfína
Distomo
48
Óros Elikón
Pétra 1526 ▲
Palovoúna 1748 ▲
3
Thíva (Thebes)
2

Pleuron
Návpaktos
8
48
Galaxídi
7
Andíkyra
4 † Moní Ósios Loukás
Vágia
Kavirion

Mesolóngi
9
Evinohóri
Psathópyrgos
Ágios Nikólaos
Eratiní
Óros
Thísvi
Elopía
907 ▲
Óros Kitherón
Erythrés

Kryonéri
Río
8
Andírio
Kamáres
Kólpos Andíkyras
Paralía
Melissóhori
Aigósthena
1
1131 ▲

Patraïkós Kólpos
Pátra
Égio
Korinthiakós Kólpos
Óri
Geránia
Pórto Germenó

Ionian Beach
Káto Ahéa
Témeni
1926 ▲
Trápeza
Kráthio
Lykoporiá
Kamári
Xilókastro
Perahóra
1351 ▲
Mégara
8 A

Kalógria
9
Vasilikó
Óros Panaheïkó
Selinoús
1779 ▲
Áno Diakoptó
Kerpiní
Moní Méga Spíleo †
1757
Soúli
Kiáto
Óri
Athína

Várda
Lápas
700 ▲
Hióna
Katarráktis
33
Flamboúra
Kalávryta
Moní Áno Sinikiá Trikala †
Trikala
Sikyóna
Kórinthos
Loutráki

Káto Vlasía
2224 ▲
Stavrodrómi
Pelopónnisos
Óros Kyllíni
Sikyóna

Map, page 166

Delphi

The ancient site of **Delphi** ❻ is 11 km (7 miles) further along, built on terraces at the base of sheer cliffs, the whole poised to topple over into the Plístos Gorge. Since its excavation by the French towards the end of the 19th century, Delphi has ranked as the most popular, memorable ruin on the mainland, attended as well by gliding birds of prey launching themselves from the palisades. A visit involves steep climbs rewarded by ever-changing viewpoints and new monumental treasures.

The first locale, on the south side of the road, is the so-called **Marmaria** (open daily same hours as main site; free), comprising a gymnasium (complete with a straight track and a round bath) and the sanctuary of Athena Pronaia. Pronaia means "guardian of the temple" and ancient visitors passed first through this shrine. The original 7th-century BC temple was destroyed by the Persians, and replaced by the present complex; the most interesting structure here is the circular, 4th-century *tholos*, whose purpose remains unknown.

On the north side of the road gushes the Castalian Spring (open daily; free). Parts of the older, rectangular fountain right next to the road date to the 6th century BC, although thin marble slabs on the floor are Hellenistic or early Roman. All pilgrims had to perform ritual ablutions here.

The main sacred precinct at Delphi is the **Sanctuary of Apollo**, above the road past the Castalian Spring (open summer Tue–Sun 7.30am–6.45pm, winter Tue–Sun 8am–5pm, all year Mon 8.30am–2.45pm; entrance fee). Many of the ruins exposed today date from Roman times, but just as many monuments, including the stadium and main temple, are earlier. For the casual visitor, highlights include the Athenian Treasury, the Athenian stoa and the Temple of Apollo.

The top sights

The Doric-order **Athenian Treasury** (late 6th- or early 5th-century) was pieced together by French archaeologists in 1904–06, using the inscriptions covering its surface as a guide. The late-6th-century **Athenian stoa**, today retaining three complete Ionic columns before a polygonal wall, was a roofed area protecting souvenirs from various Athenian naval victories, including the defeat of the Persians at Salamis in 480 BC. An inscription reads: "The Athenians have dedicated this portico with the arms and bow ornaments taken from their enemies at sea."

The **Temple of Apollo** just above the Athenian stoa is the third confirmed temple to have stood here, and there are literary rumours of three even earlier ones; two 7th- and 6th-century predecessors were done for by fire and earthquake respectively. What you see dates from 369–329 BC, and is impressive enough, measuring 66 by 26 metres (215 by 85 ft): six columns were re-erected by the French. The god Apollo was associated, among other things, with prophecy, his main function here. His oracle resided under the temple flooring in the *adyton* chamber, where a chasm in the earth belched forth noxious and possibly mind-altering vapours. Consulting the oracle of Delphi consisted of several stages. The petitioner's question would be relayed to the god Apollo by a priestess

BELOW: the Sanctuary of Athena Pronaia, Delphi.

Plays were performed at Dephi's theatre during the Pythian Festival, held every four years.

known as the Pythia, who could hear the answer only when she was in a trance – induced, conveniently enough, by residing in the vapour-filled adyton. Her ravings, in turn, could be understood only by the sanctuary's priests, who interpreted them for the supplicant – often ambiguously – for a suitable fee. One of the oracle's more memorable pronouncements was that Oedipus would kill his father and marry his mother – thereby giving the world its most tragic hero and Freud his Oedipus complex.

The small **theatre** above the temple, originally 4th-century but thoroughly restored during the Roman era, seats 5,000 people and has marvellous acoustics. The **stadium**, a long narrow oval, is well worth the somewhat steep walk beyond the theatre. It retains 12 rows of seats on the north side and six rows of seats, now mostly tumbled, on the south. You will easily find the starting and finishing lines, the limestone blocks complete with grooves for the runners' toes.

The Delphi **museum** has been undergoing a comprehensive refit in the run-up to the 2004 Athens Olympics, but future hours will probably match those of the site and, once it reopens, it is worth a visit for its magnificent collection. The bronze charioteer of 470 BC with his onyx eyes is the most famous denizen, but look out also for two huge 6th-century *kouroi*, the votive, life-sized bull made from hammered silver sheets, the Ionic Sphinx of the Naxians, dating from 565 BC, and the Siphian frieze with scenes from the Trojan War and a battle between the gods and the titans.

The coast of Fokída

BELOW: Delphi's Temple of Apollo.

Below Delphi and its namesake modern, touristic village, a vast plain of olive trees stretches south towards the Gulf of Corinth. Literally gritty **Itéa** was once

Map, page 166

the ancient port of Delphi and still ships out the odd cargo of purple-red baux-ite, strip-mined from the flanks of Mt Gióna to the west. But the real star of this often bleak coast is little **Galaxídi** ❼. With its Venetian-influenced mansions, the place seems closer in style to Koróni or Návpaktos than the rough-hewn vil-lage houses of Fokída. Local shipowners prospered during the 18th and 19th centuries when Galaxídi was, amazingly, the fourth-busiest harbour in Greece – thus the elaborate mansions. But captains refused to convert to steam after the 1890s, and the place sank into obscurity until being rediscovered by wealthy Athenians looking for a pleasant weekend bolthole. Foreign tourists are thus few, but there are plenty of comfortable lodgings and decent restaurants along the south harbour quay, where yachts congregate.

Cervantes, then a crewman on a Spanish ship, lost his left arm to a cannonball at the battle of Lepanto, fought off Návpaktos in 1571.

The coastal road of Fokída heads west, passing **Ágios Nikólaos** (regular ferries to Égio on the Peloponnese) and **Trizónia**, the only inhabited island in the Gulf of Corinth, before arriving at **Návpaktos** ❽, just inside Étolo-Akarnanía. The Ottomans used it as a base before sailing out to defeat in the naval battle of Lepanto (the Venetians name for Návpaktos), crushed by an allied Christian armada commanded by John of Austria in 1571. An Ottoman chronicler lamented, "The Imperial fleet encountered the fleet of the wretched infidels and the will of Allah turned another way." For all its res-onance in the West, however, the battle – gleefully celebrated as the first major bloodying of the "Terrible Turk" – had little local effect, since the Ottomans had already taken Cyprus that summer, quickly rebuilt their navies and went on to conquer Crete within a century. In cool weather, climb up from the little egg-shaped Venetian harbour to the sprawling, pine-tufted castle above. Much the largest place on the gulf's north shore, today Návpaktos

BELOW: a ship in the Gulf of Corinth.

The Venetian castle at Návpaktos extends to ramparts guarding the harbour.

gracefully combines the functions of low-key resort and market town. The better hotels and most restaurants stand behind plane-tree-shaded Grímbovo beach, although bathing there is dubious; retire instead to the westerly beach of Psáni.

Étolo-Akarnanía

Continuing further west into Étolo-Akarnanía from Návpaktos, the landscape becomes flatter and less dramatic; the main sight en route is the new, earthquake-proof **suspension bridge** at the **Río-Andírrio straits**, scheduled to replace the former 15-minute ferry ride over to the Peloponnese by mid-2004. The road veers inland briefly before arriving at **Mesolóngi** ❾, where Lord Byron died on 19 April 1824. The Ottomans had been trying to take the town since 1822; in April 1825 the final attack was mounted by 30,000 troops against 5,000 active insurgents. After a year of close siege, about half the population of 20,000 – combatants and civilians alike – broke out but were ambushed, with only about 1,600 surviving. Those remaining in town fired their own powder magazines, killing themselves, several thousand children and the elderly, and many Turkish attackers.

The northeast entrance to the town through the Venetian wall is known as the **Gate of the Sortie**, built by King Otho where the inhabitants defied the siege. To the west lies the **Garden of Heroes** (signposted "Heroes' Tombs"), with a tumulus covering the bodies of the anonymous defenders; the tomb of the Greek commander, Markos Botsaris; and a statue of Byron, beneath which his heart is buried. Today Mesolóngi is, more on sentimental than practical grounds, the capital of Étolo-Akarnanía, and lives mostly from the products of the vast and sometimes whiffy lagoons which surround the town on three sides: salt, *avgotáraho* or

BELOW: Návpaktos harbour.

compressed fish roe, and smoked eels. The latter two items can be sampled at several tavernas on and around Athanasíou Razikotsíka, at the heart of the old quarter.

Beyond Mesolóngi, and the enormous walls of ancient Pleuron on the mountainside, the road splits near **Etolikó** , a strange place built as a medieval refuge on an island in a lagoon. The more popular highway goes through the impressive **Klisoúra Gorge** past unsightly **Agrínio**, commercial capital of the province, and on through tobacco fields to **Amfilohía** at the southernmost point of the Amvrakikós Gulf.

A more interesting route to western Epirus veers off at Etolikó and mostly follows the coast all the way. Once across the mighty Aheloós River and over some oak-covered hills, you emerge at **Ástakos**, a minor ferry port with services to Itháki but also a major yacht anchorage. The onward road offers spectacular views over small and large members of the Ionian archipelago before cruising through **Mýtikas** and **Páleros**, two little resorts in the lee of Levkáda which make excellent meal stops. At the end of the journey is **Vónitsa** with its little castle, gulf-front tavernas and, as ever hereabouts, a merely functional beach; from here you are poised to head either southwest to Levkáda or northwest through a 2003 tunnel under the mouth of the Amvrakikós Gulf to Préveza.

North into Evrytanía

From Návpaktos, a little-used but highly scenic road goes northeast into the valley of the Évinos River, beloved of rafters, and then climbs again to the basin of Lake Trihonída, the largest natural body of fresh water in Greece. On a plateau out of sight to the northeast lies the lively town of **Thérmo** and its predecessor,

Map, page 166

Jason, who set out in his ship Argo to find the Golden Fleece, began his journey in Iolkos, an ancient site on the outskirts of Vólos.

BELOW: Welcoming Lord Byron at Mesolóngi by Theodoros Vryzakis, 1861.

ancient **Thermos** ⓫ (open Tue–Sun 8.30am–3pm; entrance fee), the main religious centre of the ancient Aetolians. Beyond Thérmo, the gradient steepens as you head north through the forest to Evrytanía province. First up are **Prousós** ⓬ village and monastery, poised on the precipitous, landslide-prone north slopes of Mt Panetolikó; its isolation made the area a haunt of revolutionary hero Karaïskakis. Some spectacular gorges bring you to the main **Karpenisiótis valley**, heart of Evrytanía and nicknamed the "Greek Switzerland". Helvetic indeed are the green slopes and fir trees, matched by Swiss-style stratospheric accommodation prices. The ski centre on Mt Veloúhi, north of the provincial capital of **Karpenísi** ⓭, is a popular target, as are day-walks up Mounts Kaliakoúda and Helidóna, the valley's 2,000-metre (6,500-ft) peaks. The main villages just outside of war-ravaged Karpenísi, more appealing for a stay or a meal, are Méga Horío, Mikró Horió, Gávros and Koryshádes.

North from Fokída to Thessaly

From the Delphi area, it is also possible to head straight north between Mounts Parnassus and Gióna towards **Lamía** ⓮, capital of its own province and a pleasant lunch stop. On the way you pass a hallowed site of Ancient Greek heroism. In antiquity, **Thermopylae** ⓯ was a narrow passage between the cliffs and the sea, although today silt from a nearby river has displaced the coastline by almost 5 km (3 miles). In 480 BC the Spartan general Leonidas held the pass for three days against a vastly larger Persian army, until the Persians, tipped off by the traitor Ephialtes, outflanked the defenders by using a higher pass. Leonidas ordered most of the Greek army to retreat, but fought to the end with his hand-picked guard of 1,300 men. A monumental statue of Leonidas now marks the spot, across the road

Orchards of cherry and apple spread out on the terraced hillsides below Mount Pílio. Look out for these fruits in bottles in the local village shops.

BELOW: Vólos seen from Mount Pílio.

from the grave mound for the Greek dead. Just beyond are the still-popular hot sulphur springs (Thermopylae means "hot gates") after which the pass is named.

Less than one hour's drive along the motorway from Lamía, **Vólos** ⓰ – capital of the Thessalian province of Magnisía – is certainly not the most photogenic of towns. Destroyed by several earthquakes between 1947 and 1957, it is a busy, modern port, a sort of compressed version of Thessaloníki and Piraeus. That said, it is also a spirited town, with (like most of Thessaly) a tradition of Communist politics, a university, and arguably the largest Greek concentration of *ouzerís* along its waterfront. This gets leafier and more Aegean as you head east towards the archeological museum (closed until 2005), which houses finds dating back to Neolithic times and Vólos' early days as ancient Iolkos.

Map, page 166

Mount Pílio

The great Thessalian plain, once the bed of an inland sea, is ringed by mountains; the only natural outlet is where the Piniós River exits through the fabled **Vale of Témbi**, a 10-km (6-mile) gorge between **Mount Olympos** (Ólymbos) and **Mount Óssa**. Looming above Vólos is **Mount Pílio**, legendary home of the centaurs. These fantastic beings had the legs and bodies of horses, the arms and heads of men, and – well-versed in magic and herbology – served as the wise tutors of several ancient heroes, including Achilles. Probably the centaurs were a mythologisation of an aboriginal tribe who, hiding in the dense Pílio forests, preserved the lore of Prehellenic ages.

Intriguingly, the entire region was a prominent centre of learning in Greece throughout the 17th and 18th centuries. Many important officials of the Austro-Hungarian Empire, of the sultan's inner circle and even of the Russian court

The Megálou Meteórou monastery contains 16th-century frescoes by Franco Catellano.

BELOW:
Pílio specialities.

Willows, planes and laurels border the Piniós River which cuts through the Vale of Témbi, making it a delightful place to hike. You can also take a boat trip through the gorge.

BELOW: Labinoú beach on Pílio.

were educated on Mount Pílio. The peninsula probably became such a nursery of Greek erudition owing to its timber-based wealth and relative inaccessibility to grasping Ottoman officials.

The Pílio Peninsula has two faces: the damp, shaggy northeast flank dropping to the Aegean, with excellent sand beaches of near-Caribbean hue; and the balmy, olive-covered slopes fringed with pebble shores lapped by the Pagasitic Gulf. Even if you go by charter flight to Vólos airport (a military base recently opened to civilian flights) and have use of a hire car, a week is realistically needed to tour it. The obvious, over-subscribed target is **Makrinítsa** ⓱, 17 km (11 miles) north of Vólos, with its large concentration of 18th-century mansions and a fountain-and-church-flanked square. But **Vyzítsa** ⓲ to the east is quieter, with nearly as many grand houses.

Zagorá ⓳ and **Tsangaráda** in the northeast each comprise four villages in one, their several parishes strung out along kilometres of road: because of abundant water, few Pílio communities form dense clusters as on the islands. The main developed resorts are **Ágios Ioánnis** ⓴ near Zagorá, **Plataniá** in the far south and **Áfissos** closer to Vólos. For contrast, try to stop at relatively unfrequented villages like **Lávkos**, **Sykí** and **Promýri** in the south. **Tríkeri** ㉑ and its port Agía Kyriakí, at the crab-claw southwest tip, lead a largely separate existence, with a strong maritime tradition. Beaches are too numerous to list, although the postcard stars tend to be **Mylopótamos** with its natural arch, and **Damoúhari** port with its tiny Venetian castle, both below Tsangaráda.

The Metéora

As you approach **Kalabáka** from Tríkala, towering rock formations – the **Metéora** ㉒ – rise before you in one of the great spectacles of mainland Greece. Some of the most extraordinary monasteries in the world cling to these massive pinnacles, whose name derives from the verb *meteorízo*, "to suspend in the air". These cones, cylinders and rounded buttresses, flecked with vegetation and caves like so many unbrushed, carious molars, are remnants of river sediment deposited at the margins of the prehistoric sea covering the plain of Thessaly some 25 million years ago. Tectonic-plate pressure and erosion by the young Piniós River are jointly responsible for their present shape.

Religious hermits were already colonising the caves here by the 10th century, but legend attributes the first rock-top monastery (Megálou Meteórou) to the Athonite monk Athanasios, midway through the 14th century. Progress was slow as materials were transported first by rope ladder, then by winches and baskets, and it took nearly three centuries to finish Megálou Meteórou, by which time it was just one of 24 religious communities that were flourishing on the summits. After the 17th century the monastic impetus slowed, and the more flimsily erected structures began to crumble on their exposed perches; the vicissitudes of modern Greek history since the Revolution further hastened decline, and today only eight survive of which just six are inhabited and open to pilgrims.

Map, page 166

Heading north out of Kalabáka through the village of **Kastráki**, set unimprovably in the shadow of the rocks, you encounter monasteries in the following order. **Agíou Nikoláou Anápavsa** (open Apr–Oct daily except Fri 9am–3.30pm, winter variable hours), built around 1388, has well-cleaned frescoes by the monk Theofanes of the Cretan School (*circa* 1527), including a stylite (column-dwelling) hermit being lifted by winch-hoist, as would have been done locally. **Megálou Meteórou** (open daily except Tue 9am–5pm) is the largest and highest monastery, although its church is overshadowed by a collection of rare icons and manuscripts in the refectory. **Varlaám** (open daily except Thu 9am–2pm, 3.20–5pm, winter Sat–Wed 9am–3pm), founded in 1517, offers 16th-century frescoes by Franco Catellano (partly retouched in 1870), including an Ascension and a Pandokrator in the two domes respectively. It is also the last monastery to preserve its old windlass mechanism, now only lifting supplies but formerly used for elevating monks as well.

Beautiful little **Roussánou** (open daily summer 9am–6pm, winter 9am–1pm, 3.20–6pm), completely occupying a knife-edge summit, was built in 1545 for monks, later abandoned, and re-occupied by nuns in the 1970s. It too has vividly gory 17th-century frescoes dwelling on martyrdom by various unpleasant means. **Agías Triádos** (open daily except Thu, summer 9am–6pm, winter 9am–12.30pm, 3–5pm) has a final approach of 130 steps tunnelled through a rock; the frescoes in its *katholikón* were thoroughly cleaned during the 1990s. Like other monastic churches here, this was built in two phases, resulting in two domes, two Pandokrators and two complete sets of Evangelists. **Agíou Stefánou** (open Tue–Sun 9am–2pm, 3.30–6pm), like Roussánou, is run as a convent but, heavily damaged by bombs during World War II, is the one to miss if time is running short. ❏

BELOW: Agíou Stefánou monastery.

EPIRUS

A spectacular mountain region of limestone peaks, wooded valleys and traditional stone villages, the northwest also offers a pristine national park where bears and wolves still roam

Map, page 178

I nland Epirus (Ípiros in Greek) is a world apart from the azure, sun-bleached Greece of the coasts. Its character is determined by the limestone peaks and deep river gorges of the Píndos range, which attains its greatest height just before the Albanian border in mounts Smólikas (2,635 metres/8,645 ft) and Grámmos (2,520 metres/8,270 ft). The winter precipitation, the highest in mainland Greece, ensures that forests are shaggy and the rivers foaming. An isolation enforced by both mountains and climate fostered the growth of medieval semi-autonomous villages built by traders and craftsmen returning from abroad. Local stone and wood has been transformed into imposing houses, with street cobbles, walls and roof slates blending in a uniform grey which, far from being depressing, is a classic example of harmonious adaptation to environment.

In antiquity, this was considered the limit of the civilised world; few ruins have been unearthed besides shadowy oracles at Dodona (Dodóni) and Ephyra. The Romans and Byzantines had scarcely more time for this rugged terrain south of the Via Egnatia, even though during the 13th and 14th centuries the Despotate of Epirus extended from the Ionian Sea to Thessaloníki. This ministate sheltered members of the Byzantine nobility who had fled the imperial capital when it was sacked by the Fourth Crusade in 1204. They left behind intriguing churches around Árta, joining earlier masterpieces at Kastoriá in western Macedonia.

Like the rest of northern Greece, Epirus was not incorporated into the modern state until March 1913, during the First Balkan War and some 80 years after the end of the initial Greek War of Independence.

LEFT: Dodona's 3rd-century BC theatre.
BELOW: the mansion of the Tositsa family in Métsovo is now a folk museum.

Eclipse – and Renaissance?

During the 20th century, the remoteness that once protected the area undermined its continued vigour. The ravages of World War II and the subsequent civil war, along with poor communications, the unviability of traditional livelihoods and apparently punitive government neglect, spurred massive emigration, particularly to North America, Germany and Australia. By the 1970s, many Epirot villages were in an advanced state of physical and social decline. Numerous houses were left to decay (or shoddily repaired), while others sheltered an ever-dwindling population of the economically inactive elderly.

But since the early 1980s, matters have slowly changed. The government has acted to integrate the region into the national economy, most obviously with frequent flights to Ioánnina and good roads, including the Via Egnatia expressway and its ambitious tunnels through the Píndos. Emigration has slowed down and just occasionally – thanks to tourism, subsidies for logging or grazing, and better infrastructure – even

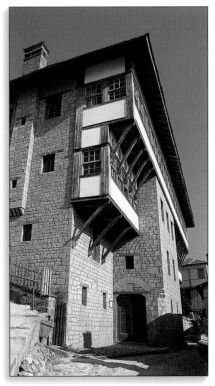

halted. Attitudes towards village life have softened, with traditional architecture and methods now viewed less as stumbling blocks to economic prosperity and more as cultural heritage to be preserved.

The core issues of this new era are most visible in the Zagóri district of Epirus. Archeological initiatives and financial incentives have led to the restoration of many buildings, so that entire villages are now preserved as homogeneous traditional settlements. Simultaneously, old roads have been widened and paved, and new ones bulldozed, giving access to the tiniest hamlets. Because of the nature of tourism here, Zagóri is one of the few places in Greece where more than lip service is paid to the idea of quality trekking routes – although trails off the most popular itineraries can be haphazardly marked and maintained at best, and facilities in the villages where you finish a day's hike can be rudimentary.

As in the whole of Greece, a touristic plum as lucrative as Zagóri has inevitably become the focus of ongoing battles between conservationists, developers and entrepreneurs. Dirt roads serving timber tracts and the high pastures

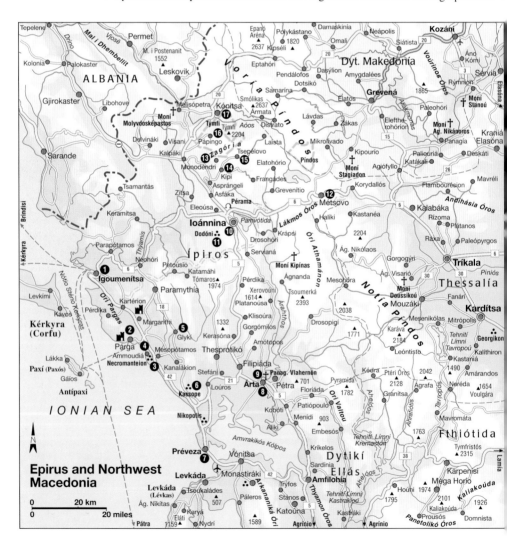

Map, page 178

scar the landscape, as does the national power corporation's reservoir at the sources of the Aóös River. Cuttings and tunnellings for the yet-to-be-opened Via Egnatia have a significant visual impact, especially near Métsovo. Yet during the late 1980s and early 1990s, not a few shepherds and villagers allied themselves with urban mountaineers, local tourism personnel, international ecologists and even the European Kayaking Federation to halt a scheme promoted by Ioánnina-based interests for a second dam on the lower Aóös, plus various ski lifts and roads which would have ruined the national park at the heart of Zagóri. Low-impact, high-quality tourism – specifically accommodation in some of the many restored houses – has been successfully promoted, particularly in the gateway villages for the park where the inhabitants sided with the conservationists.

Coastal Epirus

The modern port of **Igoumenítsa ❶**, at the very northwestern corner of mainland Greece, is the third busiest in the country after Pátra and Piraeus (Pireás), a turnstile sort of a place where an enforced halt should be avoided at all costs. Far more rewarding is the coastal road south, which after 33 km (20 miles) reaches the side road for **Karavostássi**, indisputably the finest beach in Thesprotía province. Two rivers at each end of the long strand are responsible for the ample sand, and since it is a protected area development is still limited. Just up the hill from the side-turning sits the village of **Pérdika**, whose pedestrianised centre offers a range of tavernas and a surprisingly lively night scene, courtesy of Athenian Greeks and Greeks returned from overseas.

From the Karavostássi-Pérdika junction, a few more kilometres – via the well-preserved castle of **Agiá** (open daily all day; free) – suffice to bring you to

BELOW:
the Víkos Gorge.

Local goat's cheese makes a tasty snack.

Párga ❷, Epirus's main coastal resort and deservedly so for its fine beaches, tiered houses and dominant Norman-Venetian castle. From the 14th to the late 18th centuries this was the Serene Republic's lone stronghold in Epirus, peopled by Souliot Orthodox Christians in constant conflict with their Muslim neighbours, as well as a small community of Jews who lived from the export of citrons to Europe for Jewish liturgical use. The British acquired it in 1814 and soon ceded it to the rapacious Ali Pasha of Ioánnina; the townspeople collected their relics and moved to Corfu and Paxí. Párga now enjoys 100 percent hotel occupancy (mostly from package tours) from late June through to early September, although out of season it still makes an atmospheric stop.

Some 22 km (14 miles) southeast, beside **Mesopótamos** village, lies the **Necromanteion ❸** (Nekromándio) of Ephyra (open daily 8am–3pm), the venerable oracle of the dead described by Circe in *The Odyssey*. Today the Ahérondas River (one of the legendary rivers swirling around Hades) has silted up the surrounding agricultural plain, but in Homeric times the oracle was a suitably mysterious, tree-fringed island in a lagoon. Supplicants entered the sanctuary via a maze of corridors and were then lowered by a pulley into a vaulted underground chamber to experience whatever spectral hoax the resident priests had concocted.

The Ahérondas enters the sea at **Ammoudiá ❹** just 5 km (3 miles) to the west. The river makes bathing at the beach here cold, and should you choose to stay the night, the mosquitoes are out in force after dark. But lunching at the row of tavernas on the pedestrianised quay, where tour boats for hire to the Necromanteion bob at anchor, is exceedingly pleasant, and a small but excellent "visitor information centre" at the town entrance (open Mon–Sat erratic hours; free) covers the natural history and ethnology of the area.

BELOW: a yacht moored off Párga.

Map, page 178

Inland from the Necromanteion, closer to its source, the Ahérondas squeezes through a spectacular gorge. From the village of **Glykí** ❺, a side track signposted for the "Skála Dzavélenas" dead-ends at the start of the *skála*: a spectacular 90-minute path down to the river bed and up into the realm of the Souliots, a Christian tribe never completely subdued by the Ottomans. From Glykí, continue south another 30 km (19 miles) to the combined side turning for **Zalóngo** and ancient Kassope. The former, a mountaintop monastery of little intrinsic interest, was witness to a dramatic incident in 1806 which has since become a staple of Greek nationalist legend known by every schoolchild: trapped by Ali Pasha's forces, several dozen Souliot women fled to a nearby pinnacle, where – rather than submit to the enemy – they danced off the edge into thin air clutching their children. An incongruous modern sculpture celebrates their defiance.

Nearby **Kassope** ❻ (open Tue–Sun 8.30am–3pm, may be open other times; entrance fee) is less visited and eminently rewarding: a minor Hellenistic city whose jumbled ruins are matched by a fine view over the Ionian Sea and Levkáda island. No such paeans apply to the artificial Roman city of **Nikopolis**, some 15 km (9 miles) south and 600 metres (2,000 ft) below, which promises much from the sheer extent of its ruins but offers little close up. **Áktio**, the promontory dovetailing with Préveza at the mouth of the Amvrakikós Gulf, was Roman Actium, also the name of the naval battle in which Octavian defeated Anthony and Cleopatra's forces in 31 BC. Octavian then named himself Emperor Augustus and established Nikopolis, "Victory City", nearby.

Préveza ❼, once a sleepy, shabby provincial capital, has been spruced up, partly to cater for package tourists in transit between Áktio airport and the fine

TIP

The hill-top ruins of ancient Kassope make a glorious vantage-point from which to watch the sunrise. If you're tempted, a daily bus from Préveza makes the trip at 6am.

BELOW: Nikopolis, "City of Victory", was founded by the emperor Augustus.

beaches to the north, or on Levkáda. In its old bazaar, with rather more character than Parga's, a clutch of restaurants still offer the gulf's famous sardines, and summer nightlife is loud and varied. In 2003, a new tunnel under the mouth of the gulf finally replaced the old RO-RO ferry ride across to Áktio.

Some 50 km (31 miles) over on the far side of the gulf lies **Árta ❽**, the ancient Ambracia and capital of King Pyrrhus (of the original pyrrhic victory). It later became the seat of the Despotate of Epirus, and retains a legacy of churches from that era. Most notable is the enormous, cubic **Panagía Parigorítissa** (open Tue–Sun 8.30am–3pm; entrance fee), which dates from the late 13th century and betrays Italian influences in its palazzo-like exterior. High in the dome, supported by a gravity-defying cantilever system, floats a magnificent mosaic of the Pandokrátor (Christ in Majesty), the finest on the mainland after Dafní near Athens, despite damage from World War II bombing by the Italians.

In the citrus groves around the town lie other late Byzantine churches and monasteries, the most beautiful of which is **Panagía Vlahernón** in the village of **Vlahérna ❾**, 6 km (4 miles) to the north. Despot Michael II added the domes in the 13th century, and is thought to be entombed inside; the caretaker here will lift a section of carpet to expose a part of the fine floor mosaic.

Ioánnina

Lining the shores of **Lake Pamvótis** (Pamvótida), spread below the stark face of Mount Mitsikéli, **Ioánnina ❿** has been one of Greece's great cities for over 1,000 years: a beacon of Hellenic culture, a traders' *entrepôt* and, in the 19th century (its last glorious epoch), the capital of the infamous Ali Pasha. Nicknamed "the Lion of Ioánnina", this maverick Albanian Muslim tyrant paid only minimal

TIP

During the summer, Préveza makes a good base for visiting the Ionian Islands, with frequent hydrofoil connections – although schedules often change at random.

BELOW:
Árta's graceful
18th-century
stone bridge.

allegiance to the ruling Ottoman Empire while establishing an autonomous fiefdom. Today the town remains one of Greece's liveliest provincial centres.

Unlike most large Greek centres, Ioánnina's history does not predate early Christian times, when an earthquake blocked the natural drainages of the surrounding plain and thus created the lake. Its name derives from an early church of St John the Baptist, long since vanished. After the Latin conquest of Constantinople in 1204 and the establishment of the Despotate of Epirus, Ioánnina grew in size and importance as refugees from "The City" swelled its population. It surrendered to the Ottomans in the 15th century; in 1788 Ali Pasha designated this town of 35,000 inhabitants (large for that time) his headquarters.

Ioánnina's layout is testimony to Ali's dubious legacy. While he left behind the city's most distinctive monuments (its mosques, and the redoubtable Kástro in its present form), he also had much of the city burned to deny it to a besieging Ottoman army, sent by the sultan to put down his unruly vassal in 1820. This, along with a 1960s penchant for large apartment blocks, has resulted in the relentlessly modern Ioánnina which lies outside the old town.

The wide expanse of central **Platía Pýrrou**, joined to the plazas of Akadimías and Dimokratías and lined by various public buildings, makes an obvious starting-point for a city tour. Just east of Dimokratías stands the Archeological Museum (closed until 2005), home to a fine collection of bronzes and tablets inscribed with questions for the Dodona oracle.

Except for a couple of cinemas with good first-run fare, this area is no longer the main nocturnal hub of Ioánnina. That has shifted downhill along Avérof towards the Kástro, past two shopfronts selling the famous local *bougátsa* (custard or cheese pie) at Dimokratías 2 and Avérof 3 respectively, to take better advantage of the town's setting. State-of-the-art latenight bars cluster at the far end of Ethnikís Andístasis, in a former tradesmen's bazaar by the lake, and around Platía Mavíli, on the opposite side of the citadel. On summer nights, the latter – better known as Mólos – throbs with townspeople strolling past vendors selling roast corn, *halvás* and bootleg tapes of local clarinet music from gas-lit pushcarts.

Kástro, the five-gated, walled precinct of various Epirot rulers including Ali Pasha himself, best conjures up Ioánnina's colourful past. A tangle of alleyways rises to a fortified promontory jutting out into the lake; at the lower corner looms the **Aslan Pasha Mosque**, now home to the Municipal Museum (open daily summer 8am–8.30pm; shorter winter hours; entrance fee) with its diverse collection of Epirot costumes, jewellery and relics from the city's once-large Jewish community.

One of Ali Pasha's most infamous exploits – involving Kyria Frosini, the beautiful Greek mistress of Ali's eldest son – is supposed to have taken place near the mosque-museum. In the most common variant of the tale, Ali punished the girl for resisting his advances by having her and 17 female companions tied up in weighted sacks and drowned in the lake. Xenophobic-kitsch oleograph postcards of the incident are still sold, depicting wild-eyed "barbarians" and swooning Greek maidens in the clutches of their tormentors.

Map, page 178

The Aslan Pasha Mosque, now the Municipal Museum, has fascinating relics of Ioánnina's colourful past.

BELOW: a market in Árta.

At the summit of the citadel looms the **Fethiye Tzami** (Victory Mosque) and one of Ali's restored palaces – today an indifferent Byzantine Museum (open summer Mon 12.30–7pm, Tue–Sun 8am–7pm; winter Tue–Sun 8am–5pm; entrance fee). The former treasury nearby makes an appropriate showcase for displays on the city's traditional silver industry.

After defying the sultan for three decades, Ali finally met his end on the islet of **Nisí**, on the far side of the visibly polluted lake (bus-boats make the trip from Mólos all day until 11pm). A small house in the grounds of Ágios Pandelímon monastery was his last hide-out; here, trapped on the upper storey by a Turkish assassin, Ali was shot through the floorboards then decapitated. His head was sent to Istanbul as a trophy, after having toured the provinces which it had lately so terrorised.

The monastery of Agíou Nikoláou Filanthropinón, near the island-village of Nissí, is worth a visit for its vivid frescoes.

Monasteries with more peaceful histories, and a fine island loop walk, lie in the opposite direction. The nearest Nisí village, **Agíou Nikoláou Filanthropinón**, contains vivid late-Byzantine frescoes; some depict unusually gruesome martyrdoms, while others, by the entrance, depict ancient sages such as Plutarch, Aristotle and Thucydides. Alas, the island's tavernas are touristy and poor in quality; if Ioanninans want a lakeside meal, they patronise the half-dozen restaurants which line **Pamvotídas**, the shoreline street heading northwest from Mólos.

Diversions around Ioánnina

BELOW: Ioánnina's lake and Aslan Pasha Mosque.

Some 20 km (12 miles) south of Ioánnina lies **Dodona** ⓫ (Dodóni), Epirus's main archeological site (open daily summer 8.30am–7pm; winter 8.30am–5pm; entrance fee), nestling in a valley at the foot of Mount Tómaros. According to

Herodotus, its oracle (the oldest in Greece and, until the 4th century BC, the most important) was established by a priestess abducted from a similar one in Egyptian Thebes. Zeus – considered resident in the trunk of a holy oak tree – was worshipped here, priests and priestesses deciphering the rustlings of the leaves which were the god's sacred pronouncements. The carefully restored **theatre**, dating from the 3rd-century reign of King Pyrrhus, has a capacity of 17,000 spectators – always far too large for the needs of the little town that existed here from 1000 BC until early Byzantine times. It is still occasionally used for summer performances.

Until the Via Egnatia expressway south of town opens for business (estimated for 2006), the only highway east into Thessaly is the old one curling clockwise around the lake. On this route you will pass **Pérama** (open daily summer 8am–8pm; winter 8am–sunset; entrance fee), one of Greece's most spectacular cave systems, on the outskirts of Ioánnina. Then, after a long, twisting ascent, the village of **Métsovo** ⓬, 58 km (36 miles) from Ioánnina, appears in a ravine below. It ranks as the Vlach "capital", famous for its imposing houses, handicrafts, cheeses and the traditional costumes still worn by some of the older inhabitants.

Apart from the wonderful frescoes covering the interior of the medieval monastery of Ágios Nikólaos, a short walk below town, the only other recognised sight is the **Arhondikó Tosítsa Museum** (open daily except Thu 8.30am–1pm, 4–6pm; winter 3–5pm; guided tours only; entrance fee), its reconstructed interior displaying fine woodwork and textiles.

Unlike so many Greek mountain villages, Métsovo is thriving: local worthies who made their fortunes abroad have set up endowments to encourage

Map, page 178

Exhibits in the Arhondikó Tosítsa Museum, Métsovo.

BELOW: Dodona's theatre.

local industry, such as the nearby ski resort whose clients periodically fill the dozen or so hotels – of a better standard than most in Ioánnina. And while many of the souvenirs pitched at coach tours are bogus – notably imported Albanian rugs – locally sold food is not: the red *katógi* wine, cheese, salami and *trahanás* (sourdough "pasta" for soup) all make excellent purchases.

Continuing east towards the Metéora in Thessalía (Thessaly), soon after Métsovo you negotiate the Katára Pass ("Curse Pass") – at 1,694 metres (5,557 ft) the highest paved road in the country and the main route across the central Píndos Mountains.

The Zagorohória

The road northwest out of Ioánnina leads to **Zagória,** which forms a culturally and geographically distinct region of Epirus. Its 46 villages – the Zagorohória – lie in an area bounded by the Métsovo–Ioánnina–Kónitsa highway and the Aöös River. Because of the region's infertile soil, local men emigrated to major commercial centres in Eastern Europe during the Ottoman era, subsequently returning to their homeland with considerable wealth. This allowed locals to hire a representative to send taxes to the sultan directly rather than suffer from tax-farmers, securing a large measure of autonomy.

Zagória's villages differ markedly: the east is populated largely by Vlachs (more properly, Arouman), a people rooted in Greece since antiquity, speaking a Romance language and living as caravan-drovers and shepherds driving their flocks from summer to winter pastures. Early in 1944, the occupying Germans retaliated for local resistance by burning most of the eastern villages, later rebuilt haphazardly. The western and central Zagorohória show more of a

BELOW: inside the caves at Pérama.

Map,
page
178

Slav/Albanian influence in place names and architecture; happily, most survived the war unscathed and today constitute one of Greece's showpieces.

The Zagorian landscape is dramatically varied, embracing sheer rock faces, limestone dells, dense forests, upland pasture and deep canyons. The national park at its core, comprising the Víkos Gorge and lower reaches of the Aóös, was established partly to protect a threatened population of bears, lynx, wolves and birds of prey. Yet even in the remotest corners there are signs of man: a post-Byzantine monastery with belfry, or a graceful, slender-arched bridge from the Ottoman period. Unfortunately, the pastoral culture that used to feature prominently is in sharp decline; EU subsidy policy means that few shepherds now occupy the high pastures, and unattended cattle herds are rapidly replacing the tenanted sheepfolds of yesteryear.

Central Zagória is best reached by the side road some 14 km (9 miles) out of Ioánnina, prominently marked for the **Víkos Gorge**. **Vítsa** village has fine traditional houses, a shaded central square, one of the oldest churches in the region (Ágios Nikólaos), and the easiest trail access to the floor of the gorge, the intricately engineered Skála Vítsas. Just up the road, more frequented **Monodéndri 13** supports two tavernas offering hearty local cuisine on its lower plaza, near the photogenic basilica of Ágios Athanásios flanking the classic path descending to the gorge. For the less committed, either the 1990s-vintage, rather gaudy *kalderími* (cobbled path) to the eyrie of Agía Paraskeví monastery, or the 7-km (4-mile) drive up to the Oxiá overlook, will afford breathtaking views.

From the junction below Vítsa, the easterly main road passes the turning for exquisite **Dílofo** on its way to the major villages of Kípi, Kapésovo and Tsepélovo. **Kípi 14** stands nearest to a much-photographed cluster of 18th- and 19th-century packhorse bridges, the most famous of which is the three-arched Plakída span. East of Kípi, **Negádes** has a frescoed basilica, one of the best examples of the Zagorian style, while above and to the north perches Kapésovo, with a rural museum in its enormous old school.

Kapésovo also marks the start of a one-hour path incorporating the most amazingly sinuous of all Zagorian *kalderímia*, ending at **Vradéto**, the highest – and formerly most desolate – village in the area, now enjoying a mild renaissance (although the winter population is still only seven). Continue on foot for about 40 minutes and you will reach Belói viewpoint, more or less opposite Oxiá. Twelve kilometres (7 miles) further, the paved road arrives at **Tsepélovo 15**, flanked by rural monasteries and crammed with more mansions.

Back on the Ioánnina-Kónitsa highway, you pass through **Kalpáki**, where in the early winter of 1940–41 the Greeks halted the Italian invasion, rolling Fascist troops back into the snowy Albanian Mountains for a season of hell; a small roadside museum tells the tale in full. Just beyond, a 19-km (12-mile) side road heads east to the focus of most Zagorian tourism, the paired villages of **Pápingo 16**, **Megálo** and **Mikró**. Since the early 1990s they have become quite fashionable, especially during peak holiday seasons, but there is no denying their superlative setting

BELOW: Métsovo.

at the foot of the 600-metre (1,970-ft) Pýrgi, the vertical outriders of Mount Gamíla. This massif (the heart of the national park) offers fine hiking, most notably to newt-filled **Drakólimni** (Dragon Lake).

The icy Voidomátis River, popular with kayakers, drains out of the lower Víkos canyon at Klidoniá, where a lovely old bridge marks the edge of the national park a few hundred metres in from the busy highway. An even bigger one spans the Aóös River some 10 km (6 miles) north, where it exits some narrows to a vast floodplain. A 90-minute walk along the southern bank of the Aóös Gorge leads below steep, forested slopes to the Stomíou monastery, magnificently perched on a cliff.

Kónitsa ⑰ itself offers a fine view of the floodplain; an earthquake in 1996 and massive shelling during the civil war put paid to any real architectural distinction here. For that, head 23 km (14 miles) west to the monastery and namesake village of **Molyvdosképastos**, just where the Aóös enters Albania. The monastery's early 14th-century church betrays a Serbian influence with its high, stovepipe dome and barrel-roof nave. Early in the 1990s it was reinhabited by rather zealous monks, who encourage your conversion on the spot.

Due east of Kónitsa looms 2,635-metre (8,650-ft) **Mount Smólikas**, roof of the Píndos and second summit of Greece after Mount Olympos. From several of the Vlach villages along the Aóös, trails lead up towards the peak and yet another "Dragon Lake".

The 105-km (65-mile) road from Kónitsa to **Neápolis** is the single paved connection between Epirus and western Macedonia. It follows the valley of the Sarandáporos River upstream, between Smólikas and Mount Grámmos, site of the final battles of the civil war, passing the occasional blue-painted graffiti

BELOW: Kónitsa bridge, Zagória.

Map, page 178

"Elevthería Gia Vória Ípiros!" ("Freedom for Northern Epirus!") – an expression of lingering irredentist sentiment for the Albanian portion of Epirus, home to roughly 100,000 remaining Greek Orthodox.

Hiking in the Píndos

The North Píndos offer many rewarding hiking routes, from strenuous, multiday, high-level treks to various interconnected day hikes. Landscapes vary from the limestone dells of the Gamíla uplands to the forested Víkos Gorge floor. In these days of global warming, the best seasons are no longer high summer but from mid-May to mid-June, and September to early October. Although the local trail system is extensive on paper, it is unevenly maintained and often badly waymarked; the usual method is multicoloured paint splodges or, for the long-distance O3 route, metal diamond-shaped symbols nailed to trees.

The 1:50,000 *Pindus Zagori* topographic map issued by Anavasi cartographers (available in Greece and the UK) is essential if not infallible, as is a keen sense of direction, an ability to double-check trail information from villagers, and a good sense of humour. In any month the Píndos weather can change rapidly with little warning, so rain gear and a light tent are essential – the latter also because indoor accommodation can fill up suddenly. Overnight trekkers should purchase three to four days' worth of foodstuffs in Ioánnina, as stocks in village shops remain quite limited.

The four-to-five-day hiking loop outlined below begins and ends in the Pápingo villages where there is plentiful (if slightly pricey) accommodation, as well as reliable tavernas and a regular – but not daily – bus service. You should therefore be prepared to hike into and out of Pápingo, along the trail linking it

BELOW: Drakólimni, the 'Dragon Lake'.

Map, page 178

to Klidoniá village on the Ioánnina–Kónitsa highway, if you happen not to coincide with the bus service to or from Ioánnina.

The alpine refuge on Astráka col, just visible from Megálo Pápingo, is currently inoperative (although it may reopen in 2004 from May to Oct). In any case, it is a 900-metre (2,950-ft) ascent of at least three hours, with water available at regular intervals. If the refuge is still shut, camp near the spring at the north end of the seasonal **Xiróloutsa pond** (15-minute path descent east from the col). Spend the balance of the day with a short walk (1 hr each way) up to **Drakólimni**, an alpine tarn at 2,050 metres (6,300 ft) altitude, ideal for views and picnics, just northwest of the 2,500-metre (8,195-ft) Gamíla peak.

A five-to-seven-hour hike the next day takes you between mounts Astráka and Gamíla, through alpine meadows grazed by cattle, and past the head of the Mégas Lákkos Gorge to Tsepélovo (steep final descent; net altitude loss of 850 metres/2,700 ft). Water is scarce, so plan accordingly. You should have a comfortable overnight stay in one of Tsepélovo's dozen hotels and smaller inns, although reservations are advisable during July and August.

From the ravine flanking Tsepélovo to the west, a crumbled but discernible *kalderími* climbs the cliff to the uplands towards Vradéto; after about 90 minutes you are forced onto a paved road for the final 45 minutes. From Vradéto (café serving drinks only) descend the amazing *skála* to Kapésovo (45 minutes), then use the old dirt track (not the asphalt highway) to arrive in **Koukoúli** within the next 45 minutes and in time for lunch. You can stay overnight here at one of two inns, or carry on eastwards to Kípi (another 45 minutes), which has another taverna as well as two inns.

BELOW: stone houses and cobbled streets in Zagorohória. **RIGHT:** Mikró Pápingo village in the Zagorohória.

From either Koukoúli or Kípi there are marked routes into the upper end of the Víkos Gorge, crossing it by the Misíou bridge and ascending the stair-*kalderími* to Vítsa (2 hrs), with abundant accommodation and a taverna open in the evenings. A three-hour track partly shortcuts the road up to Monodéndri, 300 metres (1,000 ft) above Kípi, with several more inns and tavernas.

A signposted, well-renovated *kalderími* takes you down to the usually dry bed of the Víkos Gorge (45 minutes). A fairly strenuous path marked as the O3 route negotiates the length of the canyon, on its true left bank after the first few minutes. At the intersection of the gorge and the Mégas Lákkos side canyon (2½ hrs), a potable spring flows (unreliable after August). Continue through thick forest, then open pasture, before reaching the movable sources of the Voidomátis River (4½ hrs from Monodéndri), which well out of the base of the Pýrgi formations.

Bearing left on an obvious cobbled path leads to **Vitsikó** (Víkos) village, 45 minutes away, where you will find two inns; the O3 route crosses the river, heading up and right, reaching either of the Pápingos within two hours, for a day's total of 6½ hours. About 90 minutes along, there is a divide in the path where you cross a stream on the left to head up to Megálo Pápingo, rather than continue straight to Mikró Pápingo. The net elevation drop amounts to only 100 metres (330 ft), but there are plenty of sharp gradients. ❑

THESSALONÍKI

*Greece's second city does not live in the shadow of Athens.
It has its own distinctive character, with many Turkish
influences and a host of splendid Byzantine churches*

Map,
pages
202–3

To a visitor approaching by sea, contemporary **Thessaloníki**  presents the uniform facade of modern apartment blocks characteristic of so many Mediterranean seaside cities. At the beginning of this century, the same view was marked by minarets rising elegantly from a tile-roofed town picturesquely climbing between medieval ramparts to an upper quarter, with vast cemeteries outside the walls. When more than half the town was destroyed by the Great Fire of August 1917, British and French architects (who were accompanying Allied expeditionary forces at the time) were promptly commissioned to produce a new town plan.

Surviving Art Deco buildings enhance the wide, sea-facing boulevards they designed, although their advice to ban high-rises was disregarded. But the fire spared much, including the old hillside quarter of **Kástra**. Roman ruins, Byzantine churches, Ottoman public and domestic buildings, and displaced Jewish tombstones lie encircled by Roman and Byzantine walls, or scattered alongside asphalt boulevards and pedestrian lanes. And after years of neglect, this great architectural heritage has finally been signposted and selectively renovated.

Thessaloníki was founded in 316–315 BC by the Macedonian king Kassander, who named it after his wife, but it rose into prominence under the Romans, boosted by their **Via Egnatia** "trunk road" which stretched from the Adriatic coast to the Hellespont (Dardanelles). Saint Paul visited twice, and wrote two Epistles to the Thessalonians; Christianity (and the city) got further boosts from the Byzantine emperors, especially Theodosius (who issued his edict here, banning paganism) and Justinian, who began new churches to supplement those adapted from Roman structures. Despite Slavic and Arab raids, frequent earthquakes, fires, adjacent malarial swamps and a spotty water supply, resilient Thessaloníki prospered. Even in temporary decline it made a rich prize for the Ottomans in 1430.

Sephardic settlers

After 1500, large numbers of Sephardic Jewish refugees from Spain and Portugal settled here, giving Salonica – as they called it – its most distinctive trait for the next four centuries. On the eve of the Balkan Wars they accounted for just over half the population of 140,000, making it the largest Jewish city of that era. In 1943, 70,000 remained to be deported to the Nazi death camps, leaving less than 1,000 today.

Following the three wars leading up to 1923, the city came to epitomise a Greek refugee town: in absolute numbers Athens may have had more, but by proportion of population, Thessaloníki contains more citizens with Turkish ancestry than anywhere else in

LEFT: the Arch of Galerius, Thessaloníki.
BELOW: a café-bar on the waterfront.

During Ottoman rule, most Byzantine churches were converted into mosques, and their interiors coated in whitewash. This fresco, from Ágios Dimítrios in Thessaloníki, was one that survived.

Greece. There are abundant Turkish surnames (such as Dereli and Mumtzis) and spicy cuisine rarely found elsewhere in Greece; indeed the city has some of the best places to eat in the country. Its own self-deprecating nicknames have long been *I Protévousa tón Prosfigón* (The Refugee Capital), after the ring of 1920s settlements, all prefixed "Néa", across eastern Macedonia, and *Ftohomána* (Mother of the Poor).

But 21st-century Thessaloníki is not all changing demographics. After years in Athens' shadow, it is finally coming into its own. The International Fair held every October in permanent grounds by the university promotes the city as a Balkan trade centre and the natural gateway to the upper Balkans. Thessaloníki is confidently on the move, with innovative restaurants and clubs occupying historic buildings, its native musicians (such as Sokratis Malamas and Nikos Papazoglou) frequently at the forefront of Greek song.

They say you can always tell a Thessalonian in the rest of the mainland; with a spring in their step, they seem a head taller than the characteristically hunchedover, downtrodden Athenians. The Thessalonians are also perhaps recognisable from their clothes, as it is said to be the best-dressed city in Greece; and so it should be, given its variety of boutiques and department stores.

The city's prosperity has an inevitable downside, with traffic-clogged streets and increasing levels of pollution. There has been a long-standing project to ameliorate this by building an underground metro system (following the line of Egnatía and then heading off towards the university). This was started in 1999, but by 2003 there was very little to show for the work, and the excavations were suspended while a new contractor was sought. Current predictions see the project being finished by 2008.

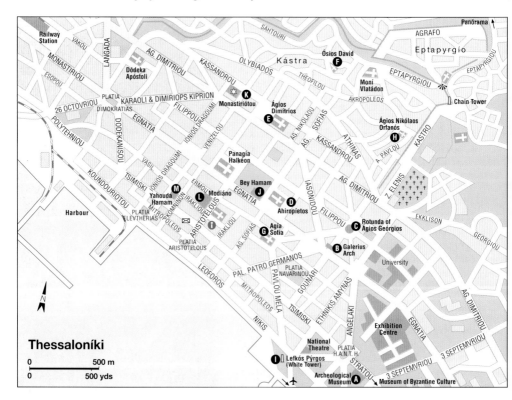

Map, page 194

A city tour

Begin at the **Archeological Museum** , which displays Macedonian, Hellenistic and Roman finds from the entire region, including the notable **Síndos** collections. Sumptuous jewellery and household effects in gold, silver and bronze vie for your attention (open summer Mon 12.30–7pm, Tue–Sun 8.30am–7pm; winter Mon 10.30am–5pm, Tue–Sun 8.30am–3pm; entrance fee). The magnificent **Vergina** treasures, of what are thought to be the royal tombs of the Macedonian king, Philip II, and his relatives, are housed in a museum at the site itself. Just beyond the Archeological Museum is the **Museum of Byzantine Culture**, opened in 1994, with artefacts from the Early Christian period (4th–7th century) through to the Middle Byzantine period (8th–12th century). The exhibits are beautifully displayed and clearly explained; among the most impressive pieces are a 5th century mosaic floor and wall paintings from a house in Thessaloníki, and some extraordinary early textiles (open Tue–Sun 8am–7pm, Mon 12.30–7pm; entrance fee).

Roman Thessaloníki is mostly subterranean. The most extensive excavations, off pedestrianised **Dimitríou Goúnari** and adjacent **Platía Navarínou**, are those of the palace of Christian-hating Emperor Galerius Caesar, he who martyred the city's patron saint Demetrius in AD 305. Above ground survives the western part of **Galerius**'s triumphal **Arch** , erected over the Via Egnatia in AD 297 to celebrate a victory over the Persians. The reliefs on the arch repay close inspection showing, as well as Galerius himself, Diocletian and Caesar. The arch was part of a large Roman complex encompassing the Rotunda (*see below*) and also the palace.

Just northwest of the arch is the **Rotunda of Ágios Geórgios**  – perhaps originally intended as Galerius's mausoleum – one of the few remaining examples of circular Roman architecture, enduring largely through conversion into a church, then a mosque. Glorious 4th-century wall mosaics partially survive, high up inside the dome and recesses; the truncated minaret is the city's last surviving one.

The **Roman agora** was located on Platía Dikastiríon. Much of this has now been excavated and remains uncovered. It is possible to get a good look at the ongoing excavations through the wire fence that surrounds the site, and there are plans to open sections of the uncovered marketplace to the public.

Byzantine Thessaloníki

A number of fine and important Byzantine churches survive in Thessaloníki, more than in any other Greek city. The earliest examples are clear adaptations of the colonnaded Roman basilica, in turn descended from Greek temples, with the outermost columns replaced by walls.

Both 5th-century **Ahiropíetos**  (open Mon–Sat 8am–noon, 5–8pm, Sun 5–7pm) and its heavily restored contemporary, **Ágios Dimítrios**  (open Mon 1.30–7.30pm, Tue–Sun 8am–7.30pm), are double-aisled basilicas with a central nave. In Ahiropíetos, hunt for fine mosaic patches under the arches, between ornate columns.

BELOW: the White Tower was added to the Roman-Byzantine walls by the Venetians.

Ágios Dimítrios was founded shortly after the saint's demise, on the site of his martyrdom. It is the largest church in Greece, almost entirely rebuilt after the 1917 fire which spared only the apse and the colonnades. Six small mosaics of the 5th to 7th century, featuring the saint, survive mostly above the columns standing on either side of the altar. The fire was responsible for the rediscovery of the crypt, which is thought to be partly constructed from the Roman baths where the saint was imprisoned; a reliquary found on the site support this. Also here are the attractive remains of a fountain that previously fed a fishpond.

At the southern end of Platía Dikastiríon is **Panagía Halkéon**, founded in 1028. The brick-built church is in the shape of a cross and contains a cycle of frescoes dating back to the 11th century. During the Ottoman occupation it served as the mosque of the local coppersmiths (no access at present).

Tiny 5th- or 6th-century **Ósios Davíd 🄵**, all that's left of the **Látomos Monastery**, is tucked away in the Kástra district (open Mon–Sat 8am–noon, 6–8pm, Sun 8–10.30am; all these Byzantine churches open according to demand, and have much shorter hours, or are closed, off season). The west end of this church has vanished, but visit for the sake of an outstanding early mosaic in the apse, only revealed in 1921 when Ottoman whitewash was removed. It depicts the vision of the Prophet Ezekiel of Christ Emmanuel, shown as a beardless youth seated on the arc of heaven, surrounded by the symbols of the Evangelists. Together, the mosaics of Ósios Davíd and Ágios Dimítrios rank as the best pre-Iconoclastic sacred art in Greece, and predate the more famous work at Ravenna in Italy.

The steep alleys of Kástra are about a 20-minute walk from the seafront. Since the late 1980s this neighbourhood of dilapidated half-timbered houses

BELOW: Panagía Halkéon, one of the city's many Byzantine churches.

has been transformed from poor, despised and "Turkish" to renovated and trendy, with scattered tavernas and cafés.

Back down in the flatlands near the waterfront, 8th-century **Agía Sofía** (Holy Wisdom) **G** (open daily 8.30am–1pm, 5.30–8pm; entrance fee) was built in conscious imitation of its namesake in Constantinople. This one, 10 metres (33 ft) wide, has a vivid Ascension, with the Apostles watching Christ borne heavenward by angels, rather than the *Pandokrátor* (Christ Enthroned) that became the rule later. In the apse and the *ikonostásis*, you can detect traces of an earlier mosaic of the Cross behind the Virgin Enthroned. It was one of a pair, and the other figural cross survives in the adjacent vault.

Another batch of churches, all well uphill from the Via Egnatia, date from the 13th and 14th centuries – examples of a cultural "golden age" at odds with the Byzantine Empire's political decline and the numerous disasters visited on Thessaloníki from the 10th to the 12th century. Financial constraints meant that frescoes, rather than mosaics, were the preferred ornamentation in these churches, most of them attached to now-extinct monasteries. By far the best of these is **Ágios Nikólaos Orfanós 𝗛**, at the northeast edge of Kástra (open Tue–Sun 8.30am–2.30pm; free). Among the better-preserved and more unusual frescoes are Christ mounting the Cross and Pilate sitting in Judgment, the very image of a Byzantine scribe; in the Washing of the Feet, it seems the talented painter inserted an image of himself on horseback, wearing a turban.

Thessaloníki's **Lefkós Pýrgos** (White Tower) **I**, effectively the city's logo, was originally built during the brief Venetian occupation as an addition to the Roman-Byzantine walls. The Ottomans used it as a prison; that, and the massacre of unruly Janissaries here in 1826, earned it the epithet "Bloody Tower". The Greeks whitewashed it post-1912 – thus the new alias – and then removed the pigment in 1985. A spiral staircase, with small windows, emerges at a lovely café and finally the crenellated roof terrace, affording fine views over the seafront and up to Kástra (open Tue–Sun 8am–7pm, Mon 12.30–7pm; free).

The vanished curtain wall leading inland from here linked the White Tower with the **Chain Tower**, the northeastern corner of the fortifications; beyond it lies the **Eptapyrgío** (Yedi Küle in Turkish), the Seven Towers Fortress, on the northeastern corner of the old walled acropolis. The seven towers on the northern side of the Eptapyrgío incorporate part of the Early Christian acropolis walls, and the six towers on the southern side were built during the Middle Byzantine period. The Ottomans made considerable additions, transforming it into a jail in the late 19th century.

Ottoman and Jewish Thessaloníki

Thessaloníki was taken by the Ottomans in 1430, just 23 years before the fall of Constantinople. The new overlords converted most churches into mosques during the first century of their rule, tacking on minarets and whitewashing over mosaics and frescoes. As a result, there are few purpose-built Ottoman mosques, though there are other interesting civic buildings. Worthy 15th-century specimens include the graceful

Map, page 194

BELOW: fish in Modiáno market.

Exhibit in the Archeological Museum, Thessaloníki.

BELOW: the Roman Rotunda, built in the 4th century AD, is now the church of Ágios Geórgios.

Ishak Pasha or **Alatza Imaret Mosque** at the base of Kástra – around the corner from the **Yeni Hamam**, or bath-house, engagingly restored as a bistro, concert hall and summer outdoor cinema – and the dilapidated **Hamza Bey Mosque** on the Via Egnatia, last used as the Alcazar cinema. Perhaps it may soon get the same treatment as the nearby **Bezesténi**, a refurbished six-domed covered market now tenanted by luxury shops. The nearby **Bey Hamam** ❿ dating from 1444 has intact stalactite vaulting over the entrance and inside.

Two more contemporary "Turkish" monuments may appeal to specialists. At the rear of the Turkish consulate stands the wooden house where Mustafa Kemal Atatürk, founder of the Turkish republic, was born in 1881. And a few hundred metres east of the Archeological Museum, at the edge of the 19th-century "New Town", is the **Yeni Cami** or "New Mosque" – an Art Nouveau folly erected by the influential Ma'min (Dönme). This so-called crypto-Jewish sect followed the 17th-century self-proclaimed Messiah, Shabbetai Zvi, into Islam. In the mass exchange of populations between Greece and Turkey in 1923, most of the Ma'min were among the 100,000 Muslims who left the city.

By contrast, there are few tangible traces of Thessaloníki's Jewish past, owing to the 1917 fire and the Nazi desecration of cemeteries and synagogues in 1943. Only the Art Deco **Monastiriótou synagogue** ⓚ, near the Ministry of Northern Greece, survived the war. Centrepiece of the vast central market – which extends to either side of **Aristotélous**, selling everything from wooden furniture to live poultry – is the covered **Modiáno** ⓛ, a fish, meat and produce-hall named after the Jewish family which established it. (Their former mansion, out beyond the Yeni Cami, now houses the Folklife Museum – currently shut for

repairs.) Though only half-occupied today, the Modiáno still supports several authentic, atmospheric *ouzerí* in the west arcade. Close by, the Louloudádika Hamam or Flower-Market Bath was also known as the **Yahouda Hamam** or Jewish Bath ; the Jewish clientele is gone, but the flowers are still outside, and a good fish taverna operates inside even as the building is being restored. In the same area, on Agíou Miná, is the **Museum of the Jewish Presence** (open Tue, Fri, Sun 11am–2pm, Wed, Thu 11am–2pm, 5pm–8pm; free). This two-storey museum presents the history of the Jewish community in Thessaloníki and contains interesting material from the ancient, destroyed, Jewish cemetery.

Maps:
City 194,
Area 202

Other attractions

The city's seafront provdes a good place for a stroll with its views, when the weather is clear, over to Mount Olympos. Better still, Níkis (the road along the harbourfront) is lined with fashionable cafés where it is easy to kill a few hours. Nearby Platías Elevtherías and Aristotélous that lead off Níkis are also pleasant places to sit and have a drink.

For an escape from the city, try a half-day excursion to **Panórama**, an affluent village 11 km (7 miles) to the east whose views justify its name; several *zaharoplastía* sell such Anatolian specialities as *salépi* (orchid-root drink), *dódurma* (Turkish ice cream) and *trígona*, triangular cream pastries. **Hortiátis**, 10 km (6 miles) north of here, has since ancient times supplied Thessaloníki with water, and retains some pines spared by arsonists, plus good tavernas. From either point, you can on a clear day look southwest across the Thermaïc Gulf to glimpse the bulk of **Mount Olympos** (Ólymbos) to the southwest, the traditional separation point between Macedonia and Thessaly. ❑

BELOW:
Thessaloníki's
waterfront.

MACEDONIA AND THRACE

Along with a landscape of fertile plains and forbidding mountains, you'll find a wondrous mix of peoples here – as well as the major holiday playground of Halkidikí

Map, pages 202–3

Standing about halfway between the Adriatic to the west and the Évros River to the east, Thessaloníki is Greece's second city, and "capital" (since 1923) of Macedonia and Thrace *(see pages 193–9)*. Scarcely 100 km (60 miles) north, the frontiers of FYROM (the Former Yugoslav Republic of Macedonia), Bulgaria and Greece meet – a boundary settled only after World War I.

Northeastern Greece does not possess the magnificent archeological sites and stunning ruined temples of the centre and the south. Its latitude spells a short summer season, a consequent dearth of cheap flights from abroad, and sparse, often overpriced accommodation (except on the Halkidikí peninsula). However, its proximity to other Balkan states and relatively recent acquisition by Greece give it greater ethnic variety, including lively music and cuisine. Ancient sites fall into two categories: either too sparse to astound, or palimpsests where layers of civilisation can be read, one after another.

Northwest Macedonia

Coming from Epirus, you officially enter Macedonia just before **Pendálofos ②**, the only place of any importance or appeal en route. Its fine stone houses – still in the Epirot style – straggle across the ravines which give the town its name ("Five-hills"). At **Neápolis ③**, the road divides: north to Kastoriá, southeast to **Siátista ④**. Perched on a bleak ridge some 20 km (12 miles) from the fork, this small town is noted for its fine 18th-century mansions or *arhondiká* – the residences of the *árhons*, or leading citizens – offering a glimpse into the self-contained society that flourished here during late Ottoman times. Then a wealthy centre for fur-trading, tanning, wine-making and a stopping point for caravans on the trade route to Vienna, Siátista declined when commercial networks changed after Greek independence.

Start with the **Nerandzópoulos mansion** on Platía Horí, whose warden has the keys to other interesting structures such as the **Manoúsi, Kanatsoúli** and **Poulikídou residences**. Visiting these will give you a good background for nearby Kastoriá, another town which prospered from the fur trade.

Returning north, the road follows the upper valley of the **Aliákmonas River**, the longest in Greece, whose 300-km (185-mile) course arcs from the Albanian border to the Thermaic Gulf. Soon you reach the **lake of Orestiáda**, or Kastoriá, almost divided in half by the eponymous town built on a peninsula. On the town's southern outskirts lies a significant military cemetery, the last resting place of government troops who were killed during the battle for Grámmos-Vítsi, which brought an end to the civil war. In the town itself, a lake-side plaza named after

LEFT: a fresco from Agíou Dionysíou, Áthos.
BELOW: waterfall at Édessa.

General James Van Fleet serves as a reminder that American equipment and advisers guaranteed a royalist victory over communist insurgency.

A Byzantine county town

Kastoriá contains no less than 54 medieval churches.

Despite extensive wartime damage, aggravated later by thoughtless modernisations, **Kastoriá ➎** remains one of northern Greece's more appealing towns. Its 54 surviving medieval churches – many erected as private chapels by rich furrier families – indicate its past as a Byzantine provincial centre and fur factory.

The half-dozen truly Byzantine specimens here represent some of Greece's finest provincial art, showing strong folk and Slav influences. You can see the best in a single morning, starting at the **Byzantine Museum** (open Tue–Sun 8.30am–3pm; entrance fee) with its good icon collection (the warden here also has control of the keys to most of the churches), and working your way south to the **Karyádis quarter**, with its fine old mansions.

Triple-aisled **Ágii Anárgyri** – built in 1018 by Emperor Basil II – sits at the northeast edge of town, overlooking the lake. Nearby **Ágios Stéfanos** is the second-oldest church in town (10th-century), again with intricately geometric masonry and an unusual women's gallery inside. South of the museum, tiny **Panagía Koumbelidíki** is unmistakeable with its disproportionately tall, drum-shaped dome, the only one in town, painstakingly rebuilt after Italian bombing in 1940. There are some fine frescoes inside and a highly unusual Holy Trinity, complete with bearded God, in the barrel vault.

Continuing south and downhill, the extensive frescoes of the single-aisled basilica **Ágios Nikólaos Kasnítsi** are the best-preserved in Kastoriá; female saints predominate in the narthex, which long served as the women's section,

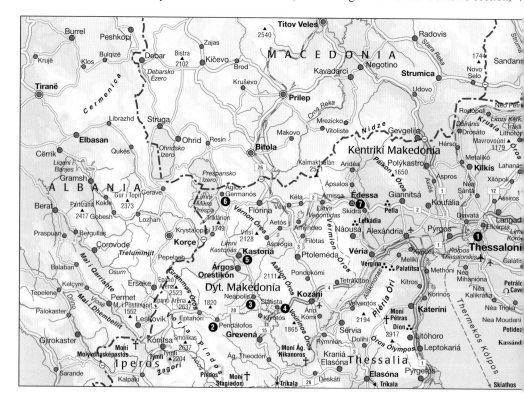

while the image of the Virgin in the Assumption on the west wall is curiously reversed right-to-left. Finally, the **Taxiárhis tis Mitropóleos** is the oldest surviving church (9th-century), with a later (14th-century) fresco of the Virgin Platýtera adored by archangels in the apse.

In the low-lying Karyádis (Dóltso) district, inland from the southern lakefront, stand the restored **Natzís** and **Immanouíl** *arhondiká*, of the same style and era as those in Siátista. Admission can be gained from the keeper of the **Folklore Museum** (open daily 10am–noon, 3–6pm; entrance fee), lodged in the Aïvazís Mansion on nearby **Kapetán Lázou**. From here, a narrow lake-shore lane heads 2.5 km (1½ miles) east to **Panagía Mavriótissa** monastery, now in ruins apart from two Siamese-twin churches – one 11th-century, the other 14th, both with fine frescoes. Peacocks strut, providing a fine view for the diners who patronise the adjacent lake-view restaurant.

Map,
pages
202–3

A gold casket found at Vergína. Its lid bears the star which was the emblem of Philip II's Macedonian dynasty.

To the Préspa Lakes and east

Some 36 km (22 miles) north of Kastoriá, following a branch of the Aliákmonas, is the side road to the Préspa Lakes basin. This atmospheric backwater where the northwestern borders of Greece meet those of FYROM and Albania was designated a Balkan Park by the governments of the three countries in 2000. There are two lakes: **Mikrá Préspa**, shallow and reedy, lying mostly in Greece, and deeper, reed-free **Megáli Préspa**, shared by Albania, FYROM and Greece. Mikrá Préspa is the nesting ground for an extraordinary bird life, notably two endangered species of pelicans and pygmy cormorants, but also for a unique trout and a hardy breed of small cattle. The society for the protection of Préspa operates two information centres, one in Ágios Germanós, the other on the shore of Megáli

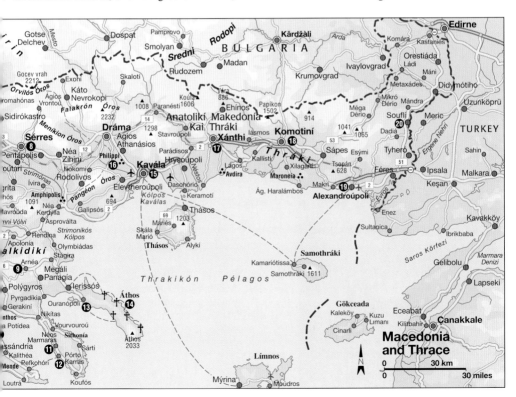

Préspa lake in Psarádes. The extraordinary bird life is most active in the spring. The surrounding hills are a haven for bears, wolves and a hardy breed of small cattle, although you will be lucky to spot them.

The best single target in the region is **Ágios Germanós** ❻, which has a visitor centre, good lodging and two frescoed Byzantine churches. **Psarádes**, the only Greek village on **Megáli Préspa**, also has an information centre and more tourist facilities and offers the opportunity to take a highly worthwhile boat excursion to the painted cave-church of **Panagía Eleoússa**. Mikrá's islet of **Ágios Ahíllios** has an evocatively ruined 10th-century basilica and is connected to the mainland by a 1-km (½-mile) long pontoon. The main road leading east passes through nondescript **Flórina**, then on towards Thessaloníki.

On the northern horizon you will notice **Mount Vóras** (Kaïmaktsalán), scene of a fierce, two-year battle during World War I between Serbs and Greeks on one side, Germans and Bulgarians on the other – neither the first nor the last campaign conducted hereabouts. Indeed, this area saw little peace during the first half of the 20th century, when the Macedonian Struggles (1903–08), the Balkan Wars (1912–13), World Wars I and II, and the civil war spelled out a narrative of strife equalled in few parts of the globe.

Macedonian sites

Traces of Alexander the Great's Macedonian Empire, which in the 4th century BC stretched as far as India, are scattered in a broad arc west to southwest of Thessaloníki, at the edges of the current flood plains of the Axiós and Aliákmonas rivers. In ancient times the Thermaïc Gulf extended much further inland, but the silt-bearing rivers have pushed the shoreline east. All of these

BELOW:
Mikrá Préspa.

MOUNT OLYMPOS

The imposing bulk of Mt Olympos (Ólympos) – Greece's highest mountain at 2,917 metres (9,568 ft) – dominates the horizon southwest of Thessaloníki. The ancient Greeks believed the mountain was the home of the gods, presided over by Zeus. Its summit defied climbers for years, not least because of the numerous bandits who lurked in the surrounding region. Sultan Mehmet IV is supposed to have attempted the mountain in 1669, but it was not until 1913 that two Swiss mountaineers with their Greek guide managed to scale the highest peak, Mýtikas ("the needle").

The climb is usually tackled from the village of Litóhoro, south of Kateríni, with an overnight stay in either the Giósos Apostolídis or Spílios Agápitos mountain refuge (book in advance during the summer through the SEO or EOS mountaineering clubs respectively, both of which have an office in Litóhoro). The climb itself is not technically difficult: the initial part is just a walk in, but the last section is steep and very exposed. You will need a good sense of balance and a head for heights, particularly when taking what is known as the Kakí Skála ("evil stairway") for the final few hundred metres. This overlooks the Kazánia chasm, a sheer drop of 500 metres (1,650 ft).

sites can be toured with your own transport in a full day out of Thessaloníki.

Dion, just northeast of Mount Olympus (Ólympos), was founded by Macedonian kings both as a military mobilisation ground and a precinct holy to the Olympian gods just overhead; its ruins, which date largely from the Roman and Byzantine eras, were buried by an earthquake-triggered mudslide in the 5th century AD (site open Mon–Sun 8am–7pm, museum open Mon 12.30–7pm, Tue–Sun 8am–7pm; entrance fee). Since 1990, well-preserved mosaics have been found here, the best – of Medusa – transferred to safe-keeping in the village museum (same hours).

Modern **Vergína**, on the south bank of the Aliákmonas, was formerly **Aigai**, the first Macedonian capital, and remained the royal necropolis. The subterranean chamber tombs of Philip of Macedonia and three others, discovered in late 1977 with their treasures intact, are impressively displayed as they were found (open Mon noon–7pm, Tue–Sun 8am–7pm; entrance fee). More modest tombs and a summer palace, the **Palatítsa**, just up the hill (the Vergína sites are open daily 8am–7pm; entrance fee). Some 18 km (11 miles) northwest on the far side of the river, **Véria** sits at one end of an escarpment running north to Édessa. Extensive Ottoman neighbourhoods of vernacular houses have been preserved in Véria, and much fine work has been done in recent years to open more than 35 Byzantine churches to the public. Begin at the Véria Byzantine Museum (open Tue-Sun 8.30am–3pm; entrance fee), wonderfully housed in a restored 19th-century flour mill at Thomedoú 1, but don't miss the 14th-century wall paintings in the Hristós Monastery (open Tue–Sun 8.30am–2pm; entrance free). North of Véria, Aristotle's School can be seen in the Mieza section of **Náousa**, and imposing Macedonian tombs can be visited at **Lefkádia** (open Tue–Sun 8:30am-3pm; entrance fee).

Some 43 km (27 miles) from Véria, **Édessa** ❼ is unlike any other Greek town, thanks to the numerous rivulets that wind through it and then over its famous waterfall. A path leads down the ravine, through cascade mist, past a cave in the cliffside; upstream, on top of the bluff, is a Roman or Byzantine bridge serving the Via Egnatia. Édessa's architecture is nothing special, but its streamside parks and wide pavements are good for strolling.

Pella, about a third of the way along the road back to Thessaloníki, was the Macedonian capital after the mid-4th century BC. From here, Philip II ruled a united Greece after 338 BC, and here also his son Alexander studied under Aristotle – and trained for his fabled campaigns in the Orient. Most of the imperial capital is yet to be unearthed, but the superb mosaics of a lion hunt, Dionysos riding a panther, and other mythological scenes, more than justify a visit to both the site and the museum (both open Tue–Sun 8am–7pm, Mon noon–7pm; entrance fee).

East to Halkidikí

Many roads lead east out of Thessaloníki. One leads initially north to the town of **Kilkís** and the Greek shore of **Lake Doïránis**, then into the Strimónas river valley towards the only paved road crossing into Bulgaria at **Promahónas**. This route is also followed by

Édessa's waterfall, plunging over a spectacular escarpment.

BELOW:
Mount Olympos.

the railway, which in this part of Macedonia traces incredible inland loops connecting relatively contiguous coastal points. Cynics assert that European contractors who built the railways for the Ottomans during the late 19th century were paid by the kilometre; in truth the sultan, having been at the wrong end of some Russian gunboat diplomacy in Constantinople, stipulated that the track was to be invulnerable to bombardment from the sea.

A more direct, northeasterly road leads to **Sérres** ❽, important since Byzantine times and still a prosperous town. It was burned down by the retreating Bulgarians in 1913 and has been largely rebuilt, but two Byzantine churches remain, much altered by war and restoration: 11th-century **Ágii Theodóri** and 14th-century **Ágios Nikólaos**. A domed Ottoman building in the central square serves as a museum.

Some 19 km (12 miles) north, in a wooded mountain valley, is another, more venerable foundation: the monastery of **Tímiou Prodrómou**, where Gennadius Scholarios, first patriarch of Constantinople after the city was captured by the Ottomans in 1453, elected to retire and is entombed.

The busiest road east of Thessaloníki skirts the lakes of **Korónia** and **Vólvi** en route to Thrace, but a slightly less travelled one veers southeast towards **Halkidikí**, a hand-like peninsula dangling three fingers out into the Aegean. Long a favoured weekend playground of Thessalonians, since the 1980s it has also seen ever-increasing foreign patronage, especially Hungarians and Czechs in search of sun, sand and sea on a cheap package or a few tanks of fuel.

Little is left to suggest the area's important role in classical times, when local colonies of various southern Greek cities served as battlefields during the first decade of the Peloponnesian War between Athens and Sparta. However, fossils and a half-million-year-old skull have been discovered in the **Petrálona Cave**, 50 km (31 miles) southeast of Thessaloníki, revealing the existence of prehistoric settlement (open daily 9am–7pm in summer; closes 5pm in winter; entrance fee).

BELOW: Pella's Lion Hunt mosaic.

The fingers of Halkidikí

At **Stágira** on the way to Áthos, a modern statue of Aristotle overlooks the Ierissós Gulf and the philosopher's birthplace, ancient Stageira. **Xerxes's Canal**, now silted up, was built around 482 BC across the neck of Áthos peninsula to help the Persians avoid the fate suffered in their previous campaign, when their fleet was wrecked sailing round Áthos cape. This and Xerxes's floating bridge over the Hellespont were considered by the Greeks to be products of Persian megalomania – "marching over the sea and sailing ships through the land." The medieval **Potídea Canal** still separates the **Kassándra** peninsula from the rest of the mainland and serves as a mooring ground for fishing boats.

The beautifully forested slopes of Mount Holomóndas cover the palm's rollingly hilly centre; **Polýgyros**, with a dull Archeological Museum, is the provincial capital, but **Arnéa** ❾ sees more tourists for the sake of its woven goods and well-preserved old houses. Kassándra, the westernmost "finger", had little life before tourism – most inhabitants were slaughtered in

1821 for participating in the independence rebellion, and the land lay deserted until resettlement by post-1923 refugees from the Sea of Marmara. **Néa Potídea** ⓾ by the canal and **Haniótis** near the tip are probably your best bets for human-scale development on a generally oversubscribed bit of real estate.

Sithonía, the middle finger, is greener, less flat and less developed; the **Mount Áthos** monasteries owned much of it before 1923, so again there are few old villages, apart from rustic **Parthenónas**, just under Mount Ítamos. The adjacent clutter of **Néos Marmarás** ⓫ and the mega-resort of **Pórto Karrás** ⓬ are exceptions to the rule of ex-fishing villages converted slowly for tourism, with ample campsites and low-rise accommodation. **Toróni** and **Aretés** on the west coast are still relatively unspoiled, while nearby **Pórto Koufós**, landlocked inside bare promontories, is a yachter's haven. **Kalamítsi beach** on the east coast has an idyllic double bay, although **Sárti** further north is the main package venue.

Following the coast north past **Pyrgadíkia** fishing hamlet brings you to the base of Áthos, the easterly finger, whose pyramidal summit rises in solitary magnificence across the gulf to the east. Several resorts, including the beach-fringed islet of **Ammoulianí** and cosmopolitan **Ouranoúpoli** ⓭, grace Áthos, but most people come here for the Holy Mountain because Ouranópoli is the entrance to Mount Áthos. For people not entering Mount Áthos, tour boats from Ouranópoli go around the peninsula, making it possible for these impressive monasteries to be seen from a respectful distance.

Pride of place in the archeological museum at Dion goes to a 1st-century BC pipe organ, unearthed at the ruins in 1992.

Mount Áthos

The fame of **Áthos** ⓮ derives from its large monastic community, today nearly 2,000 strong. In past ages these monks earned it the epithet "holy", now an intrinsic part of the Greek name: **Ágion Óros**, the Holy Mountain. Its Christian history begins with the arrival of hermits in the mid-9th century, roughly 100 years before the foundation of the first monastery. Peter the Athonite, the most famous of the early saints, is said to have lived in a cave here for 50 years.

BELOW: Ouranoúpoli on Halkidikí.

The first monastery, **Megístis Lávras**, was founded in AD 963 by St Athanasios, a friend of the Byzantine emperor, Nikiforos Fokas. Thereafter, foundations multiplied under the patronage of Byzantine emperors who supported them with money, land and treasures; in return these donors are still prayed for, and imperial charters zealously guarded in the monastery libraries.

The 20 surviving monasteries are all coenobitic, a rule in which monks keep to strict regulations under the direction of an abbot, or *igoúmenos*. Property is communal; meals are eaten together in the *trapezaría* or refectory. All monasteries observe a Greek liturgy except for the Russian **Pandelímonos**, the Serbian **Hilandaríou** and the Bulgarian **Zográfou**; all adhere to the Julian calendar, 13 days behind the Gregorian, and all (except for **Vatopedíou**) keep Byzantine time, reckoned from the hour of sunrise or sunset. Many monks prefer to live in smaller, less regimented monastic communities, the *skítes* and *kelliá* which are dotted around the peninsula but still dependent on the main monasteries. A few choose to live like hermits in an *isyhastírion*, a rough, unadorned hut or a cave, perched precipitously on a cliff edge.

In the 1970s, Áthos was perhaps at its nadir, with barely a thousand monks – many of limited educational and moral attainment – dwelling in dilapidated monasteries. Since then, a renaissance has been effected. The Holy Mountain's claims to be a commonwealth pursuing the highest form of spiritual life known in the Orthodox Christian tradition appear to have struck a chord, and the quality and quantity of novices from every corner of the globe (especially Russia, following the collapse of communism) is on the rise.

The number of pilgrims to Áthos has grown, too, even though the appropriately Byzantine process of obtaining an entry permit is expressly designed to discourage the frivolous and the gawkers. Only genuine religious pilgrims need apply; or at least that is the ideal. For – as always – political if not doctrinal strife is never far from the Holy Mountain. Most of the monks are born Greek, and prefer Greek predominance. Slavic novices and pilgrims have complained, since 1990, that they are discriminated against vis-à-vis Greeks. But divisions among Greek monks are well known, involving entire bodies of monks moving from one monastery to another in stormy disputes with abbots or civil authorities. Traditionalists decry, as elsewhere in Greece, the bulldozing of paths and the selling of timber to finance renovations – much of it in highly brutalist style.

You must phone or fax most monasteries to reserve space in guest quarters often bursting with as many as 100 visitors a night in full season and, once there, put up with the squealing of other guests' mobile phones. Accommodation and

BELOW: Dionysíou monastery, built on a rock high above the sea.

FORBIDDEN FRUITS

Áthos is probably most famous for the *ávaton* edict, promulgated in 1060 by Emperor Constantine Monomahos, which forbids access to the Holy Mountain to all females more evolved than a chicken (although an exception seems to have been made for female cats, which are kept to control the rodent population).

How did this come about? Revisionists point to prior chronic hanky-panky between monks and shepherdesses, while the religious claim that the Virgin, in numerous visions, has consecrated lush Áthos as Her private garden – and women would simply be an unnecessary temptation. Over the years, many women have tried to gatecrash in disguise, only to be ignominiously ejected; a variety of women's groups in Greece and abroad have now taken up the issue.

A more serious challenge was posed in 1998 when the (female) foreign ministers of Sweden and Finland threatened to refuse to sign a decree upholding the Mount's "special status", since it contravenes one of the European Union's most cherished laws: freedom of movement (Greece is one of 11 EU states that signed the Schengen Accord abolishing border controls among member states in 2000). The Athonite authorities have, nonetheless, vowed to resist all attempts to change the Holy Mountain's single-gender character.

food are free, but taxi rides from one monastery to another can be costly. Walking is the best way to visit the monasteries but the distances can be large and you will only get to visit a handful of monasteries anyway in your limited allotted time. Only time will tell if the Mountain can defend itself against the world.

Eastern Macedonia

North of Áthos, the coast road threads through several resorts on the Strymonic Gulf, popular with Thessalonians and Serrans, before crossing the Strimónas itself at ancient **Amphipolis**. Scant ruins remain of this city, a Thracian settlement colonised by Athens in 438 BC, top a bluff protected on three sides by the river. Most passers-by content themselves with a glimpse from the river bridge of the **Lion of Amphipolis**, a colossal statue reassembled from fragments from the 4th and 3rd century BC. On the east bank, the road forks: a faster but less scenic coast highway, or the inland road along the base of Mount Pangéo via **Elevtheroúpoli**, threading through picturesque, slate-roofed villages.

Both routes converge on **Kavála** , Macedonia's second city; as Neapolis, it was an important stop on the Via Egnatia, and a port for ancient Philippi. Well into the 1920s Kavála was a major tobacco-curing and export centre, though today the harbour sees more passenger ferries en route to Thásos and the north Aegean than it does commercial traffic. A mansion from the tobacco boom days houses the **Folk and Modern Art Museum**, featuring the Thásos-born sculptor, Polygnotos Vagis (open Mon–Fri 8am–2pm, Sat 9am–1pm; entrance fee). The treasures in the modern Archeological Museum include tomb finds from both Avdira and Amphipolis.

Overnighting is not a priority in most people's minds – hotels tend to be noisy and overpriced – but the medieval walled **Panagía** quarter, southeast of the harbour, merits a leisurely stroll up to the hilltop citadel, tethered to the modern town by a 16th-century aqueduct. Start along **Poulídou**, passing a clutch of restaurants favoured by locals, arriving soon at the gate of the **Imaret** – a sprawling domed compound, allegedly the largest Islamic public building in the Balkans. Originally an almshouse and hostel, it was radically renovated in 2003 and has since re-opened as an uncontestably atmospheric restaurant-bar.

Philippi

Some 14 km (8½ miles) northwest, ancient **Philippi** – although named after Philip II – contains little that is Macedonian. From the acropolis, where three medieval towers rise on the ruins of Macedonian walls, you have extensive views of the battlefield which made Philippi famous. Here in 42 BC, the fate of the Romans hung in the balance as the republican forces of Brutus and Cassius, participants in the assassination of Julius Caesar in 44 BC, confronted the armies of Caesar's avengers, Antony and Octavius. Upon their defeat, both Cassius and Brutus committed suicide; the Battle of Actium in 32 BC ended the struggle between the two victors.

The **Roman ruins**, mainly to the south of the highway, include foundations of both the forum and

Map, pages 202–3

TIP

The northeast has hotter summers and cooler winters than the rest of Greece. The best time to visit Halkidikí is in June or early July, when the land is still green and the hills still covered in flowers.

BELOW: the Lion of Amphipolis.

palaestra, plus a well-preserved public latrine in the southwest corner of the grounds. Philippi is reputedly the first place in Europe where St Paul preached the gospel. He arrived in AD 49, but offended the local pagans and was thrown into prison (a frescoed Roman crypt now marks the site). In AD 55, however, he got a better reception from the congregation later addressed in his *Epistle to the Philippians*. By the 6th century, Christianity was thriving here, as the remains of several early basilica-churches testify (open Tue–Sun 8am–7pm; entrance fee).

Driving east from Kavála, you soon cross the Néstos River, the boundary between Macedonia and Thrace, at the apex of its alluvial plain, a vast expanse of corn and tobacco fields. Some beautiful scenery along the Néstos Gorge can best be seen by train, or the old highway, between Dráma and Xánthi.

Thrace and its Muslims

Ancient Thrace covered much of present-day Bulgaria and European Turkey, as well as the Greek coastal strip between the Néstos and Évros rivers. Greek colonisation of the coast from 800 BC onwards often led to conflict with the native Thracian tribes. The Via Egnatia spanned the area, leaving scattered Roman and, later, Byzantine fortifications. Later, Thrace was overrun and settled by both Slavs and Ottomans. It was eventually and messily divided between Bulgaria, Turkey and Greece, between 1913 and 1923, following various wars. Although a traumatic population exchange between Turkey and Greece occurred in 1923, the Muslim inhabitants of the Greek part of Thrace were allowed to remain in return for protection granted to 125,000 Greek Orthodox living in Istanbul. (Today the Greeks in Istanbul have been reduced to a few thousand, whereas the population of Muslims of Thrace has increased slightly to about 130,000.)

An ethnic Turkish minority dwells principally in Xánthi, Komotiní and the plains southeast of the two cities; gypsies who adopted Islam and the Turkish language are also settled here. Another Muslim minority, the Pomaks, live in the Rodópi range above Xánthi and Komotiní; descended from medieval Bogomil heretics, they speak a Slavic language and traditionally cultivate tobacco on mountain terraces.

Xánthi

The open-air Saturday market at **Xánthi** , just 53 km (33 miles) from Kavála, makes a good introduction to the region's Muslim demographics. Turkish and Pomak women favour long, dull overcoats and plain-coloured yashmaks (head-scarves), now gradually being replaced by more stylish grey or brown coats and printed scarves. The gypsy women stand out in their colourful *shalvar* bloomers, their scarves tied behind the ears. Many men still wear burgundy-coloured velvet or felt fezzes, or white skullcaps. By night, the numerous, modern bars and cafés along nearby **Vasilisís Sofías** do a roaring trade, thanks to students from the University of Thrace.

Xánthi became a prosperous commercial and administrative centre in the 19th century, thanks to tobacco. Renowned masons were brought from Epirus to build merchants' mansions, tobacco warehouses and *hans* (inns). The *hans*, large square buildings around a

BELOW:
Xánthi old town.

Map, pages 202–3

central courtyard, were resting spots and trade centres near the marketplace. One old mansion at the base of the old town has become a **Folk Museum** (closed for repairs). Further uphill lie the minarets and houses of the Turkish quarter, complete with numerous satellite dishes for tuning into Turkish-language TV.

Komotini

At **Komotiní** ⓲, 56 km (35 miles) east of Xánthi via the bird-stalked lagoon of **Vistonída** and the water-girt monastery of **Ágios Nikólaos**, Muslims constitute nearly half the population. It's less immediately attractive than Xánthi, but here too is an old bazaar of cobbled lanes (Tuesday is the busiest day), complete with tiny shops, 14 functioning mosques and many old-fashioned coffee houses. A **Folk Museum** just off the central park displays local embroidery, costumes and metalwork (open Mon–Fri 10.30am–1pm; entrance fee); the **Archeological Museum** keeps finds from such Thracian sites as **Avdira**, south of Xánthi, and **Maroneia**, south of Komotiní (open daily 8.30am–6pm; free).

   Avdira itself does not repay a visit in its bedraggled state, although it nurtured two major philosophers: Democritus, who first expounded atomic theory, and the sophist Protagoras to whom is attributed the maxim "Man is the measure of all things." Odysseus legendarily called at Maroneia after leaving Troy on his return to Ithaca, procuring a sweet red wine which later saved him and his companions from the cyclops Polyphemus. Trapped in his cave, they plied Polyphemus with the wine, and then as he slept poked his single eye out with a red-hot brand and escaped by hiding under his sheep's bellies. A cave north of the sparse cliff-top site retains the name of **Polyphemus's Cave**; more rewarding, perhaps, is the medieval village of **Marónia**, preserving a few wooden mansions, and tiny Platanítis beach, with a good fish taverna.

Alexandroúpoli

The old road from Komotiní zigzags 65 km (40 miles) through barren hills before coming down to the rather drab port of **Alexandroúpoli** ⓳, gateway to Samothráki island. It's wisest to press on into the valley of the Évros River, especially if you're a birdwatcher. The delta, situated east of the Roman spa of Traianopolis, is excellent for waterfowl, while the **Dadiá Forest Reserve**, a successful venture of the WorldWild Fund for Nature (WWF), shelters black and griffin vultures. In between you can pause at **Féres** for the sake of its 12th-century church, **Panagía Kosmosótira**, whose lofty, five-domed interior is generally open to visitors.

   North of the turning for Dadiá, the first town of any size is **Souflí** ⓴, once famous for silk production. Corn fields have now replaced the mulberry trees whose leaves once nourished the silkworms, and only a small museum commemorates the vanished industry. **Didymótiho**, 30 km (18½ miles) further upstream, has a Byzantine fortress at the old town's summit, and an abandoned mosque on the square whose features speak of Seljuk (and earlier) prototypes. From here, most traffic is bound for Turkish **Edirne**, whose graceful minarets are just visible from the Greek border town of Kastaniés. ❑

BELOW: Pomak women in Xánthi market.

THE ISLANDS

Greece has more inhabited islands than any other European country – but it's anyone's guess how many there are

The poet Odysseus Elytis Once said: "Greece rests on the sea." It's an observation that few countries could claim with such authority. Some 25,000 sq. km (10,000 sq. miles) of the Aegean and Ionian seas are covered by islands. And, in characteristic Greek fashion, the exact number of them has been the topic of discussion and dispute. There may be 3,000 islands and islets, of which 167 are inhabited. Or, according to someone else's calculations, there may be only 1,000, of which fewer than 60 are populated.

The criterion that defines a populated place is open to interpretation. Does a tiny outcrop, bare save for one goatherd and six goats, constitute an inhabited island? Can an island that is totally deserted except for annual pilgrimages to a small chapel at its summit claim to be inhabited?

The arithmetic matters far more to foreigners than to the Greeks, who are interested in sea and sky, in food and festivals, rather than in facts and figures. What is indisputable, however, is the sheer variety of landscape and experience to be found lurking behind the familiar images.

This is what we attempt to show in this section – islands with an ancient past and a modern outlook, the complex choice and the pure, simple pleasures. In order to accommodate everything that is encompassed in the phrase "a Greek island", we have devoted space to tiny islands such as Kímolos and Lipsí, as well as the well-known giants like Crete and Rhodes and the holiday favourites such as Mýkonos and Corfu. We do not ignore the familiar, popular islands, of course, but we explore them to seek out the true heart of the place behind the tourist clichés.

The best way to enjoy the islands is to arrive with a certain attitude of mind. By all means, begin by uncritically enjoying the cluster of blisteringly white buildings against a shimmering sea, donkeys with a backdrop of olive groves, and so on – the vista, indeed, seared into the senses by holiday brochures. But, when the novelty wears off, or perhaps earlier, examine each island as if it were an onion and start stripping off the skins. How to strip the onion is a large part of what this book is about.

So welcome aboard the ferry and prepare for a cruise round Europe's most fascinating and welcoming islands – however many of them there might be. ❏

PRECEDING PAGES: the harbour at Sitía on Crete.
LEFT: the seafront at Mýkonos Town.

ISLANDS OF THE SARONIC GULF

Map, page 218

Salamína, Aegina, Póros, Ýdra and Spétses are all within easy reach of the mainland and popular with Greek day-trippers. But they are distinctive, rich in history and remarkably attractive

Athens and the islands of the Saronic Gulf are often lumped together in guidebooks. There is sense in this since many Athenians frequent these islands at weekends, while during the summer the islands become veritable extensions of the more fashionable Athenian neighbourhoods. Yet this view of the Argo-Saronic islands doesn't take into account their separate identities. They are islands, not suburbs. Each has its own character and deserves more of a potential visitor's attention.

Salamína (Salamis)

Salamína is best known for an ancient naval battle (480 BC) in which outnumbered Athenian ships routed the enormous Persian fleet – the ships being the "wooden walls" that the Delphic oracle had predicted would save Athens. Pride of the island is the 17th-century **Faneroméni Monastery** on the Voudóro peninsula, just 6 km (4 miles) from the capital, **Salamína Town ❶**.

The island is decidedly not posh but it is relatively undeveloped and can be reached so quickly, just a few minutes' ride across from Pérama to the port town of **Paloúkia ❷**. Most of the inhabitants live in Salamína (also called **Kouloúri**), which has an archeological and a folk museum. Cyclists may find Salamína an ideal escape from the urban jungle of Athens and Piraeus, as the island's back roads are uncrowded and untaxing on the stamina. The pleasant village of **Eándio** on the west coast has a good hotel.

Aegina (Égina)

Aegina is close enough to be within easy reach from the mainland and far enough to retain its island identity. About an hour and a half by ferry from Piraeus – or half an hour by Flying Dolphin hydrofoil – it has had little trouble attracting visitors. The island remains more popular with Athenians seeking a retreat from the city than with foreign tourists or Greeks from elsewhere. The main produce is pistachio nuts, sold all along the harbour street.

Shaped on the map like an upside-down triangle, the island's southern point is marked by the magnificent cone of **Mount Óros**, the highest peak in the Argo-Saronic islands, visible on a clear day from Athens's Acropolis. The island's centre and eastern side is mountainous; a gently sloping fertile plain runs down to the western corner where **Aegina Town ❸** overlays in part the ancient capital of the island.

The town has several 19th-century mansions constructed when the first Greek president, Ioannis

LEFT: Ýdra harbour and old town.
BELOW: bright colours on Aegina.

Aphaia.

Kapodistrias (1776–1831), lived and worked here. The **Archeological Museum** in the centre of the town displays a number of interesting artefacts from the island's history (open Tue–Sun 8.30am–3pm; entrance fee). The modern harbour, crowded with yachts and caïques, is next to the ancient harbour, now the shallow town beach north of the main quay, towards the ancient site of **Kolóna**.

Kolóna, meaning "column", is named after the one conspicuously standing column of the **Temple of Apollo**. The temple (Doric, six columns by 12, built in 520–500 BC) was superseded by a late Roman fortress, fragments of which survive on the seaward side. Although from the sea the position of the temple looks unimpressive, the view from the hill is very pleasant. There is a small museum on the site, and the reconstructed mosaic floor of an ancient synagogue (open daily 8.30am–3pm; single entrance fee for both site and museum).

The island's most famous ancient site is the **Temple of Aphaia** ❹, in the northeast, above the often packed summer resort town of **Agía Marína**. The temple stands at the top of a hill in a pine grove commanding a splendid view of the Aegean. Built in 490 BC in the years after the victory at Salamis, it has been called "the most perfectly developed of the late Archaic temples in European Hellas". It is the only surviving Greek temple with a second row of small superimposed columns in the interior of the sanctuary, it is also quite beautiful, one of the most impressive ancient temples you will see (open daily 8am–7pm; entrance fee).

On the way to the temple you will pass by the modern **Monastery of Ágios Nektários**, the most recent Orthodox saint, canonised in 1961. Across the ravine from the monastery is the ghostly site known as **Paleohóra** ("old town"), built in the 9th century as protection against piracy. Abandoned in 1826 after Greek

BELOW:
the 5th-century temple of Aphaia on Aegina.

independence, most of the 38 churches left standing are in utter disrepair, but you can still see the remains of several frescoes.

The west coast of the island is quite gentle, with a good sandy beach at **Marathóna**, but better reasons to head out here are to enjoy a meal in one of the many fish tavernas along the harbour at **Pérdika** ❺, or to go by hired boat to swim at the beautiful beach on the tiny uninhabited island of **Moní**.

Angístri

Angístri is the small island facing Aegina Town. The larger boats stop at **Skála**, while the smaller ones stop at the more attractive **Mýlos**. The island is not much developed but there are several hotels. The most attractive beach is near the salt lake on the southwestern coast by the small islet of **Doroúsa**.

Póros

The island of Póros is separated from the Peloponnese by a small passage of water – the word *póros* in Greek means "passage" or "ford". As your boat turns into the ford from the northern entrance, the channel opens ahead and lovely **Póros Town** ❻ comes into view. Almost landlocked, it is one of the most protected anchorages in the Aegean: your first glimpse will be of white houses and bright orange rooftops, with the clock tower on top of the hill. Póros can be reached not only by ship and Flying Dolphin but also (with considerably more effort) by driving via the **Isthmus of Corinth** to **Epídavros** (Epidauros) and then down to the coast at **Dryópi** and little **Galatás** across the channel.

Although a number of hotels have been built on the island, and prominent Athenians have owned vacation houses here for decades, it has never been as

Map, page 218

In the 7th century BC, Aegina became a leading maritime power, thanks to its strategic position; its silver coins – known as "tortoises" – became common currency in most of the Dorian states.

BELOW: Aegina's waterfront.

fashionable as Ýdra or Spétses (chiefly because the beaches are fewer and not as good), but during summer it gets every bit as crowded as Aegina.

In 1846 a Greek naval station was established on the northwest side of Póros, on the peninsula just before the narrow stream separating a small section of Póros Town from the main part of the island. When the station moved to Salamína in 1878, the site was used as a school; it is now used for training naval cadets. This area contains several fine family mansions with well-tended gardens and can be a refreshing place to stroll on a hot summer afternoon.

The main sight on Póros is the **Monastery of Zoödóhos Pigí** (Virgin of the Life-Giving Spring), beautifully situated on a wooded hillside (20 minutes from town by bus). Only a few monks still live there today. Noteworthy is a wooden, gold-painted iconostasis dating from the 19th century.

In front of the monastery a road encircling the heights to the east climbs through the pine woods to the ruins of the **Sanctuary of Poseidon** in a saddle between the highest hills of the island. The temple was excavated at the beginning of the 20th century and little remains, but its setting is rewarding.

The sanctuary was the headquarters of the Kalavrian League, an association of several towns that included Athens. The Athenian orator Demosthenes, who had opposed the imposition of Macedonian rule over Athens, sought refuge in the sanctuary after an Athenian revolt following the death of Alexander the Great was quelled by Antipater, Alexander's successor in Macedonia. When Demosthenes was found, he took poison but stepped outside the sanctuary before dying so he would not defile holy ground.

Ancient **Troizen** (Damalas) is about 8 km (5 miles) from Galatás across the straits on the Peloponnese. The mythological Greek hero Theseus is supposed

BELOW: Póros Town.

to have grown up here before he went off to Athens to become king. The rock he is said to have raised to prove his strength is still here, next to the Sanctuary of the Muses. Theseus is also meant to have returned to Troizen in his old age, providing Euripides with the plot for his famous play, *Hippolytus*, about the young queen Phaedra who unjustly accused Theseus's son of having violated her. Modern drama is held in the **Devil's Gorge** just above the site. For peace, go to the **Lemonódasos**, a beautiful grove consisting of some 2,000 lemon trees, about half an hour's walk on the other side of Galatás.

Map,
page
218

Ýdra (Hydra)

The island of Ýdra – once Ydrea, "the well watered" – now appears as a long, barren rock. But the harbour and the white and grey stone buildings which make up the town are still lovely; they have drawn the artistic and the fashionable since the 1950s and many, many more ever since. It is one of the few places in the country that has reined in the uncontrolled growth of cement construction, thus keeping its beauty.

A splash of Greek colour in Ýdra.

The heart of the island is its harbour-town, also called **Ýdra** ❼. All around the picturesque bay white houses climb the slope, accented by massive grey *arhondiká* (mansions built by the shipping families who made fortunes in the 18th and 19th centuries), many of them designed by architects from Venice and Genoa. Along the quay are the colourful shops of the marketplace, with the clock tower of the 18th-century **Monastery of the Panagía** in the centre; much of the stone used to build it was taken from the ancient Sanctuary of Poseidon on the island of Póros. The harbour itself, girded by a little thread of a breakwater, forms a crescent, its two ends flanked by 19th-century cannons.

BELOW: boarding the ferry at Ýdra.

The town has many good tavernas and restaurants, as well as extremely popular bars and clubs. Yet the higher reaches and the hills beyond remain surprisingly untouched, charming and full of Greek colour. Narrow alleys and steep staircases lead from one quarter to the next. The uniformity of white walls is broken again and again by a century-old doorway, a bright blue window frame, a flight of striking scarlet steps, or a green garden fence. **Mandráki** ❽, northeast of town, has the only sand beach, but the southwest is more interesting. A wide path goes along the coast to **Kamíni** and to **Vlyhós**, with its early 19th-century arched stone bridge. There are some good tavernas in both places, and water-taxis available if you've had too much good fish and wine.

Spétses

Spétses is the southernmost of the Argo-Saronic Gulf islands. In antiquity it was known as Pityousa, "pine tree" island, and it is still by far the most wooded of the group. Tourist development here is more extensive than on Ýdra but less than on either Póros or Aegina, and in recent years responsible planning has helped keep the island's charm.

Although **Spétses Town** ❾ has its share of bars and fast-food places, the Paleó Limáni (Old Harbour) still radiates a gentle grace. The 18th-century *arhondiká* you see in this part of the town are now the property of wealthy Athenian families who return to the island every summer.

Like Ýdra, Spétses' heyday was the late 18th century, when mercantile trade made it wealthy; also like Ýdra, it became a centre of activity during the Greek War of Independence, offering its merchant fleet of over 50 ships for the Greek cause. The island is distinguished for being the first in the archipelago to revolt against Ottoman rule in 1821, and the fortified main harbour, still bristling with cannons, now forms one of the town's focal points, the **Dápia**.

Bouboulina, Greece's national heroine of the Greek War of Independence, was a Spétsiot woman who took command of her husband's ships after he was killed by pirates off the North African coast. She contributed eight of the 22 Spetsiot ships that blockaded the Turks in Návplio (Nauplion) for more than a year until the garrison surrendered in December 1822.

In the September before Návplio surrendered, an Ottoman fleet attempted to lift the blockade by threatening Spétses. The fighting was indecisive but the Ottoman fleet eventually withdrew. They were encouraged to leave by fezes being placed on the asphodel plants that grew in masses along the shore (from a distance the fezes swaying in the wind looked like men, presumably armed).

This great victory is celebrated annually, every 22 September, by a *panagíri* focused on the church of the **Panagía Ármáta** on the lighthouse headland close to the Old Harbour. A mock battle is staged, a Turkish flagship made out of cardboard is burned in the middle of the harbour and there follows a display of fireworks.

Although after the War of Independence Spétses' fleet declined with the emergence of Piraeus as the main seaport, the traditions of shipbuilding continue unabated. The small **museum** in the imposing 18th-century *arhondikó* of Hatzigianni Mexi, a major shipowner in the late 18th century, contains coins, costumes, ship models, weapons and other memorabilia from the island's past, including the bones of the famous Bouboulína. The house in which she lived is behind the Dápia (open Tue–Sun 8.30am–3pm; entrance fee).

Outside the town to the northwest is **Anargýrios and Korgialénios College**, a Greek impression of an English public school. John Fowles taught here and memorialised both the institution and the island in his 1966 novel *The Magus*. The school no longer operates, and the buildings are used only occasionally as a conference centre or for special programmes. This section of town is less posh than the Old Harbour, but has some fine small tavernas.

The town beach by the church of **Ágios Mámas** and the small beach in the Old Harbour are not as nice as the beautiful beaches of **Agía Marína**, **Ágii Anárgyri**, **Agía Paraskeví** and **Zogeriá**, going around the wooden southern coast of the island from the east to the west. In addition, there are various beaches opposite Spétses on the Peloponnesian coast, of which the most accessible is at **Kósta**. For those who enjoy water-skiing, **Pórto Héli** with its protected bay provides the perfect setting.

Spétses also has occasional hydrofoil links to Návplio, and to the southern town of Monemvasía. During the summer months when the Ancient Drama Festival is held in Epídavros, a trip to one of the performances there is a delight. Yet an evening walk in the Old Harbour or in the woods of Ligonéri, a ride in a horse-drawn carriage from the Dápia to Agía Marína, and an (expensive) trip by water-taxi for an evening meal at Ágii Anárgyri are only a few of the pleasures that Spétses itself provides. ❏

Map, page 218

Spétses has been synonymous with shipping for centuries.

BELOW: in Ýdra's Byzantine Museum.

THE CYCLADES

*From the hectic nightlife of Mýkonos and Íos to the rugged beauty
of Mílos and Sérifos, and the unspoilt seclusion of Síkinos and
Kímolos, there is something for all tastes among these islands*

Map,
pages
226–7

For many people the Cyclades *are* Greece; other island chains are mere distractions from this blue Aegean essence. They were inhabited by 6000 BC; by the third millennium a fascinating island culture flourished here, with fine arts and crafts and lively commerce – as anyone who visits the excellent Goulandris Museum of Cycladic Art in Athens will appreciate (*see page 137*).

Of the 56 islands, 24 are inhabited. There are two basic ferry routes: the first, eastern and central, takes in bucolic Ándros and religious Tínos, includes Mýkonos, Páros and Náxos – the backpackers' (and everyone else's) beat – calls briefly at undeveloped islets like Donoússa and Iráklia, and concludes in spectacular Santoríni. The second, western, arches by Kýthnos, Sérifos, Sífnos and Mílos; these are somewhat less popular, with different cultural attributes. Off both ferry routes, Kéa attracts Athenian weekenders.

Ándros

Ándros was settled centuries ago by Orthodox Albanians (a few still speak Albanian); their stone dwellings of the north contrast with the whitewash and red tile of the other villages. The port town, **Gávrio**, is only that. **Batsí ❶**, 6 km (4 miles) south, is a pleasant Cycladic "fishing" town: whitewash, cafés, beaches, packaged tours, and development at the outskirts. On the east coast, **Ándros Town (Hóra) ❷** remains remarkably unspoiled. This is because so many rich Athenians have weekend houses here (less than three boat hours from Athens) that tourism has not been assiduously pursued. The prize exhibit in the **Archeological Museum** (open Tue–Sun 8.30am–3pm; entrance fee), indeed in all Greece, is the famous Hermes of Ándros, a 2nd-century copy of Praxiteles' statue. South of the Paleópolis/Hóra road is the most spectacular of Ándros's 13 Byzantine monasteries, **Panahrándou ❸**; 1, 000 years old, it still retains ties with Constantinople (Istanbul).

Ándros has many beaches – the easiest to get to are **Nimbório** just south of the port, the string of lovely strands between Gávrio and Batsí, and **Gialiá** (near Steniés, north of Ándros Town) – plus a number of beautiful and remote coves such as **Ágios Péllos**.

Kéa

Kéa-bound boats leave from the mainland port of Lávrio, some 50 km (30 miles) from Athens, and land at **Korissía**, locally called **Livádi**. The main town, **Ioulís (Hóra) ❹**, rides a rounded ridge overlooking the island's northern reach, a site chosen for its inaccessibility from foreign marauders. The famous **Lion of Kéa**, a smiling, maneless beast almost 6 metres (20 ft) long, is a 15-minute walk northeast of Hóra. Carved from grey granite; it is probably early Archaic.

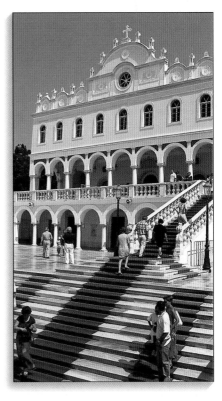

LEFT: classic architecture on Íos.
BELOW: Church of Panagía Evangelístria, Tínos.

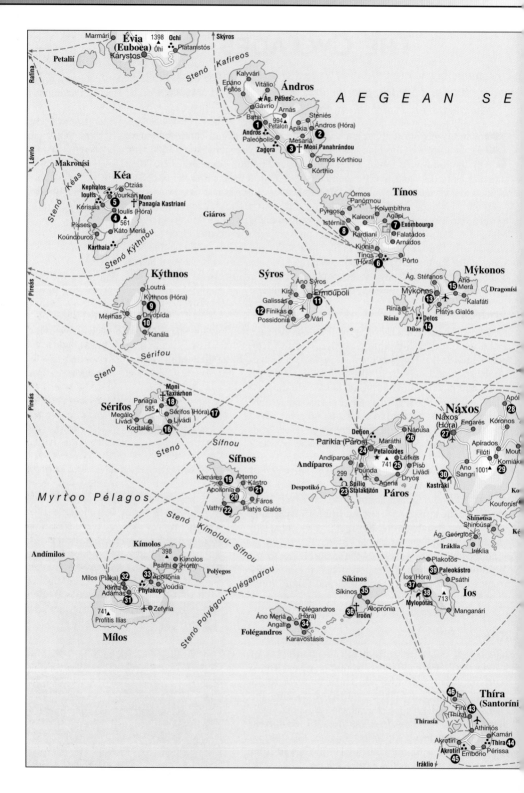

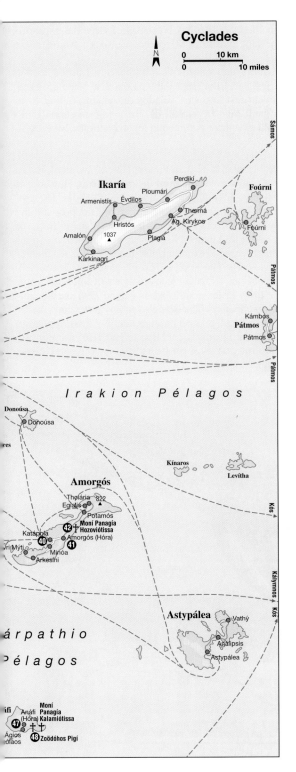

Cyclades

0   10 km
0   10 miles

Sámos

Ikaría

Perdikí

Foúrni

Ploumári

Armenístis   Évdilos

Thermá

Ag. Kírykos

Hristós

Foúrni

Amalón   1037 ▲

Plagiá

Pátmos

Karkinagrí

Kámbos

Pátmos

Pátmos

I r a k i o n   P é l a g o s

Donoúsa

Donoúsa

res

Kínaros

Levítha

Kós

Amorgós

Tholária   822 ▲

Egiáli

Potamós

Moní Panagía
Hozoviótissa

Katápola

Amorgós (Hóra)

rí Mýti

Mínoa

Arkesíni

Kálymnos   Kós

Astypálea

Vathý

á r p a t h i o

Análipsis

Astypálea

é l a g o s

ífi

Moní
Anáfi   Panagía
(Hóra)   Kalamiótissa

Ágios
ófaos   Zoödóhos Pigí

In the 19th century there were a million oak trees on well-watered Kéa, and many still provide shade. Olive trees, however, are absent; since ancient times, the island has been noted for its almonds. The jagged west coast has many sandy spits, several impossible to reach. **Písses** and **Koúndouros** are just two of the resorts that have sprung up to accommodate the Athenian escapees. Close to Korissía is **Vourkári ❺**, with **Agía Iríni** church, a Minoan excavation, and an ancient road.

Tínos

Tínos receives many thousands of tourists – but they are mostly Greeks here for the church, the **Panagía Evangelístria** (Our Lady Annunciate). In 1823, the nun Pelagía dreamt of an icon; it was duly unearthed and the church was built to house it. The icon's healing powers have made **Tínos Town (Hóra) ❻** the Lourdes of Greece. Women fall to their knees upon arrival, and crawl painfully to the church. Healing miracles often occur.

For a reminder of the Ottoman conquest, visit the peak of **Exómbourgo ❼**, 643 metres (2,110 ft), with its ruined fortress (Tínos was the last island to fall to the Turks, in 1723). A bus ride to Exómbourgo and beyond will also reveal some weird, mushroom-shaped, wind-sculpted rocks, especially above Vólax village.

Kolybíthra in the north is Tínos's best beach. **Ágios Sóstis**, near Pórto on the south coast, is also a decent stretch of beach. Of the monasteries to see, the abandoned **Katapolianí**, near **Istérnia ❽**, is exceptional. Isterníon Bay is a fabulous hike from Istérnia. **Kardianí**, the village southeast of Istérnia, is Tínos's most spectacularly set – though arcaded **Arnádos** gives it competition.

Kýthnos

After iron-mining operations ceased, Kýthnos lost its prime source of income. Foreign tourism has not supplemented it, but Athenian tourism has helped. **Mérihas** on the west coast has the biggest choice of accommodation. In summer, a "taxi-boat" runs from Mérihas to **Episkopí**, **Apókrisi** and **Kolóna** beaches. **Kýthnos Town**

Freshly-caught octopus is served in most of the Cycladic islands.

BELOW:
Ermoúpoli on Sýros.

(Hóra) **9**, 6 km (4 miles) northeast of Mérihas, is exquisite. Its streets are spanned by wood-beamed arches joining two sides of one house. Rock pavements are decorated with fish, stylised ships and flowers.

Elderly residents and visitors frequent the thermal baths at **Loutrá**, on the northeast coast 5 km (3 miles) east from Hóra. Above Loutrá, at Maroúla, excavations have revealed the earliest known Cyclades settlement, dating from before 4500 BC. A stream bed splits **Dryopída** **10** (the medieval capital) into two; the chambered Katafíki cave here is linked in legend with the Nereids.

Sýros

Sýros remains the Cyclades' capital, but when Piraeus (Pireás) overtook it as a trade centre in the late 1800s, it was cut off from the mainstream. However, it retains excellent inter-island ferry links and useful, if low-key, facilities. The capital, **Ermoúpoli** **11**, has been recently spruced up, especially the port and the government buildings. The area called **ta Vapória** ("the ships"), uphill from the shopping streets, is where you'll find many 19th-century neoclassical mansions (a few doubling as cheap hotels), especially around the marble-paved, plane-tree-shaded main square, Platía Miaoúlis. The Apollon Theatre, next to the Town Hall, was modelled on La Scala in Milan. Its recent renovation is still a point of pride.

Fínikas **12**, a beachside town in the southwest, is named after the Phoenicians, probably Sýros's first inhabitants. The island's south is softer and greener than the thinly populated north and has good beaches, namely **Possidonía** and **Vári** as well as Fínikas. Up the west coast, **Galissás** and **Kíni** are popular resorts. During the Colonels' rule, political prisoners were interned on **Giáros**, the empty island to the north.

Mýkonos

Mýkonos has made itself glamourous. Otherwise unprosperous, it has turned its rocky, treeless ruggedness into a tourist-pleasing package that works – incidentally making it more expensive than most other Greek islands. Summer draws thousands of tourists to **Mýkonos Town** 13 to sample the celebrated bars, gay scene, restaurants serving Lobster Thermidor, and the clothes and jewellery shops. Despite the glitz, the town is the prettiest and most solicitously preserved in the Cyclades, with its wooden balconies loaded with flowers, red-domed chapels and billows of whitewash. The odd-shaped **Paraportianí** (Our Lady of the Postern Gate) is probably Greece's most photographed church.

Little Venice, a row of buildings hanging over the sea at the north, is the least frenetic part of town. The **Folklore Museum** (open Mon–Sat 4–8pm, Sun 5.30–8pm; free) and the **Archeological Museum** (open Tue–Sun 8.30am–2.30pm; entrance fee), at different ends of Mýkonos's quay, are full of interesting objects. Caïques also depart from here for **Delos** 14, the sacred island that is the centre of the Cyclades (in myth Mýkonos was Delian Apollo's grandson – *see also page 241*). Or one can strike inland to **Áno Merá** 15 7 km (4 miles) east, the only real village, and visit the red-domed Tourlianí monastery, which houses some fine 16th-century icons and embroideries.

Mýkonos is famous, indeed notorious, for its all-night bars and all-day beaches. For bars, you must enquire – the scene changes all the time. For beaches, **Paradise** is half straight nude, **Super Paradise** half gay nude, and both are beautiful; **Kalafáti**, reached via Áno Merá, is quiet; **Platýs Gialós** and **Psárrou** popular with families. And the reservoir lake in the island's centre attracts thousands of migrating birds.

Pétros the pelican, mascot of Mýkonos Town.

BELOW: Little Venice on Mýkonos.

The Cycladic Bronze Age

Bronze Age Cycladic peoples left behind beautiful artefacts that provide evidence of an organised and flourishing culture, most famously in their stylised marble sculptures, all of which have been found in tombs. The settlements and cemeteries excavated on a number of islands are generally considered to be the first complex, organised, settled communities in Europe.

The Early Cycladic Bronze Age began about 3200 BC and is thought to have lasted until around 2000 BC. The later Bronze Age is divided by scholars into Middle and Late Cycladic. These latter periods increasingly display the influence of the Minoan culture of Crete, and show a move towards urban settlement. In general, the term Cycladic Culture refers to the Early Cycladic, and it is during this period that the individuality of the culture of the Cycladic islands is most evident.

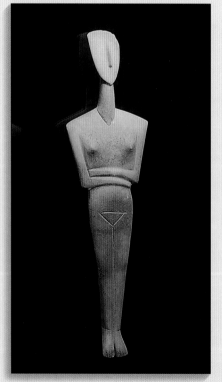

The settlements of the Early Cycladic were small, of around 50 people, comprising densely packed stone-built housing, usually only of one storey. Accompanying the settlements, outside the residential area, are cemeteries of small cist graves (rectangular graves lined with stone) and chamber tombs, clustered in family groups. The dead were inhumed in a contracted (foetal) position along with everyday objects. Much of the evidence we have of how Early Cycladic society functioned comes from these cemeteries.

The often stark differences in grave goods between tombs provides evidence of a stratified society. While some graves contain a very rich variety of artefacts, including gold and silver jewellery, others have very little, often only a single marble figure. How these differences between rich and poor played out is a matter of conjecture, but many artefacts display a high degree of skill in their manufacture, indicating a class of skilled craft workers. Hunting, fishing, animal husbandry and agriculture provided food. The islanders were practised traders, pointing to the existence of a merchant class, presumably, among the wealthier members of society. Skilled sailors, they had contact with the Greek mainland, Crete, Turkey, and even as far as the Danube Basin.

Of all the items left by these peoples, the marble figurines are perhaps both the most beautiful and intriguing. Their importance is such that they are used as a diagnostic tool by scholars to delineate the Cycladic Culture. The predominately female figures are generally around 20 cm (8 ins) in length (a few near life-sized sculptures have been discovered) and are made of white marble. Almost two-dimensional in their execution, they have flattened oval heads and folded arms; many features would have been painted on the marble (on the face, only the nose is rendered in stone). It is conjectured from the position of the feet that they were intended to lie horizontally, but there is no conclusive evidence for this, just as there is no evidence for their function. Explanations from scholars range from their being apotropaic (warding off evil), to divinities, to ancestors. ❑

LEFT: a Cycladic marble figurine.

Map,
pages
226–7

Sérifos

A long tail of land slashes out to enclose **Livádi** ⓰, Sérifos's harbour. With a half-dozen each of tavernas, hotels and disco-bars, this is a pleasant place to stay, with good beaches on either side. **Sérifos Town (Hóra)** ⓱ clings to the mountain above, which gives it a precipitous beauty. Regular buses ascend to Hóra, but the flights of old stone steps (a half-hour climb) make for a more authentic approach.

Hóra has two parts: Káto (Lower) and Áno (Upper). The upper is the more interesting; its ridge leads in the west to the old ruined **Kástro**. The view from here of the gleaming bay and the other islands is spectacular. The beach to the southwest that looks so inviting, **Psilí Ámmos**, really is.

The road is paved as far as the fortified Byzantine **Taxiárhon Monastery** ⓲ to the island's extreme north. The scenic walk there from Áno Hóra's main square takes about an hour and a half, via the village of **Kállisto**. The rustic villages of **Galáni**, **Pýrgos** and **Panagía** focus on the magnificent valley beyond the Taxiárhon. You can cross this valley by one of two footpaths around the hill that bisects it, or stick to the road.

Sérifos abounds in beaches, most accessible only on foot and so unspoiled. **Megálo Livádi** in the southwest is the island's second port (buses cross to it in the summer only). Once a mining centre, it is now rather forlorn.

Sífnos

Sífnos was and is a potter's isle. In the narrow, pretty harbour, **Kamáres** ⓳, and in Fáros, Platýs Gialós, and especially isolated Hersónisos, potters still set out long racks of earthenware to dry in the sun. Weaving and jewellery-making are the other crafts; there are fine examples of local weaving in the

BELOW:
Mýkonos nightlife.

One of Sífnos's delightful sugar-cube churches.

folklore museum in the capital, **Apollonía** ❷ (a notice on the door tells you where to find the curator). Connected to Apollonía, **Artemónas** is Sífnos's richest town, with mansions and old churches.

The oldest community, however, is **Kástro** ❹, the medieval capital, perched 100 metres (300 ft) above the sea and 3 km (2 miles) to the east of Apollonía. Catalans and Venetians once ruled the town; the walls they built are still in evidence, as are some remains of an ancient acropolis. Most of the buildings are from the 14th century. The big Venetian building in the centre of town is the **Archeological Museum** (open Tue–Sat 9am–3pm, Sun 10am–2pm; free).

Sífnos's south shore settlements make tranquil beach-side bases. A paint-blazed footpath leads from **Kataváti** just south of Apollonía to **Vathý** ❷, a potter's coastal hamlet provided with a road only in 1993. Vathý's most visually stunning feature is the **Taxiárhis** (Archangel) **Monastery**, poised as though ready to set sail. But Sífnos's most beautiful spot may well be **Hrysopigí** (Golden Wellspring) **Monastery**, built in 1653 on an islet reached by a small footbridge. No longer in monastic use, basic rooms can be rented in summer.

Andíparos

Once, 5,000 years ago, this small, pretty island was joined to Páros. A narrow channel now separates the two, plied by fishing boats and excursion boats bringing visitors to its famous cave, **Spílio Stalaktitón** (the Cave of the Stalactites) ❷. At the entrance to the cavern stands the church of Ioánnis Spiliótis (St John of the Cave). Though cement steps lessen the adventure, the cave's primordial beauty still stuns. Buses run from **Andíparos Town** to the cave; if you choose to walk, it will take about two hours.

BELOW: grand-mother and grand-son on Sífnos.

Andíparos is only 11 km by 5 km (7 miles by 3 miles), so there are no impossible distances. Good beaches and bars have lured to Andíparos some of Páros's former business. **Ágios Geórgios**, on the south coast, has two tavernas, and faces the goat island of **Despotikó**, where excavations are in progress. South of the cave the **Faneroméni chapel** stands alone on a southeastern cape.

Páros

If you arrive at this heavily trafficked island in August, expect to sleep either under the stars or expensively. The cheap rooms go fast. **Parikía (Páros)** ❷ resembles Mýkonos in appearance and in nightlife; it is gentler in spirit. The four main things to see here are the beautiful 4th–6th-century **Ekatondapylianí church** (Our Lady of a Hundred Doors), the **Archeological Museum** (open Tue–Sun 8.30am–2.30pm; entrance fee), the ancient **cemetery** (next to the post office), and the Venetian **Kástro** in the centre of town, built wholly of classical marbles. Páros is famous for the world's most translucent marble; you can still visit the ancient tunnel-quarries in **Maráthi** and pick up a chip.

A detail from Ekatondapylianí church, Parikía.

Lévkes ❷, the Turkish capital, is the largest inland village. There are several 17th-century churches, the two most prominent edged with an opaline-blue wash. In beautiful **Náousa** ❷, on the north coast, the little harbour's colourful boats seem to nudge up right against the fishermen's houses. Though the village has become fashionable, with upmarket boutiques and restaurants, the harbour is still sacrosanct. Caïques leave here for several fine beaches; the world windsurfing championship has been held at Hrýsi Aktí (Golden Beach).

In the west is the much-visited **Valley of the Butterflies**, or **Petaloúdes**, a big well-watered garden with huge trees (open daily Jun–Sep 9am–8pm). The black

BELOW: Náousa old town and harbour.

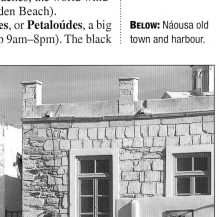

and yellow butterflies – Jersey Tiger moths actually – are colourful and countless in early summer. A big road goes there, but no bus. The bus does, however, go to **Poúnda**, from where the small ferry to Andíparos leaves.

Náxos

Náxos is the largest and most magnificent of the Cyclades. High mountains, long beaches, inaccessible villages, ruins, medieval monasteries and fascinating history make any visit here too short. **Hóra** (**Náxos Town**)  is a labyrinthine chaos of Venetian homes and castle walls, post-Byzantine churches, Cycladic to medieval ruins and garden restaurants. Hóra is divided into sections whose place names reflect the port's long Venetian occupation. Higher up, within the **Kástro**, live descendants (still Catholic) of the Venetian overlords: look for their coats of arms over doorways. The former French School, built into the

Flowering shrubs adorn the old houses climbing up the hillsides in Náxos Town. Náxos is the most fertile island of the Cyclades chain.

ramparts, now houses the **Archeological Museum** (open Tue–Sun 8.30am–3pm; entrance fee). On an islet to the north of Hóra's ferry dock, a colossal free-standing marble doorframe marks the entrance to the never-completed **Temple of Delian Apollo** of 530 BC.

On the northern shore of Náxos is the resort town of **Apóllo** ②③, a one-time hippie enclave three hours from Hóra on the daily bus. A huge 6th-century BC *kouros* – probably bearded Dionysos – lies on the hillside above the settlement, abandoned when the marble cracked.

Olive and fruit trees grow densely around the many rural villages of Náxos, concealing Byzantine churches and crumbling Venetian manors. Four villages on the road from Hóra to Apóllo are particularly worthy of attention: Komiakí, Apírados, Filóti and Halkí.

BELOW: the Temple of Delian Apollo.

Komiáki ②⑨, the highest village on the island, is extremely attractive, has wonderful views over the surrounding vineyards, and is the original home of the local *Kitrón* liqueur. **Apírados** was originally settled by Cretan refugees in the 17th and 18th centuries. The town, whose streets are marble, even looks Cretan. Its little **Archeological Museum** (if closed, ask someone for the guard) contains some rough-carved reliefs that are unique and uninterpretable.

Filóti, on the slopes of Mount Zás, is Náxos's second-largest town. If you are there for the three-day festival (from 14 August), don't bother even trying to stay sober. **Halkí**, the Trageá's main town, has several fine churches, the best being **Panagía Protóthronis** (First-Enthroned Virgin), actually 500 years older than its official foundation date, 1052. The Annunciation fresco over the sanctuary is a masterpiece.

Goats and migrating birds are southern Náxos's chief inhabitants. From Sangrí, a new paved road descends 5 km (3 miles) through a beautiful valley to the recently reconstructed Temple of Demeter (*circa* 530 BC).

It is only in the last 15 years that Náxos has become known for its beaches. Some of the best in the Cyclades are on the west coast, facing Páros. **Ágios Geórgios** south of the port is most popular. **Agía Ánna** has much developed of late; **Mikrí Vígla** beyond it has a good taverna; and further south **Kastráki** ③⓪ offers blissful solitude.

Mílos

Map, pages 226–7

Mílos is a geologist's paradise. Snaking streams of lava formed much of the island's coastline, thrusting up weirdly shaped rock formations. The island has always been extensively mined, once for obsidian, now for bentonite, perlite and china clay, among others. Gaping quarries disfigure the landscape.

Mílos has graciously adapted its growing stream of tourism, concentrated in **Adámas ❹**, the port, and Apollónia, a fishing village in the northeast. Inside the **Agía Triáda** church in Adamás, Cretan-style icons dominate; Cretan refugees founded the town in 1853. The island's capital, **Pláka** (also called **Mílos**) ❺, has both an **Archeological Museum** (open Tue–Sun 8.30am–3pm; entrance fee) and a **Folklore Museum** (open Tue–Sat 10am–1pm, 6–8pm, Sun 10am–1pm; entrance fee). A hike to the **Panagía Thalássitra** (Mariner Virgin), the chapel above Pláka (follow signs for Anna's Art Dresses), and the old **Kástro** walls gives splendid views of Mílos and, on a clear day, as far as Páros.

Southwest of Pláka lies the verdant **Vale of Klíma**, on whose seaside slope the ancient Milians built their city. Excavations undertaken in the late 19th century uncovered a Dionysian altar here, and remains of an ancient gymnasium. The **theatre** is very well preserved, probably because of its Roman renovation. Nearby, a marble plaque marks the spot where a farmer unearthed the Aphrodite of Mílos (Venus de Milo) in 1820. Below the theatre lies one of the island's prettiest villages, **Klíma**, with brightly painted boathouses lining the shore.

Further down the road from Pláka to Adamás are the only **Christian catacombs** in Greece. Carved into the hillside, they are the earliest evidence of Christian worship in the country. The 291 tombs, which probably held 8,000 bodies, have all been robbed.

When the original Venus de Milo was unearthed on the island in 1820, both arms were still intact. They were "amputated" during her clumsy removal from the island by the French.

BELOW: the tiny barren island of Folégandros.

Ten km (6 miles) northeast from Adamás lies the rubble of the ancient city of **Phylakopi**, whose script and art resemble the Minoan. It flourished for a thousand years after 2600 BC. **Apollónia** ❸, a restful base in the northeast, is a popular resort with a tree-fringed beach. It is a good starting point for several short walks that give the full measure of Mílos's strange volcanic beauty.

The tiny island of **Kímolos** – 35 sq. km (14 sq. miles), with a population of 800 – is an alluring presence for anyone who is staying in Apollónia. The caïque takes only 20 minutes to cross the narrow channel to Kímolos's only landing, **Psáthi**. Kímolos, once a pirates' hide-out, today provides refuge from the more crowded islands. Although it is blessedly undeveloped, it has several beaches, all within easy walking distance. **Hóra**, the one town, is a 20-minute walk up from the quay. The 14th-century Venetian **Kástro** above Hóra, in an advanced state of decay, looks down on a row of windmills, one of which still grinds.

Folégandros

Despite its tiny size – 32 sq. km (12 sq. miles) populated by barely 500 people – Folégandros's role in very recent history has not been insignificant: many Greeks were exiled here during the country's 1967–74 military rule.

There are buses to the capital, **Folégandros (Hóra)** ❸, a magnificently sited medieval town with an inner **kástro** high above the sea. **Hrysospiliá** (Golden Cave) near Hóra, gapes over the sea. It is rich with stalagmites and stalactites. Excavations show this was a place of refuge in the Middle Ages.

The island's second village, **Áno Meriá**, comprises stone houses and farms; the surrounding hills are dotted with chapels.

BELOW: sitting out by Ía's windmill, Santoríni.

Síkinos

Although connected by ferry to Piraeus and other Cyclades two or three times a week, and by caïque to Íos and Folégandros in summer, rocky Síkinos so far seems to have shrugged off tourism. It also escapes mention in the history books for long periods of time, but there are antiquities and churches to be seen.

The three beaches, **Aloprónia** (also the port), **Ágios Nikólaos** and **Ágios Geórgios** to the north face Íos. From Aloprónia harbour it is an hour's hike (or regular bus ride) to **Síkinos Town** ❸, which consists of the simple village (**Hóra**) and the medieval **Kástro**, with its wonderful village square arranged for defence. The abandoned convent of **Zoödóhos Pigí** sits above.

Síkinos is a sparse island with few obvious diversions. One site of note, the **Iroön** ❸, stands on what was once thought to have been a temple to Apollo; this is now reckoned to be an elaborate Roman tomb, incorporated into a church during medieval times.

Íos

A tiny island with few historic attractions, Íos is not devoid of natural beauty or charm. The harbour is one of the Aegean's prettiest. The hilltop Hóra, capped by a windmill, blazes with the blue domes of two Byzantine churches. Its layout and the palm trees that flank it look almost Levantine. But ever since the 1980s,

Íos has drawn the young and footloose, and this is its defining characteristic. Most nightlife shifts constantly about the little capital town, **Hóra** (also called **Íos**) ❸. Indeed, after the sun sets, Íos resembles a downmarket, younger Mýkonos. At around 11pm, beach stragglers break the quiet ready for night-time revels (a bus runs regularly between beach and harbour via Hóra). Once ensconced inside a bar, they could be anywhere in the Western world, with few older Greeks in sight.

However, Íos also has many good swimming beaches, including the nude beaches north of the harbour. People still sleep on the beach at **Mylopótas** ❸, although this is now less common. There are summer caïques to **Manganári bay** in the south and **Psáthi** in the east.

Beyond the church are the remains of **Paleokástro** ❸, an elevated fortress containing the marble ruins of what was the medieval capital. At a lonely spot toward the northern tip, behind the cove at **Plakotós**, is a series of prehistoric graves, one of which the islanders fiercely believe belongs to Homer, who is said to have died en route from Sámos to Athens.

Alternative transport in Amorgós.

Amorgós

A spine of mountains – the tallest is Krikelas in the northeast, at 822 metres (2,696 ft) – precludes expansive views here unless you're on top of them. The southwesterly harbour town of **Katápola** ❹ occupies a small coastal plain, while the elevated **Hóra** (or **Amorgós Town**) ❹, accessible by a regular bus service, centres on a 13th-century Venetian castle. Hóra has no fewer than 40 churches and chapels – including one that holds only two people, the smallest church in Greece.

BELOW:
traditional music
at a local festival.

Urn from the site at Akrotíri on Santoríni. The largest Minoan city outside Crete, it was destroyed in a volcanic eruption in 1500 BC – at first, archeologists thought they'd found Atlantis.

BELOW:
Firá, Santoríni.

The island's two most famous churches are outside Hóra. **Ágios Geórgios Valsamítis**, 4 km (2 miles) southwest, is on a sacred spring; this church's pagan oracle was finally closed only after World War II. Half an hour east of Hóra, spilling from a jagged cliff like milk from a jug, the 11th-century Byzantine monastery of the **Panagía Hozoviótissa** ❷ – one of the most beautiful in Greece – is home to a revered icon of the Virgin from Palestine.

Below the monastery, **Agía Ánna** beach beckons. To the southwest lie secluded coves for bathing and sunning; a line of windmills edges the ridge above. The north of the island is characterised by high-perched villages, excepting **Egiális**, a small anchorage with accommodation and good beaches nearby.

Santoríni

Entering the bay of Santoríni on a boat is one of Greece's great experiences. Broken pieces of a volcano's rim – Santoríni and its attendant islets – form a multicoloured circle around a bottomless lagoon that, before the volcano's eruption (*circa* 1650 BC), was the island's high centre. Thíra (or Thera) is the island's ancient and official name. Greeks, however, prefer its medieval name, Santoríni, after St Irene of Salonica, who died here in 304. **Firá** ❸, the capital, sits high on the rim, its white houses (many barrel-vaulted against earthquakes) blooming like asphodels. To the east of Firá, the land smoothes out into fertile fields. A few bare hills push up again in the southeast. On one of them sits **Ancient Thira** ❹ (9th century BC), where naked boys danced in a famous ritual. **Akrotíri** ❺ in the south, a Minoan town preserved in volcanic ash like Pompeii, continues to be excavated. Many of the finds – pots and frescoes – are in Firá's **Museum of Prehistoric Thera** (open Tue-Sun 8.30am–3pm; entrance fee).

Map, pages 226–7

Though Firá is most developed, many other places offer plentiful accommodation. **Ía (Oia)** , on the island's northernmost peninsula, is perhaps Greece's most photographed village. Nearby, beautiful *skaftá* ("dug") houses, rented out by the National Tourist Organisation (EOT) and a number of private hotels, are a local speciality. Each year, there are also more places available to stay and eat in **Kamári** and **Périssa**, busy resorts on the east coast. Périssa has the main campsite. Both have roasting hot black pebble beaches. They make a good starting point from which to climb up to Ancient Thira (if you don't take a taxi or bike), and then to Mount Profítis Ilías, the next hill inland. The museum in **Profítis Ilías Monastery** exhibits tools and even complete workshops of the various crafts practised here by the monks for centuries. Homemade wine and liqueur are still set out for guests. But remember that monks are not obliged to keep regular hours for tourists – the hours when Profítis Ilías admits visitors tend to be erratic.

Some boats put in below Firá at **Skála Firá**, from where you ascend by donkey, by funicular or by foot up the stone stairway. Ferries put in at **Athiniós**, 10 km (6 miles) further south.

Anáfi

Fewer than 300 people live on Anáfi in winter, surviving mainly by fishing and subsistence farming. Summer tourism, mostly Greek, has boosted the economy, but development is slow. It is served by a twice-weekly caïque from Santoríni and several ferries from Piraeus.

The south-facing harbour, **Ágios Nikólaos**, has rooms available in summer. A short bus ride or half-hour walk up, the main town, **Anáfi** (Hóra) ❼ offers a

BELOW:
colourful Cycladic architecture.

Map,
pages
226–7

wider choice, and life in the streets is still fairly untouristy. **Zoödóhos Pigí Monastery** 48 was erected over the ancient shrine to Apollo in the island's southeast corner. Extensive courses of marble masonry in its walls are believed to be remnants of the old temple. Above the monastery soars the smaller monastery of **Panagía Kalamiótissa**, high on a pinnacle that is Anáfi's most distinctive feature.

The Back Islands

The so-called "Back Islands" near Náxos were once thickly populated. Now **Donoúsa**, **Iráklia**, **Shinoúsa** and **Koufonísi** have populations of 100 to 200 each, while **Kéros** is completely uninhabited. For Iráklia, Shinoúsa and Koufonísi there are ferries twice or three times a week, and smaller boats from Náxos. Donoúsa has ferry connections four times a week, and is served by caïques from Náxos, Páros and Santoríni in summer. No boats go to Kéros. A stay on any of the Back Islands means, at least out of season, accommodation with local families and a very low-key existence.

Hilly Donoúsa is covered with vineyards; views from the harbour take in the barren Makáres islands and the grand profile of Náxos. Iráklia has two settlements: the harbour, Ágios Geórgios, and Hóra, just over an hour's hike above. Shinoúsa's hilltop Hóra has a medieval fortress at its back; Mesariá is a tiny beach settlement on the north coast. Koufonísi (its neighbour, Káto Koufonísi, belongs mainly to goats) has an actual hotel, and an east coast beach with a seasonal taverna. Kéros was a third-millennium BC burial site. Much of the Cycladic material in great museums comes from here, and if you put in to Kéros, the police will want to know why. ❑

BELOW: small fishing boats still play their part in the economy of the Cyclades.

Ancient Delos

Minuscule Delos (Dílos), to the south-west of Mýkonos, is heaven for archaeologists. Extensive Greco-Roman ruins occupying much of the island's 4 sq. km (1.5 sq. miles) make Delos the equal of Delphi and Olympia.

If you suffer from seasickness be fore-warned: the island is a "windy wasteland battered by the sea". The caïque trip takes about 40 minutes; if it is windy (it often is), it is wise to forego breakfast. In summer there are also daily trips to Delos from Tínos, Náxos and Páros.

Delos became a shrine because Leto, a Titaness pregnant by Zeus, gave birth there to Artemis (actually on adjacent Rheneia), then, clutching a palm tree, to Apollo. A floating rock, Delos was rewarded for braving Hera's jealous wrath by four diamond pillars that anchored it in the heart of the Cyclades.

Most of the ruins occupy two arms of a right angle. To the right (southern arm) are the theatre and various domestic buildings. To the left are the sanctuaries to which pilgrims from all over the Mediterranean came with votive offerings and sacrificial animals.

For nearly a thousand years, Delos was the political and religious centre of the Aegean, and host to the Delian Festival, held every four years and, until the 4th century BC, Greece's greatest religious gathering. The Romans turned it into a grand trade fair, and made Delos a free port. It also became Greece's slave market, where as many as 10,000 slaves were said to be sold daily. In 88 BC, Mithridates, king of Pontus, sacked Delos; it never recovered, and fell into disuse.

Follow the pilgrim route to a ruined, monumental gateway leading into the Sanctuary of Apollo. Within are three temples dedicated to Apollo and one to Artemis, and the remains of a colossal marble statue of the god. Close by is the Sanctuary of Dionysus, with several Dionysic friezes and phalli standing on pedestals – including a marble phallic bird, symbolising the body's immortality.

Continue to the stunning Lion Terrace, where five archaic lions squat. (These are copies; the weathered originals are in the museum.) Below this is the Sacred Lake, and a palm tree which marks the spot of Apollo's birth.

Most visitors delight in that part of Delos which was occupied by artisans rather than gods. Their houses, close to the port, are a regular warren, separated by narrow lanes lined by 2,000-year-old drains, with niches for oil-burning streetlamps. The main road leads to the theatre, which seated 5,500. It is unimpressive, but there are superb views from the uppermost of its 43 rows. On the way to the theatre are grander houses surrounded by columns and with exquisite mosaics.

From here, a gentle stroll leads to the summit of Mount Kýnthos (110 metres/368 ft), from which the views of the ruins and the Cyclades are memorable. Finish off your tour by descending first past the grotto of Hercules, and then stopping at the Sanctuaries to the Foreign Gods. In classical times practically the entire Levant traded here, under the tutelage of shrines erected to their divinities. ❏

RIGHT: one of the lean Lions, carved in the 7th century BC, which guard Delos' Sacred Lake.

THE ISLANDS IN BLOOM

The Greek islands are at their most bountiful in spring and early summer, when every hillside and valley is decorated with glorious colour

Greece in spring is a botanist's dream and a gardener's despair. Some 6,000 species of wild plant grow in Greece and the islands, and in the spring (March to May) visitors may enjoy a magnificent cornucopia of flowers and fragrances.

Hillsides resemble giant rock gardens, while brilliant patches of untended waste ground outdo Northern Europe's carefully tended herbaceous borders with ease. Winter rains, followed by a bright, hot, frost-free spring, produce a season's flowers compressed into a few, spectacular weeks before the summer's heat and drought become too much. By late May or June the flowers are over, the seeds for next year's show are ripening, and greens are fading to brown to match the tourists on the beaches.

SUMMER SURVIVAL

Except in the cooler, higher mountains, most plants go into semi-dormancy to survive the arid summer. The first rains of autumn, which could come as early as September or as late as November, tempt a few autumn bulbs into flower but also initiate the germination of seeds – plants that will grow and build up strength during the winter in preparation for the following spring, when their flowers will again colour in the waiting canvas of the hills and valleys.

The richness and diversity of the flora are due in part to the islands' location between three continents – Europe, Asia and Africa – partly to the Ice Age survival in temperate Greece of pre-glacial species, and partly to the wonderful variety of habitats. Limestone, the foundation of much of Greece, is a favoured home for plants, providing the stability, minerals, water supply and protection they need.

▷ **THE HILLS ARE ALIVE**
Sunshine, colour and quantity mark the spring flowering of the islands, as here in the mountains of Crete in mid-April.

△ **A GOOD REED**
Not bamboo – but it has similar uses. The giant reed (*Arundo donax*) can even be made into pan pipes.

▽ **CUP OF MANY COLOURS**
Ranunculus asiaticus is an unlikely buttercup, with poppy-sized flowers in shades of white, pink, orange, red – and occasionally yellow.

▽ **SCARLET MEMORIAL**
The startling reds of *Anemone coronaria* mark the arrival of spring and in myth represent the spilt blood of the dying Adonis.

▽ **HANDY BUSH**
The long flowering period of the native oleander makes it popular in gardens and as an ornamental roadside crash barrier.

BEETLES, BEES AND BUTTERFLIES

The profusion of flowers and plants provides food for an equal profusion of insects. Butterflies are conspicuous from spring to autumn, including the lovely swallowtail (*above*) whose colourful caterpillars feed on the leaves of common fennel. Its larger, paler and more angular relative, the scarce swallowtail, despite its name, is even more abundant.

Look for clouded yellows and paler cleopatras, reddish-brown painted ladies and southern commas, white admirals, and a myriad of smaller blue butterflies.

Butterflies, bees and day-flying hawk moths tend to go for flowers with nectar, while beetles and flies go for the pollen. Some insects even use the heat accumulated in the solar cup of many flowers in order to warm up their sex lives.

The leaves of plants feed armies of insect herbivores, which themselves are eaten by more aggressive insects. Some of the omnivorous Greek grasshoppers and crickets are as happy munching through a caterpillar, or even another grasshopper, as the grass it was sitting on.

◁ **FIRE FENNEL**
According to legend, fire was brought to earth by Prometheus hidden in the smouldering stem of a giant fennel (*Ferula communis*).

▽ **NATURAL FOOD**
Wild artichokes are painfully spiny to prepare for the pot; but their flavour is prized by Greek country folk over the spineless cultivated variety, and their market price increases accordingly.

RHODES

According to the ancient Greeks, Rhodes is "more beautiful than the sun". Even today's brash resorts cannot dim the appeal of its benign climate, entrancing countryside and unique history

Maps:
City 247
Island 248

The largest and best-known of the Dodecanese islands, Rhodes (Ródos) is endowed with a balmy climate and a wealth of monuments from many eras. Ancient Rhodes originally consisted of three city-states: Kameiros, Ialyssos and Lindos. Following Athenian attacks they decided to unite, founding the city of Rodos at the island's northeast tip, separated from Asia Minor by only a 13-km (7-mile) strait. Fortifications were completed by 408 BC, and the town laid out in the popular grid plan of that era, championed by a certain Hippodamus.

Well-defended by its fleet and strategically positioned, Rhodes prospered as a trading-station and led a charmed life despite fickle alliances, as the moment suited, with Athens, Sparta, Alexander the Great, or the Persians. Under Alexander, Rhodes forged links with the Ptolemies; consequently, the Rhodians refused to fight the Egyptians alongside King Antigonos. After Alexander's death, Antigonos sent his son, Demetrios Polyorketes, along with 40,000 men to attack the city in 305 BC; he failed after a year-long siege. The leftover bronze military hardware was melted down to make the island's most famous landmark, the Colossus of Rhodes, a representation of Apollo. A beacon to passing ships, it stood over 30 metres (100 ft) tall, somewhere near the harbour entrance, for nearly 70 years before it collapsed during an earthquake in 226 BC.

LEFT: Agathí beach, on the east coast.
BELOW: Ágios Nikólaos fort guards Mandráki harbour.

The city emerged from the siege with prestige and prosperity enhanced, eclipsing Athens as the cultural beacon of the east Mediterranean. However, it got ideas above its station when it unwisely tried to reconcile the warring Romans and Macedonians. Rome retaliated in 168 BC by effectively making Rhodes a Roman vassal; involvement in Rome's civil wars a century later saw Rhodes sacked by Cassius and its fleet destroyed. After Octavius's victory in 42 BC and the establishment of imperial Rome, Rhodes regained some autonomy, and again served as a finishing school and sybaritic posting for officialdom. But its glory days were over. In late Roman and Byzantine times the island endured second-rate status, prone to barbarian raids.

Early in the 14th century, the Knights of St John – expelled from Palestine and Cyprus – settled on Rhodes, ejecting the Genoese who had been holding the island on sufferance of the Byzantines. They proceeded to occupy and fortify virtually all of the Dodecanese, rebuilding Rhodes Town's rickety Byzantine city walls and acting as a major irritant to the sultan with their depredations of Ottoman shipping. Finally, in the spring of 1522, Süleyman the Magnificent landed an army of 200,000 on Rhodes to end the problem; Rhodes's second siege was shorter and more conclusive than the first, but only just. The Knights resisted valiantly, but finally were forced to surrender.

On New Year's Day 1523, 180 survivors concluded honourable terms of surrender and sailed off to exile on Malta.

The Ottomans suitably appreciated their hard-won possession, at least initially, and instituted the regime common to fortified cities in their empire: Christians were forbidden from staying overnight within the walled old town, although Jews were tolerated in their small quarter to the east. This exclusionary edict gave rise to the *marásia* or Orthodox suburb villages which hem Rhodes Town on three sides, often bearing the names of their main parish churches. The Ottomans built a few grand mosques from scratch within the walls, but more usually appropriated small Byzantine and Crusader churches as *mescids* (the Muslim equivalent of a chapel). Even at the zenith of Ottoman power, the Muslim population of the entire island never much exceeded 15 percent. Ottoman rule became increasingly desultory and inefficient until the Italians effectively annexed Rhodes in spring 1912 (*see page 48*).

Legend has it that the Colossus stood with one foot on either side of Mandráki harbour entrance. But to do so it would have had to have been over 10 times its probable size – an impossible feat of engineering.

The Old City

Despite still-visible damage from Allied bombing in early 1945, the Old City of **Rhodes ❶** is one of the architectural treasures of the Mediterranean, a remarkably complete walled medieval town. The ramparts themselves (one-hour tours only; Tue, Sat 2.45pm; entrance from gate beside Palace of the Grand Masters; entrance fee) give a good perspective over the palm-and-minaret-studded lanes. At the northwest summit stands the **Palace of the Grand Masters Ⓐ** (open summer Mon 2.30–9pm, Tue–Fri 8.30am–9pm, Sat–Sun 8.30am–3pm; winter Mon 12.30–3pm, Tue–Sun 8.30am–3pm; entrance fee), destroyed in 1856 by an ammunition explosion and hastily reconstructed by the Italians during the 1930s.

BELOW: a mosaic floor in the Palace of the Grand Masters.

On the ground floor are two excellent galleries detailing medieval and ancient Rhodes, with exemplary layout and labelling.

From outside, the better-restored **Street of the Knights (Odós Ippotón) ⑧**, where the chivalric order once housed its members according to their native language, leads downhill to the badly labelled **Archeological Museum ⑨** (open Tue–Sun 8.30am–2.45pm; entrance fee) with its "Marine Venus" beloved of Lawrence Durrell; the **Byzantine Museum ⑩**, opposite in the former cathedral of the Knights (open Tue–Sun 8.30am–2.45pm; entrance fee), with its exhibits of local icons and frescoes; and the ethnographic **Decorative Arts Collection** (Tue–Sun 8am–2.30pm; entrance fee), with doors and chests salvaged from Dodecanesian village dwellings.

Despite an enduring resident Turkish minority, Ottoman monuments are not much highlighted except for the **Ottoman Library** (open Mon–Sat 9.30am–4pm; tip custodian) and a wonderful, still-functioning **Turkish Bath ⑧** (open Mon–Fri 11am–6pm, Sat 8am–6pm) on Platía Ariónos. The arcaded synagogue of **Kal Kadosh Shalom ⑨** (open daily 10am–5pm; donation), in the former Jewish quarter, can also be visited; it serves largely as a memorial to the more than 1,800 Jews of Rhodes and Kós who were deported to Nazi death camps in June 1944.

The New Town

Established by the Orthodox Greeks who were banished from the Old City by the Ottomans, and developed by the Italians when they took control in the early 20th century, the New Town (**Neohóri**) is the commercial centre of Rhodes and the administrative capital of the Dodecanese. Here, smart shops abound, peddling Lacoste, Benetton and Trussardi. Watch the world go by and the yachts bobbing

Maps:
City 247
Island 248

Rhodes' most famous statue: the Aphrodite Thalassia (Marine Venus) in the Archeological Museum.

BELOW:
Líndos beach and acropolis.

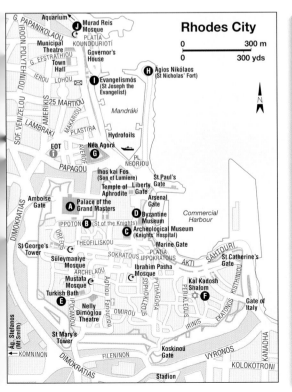

Ancient Kameiros.

from one of the pricey, touristy pavement cafés at **Mandráki** port. Marginally cheaper are the cafés inside the **covered market (Néa Agorá)** Ⓖ among fishmongers, butchers and wonderfully heaped-up produce. Cheap *souvlákia* and fresh orange juice are available, and there's a good bakery.

Mandráki's quay buzzes night and day with caricature artists, popcorn vendors, sponge-sellers and touts hawking boat trips. Excursion boats leave by 9am for the island of Sými, calling first at Panormítis Monastery, or down the east coast to Líndos. Hydrofoils depart from the base of the jetty, while full-sized ferries leave from the commercial harbour, a 15-minute walk east.

Mandráki, guarded by the round bastion-lighthouse of **Ágios Nikólaos (St Nicholas' Fort)** Ⓗ, is also an established port of call for the international yachting circuit, with local charters, too. By the harbour entrance stands a cluster of Italian Art Deco: the Governor's House with its Gothic arches, the **church of St Joseph the Evangelist (Evangelismós)** Ⓘ next door and, across the way, the post office, Town Hall and Municipal Theatre. Opposite the theatre, the **Mosque of**

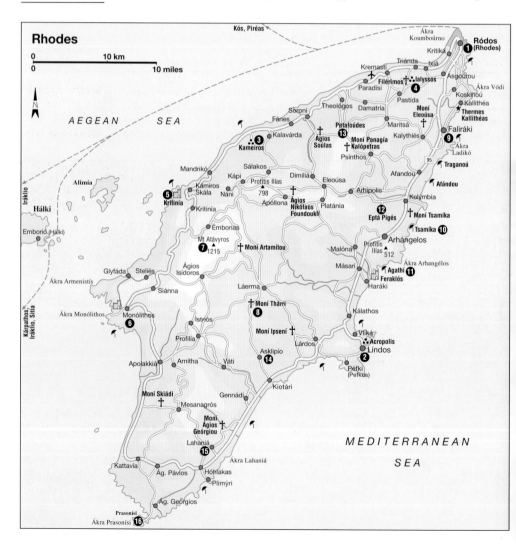

Murad Reis **❶** stands beside one of the island's larger Muslim graveyards. Beyond this is the **Villa Cleobolus**, where Lawrence Durrell lived from 1945 to 1947.

Away from the harbour, Neohóri throbs with nightlife, revellers spilling out of the bars on to the pavements in high season. There are said to be over 200 bars packed into an area measuring less than a square kilometre. Orfanídou in particular is informally dubbed "Skandi Street" after the new Vikings.

Maps:
City 247
Island 248

Three ancient city-states

One of the original Dorian city-states, **Líndos ❷**, 44 km (27 miles) south along the east coast, is the island's other big tourist magnet. Settled early thanks to its fine natural harbour – the island's only one aside from Mandráki at Rhodes Town – its strong acropolis supports a scaffolded Hellenistic Athena temple and another Knights' castle. Clustered below is the late-Medieval village of imposing mansions built by local sea-captains; with its barren surroundings, the place has always lived from the sea. Italian, German and British bohemians first rediscovered Líndos in the 1960s, attracted by the pellucid light, but its role as an artists' colony has long since been replaced by one as a package-tour dormitory; midsummer visits are not recommended, when you can hardly move down the narrow, cobbled streets.

Tsambíka monastery is a magnet for childless women.

The second of the original city-states, **Kameiros ❸**, 33 km (20 miles) down the windswept west coast from Rhodes Town, merits a visit for displaying a perfectly preserved classical townscape, without the usual later accretions (open summer Tue–Sun 8am–7pm; winter Tue–Sun 8.30am–3pm; entrance fee). Unlike old Lindos, it was abandoned shortly after 408 BC. Not so ancient **Ialyssos ❹** (open Tue–Fri 8.30am–6pm, Sat–Sun 8.30am–3pm; entrance fee),

BELOW: the castle at Monólithos, built by the Knights of St John.

Map, page 248

12 km (7½ miles) is southwest of Rhodes Town. Only a Doric fountain and some Hellenistic temple foundations are evident from the ancient city-state. Today the town is best known for its appealing medieval monastery of **Filérimos**, now well restored after being damaged during World War II.

Island sights

Although bus frequencies have actually improved in recent years, Rhodes is most easily explored by hire car. Superbly sited Knights' castles at **Kritinía ❺** and **Monólithos ❻**, both beyond Kámiros, make suitable targets, along with the village of **Siána** in between, well equipped for visitors, with numerous tavernas. All lie under the shadow of 1,215-metre (4,000-ft) **Mount Atávyros ❼**, the highest point on Rhodes; from just north of Ágios Isídoros a marked path goes to the summit with its foundations of a Zeus temple. The best Byzantine monuments in the interior are the late Byzantine church of **Ágios Nikólaos Foundoukli** with smudged frescoes, just below 798-metre (2,600-ft) Profítis Ilías, and the monastery of **Thárri ❽**, with its glorious, cleaned 14th-century frescoes, hidden amid unburned pine forest between Líndos and Monólithos.

The southern tip of Rhodes is popular with windsurfers.

The best beaches cluster on the more sheltered east coast. The first resort travelling south from Rhodes Town is **Kallithéa**, which sprang up around the spa established there by the Italians. Round the headland is Kallithéa Bay, one of the best beaches on the island and the most energetically exploited for tourism. On the south side of the bay is **Faliráki ❾**, one of Greece's more notorious resorts and very popular with young package tourists. By day, every possible form of watersport is available; by night, when the neon lights are switched on, bars compete with loud music and improbably alchoholic cocktails.

BELOW: a local in Rhodes Town.

Pebbly **Traganoú**, at the north end of Afándou bay, has caves and overhangs, and is mostly patronised by Rhodians. **Tsamíka ❿** huddles beneath a giant promontory on which stands a tiny monastery of the Virgin in her avatar of fertility goddess – hundreds of *ex-votos* testify to her successful intervention for childless couples. **Agáthi ⓫**, just north of ruinous Feraklós castle and Haráki port, remains miraculously undeveloped.

Inland from Tsambíka, **Eptá Pigés ⓬** is an enduringly popular oasis, its reservoir an Italian legacy. Northwest of there, the **Petaloúdes (Butterfly Valley) ⓭** is the home of millions of Jersey Tiger moths, attracted by the *Liquidambar orientalis* trees in this secluded stream canyon.

Beyond the Líndos promontory, there are few specific sights aside from the wonderfully frescoed 11th-century church at **Asklipío** village ⓮, just inland from the mushrooming resort of Kiotári. There are more, usually empty beaches at Gennádi; and below, the ravine-hidden, well-watered village of **Lahaniá ⓯** has attracted a second generation of drop-outs after the original Líndos scene, who renovate traditional houses here under long-lease agreements. Land's End for Rhodes is the sandspit-tethered islet of **Prasonísi ⓰**, reached from Kattaviá village; topography and winds combine to make the broad, flat beach here one of the premier venues for windsurfing in Greece, with at least two schools operating every season. ❏

Italian Architecture in the Dodecanese

The Italians, who occupied the Dodecanese from 1912 until 1943, adorned the historic centres of Rhodes and Kós towns with grandiose public buildings, constructed a huge naval base and the planned town of Porto Lago (Lakkí) on Léros, and did much to reconstruct Kós after the earthquake of 1933. Because of its associations with Fascism, anything linked to this period, whatever its quality, had been disparaged if not neglected.

In Rhodes, a new administrative centre – the Foro Italica – was created, comprising all public services, and centred on the all-important Fascist Party Headquarters with its tower and speaker's balcony. Beyond lay the new city's tourist area, which included La Ronda Sea Baths (today Élli), the Albergo delle Rose (now the casino) and the aquarium at the far cape.

Art Deco style featured in the Fascist Youth Building and the football stadium; other buildings, such as La Ronda, the aquarium and the Customs House mixed elements of Art Deco with abstract Ottoman motifs. Out in the countryside, the Kallithéa Baths (*shown below*) are the best example of Dodecanesian Art Deco, stylishly blending with their surroundings.

The later phase of Fascist rule, from 1936, coinciding with the harsh tenure of Governor Cesare de Vecchio, stressed the perceived continuity between the Knights Hospitallers and the Italians. Many monuments of the Knights were restored, and new buildings in a "neo-Crusader" style, such as the Bank of Rome, were erected. At the same time, buildings such as the Albergo delle Rose and the Courthouse were "purified" by removing the allegedly superfluous, orientalising features of Art Deco, and replacing these with a cladding of Póros stone. In this final stage, Italian architecture in the Dodecanese conformed to rationalist-internationalist canons of the decade, with more monumental and rigidly symmetrical structures. The Puccini Theatre (now the Municipal Theatre) on the Piazza del'Impero was the best example of many such around this square. ❑

BELOW: orientalised Art Deco, complete with palm trees, at Kallithéa.

THE DODECANESE

Closer to Turkey than Greece, the archipelago has enormous variety, from holy Pátmos to busy Kós, from wild Kárpathos to tranquil Tínos, from fertile Tílos to the volcano that is Nísyros

Map, page 254

G reek place names often reveal history, and "Dodecanese" (Dodekánisos), a new name by Greek standards, is no exception. Through four centuries of Ottoman rule these islands were known as the Southern Sporades, a name still appearing on older maps. During this period, smaller, more barren islands here were granted considerable privileges – in effect, being invited to look after themselves – while larger, more fertile Rhodes and Kós were more strictly governed and colonised by Muslims. After the establishment of an independent Greece in 1830, and periodic armed hostilities between it and the Ottoman Empire, such privileges were gradually withdrawn. The 12 larger islands (*dódeka nisiá* in Greek) submitted a joint objection against these infringements in 1908; it failed but the new name stuck, despite there being – depending on how one counts – 14 or even 18 inhabited isles in this chain, extending northwest to southeast in an arc along the Turkish coast.

In 1912 the Italians, as part of a larger war against the Turks, took this group to cut the Ottoman supply lines to Libya. Despite initial promises to relinquish the archipelago once the Turks left Tripoli, the Italian annexation was consolidated by World War I and the subsequent rise of the Fascist regime after 1923, when the group was officially renamed the "Italian Islands of the Aegean". The Fascists were busy colonialists, erecting numerous distinctive edifices *(see page 251)*, planting eucalyptus to drain swamps, building roads and imposing their language, religion and political culture on public life. Repression was stepped up considerably in 1936 when governor Mario Lago was replaced by Cesare de Vecchi, such a zealous Fascist that he came to a sticky end at the hands of his own people when the Italians capitulated in September 1943. In a series of bloody actions against now pro-Allied Italian forces, the Germans assumed control of the Dodecanese in late 1943, but in turn surrendered the islands to the British two years later.

LEFT: windmill on Kárpathos.
BELOW: evening light on Léros.

Finally, in early 1948, after a 10-month interlude of Greek military rule imposed to weed out local collaborators with the Italians, the Dodecanese were united with Greece to become the country's southeasternmost, and most recent, territorial acquisition. Massive emigration to Australia, South Africa and North America ensued, as in chaotic post-war Greece union with the "mother" country initially brought little other than freedom of movement. Today the islanders live – as they always have – largely off the sea, which has brought them a catch of vital importance to the local economy: tourists.

Kárpathos, Kásos and Hálki

The most dramatic way to arrive at **Kárpathos** is by ship from Rhodes, invariably departing before dawn. After several hours' journey, the island appears with

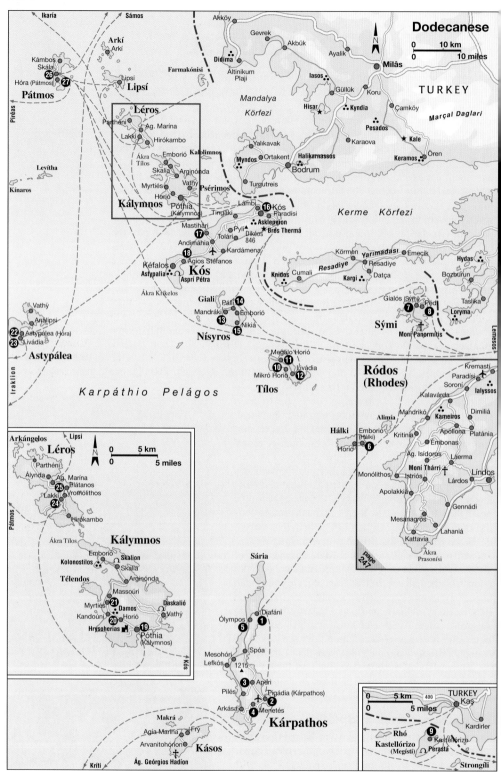

Dodecanese

its imposing, often cloud-flecked summit-ridge. Boats stop at **Diafáni** ❶, the northerly port given a jetty only in 1996. By the mid-morning light, onward passengers have an hour to get acquainted with Kárpathos. Its eastern shore drops steeply to the sea, baby pines sprouting from slopes denuded during the fierce blazes of the 1980s; occasionally, the cliffs relent at large, white, empty beaches.

After these first impressions, the main port of **Pigádia** ❷ is inevitably a disappointment, with little to recommend it other than its fine setting; it dates only from the 19th century, but the islanders themselves – not invading forces – effectively wrecked it with concrete constructions from the 1960s onwards. This lack of distinction also has something to do with Kárpathos's status as a backwater since ancient times; neither the Knights of St John nor the Ottomans bothered much with it, leaving it to the Genoese and Venetians, who called it Scarpanto.

Getting to a beach is apt to be a top priority. An excellent one stretches immediately north for 3 km (1¾ miles) along Vróndi Bay. More secluded ones, visible on the ferry ride in, prove close-up to have aquamarine water and white-sand or pebble shores, guarded by half-submerged rock formations. The best of these are Ápella, Aháta and Kyrá Panagiá, accessible either on small-boat excursions or overland – although many Kárpathiot roads are appalling (the east-coast road is being paved) and hire cars expensive. The west coast is served by good roads but far more exposed, though at remote Levkós, a series of three bays tucked in between headlands, there are excellent beaches and a busy resort.

Most villages are well inland and high up, the standard medieval strategy against pirates, of whom Kárpathos had more than its fair share. The wealthiest settlements are a trio – **Apéri** ❸, Óthos and Voláda – just south of cloud-capped Mount Kalilímni, 1,215 metres (4,000 ft) high, plus **Menetés** ❹ near Pigádia, all studded with a variety of traditional and contemporary villas.

The source of the wealth seems mysterious at first, since there is little fertile lowland, no industry, and mass tourism began only in the late 1980s. In fact, Kárpathos lives largely off remittances from seamen and emigrants (mostly in the US); this economy has profoundly affected local culture, architecture and attitudes. It has deliberately slowed the development of tourism and, paradoxically, also enhanced the position of women who stayed behind. Overseas values have left their mark on house-building, although even the most vulgar modern pile may sport a date of construction, the owner's initials and a traditional emblem, perhaps a mermaid or double-headed Byzantine eagle.

In its original form, the vernacular Karpathiot house consists of a single, mud-floored space appropriately divided; to one side a raised wooden platform or *dórva*, where the bride's dowry linen, festival clothing and mattresses are kept, the latter rolled out at night. In the centre, a wooden pole – the "pillar of the house" – upholds the ceiling, and to complete the symbolism a painting or photograph of the couple is pinned to the pole under their wedding-wreath – a custom perhaps developed to acquaint children with chronically absent fathers. The walls are decked with shelves and plate-racks, containing hundreds of kitsch and near-kitsch ornaments: not local handicrafts, but ethnic dolls,

Map, page 254

BELOW: a young woman in traditional dress, Ólympos.

gaudy pottery and other baubles collected by wandering Karpathiot sailors. Even modern, multi-room villas still model their *salóni* (sitting room) on this pattern.

Many Dodecanese islands are matrilineal (as opposed to matriarchal). On Kárpathos it's merely more evident, at least in the northernmost villages of **Ólympos** ❺ and **Diafáni**, where the women still wear traditional dress; the well-travelled men have worn approximations of Western garb for as long as anyone can remember. The women's pantaloons, aprons, headscarves and boots are still locally made, but this everyday costume is completed by Irish wool scarves and imported sequins and embroidery, much of it Chinese and Bulgarian. Festival dress is rather more colourful and includes a gold-coin collar, the number of coins signalling a girl's wealth to prospective suitors.

Bougainvillea brightens Ólympos village.

Two of the most renowned festivals – Easter and Assumption Day – are still celebrated with special verve at Ólympos, which is draped over a windswept ridge. It has long been something of a honeypot for anthropologists, academic and amateur, owing to its relict Dorian dialect, the aforesaid costumes, music and communal ovens. But conventional tourism has been as distorting – and rescuing – here as subsidies from abroad have been elsewhere on Kárpathos; the last of several windmills stopped working as a real accessory to life late in the 1970s, but one was restored as a functioning museum-piece a few years later.

If you stay in either Diafáni or Ólympos, much the best way to spend time is to go for walks on the path network across the north of the island; Avlóna farm hamlet, the beach and ruins at Vrykoúnda, more ambitiously to Trístomo inlet, or simply down the canyons to Diafáni are popular targets.

BELOW: Ólympos village, Kárpathos.

Just southwest of Kárpathos, **Kásos** is its bleak satellite, devastated by an Ottoman massacre in 1824 and totally dependent ever since on seafaring.

Map, page 254

Effectively protected from conventional tourism by its lack of beaches, it consequently has limited tourist facilities – especially off-season – and is thus frequented mostly by overseas-based Kassiots during the summer festival period.

Hálki, just off Rhodes, is another bare speck of limestone enlivened by the colourful port of **Emborió** ❻; formerly home to sponge-divers, most of it was restored in the late 1980s and it is now packed from April to October with upmarket package tourists.

Sými

Sými lies northeast of Rhodes, between the outstretched "claws" of Turkey's Datcá Peninsula. Although still retaining some forest, it is waterless and dependent on cisterns or tanker-boats, which has limited tourism. Most visitors come for the day to the photogenic harbour, which at the end of the 19th century supported a greater population (25,000) than Rhodes Town. Prosperity rested on sponge-diving, for which the island long held the Ottoman monopoly, and the related caïque-building industry. Although the Italian takeover of both the Dodecanese and the Libyan coast (where the sponges were harvested) failed to break the Greek hold on the sponge industry, World War II and the rise of synthetic sponges brought down the curtain on an era. War-related privations scattered the population to Rhodes, Athens and overseas, and today fewer than 3,000 call **Gialós** ❼ (the quayside settlement) and Horió (the hillside village) home. Some caïques are still fashioned in the Haráni boatyards, but the sponges sold from Gialós's souvenir-stalls are mostly imported from Florida and the Philippines.

Sými's self-government during the Ottoman period was typical of "infidel" communities providing a desirable commodity, generally left to themselves as

Gialós hospitality featuring traditional dress.

BELOW:
Sými harbour.

long as they paid a yearly tribute-tax (in Sými's case, a boatload of sponges for the sultan's harem). Two *dimogérondes*, or municipal elders, were elected for one-year terms each January: one presided over the local council and outstanding judicial matters, and managed relations with the Ottoman bureaucracy, while the other oversaw community revenues. The number of (male) voters was unlimited, although they had to be over 21 and under 80, literate, of sound mind, with their taxes paid up and no penal sentence pending. The local council was elected initially by acclamation, but by secret ballot after 1902.

Pédi ❽, the valley south of Horió ridge, is the only arable patch of land on the island; there is a small waterside hamlet, too, and some scraps of sand beach. Emborió bay, north of Gialós, offers a supplemented beach, a Byzantine mosaic floor and a small catacomb complex. However, most of the island's beaches are pebbly, and accessible only by arduous hikes or boat excursions; the favourites are Ágios Vassílios, Marathoúnda and Nanoú (the latter two have tavernas). Among rural monasteries, the most artistically distinguished are **Mihaïl Roukouniótis**, due west of town, with its vivid 18th-century frescoes, and (even better) **Sotíras Megálos Nerás**, south along the paved road to the gargantuan monastery of **Mihaïl Panormítis**. Being on the sea-lane in from Rhodes, this gets the most visitors, irrespective of merit; a small museum, a large pebble courtyard and a sombre memorial to resistance fighters executed here in 1944 are the main sights.

Kastellórizo (Megísti)

Kastellórizo, some 70 nautical miles east of Rhodes in the shadow of Anatolia, has similarly come down in the world. At the turn of the 19th century, this limestone dot on the map had a population of over 10,000 thanks to the best natural harbour between Piraeus and Beirut, and the schooner fleet based here. But the fleet was sold rather than motorised; the island was heavily shelled during World War I while occupied by the French, then rocked by a 1926 earthquake and a 1944 munitions blast, which together destroyed three-quarters of the houses.

Most "Kassies" emigrated after the war to Rhodes and Western Australia. Barely clinging to life in a virtual ghost town, the US Government even tried to convince Greece to cede the island to Turkey in 1964, in return for limited hegemony in Cyprus. Geopolitical realities still prevail; the islanders are obliged to get everything from haircuts to fresh vegetables across the way in Turkish Kaş, where a number of Turks are of part-Kassie ancestry.

In the end, it was pleasure-yachting and a film (*Mediterraneo*, filmed here in 1989) that probably saved Kastellórizo from desolation. A steady stream of (initially Italian) tourists has revived its fortunes, along with an airport and other government subsidies. There are no beaches and little to see other than rural monasteries, an ancient acropolis, a sea-cave entered only by boat and a tiny red-stone Crusader castle that gives the island its Italianate name. But the social scale of **Kastellórizo Town** ❾ is cosy, and the nightlife surprisingly lively.

TIP

If you decide to buy a natural sponge as a souvenir of Sými, make sure to ask for one that has not been bleached. Bleach is used to make the sponge look more inviting, but it also weakens the fibres.

BELOW: the huge monastery of Mihaïl Panormítis, Sými.

Tílos and Nísyros

Map, page 254

Seahorse-shaped **Tílos**, north of Hálki and west of Rhodes, is the least maritime of these islands. With fertile volcanic soil and sufficient ground water, the islanders instead made Tílos the granary of the Dodecanese. Since the late 1980s, discerning tourists have been attracted by tranquillity, some fine beaches and good hiking opportunities. Historically there were just two villages, imaginatively named **Mikró Horió ⑩** (Little Village, in the east) and **Megálo Horió ⑪** (Big Village, in the west), continually at odds with each other. Mikró was abandoned after World War II in favour of **Livádia ⑫**, the port and main tourist resort. The rivalry supposedly ended with the election in 1998 of a single municipal council – the only sensible solution for a registered population of 500.

The crags above the plains hide seven small castles of the Knights of St John, as well as several medieval chapels. Éristos in the west is the largest and (arguably) best beach; inland extends a great *kámbos* planted with citrus, the whole surveyed by Megálo Horió. In the far west, **Agíou Pandelímona** is the main monastery, and venue for the principal festival (25–7 July, annually).

Circular **Nísyros**, between Tílos and Kós, is not merely "volcanic", as it is often described, but is actually a volcano – a dormant one that last erupted in 1933. Accordingly, what water exists here is sulphur-tainted, but the island is paradoxically green with oak, almond and other plants that thrive on volcanic soil. Once you're away from the harbour, **Mandráki ⑬**, the port and capital, is attractive with its close-packed houses overawed by Panagí Spilianí, installed in the inevitable Knights' castle, and the even more imposing remains of the 7th-century BC Doric citadel of **Paleókastro** just south. **Pálli ⑭** is the alternative port for fishermen and yachties, just east of the mineral-water spa. You don't

Nísyros is nicknamed the "Polo Mint island", thanks to its clusters of white cube houses and its hole in the middle – the hissing crater of Polyvótis volcano.

BELOW: Kastellórizo.

come to Nísyros for beach life, but on the east coast Liés and Pahiá Ámmos are more than decent.

There are two inland villages: **Emborió**, essentially abandoned and bought up by outsiders, and the more thriving **Nikiá** ⓯ in the southwest, at the edge of the volcanic caldera created in 1422 when the (originally much taller) island blew its top. Coach tours of tourists based in Kós descend periodically, but otherwise the lifeless crater-floor, with its hissing steam-vents and sulphurous smell, is deserted.

Kós

The second-largest Dodecanese island in population, **Kós** is also tied for second in size with Kárpathos. It follows the lead of Rhodes in most things: a shared history, give or take a few years; a similar Knights' castle guarding the harbour, plus a skyline of palms and minarets; and an agricultural economy displaced by tourism. However, Kós is much smaller than Rhodes, and much flatter – amazingly so – with only one mountain, Díkeos. The margin of the island is fringed by excellent beaches, most easily reached by motorbike or even pushbike.

An earthquake in 1933 devastated most of **Kós Town** ⓰, but gave Italian archeologists a perfect excuse to comprehensively excavate the ancient city. Hence much of the town centre is an archeological park, with the ruins of the **Roman agora** (the eastern excavation) lapping up to the 18th-century **Loggia Mosque** and the millennial **Plane Tree of Hippocrates**, not really quite old enough to be contemporary with the great ancient healer. The western digs offer covered mosaics and the colonnade of an indoor running-track; just south stand an odeion and the **Casa Romana**, a restored Roman villa with more mosaics and murals (open Tue–Sun 8.30am–3pm; entrance fee).

BELOW: mosaic in the Hellenistic Asklepeion, Kós.

The Italian-founded **Archeological Museum** (open Tue–Sun 8am–2.30pm; entrance fee) has a predictable Latin bias in exhibits, although the highlighted statue, purportedly of Hippocrates the father of medicine, is in fact Hellenistic. Hippocrates himself (*circa* 460–370 BC) was born and practised here, but probably died just before the **Asklepeion**, the ancient medical school 4 km (2½ miles) southwest of town, was established. The site (open Tue–Sun 8am–7pm; closing earlier in winter; entrance fee) impresses more for its position overlooking the straits with Turkey than any structures, for the masonry was thoroughly pilfered by the Knights to build their enormous castle, which – unlike the one at Rhodes – was strictly military.

Between the Asklepeion and Kós Town, pause at **Platáni**, roughly halfway, to dine at one of three excellent Turkish-run tavernas – although as on Rhodes, most local Muslims have chosen to emigrate to Turkey since the 1960s. There was a small Jewish community here too, wiped out with the Rhodian one in 1944, leaving behind only the marvellous Art Deco **synagogue** by the town agora.

The road east of town dead-ends at **Brós Thermá**, enjoyable hot springs which run directly into the sea. West of town are the package resorts of **Tingáki** and **Marmári** with long white beaches, and the less frantic **Mastihári** ⓱, with a broader beach and a commuter boat to Kálymnos. In the far southwest, facing

Nísyros, are the most scenic and sheltered beaches, with names like "Sunny" and "Magic"; at nearby **Ágios Stéfanos** , twin 6th-century basilicas are the best of several early Christian monuments on the island. The Kéfalos headland beyond saw the earliest habitation of Kós: Asprí Pétra cave, home to Neolithic man, and Classical Astypalia, birthplace of Hippocrates, with its remaining little theatre.

On the western flank of Mount Díkeos, the Byzantines had their island capital at old Pýli, today a jumble of ruins below a castle at the head of a spring-fed canyon. Closer to the 846-metre (2,776-ft) peak cluster the appealing villages collectively known as **Asfendioú**, on the forested north-facing slopes looking to Anatolia. At Ziá, tavernas seem more numerous than permanent inhabitants. Asómati's vernacular houses are slowly being bought up and restored by foreigners.

Kálymnos

First impressions of **Kálymnos**, north of Kós, are of an arid, mountainous landmass, and a decidedly masculine energy to the main port town of **Póthia** . The now almost-vanished sponge industry has left many reminders: Kálymniot *salónia* crowded with huge sponges and shell-encrusted amphoras, souvenir shops overflowing with smaller sponges, and, more ominously, various crippled old men.

In the old days, divers used to submerge themselves by tying heavy stones to their waists. Holding their breath, they retrieved the rock-bound sponges spied from the surface; they could usually get two or three before they had to resurface. Better divers could reach a depth of 10 fathoms before the "machine" was introduced late in the 19th century. The "machine" is the local term for the first diving apparatus, a rubber suit with a bronze helmet connected to a long

Map, page 254

Brightly coloured embroidered cushions in Kós Town's Old Bazaar.

BELOW: the Plane Tree of Hippocrates and the minaret of the Loggia Mosque.

rubber hose and a hand-powered air pump. The diver was given enough air-hose for his final depth, where he could stay a long time owing to the constant air supply.

Too long, as it soon turned out – compressed air delivered to divers at the new, greater depths bubbled out of solution in their bloodstream as they rose, invariably too rapidly. The results of this nitrogen embolism – informally known as "the bends" – included deafness, incontinence, paralysis and often death. By the 1950s this had been understood and the carnage halted, but it was too late for hundreds of Kalymniot crewmen.

To the northwest loom two castles: Hrysoherías, the Knight's stronghold, and the originally Byzantine fort of Péra Kástro, above the medieval capital of **Horió** ⓴, still the island's second town. Most visitors stay at the beach resorts on the gentler west coast between Kandoúni and Massoúri, with **Myrtiés** ㉑ the most developed of these, and also the port for the idyllic, car-free islet of **Télendos**. The east coast is harsh and uninhabited except for the green, citrus-planted valley extending inland from the fjord of Vathýs.

Astypálea

Lonely, butterfly-shaped **Astypálea**, stuck out on a subsidised ferry line between the Dodecanese and the Cyclades, would be probably more at home among the latter archipelago. The Knights did not make it this far; a Venetian clan is responsible for the fine castle at the summit of **Astypálea Town** (**Hóra**) ㉒, the most dazzling Dodecanese hill-village aside from a namesake on Pátmos. Houses with colourful wooden *poúndia* (balconies with privies) adorn the steep streets and until the 1950s there was also a separate hamlet inside the upper castle.

BELOW: preparing sponges on Kálymnos.

Map, page 254

Hóra aside, however, Astypálea is rather bleak, with only a few good beaches to the southwest (Tzanáki, Ágios Konstandínos and Vátses) plus a few more like those at Marmári and Stenó along the island's narrow middle. Most travellers stay at the uninspiring port of Skála, at more congenial **Livádi ㉓** west of Hóra, or at Análipsi (Maltezána) by the airport.

Léros

Léros, with its half-dozen deeply indented bays, looks like a jigsaw-puzzle piece gone astray. The deepest inlet, Lakkí, sheltered an important Italian naval base from the early 1930s onward, and from here was launched the submarine that torpedoed the Greek battleship *Elli* in Tínos harbour on 15 August 1940.

Today the main ferry port, **Lakkí ㉔** seems incongruous, an Internationalist-Rationalist-style planned town far too grand for the present token population. Its institutional buildings, long neglected as reminders of colonial subjugation, were finally restored in 2001. The local atmosphere is not cheered by the presence of three asylums for handicapped children and mentally ill adults. Substandard conditions in all of these prompted an uproar when exposed by the international press in 1988.

Mailboxes are highly visible.

The rest of Léros is more inviting, particularly **Pandéli** with its waterfront tavernas, just downhill from the capital of **Plátanos ㉕**, draped over a saddle culminating in a well-preserved Knights' castle. South of both, **Vromólithos** has the best, easily accessible car-free beach on an island not known for soft sand. **Ágia Marína**, beyond Plátanos, is the hydrofoil harbour; like Pandéli, it offers good tavernas. **Álynda**, to the north around the same bay, is the oldest established resort and has a long beach.

BELOW:
windmill on Léros.

Lipsí and baby islets

Lipsí, the small island just north of Léros, has like Tílos awakened to tourism since the 1980s. Lately it has also awakened to unwanted notoriety as the "Island of Terrorism", since alleged November 17 supremo Alexandros Giotopoulos was arrested at his villa here in July 2002. The island's fertile appearance is deceptive – there is only one spring, and up to four times the current impoverished local community have emigrated (mostly to Tasmania) since the 1950s. All facilities are in the single port town, built around the best natural harbour; smaller bays, with beaches, are found at Katsadiá in the south and Platýs Gialós in the northwest.

Beyond Lipsí are other tiny islets, which see few visitors outside of high summer. **Arkí** (pop. 40) clings gamely to life, its scattered houses dependent on solar panels and visits from yachts to the sheltered Port Augusta, with all tourist facilities. Across the way sprawls **Maráthi**, with a long sandy beach and two taverna-rooms. **Agathoníssi**, halfway to Sámos, is a metropolis in comparison, with 140 year-round inhabitants scattered in three hamlets; goats graze the mastic-and-carob-covered hills sloping down to pebble beaches.

Pátmos

Pátmos has been indelibly linked to the Bible's Book of Revelations (Apocalypse) ever since tradition placed its authorship here, in AD 95, by John the Evangelist. The volcanic landscape, with its eerie rock formations and sweeping views, seems suitably apocalyptic. **Skála** ㉖ is the port and largest village, best appreciated late at night when crickets serenade and yacht-masts glimmer against a dark sky. By day Skála sacrifices any charm to stampeding cruise-ship patrons; all island commerce, whether shops, banks or travel agencies, is here. Buses

BELOW:
monks in the
monastery of Ágios
Ioánnis Theológou.

leave regularly from the quay for the hilltop **Hóra** , but a 40-minute walk along a cobbled path – a short-cut avoiding the road – is preferable.

Just over halfway stands the **Monastery of the Apocalypse** (open daily 8am–1pm, Tue, Thu, Sun 4–6pm; free), built on the grotto where John had his Revelation. A silver band on the wall marks the spot where John laid his head to sleep; in the ceiling yawns a great cleft through which the divine voice spoke.

Hóra's core, protected by a huge, pirate-proof fortress and visible from a great distance, is the **Monastery of Agíou Ioánnou Theológou** (same hours), founded in 1088 by the monk Hristodoulos. A photogenic maze of interlinked courtyards, stairways, chapels and passageways, it occupies the site of an ancient temple to Artemis. The Treasury (entrance fee) houses Greece's most impressive monastic collection outside of Mount Áthos: priceless icons and jewellery are on display, although the prize exhibit is the edict of Emperor Alexios Komnenos granting the island to Hristodoulos. The Library, closed to all but ecclesiastical scholars, contains over 4,000 books and manuscripts.

Away from the tourist-beaten track, Hóra is filled with a pregnant silence, its thick-walled mansions with their pebble courtyards and arcades the preserve of wealthy foreigners. From Platía Lótzia on the north side, one of the finest views in the Aegean takes in at least six islands on clear days.

The rest of the island is inevitably anticlimactic, but the beaches are good. The biggest sandy one is **Psilí Ámmos** in the far south, accessible by boat trip or a half-hour walk from the road's end, and favoured by naturists. Beaches north of Skála include Melóï, with a good taverna; Agriolivádi; Kámbos, popular with Greek families; isolated Livádi Yeranoú, with an islet to swim to; and finally Lámbi, sprinkled with colourful volcanic pebbles, and an excellent taverna. ❑

Map, page 254

The Monastery of St John was built as a fortress to protect its treasures from pirates: there are even slits in the walls for pouring boiling oil over attackers.

BELOW: the monastery walls.

THE NORTHEAST AEGEAN

While the cosmopolitan eastern islands of Sámos, Híos and Lésvos once played a leading role on the world's stage, the scattered isles of the northeast are still relatively untouched by tourism

T he islands of the northeast Aegean have little in common other than a history of medieval Genoese rule. The northerly group, comprising Thásos, Samothráki and Límnos, has few connections with the south Aegean; indeed Thásos belongs to the Macedonian province of Kavála, and Samothráki to Thracian Évros. These islands, so conveniently close to the mainland, with a short summer season, inevitably attract Greek vacationers far more than tourists from overseas.

Lésvos, Híos and Sámos to the southeast once played leading roles in antiquity, establishing colonies across the Mediterranean and promoting the arts and sciences, though little tangible evidence of ancient glory remains. All three islands served as bridges between Asia Minor and the rest of the Hellenic world and were, in fact, once joined to the coast of Asia Minor until Ice Age cataclysms isolated them. Turkey is still omnipresent on the horizon, a mere 2 km (1 mile) across the Mykale straits at Sámos. Politically and legally, however, the two countries have often been light years apart, something reflected in the frequent unreliability of the absurdly overpriced short boat trips across.

LEFT: gold-leaf mosaic in Néa Moní monastery, Híos.
BELOW: a helicopter drops water on a forest fire on Thásos.

Thásos

Just seven nautical miles from mainland Macedonia, mountainous and almost circular **Thásos** is essentially a giant lump of marble, mixed with granite and schist, crumbling into white beach sand at the island's margins. Along with numerous illegal ones scarring the landscape, Greece's largest legal marble quarry provides employment for many; the cut slabs, lying stacked or being trucked about, are a common sight. In antiquity, gold, silver and precious stones were also mined here.

Ferries and hydrofoils for Thásos leave regularly from Kavála; there are also ro-ro services for drivers from Keramotí further east. Bus services around the coastal ring road are adequate, though most visitors hire motorbikes – Thásos is small enough for a long-day tour – or cars. The east and south coasts have the better beaches; the west coast has access to most inland villages. Honey, preserved walnuts and *tsípouro*, the northern Greek firewater, are favourite souvenirs.

Thásos's past glory as a wealthy mining island and regional seafaring power is most evident at the harbour capital of **Liménas** (or **Thásos Town**) ❶, where substantial remnants of the ancient town have been excavated by the French School; choice bits of the ancient acropolis overhead are nocturnally illuminated. The biggest area, behind the picturesque fishing harbour, is the agora; the nearby Archeological Museum is closed indefinitely for a major overhaul.

Beginning at the **Temple of Dionysos**, a path permits a rewarding walking tour of the ancient **acropolis**. First stop is the Hellenistic **theatre** (currently being re-excavated), a future venue for summer-festival performances; continue to the medieval **fortress**, built by a succession of occupiers from the masonry of an Apollo temple. Tracing the course of massive 5th-century BC walls brings you next to the foundations of an **Athena temple**, beyond which a rock outcrop bears a shrine of Pan, visible in badly-eroded relief. From here a vertiginous "secret" stairway plunges to the **Gate of Parmenon** – the only ancient entry still intact – at the southern extreme of town.

The first village south from Liménas, slate-roofed **Panagía ❷** is a busy place whose life revolves around the plane-tree-filled square with its four-spouted fountain. **Potamiá ❸**, further down the valley, is less architecturally distinguished; visitors come mainly for the **Polygnotos Vagis Museum** (open Tue–Sat 9.30am–12.30pm, summer also 6–9pm, Sun 10am–1pm; entrance fee), featuring the work of this locally born sculptor. Beyond, the road plunges to the coast

Thanks to frequent forest fires during the 1980s and early 1990s, Thásos is now three-quarters denuded of its original pine forest, which survives only in the northeast.

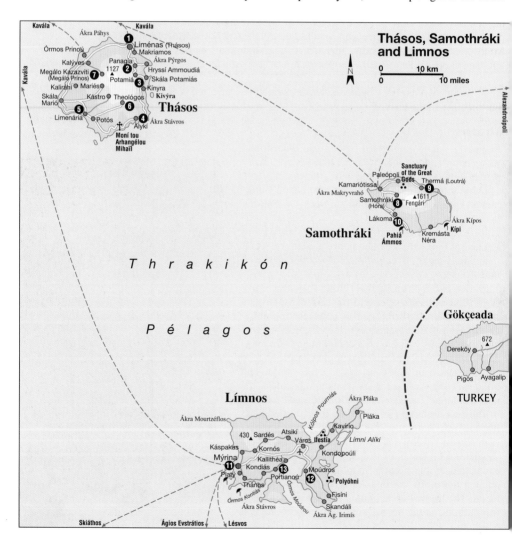

at Potamiá Bay. **Skála Potamiás**, at its south end, is purely lodging and tavernas, with more of that just north at Hryssí Ammoudiá; in between stretches a fine, blonde-sand beach. There are even better strands at **Kínyra**, 24 km (15 miles) from Liménas, but most one-day tourists schedule a lunch stop at the several beachfront tavernas in the hamlet of **Alykí ❹**, architecturally preserved thanks to adjacent ruins: an ancient temple and two atmospheric Byzantine basilicas.

Rounding the southern tip of Thásos, you pass three beach resorts at Astrída, Potós and Pefkári; only **Astrída** remains attractive, Potós in particular being an overbuilt package dormitory. At **Limenária ❺**, now the island's second town, mansions of the departed German mining executives survive; more intriguingly perhaps, it's the start-point for a safari up to hilltop Kástro, the most naturally pirate-proof of the inland villages. Beyond Limenária, there's little to compel a stop on the coast.

Theológos ❻, actually reached from Potós, was the island's Ottoman capital, a linear place where most houses have walled gardens. **Mariés** sits piled up at the top of a wooded valley, just glimpsing the sea; by contrast **Sotíros** enjoys phenomenal sunsets, best enjoyed from its central taverna shaded by enormous plane trees. Of all the inland settlements, **Megálo Kazazvíti ❼** (officially Megálo Prínos) has the grandest *platía* and the most numerous traditional houses, snapped up and restored in variable taste by outsiders.

Tomatoes drying in the sun – growing them is a cottage industry here.

Samothráki (Samothrace)

Samothráki raises forbidding granite heights above stony shores and storm-lashed waters, both offering poor natural anchorage. Homer had Poseidon perched on top of 1,611-metre (5,000-ft) **Mount Fengári**, the Aegean's highest summit,

BELOW:
a stunning bay
on Thásos.

to watch the action of the Trojan War to the east. Over time, the forest cover has receded from the now-barren peak, where modern climbers – on rare occasions – still have the same view, extending from northwestern Turkey to Mount Áthos.

Fengári (Mount Moon) and its foothills occupy much of the island, with little level terrain except in the far west. Tourism is barely developed, and the remaining islanders prefer it that way; in its absence the permanent population has dipped below 3,000, as farming can support only so many. Certainly an overpriced car-ferry from Alexandroúpoli on the Thracian mainland does not help matters. Boats and occasional hydrofoils dock at **Kamariótissa**, the functional port where hire vehicles are in short supply; although most roads are now paved, only the west of the island has a rudimentary bus service. **Samothráki (Hóra)** ❽, 5 km (3 miles) east, is more rewarding, nestled almost invisibly in a circular hollow. A cobbled commercial street serpentines past sturdy, basalt-built houses. From outdoor tables at the two tavernas on Hóra's large *platía*, you glimpse the sea beyond a crumbled Byzantine-Genoese fort at the edge of town.

Samothráki's other great sight is the **Sanctuary of the Great Gods**, tucked into a ravine some 6 km (4 miles) from Kamariótissa along the north-coast road. From the late Bronze Age until the coming of Christianity, this was the major religious centre of the Aegean. Local deities of the original Thracian settlers were easily syncretised with the Olympian gods of the later Aeolian colonists, in particular the *Kabiri*, or divine twins Castor and Pollux, patrons of seafarers – who needed all the help they could get in the rough seas hereabouts.

The sanctuary ruins (open Tue–Sun 8.30am–sunset; entrance fee) visible today are mostly late Hellenistic, and still eerily impressive if overgrown. Obvious monuments include a partly re-erected temple of the second initia-

A May Day wreath hangs on a door in Samothráki.

BELOW: looking back from the ferry leaving Thásos.

Map, page 268

tion; the odd, round **Arsinoeion**, used for sacrifices; a round theatral area for performances during the summer festival; and the fountain niche where the celebrated Winged Victory of Samothrace (now in the Louvre) was discovered.

Some 6 km (4 miles) further east, hot springs, cool cascades and a dense canopy of plane trees make the spa hamlet of **Thermá** ❾ the most popular base on the island, patronised by an unlikely mix of the elderly infirm and young bohemian types from several nations. Hot baths come in three temperatures and styles – including outdoor pools under a wooden shelter – while cold-plunge fanatics make for **Krýa Váthra** canyon to the east. Thermá is also the base camp for the climb of Mount Fengári, a six-hour round trip.

Villages south of Hóra see few visitors, though they lie astride the route to **Pahiá Ámmos**, the island's only sandy beach. From **Lákoma** village ❿, it's about 8 km (5 miles) by unpaved road to the beach, where a single seasonal taverna operates. Beyond Pahiá Ámmos, you can walk to smaller **Vátos** nudist beach, but you'll need a boat – or to drive clockwise completely around Samothráki – to reach the gravel beach of **Kípi** in the far southeast.

Límnos

Nowhere in the Aegean does legend match landscape so closely as here. In mythology, Zeus cast hapless Hephaistos from Mount Olympos (Ólymbos) onto Límnos with such force that the fall lamed him permanently. The islanders rescued the god, revering him as a fire deity and patron of metallurgy, an understandable allegiance given the overtly volcanic terrain of Límnos. Hephaistos re-established his forge here; now-solidified lava crags in the west oozed forth as late as the Classical period, reassuring Limnians that Hephaistos was at work.

The 4th-century BC statue of Victory (Athena Nike) was discovered in 1863 by a French diplomat, Charles Champoiseau, who immediately sent it to Paris. The Greek government has long demanded its return, but so far has had to settle for a plaster copy.

BELOW: goat herding on Thásos.

Garden urn in Plomári, Lésvos's second town.

BELOW: the poet Sappho looks over the waterfront in Mytilíni.

Dominating the sea approaches to the Dardanelles, Límnos has been occupied since Neolithic times, and has always prospered as a trading station and military outpost, rather than a major political power. The Greek military still controls much of the island's extent, including half of the huge airport, belying an otherwise peaceful atmosphere. The volcanic soil crumbles to form excellent sandy beaches, or produces excellent wine and a variety of other farm products; the surrounding seas yield plenty of fish, thanks to periodic migrations through the Dardanelles.

Most things of interest are found in the port-capital, **Mýrina** ⑪, or a short distance to either side – luckily, since the bus service is appalling. Volcanic stone has been put to good use in the older houses and street cobbles of Mýrina, while elaborate Ottoman mansions face the northerly town beach of Romeïkós Gialós with its cafés; the southerly beach of Toúrkikos Gialós abuts the fishing port with its seafood tavernas. Public evidence of the Ottoman period is limited to an inscribed fountain and a dilapidated octagonal structure – probably a dervish *tekke* (lodge) – behind a supermarket, both near the harbour end of the long market street. Festooned engagingly over the headland above town, the ruined **kástro** is worth the climb for sunset views. Mýrina's admirably presented **Archeological Museum** (open daily 8am–7pm; entrance fee) holds finds from the island's major archeological sites: Kabeirio (Kavírio), Hephaistia (Ifestía) and Polyochni (Polyóhni). These are all a long trip away in the far east of Límnos, and of essentially specialist interest.

Sadder relics of more recent history flank the drab port town of **Moúdros** ⑫ – two Allied cemeteries maintained by the Commonwealth War Graves Commission. During World War I, Moúdros was the principal base for the disastrous Gallipoli campaign; of about 36,000 casualties, 887 are interred outside of Moúdros on the way to Roussopoúli, while 348 more lie behind the village church at **Portianoú** ⑬, across the bay.

The road north from Mýrina passes the Italian-dominated Aktí Mýrina resort en route to good beaches at **Avlónas** and **Ágios Ioánnis**. In the opposite direction lie even better ones at **Platý** and **Thános**, with tiered namesake villages on the hillsides just above; continuing southeast from Thános brings you to **Nevgátis**, justifiably acclaimed as the island's best beach.

Ágios Efstrátios (Aï Strátis)

A tiny wedge of land south of Límnos, **Ágios Efstrátios** (Aï Strátis) is doubtless the most desolate spot in the northeast Aegean – all the more so since a 1967 earthquake devastated the single village. Thanks to junta-era corruption, reparable dwellings were bulldozed and the surviving inhabitants (nearly half were killed) provided with ugly, pre-fab replacement housing laid out on a grid plan. This, plus two dozen surviving older buildings, is all you see as you disembark the regular ferries stopping here on the Rafína–Límnos–Kavála route, or (in summer) the small Límnos-based ferry. Despite all this, the island has grown in popularity as a summer retreat, and you may just have company at the several beaches; the remotest are a tough 90 minutes' walk north or south of "town".

Lésvos (Mytilíni)

Greece's third-largest island, measuring 70 by 40 km (44 by 24 miles) at its extremities, distant, fertile **Lésvos** is the antithesis of the *nisáki*, or quaint little islet. Between its far-flung villages lie 11 million olive trees producing 45,000 liquid tonnes of oil a year. Shipbuilding, carpentry, *oúzo*-distilling and pottery remain important, but none rivals the olive, especially since it complements the second industry, tourism. Nets to catch the "black gold" are spread in autumn, after the last charter flight has left.

Early inhabitants were related to the Trojans; in *The Iliad* the Achaeans punished Lesbos for siding with Troy. Natives were later supplemented by Aeolian colonists, who – in a convoluted topography created by two penetrating gulfs – founded six city-states, the most important being Eressos, Mithymna, Antissa and Mytilene. Although they vied for political supremacy, Lesbos developed a uniform culture, nurturing such bards as Terpander and Arion well before Alcaeus and Sappho in the 6th century pushed lyric poetry to new heights, while their contemporary Pittacus (no friend of aristocrats like Alcaeus or Sappho) initiated democratic reforms.

With its thick southern forests and idyllic orchards, Lésvos was a preferred Roman holiday spot; the Byzantines considered it a humane exile for deposed nobility, while the Genoese Gattilusi clan kept a thriving court here for a century. To the Ottomans it was "The Garden of the Aegean", their most productive, strictly governed and heavily colonised Aegean island. Following 18th-century reforms within the empire, a Christian land-owning aristocracy developed, served by a large population of labouring peasants. This quasi-feudal system made Lésvos fertile ground for post-1912 Leftist movements, and its

Maps, pages 268, 274

The ancient city-state of Eressos in western Lésvos is thought to be the birthplace of the poetess Sappho; it has subsequently become something of a place of pilgrimage for gay women from all over the world.

BELOW: the harbour at Mytilíni.

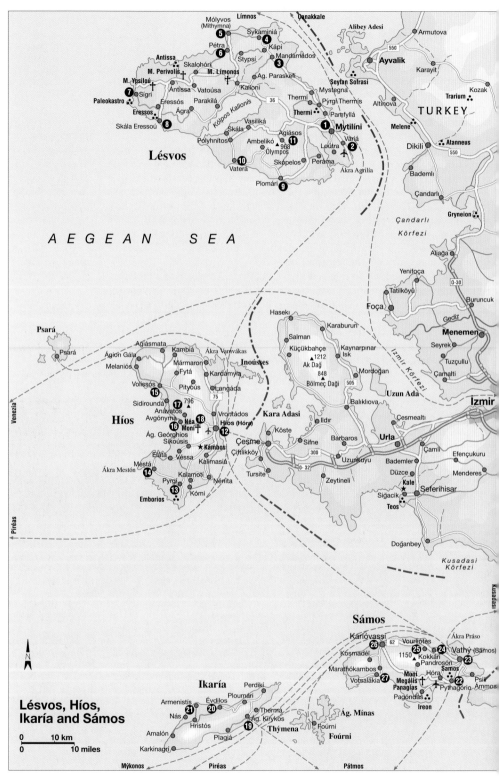

**Lésvos, Híos,
Ikaría and Sámos**

0   10 km
0   10 miles

Map, page 274

habit of returning Communist MPs since the junta fell has earned it the epithet of "Red Island" among fellow Greeks.

The years after 1912 also saw a vital local intelligentsia emerge, but since World War II Lésvos's socioeconomic fabric has shrunk considerably with emigration to Athens, Australia and America. However, the founding here in 1987 of the University of the Aegean brought hope for a cultural revival.

Mytilíni ❶, the capital (its name is a popular alias for the entire island), has a revved-up, slightly gritty atmosphere, as befits a port town of 30,000; it is interesting to stroll around, though few outsiders stay. Behind the waterfront, assorted church domes and spires enliven the skyline, while **Odós Ermoú**, one street inland, threads the entire bazaar, from the fish market to the now-disused north harbour of Epáno Skála, passing a mosque (ruined) and Turkish baths (well restored) en route. Behind the ferry dock stands the **Archeological Museum** (open May–Sep daily 8am–7pm, Oct–Apr Tue–Sun 8.30am–3pm; admission fee), spread over two premises; the new, uphill annexe features superb mosaics rescued from local Roman villas.

Also noteworthy are a pair of museums in **Variá ❷**, 5 km (3 miles) south of town. The **Theophilos Museum** (open May–Sep Tue–Sun 9am–2pm, 6–8pm; entrance fee) contains over 60 paintings by locally born Theophilos Hazimihaïl, Greece's most celebrated naive painter. The nearby **Theriade Museum** (open Tue–Sun 9am–2pm, 5–8pm; entrance fee) was founded by another native son who, while an avant-garde art publisher in Paris, assembled this collection, with work by Chagall, Picasso, Rouault and Léger.

The road running northwest from Mytilíni follows the coast facing Turkey. **Mandamádos ❸**, 37 km (23 miles) from Mytilíni, has on its outskirts the

Mytilíni's castle, one of the largest in the eastern Mediterranean, has been used and rebuilt by the Romans, Byzantines, Venetians and Ottomans.

BELOW: the Roman aqueduct that supplied Mytilíni.

A painting in the Theophilos Museum, Variá. A wandering tramp, Theophilos painted murals to earn a crust. After he died in 1934, his naive paintings became internationally known.

BELOW: the rooftops of Agiásos village, Lésvos.

enormous **Taxiárhis Monastery** with its much-revered black icon. At Kápi the road divides; the northerly fork is wider, better paved and more scenic as it curls across the flanks of Mount Lepétymnos, passing by the handsome village of **Sykaminiá** ❹ and its photogenic, taverna-studded fishing port. You descend to sea level at **Mólyvos** ❺, linchpin of Lésvos tourism and understandably so: the ranks of sturdy tiled houses climbing to the medieval castle are an appealing sight, as is the stone-paved fishing harbour. Its days as a bohemian artists' and alternative activities colony are over, however, with package tourism dominant since the late 1980s. **Pétra** ❻, 5 km (3 miles) south, accommodates the overflow on its long beach, while inland at the village centre looms a rock plug crowned with the Panagía Glykofiloússa church. At its foot the 18th-century **Vareltzídena Mansion** (open Tue–Sun 8.30am–7pm; free) is worth a look, as is the frescoed church of **Ágios Nikólaos**.

From Pétra, head 17 km (10 miles) south to the turning for **Límonos Monastery**, home to an ecclesiastical museum, before continuing west towards the more rugged half of the island, with its lunar volcanic terrain. Stream valleys foster little oases, such as the one around **Perivolís Monastery**, 30 km (19 miles) from Limónos (open daily 8am–1hr before sunset), decorated with wonderful frescoes. Beyond 10 km (6 miles), atop an extinct volcano, the **Monastery of Ypsiloú** contemplates the abomination of desolation – complete with scattered trunks of the "Petrified Forest", prehistoric sequoias mineralised by volcanic ash.

Sígri ❼ (90 km/56 miles from Mytilíni), a sleepy place flanked by good beaches, is very much the end of the line, though lately an alternate ferry port; most prefer **Skála Eressoú** ❽, 14 km (9 miles) south of Ypsiloú, for its beach; in particular numerous lesbians come to honour Sappho, who was born here.

Map, page 274

Southern Lésvos, between the two gulfs, is home to olive groves rolling up to 968-metre (3,173-ft) Mount Ólympos. **Plomári** ❾ on the coast is Lésvos's second town, famous for its *oúzo* industry; most tourists stay at pebble-beach **Ágios Isídoros** 3 km (2 miles) east, though **Melínda** 6 km (4 miles) west is more scenic. **Vaterá** ❿, whose 7-km (4-mile) sand beach is reckoned the best on the island, lies still further west; en route, you can stop for a soak at restored medieval spas outside Lisvóri and Polyhnítos, 45 km (28 miles) from Mytilíni.

Inland from Plomári, the remarkable hill village of **Agiásos** ⓫ nestles in a wooded valley under Ólympos. Its heart is the major pilgrimage church of Panagía Vrefokratoússa, which comes alive for the 15 August festival, Lésvos's biggest.

Psará

Scarcely 350 inhabitants remain on melancholy **Psará**, its bleakness relieved only by occasional fig trees and the odd cultivated field. Besides the lone port village, there's just one deserted monastery in the far north. Six beaches lie northeast of the port, each better than the preceding, though all catch tide-wrack on this exposed coast. A few tourists trickle over from Híos, on regular Miniotis Line ferries calling from both Híos Town and Limniá, near Volissós; big ferries call weekly from Rafína or Lésvos.

Híos (Chíos)

Although the island had been important and prosperous since antiquity, the Middle Ages made the **Híos** of today. The Genoese seized control here in 1346; the Giustiniani clan established a cartel, the *maona*, which controlled the highly profitable trade in gum mastic. During their rule, which also saw the introduction

BELOW: harvesting resin from the mastic trees, Híos.

A STICKY BUSINESS

The mastic bushes of southern Híos are the unique source of gum mastic, the basis for many products before petroleum was refined. It was popular in Constantinople as chewing-gum, and allegedly freshened the breath of the sultan's concubines. The Romans made mastic toothpicks to keep their teeth white and prevent cavities; Hippocrates praised its therapeutic value for coughs and colds; and lately practitioners of alternative medicine make even more ambitious claims on its behalf.

In the 14th and 15th centuries, the Genoese set up a monopoly in the substance; at its peak, the trade generated enough wealth to support half-a-dozen *mastihohoriá* (mastic villages). However, the coming of the Industrial Revolution and the demise of the Ottoman Empire was the end of large-scale mastic production.

Today, smaller amounts are generated in a process which has not really changed since ancient times. In late summer, incisions made in the bark weep resin "tears", which are scraped off and cleaned. Finally, the raw gum is sent to a central processing-plant where it is washed, baked and formed into "chiclets" of gum. Some 150 tons are produced annually, most of it exported to France, Bulgaria and Saudi Arabia for prices of up to $35 a kilo.

Tomatoes are strung out for drying in September.

of mandarin fruit, Híos became one of the wealthiest and most cultured islands in the Mediterranean. Local prowess in navigation was exploited by 150 ships calling here annually; Christopher Columbus apocryphally came to study with Hiot captains prior to his voyages.

In 1566 the Ottomans expelled the Genoese, but granted the islanders numerous privileges, so that Híos continued to flourish until March 1822, when poorly armed agitators from Sámos convinced the reluctant Hiots to participate in the independence uprising. Sultan Mahmut II, enraged at this ingratitude, exacted a terrible revenge; a two-month rampage commanded by Admiral Kara Ali killed 30,000 islanders, enslaved 45,000 more, and saw all settlements except the mastic-producing villages razed. Híos had only partly recovered when a strong earthquake in March 1881 destroyed much of what remained and killed 4,000. Today Híos and its satellite islet Inoússes are home to some of Greece's wealthiest shipping families.

Its catastrophic 19th-century history ensures that **Híos Town** or **Hóra ⓬** (pop. 25,000) seems at first off-puttingly modern; scratch the ferroconcrete surface, however, and you'll find traces of the Genoese and Ottoman years. The most obvious medieval feature is the **Kástro**; moated on the landward side, it lacks a seaward rampart, destroyed after the 1881 quake. Just inside the imposing Porta Maggiora stands the **Giustiniani Museum** (open Tue–Sun 9am–3pm; entrance fee), a good collection of religious art rescued from rural churches. Off a small nearby square is a Muslim cemetery with the tomb of Kara Ali – he of the massacres, blown up along with his flagship by one of Admiral Kanarís's fireboats in June 1822. Further in lies the old Muslim and Jewish quarter with its derelict mosque and overhanging houses; Christians had to settle outside the walls.

BELOW: a typical example of *xystá* decorations on a house in Mestá.

South of Hóra you pass through **Kámbos**, a broad plain of high-walled citrus groves dotted with the imposing sandstone mansions of the medieval aristocracy, standing along narrow, unmarked lanes. Many were destroyed by the earthquake, while a few have been restored as accommodation or restaurants. Irrigation water was originally drawn up by *manganós* or waterwheel; a few survive in ornately paved courtyards.

The onward road heads southwest towards southern Híos, with its 20 villages known as the **mastihohoriá**, built as pirate-proof strongholds by the Genoese during the 14th and 15th centuries. Laid out on a dense, rectangular plan, their narrow passages are overarched by earthquake buttresses, with the backs of the outer houses doubling as the perimeter wall.

Pyrgí ⓭, 21 km (13 miles) from Hóra, is one of the best-preserved *mastihohoriá*; most of its façades are adorned with black-and-white geometric patterns called *xystá*. A passageway off the central square leads to the Byzantine Ágii Apóstoli church, decorated with later frescoes. In the back alleys, tomatoes are laboriously strung for drying in September by teams of local women.

Some 11 km (7 miles) west, **Mestá ⓮** seems a more sombre, monochrome labyrinth, which retains defensive towers at its corners; several three-storeyed houses have been restored as accommodation. Such quarters are typically claustrophobic, so guests will appreciate the nearby beach resorts of **Kómi** (sand) and **Emboriós** (volcanic pebbles).

With your own car, the beautiful, deserted west coast with its many coves is accessible via attractive **Véssa**, the paved road eventually taking you to castle-crowned **Volissós** ⓯ in the far northwest. Around this half-empty village are the island's finest beaches – and scars from a series of 1980s fires which burnt two-thirds of Híos's forests. Between Kastélla and Elínda bays, a good road snakes east uphill to **Avgónyma** ⓰, a clustered village well restored by returned Greek-Americans. Just 4 km (2½ miles) north perches almost-deserted, crumbling **Anávatos** ⓱, well camouflaged against its cliff; from this in 1822, 400 Hiots leapt to their deaths rather than be captured.

Some 5 km (3 miles) east, the monastery of **Néa Moní** ⓲ (open daily 8am–1pm, 4–8pm) forms one of the finest surviving examples of mid-Byzantine architecture, founded in 1049 by Emperor Constantine Monomachus IX on a spot where a miraculous icon of the Virgin had appeared. It suffered heavily in 1822 and 1881, first with the murder of its monks and the pillage of its treasures, and then with the collapse of its dome. Despite the damage, its mosaics of scenes from the life of Christ are outstanding.

Map,
page
274

Detail from the Byzantine monastery of Néa Moní, Híos.

Ikaría and Foúrni

The narrow, wing-shaped island of **Ikaría** is named after mythical Icarus, who supposedly fell into the sea nearby when his wax wings melted (the Greek Air Force has adopted him as patron, apparently impervious to the irony). One of the least developed large islands in the Aegean, Ikaría has little to offer anyone intent on ticking off four-star sights, but appeals to those disposed to a decidedly eccentric environment. For three brief months after 17 July 1912, when a certain

BELOW:
local fishermen.

Dr Malahias declared the island liberated, it was an independent republic, with its own money and stamps. In later decades, Ikaría served as a place of exile for hundreds of communists; the locals thought they were the most noble, humanitarian folk they'd ever met and still vote Communist in droves – not quite what Athens intended.

Composer and former communist Mikis Theodorakis, best known for his 1964 film score for **Zorba the Greek**, *was held in a concentration camp on Ikaría during the Greek civil war.*

Ágios Kírykos  is the capital and main southerly port, its tourist facilities geared to the clientele at the neighbouring spa of Thermá. Taxis are more reliable than the bus for the 41-km (25-mile) drive over the 1,000-metre (3,300-ft) Atherás ridge to **Évdilos**, the north-facing second port. Another 16 km (10 miles) takes you past **Kámbos**, with its sandy beach and ruined Byzantine palace, to the end of the asphalt at **Armenistís**. Here only do foreigners congregate, for the sake of excellent beaches – Livádi and Mesahtí – just east, though the surf can be deadly. **Nás**, 4 km (2½ miles) west, is named for the *naos* or temple of Artemis Tavropolio on the banks of the river draining to a popular pebble cove. **Gialiskári**, a fishing port 4 km (2½ miles) east, is distinguished by its photogenic jetty chapel.

There are few bona fide inland villages, as the proud Ikarians hate to live on top of each other, keeping plenty of room for orchards between their houses. Above Armenistís are four hamlets lost in pine forest, collectively known as **Ráhes**; at Hristós, the largest, people cram the café-bars all night, sleep until noon and carry belongings (or store potent wine) in hairy goatskin bags. The surrounding countryside completes the hobbit-like image, with vertical natural monoliths and troglodytic cottages for livestock made entirely of gigantic slate slabs.

BELOW: the castle and harbour of Pythagório, Sámos.

Foúrni, one of several islets southeast of Ikaría, lives from its thriving fishing fleet and boatyards; seafood dinners figure high in the ambitions of arriving tourists, who mostly stay in the surprisingly large port town. A road links this with Ágios Ioánnis Hrysóstomos in the south and remote Hrysomiliá in the far north, the only other villages, but path-walking (where possible) and boat-riding are more relaxing ways of getting around. Best of many beaches are at **Kámbi**, one ridge south of port, or at **Psilí Ámmos** just north.

Map, page 274

Sámos

Almost subtropical **Sámos**, with vine terraces, cypress and olive groves, surviving stands of black and Calabrian pine, hillside villages and beaches of every size and consistency, appeals to numerous package tourists. Forest fires – the worst of these in July 2000 – and development have blighted much of the island, but impassable gorges, the Aegean's second-highest mountain and beaches accessible only on foot hold sway in the far west.

Sponges on sale, Pythagório harbour.

From the immense harbour mole at heavily commercialised **Pythagório ㉒**, constructed by Classical slaves and scarcely changed, you can watch majestic Mount Mykale in Turkey change colour at dusk. The port's shape suggested a frying-pan, hence Tigáni, the town's former name – perhaps too prophetic of what it's become: a casserole of lobster-red Scandinavians fried in suntan-oil. The authorities changed the name in 1955 in honour of native son Pythagoras.

The 1,040-metre (3,200-ft) **Evpalínio Órygma** (Eupalinos's Tunnel; open Tue–Sun 8.30am–2.30pm; entrance fee), an aqueduct built during the rule of the brilliant but unscrupulous tyrant Polykratis (538–522 BC), cuts through the hillside northwest of town. It is one of the technological marvels of the ancient world; surveying was so good that two work crews beginning from each end met with no vertical error, and a horizontal one of less than 1 percent. You can visit much of

BELOW:
the frescoes at
Megális Panagías.

The Archeological Museum in Vathý has a rich trove of finds from the ancient Sanctuary of Hera.

it, along the catwalk used to remove spoil from the water channel far below. One re-erected column and sundry foundations – the ruins of what was once a vast **Sanctuary of Hera** – lie 8 km (5 miles) to the west of Pythagório, past coastal Roman baths and the airport (open Tue–Sun 8.30am–3pm; admission fee).

Vathý or **Sámos Town ㉓**, built along an inlet on the north coast, is the main port, founded in 1832. Tourism is less pervasive here; the main attraction is the excellent, two-wing **Archeological Museum** (open Tue–Sun 8.30am–2.30pm; admission fee), with a rich trove of finds from the Sanctuary of Hera. Star exhibit is a 5-metre (16-ft) high, nearly intact *kouros* (male votive statue), the largest ever found. The small-objects collection confirms the temple's Middle Eastern slant of worship and clientele: orientalised ivories and locally cast griffin's heads.

Áno Vathý, the large village clinging to the hillside 1.5 km (1 mile) southeast, existed for two centuries before the harbour settlement; a stroll will take you through steep cobbled streets separating 300-year-old houses, their overhanging second stories and plaster-lath construction akin to those of northern Greece and Anatolia, though many are senselessly destroyed annually.

First stop of note on the north-coast road (12 km/7 miles) is **Kokkári ㉔**, a former fishing village now devoted to tourism. The original centre is cradled between twin headlands, while windsurfers launch themselves from the long, westerly pebble beach. Overhead loom the scorched crags of Mount Ámbelos (1,150 metres/3,800 ft); just past Avlákia a road climbs to the attractive and thriving little village of **Vourliótes ㉕**, named after its first inhabitants, who came from Vourla in Asia Minor, and justly famous for its wine production.

The coastal highway continues west, sometimes as a sea-level corniche route, to **Karlóvassi ㉖**, 31 km (19 miles) from Vathý. It's a sprawling, somewhat

BELOW: Vathý.

dishevelled place, little touristed and lumped into four districts. Néo, the biggest, houses post-1923 refugees and has cavernous, derelict warehouses down by the water, vestiges of a leather-tanning trade which thrived here before 1970. Meséo is more villagey, as are Áno and Paleó, lining a green valley behind the sentinel church of Ágia Triáda. Limín, below Áno, has most local tourist facilities, including a ferry service. The shore west of here has some of Sámos's best beaches, including sand-and-pebble **Potámi**, visited by most of Karlóvassi at weekends. Beyond here, you must walk to a pair of remote, scenic beaches at **Seïtáni**.

Karlóvassi lies roughly halfway around an anticlockwise loop of the island; head south, then east through an interior dotted with small villages of tiled, shuttered houses and stripey-domed churches. At **Ágii Theodóri** junction, choose southwest or east.

Going southwest takes you through Marathókambos and its sleepy, atmospheric port, Órmos, to **Votsalákia** ㉗, Sámos's fastest-growing beach resort. Less busy beaches like Psilí Ámmos and Limniónas can be found further west along the road curling around the base of Mount Kérkis (1,437 metres/4,725 ft), which forms the west end of the island. The mountain is usually climbed from the **Evangelístria convent** on the south or Kosmadéï on the north – either way it is a full day's outing. Returning to Pythagório, schedule stops at the roadside stalls before **Pýrgos** for a jar of local honey, and just below Mavratzéï, at the monastery of **Megális Panagías** ㉘, with the oldest (if rather smudged) frescoes on Sámos, dating from after 1586. The vast *platía* of **Pagóndas** village nearby hosts the island's liveliest *panegýri*, on the Sunday night of *Agíou Pnévmatos* (Pentecost). ❑

Map, page 274

BELOW:
Posidónio beach.

THE SPORÁDES AND ÉVIA

*The four "scattered islands" (Sporádes) are all different –
Skiáthos lively and busy, Skópelos quieter and beautiful, Alónisos
the least developed, and Skýros with its own unique culture*

Map
on page
286

T he scythe of **Koukounariés** ❶ on **Skiáthos** is used as evidence on thousands of postcards that the Aegean can produce the kind of beach normally associated with the Caribbean. Propriety would prevent as many postcards from featuring **Krasás** (colloquially "Banana Beach") because it caters for nudists. The fact that no one cares whether bathers at Banana Beach strip off or not is typical of the easy-going nature of the people of Skiáthos as a whole. The island has beaches for all occasions: some among the supposed 60 will always be sheltered wherever the wind is coming from.

Koukounariés and Banana are near-neighbours at the end of the twisting, busy 18-km (11-mile) road that runs along the south coast of Skiáthos. There are dozens of beaches along it and several more beyond it, many with a taverna or at least a kiosk selling drinks and sandwiches – a few now have lively beach bars and even bungee jumping. A path leading down from the road usually promises a beach at the end; with luck it won't be as crowded as Koukounariés. Round-the-island boat trips pass the rocky and otherwise inaccessible northern shoreline where the only human construction is the **Kástro** ❷, the abandoned 16th-century capital once connected to the rest of the island by a single drawbridge. For 300 years the islanders huddled on this wind-buffeted crag, hoping the pirates would pass them by. In World War II, Allied soldiers hid out there, waiting for evacuation. Today it is an obligatory stop for the excursion caïques after they have dipped into three technicolour grottoes and dropped anchor at **Lalária**, a cove famous for its smooth, round stones, and before proceeding to a beach taverna for lunch.

LEFT: Pánormos beach on Skópelos.
BELOW: Óhi Day celebrations, Skópelos.

Skiáthos Town

The bluff above the under-used beach at the end of the very busy airport runway has produced fragments suggesting a prehistoric settlement, but neither it nor the rest of the island have ever been properly excavated. Fires set by the Nazis destroyed most of the pretty pre-war town. But **Skiáthos Town** ❸ makes up in liveliness what it may lack in architectural merit. In fact, its nightlife is probably the most important consideration after the beaches for the type of visitor that Skiáthos attracts in intimidating numbers in August.

The preferences of the fast-living set change constantly, but it is not difficult to spot which places are in vogue, whether one's preference is for beer and blues, wine and Vivaldi, or tequila and 1950s rock. The lights are brightest but also the tackiest along **Papadiamántis**, the paved pedestrian street which bisects the two hills on which the town stands, and along the *paralía* or waterfront. The atmosphere is more pub and bar oriented around **Polytehníou** and the cobbled alleys above the port. Expect restaurants,

with international flavours as well as Greek, rather than tavernas, and be prepared to pay accordingly, especially along the seafront.

A moped or hired car – or perhaps a mule and a desperate craving to get away from it all – would be necessary to follow the unpaved roads looping through the mountains. They provide stunning views as well as the chance to pop into monasteries which, with Kástro, are more or less the only buildings of historic interest. Of these, the grandest and closest to town is **Evangelistrías**, with **Panagía Kehrías** and **Kounístra** also pilgrimage-worthy if the beaches should pall.

The permanent population of 5,100 also includes an expatriate colony in lovely houses on the **Kanapítsa peninsula**. The fact that they want nothing done to improve the deplorable state of the access road says something, as do doubts about the new – larger – airport terminal building. The island hardly needs to be able to admit more visitors than already arrive between mid-July and mid-September. Skiáthos has many devotees who return year after year – they know better and adjust their timing to suit.

The Church of Christ, a Skópelos landmark.

Skópelos

Skópelos's distinguished past is not so much demonstrated by prominent historical sites as by the exceptionally fine houses in **Skópelos Town ④**, a handsome amphitheatre around a harbour lined with bars and tavernas under mulberry trees. The island escaped earthquakes and Nazi vindictiveness and is therefore the most "authentic" and traditional of the three northern Sporádes (Skýros being in a class by itself). Slate roofs, wooden balconies, hand-painted shop signs and flagstone streets give it a serenity and dignity rarely found in Skiáthos in season. On the other hand, beaches are not the island's forte. It has far fewer than Skiáthos

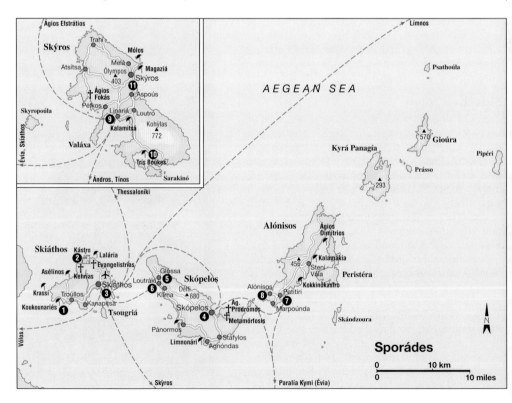

and Alónisos – mostly on the south and west coasts – though nudists are welcomed at **Velánio** just beyond the family beach at **Stáfylos** (where a gold crown and ornate weapons dating from Minoan times were found).

As compensation, Skópelos offers forested hills for spectacular walks to 40 monasteries and 360 churches, 123 of which are tucked among the houses above the port, which in turn is crowned by a Venetian castle planted on ancient foundations. **Glóssa 5**, the island's other town, is something of an oddity in that the people who live there have a pronounced dialect which, together with houses whose features are not like other island architecture, suggests that they immigrated from Thessaly. They seem to have made themselves welcome; other islanders refer approvingly to their "exaggerated hospitality". The main road on the island runs between the port of **Loutráki 6**, where Glóssa used to stand before it moved up the mountain for safety's sake, and Skópelos Town. It is an attractive run which includes a number of hamlets, beaches and **Pánormos Bay**, where there are a few remains of a city which probably existed in 500 BC. Now yachts park in one of its fjord-like inlets, and tavernas ring its shores.

Map
on page
286

Alónisos

On the hill above **Patitíri 7**, the last port on the Vólos–Ágios Konstandínos ferry and hydrofoil routes, is the **Hóra** (also called **Alónisos Town**) **8**, the former capital destroyed by an earthquake in 1965. This compounded the blow the islanders had already suffered when all their grapevines withered and died from phylloxera only a few years earlier. Alónisos seems to have been ever thus: the previous capital, Ikos, the name by which the island was known in Classical times, literally disappeared when the ground on which it stood toppled into the sea.

Children on Skópelos at the annual 28 October parade marking Greece's defiance of Italy's invasion in 1940.

BELOW: Glóssa is Skópelos's second town.

The submerged remains of the capital, off **Kokkinókastro** beach, are an important part of a Marine Conservation Park which may be explored with a snorkel but not with scuba tanks (this is a general rule in the Aegean to prevent pilfering and damage). The way the island has adjusted to its unrealised potential and bad luck is something for which many visitors should be grateful. Its people are laid-back and charming, its atmosphere cheerful and unpretentious. It is also the least developed of the Sporádes, a much quieter island surrounded by an interesting collection of islets. Some of them are off-limits to tourists and fishermen alike, protected areas within the Marine Park reserved for the endangered monk seal and other rare fauna. **Gioúra**, for example, is home to a unique breed of wild goat and also has a cave that is full of stalactites and stalagmites. It and **Pipéri** may not be visited but caïques leave Patitíri on calm days for excursions to the closer islets of **Peristéra** and **Kyrá Panagía**, where sheep flocks roam and there are a couple of monasteries to glimpse.

A good but winding paved road links the south with the north of the island, including an offshoot to the little yacht harbour of **Stení Vála** (which is the island's centre for research and protection of the Mediterranean monk seal) and the excellent, pebbly beach on a small, flat promontery at **Ágios Dimítrios**, 10km (6 miles) beyond Stení Vála. Otherwise caïques are an alternative form of transport, and there is a fleet of them waiting every morning at Patitíri to take bathers to the beach of their choice. The terrain is rugged and walking accordingly quite demanding, but exploring by motorbike or car is much safer here than it is on the winding gravel roads of Skiáthos and Skópelos.

The paved path from Patitíri up to the site of the 1965 earthquake looks and is steep, but the Old Town is served by a bus and is well worth a visit. Thanks

BELOW:
feline fulfilment.

largely to the efforts of foreigners who spied a bargain and bought up the old ruins, it is fast coming back to life. Boutiques are springing up in once-abandoned courtyards, and there are several bars and tavernas commanding stunning views as well as providing restorative drinks and delicious food.

Map on page 286

Skýros

Skýros was probably two islands originally, the halves joining near where there is now a road linking **Linariá ❾**, the main port, with the little village of **Aspoús** on the way to Skýros Town. The southern part of the island is mountainous and largely barren, and visitors are unlikely to venture below **Kolybáda** unless they are heading for **Pénnes** beach or the poet Rupert Brooke's grave in an olive grove at **Trís Boúkes ❿**. Trís Boúkes is about a 30-minute drive from Kolybáda, and Pénnes another 15 minutes more over a reasonably well-tended, wide dirt road.

The beaches at **Pagiá** and **Skloúka** just north of Kolybáda are lined with a growing number of summer homes, but have none of the appeal of the beaches in the northern half of the island. The real appeal of the southern part of the island is from the sea, for cliffs along most of the coast from Pénnes all the way around to **Ahílli Bay** near Aspoús fall straight down into the sea. These cliffs are inhabited by a few wild goats and seemingly innumerable Eleanora's falcons, which can be seen darting around the heights all the way over to Skýros Town. Excursions by boat can be arranged at the port of Linariá, where the island-owned ferry comes in to land.

The annual Skýros carnival takes place just before Lent, but in fact has its roots in a pre-Christian pagan festival.

Skýros Town ⓫ is on the northern half of the island on the east coast, high above the long sand beach that runs between the now contiguous settlements of Magaziá to the south and Mólos at the north end. Life in the town is played out

BELOW: Skýros Town.

A CORNER OF A FOREIGN FIELD...

It was quite by chance that Skýros became the burial place of the poet Rupert Brooke. When war broke out in 1914, Brooke first thought of becoming a war correspondent, but soon changed his mind and decided to join up. He enlisted as a second lieutenant in the newly formed Royal Naval Division, and briefly saw action at the fall of Antwerp. In the spring of 1915, he arrived on the island of Limnos, where ships and men had begun massing in preparation for the ill-fated assault on Gallipoli.

Moúdros Bay became so crowded that Brooke's detachment was ordered to wait instead off the bay of Trís Boúkes, in the far south of Skýros. Between manoeuvres, he and some fellow officers rested on shore in a small olive grove above the bay which, the others remembered, the poet particularly liked. Three days later he died of blood-poisoning on a hospital ship, aged 27; his fellow officers buried him in the olive grove.

Brooke was subsequently beatified in the eyes of a nation mourning its youthful heroes, even though he never lived to see the horrors of trench warfare. Today, the site can be reached by caique, a long walk from Kolybáda, or by taxi. There is also a memorial to Brooke in Skýros Town – a highly romanticised bronze statue of "Immortal Poetry".

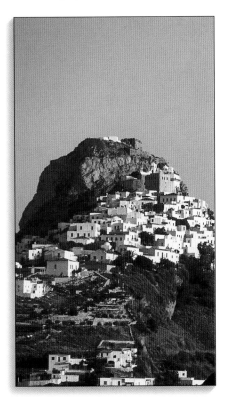

all along the meandering main street, which runs from the telephone exchange (OTE) to the raised, largely ignored square to the northern edge of town where the highly romantic statue of Rupert Brooke commands the view. A series of small side streets wander up to the **kástro**, the old Byzantine/Venetian castle on the heights.

The beach below town runs from Magaziá all the way down to **Mólos**, with more stretches of beach – not as attractive – farther along the northeast coast near **Polýhri**. On the east side of the island there are pleasant sandy coves at Linariá just past the port and Pévkos. The central section of this part of the island is wooded, as is the northern coast from just past the airport down to the little bay of **Atsítsa** which has, as required, a small taverna by the water. Beyond Atsítsa a driveable dirt road leads to the pebbly cove at Ágios Fokás with its excellent taverna and a few rooms leading eventually to the Skýros Town–Livariá road.

Évia (Euboea)

Évia, Greece's second-largest island (after Crete) lies just off the coast of mainland Greece, looking on the map like a large jigsaw-puzzle piece just slightly out of position. The island's main town, **Halkída ❶**, is close enough to the mainland for a small drawbridge and a new, far larger suspension bridge to make easy connection. Aristotle is supposed to have been so frustrated in trying to understand the tides here in the narrow channel, which are highly irregular and sometimes quite fast, that he jumped into the waters.

Halkída is a brash industrial town, but the **kástro** with its mosque and church of **Agía Paraskeví** are worth visiting, as is the Archeological Museum in the new town. There is also a synagogue, built in the middle of the 19th century and still

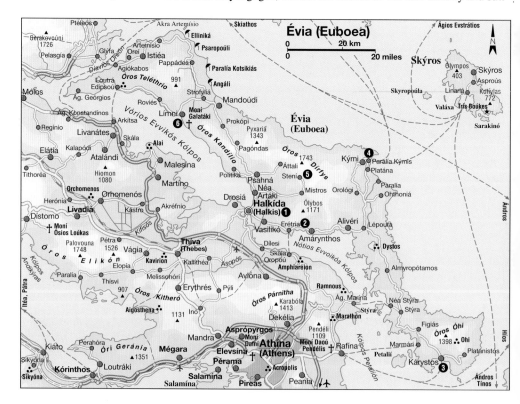

Map on page 290

used by the very small but active Jewish Romaniote community. **Erétria ❷** to the south is a crowded summer resort town where the ferries land from **Skála Oropoú** on the mainland. As with Halkída, Erétria is a town to pass through, but the small **Archeological Museum** on the west side of town is very good.

In general, the southern part of the island is drier and less green. The coastal road from Erétria is dotted with villages and summer homes until just before **Alivéri** where it turns inland. The turning for the south, notably the prosperous seaside town of **Kárystos ❸**, is at **Lépoura**. From here the main road forges eastwards through the hamlet of **Háni Avlonaríou**, with the large and unusual 14th-century church of **Ágios Dimítrios**, before continuing through often beautiful hilly farmland to drop down on the east coast to **Paralía** (or **Stómio**) where a small river reaches the sea. The wide road then runs along the shore through **Platána** to the harbour at **Paralía Kýmis ❹** and the boat to Skýros. North of Halkída, the small village of **Stení ❺** on the slopes of **Mount Dírfys** is a favourite goal for Athenians seeking clean air and grill restaurants. **Límni ❻** on the west coast is a pretty and convenient 19th-century seaside village, although the beaches are unimpressive.

A long stretch of truly outstanding beach lies farther north, after the ancient but still functioning baths at **Loutrá Edipsoú**, from **Gregolímano** and **Ágios Geórgios** all the way around the triangular point of the peninsula. The east coast is mountainous, with rocky shoulders dropping sharply down to the sea, but there are a few beaches worth seeking out. They include **Angáli**, **Paralía Kotsikiás**, **Psaropoúli** and **Ellinká**, of which the last is the smallest and prettiest. The famous bronze statue of Poseidon poised to throw a spear, now in the National Museum, was found in the sea off **Cape Artemesion** on the northern coast in 1928. ❑

BELOW:
Halkída, Évia.

CORFU

Few places have been as exploited and developed for tourism as Corfu. Yet, away from the package-tour resorts, there is much to savour on this beautiful green island

Maps:
Town 294
Island 296

S trategically poised between the Ionian and Adriatic seas, just off the Greek mainland, Corfu (Kérkyra) has an unsurprisingly turbulent history and a long catalogue of invaders. The Venetians in particular left a rich legacy of olive groves, which still form much of the island's vegetation. Despite a million-plus visitors a year, tourism has not entirely steamrolled the entire island: 10 km (6 miles) from the most brazen fleshpots you can drive along a one-lane potholed road through sleepy villages whose inhabitants stare or wave at you.

Habitation dates back 50,000 years, although Corfu enters history as "Corcyra" in the 8th century BC, when it was colonised by ancient Corinth. By the 5th century BC, Corcyra had become a major, independent naval power, siding with Athens against Sparta (and Corinth) in the Peloponnesian Wars.

Nearly eight centuries of Byzantine tenure from AD 395 brought a measure of stability and prosperity; but latter years saw incursions by "barbarians", the Norman-Angevin Kingdom of the Two Sicilies, the Despotate of Epirus, and the Venetians. Weary of misrule and piracy, in 1386 the Corfiots submitted voluntarily to Venetian rule, in place for 411 years despite four Ottoman sieges. Napoleon dissolved what remained of the Venetian Empire in 1797, and the French held the island until 1814 (except for the brief reign of the Ottoman-Russian-controlled "Septinsular Republic"). The British held sway between 1814 and 1864, when all the Ionian Islands were ceded as a sweetener for George I's ascent of the Greek throne.

During World War I, Corfu was the final destination of a retreating Serbian army; memorials and cemeteries from that era remain. World War II saw Kérkyra Town suffer extensive damage under a German bombardment to displace the Italian occupiers, who had surrendered to the Allies. During a brief but brutal occupation, the Nazis deported Corfu's significant Jewish community.

LEFT: clear water off Corfu.
BELOW: Corfu Town's Listón.

A historic capital

Corfu Town, also known as **Kérkyra ❶**, occupies a central east-coast location. "Corfu" is a corruption of *koryfí*, "peak", of which there are two on a Byzantine-fortified outcrop transformed into the **Paleó Froúrio ❹** (**Old Fort**; open daily summer 9am–7pm, winter 9am– 3pm; entrance fee) by the Venetians during the 15th and 16th centuries, when they cut a canal to make the citadel an island. The Old Fort overlooks the **Old Port**, where the ferries from the mainland dock. The more complete **Néo Froúrio** (**New Fort**) ❸ to the west (open daily 9am–7pm; entrance fee) is strictly Venetian and offers superb views.

With its tottering, multistoreyed apartments and maze-like lanes ending in quiet plazas, the Old Town

constitutes a *flâneur*'s paradise. Vacant bomb sites still yawn near the Néo Froúrio, and many main thoroughfares are brashly commercialised, but the backstreets are surprisingly unspoilt, festooned with washing lines and echoing to pigeon coos. An elegant counterpoint is the **Listón ❻**, to the east, built by the French as a replica of the Parisian Rue de Rivoli. The name refers to local aristocrats listed in the Venetian Libro d'Oro, who were the only citizens with sufficient social standing to walk beneath the arcades.

The Listón faces the **Spianáda** (Esplanade) ❼, a large and grassy open space cleared by the Venetians to deprive attackers of cover. On the southern half of the Esplanade is the plain **Ionian Monument**, which celebrates the island's union with Greece in 1864. It is surrounded by marble reliefs displaying the symbols of the seven Ionian Islands (the *Eptánisa*). Nearby is the Victorian bandstand, where Sunday concerts are held in summer, and the Maitland Rotunda, dedicated to the first British High Commissioner. At the far end is the statue of Greece's first president (1827–31) and Corfu's greatest son, Ioannis Kapodistrias. Today the Spianáda hosts idiosyncratic cricket matches, an enduring British legacy, as is the enormous Victorian cemetery outside town, and the ginger beer that is still available at some of the Listón's cafés.

The Spianáda is also the focus for Corfu's famous Orthodox Easter celebrations. On Good Friday, each parish parades its *Epitávios* (Bier of Christ) to the accompaniment of uniformed brass bands, playing dirges that can make grown men weep. On Saturday morning the relics of local patron saint Spyrídon go walkabout, and the tunes gets jollier as people shower crockery from their balconies to banish misfortune. Fireworks top off the Saturday midnight Resurrection Mass.

*The Greeks call these west-coast islands the **Eptanísa** – the seven isles. But as Kýthira, the seventh isle, lies off the southern tip of the Peloponnese, it remains quite isolated from the others.*

BELOW: Paleó Froúrio, one of Kérkyra's two Venetian fortresses.

Corfu Town

0   200 m
0   200 yds

Map on page 294

Both music and Saint Spyrídon are integral parts of Corfiot life. Until it was destroyed by Nazi bombs, Kérkyra had the world's largest opera house after Milan's La Scala; there are still regular opera performances and thriving conservatories. A few blocks back in the streets behind the Listón is the 16th-century **Church of Ágios Spyrídon ⑤**. Spyrídon, after whom seemingly half the male population is named "Spýros", was a 4th-century Cypriot bishop whose remains were taken to Constantinople in the 7th century and then, in the 15th, smuggled to Corfu, where he is credited with saving the island from several disasters. His casket, prominently displayed in the church, is processed around town four times a year.

Across the north side of the Spianáda stands the imposing **Palace of St Michael and St George ⑥**, erected in 1818–23 as the residence for the British High Commissioners. When the British left, Greek royalty used it as a summer residence. The bronze toga-clad figure who stands above a lily pond in front of the palace is Sir Frederick Adam, Britain's second High Commissioner. The pool and its water spouts are there to remind people that Adam was the first to ensure Kérkyra Town a reliable water supply, with an aqueduct system still in use today. The palace's state rooms now house the **Museum of Asiatic Art** (open Tue–Sun 8.30am–3pm; entrance fee). Its collection of over 10,000 Asian artefacts is one of the most comprehensive collections of its kind in the world.

But the town's one unmissable indoor sight is the **Archeological Museum ⑦** (open Tue–Sun 8.30am–3pm; entrance fee), with superb late Archaic art. The star exhibit is the massive Gorgon pediment from a 6th-century BC temple of Artemis at Paleopolis, but for some the smaller, more detailed pediment of a Dionysiac symposium, equals it. Both came from excavations in Mon Repos

There was an old man of Corfu/Who never knew what he should do/So he rushed up and down/ Till the sun turned him brown/That bewildered old man of Corfu.

—EDWARD LEAR

BELOW: a Corfu brass band.

The Gorgon Pediment in the Archeological Museum of Corfu.

BELOW: the 13th-century Angelókastro.

estate, the birthplace of Britain's Prince Philip. Just south of this at Kanóni are the photogenic islets of **Vlahérna**, with a little monastery and causeway to it, and **Pondikonísi**, said to be a local ship petrified by Poseidon in revenge for the ancient Phaecians helping Odysseus.

The north of the island

The coast northwest of town supports busy resorts such as **Kondokáli**, **Komméno**, **Dasiá** and **Ýpsos**. The best beach along this coast is the farthest, at **Barbáti**. Beyond it, the mountains plunge more sharply to the sea and the landscape becomes more stereotypically Mediterranean, mingling cypress with olive trees. To escape the bustle of the resorts, wander inland on an uphill journey past quiet villas and olive groves to **Káto Korakiána**. Here, set in the grounds of an old Venetian villa, is the **Kastello Art Gallery** (open Mon, Wed, Fri 10am–2pm, 6–9pm, Thu, Sat 10am–2pm; free), which exhibits works on loan from the Greek National Art Gallery.

The mini-Riviera between **Nisáki 2** and **Ágios Stéfanos Sinión 3** basks in the nickname of "Kensington-on-Sea" after a clientele who stay in villas – there are almost no hotels – and enjoy secluded pebble coves. The adjacent villages of **Kalámi** and **Kouloúra** were beloved of the Durrell family. Lawrence Durrell wrote *Prospero's Cell* while living in the White House in Kalámi (now a taverna), while Kouloúra was the birthplace of his brother Gerald's *My Family and Other Animals*. Mass tourism resumes at **Kassiópi 4**, once a small fishing village and now a busy resort. The Roman emperor Nero gave a song recital here in AD 67, but only the crumbled Angevin castle recalls past prominence. There are several wonderful pebble beaches.

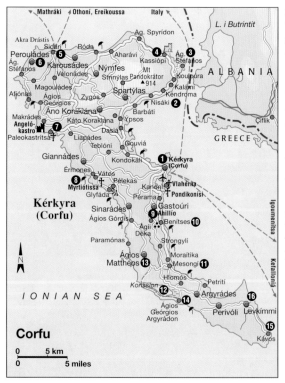

Map
on page
296

Alternatively, head up the north slopes of 914-metre (2,950-ft) **Mt Pandokrátor** to **Paleá Períthia**, a well-preserved Venetian-era village. Back on the coast, **Aharávi**, **Róda** and **Sidári** ❺ are three over-developed resorts. From Sidári ply the most reliable boats to the three small inhabited Diapóndia islets, Mathráki, Erikoússa and Othoní (the westernmost point of Greece). The town's finest feature is the series of striking rock formations that rise out of the sea at the western end of the resort.

The west-coast beaches beyond Sidári are calmer, beginning below **Perouládes** ❻ with its superlative sunsets, continuing through Ágios Stéfanos Avliotón, Arílas and Ágios Geórgios Págon. Beyond **Kríni** looms the shattered but still impressive Byzantine-Angevin **Angelókastro**, guarding the approach to the beautiful double bay of **Paleokastrítsa** ❼, once idyllic but now swamped. The best view of Paleokastrítsa is from the mountain above it, at the Bella Vista café outside the village of **Lákones**. Beaches resume at **Érmones**, but the small **Myrtiótissa** ❽ – beloved of naturists – or the big sandy beach at **Glyfáda** are better, while **Ágios Górdis** is a backpackers' paradise. Inland, **Pélekas** offers island panoramas from the "Kaiser's Throne".

The south of the island

Inland and south of Kérkyra stands the pretentious **Achilleion Palace** ❾, built in 1890 for Empress Elisabeth of Austria, then acquired after her assassination by Kaiser Wilhelm II. It once housed a casino, has also hosted European Union meetings, and is now a museum (open daily 9am–4pm; entrance fee). **Benítses** ❿ resort has seen its heyday come and go. The main street in **Moraítika** is one line of restaurants/bars/shops, but the beach is good. The older part of Moraítika is up on a hill just off the main road, and has no tourist development, just an attractive taverna or two providing a pleasant antidote to the hectic resort below. **Mesongí** ⓫ is marginally more pleasant, although an increasing amount of development now spreads back from the long but very narrow beaches. Behind the beach, Mesongí has some of Corfu's oldest olive groves, planted by the Venetians more than 500 years ago.

The main road turns inland here and reaches a crossroads at Áno Mesongí. Continue straight on to Halikoúna beach at the northwest end of the **Korissíon lagoon** ⓬, a protected nature reserve. From the village of **Ágios Matthéos** ⓭, you can access long, sandy **Paramónas** beach.

Turning left at Áno Mesongí, then leaving the main road at **Argyrádes** takes you to the coastal hamlet of **Boúkari**, spared exploitation by an utter lack of beaches. On the opposite shore lies **Ágios Geórgios Argyrádon** ⓮, a frankly unpleasant sprawl with only a splendid beach to its credit. The northernmost part of the beach is **Íssos**, which borders the southwest end of the Korissíon Lagoon. The Corfiots have deliberately quarantined the Club 18–30 at the far southeast tip of the island, at **Kávos** ⓯. **Levkímmi** ⓰, the underrated second-largest town on Corfu, with a picturesque river, goes about its business just inland, seemingly oblivious to its neighbour. ❏

BELOW: fruit seller.

THE IONIAN ISLANDS

Lushest of all the Greek island chains, the Ionians offer
superb beaches, great natural beauty and a distinct culture –
including a graceful Venetian influence in the local architecture

Throughout the Ionian archipelago, as on Corfu, the long Venetian domination (1396–1797) left an indelible mark. Culturally, these islands look west to Europe rather than north to the Balkans or east to Anatolia; only Levkáda had a brief period of Ottoman rule.

A heavy rainfall makes the Ionians among the greenest of Greek island chains. Olive groves and vineyards are reminders that agriculture, rather than tourism, still claim a part in the economy. However, this same unsettled weather has dampened many a traveller's holiday; from mid-September until mid-May, rains can wash out any beach visit quite without warning. The rest of the year, the northwest wind or *máïstros* substitutes for the *meltémi* blowing elsewhere in Greece.

Paxí (Paxós)

Small, hilly and green, **Paxí** (or **Paxós**) has a rugged west coast with cliffs and sea caves, and various pebble beaches on the gentler east shore. Paxí figures little in ancient history and mythology, and was systematically populated only during the 15th century. Here too the Venetians left a legacy of olive trees, and Paxiot oil ranks among the best in Greece.

All boats dock at the small capital, **Gáïos ❶**, arrayed around its main square and sheltered by the two islets of **Ágios Nikólaos** (castle) and **Panagía** (small monastery). Gáïos offers narrow streets and a few 19th-century buildings with Venetian-style balconies and shutters, plus most island shops.

Paxí's single main road meanders northwest through olive groves and tiny hamlets consisting of a few houses and perhaps a *kafení o* at lane junctions. Walking is still the best way to explore the maze of old walled paths, dirt tracks and paved lanes criss-crossing the island. **Longós ❷** on the northwest coast is the most exclusive resort, flanked by the popular beaches of Levréhio and Monodéndri. The "motorway" ends at **Lákka ❸**, favoured by yachts and the majority of landbound tourists; small beaches like Orkós lie nearby.

The satellite islet of **Andípaxi (Andípaxos) ❹** shelters two excellent beaches, mobbed by daytrippers in season, when three tavernas operate. Andípaxi's vineyards produce a heavy red wine favoured for local festivals, and a lighter tawny white.

Levkáda (Lévkas)

Levkáda is barely an island, joined to the mainland by a floating drawbridge over a canal dredged in ancient times. Yet Levkáda feels like one of the Ionians, with predictable Venetian influences on speech

LEFT: Navágio beach, Zákynthos.
BELOW: Vasilikí harbour, Lefkáda.

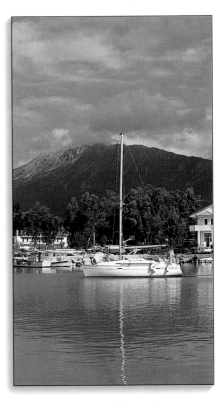

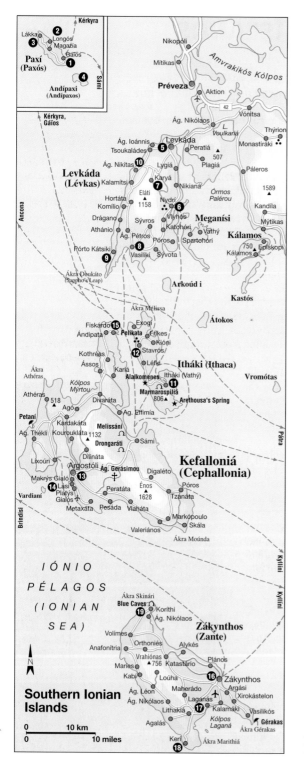

Southern Ionian Islands

and cuisine, plus the imposing fort of Santa Maura by the bridge. Levkáda's rugged landscape has preserved rural lifestyles in the hill villages; older women still wear traditional dress, while local crafts and foodstuffs are avidly promoted.

Levkáda Town 5 faces the canal and the lagoon enclosed by Gíra sand-spit, with safe mooring for numerous yachts on the southeast quay. Much of downtown is off-limits to cars; part of the main walkway is named for Wilhelm Dorpfeld, the early 20th-century German archeologist whose quixotic life's work attempted to prove that Levkáda was in fact Homeric Ithaca. Several ornate Italianate churches date from the late 17th or early 18th century; their Baroque relief work sits oddly beside antiseismic belfries modelled on oil derricks. Secular architectural responses to the 1953 earthquake could be termed "Caribbean-Tudor"; stone-built ground floors are often preserved, supporting lighter, half-timbered upper stories sheathed in corrugated tin.

Heading down Levkáda's east coast, the little port-resorts of **Lygiá** and **Nikiána**, with pebble coves and fish tavernas, are calmer than **Nydrí 6**, 20 km (12 miles) south of Levkáda, opposite a mini-archipelago of four islets. Until the 1970s it was a tiny fishing village, where Aristotle Onassis used to pop over for dinner from Skorpiós, his private island; now Nydrí is a busy package resort despite poor beaches. Some 3 km (1½ miles) inland, the Roniés waterfalls prove suprisingly impressive, revealing abundant water at the heart of Levkáda. Beyond this stretches a fertile upland, studded by churches with Venetian belfries. The main village here is **Karyá 7**, its vast central *platía* shaded by several giant plane trees.

Beyond Nydrí, Dorpfeld excavated at Stenó and is buried on the far side of sumpy Vlyhó bay. The island ring road curls past **Mikrós Gialós** and **Sývota** bays before descending to **Vasilikí 8**, 40 km (25 miles) from town, one of Europe's premier windsurfing resorts.

Map,
page
300

Beyond Cape Levkátas (Ákr. Doukáto) – from where Sappho legendarily leaped to her death – lie spectacular west-coast beaches, accessible by roads of varying steepness. **Pórto Kátsiki** ❾ stars on every third postcard of Levkáda; **Egremní** and **Gialós** are less frequented but nearly as good, while panoramic **Atháni** village has the closest tourist facilities. Further on, **Drymónas** has the best rural architecture, while **Kalamítsi** has an eponymous beach and "shares" Káthisma, Levkáda's longest, with **Ágios Nikítas (Aï Nikítas)** ❿. The only port actually on the west coast has become its main resort, worth avoiding in peak season.

Itháki (Ithaca)

Most boats dock at the main town, **Vathý** ⓫, at the end of a deeply inset bay. The town was badly damaged by an earthquake in 1953, but much has been restored. The attractive harbour front is known for its huge number of tavernas. To the south of the town are a number of sites supposedly associated with events in Homer's Odyssey. These include the **Arethoúsa Spring**, the **Cave of the Nymphs** and, near the port of **Píso Aetós**, ancient **Alalkomenes**. Above Píso Aetós is the island's deserted medieval capital of **Perahóri**. The route across the isthmus and along the west coast to the villages of **Lévki** and **Stavrós** in the northern half of the island is particularly beautiful.

Stavrós ⓬ is a pleasant but undistinguished town above the nearby beach and port at **Pólis**. Remains of the island's oldest settlement are on **Pelikáta hill** here. A road winds up past the little hill-village of **Exogí** to a chapel, from where there are spectacular views over the bay of **Afáles**. Another road from Stavrós leads to **Platrithiás**, which also has Mycenaean remains. The two lovely port villages of **Fríkes** and **Kióni** are ideal places to stay, but very popular.

In 1939 Itháki had a population of around 15,000; now it is nearer 3,000, thanks to mass emigration – particularly to Australia and South Africa – following the 1953 earthquake.

BELOW:
Itháki's main town, Vathý, by night.

Mountain goat, Kefalloniá.

Kefalloniá (Cephalonia)

Kefalloniá is the largest and second most mountainous of the Ionian Islands. Mount Énos, at 1,628 metres (5,340 ft), is the highest peak in the Ionian Islands; the summit is set aside as a national park to preserve the native Cephalonian fir.

Argostóli ⑬, the island's capital, is on the west coast on the large Argostóli Gulf. Almost completely destroyed in a huge earthquake in 1953, it has now been rebuilt and is a convenient base from which to explore. The town itself has a few attractions – a small but well-laid-out **archeological museum** (open Tue–Sun 8.30am–3pm; entrance fee), the fascinating **Korgialenios Museum** with its exhibits of bourgeois island life (open Mon–Sat 9am–2pm; entrance fee), and the **Foka-Kosmetatou Foundation** in a beautifully restored neoclassical mansion (open Mon–Sat 9.30am–1pm, 7–10pm; entrance fee). Just south of the town is **Votanókypos Kefaloniás**, a botanical garden set in an old olive grove which aims to preserve rare species from the island's flora (open Tue–Sat 10am–2pm, 6–8pm; entrance fee). Further south, across the Livathó plain, are the ruins of the island's Venetian capital, **Ágios Geórgios** (open Jun–Oct daily 8am–2.30pm; entrance fee), perched on a hill above the village of Peratáta. The views from the citadel's ramparts are superb.

To the north of Argostóli are the *katavóthres* ("sea mills"). Here seawater sinks into swallow holes, only to appear in the Melissáni Cave *(see below)* on the other side of the island. Although now just a trickle, before the 1953 earthquake the flow was strong enough to power flour mills. Continuing on along the western coast there are some good beaches beginning with Makrýs and Platýs Gialós at **Lási** ⑭, Kefalloniá's largest resort, and continuing all the way down the coast to **Kateliós** and **Skála** (the site of a Roman villa) on the south coast.

BELOW: in the huge Drongaráti Cave.
RIGHT: Melissáni is an underground lake.

Lixoúri on the Palliкí Peninsula the western side of the Argostóli Gulf can be reached by a frequent car ferry from Argostóli. The town itself is rather sleepy, but the **Museum and Library** (open Tue–Sat 9.30am–1pm; entrance fee) is worth a look. South of Lixoúri, across the earthquake-ruptured plain of Katogís, are the wonderful red sand beaches of **Mégas Lákkos** and **Xí**. Beyond Xí is **Kounopé-tra**, the huge boulder that used to rock on its bed until the 1953 earthquake set it still. The beautiful fine-pebble beach at **Petaní** is in the northwest of the peninsula.

Crossing the island, by the spectacular road over the col between Mount Énos and Roúdi, brings you to the port of **Sámi**. The harbour and the wonderful nearby beach of **Andísamos** were the locations for much of the filming of *Captain Corelli's Mandolin*, the book of which was set on the island. Close by Sámi are the caves of **Melissáni** and **Drongaráti**. The **Melissáni Cave** (open May–Oct daily 9am–7pm, Nov–Apr Fri–Sun 10am–4pm; entrance fee) is an underground lake with part of the roof open to the sky; when the sun shines down on the water it becomes a bright translucent blue. The large chamber of **Drongaráti** (open summer only daily 8am–8pm) is decorated with hundreds of stalactites and stalagmites. The main road south from Sámi leads to the pleasant resort of **Póros** and the excavated Mycenean tholos tomb at **Tzanáta**.

The northern part of Kefalloniá comprises sheer mountains whose cliffs fall preciptiously to the sea, as well as pretty villages that largely escaped the 1953 earthquake. The west-coast road is a spectacular, if rather worrying, ride. The famous beach at **Mýrtos** is impressive from above but consists of coarse pebbles and has a dangerous undertow. Further north is the perfect horseshoe harbour of **Ásos**. On the isthmus leading to a large hill that rises sharply out of the sea is a large 16th-century Venetian fort. However, the island's most upmarket resort is

Map on page 300

Kefalloniá is noted for its honey (thyme-scented), quince jelly, rabbit stew and a local speciality called riganáta – féta cheese mixed with bread, oil and oregano.

BELOW: the clear waters of Eblísi beach, Fiskárdo.

*A good catch
in Zákynthos.*

the small port of **Fiskárdo** ⑮, slightly too pretty and popular as a yachting harbour for its own good. There are many wonderful small pebble beaches, many of them backed by cypress trees, all around this northern part of the island.

Zákynthos (Zante)

Dubbed "Zante, Fior di Levante" by the Venetians, the central plain and eastern hills of Zákynthos still support luxuriant vegetation. The south and east coasts shelter excellent beaches, some almost undeveloped, others home to rampant and unsavoury tourism. The once-elegant harbour town of **Zákynthos** ⑯ was rebuilt after the 1953 earthquake in the same style; it may be not quite convincing but the Venetian atmosphere is still pleasant. At the southern end of the harbour is the church of **Ágios Dionýsios**, the island's patron saint, rebuilt after an earthquake in 1893. At the harbour's northern end is Platía Solomoú, surrounding which are the town's other main attractions: the church of **Ágios Nikólaos tou Mólou**; the **Museum of Post-Byzantine Art** with its superb 17th- and 18th-century paintings (open Tue–Sun 8am–2.30pm; entrance fee); and, tucked behind on Platía Márkou, the **Museum of Eminent Zakynthians**, chiefly dedicated to the poet Dionysios Solomos (open daily 9am–2pm; entrance fee). Above the town is the Venetian fort at **Bóhali** (open daily 8am–2pm; entrance fee): the pine-filled interior is very attractive and the views are wonderful.

At the southeastern tip of the island is the beautiful **Vasilikós Peninsula**, location of some of the best beaches on the island. The best of these is **Gérakas** on its western side. However, the beaches on Laganás Bay are some of the last few nesting sites of the Mediterranean loggerhead turtle. As the majority of visitors to the island are flown into the brash and raucous resort of **Laganás** ⑰,

there is an agglomeration of hotels, restaurants and bars, fast-food joints and discos along this coast, severely endangering the survival of the turtles. In response the **National Marine Park of Zákynthos** has been set up, encompassing the whole gulf between capes Gérakas to Kerí. All affected beaches have wardens to protect the nests, dawn-to-dusk curfews, and boating and land access are restricted.

The broad Central Plain is the most fertile region in the Ionians and is given over to intensive agriculture. One highlight is the **Skaliá Cultural Centre/Théatro Avoúri** near Tragáki, a series of stone-built auditoria where storytelling events are held. The village of **Maherádo** to the west has the pilgrimage church of Agías Mávras with its ornate gilded Baroque interior. Over on the east coast are the popular, and slightly tacky, resorts of **Tsiliví** and **Alykés**.

The mountainous west coast is much wilder, and sees far fewer tourists. From the cliffs at **Kerí ⑱**, on the southwest peninsula, there are incomparable views of the sea. A string of pretty hill villages runs along the western side of the mountains. The most attractive is **Loúha**, one of the highest settlements on the island. From **Kilioméno** the road runs north past **Kábi** where a huge cross on a headland commemorates a wartime massacre. Before Kábi, down by the sea is a beautifully situated *tavérna* at **Limniónas** where you can swim off the rocks. Further north, past the monasteries of **Anafonítria** and **Ágios Geórgios tou Krimnón**, is perhaps the Ionians most iconic tourist sight, the shipwreck at **Navágio Bay**, surrounded by towering white cliffs. Further on are the mountain villages of **Volímes**, noted for their honey and textiles. At the very northern tip of the island (Cape Skinári) are the **Blue Caves**; sun on the clear water here reflects an iridescent blue on the cave walls (boats run from the small port of Ágios Nikólaos and Alykés).

Kýthira – bridge to Crete

The island of **Kýthira** sees at least one ferry boat daily. Essentially a bleak plateau slashed by well-watered ravines, the island forms part of a sunken land-bridge between the Peloponnese and Crete. It is very much an in-between sort of place, with a history of Venetian and British rule like the other Ionian isles with which it, in theory, belongs; although it is now lumped administratively with the Argo-Saronics under Pireás. Architecturally, it's a hybrid of Cycladic and Venetian styles with an Australian accent, courtesy of remittances from the 60,000-odd locals who headed Down Under in the 1950s.

The island does not put itself out for visitors: accommodation is dear and oversubscribed, the season short, and good tavernas thin on the ground. Yet Kýthira seems increasingly popular, thanks to regular hydrofoils and flights from Athens. **Kýthira Town** is also one of the finest island capitals of the Aegean, with medieval mansions and Venetian fortifications. Far below, **Kapsáli** is the yacht berth, though better beaches are found on the east coast, as far as the fishing anchorage of **Avlémonas**. There are more castles to be found there and at Venetian **Káto Hóra**, just above **Agía Sofía cavern**, the principal west-coast attraction; the ravine-edge ghost village of **Paleohóra** in the northeast was the capital from 1248 until 1537, when it failed the pirate-proof test. ❑

The National Marine Park of Zákynthos was set up to protect nesting turtles.

BELOW:
old women in Vólimes, Zákynthos.

Map on page 300

CRETE

Greece's largest and southernmost island is characterised by soaring mountains, Venetian cities, a proudly independent people and unique remains of Europe's first great civilisation

Maps:
Island 308
City 310

Megalónisos (Great Island) is what Cretans call their home, and "great" refers to far more than size. It can certainly be applied to the Minoan civilisation, the first in Europe and the core of Cretan history. Visitors by the thousand pour into the ruins of Knossos, Phaistos, Malia and Zakros, before heading towards one of the scores of excellent beaches. With two major airports, Crete cannot be classified as undiscovered, but through its size and scale it manages to contain the crowds and to please visitors with widely divergent tastes. While a car is essential for discovering the best of the island, car hire is, unfortunately, comparatively expensive.

For more than half the year, snow lies on the highest peaks which provide a dramatic backdrop to verdant spring meadows ablaze with flowers. This, as botanists and ornithologists know well, is by far the best time to visit. The former arrive to view more than 150 species which are unique to the island, while the latter are thrilled by more than 250 types of birds heading north. It is in spring that the island is redolent with sage, savory, thyme, oregano – and dittany, the endemic Cretan herb. Bathing in an infusion of dittany is rumoured to increase sexual desire.

Crete, much more than other Greek islands, is a place both for sightseeing and for being on the beach. Minoan ruins are the major magnets, but there are also Greek, Roman and Venetian remains, and a score of museums. There are hundreds of Byzantine churches, many with rare and precious frescoes. If the church is locked; enquire at the nearest café. Even if you don't track down the key, you will enjoy the encounter with local people.

LEFT:
the harbour at Sitía.
BELOW: Iráklio
harbour and the
Koúles fortress.

Iráklio (Heráklion)

The capital of Crete since 1971, **Iráklio** has nearly a third of the island's population and is Greece's fifth-largest city. Although it vaunts the highest per capita income of any Greek city, this wealth does not show in the civic infrastructure. Indeed, much of Iráklio is a building site, thanks to a tendency to spend money on starting buildings without sufficient capital for completion.

Most tourists head for the Minoan site of **Knossos** ❷ (open daily 8am–7pm; entrance fee; *see also pages 318–19*). To fully comprehend the site and its contents, this should be combined with a visit to the Iráklio's outstanding **Archeological Museum Ⓐ** (open daily 8am–7pm, except Mon mornings; entrance fee). The tourist office is almost next door, and both are moments from the cafés and restaurants of **Platía Elevtherías** (Freedom Square) Ⓑ.

Iráklio's other major attractions are from the Venetian era, testifying that this was Crete's most

prosperous period in historical times. Head seawards to the old harbour and visit the **Venetian *arsenali*** (covered boat-building yards) ❍ and the restored **Koúles fortress** ❍ (open Tue–Sun 8.30am–3pm; entrance fee) whose three high-reliefs of the Lion of St Mark confirm its provenance.

A few minutes to the west of the old harbour on S. Venizélou is the **Historical Museum** ❍ with collections from early Christian times onwards (open Mon–Sat 9am–2pm; entrance fee). Head towards the city centre and the upmarket cafés of **Venizélou** (also Lion or Fountain) Square which takes its popular names from the stylish 17th-century **Morosíni fountain** ❍ and guardian marble lions. Overlooking the square is the handsome, rebuilt, Venetian *loggia* (city hall) ❍, flanked by the churches of **Ágios Márkos** ❍ and **Ágios Títos** ❍. Since 1966, when it was returned from St Mark's in Venice, the skull of St Titus, St Paul's apostle to Crete and its first bishop, has been housed in Ágios Títos.

Walk south through Odós 1866, "market street", redolent with tantalising smells, jammed with people and resonant with decibels, but now very touristy (the true city markets take place in Iráklio's suburban streets) and then west to the **Icon Museum** (open Mon–Sat 9am–1pm; entrance fee), housed in the small church of **Agía Ekateríni** ❍. It contains some exquisite icons, six of them by the 16th-century master, Mihaïl Damaskinos.

Challenging but rewarding is a circumambulation of the 15th-century **city walls**, in their day the most formidable in the Mediterranean, once besieged for 21 years. They stretch for nearly 4 km (2½ miles) and in parts are 29 metres (95 ft) thick. En route, pause a moment at the tomb of the great Irákliot author and iconoclast **Níkos Kazantzákis** to enjoy the spectacular views.

Walk Iráklio's Venetian walls and you will reach the tomb of local author Nikos Kazantzakis, of Zorba the Greek fame. His epitaph reads: "I believe in nothing, I hope for nothing, I am free."

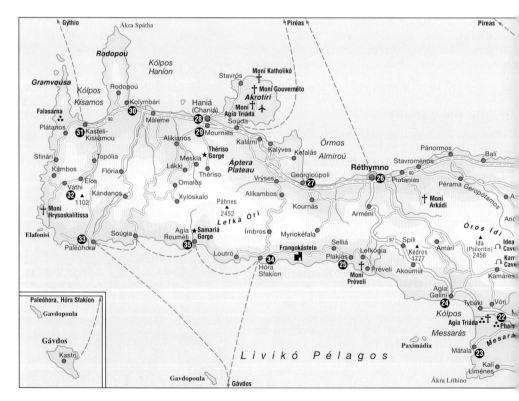

In and around the village of **Arhánes** ❸, 12 km (8 miles) south of Knossos, are three churches with interesting frescoes and icons, and three Minoan sites. Evidence suggests that when the **Anemóspilia** temple was destroyed, by an earthquake, a priest was in the ritual act of sacrificing a youth. This conjecture has outraged some scholars as much as Nikos Kazantzakis's books outraged the established Orthodox Church.

A steep climb from Arhánes (allow one hour) leads to the summit of **Mount Gioúhtas** (811 metres/2,660 ft), from where you can admire the panorama while griffin vultures soar overhead. Resembling a recumbent figure, said to be Zeus, the mountaintop has a Minoan peak sanctuary, a 14th-century chapel, and caves in which Zeus is buried. Perhaps this proves the truth of the aphorism that "all Cretans are liars" because to most Greeks, Zeus is, after all, immortal.

Týlisos ❹, 13 km (8 miles) southwest of Iráklio, possesses three well-preserved Minoan manor houses (open daily 8.30am–3pm; entrance fee) and is one of the few present-day villages to retain its original Prehellenic name. Twenty km (13 miles) further west on the same road, the village of **Anógia** ❺ is a weaving and embroidery centre. Many locals wear native dress but this is no stage setting: Anógia has a long tradition of resistance and revolt – the village was razed in 1944 – and its men and women are among the fiercest and bravest in Crete.

From Anógia the road climbs to the magnificent **Nída plateau** from where it is a 20-minute uphill stroll to the **Idean Cave** which was the nursery, if not the birthplace, of Zeus. Here the infant god was hidden by the Kouretes, who clashed their weapons to drown the sound of his cries, while the nymph Amaltheë fed him goat's milk. Strong walkers might wish to push on to the summit of **Mount Psilorítis**, at 2,456 metres (8,060 ft) the highest point on Crete.

Maps:
Island 308
City 310

TIP

It's usually possible to arrange for a taxi driver to drop you off somewhere and pick you up a few hours later. Alternatively, you can negotiate a private sightseeing tour.

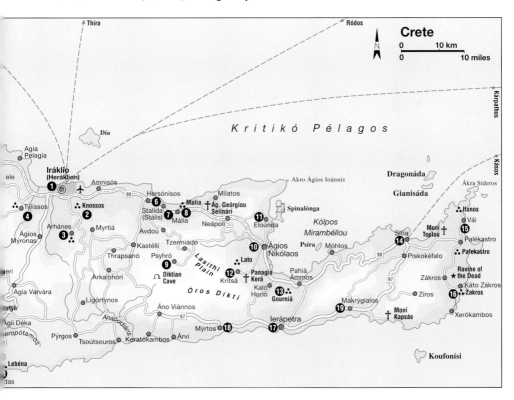

The Diktian Cave,
supposedly the birth-
place of Zeus. His
father, the Titan Kro-
nos, had been told
he'd be overthrown
by a son, so he ate all
his offspring. Only
Zeus survived, as he
was hidden here for
protection.

East from Iráklio

Return to Iráklio and continue eastwards along the national highway for 24 km (15 miles). You have reached the Cretan Riviera – a stretch reminiscent of Blackpool or Coney Island – with the resorts of **Hersónisos** ❻, **Stalída** (Stális) ❼ and **Mália** ❽. It is neither elegant nor ethnic: bars, heavy rock, pizzerias and fast food abound. However, the beaches are among the best and busiest.

The **Palace** at Mália (open daily 8.30am–3pm; entrance fee), traditionally associated with King Sarpedon, brother of Minos, is contemporary with Knossos. The ruins are not as extensive as Knossos or Phaistos, but even without reconstruction, they are more readily understood. The remarkable number of store- and workrooms suggests a wealthy country villa more than a palace. Recent excavations have unearthed the **Hrysólakkos** (Golden Pit) from the proto-palatial period (2000–1700 BC), an enormous necropolis with numerous gold artefacts.

From either Mália or Hersónisos, twisting mountain roads lead up to the **Lasíthi Plain**, 840 metres (2,750 ft) above sea level and 57 km (36 miles) from Iráklio. This fertile and impeccably cultivated land supports a cornucopia of potatoes and grain crops, apples and pears. For many years the 10,000 windmills here, with their canvas sails, served to pump up water from the limestone below. More recently, however, they have been replaced by diesel pumps. **Psyhró** ❾ is the starting point for the giant **Diktian Cave**, another birthplace of Zeus.

Onwards to **Ágios Nikólaos** ❿, 69 km (43 miles) from Iráklio, invariably abbreviated by tourists to "Ag Nik". Magnificently situated on the Gulf of Mirabello and overlooked by the eastern mountains, this was once the St Tropez of Crete. Between here and **Eloúnda** ⓫ (10 km/6 miles away) are some of the

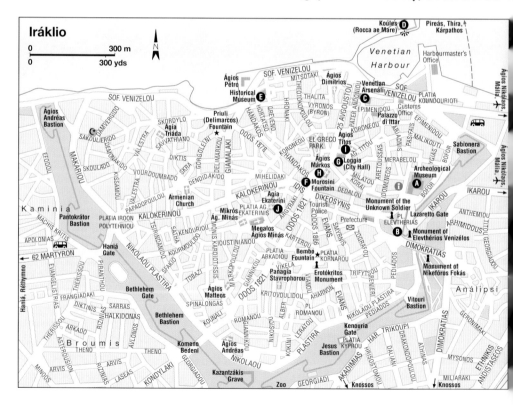

island's best and most expensive hotels, although Ag Nik does lack a decent beach, having built a football pitch over its best one. Hotels, discos and cafés cluster around Ag Nik's **Mandráki** harbour and **Lake Voulisméni**, 64 metres (210 ft) deep and once believed to be bottomless. Eloúnda's **Spinalónga** island, an isolated leper colony until 1957 (the last in Europe), with a ruined Venetian fortress and poignant memories, is readily reached from Ag Nik by boat.

Clinging to the hillside 11 km (7 miles) from Ag Nik is **Kritsá** ⓬, said to be the home of the best weavers on the island. Their brilliantly coloured work hangs everywhere – for sale – complementing the flowers and contrasting with the whitewashed homes that line the narrow village alleyways. Immediately below is the church of **Panagía Kerá**, Crete's greatest Byzantine treasure. The entire interior is an illustrated bible of 12th- to 15th-century frescoes. Until a few years ago Panagía Kerá was a functioning church; with changing times, it is now a museum (open Mon–Sat 9am–3pm, Sun 9am–2pm; entrance fee).

Leave Ag Nik and head southeast. After 19 km (12 miles), **Gournia** ⓭ (open Tue–Sun 8.30am–3pm; entrance fee), the remains of the streets and houses of a Minoan town, is spread over a ridge that overlooks the sea. In spring, when the site is covered with a riot of flowers and filled with their perfume, even those bored with old stones will be delighted to be here.

Sitía ⓮, 70 km (44 miles) from Ag Nik, is a laid-back town which, to the delight of visitors and the chagrin of locals, has not yet hit the big time. Here are the almost obligatory Venetian fort, **Archeological Museum** (open Tue–Sun 9am–3pm; entrance fee) and **Folklore Museum** (open Tue–Sun 9.30am–2.30pm; entrance fee), and an unimpressive beach. After a further 24 km (15 miles) is **Vái** ⓯, renowned for its myriad palm trees, large sandy beach and

Map, pages 308–9

The remains of the leper colony on Spinalónga island.

BELOW:
Ágios Nikólaos.

*The minaret of
Ierápetra's
Turkish mosque.*

tropical ambience. The palm trees are native, not from a desert island, and the beach is usually crowded.

Kato Zakros ⑯, 43 km (27 miles) from Sitía, is the fourth great Minoan site (open daily 8am–7pm; entrance fee), situated below the spectacular **Ravine of the Dead**, where caves were used for Minoan burials. The main dig has the customary central courtyard with royal, religious and domestic buildings and workshops radiating outwards; most date from 1900–1600 BC, the apogee of Minoan civilisation. Crete's eastern end is sinking below the water table, however, so they are often waterlogged.

Back at Gournia, a flat road crosses the island to **Ierápetra** ⑰ (35 km/22 miles from Ag Nik), the south coast's only large town and Europe's southernmost. Recently, Ierápetra has enjoyed a boom in both market gardening and in tourism, although it is hardly atmospheric; there is a promenade behind an average beach and a tiny Venetian fort. Fifteen km (9 miles) to the west lies the pretty village resort of **Mýrtos** ⑱, which takes advantage of mild weather to remain open throughout the winter. Eastwards 24 km (15 miles) from Ierápetra is the summer resort (and reasonable beach) of **Makrýgialos** ⑲, from where a side road leads to the 14th-century **Kapsás Monastery** set snugly into the cliffs at a gorge entrance.

South from Iráklio

Head south from Iráklio over the island's spine and you reach a breathtaking view of the **Plain of Mesará**, whose rich soil and benign climate make it an agricultural cornucopia. At the edge of the plain, 40 km (25 miles) from Iráklio, is the village of **Ágii Déka** (Holy Ten) with its heavily restored medieval church; fragments from nearby Gortys have been incorporated into its walls.

Map, pages 308–9

Gortys (Górtyn) ⑳ is 1 km (½ mile) further. This was the capital of the Romans, who came to Crete in the 1st century BC to settle feuds but who stayed and conquered the island. Outstanding are the Roman *odeon* and a triple-naved basilica, the latter by far the best-preserved early church in Crete, built to house the tomb of St Titus (open daily 8am–7pm; entrance fee). But the most renowned artefacts are some stone blocks incorporated into the *odeon*. About 2,500 years ago a 17,000 character text, the Code of Gortys, was incised on these – rules governing the behaviour of the people. The script is written in ox-plough manner – reading left to right along one line, then right to left along the next.

Those in search of more classical ruins, of health and of good swimming might wish to turn off and drive south to **Léndas** ㉑ (72 km/45 miles from Iráklio), before continuing to Phaistos. Nearby **ancient Lebena** was the port for Górtyn, and its therapeutic springs made it a renowned sanctuary with a temple to Asclepios, the god of healing. Traces of this, with mosaic floors and large baths, can be seen. **Phaistos** (modern Festós) ㉒, Crete's second great Minoan site (open daily 8am–7pm; entrance fee), occupies a magnificent location 16 km (10 miles) west of Gortys. State-rooms, religious quarters, workshops, storerooms and functional plumbing can all be identified; those purists who bristle at Knossos's reconstruction can let their imaginations run riot unhindered here.

Church bells at Mátala resort.

Next, on to **Mátala** ㉓, 70 km (44 miles) from Iráklio. The resort first gained renown when the sandstone caves in the cliffs around the small sandy beach became home to the world's hippies; Joni Mitchell stayed and wrote a song about it. The scenic 30-minute walk south to Red Beach is highly recommended, though **Kómmos** beach to the north is much larger and has a recently excavated Minoan site. The larger south-coast resort of **Agía Galíni** ㉔ also lies on

BELOW: the mountainous interior.

Arkádi Monastery,
Crete's most
sacred shrine.

BELOW: Haniá's
Venetian-built
waterfront.

the Gulf of Mesará, though a little further west. The harbour, with a short wide quay and a tiny main street jammed with tavernas and bars, is enclosed within a crescent of steep hills covered with modest hotels. Further into western Crete is **Plakiás** ㉕, with its five large beaches and spectacular mountain backdrop, 112 km (70 miles) from Iráklio.

West from Iráklio

Back in Iráklio, an oleander-lined expressway runs west towards Réthymno. Leave the new road 25 km (16 miles) from the capital to arrive in **Fódele**, a small village rich in orange trees and locally made embroidery. A restored house here is said to be the birthplace in 1545 of Dominikos Theotokopoulos, better known as **El Greco**. Fódele's fame may be fleeting for the latest word is that El Greco was probably born in Iráklio.

At Stavroménos or Plataniás, just before Réthymno, turn southeast for the beautifully situated **Arkádi Monastery** (80 km/50 miles from Iráklio), Crete's most sacred shrine for its resistance to the Turks. The elaborate 16th-century western façade of the church figured on the 100-drachma note.

Réthymno (Réthimno) ㉖, which prides itself on being Crete's intellectual capital, has an intact old town with a small, picturesque Venetian harbour; the quayside – choc-a-bloc with colourful fish restaurants – is guarded by an elegant lighthouse. To the west is the immense ruined **Fortétsa**, said to be the largest extant Venetian castle, with excellent views (open Tue–Sun 8am–8pm; entrance fee). The town's other attractions – the **Rimóndi Fountain**, the **Archeological Museum** (open Tue–Sun 8.30am–3pm; entrance fee) and the **Neratzés Mosque** – all lie between the harbour and the fortress. Venet-

ICONS AND EL GRECO

The artist El Greco (1545–1614), a Cretan native who studied under Titian, is best known for his portraits and religious pictures painted in Rome and Toledo. His highly distinctive style anticipated modern impressionism by his use of cold white, blue and grey colour schemes, and by his sacrifice of realism to emotional effect. His work also strikingly fuses Byzantine and Renaissance influences, a legacy of his early training as an icon-painter in Iráklio.

These icons were not objects of idolatrous worship, but this was precisely the indictment of the so-called iconoclasts in the 7th and 8th centuries. In an effort to purify the religion they proceeded literally to deface thousands of icons throughout Byzantium. Intact pre-9th-century icons are consequently very rare. The church of Agía Ekateríni here has a fine collection of icons, including a group by Mihaïl Damaskinos, a contemporary of El Greco. Both artists are thought to have studied at the church, all that remains of the Mount Sinai Monastery School, founded by exiles from Constantinople after the fall of "the City".

Only one work by El Greco can be viewed on Crete – *View of Mount Sinai and the Monastery of St Catherine*, in the Historical Museum (*for details, see page 308*).

ian houses with unexpected architectural delights line the narrow streets linking these sights, while minarets and overhanging wooden oriels give the place a Turkish-style raffishness.

Réthymno and – to the west – Haniá are joined by an expressway and an old road. Leave the highway after 23 km (14 miles) to enter **Georgioúpoli** ㉗ at the mouth of the River Armyrós. This delightful, princely hideaway has a good long beach and a eucalyptus-shaded square.

Haniá (Chaniá) ㉘, 59 km (37 miles) from Réthymno, is Crete's second city and its capital until 1971. It is a larger version of Réthymno and claims to be one of the oldest continuously inhabited cities in the world; its jewel is the outer **Venetian harbour**. Here, the quayside is wide and backed by characterful, colourful old buildings whose reflections shimmer in the water. The ambience is of the Levant and this is *the* place for the *vólta* – the evening stroll. The **Archeological Museum** (open Tue–Sun 8.30am–3pm; entrance fee) occupies the church of the Franciscan Friary, one of the best-preserved and largest of a score of still-standing Venetian churches. The medieval synagogue has been wonderfully reconstructed.

Those with a sense of history will visit Mourniés and Thériso, villages south of Haniá. The house in which Elevtherios Venizelos, father of the modern Greek nation, was born, now a museum, is in **Mourniés** ㉙.

West from Haniá

The road west from Haniá hugs the coast, passing several busy small resorts that merge imperceptibly, before arriving at **Kolybári** ㉚. Proceed westwards, passing memorable views of the plain of Kastéli and the Bay of Kísamos enclosed

Map, pages 308–9

Cans of olive oil in Haniá's covered market make colourful souvenirs.

BELOW: fruit and veg for sale in Réthymno old town.

within the peninsulas of Rodopoú and Gramvoúsa. The road makes a tortuous descent to the plain and to pleasant but rather characterless **Kastéli-Kissámou ③** (42 km/26 miles from Haniá).

Turn left at **Plátanos** and a twisting corniche leads after 44 km (28 miles) from Kastéli to **Váthi ㉜** and several splendidly frescoed Byzantine churches. From Váthi a poor road through a ravine leads in a dusty 10 km (6 miles) to the **Hrysoskalítissa Convent**. The name, meaning "Golden Stairway", comes from the legend that one of the 90 steps descending from the terrace is made of solid gold, invisible to sinners. From here, a barely negotiable road terminates at the broad sands of **Elafonísi**, bordering a shallow lagoon. Wade across to the island of the same name which has excellent beaches – hence very busy in high season – and you are at westernmost Crete.

Around the corner to the southwest lies **Paleóhora ㉝** (76 km/48 miles from Haniá), a relatively unspoiled resort with a choice of accommodation and restaurants and both sand and shingle beaches. **Hóra Sfakíon** (Sfakiá) **㉞**, 75 km (47 miles) from Haniá, is the capital of the Sfakians, who epitomise the independent and unmanageable Cretans. A small, picturesque port with a brave past, its sole *raison d'être* today – but don't tell this to the Sfakians – is a transfer point for exhausted tourists returning by ferry from their Samariá Gorge excursion.

The Samariá Gorge

Crete offers an exciting and spectacular walk through the **gorge of Samariá**, the longest (18 km/11 miles) in Europe. The walk starts by descending a steep stairway at **Xylóskalo**, 1,200 metres (3936 ft) above the sea, at the southern end of the vast Omalós plain, itself a 45 km (28 miles) tortuous drive from Haniá.

Taking it easy in Hóra Sfakíon.

BELOW: the "Iron Gates" in the Samariá Gorge.

LOCAL SUPERSTITIONS

The Cretans still observe countless practices that could be summarily dismissed as superstition, but which derive from ancient pagan religions, or early Christian observance, or actual historical events. Some examples:

● After Mass early on Easter Day, believers take home candles lit from the holy flame and use their smoke to mark a cross on the door lintel. This protects the house from bad luck and evil spirits for the rest of the year.

● Hard-boiled eggs are painted red on Holy Thursday to symbolise the blood of Christ. On Easter Day, people strike their eggs against other people's: the owner of the last egg to remain unbroken is considered lucky.

● A knife that was made during Holy Week offers protection against evil spirits.

● In eastern Crete, it is bad luck to give a knife as a present; but in western Crete, giving a knife to the best man at a wedding brings good luck.

● If an unexpected and unwanted guest arrives, someone creeps outside the door and spills salt on the ground. This is supposed to ensure the speedy departure of the visitor.

● Constantinople fell to the Turks on 29 May 1453 – a Tuesday. Many Cretans still believe in Unlucky Tuesday and are reluctant to do important business on that day.

Map, pages 308–9

After about 10 km (6 miles), with most of the steeper descent over, the abandoned **village of Samariá** and its church come into view. Stop and admire the church's lovely 14th-century frescoes – an opportunity to regain your breath without loss of face. The going now gets tough and involves criss-crossing the river-bed (be warned: flash floods can occur and wardens' warnings should be heeded). There is a lot of scree on the way, so you should wear sturdy walking shoes and be careful you don't slip. As the gorge narrows, the walls soar straight upwards for 300–600 metres (1,000–2,000 ft). Soon after passing the church of Avéndis Hristós, the **Sideróportes** (Iron Gates) are reached; here the gorge – scarcely penetrated by sunlight – is little more than 3.5 metres (11 ft) wide.

The park is under the strict aegis of the Haniá Forest Service, which specifically forbids certain activities, including singing. While you are walking, the elusive Cretan wild goat, the *agrími*, will probably be nearby, though it is unlikely that you will see many. On the other hand, you may spot bearded vultures overhead.

And so to old Agía Rouméli and the church of the Panagía. However, there is a further 3 km (2 miles) of hot and anticlimactic walking before celebrating with a longed-for swim or cold drink at new, coastal **Agía Rouméli ㉟**, with its tavernas and pensions. In ancient times, this is where Cretan cypress wood – much coveted in the ancient world – was exported to Egypt. Once refreshed, the only practical exit from the gorge – other than retracing the same route – is by boat eastwards to Hóra Sfakíon or westwards to Soúgia and Paleóhora. There are no roads.

The gorge is open from about the beginning of May until the end of September (entrance fee). Allow four to six hours for the walk.   ❑

Cross-country transport, Samariá Gorge.

BELOW:
Agía Rouméli.

CENTRE OF EUROPE'S FIRST CIVILISATION

Until a century ago, Crete's Minoan civilisation was little more than a myth. Now its capital is one of the largest and best restored sites in Greece

Knossos is a place of questions, many unanswered. Many visitors to the site find the concrete reconstructions and repainted frescoes (often from very small existing fragments) aid comprehension. But for many, used to other, more recent ruins that are clearly defensive or overtly religious, the site is mysterious. Can we hope to look back at fragments of a culture from 3,500 years ago and understand its imperatives and subtleties?

In legend, Knossos was the labyrinth of King Minos, where he imprisoned the minotaur, the human-bovine child of his wife Pasiphae. In reality, the role of the Minoan palace was probably not in the modern sense of a palace, but perhaps as an administrative and economic centre, unified by spiritual leaders.

Among the 1,300 rooms of the main palace were both the sacred and the commercial: lustral baths for holy ceremonies; store rooms for agricultural produce; workshops for metallurgy and stone-cutting. Nearby are the Royal Villa and the Little Palace.

Try to visit earlier or later in the day, to avoid the worst of the crowds, and to avoid being swept along by the flow. Look for the subtle architectural delights – light wells to illuminate the larger rooms; hydraulic controls providing water for drinking, bathing and flushing away sewage; drains with parabolic curves at the bends to prevent overflow.

Combine that with a afternoon visit to the archeological museum – to take full advantage of the air-conditioning inside the building.

△ **OVERVIEW**
The scale of the site is most apparent from the air – nearly 2 hectares (4 acres) of palaces ruled a population of perhaps 100,000.

▽ **EMPTY VESSELS**
Huge earthenware jars, *pithoi*, were used to store grain, olive oil, wine or water. Similar jars are still made in a few Cretan villages today.

△ **CHAIR OF STATE**
The throne room, possibly a court or council room, has a gypsum throne flanked by benches, and frescoes of griffins. These may have symbolised the heavenly, earthly and underworldly aspects of the rulers.

△ THE PLAY'S THE THING
The theatre was used for plays and processions. An engineered road, one of the oldest in Europe, leads from here to the Little Palace.

▽ ALL AT SEA
The fresco in the Queen's apartments (which included an en suite bathroom) features dolphins, fishes and sea urchins.

◁ BULL AND GATE
A (replica) fresco depicting the capture of a wild bull decorates the ramparts of the north entrance, leading to the road to Knossos' harbour at Amnissos.

▽ DILEMMA OF HORNS
The famous double horns now sitting on the south facade were once regarded as sacred symbols, though perhaps this is an overworking of the bull motif of the site.

◁ COLOUR CODING
The South Propylon (pillared gateway) has near life-size frescoes of processionary youths, including the famous slender-waisted cup-bearer. In Minoan art, male figures were coloured red, female white.

CONTROVERSIAL EXCAVATIONS

In 1878 a local merchant, Minos Kalokairinos, uncovered a fragment of the remains at Knossos, but the Turkish owners of the land prevented further excavation and even the wealthy German Heinrich Schliemann couldn't afford their asking price when he attempted to buy the site.

However, once Crete gained autonomy from the Turks in 1898, the way was open for the English archeologist Arthur Evans (later knighted) to purchase the area and begin excavating. He soon realised that this was a major discovery. He worked at Knossos over a period of 35 years, though by 1903 most of the site had been uncovered.

Evans' methods of using concrete to reconstruct the long-gone timber columns, and to support excavated sections of wall have received much criticism. While these preserved some of the structure *in situ*, it also involved much interpretative conjecture on the part of Evans (pictured above with a 1600 BC steatite bull's head from the Little Palace).

Excavation continues to this day, under subtler management.

INSIGHT GUIDES

Travel Tips

☀ INSIGHT GUIDES Phonecard

One global card to keep travellers in touch.
Easy. Convenient. Saves you time and money.

It's a global phonecard

Save up to 70%* on international calls from over 55 countries

Free 24 hour global customer service

Recharge your card at any time via customer service or online

It's a message service

Family and friends can send you voice messages for free.

Listen to these messages using the phone* or online

Free email service - you can even listen to your email over the phone*

It's a travel assistance service

24 hour emergency travel assistance – if and when you need it.

Store important travel documents online in your own secure vault

For more information, call rates, and all Access Numbers in over 55 countries, (check your destination is covered) go to www.insightguides.ekit.com or call Customer Service.

JOIN now and receive US$ 5 bonus when you join for US$ 20 or more.

Join today at

www.insightguides.ekit.com

When requested use ref code: **INSAD0103**

OR SIMPLY FREE CALL 24 HOUR CUSTOMER SERVICE

UK	0800 376 1705
USA	1800 706 1333
Canada	1800 808 5773
Australia	1800 11 44 78
South Africa	0800 997 285

THEN PRESS ⓪

For all other countries please go to "Access Numbers" at www.insightguides.ekit.com

* Retrieval rates apply for listening to messages. Savings based on using a hotel or payphone and calling to a landline. Correct at time of printing 01.03

(INS001)

powered by ⊛ *ekit*

"The easiest way to make calls and receive messages around the world"

CONTENTS

Getting Acquainted

The Place 322
Geography 322
Government 322
Economy...............................322
The People 322
Climate 322
Religion 323

Planning the Trip

Visas and Passports 323
Customs 323
Health...................................323
Money Matters......................324
What To Pack 324
Getting There 324
Specialist Operators..............325

Practical Tips

Tourist Information 326
Business Hours 326
Telecommunications 326
Postal Services 326
Emergency Numbers..............326
Medical Treatment 327
Security and Crime 327
Media 327
Tipping 327
Etiquette 328
Women Travellers..................328
Travelling With Kids...............328
Public Holidays 328

Getting Around

Public Transport 329
Private Transport...................330
Timetables............................330
Car Hire 331
Cruises 332

Where to Stay

How to Choose......................333
Hotel Listings 333
Youth Hostels 356
Traditional Settlements..........356
Camping 356

Where To Eat

What To Eat...........................356
Restaurant Listings 357
The Wines of Greece 370
Coffee, Chocolate and Tea.....372

Culture

Theatre 374
Cinema 374
Music and Dance 374
Cultural Events......................374

Nightlife

Religious and Other Festivals 375
Gay Life 375

Sport

Participant Sports..................375
Spectator Sports 376
Sailing 376

Language

The Greek Language 371
Common Expressions............372

Further Reading

History 380
Anthropology and Culture......381
Literature 381
Useful Websites 382

Getting Acquainted

The Place

Situation Eastern Mediterranean, stretching from 39° to 35°N, 20° to 28°E.
Area 131,950 sq km (50,950 sq miles), including around 25,050 sq km (9,670 sq miles) of islands.
Capital Athens
Population nearly 11 million. Greater Athens and Piraeus have a population of over 4 million. Thessaloníki, the second largest city, has nearly 1 million residents. The most populated island is Crete, with just over ½ million inhabitants.
Language Modern Greek.
Literacy 95 percent.
Religion Predominantly Greek Orthodox Christianity, with small minorities of Muslims, Catholics, evangelical sects and Jews.
Currency Euro.
Weights and measures Metric.

The People

Although about 40 percent of the country's population lives in Athens, the city is often called Greece's largest village. Greeks rarely move far from their village roots, even though – with more and more young people moving to cities – chronic depopulation of the countryside has become a serious problem.

Even the most jet-setting businessman is home-loving and much of the Greeks' social life is centred round the family. Children are adored (and given more licence than you might allow your own).

A nation of many passions, from football and basketball to politics, which can be very partisan, the Greeks love nothing better than discussing the meaning of life. If you strike up a conversation in a taverna, expect to while away an hour or two – especially during election time, when the whole country buzzes with political fervour and speculation.

Electricity 220V, round two-pin plugs (*see also What to Pack*).
International Dialling 30 (country code for Greece), followed by the entire 10-digit number, starting with 2 for landlines and 6 for mobiles.
Time Zones Two hours ahead of Greenwich Mean Time. As in the entire EU, the clock is advanced one hour from the last weekend in March to the end of September.

Geography

Mainland Greece is made up of Attica, the Peloponnese, central Greece (more poetically known as Roúmeli), Thessaly, Epirus, Macedonia and Thrace. Its backbone is formed by the Píndos (Pindus) mountains, extending northwest from Roúmeli to the Albanian border in Epirus reaching its highest point at Smolikas, but the highest mountain is Olympos, straddling the border between Thessaly and Macedonia, at a height of 2,917 metres (9,570ft).

The coast is a series of so many coves and inlets that it runs to 15,000 km (9,320 miles), and the Mediterranean reaches its deepest point at the 4,850 metres (15,912ft) Oinoussa Pit off the south coast of the Peloponnese.

The hundreds of islands that spill out into the Mediterranean and Aegean are divided into groups: the Ionian archipelago to the west, the Sporades and Évvia in the central Aegean, the Cyclades and Dodecanese running out southeast from Athens, and the northeast Aegean islands just off the Turkish coast. The largest islands are Crete, Corfu, Kefalloniá, Rhodes, Lésvos and Sámos, all famous for their vegetation, though the flora throughout all Greece is remarkable.

Government

Greece is a republic with a president, elected by parliament, who holds ceremonial executive power. The parliament has 300 elected members led by the prime minister.

King Constantine went into exile in December 1967 following the April seizure of power by the infamous colonels' junta, and the monarchy was abolished by a referendum held after the collapse of the dictatorship in 1974. Since then two parties, New Democracy (conservative) and PASOK (socialist) have taken turns at governing; PASOK was in power from 1993 to 2004, winning in both the 1996 and the (extremely close) 2000 elections under Kostas Simitis. The spring 2004 poll was won by ND under Kostas Karamanlis.

Economy

About 23 percent of the land is arable, and the country produces fruit, vegetables, olives, olive oil, wine, currants, grain, cotton and tobacco. Its natural resources include the minerals bauxite, lignite and magnesite, while building slate and marble are extensively quarried. Crude oil deposits are limited, with just a single field off Thásos currently exploited. About 15 percent of the labour force works in mining and manufacturing, producing textiles, chemicals and food products. Shipping is still an important source of revenue, but tourism is the largest foreign currency earner.

In 1981 Greece became the 10th member of the European Union, with full integration at the end of 1993; it adopted the euro as currency in February 2002. The late 1980s and 1990s had already seen a huge rise in the cost of living throughout the country, and the euro seems to have only accentuated this – a shock for anyone who remembers it as a "cheap & cheerful" destination. Although it is no longer the place for bargain-basement holidays, Greece remains good value for foreign travellers, with restaurant meals and accommodation about the same as rural Spain or France.

Climate

The Greece seen in tourist posters is a perennially warm and sunny place – and it is, by European standards. But this picture does not reflect the considerable climatic variety. The north and inland regions have a modified continental climate, so winters are quite cold and summers extremely hot. In Ioánnina, Trípoli and Kastoriá, for example, snow and freezing temperatures are not uncommon. In mountainous regions, winters are even more inclement.

The southern islands, the coastal Peloponnese and the Attic Peninsula conform more to the traditional Mediterranean image: a long, warm season of rainless, sunny days extending roughly from early May to mid-October. But here too the winters are cool, with rain falling in unpredictable spells between December and April.

In general, late spring (late April–June) and autumn (September–October) are the best times to visit. During these periods, you will find mild to warm temperatures, sunny days and fewer tourists. Throughout July and August Greece is at its sultriest and most crowded. Still, millions of tourists seem to prefer the heat and the company, choosing this busiest period for their holiday.

Religion

The Greek Orthodox Church still exerts enormous influence on contemporary life, both in mainland Greece (including Athens) and the islands. Sunday is the official day of rest, and even in mid-season in some tourist areas, shops and activities are suspended. Excursion boats from island to island, for example, might well be running to schedule, but what no one bothers to point out is that nothing on the destination island will be open when you arrive. Always enquire beforehand when planning anything on Sundays.

The most important holiday in Greece is Easter, celebrated by the Greek Orthodox calendar and usually a week or two to either side of Catholic Easter. It is advisable to find out before booking a spring holiday exactly when Easter is, as services, shops and even flights experience disruptions during Easter period.

On 15 August, the Assumption of the Virgin Mary, many places hold a *panigýri* (celebration) to mark the reception into heaven of the *Panagía*, as the Madonna is known in Greek. Greeks make pilgrimages from all over the country to Tínos in the Cyclades where the icon of the Panagía Evangelístria is said to work miracles. The most colourful festival of the Virgin, however, takes place on 15 August in the hillside town of Ólymbos on the island of Kárpathos, where the women wear brilliant traditional dress and the *panigyriá* can last for days.

Nearly every day is a cause for celebration for someone in Greece. Instead of marking birthdays, Greeks have *giortés*, name days, which celebrate Orthodox baptismal names. When the day commemorates a popular name-saint like John or Helen, a quarter of the nation has a party. You'll hear locals say: "*Giortázo símera*" (I'm celebrating today). To which you may reply: "*Hrónia pollá*" ("many years", in other words, many happy returns).

Seasonal Averages

- January–March
6–16°C (43–61°F)
- April–June
11–29°C (52–84°F)
- July–September
19–32°C (66–90°F)
- October–December
8–23°C (46–73°F)

Planning the Trip

Visas and Passports

Citizens of EU nations, as well as Switzerland and EEA countries, have unlimited visitation rights to Greece; your passport will not be stamped on entry or exit. With a valid passport, citizens of the USA, Canada, Australia and New Zealand can stay in the country for up to three months (cumulative) within any six-month period, with no visa necessary. To stay longer, you must obtain a permit from the nearest Aliens' Bureau; however this is lately proving nearly impossible (and very expensive) to obtain. Citizens of all non-EU/EEA countries should contact the nearest Greek embassy or consulate about visa and permitted length-of-stay requirements, which are liable to change again in future.

Customs

There are no official restrictions on the movement of goods within the European Union, provided the goods were purchased within the EU. It is no longer necessary for EU nationals to exit their home-country Customs through a red or green channel.

Duty-paid goods

If you buy goods in Greece for which you pay tax, there are no restrictions on the amounts you can take home. EU law has set "guidance levels", however, on the following:
- **Tobacco** 800 cigarettes, or 400 cigarillos, or 200 cigars or 1kg of tobacco.
- **Spirits** 10 litres
- **Fortified wine/wine** 90 litres
- **Beer** 110 litres
  If you exceed these amounts you must be able to prove the goods are for personal use.

Duty-free goods

Since the abolition of duty-free concession within the European Union, all goods brought into Greece from EU countries must be duty-paid. In theory there are no limitations to the amount of duty-paid goods that

can be brought into the country. However, cigarettes and most spirits are much cheaper in Greece than in Britain and Ireland (government duty is much lower), so waiting until you reach your destination to buy these goods will save you money.

For travellers from non-EU countries, allowances for duty-free goods brought into Greece are:
- **Tobacco** 200 cigarettes, or 100 cigarillos, or 50 cigars, or 250g of tobacco.
- **Alcohol** 1 litre of spirits or liqueurs over 22 percent volume, or 2 litres of fortified, sparkling wine or other liqueurs.
- **Perfume** 60cc of perfume, plus 250cc of *eau de toilette*.

Non-EU residents can claim back Value Added Tax (currently between 6 and 18 percent) on any items costing over €120, provided they export the item within 90 days of purchase. Tax-free forms are available at tourist shops and department stores. Keep the receipt and form. Make your claim at the customs area of the airport when departing.

Currency restrictions

There are no limits on the amount of euros visitors can import or export. There are no restrictions on travellers' cheques, but cash sums of more than $10,000 or its equivalent should be declared on entry.

Importing cars

Visitors arriving with their own car are allowed to circulate for up to six months without formality; after that the bureaucratic fun begins, and people intending to establish residence will find that it's usually cheaper and easier to buy a Greek-registered car than try to import their overseas motor. Cars detected circulating after the initial six-month period without valid road tax are liable to seizure by customs/tax undercover agents.

Health

Greece has few serious diseases apart from those that you can contract in the United States or the rest of Europe. Citizens of the USA, Canada and United Kingdom do not need any immunisations to enter the country.

Insurance

British and EU residents are entitled to free medical treatment in Greece as long as they carry an E111 form (obtainable from post offices). However, this guarantees only the most basic health care: you are only entitled to use one of the lowest-grade state hospitals, and will have to pay for your own medicine. So it is advisable to take out private medical insurance. You will have to pay for private treatment up front, so you must keep receipts for any bills or medicines you pay for to make a claim. If you plan to hire a motor scooter in Greece, you may have to pay a insurance supplement to cover you for accidents.

Money Matters

The Greek currency is the euro (*evró* in Greek), which comes in coins of 1, 2, 5, 10, 20 and 50 cents (*leptá*), plus 1 and 2 euro, as well as notes of 5, 10, 20, 50, 100, 200 and 500 euro (the latter two denominations rarely seen).

All banks and most hotels buy foreign currency at the official rate of exchange fixed by the Bank of Greece. Though it's safer to carry most of your currency in travellers' cheques, it is also worth carrying a limited sum in US dollars or sterling. When you can't find a place to cash cheques, there will usually be a shop or post office able to convert those currencies into euros. Exchange rates go up or down daily. To find the current rate, check displays in bank windows, or the newspapers; you can read the tables even in Greek.

Credit/debit cards

Many of the better-established hotels, restaurants and shops accept major credit cards, as does Olympic Airways and the larger ferry companies or travel agents. The average pension or taverna does not, however, so be sure to enquire if that is how you intend to pay. You will find that most brands of card are accepted by the numerous autoteller machines, upon entry of your PIN number. However, use debit rather than credit cards in ATMs, as the latter

tend to have ruinous surcharges, often amounting to over 4 percent of the transaction value. This caveat aside, you will find that this is the most convenient and least expensive way of getting funds, and many of the machines operate around the clock.

What To Pack

Clothes

If you visit Greece during the summer months, you will want to bring lightweight, casual clothing. Add a pullover or jacket to this and you will be prepared for the occasional cool night breezes. Lightweight shoes and sandals are ideal in the summer, but you will also need a pair of comfortable walking shoes that have already been broken in. If you plan to do any rigorous hiking in the mountains or on the islands, bring sturdy, over-the-ankle boots with a good tread; leather will be more comfortable in summer temperatures than high-tech synthetic materials.

In general, both Greeks and tourists dine in casual dress. You will only need formal dress if you plan to go to fancy establishments, casinos, formal affairs and so on. If you visit Greece during the winter months, which can be surprisingly cold, bring the same kind of clothes you would wear during spring in the northern part of the United States or central Europe.

Toiletries

Most international brands are widely available, except on the smallest islands. Feminine hygiene products are more likely to be sold in supermarkets than pharmacies.

Sun protection

A hat, sun cream and sunglasses are also highly recommended for

protection from the intense midday sun (sophisticated sun creams of up to SPF30 are widely available in pharmacies and cosmetics shops).

Adaptors

220v AC is the standard household electric current throughout Greece. Non-dual-voltage shavers and hair dryers from North America should be left at home in favour of versatile travel models – they can be bought on the spot in Greece. Greek plugs are the standard round, two-pin European continental type, different from those in North America and the UK; plug adaptors for American appliances are easy to find, three-pin-to-two-pin adaptors for UK appliances much less so, so these are best purchased before departure.

Universal plug

Greek basins often aren't equipped with plugs, so if you want water in your sink a universal plug is essential.

Film

Film is widely available in a range of formats and speeds, at competitive prices, though if you require something esoteric, it's best to bring your own.

Torch

If you're planning a trip to one of the islands, pack one, as walking home from the taverna can be tricky if there's no moon. If you forget, Maglites or the like are widely sold.

Getting There

By Air

Greece has good air connections with all six continents and is serviced by numerous international airlines. Charter flights generally operate from mid-April to the end of October, even into November into Rhodes and Crete. There are ways of flying in at a much lower cost than the standard airline fares (such as internet e-tickets, last-minute seats or "bucket shop" tickets), and you may want to familiarise yourself with the different possibilities, and their related advantages and disadvantages before buying a ticket. The airlines' own websites are often a good source of discount tickets, matching (or nearly so) the prices offered by general websites like Expedia or Travelocity, and being e-tickets are loss-proof.

The majority of schedule airline passengers travelling to Greece make Athens' Eleftherios Venizelos Airport their point of entry, though a number of services (from the rest of Europe only) arrive at Thessaloníki's

Drugs and Medicines

Greek pharmacies stock most over-the-counter drugs, and pharmacists are well trained. The Greeks themselves are some of the champion hypochondriacs and potion-poppers of Europe, and all manner of homeopathic or herbal remedies and premium-ingredient dietary supplements are available. Many formulas that would have to be obtainable only on prescription elsewhere, if at all, are freely obtainable in Greece. So you should have no problem obtaining most medicines (except in remote areas and islands).

Essential drugs, made locally under licence, are price-controlled,

with uniform rates all over the country – eg a tube of 1% hydrocortisone cream costs less than €1.50 – but discretional sundries and anything imported can be pricey (eg, a packet of four water-resistant French-made bandages for €3.50). If you want to be absolutely sure, pack a supply of your favourite remedies to last out the trip, but check labels carefully – codeine (a key ingredient in some painkillers such as Panadol and Solpadeine) is banned in Greece.

Greek authorities take the unauthorised use of drugs very seriously indeed; this is not the country in which to carry cannabis.

Dress Codes

The Greeks will not expect you as a tourist to dress as they do, but scuffed shoes, ripped jeans or visibly out-of-date clothing are considered offensive.

In certain places and regions, you will encounter explicit requirements or conventions concerning the way you dress. To enter a church, men must wear long trousers, and women sleeved dresses. Often dresses or wraps will be provided at the church entrance if you do not have them. Not complying with this code will be taken as insulting irreverence.

Some specific areas have their own dress codes. On Mýkonos, for example, male and female tourists alike will shock no one by wearing shorts or a swimsuit in most public places. But this same apparel will be severely alienating in a mountain village in Epirus or Crete, or in any other area that is less accustomed to tourists. The best approach is to observe what other people are wearing and dress accordingly.

Macedonia Airport.

Between Eleftherios Venizelos Airport, central Athens and Piraeus there are various connecting services. As of July 2004, a light-rail line should whisk you from the airport to Stavrós station, new terminus of the metro network. Tickets into town cost €2.90 and are valid on all Athens public transport for 24 hours. Until the light-rail link opens, take E94 express bus (every 15–30min 6am–midnight) from outside arrivals to metro station Ethnikí Ámyna and then continue by metro. Alternatively, take the E95 express bus all the way to central Sýndagma Square (every 25–35min), or the E96 express bus to Pireás port (every 20–40min).

Should you need to use one, a taxi from Venizelos Airport into Athens will cost €12–20 depending on time of day/night and your final destination, but including airport supplement and per-bag fee. Traffic congestion has improved since the opening of the Attikí Odós or ring highway around northern Athens, but the journey time can still be over an hour.

By Sea

Most visitors entering Greece by sea do so from the west, from Italy. You can catch a boat to Greece from Venice, Ancona, Trieste and Bari, but the most regular service is from Brindisi. Daily ferry lines (less frequent in the low-season) connect Brindisi with the three main western Greek ports: Corfu, Igoumenítsa and Pátras. Corfu is a 9-hour trip; Igoumenítsa 11 hours; and Pátras 16 to 18 hours, depending on whether you take a direct boat or one that makes stops in Corfu and Igoumenítsa. The "Superfast" ferries between Ancona and Pátras offer an efficient 22-hour crossing.

Igoumenítsa is the ideal port of call for those setting off to see central-western Greece. Pátras is best if you want to head directly to Athens or into the Peloponnese. Regular buses and trains connect Pátras and Athens (4 hours by bus, 5 hours by train). If you plan to take your car with you on the boat, you should definitely make reservations well in advance. Otherwise, arriving a few hours before the departure time should suffice, except during peak seasons when booking in advance is essential for seats or berths.

By Land

From Europe The most direct overland route from northwestern Europe to Greece is a long one: 3,000 km (1,900 miles) from London to Athens. It has always been a rather arduous and impractical travel option if you're just trying to get to Greece for a brief holiday; sporadic troubles in former Yugoslavia now may mean even longer detours through Hungary, Romania and Bulgaria. Check with your local Greek tourist office or motoring organisation for the latest information before leaving.

There is also the option of making use of the one or two remaining, reputable **bus** lines that connect Athens and Thessaloníki with many European cities (taking 3½ days from London, for example).

The various **trains** you can take from northwest Europe will take about as long as the bus, and cost considerably more, but fares include the Italy-Greece ferry crossing, and may get you to Greece feeling more intact.

From Asia via Turkey If you are travelling strictly overland to Greece from Asia you will pass through Istanbul and cross into Greece at the Évros River. The best way to do this is by car or bus. The road is good and the journey from Istanbul to Thessaloníki takes approximately 15 hours; several bus companies serve the route.

The train has the appeal of following the route of the old Orient Express, with better scenery than the road. But, unless you're a great rail fan, the travel time can be off-putting: 17 hours by the timetables, up to 19 hours in practice, including long halts at the border.

Another popular option is to take one of the small boats between western Turkish ports and select Greek islands just opposite. Fares are overpriced for the distance involved, but it is undeniably convenient. The most reliable links are from Çesme to Híos and Kusadasi to Sámos.

Specialist Operators

Your local overseas branch of the Greek National Tourist Organisation (see page xxx) can usually provide a list of that country's tour operators and specialist agents offering holidays in Greece. Otherwise, here are a few suggestions for something unusual:

- **Archaeological tours**
British Museum Traveller, London, UK; tel: 020 7436 7575, www.britishmuseumtraveller.co.uk
- **Bicycle tours**
Classic Adventures, USA; tel: 1-800-935-5000; www.classicadventures.com
- **Birdwatching**
Limosa Holidays, UK; tel: 01263 578143
- **Botanical tours**
Marengo Guided Walks, Hunstanton, UK; tel: 01485 532710; www.marengowalks.com
- **Horse-riding**
Equitour, a division of Peregrine Holidays, Oxford, UK; tel: 01865 511642; www.peregrineholidays.com
- **Sail-and-trek mixed tours**
Hellenic Adventures, USA; tel: 1-800-225-2380; www.hellenicadventures.com
- **Walking holidays**
ATG Oxford, UK; tel: 01865 315678; www.atg-oxford.co.uk
Exodus London, UK; tel: 020 8675 5550 www.exodus.co.uk
Himalayan Travel, USA; tel: 1-800-225-2380; www.gorp.com/himtravel.htm
Ramblers Holidays, Welwyn Garden City, UK; tel: 01707 331133; www.ramblersholidays.co.uk
Waymark Holidays, Slough, UK; tel: 01753 516477; www.waymarkholidays.co.uk
- **Writing workshops/holistic holidays**
Skyros Centre, London, UK; tel: (020) 7267 4424; www.skyros.com

Practical Tips

Tourist Information

Tourist offices

If you would like tourist information about Greece during your trip, visit the nearest Greek National Tourist Organisation – GNTO, or EOT in Greek. They provide information on public transport, as well as leaflets and details about sites and museums. There are over a dozen regional GNTO offices across the country. The new head office in Athens is at Amalías 26; tel: (210) 33 10 392.

In some tourist areas, especially many of the islands, there are semi-official municipal tourist information centres open from June to September. These are usually prominently sited near the centre of the main town, and provide all the local information you might need. Some can even help with finding accommodation.

Tourist Police

The Greek Tourist Police are often a mine of information too. A branch of the local police and found in most large towns, they can be helpful in providing information about hotels as well as fielding a wide variety of travel questions.

Business Hours

All banks are open 8am–2.30pm Monday to Thursday, and close at 2pm on Friday. ATMs are now everywhere – even the smaller islands will have at least one – and this is how most people obtain cash nowadays.

The schedule for business and shop hours is more complicated. Business hours vary according to the type of business and the day of the week. The main thing to remember is that businesses generally open at 8.30 or 9am and close on Monday, Wednesday and Saturday at 2.30pm. On Tuesday, Thursday and Friday most businesses close at 2pm and reopen in the afternoon from 5pm to 8.30pm (winter), 5.30 or 6pm to 9pm (summer).

You'll soon learn that schedules are very flexible in Greece (both in business and personal affairs). To avoid disappointment, allow ample time when shopping and doing business. That way, you may also enter into the Greek spirit of negotiation, in which a good chat can be as important as the matter of business itself.

Telecommunications

The cheapest way to make telephone calls is to buy a telephone card from a kiosk and use a (usually noisy) phone booth. Cards come in three sizes: 100 units, 500 units and 1,000 units, with the largest ones representing the best value. Otherwise, you may still find a telephone kiosk at which you can pay a few euro-cents for a local call.

You can also make long-distance calls from the dwindling number of kiosks which have a cardphone, free-standing street-corner cardphones, or from the new-style coin-op counter phones which take assorted euro coins, often found in hotel lobbies and restaurants. Calls from hotel rooms typically have a minimum 200 percent surcharge on top of the standard rates – to be avoided for anything other than brief local calls.

Many post offices offer fax services; larger towns usually have at least two cybercafés – rates range from €4 to €7 per hour.

Greece has one of the highest per-capita mobile-phone usage rates in the world, and a mobile is an essential fashion accessory for any

self-respecting Greek. Foreign mobile owners will find themselves well catered for, with thorough coverage and reciprocal agreements for most UK-based services. Calls within Greece are affordable, but the cost of overseas calls mounts up quickly. North American users will have to bring a tri-band apparatus to get any joy. If you're staying for any amount of time, you will find it better to either buy a pay-as-you-go phone from one of the four Greek providers (Vodaphone, Cosmote, Telestet, Q-Telecom) or, if feasible, buy just a SIM card for the apparatus you've brought along.

Emergency Numbers

The following numbers work country-wide:
- **Police** 100
- **Ambulance** 161
- **Fire brigade, urban** 199
- **Forest fire reporting** 191
- **Tourist police 171** (Athens only; in other parts of Greece, ring 210 171)

Elsewhere, hotel staff will give you details of the nearest hospital or English-speaking doctor.

Postal Services

Most local post offices are open weekdays from 7.30am until 2pm. However, the main post offices in central Athens (on Eólou near Omónia Square and on Sýndagma Square at the corner of Mitropóleos Street) are open longer hours on weekdays, as well as short schedules on Saturday and Sunday.

Postal rates are subject to fairly frequent change; currently a postcard or light letter costs 65 euro-cents to any overseas destination. Stamps are available from the post office or from many kiosks (perίptera) and hotels, which may charge a 10–15 percent commission. But make sure you know how much it is to send a letter or postcard, as kiosk owners tend not to be up to date with latest international postal rates.

If you want to send a parcel from Greece, do not to wrap it until a post office clerk has inspected it, unless it's going to another EU country, in which case you can present it sealed. Major post offices stock various sizes of cardboard boxes for sale in which you can pack your material, as well as twine, but you had best bring your own tape and scissors.

Letters from abroad can be sent Post Restante to any post office. Take your passport or other convincing ID when you go to pick up mail.

Greek National Tourist Organisation Offices

United Kingdom
4 Conduit Street, London WIR ODJ
Tel: (020) 7499 4976
Fax: (020) 7287 1369
Email: EOT-greektouristoffice
@btinternet.com

United States
Olympic Tower, 645 Fifth Avenue, 9th Floor, New York, NY 10022
Tel: (212) 421 5777
Fax: (212) 826 6940
E-mail: info@greektourism.com

Australia
51 Pitt Street, Sydney NSW 2000
Tel: (02) 9241 1663/5
Fax: (02) 9235 2174
Email: hto@tpg.com.au

Canada
91 Scollard Street, 2nd Floor, Toronto, ON M5R 1G4
Tel: (416) 968 2220
Fax: (416) 968 6533
E-mail: grnto.tor@on.aibn.com
Website: www.greektourism.com

Medical Treatment

For minor ailments your best port of call is a pharmacy. Greek chemists usually speak good English and are well-trained and helpful, and pharmacies stock a good range of medicines (including contraceptives) as well as bandages and dressings for minor wounds.

Certain pharmacies are open outside of normal shop hours and at weekends, on a rotating basis. You can find out which are open either by looking at the bilingual (Greek/English) card posted in pharmacy windows or by consulting a local newspaper. In big cities, and major tourist resorts such as Crete or Rhodes, one or two pharmacies will be open 24 hours a day.

There are English-speaking GPs in all the bigger towns and resorts, whose rates are usually reasonable. Ask your hotel or the tourist office for details.

In Athens, the doctors' roster can be obtained by dialling 105; get the 24-hour pharmacy roster by dialling 107.

Treatment for broken bones and similar mishaps is given free of charge in the state-run Greek hospitals – go straight to the casualty/emergency ward. The EU form E111 is generally not even requested, your statement of EU nationality usually being sufficient. For more serious problems you should have private medical insurance. If you have a serious injury or illness, you are better off travelling home for treatment if you can. Greek public hospitals lag behind northern Europe and the US in both their hygiene and standard of care; the Greeks bring food and bedding when visiting sick relatives, and must bribe nurses for anything beyond the bare minimum in care.

Security and Crime

Greece is still one of the safest countries in Europe. Despite the luridly publicised antics of certain Albanians and Romanians, violent crime remains relatively rare. Sadly, however, petty theft does occur, and it is now the norm to lock cars and front doors in the countryside.

Because of security considerations after the September 11 attacks in New York, and the Olympics, it is unwise to leave luggage unattended anywhere except perhaps in a hotel lobby, under the gaze of the desk staff. Belongings inadvertently left behind in a café will still usually be put aside for you to collect.

Animal Hazards

Nearly half the stray dogs in rural areas carry echinococcosis (treatable by surgery only) or kala-azar disease (leishmaniasis), a protozoan blood disease spread by sandfleas.

Mosquitos can be a nuisance in some areas of Greece, but topical repellents are readily available in pharmacies. For safeguarding rooms, accommodation proprietors often supply a plug-in electric pad, which vapourises smokeless, odourless rectangular tablets. If you see them by the bed, it's a good bet they'll be needed; refills can be found in any supermarket.

On the islands, poisonous baby pit vipers and scorpions are a problem in spring and summer. They will not strike you unless disturbed, but do not put your hands or feet in places (such as drystone walls) that you haven't checked first. If you swim in the sea, beware jellyfish whose sting is usually harmless but which can swell and hurt for days.

On beaches, it is worth wearing plastic or trekking sandals to avoid sea urchins (those little black pincushions on rocks that can embed their very sharp and tiny spines into unwary feet, which then break off). A local Greek remedy is to douse the wound with olive oil and then gently massage the foot until the spines pop out, but this rarely works unless you're willing to perform minor surgery with pen-knife and sewing needle – which should be done, as spine fragments tend to go septic.

Tipping

Menu prices at most cafés, restaurants and *tavérnes* include a service charge, but it is still customary to leave an extra 5–10 percent on the table for the waiters.

Just as important as any such gratuity, however, is your appreciation of the food you eat. Greek waiters and restaurant owners are proud when you tell them you like a particular dish.

Drinking Water

Carrying a large plastic bottle of mineral water is a common sight in Greece, but it is rather deplorable, as sunlight releases toxic chemicals from the plastic into the water, and the spent bottles contribute enormously to Greece's litter problem. Buy a sturdy, porcelain-lined canteen and fill it from the cool-water supply of bars and restaurants you've patronised; nobody will begrudge you this. Although unfiltered tap water is generally safe to drink, it may be brackish, and having a private water supply is much handier. On the mainland and larger islands, certain springs are particularly esteemed by the locals – queues of cars, and people with jerry-cans, tip you off. If you do want bottled water, it can be bought almost anywhere that sells food, even in beach cafés and tavernas.

Media

Print

Many kiosks throughout Athens and other major resorts receive British newspapers, plus the *International Herald Tribune*, either late the same afternoon or, more usually, the next *Athens News* in colour (online at www.athensnews.gr) is interesting and informative, with both international and local news, particularly good for the Balkans, and complete TV and cinema listings. *Odyssey* is a glossy, bi-monthly magazine created by and for the wealthy Greek diaspora, somewhat more interesting than the usual airline in-flight mag.

Radio and TV

ER 1 and ER 2 are the two Greek state-owned radio channels. ER 1 is divided into three different "programmes". The First (728 KHz) and Second (1385 KHz) both have abundant Greek popular music and news, some foreign pop and occasional jazz and blues. Third (665 KHz) plays a lot of western classical

Foreign Embassies in Athens

All embassies are open from Monday to Friday only, usually from 8am until 2pm, except for their national holidays (as well as Greek ones).

• **Australia** Anastasíou Tsohá 24, corner Soútsou (Ambelókipi metro); tel: 64 50 404.

• **Canada** Gennadíou 4, Kolonáki, (Evangelismós metro); tel: 72 73 400.

• **Ireland** Vassiléos Konstandínou 7 (by National Gardens); tel: 72 32 771.

• **South Africa** Kifissiás 60, Maroússi; tel: 210 61 06 645.

• **UK** Ploutárhou 1, Kolonáki (Evangelismós metro); tel: 72 72 600.

• **USA** Vasilísis Sofías 91, Ambelókipi (Mégaro Mousikís metro); tel: 72 12 951.

music. ER 2 (98 KHz) is much like the first two programmes.

The BBC World Service offers news on the hour (plus other interesting programmes and features). The best short-wave (MHz) frequencies to pick up the BBC in Athens are as follows: 3–7.30am GMT: 9.41 (31 m), 6.05 (49 m), 15.07 (19 m) 7.30am–6pm: GMT–15.07 (19 m) 6.30pm–11.15pm GMT–9.41 (31 m), 6.05 (49 m). Additionally, a plethora of private stations broadcast locally from just about every island or provincial town, no matter how tiny.

There are two state-owned and operated television channels (ET1 in Athens, ET3 in Thessaloniki) and a half-dozen private television channels (Antenna, Net, Mega, Star, Alpha and Alter). Often they transmit foreign movies and programmes with Greek subtitles rather than being dubbed. Several cable and satellite channels are also broadcast, including Sky, CNN and Super Channel.

Etiquette

The Greeks are at heart a very traditional nation, protective of their families and traditions. So to avoid giving offence it is essential to follow their codes of conduct.

Locals rarely drink to excess, so drunken and/or lewd behaviour is treated with at best bewilderment, at worse severe distaste (or criminal prosecution, as many young louts on Rhodes have learned to their cost).

Nude bathing is legal at only a few beaches (such as on the island of Mýkonos), but it is deeply offensive to Greeks. Even topless sunbathing is sometimes not sanctioned, so watch

for signs forbidding it on beaches. The main rule of thumb is this: if it is a secluded beach and/or a beach that has become a commonly accepted locale for nude bathing, you probably won't offend anyone.

Despite assorted scandals and embarrassing espousal of retrograde issues in recent years, the Greek Orthodox Church still commands considerable respect in Greece, so keep any unfavourable comments about the clergy or even Greek civil servants to yourself.

Women Travellers

Lone female visitors may still be targeted for attention by predatory Greek males, especially around beach bars and after-hours discos, but in general machismo is no longer any more a problem than anywhere else in southern Europe. Inexorable changes in Greek culture mean that Greek women have much more sexual freedom than previously, especially in the cities. There is now little controversy in their spending time with their male counterparts, up to and including cohabiting before (or instead of) marriage.

In remote areas, many Greeks are still highly traditional and may find it hard to understand why you are travelling alone. You will not feel comfortable in their all-male drinking cafés.

Travelling with Kids

Children are adored in Greece, and many families are still highly superstitious about their welfare – don't be surprised to see kids with

Public Holidays

The Greeks like their festivals and celebrate them in style, so most business and shops close during the afternoon before and the morning after a religious holiday, as well as the day itself.

- **1 January** Protohroniá/New Year's Day
- **6 January** Agía Theofánia/ Epiphany
- **Moveable** Katharí Deftéra Clean Monday (First Day of Lent)
- **25 March** Evangelismós/ Annunciation
- **1 May** Labour Day
- **Moveable** Megáli Paraskeví/ Good Friday
- **Moveable** Orthodox Easter (Pásha), Easter Monday
- **Moveable** Agíou Pnévmatos/ Pentecost Monday (50 days after Easter)
- **15 August** Assumption (Apokímisis) of the Holy Virgin
- **28 October** "Ohi" Day, National Holiday
- **25 December** Hristoúgenna/ Christmas Day
- **26 December** Sýnaxis tis Theotókou/Gathering of the Virgin's Entourage

amulets pinned to their clothes to ward off the evil eye. So expect your own kids to be the centre of attention. Children are given quite a bit of leeway in Greece and treated very indulgently. they are allowed to stay up late and are routinely taken out to eat in tavernas. You may have to put your foot down when shop owners offer free sweets or strangers are over-indulgent towards your own children.

Photography

Although Greece is a photographer's paradise, taking photographs at will is not recommended. Cameras are not allowed in museums, and you may have to pay a fee to take photographs or use your camcorder at archaeological sites. Watch out for signs showing a bellows camera with a red "X" through it, and do not point your camera at anything in or near airports – most of which double as military bases.

Prints can be processed just about anywhere in Greece, but slides are usually sent to Athens or Thessaloníki, so wait until you get home to have them processed. Most university towns (Iráklio, Ioánnina, Pátra) do have at least one lab that will do E-6 processing.

"Greek Time"

Beware Greek schedules. Although shops and businesses generally operate the hours indicated on page 327, there is no guarantee that when you want to book a ferry or buy a gift, the office or shop will actually be open.

Siesta (mikró ýpno in Greek) is observed throughout Greece, and even in Athens the majority of people retire behind closed doors between the hours of 3pm and 6pm. Shops and businesses also close, and it is usually impossible to get much done that day until late-afternoon or early evening. To avoid frustration and disappointment, shop and book things between 10am and 1pm Monday to Friday.

Since 1994 Athens has experimented with "straight" hours

during the winter to bring the country more in line with the EU, but this seems to be discretionary rather than obligatory, with some stores observing the hours and others adhering to traditional schedules – which can be rather confusing. So far it has not caught on across the rest of the country.

The shops in Athens' Pláka district remain open until 10pm or longer to take advantage of browsers, and tourist shops throughout the country usually trade well into the evening in summer. But butchers and fishmongers are not allowed to open on summer evenings (although a few disregard the law), and pharmacies (except for those on rota duty) are never open on Saturday mornings.

Getting Around

By air

Flying is considerably more expensive than travelling by boat, bus or train (three times more than a ferry seat, just under double the price of a boat berth), though still reasonable when compared to the price of domestic flights in other countries. For example, the 50-minute ATR flight between Athens and Samos costs about €80.

Greece's national airline, Olympic Airways, has had management and labour troubles for years, and is perennially up for sale (no takers to date). Strikes, mechanical faults and working to rule have in the past caused some flights to be cancelled or delayed, so leave plenty of leeway in your domestic flight arrangements if you have to be back in Athens for an international flight. You can reserve seats, pay fares and collect timetables at any Olympic office, and at numerous on-line travel agents. Island flights are often fully booked over the summer, so book at least a week in advance. Olympic can be reached nationwide on low-cost number 801 11 44444, or on the web (info only, no booking possible) at: www.olympic-airways.gr

Currently the only private alternative is Aegean Airlines, which flies from Athens and Thessaloníki to ten major domestic destinations. Their nationwide low-cost number is 801 11 20000, or you can book online: www.aegeanair.com

By bus

A vast network of bus routes spreads across Greece; the KTEL is a syndicate of bus companies whose buses are cheap, generally punctual and (eventually) will take you to almost any destination that can be reached on wheels. KTEL buses on the more idiosyncratic rural routes often have a distinct personal touch, their drivers decorating and treating the bus with great care.

In the larger cities there may be different KTEL stations for different destinations. Travelling from Thessaloníki to Halkidikí, for example, you will leave from a remote eastern station, though all other destinations are served by a new unitary terminal opened in 2002; Athens has two terminals, while Iráklio in Crete has three.

An additional bus service is provided by OSE, the state railway organisation. Their coaches run only along the major routes, but often dovetail usefully with the KTEL for departure times.

City buses With an influx of new, air-conditioned vehicles, travelling by the regular Athens blue-and-white buses is much less an ordeal than it used to be. They are still usually overcrowded, and the routes are a mystery even to residents. But they are eminently reasonable, at 45 cents per ticket, or €2.90 for an all-day pass. Tickets, valid on trolleys as well, are sold individually or in books of 10, from specific news kiosks and special booths at bus and metro stations, and at various points around the city. Most bus services run until nearly midnight.

Trolley buses, with an overhead pantograph, are marginally faster and more frequent, and serve points of tourist interest; number 1 links the centre of Athens with the railway stations, number 5 passes the Archaelogical Museum, and number 7 does a triangular circuit of the central districts.

The most useful suburban services for tourists are the orange-and-white KTEL Attica buses going from 14 Mavromatéon Street, Pédio toú Áreos Park, to Rafína (an alternative ferry port for the Cyclades and northeast Aegean) and Soúnio (for the famous Poseidon temple there).

Rural buses In the countryside and on islands buses can be converted school buses or modern coaches, or even pick-up trucks with seats installed in the payload space to transport tourists. Some drivers ricochet through mountain roads at death-defying speeds; accidents, however, appear to be rare. Just stow your luggage carefully to be on the safe side.

On islands, a bus of some description will usually meet arriving ferries (even if a boat is delayed) to transport passengers up the hill to the island's *hóra*, or capital. Bus stops are usually in main squares or by the waterfront in harbours and vehicles may or may not run to schedule. A conductor dispenses tickets on the bus itself; often the fare required and the ticket will not show the same price, with the lower old price over-stamped. This isn't a con, but merely

Airport At Level 0 of Arrivals at Eleftherios Venizelos airport, Pacific Left Luggage offers service (tel: 210 35 30 352)

Hotels Most hotels in Greece are willing to store locked suitcases for up to a week if you want to take any short excursions. This is usually a free service, provided you've stayed a night or two, but the hotel accepts no responsibility in the highly unlikely event of theft.

Commercial offices On the islands there are left-luggage offices in many harbour towns. For a small charge space can be hired by the hour, day, week or longer. Although contents will probably be safe, take small valuables with you.

a practice – bus companies use pre-printed tickets until the supply is gone, which may take several years.

By metro

The Athens metro system opened in January 2000, halving travel times around the city and making a visible reduction in surface traffic. The stations themselves are palatial and squeaky-clean, with advertising placards kept to a minimum. The old ISAP electric line, in existence since the 1930s, has been refurbished and designated line M1 (green on maps); it links Piraeus with Kifisiá via the city centre. Line M2 (red) links Dáfni in the south with Sepólia in the northwest of town, with extensions planned all the way down to Glyfáda and up to Thivón. Line M3 (blue) joins Monastiráki with Ethnikí Ámyna in the far east, with the extension to Stavrós set to be finished before the Olympic Games, and a later extension west to Egáleo. The main junction stations of the various lines are Omónia, Sýndagma and Monastiráki.

The best strategy for visitors is to buy a day pass for €2.90, which includes one journey to or from the airport; the ISAP line M1 and lines M2/M3 have separate pricing structures, with M1 tickets not valid on M2/M3, and if you're caught by the ubiquitous plainclothes inspectors with the wrong ticket, or no ticket, you get a spot fine of twenty times the standard fare.

Thessaloníki has recently begun construction of its own metro/light rail system, but inauguration is several years away.

By train

The best thing about rail travel in Greece is the price – even cheaper

Ferry/Catamaran/Hydrofoil Timetables

Since 1997, the GNTO and GTP (Greek Travel Pages) have co-produced a comprehensive, fairly impartial, printed sea transport timetable, *Greek Travel Routes*. Alas, it appeared only sporadically and usually fairly late in the season, though it may revive again for the Olympic year. The best resource at present is the GTP'S websites, www.gtp.gr and www.gtpweb.com, which are fairly accurate, with updates at least every few weeks.

Alternatively, major tourist information offices (Rhodes, Iráklio, etc) supply a weekly schedule, and

most offices hang a timetable in a conspicuous place so you can look up times even if the branch is closed. This should, however, not be relied on implicitly – you may miss your boat. In general, for the most complete and up-to-date information on each port's sailings the best source is the Port Police (in Piraeus and most other ports), known as the *limenarhío*.

Be aware that when you enquire about ferries at a travel agent, they will sometimes inform you only of the lines with which they are affiliated.

than the bus. Otherwise, the Greek rail service, known as OSE, is quite limited, both in the areas it reaches and frequency of departures. Trains are also fairly slow and, unless you are doing the Athens–Thessaloníki run overnight in a couchette, or the quickish run down to Pátra (where the station is virtually opposite the docks), you will probably find the bus more convenient.

You can speed things up by taking an Intercity express train for a considerable surcharge. If you're on a tight budget you can really cut costs by taking the train round-trip, in which case there is a 20 percent reduction. Students and people under 26 are usually eligible for certain discounts. All the common railpasses are honoured in Greece, though you may still have to pay certain supplements and queue for seat reservations.

By sea

Ferries Piraeus is the nerve centre of the Greek ferry network, and chances are you will pass through it at least once; in diminishing order of importance, Rafína, Thessaloníki, Pátra and Kavála are also used. In high season, routes vary from "milk runs" stopping at five islands en route to your destination, to "express" direct ones, so it is worth shopping around before purchasing your ticket. It is also advisable not to purchase your ticket too far in advance: very rarely do tickets for the boat ride actually sell out, but there are frequent changes to schedules which may leave you trying to get a refund.

Personalised ticketing for all boats has been the rule since 2001, so it is no longer possible to purchase tickets on board as in the past. The only exceptions seem to be a few of the ro-ro short-haul ferries (eg Igoumenítsa-Levkímmi).

When you buy your ticket, get

detailed instructions on how to find its berth – the Piraeus quays are long and convoluted; the staff who take your ticket should make sure you are on the right boat.

Above all, be flexible when travelling the Greek seas. Apart from schedule changes, a bad stretch of weather can keep you island-bound for as long as the wind blows. Strikes too are often called during the summer, and usually last for a few days. Out on the islands in particular, the best way to secure accurate, up-to-the-minute information on the erratic ways of ferries is to contact the Port Authority (*limenarhío*), which monitors the movements of individual boats. Port Authority offices are usually located on the waterfront of each island's principal harbour, away from the cafés.

If you are travelling by car, especially during the high season, you will have to plan much further ahead because during the peak season, since car space is sometimes booked many weeks in advance. The same applies to booking a cabin for an overnight trip during summer.

Gamma class – also known as deck, tourist or third – is the classic, cheap way to voyage the Greek seas. There is usually a seat of one sort or another – in community with an international multitude, singing with a guitar, passing a bottle around under the stars. And if the weather turns bad you can always go inside to the "low-class" lounge or the snack bar.

Catamarans/"high speeds"

Fleets of sleek new "high speed" ferries or true catamarans, made in France or Scandanavia, are steadily edging out most ordinary craft (as a stroll around the quays at Piraeus will confirm). They have some advantages over hydrofoils (see below) – they can be even faster, most of them carry lots of cars, and they're permitted to sail in wind conditions of up to Force 7,

whereas "dolphins" are confined to port at 6. The bad news: there are no cabins (because they mostly finish their runs before midnight), food service is even worse than on the old ferries and there are no exterior decks. The aeroplane-seating salons are ruthlessly air-conditioned and subject to a steady, unavoidable barrage of banal Greek TV on overhead monitors (even in *diakikriméni* or "distinguished" class). Cars cost roughly the same to convey as on the old-style boats, but seats are priced at hydrofoil levels. Catamarans come in all shapes and sizes, from the 300-car-carrying behemoths of NEL Lines in the northeast Aegean, Cyclades and central Dodecanese, to the tiny *Sea Star* in the Dodecanese. The useful Dodekanisos Express serves more of the Dodecanese, and can take five cars.

Hydrofoils Though catamarans are undoubtedly the wave of the future, there is still a network of scheduled hydrofoil services to many islands. Like catamarans, hydrofoils are more than twice as fast as the ferries and about twice as expensive, but as ex-Polish or ex-Russian river craft, are not really designed for the Aegean, and prone to cancellation in conditions above wind Force 6.

Hydrofoils (nicknamed *delfínia* or "dolphins" in Greek) connect Piraeus with most of the Argo-Saronic region (Égina, Póros, Ýdra, Spétses and Peloponnese mainland ports as far as Monemvasía), as well as Vólos and the three northerly Sporades (Alónissos, Skíathos, Skópelos). In the Ionian archipelago, there are hydrofoil services from Igoumenítsa to Paxí. In the northeast Aegean, there are local, peak-season services between Thásos or Samothráki and the mainland, while in the Dodecanese all the islands between Sámos and Rhodes, inclusive, are well served.

Phone numbers for the few surviving hydrofoil companies are constantly engaged, or spew out only pre-recorded information in rapid-fire Greek, so the best strategy is to approach the embarkation booths in person. In Piraeus these are on Aktí Miaoúli quay (for Saronic Dolphins and Hellas Dolphins); despite what you may read elsewhere, no services depart any longer from Zéa marina. At Vólos, apply to the gatehouse for the harbour precinct; elsewhere tickets are best obtained from in-town travel agents.

Private Transport

Taxis

Taxis in Greece, especially in Athens, merit a guidebook to themselves.

Drive at your peril in Athens during its multiple rush hours (8–10am, 2–3pm, 4.30–5.30pm, 8–10pm). The twin perils of traffic jams and pollution reached such heights in the capital that a law was introduced during the 1980s: on even days of the month only cars with even-numbered licence plates are allowed in the centre; on odd days only those with odd-numbered plates. This has done little to improve the congestion, noise and smog in Athens, as many families have two cars (one of each type of number plate) and alternate according to the day of the week.

There are three stages to the experience.

First: getting a taxi. It's almost impossible at certain times of the day in Athens, and probably worst before the early afternoon meal. When you hail a taxi, try to get in before stating your destination. The drivers are very picky and often won't let you in unless you're going in their direction. If you see an empty taxi, run for it, be aggressive – otherwise you'll find that some quick Athenian has beaten you to it.

Second: the ride. Make sure the taxi meter is on "1" when you start out, and not on "2" – that's the double fare, which is only permitted from midnight to 5am, or outside designated city limits. Once inside, you may find yourself with company. Don't be alarmed. It is traditional practice for drivers to pick up two, three, even four individual riders, provided they're going roughly in the same direction. In these cases, make a note of the meter count when you get in. In fact, because taxis are so cheap, they can end up functioning as minibus services.

Third: paying up. If you've travelled with other passengers, make sure you aren't paying for the part of the trip that happened before you got in. You should pay the difference in meter reading between embarking and alighting, plus the €0.74 minimum. Otherwise, the meter will tell you the straight price, which may be adjusted according to the tariff that should be on a laminated placard clipped to the dashboard. There are extra charges for each piece of luggage in the boot, for leaving or entering an airport or seaport, plus bonuses around Christmas and Easter.

Some drivers will quote you the correct price, but many others will try to rip you off, especially if it seems that you're a novice. If the fare you're

charged is clearly above the correct price, don't hesitate to argue your way, in whichever language, back down to a normal price.

These rules apply more to Athens than to the islands, although it's still necessary to be pretty assertive on Crete and Rhodes. On the smaller islands, expect to share your taxi, not only with other passengers, but also with an animal or two.

In recent years various radio taxi services have started up in Athens and most other larger towns. They can pick you up within a short time of your call to a central booking number.

Cars

Having a car in rural Greece enables you to reach a lot of otherwise inaccessible corners of the country; however, driving a car in Athens or Thessaloníki is unpleasant and confusing. Tempers run short, while road signs, or warnings of mandatory turning lanes, are practically non-existent.

EU-registered cars are no longer stamped into your passport on entry to the country, can circulate freely for up to six months, and are exempt from road tax as long as this has been paid in the home country – however, you are not allowed to sell the vehicle. Non-EU/EEA nationals will find that a bizarre litany of rules apply to importing cars, chief among them that you must re-export the car when you depart, or have it sealed by Customs in an off-road facility of your choosing.

Driving in Greece All EU/EEA licences, and licences held by returning diaspora Greeks irrespective of issuing country, are honoured in Greece. Conversely, all other licences – this includes North American and Australian ones – are not valid, as many tourists from those

nations attempting to hire cars have discovered to their cost. These motorists must obtain an International Driving Permit before departure (issued by the AAA or CAA in North America on the spot for a nominal cost); the Greek Automobile and Touring Club (ELPA) no longer issues them to foreign nationals in Greece. Similarly, with the advent of the single European market, insurance Green Cards are no longer required, though you should check with your home insurer about the need for any supplementary premiums – many policies now include pan-European cover anyway.

Greek traffic control and signals are basically the same as in the rest of continental Europe, though roundabouts are handled bizarrely by French or English standards – in most cases the traffic entering from the slip road, not that already in the circle, has the right of way.

Motorways speeds are routinely in excess of the nominal 100–120kph (62–75 mph) limits, and drivers overtake with abandon. A red light is often considered not so much an obligation as a suggestion, and oncoming drivers flashing lights at you on one-lane roads means the opposite of what it does in the UK. Here, it means: "I'm coming through." Greece has the highest accident rate in Europe after Portugal, so drive defensively.

Greece has a mandatory seatbelt law, and children under 10 are not allowed to sit in the front seat. It is an offence to drive without your licence on your person (€83 fine). Every car must also carry a first-aid kit in the boot (though hire companies tend to skimp on this). Police checkpoints at major (and minor) junctions are frequent, and in addition to the above offences you can be done for not having evidence of insurance, paid

Hiring a car in Greece is not as cheap as you might hope, owing to high insurance premiums and import duties. Prices vary according to the type of car, season and length of rental and should include CDW (collision damage waiver) and VAT at 18 percent. Payment can, and often must, be made with a major credit card. A full home-country driving licence (for EU/EEA residents) or an International Driving Permit (for all others) is required and you must be at least 21 years old.

In the UK and North America, you can book a car in advance through major international chains such as Hertz, Avis, Budget or Sixt – their

websites have all-inclusive quotes and booking/payment facilities. But there are many reputable, smaller chains, some particular to Greece, that offer a comparable service at lower rates. In Athens most are on, or just off, Syngroú Avenue in the district known as Makrigiánni.

Antena
Syngroú 52, tel: 210 92 24 000
Autorent
Syngroú 11, tel: 210 92 32 514
Just
Syngroú 43, tel: 210 92 39 104
Kosmos
Syngroú 9, tel: 210 92 34 695
Reliable
Syngroú 3, tel: 210 92 49 000

road tax or registration papers in/on the vehicle.

Super and normal unleaded petrol, as well as lead-substitute super, are readily available throughout Greece, though filling up after dark can be difficult. Most garages close around 8pm and, although a rota system operates in larger towns, it is often difficult to find out which station is open. International petrol stations operated by companies like BP and Shell usually take credit cards, but Greek ones often don't.

Road maps Gone are the days when visitors had to suffer with mendacious or comical maps which seemed based more on wishful thinking (especially projected but unbuilt roads) than facts on the ground. There are now three commercial Greek companies producing largely accurate maps to the Greek mainland, mountain areas and islands: Road Editions, Emvelia and Anavasis. They can be found country-wide, in tourist-shop racks and better bookshop chains like Newsstand or Papasotiriou.

Motorcycles and bicycles

On most Greek islands and in many mainland tourist areas, you'll find agencies that hire small motorcycles, various types of scooters, 50cc and under, and even mountain bikes. These give you the freedom to wander where you will, and weekly rates are reasonable.

For any bike of over 50cc, helmets and a motorcycle driving licence are both theoretically required, and increasingly these rules are enforced. The ill-fitting helmets offered are a bit of a joke, but if you refuse them you may have to sign a waiver absolving the dealer of criminal/civil liability – and police checkpoints (see above) can be zealous, levying €88 fines on locals and visitors alike.

Before you set off, make sure the bike of whichever sort works by taking

Breakdowns

The Greek Automobile Association (ELPA) offers a breakdown service for motorists, which is free to AA/RAC members (on production of their membership cards). Phone 104 for assistance nationwide. Some car-hire companies have agreements instead with competitors Hellas Service (dial 1057) or Express Service (dial 154), but these call centres can be slow to dispatch aid. Always ring a local garage number if this is what the hire company instructs you to do.

Cruises

Apparently one in six of all visitors to Greece embarks on an Aegean cruise. These cruises can range from simple one-day trips to the Saronic Gulf islands close to Athens and Piraeus, to luxury four-day journeys taking in the part of the Turkish coast, Rhodes and Crete. Many people opt for a seven-day excursion, which offers an opportunity to see a couple of islands in the Cyclades, a few of the Dodecanese islands, and a foray over to Istanbul for good measure.

Accommodation, prices and standards on board ship vary widely and it would be a very good idea to shop around for a good price.

Ticket agencies in Athens are the places to visit, with cruise opportunities prominently displayed in windows. (However, if you have ever been at Mýkonos harbour

it for a test spin down the street. Brakes in particular are badly set, lights may need new fuses or bulbs, and spark-plugs get fouled – ask for a spare and the small spanner (wrench) to change them. Otherwise, you may get stuck with a lemon, and be held responsible for its malfunctioning when you return it.

Reputable agencies now often furnish you with a phone number for a breakdown pickup service.

Above all, don't take unnecessary chances, like riding two on a bike designed for one. More than one holiday in Greece has been ruined by a serious scooter accident. It is strongly suggested that where possible you stick with the traditional, manual-transmission Honda/Yamaha/Suzuki scooters of 50–100cc, with skinny, large-radius, well-treaded tyres. The new generation of automatic, button-start *mihanákia/papákia* (as they're called in Greek slang), with their sexy fairings and tiny, fat, no-tread tyres, look the business but are unstable and unsafe once off level asphalt. In particular, if you hit a gravel-strewn curve on one of these you will go for a spill, and at the very least lose most of the skin on your hands and knees.

Yacht charter

Chartering a yacht is one of the more exotic ways of island-hopping in Greece. It is by no means cheap, although hiring a boat with a group of friends may not far exceed the price of renting rooms every night for the

when the ships arrive and watched the frantic preparations of shop managers adjusting their prices upwards, it may change your mind about a cruise entirely.)

The most comprehensive company is **Royal Olympic Cruises**; it is accustomed to dealing with foreigners, and offers a variety of cruise durations. Details can be found from most Greek travel agents or by contacting Royal Olympic's headquarters at 87 Aktí Miaoúli, 185 38, Piraeus, tel: 210 42 91 000.

London-based **Swan Hellenic Cruises** offer more upmarket, all-inclusive holidays on large luxury liners, with guest speakers instructing passengers on anything from archaelogy to marine biology. Swan Hellenic are at 77 New Oxford Street, London WC1A 1PP; tel: (020) 7800 2200; www.swanhellenic.com

same number of people.

Depending on your nautical qualifications and your taste for autonomy, you can either take the helm yourself or let a hired crew do so for you. There are over a thousand yachts available for charter in Greece, all of which are registered and inspected by the Ministry of the Merchant Marine. For more information about chartering contact: **The Hellenic Professional Yacht Owners' Association** 43 Freattýdos Street, Zéa Marina, Piraeus; tel: 210 45 26 335. **The Greek Yacht Brokers and Consultants Association** 36 Alkyónis Street, Paleó Fáliron, Athens; tel: 210 98 16 582.

Kaïkia

Apart from conventional ferries, most of which carry cars, there are swarms of small *kaïkia* (caiques) which in season offer inter-island excursions pitched mostly at day-trippers. Since they are chartered by travel agencies, they are exempt from Ministry of Transport fare controls – as well as the 30-year-old, scrap-it rule now enforced in Greece for scheduled ferries – and can be very pricey if used as a one-way ticket from, say, Sámos to Pátmos. The stereotypical emergency transfer by friendly fisherman is, alas, largely a thing of the past; never comfortable at the best of times, it is now highly illegal – knowing this, skippers quote exorbitant prices if approached, and must undertake the journey when the port policeman's gaze is averted.

Where to Stay

How to Choose

There is a broad range of accommodation in Greece, from deluxe hotels to student hostels. Listed are a sample of different categories across the country.

On the islands and in many parts of the mainland, the main type of affordable lodging is private rented rooms (*domátia*) and, increasingly common these days, self-catering studios or apartments (*diamerís-mata*). These are classified separately from hotels, but also subject to official regulation.

In general, when looking for any kind of accommodation, local tourist offices or the Tourist Police, can be of help if you're in a fix – most obviously if no rooms are on offer when you disembark at the dock. The best system, though, increasingly used even by backpackers equipped with mobile phones, is booking a room yourself a few days (or weeks) in advance.

Athens

Andromeda Athens
T. Vássou 22, Abelókipi
Tel: 210 641 5000
Fax: 210 646 6361
www.andromedahotels.gr
A little out of the way, just beyond the Mégaro Mousikís, but small and chic, and very pricey. The well designed rooms and suites have Persian carpets, rather generic bits of art, and modern furnishings. There is a nice swimming pool and the well-regarded Etrusco restaurant. €€€

Athens Hilton
Vas. Sofías 46
Tel: 210 728 1000
Fax: 210 728 1111
www.athens.hilton.com
The new-look Hilton is both extremely plush and hideously expensive. Now open after a €96-million refit, everything is glitzy, from the grand lobby, to the luxuriously carpeted hallways, to the rooms with their marbles bathrooms. Four restaurants, including the rooftop Galaxy with stupendous views. €€€€

Grande Bretagne
Sýndagma Square
Tel: 210 333 0000
Fax: 210 332 8034
www.grandebretagne.gr
Almost as expensive and just as plush in its own special way, the Grande Bretagne is the doyen of Athenian hotels. Also just emerged from a refit, this historic building oozes class, from its luxurious rooms, to its beautiful spa, to its highly recommended restaurant (*see page 366*). €€€

St George Lycabettus
Kleoménous 2, Kolonáki
Tel: 210 729 0711
Fax: 210 729 0439
www.sglycabettus.gr
In a pre-Olympic fit of enthusiasm, the St George has also undergone renovation. Now styling itself a "boutique hotel", the external (more expensive) rooms have one of the best views in the city. The cool, comfortable rooms and suites are elegant and subdued, and the rooftop swimming pool is a delight. There are also two good restaurants, one with a superb view over the Acropolis. €€€

Museum
Bouboulínas 16 and Tosítsa
Tel: 210 380 5611
Fax: 210 380 0507
www.bestwestern.com
Perhaps the best thing about this well-run hotel, is its location close to the Archaeological Museum. The rooms are plain and comfortable, but a little over-priced. There is no restaurant (good ones nearby) but breakfast is included. €€€

NJV Athens Plaza
Sýndagma Square
Tel: 210 33 52 400
Fax: 210 32 35 856
www.grecotel.gr

Modern, swish, and just a bit corporate, the Plaza does, however, kit out its rooms with fabrics by Ralph Lauren and Versace and tries hard to pander to your every whim. The lobby café is a good retreat from the heat or cold. €€€

Royal Olympic
Ath. Diákou 28–34
Tel: 210 928 8413
www.royalolympic.com
A long-standing hotel, now spruced up, with comfortable, if slightly anonymous rooms. The 1960s lobby with a huge chandalier is quite amusing, as is the equally dated dining room, but this is due to period charm rather than it beng run-down. €€€

Acropolis View
Webster 10 and Robértou Gáli
Tel: 210 921 7303
www.acropolisview.gr
The implied view of the Acropolis is available from only a few of the 32 rooms, but also from the roof terrace. The rooms themselves are small but clean and well-cared-for, and the hotel has had the inevitable pre-Olympic makeover. The location is excellent with nearby metro. €€

Attalos
Athinás 29
Tel: 210 321 2801–3
Fax: 210 324 3124
www.attalos.gr
Fairly standard but comfortable rooms close to Monastiráki Square (noisy during the day but quietens down at night). The staff are attentive and friendly, and there is a fine view of the city and the Acropolis from the roof terrace. €€

Austria
Moúson 7, Filopáppou
Tel: 210 923 5151

Hotel Categories

The Greek authorities have six categories for hotels, this is currently expressed as letters but is due to be replaced by a star system (no-star=E, five-star=deluxe), although this is being resisted by hoteliers. Although the current letters are supposed to accurately reflect the hotels' amenities, a swimming pool or tennis court could place an establishment in the A or B bracket even though in every other respect it has indifferent facilities. Also, the number of rooms can limit one's maximum rating, so you commonly encounter 14-room C-class hotels which are superior in every respect to a nearby 50-room B-class.

The following general principles apply, though: Luxury, A-, B- and C-

class hotels all have private bathrooms. Most D-class hotels have en-suite bathrooms, while the dwindling number of E-class hotels don't.

Luxury and A-class hotels must have a bar and restaurant and offer a full choice of breakfasts. B- and C-class should provide a buffet breakfast in a separate dining room, but classes below that will often offer little better than a bread roll, jam and coffee, if even that.

Luxury and A-class hotels should have some or all of these auxiliary facilities: a swimming pool, fitness centre, "private" beach, conference hall, internet access from the rooms, 24-hour desk attendance, "tamed" taxi service.

Price Guide

Price categories are based on the cost of a double room for one night in the high season:
€€€ Expensive over €100
€€ Moderate €50–100
€ Inexpensive under €50
For details of the Greek Tourist Authority's hotel classification system see Hotel Categories on page 333.

Fax: 210 924 7350
www.austriahotel.com
Well-placed, clean and quiet, and for all its name very Greek, though it is popular with German-speaking visitors. The air-conditioned rooms are plain with small en-suite bathrooms and balconies.A good buffet breakfast included in the price. €€
Cecil
Athinás 39
Tel/fax: 210 321 7079
www.cecil.gr
Close by the Attalos, and almost identical in price, the rooms in this hotel are a little more spartan than in its neighbour, but clean, with wooden floors. Breakfast is included in the cost of your stay and the price reflects the hotel's location rather than its facilities. €€
Aphrodite
Einárdou 12 and M. Vóda 65
Tel: 210 881 0589/881 6574
www.hostelaphrodite.com
Clean, unpretentious and friendly, this small hotel is a good deal. Slightly off the beaten track but midway between Viktoria and Stathmos Lárisas metro stations. There is a pleasant basement bar and an excellent deal on the inter-island pass. €
Marble House
A. Zínni 35, Koukáki
Tel: 210 922 8294/923 4058
Fax: 210 922 6461
www.marblehouse.gr
This inexpensive, clean and friendly hotel is probably the best deal in Athens. Close to the Syngroú-Fix metro. Some rooms now have air-conditioning (the others have powerful ceiling fans) and breakfast is available for an extra charge. It has been done up recently and the prices remain low for the city. €
YHA
Victor Hugo 16
Tel: 210 523 2540
Fax: 210 523 2540
www.hihostels.com
A very cheap and well-maintained (the hostel was renovated in 2002) place to stay close to Omónia Square, the railway stations and the National Museum. The four- or twin- bedded

rooms are clean, and the in-house travel service offers discount tickets. Other facilities include a kitchen and luggage store. €
XEN/YWCA
Amerikís 11
Tel: 210 362 4291–4
Fax: 210 362 2400
xene7@hol.gr
This central, women-only hostel is a clean, safe place to stay. It is very good value and some of the rooms (shared triples or doubles) have attached baths. All of them have ceiling fans. There is also a basic restaurant. €

Peloponnese

Areópoli
Pyrgos Kapetanakou
Tel: 27530 51479
One of the better executed EOT restoration projects, this three-storey tower, set in a walled garden, comprises various sized rooms; with communal balconies and a ground-floor refectory. €€

Arhéa Kórinthos
Shadow
approach road
Tel: 27410 31481
Rear rooms at this simple inn, with their views over the lush plain, are best; some noise from live music at weekends in the restaurant. €

Diakoftó
Chris-Paul Hotel
Tel: 26910 41715
Fax: 26910 42128
www.chrispaul-hotel.gr
Named after the family's two children, this friendly hotel is well positioned for the start of the journey up through the Vouraïkós Gorge. €€

Dimitsána
Xenonas Kazakou
Tel/Fax: 27950 31660
A traditional guesthouse in an attractively restored stone house, towards the top of the village. €€

Kalamáta
Haïkos Hotel
Navarínou 115
Tel: 07210 88902
Friendly staff and good-sized rooms in this modern hotel on the seafront. €€
Iviskos Hotel
Fáron 196
Tel: 27210 62511
fax 27210 82323
Set in one of the Neo-Classical buildings with which Kalamáta is richly endowed; this one is lovingly cared for. €€

Kalávryta
Filoxenia Hotel.
Ethnikís Andistásis 20
Tel: 26920 22422
Fax: 26920 23009
www.hotelfiloxenia.gr
Traditional hospitality and efficient service; one of the main hotels for the winter ski season on Mt Helmós. €€

Kórinthos
Ephira
Ethnikís Andistásis 52
Tel: 27410 22434
Fax: 27410 24514
www.ephirahotel.gr
A pleasant modern hotel, well-priced and very near the bus station and the centre of town. Internal rooms have less traffic noise. €€

Koróni
Auberge de la Plage
Zánga Beach
Tel: 27250 22401
Fax: 27250 22508
No prizes for its 1970s modernist architecture, but an incomparable setting overlooking sand and sea. €€

Kosmás
Xenonas Maleatis Apollo
Tel: 27570 31494
Another place to escape some of the summer's heat, this traditional guesthouse is 1,150 m (3,775 ft) up in a delightful village on Mt Párnon. A great base for touring this remote part of Arkadía. Simply decorated rooms, with some kitchen facilities. €€

Loutráki
Acropole
Tsaldári 11
Tel: 27440 22265
Fax: 27440 61171
A hospitable family hotel, convenient for the centre, spa and beach. €€

Monemvasiá
Lazareto
Tel: 27320 61991
Fax: 27320 61992
lazaretohotel@yahoo.com
At the foot of the Monemvasiá rock, overlooking the causeway, the stone-walled ruins of the old hospital have been converted into a discreetly luxurious hotel with a good restaurant. €€€
Malvasia
Tel: 27320 61323
Fax: 27320 61722
The scattered units of this restoration complex are some of the best in town; each room, well furnished in wood and marble, is unique, with features such as fireplaces and balconies. Unit size varies from simple doubles to a family-sized apartment. €€€

Mykínes (Mycenae)
La Belle Hélène
main road
Tel: 27510 76225
Fax: 27510 76179
Reasonable, with the feel of an English country B&B, as conservation rules mean no en-suite bathrooms. Attached restaurant has guestbook with celebrity signatures. (The archaelogist Schliemann lived here while excavating Mycenae.) €€

Návplio
Ilion Hotel and Apartments
Evthimiopoúlou 4/Kapodistríou 6
Tel: 27520 22010
Fax: 27520 24497
www.ilionhotel.gr
Spectacularly decorated rooms and suites, some self-catering, on the hill slope below the Acronavplía. €€€
Nafplio Palace
Akronavplía
Tel: 27520 70800
Fax: 27520 28783
www.nafplionhotels.gr
Low-key but luxurious, set inside the walls of the Akronavplía fortress, and with fabulous views out across the sea to Boúrtzi island. €€€
Marianna Pension
Potamaníou 9
Tel: 27520 24256
Fax: 2752099365
www.pensionmarianna.gr
A beautifully refurbished pension, tucked in under the walls of the Akronavplía fortress. The breakfast terrace has wonderful views of the town. €€

Néos Mystrás
Vyzantion
Tel: 27310 83309
Fax: 27310 20019
byzanhtl@otenet.gr
A recently refurbished hotel; most bathrooms have full-sized tubs, and most rooms enjoy an unbeatable view of the Byzantine ruins. €€

Olybía (Olympia)
Hercules
Tel: 26240 22696
Fax: 26240 22213
Quiet location near the church, with welcoming management. €€
Olympia Youth Hostel
Praxitéles Kondýli 18
Tel: 26240 22580
Nondescript and fairly basic, but the beds are comfortable and the showers are warm. Conveniently close to the ancient site. €

Parálio Ástrous
Chryssi Akti (Golden Beach)
Tel: 27550 51294
Not the most luxurious hotel in town,

indeed with hospital decor, but large rooms, reasonably priced, central and overlooking the beach. Open all year. €

Pátra
Byzantino
Ríga Feréou 106
Tel: 2610 243000
Fax: 2610 622150
www.byzantino-hotel.gr
A beautifully decorated, high-class hotel near the centre of town; open all year. €€€
Galaxy
Agíou Nikoláou 9
Tel: 2610 275 981
Fax: 2610 278 815
A hospital, good quality hotel, on a pedestrianised street at the very heart of the city. Some street noise from Pátra's trendiest street cafés and bars. €€€

Pýrgos
Marily
Deligiánni 48
Tel: 26210 28133
Fax: 26210 27066
Near the railway station and less than 10 minutes' walk from the bus station, so a good base for exploration of the area. €€

Río
Porto Rio
Tel: 2610 992102
Fax: 2610 992115
www.portorio-casino.gr
Very swish, accommodating Pátra's casino, and with small beaches nearby. €€€

Spárti
Cecil
Paleológou 125
Tel: 27310 24980
Fax: 27310 81318
Set on a corner near the top of the main street, this small hotel is well-placed for both Spárti's archaeology and the city life. Extremely friendly and informative management. €€

Stemnítsa
Trikolonion
Tel: 27950 81297
Two 19th-century mansions mated to a modern annexe have bred this underrated C-class hotel with an excellent restaurant; the best accommodation for some distance around. 1,050 metres (3,500 ft) up, so cooler in summer. €€

Stoúpa
Lefktron
Tel: 27210 77322
Fax: 27210 77700
www.lefktron-hotel.gr

A well-sited hotel in the centre of the resort and 5 minutes' walk from the beach. Comfortable rooms, friendly management, and a pool. €€

Taÿgetos
Touristiko Taïgetou
Selibovés, the pass between Kalamáta and Spárti
Tel: 27210 99236
Fax: 27210 98198
A high-altitude refuge, at 1,375 metres (4,500 ft), at the hub of numerous tracks leading into the mountains. The restaurant provides both panoramic views over alpine fir forest and 2,000-metre peaks and tasty home-cooking. Open all year. €

Trípoli
Anactoricon
Ethnikís Andistásis 48
Tel: 2710 222 545
Friendly, professional staff in a comfortable hotel near the centre of town; spacious rooms, recently renovated. €€

Vytína
Mainalon Hotel
Areos Square
Tel: 27950 22217
Fax: 27950 22200
A stylishly elegant hotel, in the centre of this small ski-resort. A good summer base for exploration of central Arkadía. €€€

Giálova
Helonaki
Tel/Fax: 27230 23080
Very hospitable small hotel, with a very popular restaurant underneath (so not for light sleepers). Fabulous sea-views over Navarino Bay. Rooms have a fridge. €

Gýthio
Aktaion
Vassiléos Pávlou 39
Tel: 27330 23500
Fax: 27330 22294
Refurbished neo-classical pile at the north end of the quay; some traffic noise, but all balconied rooms have sea view and air-conditioning. €€€
Zafiro Apartments
Mavrovoúni Beach
Tel: 27330 22991
Spacious apartments set in a quiet orchard, 4 km (2 1/2 miles) from Gýthio; very clean and spacious, with large balconies; hospitable owners. €€

Central Greece

Aráhova
Xenonas Maria
Just above through road
Tel: 22670 31803

The only restored-mansion inn here; currently five tasteful rooms of various sizes, with more being added next door for 2004. €€

Xenonas Petrino
Town centre
Tel: 22670 31384
Modern but stone-clad building (thus the name) with a variety of doubles, triples, quads; upper-storey rooms more exciting than ground-floor ones. €€

Delfí (Delphi)

Athina
Vassiléon Pávlou and Frederíkis 55
Tel/fax: 22650 82239
The best backpackers' hotel: simple wood-decor, en-suite rooms, many with rooms of the Itéa Gulf. Heated in winter; closed Nov–Christmas and weekdays Christmas–end March. €

Pan
Vassiléon Pávlou and Frederíkis 53
Tel: 22650 82294
Fax: 22650 83244
An excellent mid-range hotel, with plain doubles but excellent family suites with large bathtubs. Their 2002-built annexe across the road, Artemis, has a higher standard – most of the baths here have mini-tubs – but you sacrifice the view. €

Sun View
Apóllonos 84
Tel: 22650 82349
Fax: 22650 82815
dalentzis@internet.gr
Very quietly located pension on the uppermost street; rooms acquired pastel shades in 2002, plus art on the walls. There's a breakfast salon downstairs, and parking outside. €

Galaxídi

Galaxa
Hillside above Hirólakas bay
Tel: 22650 41620
Fax: 22650 42053
Rooms here are somewhat casually maintained, but the views are superb and the welcome friendly at this restored-house hotel. The best bit is the breakfast and drinks garden bar, under the vines across the way. €€

Ganymede
E. Vlami Street, town centre, about 500m from the main port
Tel 22650 41328
Fax 22650 42160
www.gsp.gr/ganimede.gr
Galaxídi's oldest restoration hotel, under the management of delightfully entertaining Italian owner Brunello Perocco. Just six en-suite rooms in an old house (plus two modern studios), but it's Bruno, his garden bar and the famous breakfasts that keep people returning – reservations mandatory. Closed November. €€

Návpaktos

Akti
Grímbovo, by the fountain-stream
Tel: 26340 28464
Fax: 26340 24171
akti@otenet.gr
This hotel is the town's clear winner, set behind the town's easterly beach: it is the little touches like insect screens and oblique sea views from about half the rooms that make the difference. The breakfast is of a good standard, and the top-floor suites are palatial. €€

Ilion
Inland at the base of the *kástro*
Tel: 26340 21222
For a stay in the old town, try this quiet little ten-room inn, though it's best to be lightly laden, as you're some way distant from the nearest parking. €€

Karpenisiótis valley

Helidona
Old Mikró Horió
Tel: 22370 41221/697 2555637
In a region known for very pricey lodging, this 2001-reburbished hotel remains affordable, and is superbly set on the old *platía*, with a ground floor restaurant. €€

Agrambeli
Gávros
Tel: 22370 41148
A riverside pension with cool, cavernous rooms; there's a breakfast bar and large swimming pool in the middle of the lawn. €

Messolóngi

Theoxenia
Tourlídos 2, south edge of town
Tel: 26310 22493
Fax: 26310 22230
The most attractive and best-equipped hotel here, more by virtue of position and pleasant grounds than anything else. €€

Vólos

Aigli
Argonavtón 24
Tel: 24210 24171
Fax: 24210 33006
This is the best city-centre hotel. It occupies a well-restored early-20th-century building, but the price is only worth it if you can get a sea-view room. €€

Roussas I
Iatroú Tzánou 11
Tel: 24210 21732
Fax: 24210 22987
At the east end of the seafront, this is the city's most secluded hotel, and under-rated at E-class, which makes it a bargain. Well-kept en-suite rooms, and free parking nearby, though no breakfast. €

Makrinítsa

Arhondiko Repana
on main lane
Tel: 24280 99067
Fax: 24280 99548
The best value in this rather touristy village; slightly over-restored but comfortable rooms with all mod cons. €€

Portariá

Kritsa
Central *platía*
Tel: 24280 99121
Fax: 24280 90006
www.hotel-kritsa.gr
Taste is the key word here; an indifferent, interwar hotel building has been transformed into something worth going out of your way for. It has just 8 rooms (some of these are suites), 4 with balconies and views over the square. The massive breakfast puts to shame bog-standard continentals offered elsewhere at the same price. €€

Zagorá

Arhondiko Konstantinidi
Tel: 24260 23391
Fax: 24260 22671
One of the few surviving 18th-century mansions in the north of Pílio, this offers well-converted rooms, spacious common areas (including the courtyard) and a good buffet breakfast. €€

Ágios Ioánnis

Anesis
shore road
Tel: 24260 31123
Fax: 24260 31223
anesis@otenet.gr
One of the first hotels here, renovated in the 1990s, and one of the few still welcoming walk-in trade; civilised management presides over good-taste, pastel-decor rooms. €€

Moúressi

The Old Silk Store
curve in access road by bakery
Tel/fax: 24260 49086
www.pelionet.gr/oldsilkstore
Nineteenth-century silk-merchant's mansion lovingly converted into a B&B by Cornishwoman Jill Sleeman, who also leads walks in the area. Excellent breakfasts (own-made jams and

wholemeal breads), served in the idyllic garden. €€

Damoúhari
Damouhari Hotel
centre bay
Tel: 24260 49840
Fax: 24260 49841
Most of this mock-trad, stone-built studio complex is taken up by package companies, but the bayside annexe, five state-of-the-art rooms over the restaurant, is kept back for walk-ins. You still have access to the hillside pool, and the eclectically decorated bar. €€

Tsangaráda
Kastanies
Ágios Stéfanos district, the last building in town heading northwest
Tel: 24260 49135
Fax: 24260 49169
www.kastanies.gr
The rooms in this restored mansion, which is set in a terraced garden, are expertly furnished in good taste, and the spotless bathrooms are all of an exceptional standard; they all have tubs. The excellent breakfast is famously rich, and the attached restaurant (Evohia) has an equally good reputation. €€
Konaki
Agía Paraskeví district, below the through highway
Tel: 24260 49481
All rooms here have fridges and views of some sort, some have iron beds and balconies; pleasant basement breakfast area. €€

Vyzítsa
Kondou
up the slope from the car park
Tel: 24230 86793
vikonto@otenet.gr
A good standard of restored accommodation (dating from 1792) on two floors, at an affordable price; mind your head going in the low room-doors. €€
Thetis
by the church and central car park
Tel: 24230 86111
Maybe not the grandest restored arhondikó here, but the most popular, thanks to its kafenío (where breakfast is available) and excellent value. A mix of wood-trimmed rooms, both en-suite and not. €

Potistiká
Elytis
on slope above the beach
Tel: 24230 54482
If you just want a seaside holiday without cultural distractions, this is probably the best place on Pílio to do it: a pristine, undeveloped bay, and

this welcoming, if bland-roomed hotel just inland, with an attached full-service restaurant. €

Argalastí
Agamemnon
village centre
Tel/fax: 24230 54557
www.agamemnon.gr
Yet another restored mansion, with exposed stonework and fireplaces in the rooms, antiques in the common areas and a large pool outside – and used by packages. Still, worth a try as a base in the south of the peninsula. €€
Karýtsa
Dóhos Katalymáta, between Karýtsa and Stómio
Tel: 24950 92001
On the slopes of Mount Kíssavos, this 2002-built hotel nestles in the forest above some of the best and least visited beaches in Greece. Huge wood-floored rooms or suites, all have sea-facing balconies and full bathtubs, while some have cooking facilities. The stone-floored common areas include a concert hall, hosting special events all summer, a pool, and the bar/breakfast salon. €€

Kalambáka
Elena
Kanári 3, in the old village centre
Tel: 24320 77789
2002-built xenónas with just four large, superior-standard, air-conditioned rooms. A bit pricey, but quiet and just a few steps from the wonderful Byzantine cathedral. €€
Meteora
Ploutárhou 13, west end of town
Tel: 24320 22367
Fax: 24320 75550
Air-conditioned rooms, adequate parking, breakfast augmented with cake and cheeses, and the Gekas brothers' unfailing helpfulness gives this nominally E-class hotel the edge over the noise-plagued behemoths on the main drag. €

Kastráki
Doupiani House
west edge of village, well-signed above road to monasteries
Tel: 24320 77555
Fax: 24320 75326
doupiani-house@kmp.forthnet.gr
The in-your-face views of the rock formations, already decent air conditioned rooms set for upgrading in 2004, and Thanassis' and Toula's welcome mean you always have to reserve in advance here. €
Ziogas Rooms
set well off noisy through road
Tel: 24320 24037
Most of the large balconied units face

on to the rocks; there is heating for the winter, as well as a combination breakfast salon and taverna on the ground floor. €

Aspropótamos
Pyrgos Mantania (Mantania Tower)
near Kalliroe village
Tel: 24320 87351/87600
www.mantania-ae.gr
A superb inn, new but stone-built, poised to take advantage of river-kayaking and forest-walking aficionados who visit this area. Families are catered for in the upstairs 4-bedded suites, with fireplaces; cheaper but still large standard rooms on the lower floors. Well-regarded restaurant -bar in a separate building. €€

Epirus

Ioánnina
Kastro
Androníkou Paleológou 57
Tel: 26510 22866
Fax: 26510 22780 www.epirus.com/hotel-kastro
Small, cosy restoration inn on the way to the inner citadel, with seven varied rooms (ground-floor ones, with fans but no air-con, are a tad cheaper). Limited street parking; open all year. €€
Orizon/Horizon
Lykiades village, 12km out of town
Tel: 26510 86180,
www.epirus.com/horizon
Stunning views over the entire lake valley from this well-designed, 2000-built hotel. Rooms vary but are all huge, with wood floors and some with fireplaces. It's very popular with Greek weekenders, so reservations are mandatory. €€
Politeia
Anexartisías 109A
Tel: 26510 22235
www.etip.gr
Studio-hotel on the site of an old tradesmen's hall. Though units are self-catering, breakfast is offered in the courtyard. Pretty quiet, despite the location; open all year. €€
Xenia
Dodónis 35
Tel: 26510 47301
Fax: 26510 47189
Most of the Xenia chain in Greece are to be scrupulously avoided, but this one's a goodie, and solves two major Ioánnina problems: street noise and parking. Set back from the street in pleasant, park-like grounds, its common areas are the hotel's main plus; the parquet-floored rooms, lightly redone in 2001, remain essentially well worn and resolutely 1960s. Open all year. €€

Métsovo

Filoxenia
near the central plaza
Tel: 26560 41021
Fax: 26560 42009
An excellent-value inn on the side of the square. Comfortable rooms, the rear ones have stunning views. €

Bitounis
main street
Tel: 26560 41217
Fax: 26560 41545
bitounis@met.forthnet.gr
Luxurious digs managed by energetic English-speaking brothers long resident in London. All rooms got a thorough overhaul in 2001, most have balconies, plus there are attic family suites and a sauna for ski season. €

Kónitsa

Yefiri
riverside district
Tel: 26550 23780
Fax: 26550 22783
gefyri@yahoo.com
The best standard offered in town, with large wood-floored rooms and extensive common areas; there's a pool too, if the adjacent river with its sporting opportunities for some reason doesn't appeal. €€

Pápingo (Megálo)

Papaevangelou
north end of the village
Tel: 26530 41135
Fax: 26530 41988
The best traditional-style inn here, with enormous rooms (some self-catering), and equally spacious bar, where the better-than-average breakfast is served. Friendly, willing management. €€€

Kalliopi
south side of the village
Tel: 26530 41081
Cosy *xenónas* with heated rooms furnished in good taste; attached to the recommended namesake restaurant (*see page 369*). €€

Nikos Tsoumanis
village centre
Tel: 26530 42237
Attached to the namesake restaurant, these five new units built in traditional style are comfortable if a bit dark; more are planned. €€

Pension Koulis
behind central *kafenío*
Tel: 26530 41138
The original village inn, converted in 1993 to en-suite rooms; Koulis himself has retired and sons Nikos and Dimitris are now at the helm. €

Pápingo (Mikró)

O Dias
Tel: 26530 41257
Fax: 26530 41892

An excellent renovation inn spread over two traditional buildings, bracketing a terrace restaurant and a bar; the proprietor is particularly trekker-friendly and helpful, as mountaineering is the main enterprise hereabouts. €€

Koukoúli
village centre
Tel: 26530 71743
Lovingly restored village house kept by an entertaining English couple, just three units so far but two larger ones planned, along with breakfast salon (currently you eat in the lovely garden). Reservations advised. €€

Ano Pedina

To Spiti tou Oresti
near top of village
Tel/fax: 26530 71202
Dutch/Greek co-managed, this restoration inn has warmly furnished, double-glazed rooms, most en-suite. The attached restaurant can be uneven. €€

Elati

Iy Elati
village centre
Tel: 26530 61492
Fax: 26530 71181
A bit away from the heart of the national park, but that means you're more likely to happen on a vacancy, and there are stunning views of Mount Gamíla from the outdoor terrace. The manager is returned Greek-Canadian; the restaurant is competent. €€

Tsepélovo

Gouris
east side of village
Tel: 26530 81214/81288
Run by Anthoula and daughters, this welcoming, 1996-renovated en-suite inn has long been popular with walkers in the region, thanks to the late Alekos Gouris' efforts to promote local trekking. If you're offered half board, accept it, as the *platía* tavernas are moderate. €

Mountain Refuges

Mountain refuges are run by the various Greek mountaineering clubs and can range from a small 12-bed ski hut where you need to bring your own food and supplies to 100-bed lodges where all meals are provided. There are over 40 of them, but very few are permanently staffed – most conspicuously, two on Mount Olympus and one in Crete's White Mountains – and getting the key for the others from the controlling club is generally more trouble than it's worth.

Párga

Magda's Apartments
below road to Agiá
Tel: 26840 31728
Fax: 26840 31690
magdas@otenet.gr
The best standard within the town: several ranks of self-catering rooms in an olive grove, with a bar and pool terrace. There is some package allotment, so book early; open Greek Easter–late October. €€

Golfo Beach
Kryonéri beach
Tel: 26840 32336
Fax: 26840 31347
The diametric opposite of Magda's (above): a slice of 1970s Greece, the oldest inn at Párga. Rooms are basic, about half en-suite. Half of them face the sea, the others a pleasant garden. Good restaurant downstairs. Open May–October. €

Karavostási

Karavostasi Beach
back from the middle of the beach
Tel: 26650 91104
Fax: 26650 91568
karavost@otennet.gr
Well designed, sympathetic beach hotel with large pool, well-kept gardens and decent breakfasts. The rooms are all-white spartan, but perfectly adequate. Open end of May to early October. €€

Ammoudiá

Glaros
right by river, 200m behind beach Tel: 26840 41300
Fax: 26840 41118
No great character – the village was only built in the 1960s – but air-conditioned, en-suite and quiet, this little hotel makes a good base for the nearby beaches and quayside tavernas. Open May–September. €

Thessaloníki

Bristol Capsis
Oplopioú & Katoúni 2
Tel: 2310 506500
Fax: 2310 515777
www.capsishotel.gr
Perhaps Thessaloníki's most sumptuous boutique hotel. Sixteen individually named rooms each immaculately restored in the shell of the former Bristol Hotel. €€€

Capsis Hotel
Monastiríou 18
Tel: 2310 52321
Fax: 2310 510555
www.capsishotel.gr
This modern city-centre hotel offers all the expected luxury facilities including a roof garden, gym swimming pool and sauna. €€€

Price Guide

Price categories are based on the cost of a double room for one night in the high season:
€€€ Expensive over €100
€€ Moderate €50–100
€ Inexpensive under €50
For details of the Greek Tourist Authority's hotel classification system see Hotel Categories on page 333.

Electra Palace
Plateía Aristotélous 9
Tel: 2310 294000
Fax: 2310 294001
www.forthnet.gr/electrapalace
Another central hotel, overlooking the broad Platía Aristotélous. Neo-classical façade, very imposing and very comfortable. €€€

Kinissis Palace
Egnatías 41 & Syngroú
Tel: 2310 508082
Fax: 2310 523904
www.kinissi-palace.gr
A renovated city-centre hotel retaining its original style and atmosphere. Rooms are large and airy with double glazing; there's also a small sauna and massage centre. €€€

Macedonia Palace
Megálou Alexándrou 2
Tel: 2310 897197
Fax: 2310 897210
www.grecotelcity.gr
A short way south of the White Tower is another landmark luxury hotel that draws many business travellers and VIPs. Oozes distinguished class. €€€

Mediterranean Palace
Salamínos 3 & Karatásou
Tel: 2310 552554
Fax: 2310 552622
www.mediterranean-palace.gr
You can't get closer to the port or the Ladádika district than with this imposing belle époque hotel. Large, lavishly furnished rooms and airy public areas. €€€

Minerva Premier
Egnatías 44 & Syngroú 12
Tel: 2310 566440
Fax: 2310 566436
info@minervapremier.gr
Built within a 1929 neo-classical building, the hotel's standard rooms are comfortable enough and its business rooms are mini-offices. Lots or marble, crystal and wood. €€€

Philippeion Hotel
Dásos Séich-Soú
Tel: 2310 203320
Fax: 2310 218528
www.philippion.gr
Out of reach of the bustling city, in the Séih-Soú forest. Excellent views down to the city, more than comfortable

rooms and a free shuttle service to/from the centre. €€€

ABC Hotel
Angeláki 41
Tel: 2310 265421
Fax: 2310 276542
Very handy for the Thessaloníki Annual Fair, this east side business hotel is smartly functional, sporting renovated rooms with most mod cons for a mid-range hotel. €€

Hotel Tourist
Mitropóleos 21
Tel: 2310 270501
Fax: 2310 226865
Despite the small reception area the Tourist is a comfortable mid-range hotel with standard-sized and reasonably well appointed rooms. Very central. €€

Le Palace
Tsimiskí 12
Tel: 2310 257300
Fax: 2310 221270
www.lepalace.gr
Another central hotel in an old (1926) building. Fully renovated in 2002, Le Palace has a style reminiscent of Paris in the '30s. There's a relaxing in-house cafeteria called the Deli Deli. €€

Luxembourg
Komninón 6
Tel: 2310 252600
Fax: 2310 252605
In the heart of the commercial district, this hotel is vaguely art deco in style. Rooms are standard but comfortable enough. €€

Best Western Vergina
Monastiríou 19
Tel: 2310 516021
Fax: 2310 529308
www.vergina-hotel.gr
Part of the Best Western chain, the Vergina is very close to the port and the train station. Comfortable, businesslike and similar to other hotels in the chain. €€

Hotel Alexandria
Egnatía 18
Tel: 2310 536185
Fax: 2310 536154
A good budget choice from among the many cheapies at the western end of Egnatía. The management is a bit sullen, but the rooms are very decent. €

Hotel Ilysia
Egnatía 24
Tel: 2310 528492
Another reasonable budget choice. Rooms are a little more basic than its neighbour the Alexandria, but have TVs, fridge, telephone and private bathroom. €

Orestias Kastoria
Agnóstou Stratiótou 14
Tel: 2310 276517
Fax: 2310 276572

Of all the budget choices, this one stands out from the others. Away from the noise of Egnatía this hotel, in a neo-classical building, has light, clean and airy rooms that are very presentable. €

Panórama

Hotel Panorama
Analípseos 26
Tel: 2310 341229
Fax: 2310 344871
www.hotelpanorama.gr
A 70s-era renovated hotel in the hills above Thessaloníki, the Panorama is good for travellers with their own transport. Comfortable rooms and excellent panoramic views over the city. €€€

Nefeli
Komninón 1
Tel: 2310 342002
Fax: 2310 342080
nepheli@otenet.gr
Another good, out-of-town choice for people who like a little more breathing space. Pretty roof garden, splendid views and comfortable rooms. Excellent restaurant. €€€

Macedonia and Thrace

Kastoriá

Arhondikó tou Vérgoula
Aidístras 14
Tel: 24670 23415
Fax: 24670 23676
A converted old mansion on the quiet side of town. Ideal for a weekend getaway, the old-fashioned rooms in this mansion simply ooze old-world style. There is a large yet homely breakfast room and wine bar downstairs. €€

Eolís
Agíou Athanasíou 30
Tel: 24670 21070
Closer to the centre of town, a delightful restored German-style mansion, once used as a consulate. A neat boutique hotel, with lavishly furnished rooms and all the expected mod cons. There is a welcoming cafeteria and bar. €€

Alexandroúpoli

Thraki Palace
4km (2 /2 miles) along Alexandroúpoli-Thessaloníki road
Tel: 25510 89100
Fax: 25510 89119
www.thrakipalace.gr
The latest in string of upper market hotels that have blossomed in Alexandroúpoli. A little out of the city centre for travellers without transport, but self-contained and with its own private beach. A nicely designed place with well-thought-out public areas, restaurant and bar. €€€

Monastery Stays

Monasteries and convents can occasionally provide lodging for travellers, though their *xenónes* (guest lodges) are intended primarily for Orthodox pilgrims. Mount Áthos, of course, has a long tradition of this hospitality (for men only). If you have found a monastery that does accept overnight guests, you will have to dress appropriately and behave accordingly. The doors may close as early as sunset and some kind of donation may be expected.

Amouliani

Agionísi Resort
1.5km (1 mile) from the port
Tel: 23770 51102
Fax: 23770 51180
www.papcorp.gr
Top-class accommodation in this low-key bungalow-style resort. Built amphitheatrically close to a sandy beach, the individual bungalows are spacious and well-appointed, with local furnishing touches from Halkidikí. There's a pool and manicured garden, and a private ferry service to and from the Athos coastline opposite. €€

Arnéa

Oikia Alexandrou
Platía Patriárhou Vartholoméou 1st
Tel: 23720 23210
www.oikia-alexandrou.gr
A family home turned into a boutique pension. The immaculately decorated interior features cosy, wood-floored rooms with all modern conveniences. The bar-cum-restaurant downstairs serves up wholesome Macedonian dishes and in winter there is a welcoming log fire. €€€

Dadiá

Ecotourism Hostel
1 km (1/2 mile) beyond Dadiá village
Tel: 22540 32263
Run by the Visitors' Centre for WWF's Dadiá Wildlife Refuge, each of the simply furnished en-suite rooms has been named after birds that frequent the Dadiá Forest. This is the best place to stay if you want to get up early to views the raptors soaring and feeding in the Refuge, an hour's brisk uphill hike deep into the forest. There are a couple of decent tavernas in the village. €

Édessa

Varósi
Arhieréos Meletíou 45-47
Tel: 23810 21865
Fax: 23810 28872

Tucked away in the back streets of the town's Ottoman quarter this faithfully refurbished old home is now a cosy, inexpensive boutique pension. The modern yet traditional-styled rooms are wooden-floored and stone-walled. Enormous optional breakfast in the fireplace-equipped dining/sitting area. €

Kavála

Hotel Nefeli
Erythroú Stavroú 50
Tel: 2510 227441
Fax: 2510 227440
For a town not noted for its hotel accommodation, this one breaks the rules. Renovated thoroughly in 2002, the Esperia manages to combine convenience of location (it's very central) with comfort. As a business hotel it provides all the expected amenities. For travellers it's as close as you can get to bus and ferry links onwards. €€

Komotiní

Olympos Hotel
Orféos 37
Tel: 23510 37690
holympus@otenet.gr
Most of Komotiní's hotels are business-oriented and impersonal. The Olympos is an exception – friendly and welcoming, but modern and up to date after recent renovation. It's very handy to the centre of town and a clutch of good-quality local restaurants. €€

Litóhoro

Villa Pantheon
West end of Litóhoro village
Tel: 23520 83931
Fax: 23520 83932
Claiming possibly the best location in this small base village for Mt Olympus, this is a very pleasant and well-appointed family-style hotel. Rooms are all solidly furnished, with small kitchenettes, minibars, satellite TV and air-conditioning. €€

Préspa

Ágios Germanós Hostel
centre of Ágios Germanós village
Tel: 23850 51357
www.prespa.com.gr
A fairly new offering to an area with limited accommodation. There are only eight rooms in this converted stone and wood farmhouse, but they are all well equipped and very comfortable. All are centrally heated, while two have working open fireplaces. €€

Xánthi

Hotel Dimokritos
28 Oktovríou 41

Tel: 25410 25411
Fax: 25410 25537
Xánthi is a business-oriented town and its hotels reflect the clientele. The Dimokritos has gone to some lengths to make itself appealing to travellers too. All rooms have fridges and TVs (and dedicated ISDN lines). It's also very central with most places of interest and good places to eat no more than a 10-minute walk away. €€

Saronic Gulf

Salamína

Gabriel
Eándio
Tel: 210 466 2275
Not plush but the best hotel on the island, in the seaside village of Eándio, right by the water. Standard facilities and comfortable enough should you stay on Salamína. €€

Aegina

Apollo
Agía Marína
Tel: 22970 32271
Fax: 22970 32688
apolo@otenet.gr
On the east side of the island in Égina's main resort. Apollo is a large, somewhat ageing but still comfortable choice if you want to be near a decent beach. Good facilities and a restaurant. €€
Hotel Brown
Égina Town
Tel: 22970 22271
Fax: 22970 25838
brownhotel@aig.forthnet.gr
Right on the southern waterfront a five-minute walk from the ferry quay is this converted sponge factory, now a hotel still owned by the original family whose ancestry was partly English (hence the name). Rooms are spacious and tidy and there's a large leafy garden. €€
To Petrino Spiti
Égina Town
Tel: 22970 23837
A three-floored stone house (*pétrino spíti*) a 10-minute walk from the harbour. Very comfortable and distinctive. There are nine studios all done out in different styles – a couple of them in antique style. €

Angístri

Yana Hotel
Skála, Angístri
Tel: 22970 91356
Fax: 22970 91342
One of Angístri's better budget hotels, comprising only 15 rooms, each offering comfort and space. Located in the port settlement of Skála, its location means you don't need a taxi to get there. Open April–November. €

Póros

Hotel Manessi
Póros Town
Tel: 22980 22273
Fax: 22980 24345
manessis@otenet.gr
A very pleasant waterfront choice right
in the middle of the action. Housed in
a neo-classical building all rooms are
well equipped with central heating and
air-conditioning, TV and fridge and
most have balconies looking over the
port. €

Sto Roloi
Hatzopoúlou & Karrá 13,
Póros Town
Tel: 22980 25808
Fax: 210 963 3705
www.storoloi-poros.gr
Sto Roloi ("at the clock") is located
near the prominent clock tower on top
of the hill behind Poros town, in a
200-year-old house converted into
three apartments, with two more next
door at Anemone House and the Little
Tower. All decorated with traditional
furnishings. €€€

Seven Brothers Hotel
Platía Iróon, Póros Town
Tel: 22980 23412
Fax: 22980 23413
www.poros.com.gr/7brothers
A small family-run hotel with a
restaurant. Rooms are large and very
comfortable, with TV and air-
conditioning. Very handy for the centre
of Póros Town and the ferry and
hydrofoil quay. €€

Ýdra

Orlof
Ýdra Town
Tel: 22980 52564
Fax: 22980 53532
orloff@internet.gr
A very comfortable mansion turned
hotel with all creature comforts. All
rooms are individual, in different
shapes and sizes. Some look out over
the town, others onto the flower-filled
garden, where a large buffet breakfast
is served. €€€

Leto
Ýdra Town
Tel: 22980 53386
Fax: 22980 53806
leto@sofianos.gr
A traditional style Hydriot house
turned boutique hotel. All rooms are
tastefully designed in Hydriot naval
style and all are air-conditioned.
Facilities include an attractive
breakfast room and a separate area
for smokers – unusual in Greece. €€

Miranda
Ýdra Town
Tel: 22980 52230
Fax: 22980 53510
Set in a mansion built in 1810
Miranda is a traditional style hotel

with 14 differently decorated rooms,
some traditional, others art deco. The
classy atmosphere is enhanced by the
in-house art gallery. Breakfast is
served in the garden. €€

Spétses

Nissia Hotel
Spétses Town
Tel: 22980 75000
Fax: 22980 75012
www.nissia.gr
Perhaps the classiest hotel on the
island, the Nissia is 500 metres (550
yds) west of the main ferry quay,
overlooking the promenade. Consists
of 31 comfortable single-floor and two-
floored apartments built in traditional
island style, all with sea views. An
extensive buffet breakfast is included.
€€€

Spetses
Spétses Town
Tel: 22980 72602
Fax: 22980 72494
www.spetses-hotel.gr
Located on its own beach 800 metres
(½ mile) west of the ferry quay.
Rooms are large and amply furnished,
and all have balconies overlooking the
sea, TV, music system, air-
conditioning and minibar. There is an
in-house restaurant. €€€

Lefka Palace
Spétses Town
Tel: 22980 72311
Fax: 22980 72161
lefkapalace@hotmail.com
The Lefka Palace is in a class of its
own with large airy rooms and ample
verandas. Close to the sea, there is
also a large swimming pool, tennis
courts and extensive gardens. €€

Cyclades

Ándros

Paradisos
Ándros town
Tel: 22820 22187
An elegant neo-classical mansion near
the centre of town, 700 metres (760
yds) from the beach. Airy rooms with
superb views from the balconies.
€€€

Andros Holiday Hotel
Gávrio
Tel: 22820 71384
Fax: 22820 71097
androshol@otenet.gr

Right on the beach just outside town.
Attractive rooms with sea-view
terraces, swimming pool, tennis
courts, restaurant. €€

Mare e Vista – Epaminondas
Batsí
Tel: 22820 41682
www.mare-vista.com
The island's best hotel, with big
rooms and terraces, a big pool,
gardens and a garage; 15 minutes'
walk from the town, closer to the
beach. €€

Niki
Ándros town
Tel/fax: 2282 29155
Opened in 2002, this redone
mainstreet mansion is convenient,
elegant and inexpensive. All rooms
have balconies, some facing the main
street, some the sea. €

Kéa

Ioulis
Ioulís (Hóra)
Tel: 22880 22177
Delightfully quiet spot in the kástro,
with lovely views from the terrace.
Basic but serviceable. €€

Kéa Beach
Koúndouros Bay
Tel: 22880 31230
Fax: 22880 31234
Luxury bungalow complex 5 km (3
miles) south of Písses, built in
traditional Cycladic style, with all
facilities from a nightclub to
watersports. €€

Tínos

Alonia
Hóra (3 km/1½ miles towards Pórto)
Tel: 22830 23541
Fax: 22280 23544
Unprepossessing from the outside,
this is Tinos' most welcoming hotel.
The pool is big and surrounded by
greenery, the rooms' balconies have
beautiful views, and the food is good.
€€

Tinion
Hóra
Tel: 22830 22261
Fax: 22830 24754
Charming old-world hotel in the centre
of town, with tiled floors, lace curtains
and a large balcony. €€

Kýthnos

Kythnos
Mérihas Bay
Tel: 22810 32247
Basic but friendly hotel right on the
waterfront. Rooms at the front have
balconies overlooking the sea. €

Sýos

Dolphin Bay Hotel
Galissás
Tel: 22810 42924

Price Guide

Price categories are based on the cost of a double room for one night in the high season:
€€€ Expensive over €100
€€ Moderate €50–100
€ Inexpensive under €50
For details of the Greek Tourist Authority's hotel classification system see Hotel Categories on page 333.

Fax: 22810 42843
www.dolphin-bay.gr
The largest and most modern resort-hotel on the island, with all facilities, large swimming pool, restaurant, and beautiful views over the bay. €€€
Hotel Faros Village
Azólimnos
Tel: 22810 61661
Fax: 22810 61660
mavross@otenet.gr
This large hotel by the beach is five minutes' drive away from the capital. It has all the usual facilities, including two pools and restaurant. All rooms have verandas with either sea or garden views. €€€
Omiros
Ermoúpoli
Tel: 22810 24910
Fax: 22810 86266
150-year-old neo-classical mansion restored to a high standard. Rooms furnished in traditional style, with views of the lively harbour. €€

Mýkonos

Cavo Tagoo
Hóra
Tel: 22890 23692
Fax: 22890 24923
www.cavotagoo.gr
Jet-set luxurious, set on a hillside 500 metres (550 yds) north of Hóra. Prize-winning Cycladic architecture, beautiful furnishings, impeccable service, friendly atmosphere, good views, pool, and Mykonos' best restaurant. €€€
Deliades
Ornós
Tel: 22890 79430
Fax: 22890 26996
www.hoteldeliadesmykonos.com
Built in 2001 with quiet taste, a short walk up the hill from Ornós beach. Every room has a big terrace with sea view. Relaxed atmosphere, pool, port and airport transfer. €€€
Villa Konstantin
Ágios Vasílios
Tel: 22890 26204
Fax: 22890 26205
www.villakonstantin-mykonos.gr
700 metres from the town, in authentic island style but with all the

luxuries. All rooms have terraces or balconies, most with sea views, and some have kitchens. €€
Myconian Inn
Hóra
Tel: 22890 23420
Fax: 22890 27269
mycinn@hotmail.com
Right on the upper edge of town, this hotel is convenient, quiet, unpretentious and tasteful. Balconies overlook the port. €

Sérifos

Areti
Livádi
Tel: 22810) 51 47 9
Fax: 22810) 51 54 7
Family-run hotel (and cake-shop) near the ferry landing, built on a hill with superb views. Peaceful terraced garden overlooking the sea. €€

Sífnos

Platis Gialos Hotel
Platýs Gialós
Tel: 22840 71324
Fax: 22840 31325
Large, Cycladic-style hotel at the far end of the beach. Well furnished and tastefully decorated with wood-carvings and wall paintings. The flagstone terrace reaches to the sea. All amenities, including a restaurant with the same view. €€€
Artemon Hotel
Artemónas
Tel: 22840 31303
Fax: 22840 32385
Simple, attractive family hotel with rooms that overlook fields rolling towards the sea. €€
Apollonia
Apollonía
Tel: 22840 31490
Charming small hotel (only 9 rooms) with traditional island architecture and friendly service. €
Moní Hrysopigí
Apókofto
Tel: 22840 31255
This 17th-century monastery, situated on an islet reached by footbridge, rents out simple cells in summer. Book well in advance. €

Andíparos

Hryssi Akti
near Kástro
Tel: 222840 61206
Fax: 22840 61105
Elegant hotel with good rooms right on the beach on the east coast. €€
Mantalena
Kástro
Tel: 22840 61 20 6
Fax: 22840 61550
Clean but simple rooms on the waterfront, with good views of the harbour and across to Páros. €

Páros

Astir of Paros
Náousa
Tel: 22840 51986
Fax: 22840 51985
www.ila-chateau.com/astir/index.htm
One of Greece's finest deluxe hotels, right on the beach, across the bay from the town. Spacious rooms with balconies, and bathrooms lined with Parian marble. Large pool, golf course, extensive gardens. €€€
Pandrossos Hotel
Parikía
Tel: 22840 21394
Fax: 22840 23501
www.pandrossoshotel.gr
On a pretty hill at Parikia's edge, yet in town. Beautiful views of the bay, pool, good restaurant, marble lobby. €€
Dina
Parikía
Tel: 22840 21325
Fax: 22840 23525
Friendly hotel in the heart of the old town. Spotlessly clean rooms set around a lovely flowered courtyard. Only 8 rooms, so book early. €

Náxos

Apollon
Hóra
Tel. 22850 22468
Fax: 22850 25200
apollon-hotel@naxos-island.com
An efficient, convenient place to stay in town with parking, on the picturesque pedestrian museum square by the cathedral. €€
Chateau Zevgoli
Hóra
Tel: 22850 22993
Fax: 22850 22600
chateau-zevgoli@nax.forthnet.gr
Quiet, plush and exclusive, high up in the old town. A Venetian mansion with only 10 rooms, each lovingly decorated. One has a four-poster bed, most have great views. €€

Mílos

Kapetan Tassos
Apollónia
Tel: 22870 41287
Modern apartments in traditional blue-and-white island architecture, with good sea views. 11 km (7 miles) from Adamás, so you need transportation. €€
Popi's Windmill
Trypití
Tel: 22870 22286
A luxuriously converted windmill with all the amenities of an elegant hotel, plus beautiful views towards Adamás port. Actually two windmills, each with two bedrooms. €€
Panorama
Klíma

Tel: 22870 21623
Fax: 22870 22112
Small seafront hotel, family-run with
friendly service. The owner sometimes
takes guests fishing. €

Folégandros
Anemomylos
Hóra
Tel: 22860 41309
Fax: 22860 41407
anemomil@otenet.gr
A fully-equipped apartment complex
built in traditional Cycladic style
around a courtyard. Stunning views
from the balconies overhanging the
cliff edge. €€€
Fani-Vevis
Hóra
Tel: 22860 41237
Comfortable hotel in a neo-classical
mansion with rooms overlooking the
sea. €€
Kastro
Hóra
Tel/fax: 22860 41230
A 500-year-old traditional house that
is actually part of the ancient Kástro
walls. Quaint rooms have pebble
mosaic floors, barrel ceilings and
spectacular views down sheer cliffs to
the sea. €

Síkinos
Kamares
Aloprónia
Tel: 22860 51234
Traditional-style, affordable hotel with
average but comfortable rooms. €€
Porto Sikinos
Aloprónia
Tel/fax: 22860 51220
The best accommodation on the
island: a complex of 18 Cycladic-style
buildings right on the beach. Bar and
restaurant. €€
Flora
Aloprónia
Tel: 22860 51214
Simple rooms built round courtyards
on the hillside above the port. Great
sea views. 10-minute walk from the
beach. Most rooms face the sea. €

Íos
Íos Palace
Mylopótas
Tel: 22860 91269
Fax: 22860 91082
iospalas@otenet.gr
Modern hotel designed and decorated
in the traditional style. Near the
beach, with very comfortable rooms,
marble-lined bathrooms and balconies
overlooking the sea. €€€
Philippou
Hóra
Tel: 22860 91290
Small, comfortable hotel in the centre
of Íos's hectic nightlife. Great location

if you plan to party all night.
Otherwise, bring earplugs or choose
somewhere out of town. €€
Acropolis
Mylopótas
Tel/fax: 22860 91303
Clean, simple rooms with balconies
overlooking the beach below. €

Amórgos
Aigialis
Órmos Egiális
Tel: 22850 73393
Fax : 22850 73395
www.amorgos-aegialis.com
Smart modern hotel complex with
good facilities, including a taverna and
large swimming pool. Lovely views
over the bay from the veranda. €€
Minoa
Katápola
Tel: 22850 71480
Fax: 22850 71003
Traditional-style hotel on the harbour
square. Can be noisy. €

Santoríni
Aigialos Houses
Firá
Tel: 22860 25191
Fax: 22860 22856
www.aigialos.gr
Every house is different in this
complex; all are tastefully luxurious,
quiet and convenient, and have
spectacular views, with balconies or
terraces overlooking the caldera. A fine
restaurant (residents only). €€€
Atlantis Villas
Ía
Tel: 22860 71214
FAX: 22860 71312
www.atlantisvillas.com
These traditionally furnished cave-
apartments are many white steps
down the Ía cliffside. Very friendly,
with all services, and caldera views
from terrace and pool. €€€
Fanari Villas
Ía
Tel: 22860 71008
Traditional *skaftá* cave houses
converted into luxury accommodation.
Pool, breakfast terrace, bar and 240
steps down to Ammoudiá Bay.
Attentive, friendly service. €€€
Katikies
Ía
Tel: 22860 71401
katikies@slh.com
One of the best on the island. Lovely
new apartments built in traditional
style, spectacular views and a
wonderful pool. Excellent service.
€€€
Theoxenia Hotel
Firá
Tel: 22860 22740
Fax: 22860 22950
www.theoxenia.net

Right on the main cliifside street, this
attractive small hotel is friendly and
efficient, and has all amenities,
including a pool. Upstairs rooms have
caldera views. €€€
Hermes
Kamári
Tel: 22860 31 66 4
Fax: 22860 33 24 0
www.hermeshotel-santorini.com
Friendly, family-run hotel set in
beautiful gardens not far from the
town centre and the black beach.
Pool, comfortable rooms, and all the
amenities. €€

Rhodes

Marco Polo Mansion
Agíou Fanouríou 42, Rhodes
Old Town
Tel/fax: 22410 25562
www.marcopolomansion.web.com Superb
conversion of an old Turkish mansion;
all rooms are en-suite and furnished
with antiques from the nearby
eponymous gallery. Large buffet
breakfasts included, one-week
minimum stay, advance booking
required. €€€
Miramare Wonderland
Ixiá
Tel: 22410 96251
Fax: 22410 95954
Fake-vernacular bungalows painted in
traditional colours, in a landscaped
setting just behind the beach. Tasteful
mock-antique furnishings and jacuzzis
in some tubs. A private mini-railway
salvaged from a Welsh mine shuttles
guests around the huge grounds.
€€€
Andreas
Omírou 28D, Rhodes Old Town
Tel: 22410 34156
Fax: 22410 74285 www.hotelandreas.com
An old favourite under dynamic new
management, this pension in an old
Turkish mansion was thoroughly
refurbished in 2003. En-suite rooms
are in a variety of formats (including
family-size, and a spectacular tower
unit for two). A terrace bar serves
evening drinks and excellent
breakfasts. Two-night minimum stay.
Open late March–end October. €€
Ganymedes
Perikléous 68, Rhodes Old Town
Tel: 22410 78631
Fax: 22410 78632
www.hotel-ganymedes.com
Just four rooms at this 2003-built
boutique hotel, three of them large
and airy, one best as a single, all
exquisitely furnished. There's a roof
terrace for evenings, and a genuine
French patisserie on the ground floor
for breakfast and cakes. €€
S. Nikolis
Ippodámou 61, Rhodes Old Town

Tel: 22410 34561
www.s-nikolis.gr
A variety of restoration premises, of which the "honeymoon suites" are the best executed, while self-catering apartments are excellent value for groups or families. Open April–November, booking essential. €€

Niki's
Sofokléous 39, Rhodes Old Town. Tel: 22410 25115
Fax: 22410 36033
An excellent budget hotel, most rooms having balconies and air-con. Helpful management and credit-card acceptance are other bonuses. €

Spot
Perikléous 21, Rhodes Old Town
Tel/fax: 22410 34737
spothot@otenet.gr
Another good budget/backpacker hotel, a modern building containing cheerful en-suite rooms with air-con/heating (extra charge) or fans. Internet facilities, free luggage storage; open March-November. €

Dodecanese

Kásos

Anessis
Frý
Tel: 02450 41234 and
Anagenessis
Frý
Tel: 02450 41495
Exceedingly modest though they are, these two hotels represent nearly half the beds available in Frý, the port town. Comfortable rooms, some with sea views. €

Kárpathos

Atlantis
by the Italian "palace", Pigádia
Tel: 22450 22777
Fax: 22450 22780 htlatlantis@yahoo.com
Helpful, well-appointed hotel with quiet setting, easy parking, space held back for non-package travellers and a small pool. €€

Akrogiali Studios
Potáli bay, Paralía Lefkoú
Tel: 22450 71263
Fax: 22450 71178l
Just eight, spacious units, all with views towards the pebble beach; friendly management, minimarket downstairs for restocking. €

Astro
Ólymbos
Tel: 22450 51421
A good, relatively comfortable en-suite "hotel" in this traditional village, kept by the two sisters who manage the Café Restaurant Zefiros where breakfast is served. €

Glaros
Diafáni
Tel: 22450 51501

Fax: 22450 51259
The most comfortable lodgings here, 16 tiered studio units on the south hillside, some with four beds. €

Pine Tree
Ádia hamlet, west coast
Tel: 697 73 69 948
pinetree_adia@hotmail.com
Ideal place to hide away, in a lovely oasis setting, but you must have your own transport. Units are basic but serviceable. €

Vardes Studios
Amopí beach
Tel: 22450 811111 or 697 2152901
The best standard here among outfits accepting walk-in trade, with huge units (they can fit two adults and two children at a pinch) overlooking well-tended gardens some way inland. €

Sými

Aliki
Haráni quay, Gialós
Tel: 22460 71665
www.simi-hotelaliki.gr
An overhauled 1895 mansion, and Sými's poshest hotel: tasteful rooms with wood floors and some antique furnishings, plus air-con and large bathrooms, though few sea views. €€

Les Catherinettes
north quay, Gialós
Tel: 22460 72698
marina-epe@rho.forthnet.gr
Creaky but spotless en-suite pension above restaurant of the same name, in a historic building with painted ceilings and sea-view balconies for most rooms. €€

Fiona
top of the Kalí Stráta, Horió
Tel: 22460 72088
Mock-traditional hotel building, large airy rooms with double beds and stunning views; breakfast in mid-air on the communal terrace. €€

Sými Specials

Symi Visitor in Gialós square is an agency run by affable Greek-Australian Nikos Halkitis and his partner Wendy Wilcox, offering a variety of accommodation at all price ranges, from double studios to entire houses, mostly in Horió; tel: 22460 72755; www.symivisitor.com

Albatros
Gialós marketplace
Tel: 22460 71707/71829
Partial sea views from this exquisite, small hotel with French co-management; pleasant second-floor breakfast salon, air-con. Families should ask also about their more expensive Villa Symeria. €

Kastellórizo

Mediterraneo Pension
north end of the west quay
Tel: 22460 49007
www.mediterraneopension.org
Another architect-executed refurbishment, this offers simple but well-appointed rooms with mosquito nets and wall art, half with sea views, plus an arcaded ground-floor suite and optional breakfast with proprietress Marie's homemade marmalade. Unusually, open all year. €€

Karnayo
platía at west end of the south quay
Tel: 22460 49225
Fax: 22460 49266
The best restoration accommodation on the island, designed by a trained architect. Rooms, studios and a four-bed apartment occupy two separate buildings, with wood-and-stone interiors. €€

Kastellorizo Hotel Apartments
west quay
Tel: 22460 49044
www.kastellorizohotel.gr
These air-conditioned, quality-fitted studios or galleried maisonettes, some with sea view, offer the best facilities on the island. Tiny plunge pool, and its own lido in the bay. €€

Hálki

Most accommodation is block-booked by package companies from April to October; here are two exceptions.

Captain's House
north of the church and inland
Tel: 22460 45201
Five-room, en-suite pension in a converted mansion with garden bar and helpful management. €

Pension Keanthi
inland near the school
Tel: 22460 45334
Bland, pine-furnished rooms with high ceilings, plus a few galleried studios. €

Tílos

Eleni Beach
about halfway around the bay Tel: 22460 44062
Fax: 22460 44063
Willing management for large, airy, white-decor hotel rooms requiring advance booking. €€

Blue Sky Apartments
ferry dock, above Blue Sky taverna
Tel: 22460 44294
Fax: 22460 44184
www.tilostravel.co.uk
Well-appointed, galleried two-person units, built in 2002. €

Irini
200m inland from mid-beach
Tel: 22460 44293
Fax: 22460 44238, www.tilosholidays.gr
Long the top hotel on Tilos, Irini still

wins points for its beautiful grounds and common areas, including large pool. Package patronage is heaviest in May and September; otherwise individual travellers can usually find a vacancy. The same management keeps the hillside **Ilidi Studios**, with both 2- and 4-person units. €€

Miliou Studios
Megálo Horió
Tel: 22460 44204
Fax: 22460 44265
The best-value accommodation this end of the island, in a leafy setting near the base of the village. A variety of units, from basic rooms to two-room apartments, fill quickly during July–August. €

Nísyros

Porfyris
Mandráki centre
Tel: 22420 31376
Fax: 22420 31176
By default, the best hotel here; in 2001 fridges and air-conditioning were added to the 1980s rooms, which overlook either orchards and the sea or the large pool. €

Xenon Polyvotis
Mandráki port
Tel: 22420 31011
Fax: 22420 31204
This municipally-run inn offers the best standard on the harbour, with biggish, neutral-decor rooms and knockout sea views. €

Kós

Grecotel Royal Park
Marmári
Tel: 22420 41488
Fax: 22420 41373
rpark1@otenet.gr
Garden- or sea-view bungalow units are a maximum 300 m (330 yds) from the beach, with fridges, air-conditioning, bathtubs. €€

Afendoulis
Evrypýlou 1, Kós Town
Tel: 22420 25321
Fax: 22420 25797
afendoulishotel@kos.forthnet.gr
Welcoming, family-run C-class hotel: cheerful en-suite rooms with fans, most with balconies, plus some cooler basement "caves" much sought after in summer. Open April–late October. €

Alexis
Irodótou 9, Kós Town
Tel: 22420 25594
A backpackers' home-from-home in a villa overlooking the Hellenistic baths. Rooms large, though most not en-suite. Self-catering kitchen and terrace; open late March to early November. €

Fenareti
Mastihári
Tel: 22420 59028

Fax: 22420 59129
Hillside hotel in the least packaged of Kós's coastal settlements, overlooking the widest part of the beach; rooms and studios in a peaceful garden environment. €

Kamelia
Artemisías 3, Kós Town
Tel: 22420 28983
Fax: 22420 27391
Another friendly, well-placed, family-run hotel, which the Afendoulis refers to when full; rear rooms have an orchard view. Open April– October, with heating. €

Astypálea

Kilindra Studios
west slope of Hóra
Tel: 22430 61966
Fax: 22430 61131
www.astipalea.com.gr
Mock-traditional units built in 2000 in the shadow of the castle, offering all luxury amenities including a swimming pool; open all year. €€€

Astypálea Options

Restored studios or entire houses up in Hóra are beginning to show their 1980s vintage – upgrading works began in 2003 – but still make for an atmospheric stay. Prices from €45 to €85 for two people, according to season. Inquire at Kostas Vaïkousis' antique shop on the quay or reserve on 22430 61430 or 697 7477800.

Australia
Skála
Tel: 22430 61067
Fax: 22430 59812
2002-upgraded rooms and studios in separate blocks, with phones, fans, air (on); good affiliated restaurant. €€

Maltezana Beach
Análipsi (Maltezána)
Tel: 22430 61558
Fax: 22430 61669,
www.maltezanabeach.gr
A state-of-the-art bungalow hotel, the island's newest and largest, with spacious, well-appointed standard rooms and even bigger suites arrayed around gardens and a pool. On-site restaurant; open Easter–end September. €€

Venetos Studios
base of west hillside, Livádia
Tel: 22430 61490
Fax: 61423
venetos@otenet.gr
Units in several buildings scattered across an orchard; facilities range from basic rooms to four-person apartments. €

Price Guide

Price categories are based on the cost of a double room for one night in the high season:
€€€ Expensive over €100
€€ Moderate €50–100
€ Inexpensive under €50

Kálymnos

Maria's Studios
above Melitsahás cove
Tel: 22430 48135
Spacious units with proper kitchens fit three, don't get packages, and overlook one of the better beaches on the west coast. €

Pension Plati Gialos
Platý-Gialós
Tel/fax: 22430 47029
www.pension-plati-gialos.de
Ever-popular family-run backpacker haven overlooks Linária cove, and beyond to Kandoúni. Units are basic but everything works (including wall fans and American-style showers); extended balconies, mosquito nets and breakfast terrace. €

Villa Themelina
Evangelístria district, Póthia
Tel: 22430 22682
The town's top choice: en-suite rooms in a 19th-century mansion, plus an annexe of modern studios behind the pool and gardens. No air-con, but very good breakfasts served on the patio; open all year. €

Télendos

On the Rocks
Tel: 2243 48260
www.telendos.com/otr
Just four smartly appointed rooms with double glazing, mosquito nets etc, above amiable Greek-Australian-run bar of the same name. €

Porto Potha
Tel: 22430 47321
portopotha@klm.forthnet.gr
At the very edge of things, but this hotel has a large pool and friendly managing family. €

Léros

Castle Vigla
hill south of Vromólithos
Tel: 22470 24083
Fax: 22470 24744
Cottage and studio complex with some of the island's best views (vígla means "watchpoint"). €€

Crithoni Paradise
Krithóni
Tel: 22470 25120
Fax: 22747O 24680
Léros' top-rated accommodation, a low-rise complex with a smallish pool, disabled access and smallish but sea-view rooms (go for the suites if money

permits). Buffet breakfast; open all year. €€

Tony's Beach
Vromólithos
Tel: 22470 24742
Fax: 22470 24743
Spacious, simply appointed units behind the best beach on the island; handicapped access, ample parking, very quiet. Open June– September only. €€

Alinda
Álynda beach
Tel: 22470 23266
Fax: 22470 23383
The first hotel established here, this has well-kept 1970s vintage rooms with a mix of sea and mountain views and a respected restaurant with garden seating. €

Rodon
between Pandéli and Vromólithos in Spiliá district
Tel: 22470 23524/22075
Small but well-kept, mostly balconied rooms better than this hotel's official E-class rating; also ground-floor 3-person studios, with less of a sea view. €

Lipsí

Aphrodite
behind Liendoú beach
Tel: 22470 4100
A 1997-built, attractive studio bungalow-hotel complex, with large units; tends to get package clients but usually there's a vacancy. €

Galini Apartments
by the ferry jetty
Tel: 22470 41212
Fax: 22470 41012
Well-appointed rooms with balconies and fridges, very welcoming family. €

Studios Kalymnos
inland side of town on way to Monodéndri beach
Tel: 22470 41141
Fax: 22470 41343
studios_kalymnos@lipsi-island.gr
Fairly spartan but quiet rooms with cooking facilities, in a garden setting. €

Pátmos

Porto Scoutari
hillside above Melóï beach
Tel: 22470 33124
Fax: 22470 33175
www.portoscoutari.com
The island's top digs: enormous self-catering suites, arrayed around the pool area, have sea views and air-con/heating, as well as mock-antique furnishings and original wall art. Elina the proprietress is a font of island knowledge. €€€

Blue Bay
Skála, Konsoláto district
Tel: 22470 31165

Fax: 22470 32303
www.bluebay.50g.com
The last building on the way out of town towards Gríkou, and spared the late-night ferry noise that plagues most hotels here. Rooms were refurnished in 2001. Friendly Australian-Greek management, on-site internet café. €€

Effie
Skála, Kastélli hillside
Tel: 22470 32500
Fax: 22470 32700
Bland, blonde-pine-and-tile rooms spread over two hotel wings, but with balconies and air-conditioning they're good value in a quiet setting. Open all year. €€

Galini
Skála
Tel: 22470 31240
Fax: 22740 31705
In a quiet cul-de-sac near the ferry quay, this C-class hotel offers B-class standards in furnishings and bathrooms, and excellent value. €€

Golden Sun
Gríkou
Tel: 22470 32318
Fax: 22470 34019
Hillside setting with most rooms facing water; stays open into autumn (unusual at Gríkou) and not monopolised by packages (though there are German "special interest" groups). €€

Maria
Hóhlakas Bay, near Skála
Tel: 22470 31201
Fax: 22470 32018
Very quiet, garden-set small hotel with all air-con, balconied rooms facing the sea (bathrooms are tiny though). €€

Northeastern Aegean

Sámos

Arion
1km (½ mile) west of Kokkári
Tel: 22370 92020
www.arion-hotel.gr
The best accommodation on Sámos' north coast, a well-designed hotel-wing and bungalow complex on a hillside. Famously good breakfasts. €€€

Doryssa Bay Hotel-Village
Potokáki, near airport
Tel: 22730 61360
Fax: 22730 61463
www.doryssa-bay.gr
One of the few actual beachfront resorts on Sámos, with a saltwater pool just in from the sand if the sea's too cold. If budget permits, skip the dull 1970s hotel wing in favour of the meticulously constructed fake "village", no two houses alike and incorporating all the vernacular styles of Greece. €€€

Kerveli Village
approach to Kérveli beach
Tel: 22730 23631
Fax: 22730 23006
www.kerveli-village.gr
This is a well-executed, smallish bungalow hotel set among olive trees and cypresses, with superb views across to Turkey and over Kérveli Bay. A good selection of beaches and tavernas within walking distance. €€€

Aïdonokastro
Platanáki/Aïdónia district, near Ágios Konstandínos
Tel: 22730 94686
Fax: 22730 94404
About half the abandoned hillside hamlet of Valeondádes has been renovated as a unique cottage-hotel, each former house now a pair of two- or four-person units with traditional touches. €€

Amfilisos
Bállos beach, near Órmos Marathókambos
Tel: 22730 31669
Fax: 22730 31668
The hotel itself is nothing extraordinary, but Bállos is a deliciously sleepy place for doing very little except exploring the coast to the southeast and sampling some good local tavernas. €€

Avli Pension
Áreos 2, Sámos Town
Tel: 22730 22939
Housed in the former convent school of French nuns who staffed the local Catholic church until 1973, this is the best budget choice in town. Just over half of the rooms round the courtyard (avlí) are en-suite. Affable owner Spyros is a reliable source of information on local tavernas and nightspots. €

Ikaría

Erofili Beach
right at the entrance to Armenistís Tel: 22750 71058
Fax: 22750 71483
www.erofili.gr
Considered the best-standard hotel on the island, with designer rooms and ample common areas. A small

saltwater pool perches dramatically over Livádi beach. €€

Messakhti Village
Messakhtí beach, Armenistís
Tel: 22750 71331
Fax: 22750 71330
www.messakti-village.com
Imposing common areas, large private terraces and equally spacious studios (fit 3 to 6), but poor breakfast and rather plain furnishings at this architect-designed hillside complex. The large pool is a necessity in August, when the sea here can be dangerously rough. €€

Akti
on a knoll east of the hydrofoil and *kaïki* quay, Ágios Kírykos
Tel: 22750 22694
Not a place for a long stay, but ideal if waiting for an early ferry or hydrofoil; friendly, basic spotless, with rooms both en-suite and not. €

Híos

Kyma
east end of Evgenías Handrí
Tel: 22710 44500
Fax: 22710 44600
B-class hotel inside a converted neoclassical mansion (plus less attractive modern extension); very helpful management, good breakfasts in the original salon with painted ceiling. €€

Mavrokordatiko
Kámbos district, 1.5 km (1 mile) south of the airport on Mitaráki lane
Tel: 22710 32900
www.mavrokordatiko.com
Best and most popular restoration project in the Kámbos, with heated, wood-panelled rooms and breakfast (included) served by the courtyard with its *mánganos* (waterwheel). €€

Spitakia
Avgónyma
Tel: 22710 20513
Fax: 22710 43052
kratisis@spitakia.gr
A cluster of small but well-restored houses taking up to five people, near the edge of this stunningly set west-coast village. €€

Chios Rooms
Egéou 110, Híos Town
Tel: 22710 20198
chiosrooms@hotmail.com
Upstairs rooms with high ceilings and

Híos Houses

Omiros Travel in Volissós is a little booking office that handles 16 old village houses restored in the early 1990s. Units, all with period features, usually accommodate two people, prices €–€€. Tel: 22740 21413; fax: 22740 21521.

tile-and-wood floors, some en-suite, in lovingly restored building managed by a New Zealand/Greek couple. Best is the "penthouse", with a private terrace. €

Markos' Place
south hillside, Karfás beach
Tel: 22710 31990 or 697 32 39 706
www.marcos-place.gr
Inside a disused monastery, Markos Kostalas has created a uniquely peaceful, leafy environment. Guests are lodged in the former pilgrims' cells; individuals are welcome (several single "cells") as are families (two "tower" rooms sleep four). Minimum stay 4 days; open April–November. €

Lésvos

Pyrgos
Eleftheríou Venizélou 49, Mytilíni
Tel: 22510 25 069
www.pyrgoshotel.gr
The town's premier restoration accommodation, with over-the-top kitsch decor in the common areas. Rooms, most with balcony, are perfectly acceptable, and there are three round units in the tower. €€€

Clara
Avláki, 2km south of Pétra
Tel: 22530 41532
Fax: 22530 41535
www.clarahotel.gr
The large, designer-furnished rooms of this pastel-coloured bungalow complex look north to Pétra and Mólyvos; particularly renowned for its ample buffet breakfasts relying on local products. Tennis courts and pool. €€–€€€

Malemi
Skála Kallonís
Tel: 22530 22594
Fax: 22530 22838
malemi@otenet.gr
Pleasant bungalow complex, the most welcoming of half a dozen here, with units from doubles to family suites, attractive grounds, tennis court and a large pool. €€

Molyvos I
Mólyvos beach lane
Tel: 22530 71496
Fax: 22530 71460
Nominally B-class outfit on the pebble shore, behind the tamarisks and a stone-paved terrace where breakfast is served. Large, tile-floored, 1980s rooms; reasonable buffet breakfast. You get the use of (and shuttle to) the pool and sports facilities at sister hotel Molyvos II at Eftaloú, though there is a "private" beach area here. €€

Vatera Beach
Vaterá
Tel: 22520 61212
Fax: 22520 61164
www.vaterabeach.gr

Rambling, Greek/American-run hotel behind the best beach on the island. Rooms with air-con and minibar fridges, free sunbeds, in-house restaurant relying on own-grown produce and free advice from Barbara the proprietress. €€

Pension Lida
Plomári
Tel/fax: 22520 32507
Welcoming restoration inn in two adjacent old mansions formerly belonging to a soap-manufacturing magnate; sea-view balconies for most units, enthusiastic management. €

Límnos

Porto Myrina Palace
Ávlonas beach, 2km N of Mýrina
Tel: 22540 24805
Fax: 22540 24858
Considered the best, and most easily bookable, luxury hotel on the island, with grounds incorporating a small Artemis temple. €€€

Villa Afrodite
Platý beach
Tel: 22540 23141
Fax: 22540 25031
Run by returned South African Greeks, this comfortable small hotel has a poolside bar and sumptuous buffet breakfasts. €€

Ifestos
Andróni district, Mýrina
Tel: 22540 24960
Fax: 22540 23623
Attractive small hotel whose rooms have a mix of seaward and hillside views, balconies, fridges, air-con. €€

Thásos

Myrioni
Liménas
Tel: 25930 23256
Very well priced and comfortable spot with a large breakfast salon; also with a cheaper annexe. €€

Thassos Inn
Panagía village
Tel: 25930 61612
Quiet except for the sound of water in runnels all around, this modern building in traditional style has most rooms facing the sea. €€

Alkyon
Liménas
Tel: 25930 22148
Spacious rooms, with harbour or garden view, plus gregarious Anglo-Greek management and afternoon tea, make this a firm favourite with English-speaking travellers. €

Samothráki

Eolos
Kamariótissa
Tel: 25510 41595
Fax: 25510 41810
Samothráki's port and capital is home

to a few hotels including this decent budget to mid-range choice. Rooms are simple but clean and welcoming. Some have views overlooking the hills, others towards the sea. Continental breakfast is included. Cash only. €€

Mariva Bungalows
Loutrá Thermá
Tel: 25510 98230
Fax: 25510 98374
Situated in the island's resort centre, these lovely flower-shrouded bungalows are built on a gentle hillside. All units are self-contained, comfortable and reasonably spacious. Ideal for a longer stay. Cash only. €€

Skiáthos

Atrium
Plataniás
Tel: 24270 49345
Fax: 24270 49444
www.atriumhotel.gr
The Atrium Hotel combines casual elegance with traditional architecture, somewhat like a monastery. It's chic, beautiful and enjoys a splendid view. Rooms are more than comfortable and some have private balconies or patios. There's a pool and a poolside restaurant. €€€

Skiathos Palace
Koukounariés
Tel: 24270 49700
Fax: 24270 49666
www.skiathos-palace.gr
One the isand's largest resort hotels, overlooking the eastern end of Koukounariés beach. The standard rooms are average in size and all have balconies, the superior rooms and suites are worth the extra. Facilities include pool, sauna and in-house restaurant. €€€

Nostos Village
Tzanéria
Tel: 24270 22520
Fax: 24270 22525
www.center.gr/nostos
A large complex on the Kanapítsa peninsula midway between Skiáthos Town and Koukounariés. Built into a verdant hillside, one of the better and more popular resort choices for visitors to the island. Choose from simpler rooms or self-catering bungalows among pine trees. €€

Skópelos

Adrina Beach
Pánormos
Tel: 24240 23373
Fax: 24240 23372
www.adrina.gr
This expansive hotel complex (42 standard rooms and 10 bungalows) occupies a large tract of hillside just to the north of Pánormos Bay, looking

out onto its own virtually private beach. If you want to get married while on holiday, there is even a small on-site chapel. €€

Dionysos
Skópelos Town
Tel: 24240 23210
Fax: 24240 22954
dionysco@otenet.gr
The Dionysos is ideal for visitors wishing to stay as close as possible to town. The 52 rooms are furnished in traditional dark pine and have air-con, TV and balconies. The hotel also has a pool with a shallow end for children. €€

Skopelos Village
Skópelos Town
Tel: 24240 22517
Fax: 24240 22958
A complex of self-catering bungalows about 500 m across the bay, with a large grassy area and a pool. Living areas are large and contain tasteful local furnishings. €€

Alónisos

Konstantina's Studios
Hóra (Old Alónisos)
Tel: 24240 66165
Fax: 24240 66165
High up in the old renovated village this small traditionally renovated building houses eight studios and one apartment. All have exceptional sea views and wooden balconies with canvas deckchairs. €€

Liadromia
Patitíri
Tel: 24240 65160
Fax: 24240 65096
liadromia@alonnisos.com
One of the first hotels to open in Alónisos, it maintains an air of old-world charm with a dash of modernity. Rooms have stucco walls, stone floors and tasteful decoration. Overlooking the harbour at the north side of Patitíri Bay, handy for all island facilities. €€

Milia Bay
Miliá
Tel: 24240 66035
Fax: 24240 66037
milia-bay@vol.forthnet.gr
Tucked away overlooking the sandy Miliá Bay, this quiet retreat consists of 12 ecologically constructed self-catering apartments, all very spacious and tastefully decorated. If you don't fancy the short walk to the beach there's a pool, as well as the in-house restaurant. €€

Skýros

Nefeli – Skyriana Spitia
Hóra
Tel: 22220 91964
Fax: 22220 92061
Combing standard hotel rooms and a stand-alone group of Skyrian houses

Price categories are based on the cost of a double room for one night in the high season:
€€€ Expensive over €100
€€ Moderate €50–100
€ Inexpensive under €50

(in practice 2-3 person studios) this is a tidy complex at the entrance to Hóra. The self-contained studios are very cosy. Good deals out of season. €€

Skyros Palace
Gyrísmata, Péra Kámbou
Tel: 22220 91994
Fax: 22220 92070
www.skiros-palace.gr
Tucked away at the northeastern end of the Magaziá-Mólos strip, down on the beach, the Skyros Palace is a fairly sumptuous place to stay, though its location may be a little inconvenient for some. Free bus shuttles ply between the hotel and Hóra. Open summer only. €€

Xenia
Magaziá
Tel: 22220 91209
Fax: 22220 92062
A rather obvious cement box on Magaziá beach. Aesthetics aside, the location is excellent and the hotel service is good, while the spacious rooms have been kept up to date with recent renovations. €€

Évia

Dreams Island
Erétria
Tel: 22290 61224
Fax: 22290 61268
Email: pezonisi@otenet.gr
www.dreams-island.gr
An unusual resort hotel on an island connected to the mainland by a short causeway. Accommodation is individual bungalows set among olive trees and all within minutes' walk of a sandy beach. €€€

Thermai Sylla Spa Wellness Hotel
Loutrá Edipsoú
Tel: 22260 60100
Fax: 22260 22055
www.thermaesylla.gr
Perhaps Greece's only official anti-stress hotel, this magnificent edifice at the northern end of the promenade is a turn-of-the-century experience brought up to date, offering beauty and therapy treatments based on the waters of the ancient spa. €€€

Hotel Karystion
Kriezótou 2, Kárystos
Tel: 22240 22391
Fax: 22240 22727
A busy foreigner-friendly hotel in the far south of Évia, close to the fortress

on the south side of town. Neat, air-
conditioned rooms, all with balconies,
TVs and phones. The town's best
bathing spots are a few minutes' walk
way. €€

Corfu

The official Greek Hotel guide lists
over 400 licensed hotels on the
island. Many of these remain in the
firm grip of tour operators from May to
October, closing in winter. The
following are open off-season and/or
to independent travellers. Additionally,
if you have a car, you can usually find
domátia or apartments on a walk-in
basis at the less packaged resorts of
Astrakerí, Kalamáki, Afiónas and
Aríllas in the north, plus Paramónas
and Boúkari in the southwest.

Kérkyra Town and around
Corfu Palace
Dimokratías 2, north end of Garítsa
Bay
Tel: 26610 39485
www.corfupalace.com
The town's only "lux" class
establishment, which enjoys a high
level of repeat clientele, including VIPs
and foreign dignitaries, especially in
May and September. They come for
the huge rooms (renovated in 1995)
with marble bathtubs, the big
breakfasts and the assiduous level of
service. Open all year. €€€
Kontokali Bay
Tel: 26610 90002
Fax: 26610 91901
www.kontokalibay.com
Slightly more affordable and larger
than the Corfu Palace, consisting of a
hotel wing and bungalows in a leafy
environment with two "private"
beaches. Recently renovated, with lots
of facilities for kids. €€€
Grecotel Corfu Imperial
Komméno
Tel: 26610 88400
Fax: 2661 91881
gman.nht@ci.grecotel.gr
Perhaps the best and most
contemporarily decorated hotel on the
island, and stratospherically
expensive. Three grades of
accommodation: standard rooms,
bungalows, and a few super-luxe villas
with their own pool. All the facilities
you'd expect for the price. €€€
Bella Venezia
Napoleóntos Zambéli 4
Tel: 26610 46500/20708
belvnht@hol.gr
Neo-classical mansion well adapted
as a B-class hotel in a central yet
quiet location at the south edge of the
old town; no pool or extra amenities
other than a large patio garden with
bar. €€

Kavalieri
Kapodistriou 4, Kérkyra
Tel: 26610 39041
Fax: 26610 39283
A-class hotel in a 17th-century building
overlooking the Spianáda. Frankly
overpriced, with smallish rooms, but all
have sea views, and the roof garden
makes the place. €€
Konstantinoupolis
Zavitsiánou 11, Old Port
Tel: 26610 48716
Fax: 26610 48718
polis@ker.forthnet.gr.
1862 building, once a backpackers'
dosshouse, now lovingly restored as a
well-priced C-class hotel with sea and
mountain views. Comfortable rooms
and common areas, lift; open all year.
€€
Nefeli
Komméno
Tel: 26610 91033
Fax: 26610 90290
This small inland hotel in mock neo-
classical style, spread over three
buildings among olive groves, has a
loyal clientele, good service and air-
conditioning in most units. Open
May–October. €€
Palace Mon Repos
Anemómylos district, Garítsa Bay
Tel: 26610 32783
Fax: 26610 23459
Renovated in the late 1990s, this
hotel is the closest thing Kérkyra Town
has to a beach resort. The lido
opposite is of indifferent quality, but
you've views to the sea, Old Fort and
Mon Repos woods, and a small
swimming pool. Open May–October.
€€

Centre-west of Corfu
Pelekas Country Club
Km 8 of Kérkyra–Pélekas road
Tel: 26610 52239
Fax: 26610 52919
reservations@country-club.gr
Corfu's most exclusive rural hotel,
just 26 units occupying an 18th-
century mansion set in over 25
hectares (60 acres) of landscaped
grounds. Outbuildings such as the
stables and olive press are now self-
catering studios and suites, all
different and antique-furnished.
Stylish breakfasts in the central
refectory, pool, tennis, helipad. Open
January–November. €€€
Casa Lucia
Sgómbou hamlet, at Km 12 of
Kérkyra–Paleokastrítsa road
Tel: 26610 91419
Fax: 26610 91732
caslucia@otenet.gr
Peaceful setting at the very centre of
the island. A restored olive-mill
complex set among lovingly tended
gardens comprises 11 units ranging

from studios to family cottages. Most
have kitchens, all share a large pool,
though furnishings are resolutely
1980s. Open April– November. €€
Fundana Villas
accessed by side road from Km 17 of
Kérkyra–Paleokastrítsa highway
Tel: 26630 22532
Fax: 26630 22453,
www.fundanavillas.com
Another 1980s restoration inn, this
time converted from a 17th-century
manor, with a commanding ridgetop
position in the middle of a gorgeous
nowhere. Units from double studios to
family apartments; most have brick-
and-flagstone floors; several were
added next to the pool in 2002. Open
April–October. €€

Northern Delights

Falcon Travel, a British-owned
travel agency based in Nisáki,
arranges stays in a dozen beach-
side apartments and villas in the
north of Corfu, or two sensitively
restored houses which they own in
the idyllic (and remote) Mt
Pandokrátor hamlet of Tritsí. Car
hire arranged for the latter; open
April–October.
Apartments €, villas €€, houses
€400–600 per week.
Tel: 26630 91318
Fax: 26630 91070
www.falcon-travel-corfu.com

Levant Hotel
above Pélekas, right beside "Kaiser's
Throne"
Tel: 26610 94230
Fax: 26610 94115
www.levant-hotel.com
1990s-built hotel in mock-traditional
style, with superb views both east and
west over the island. Rooms are
wood-floored, baths marble-trimmed,
ground-floor common areas faux-
rustic. There's a small pool, and some
of the island's best beaches a few
kilometers away. Open April–October.
€€
Liapades Beach Hotel
Liapádes
Tel: 06630 41294
Two smallish wings make up this
amiable C-class at one of the quieter
beach resorts on this coast. Open
April–October. €€

The north of the island
Nisaki Beach
Krouzéri Bay, between Nissáki and
Kalámi
Tel: 22630 91232
Fax: 22630 22079
www.nissakibeach.gr
A-class hotel with brutal 1970s

architecture but popular for its open buffet restaurant, varied watersports and children's beach activities. Rooms, mostly with sea views, are large and recently redone. €€€

Villa de Loulia
Perouládes, 500m from beach
Tel: 26630 95394
Fax: 26630 95145
villadeloulia@yahoo.com
The third of Corfu's rural restoration inns, this 1803 mansion has been refurbished with high-standard furnishings and fittings in excellent taste. The bar, lounge and breakfast area are in a separate purpose-built structure flanking the large pool. Heating but only fans, no air-con. You're paying for the exclusivity – better value out of peak season. Open March–October. €€–€€€

The south of the island

Boukari Beach
Boúkari, 4km beyond Messongí
Tel: 26620 51791
Fax: 26620 51792
www.boukaribeach.gr
Two sets of sea-view A-class apartments sleeping up to four, with all amenities including coffee machines, a few paces from the excellent co-managed restaurant. Open April–October. €€

The Ionians

Paxí

Planos Tours
Lákka
Tel: 26620 31744
Fax: 26620 31010
One of two agencies in this little port, efficiently handling everything from basic rooms to luxury villas.

Paxos Beach Hotel
Gáïos
Tel: 26620 31211
Fax: 26620 32695
www.paxosbeachhotel.gr
Hillside bungalow complex leading down through trees to its own small pebble beach about 2 km (1 mile) east of town. €€–€€€

Lefkáda

Olive Tree/Liodendro
north approach road, Ágios Nikítas
Tel: 26450 97453
olivetreehotel@hotmail.com
Halfway up the hill, with oblique sea views from most rooms, this C-class hotel avoids the airless gulch of most accommodation at this otherwise attractive resort. Rooms are typical anodyne pine-and-white-tile decor, but no package allotment so good chance of vacancies. €€

Santa Maura/Ayia Mavra
Spyridónos Viánda 2, Lefkáda Town

Tel: 26450 21308
Fax: 26450 26253
Pagoda-like period piece: pre-earthquake ground floor, wood and corrugated tin upstairs. Rooms have air-con, double glazing, traditional shutters, balconies; lovely breakfast salon and garden patio. €€

Ostria
north approach road, Ágios Nikítas
Tel: 26450 97483
Fax: 26450 97300
The 1970s-built rooms of this pension can be cell-like, but are enlivened by terracotta floor tiles, dried flowers and wall art. It's the unobstructed balcony views of the Ionian (save from four rooms) and the cool, trendy common areas (including a terrace bar open to all) that make the place a delight. The breakfast isn't always up to scratch. €–€€

Fantastiko Balkoni sto Ionio
Kalamítsi
Tel: 26450 99390
The name (accurately) means: "Fantastic Overlook of the Ionian Sea". At the far west edge of this quiet village, these state-of-the-art (mosquito screens, Italian tiling, tended garden) rooms with communal kitchen are idyllic, with friendly returned South African/ Greek management. €

Nefeli
Póndi Beach
Tel: 26450 31515
clubnefeli@hotmail.com
This beachfront hotel makes a good alternative to staying in nearby, congested Vasilikí; popular outdoor bar and windsurf facilities on site are pluses. €€

Porto Lygia
Lygiá
Tel: 26450 71441
Fax: 26450 71900
Perched on promontory away from traffic, with a lawn leading down to its own pebble beach, this is a good choice for a seaside stay near (but not in) Lefkáda Town. €€

Itháki

For rooms or villas across the island, contact one of these two travel agencies:

Delas
Tel: 26740 32104
delas@otenet.gr
Polyctor
Tel: 26740 33120
polyctor@otenet.gr
Captain Yiannis
on east quay, Vathý
Tel: 26740 33173
Fax: 26740 32849
The closest thing to an exclusive "resort" on the island, with just 11 self-catering units set in ample walled

grounds with a pool and tennis court. €€€

Perantzatha 1811 Art Hotel
Odyssea Androutsou, Vathý
Tel: 26740 33
Fax: 26740 334
www.arthotel.gr
Chic and fairly pricey but by far the loveliest hotel in Vathý. The 12 understated and tasteful rooms have been individually designed and are very comfortable. Not on the harbourfront itself (and so quieter than some other places), the rooms look out over the Vathy's pretty rooftops to the sea. The breakfasts are excellent. €€€

Nostos
about 200 metres (220 yds) inland from the quay, Fríkes
Tel: 26740 31644
Fax: 26740 31716
Smallish but upmarket C-class hotel where all rooms look over a field towards the sunrise. €€

Kostas Raftopoulos
last house on yacht quay opposite beacon, Kióni
Tel: 26740 31654 May–Oct
Tel: 210 779 8539 winter
There are just four colonial-style rooms, with big beds and mosquito nets, upstairs at this imposing mansion built in 1894 for the niece of Lord Nelson's mistress Lady Hamilton. Returned South African Kostas, who bought it in 1965, is quite a raconteur. €–€€

Kefalloniá

Agnantia Apartments
280 84 Tselendáta, Fiskárdo
Tel: 26740 51802–3
Fax: 26740 51801
www.agnantia.com
Very well maintained and beautifully located (although a little way out of Fiskárdo), these new rooms stacked up on a hillside are a lovely place to stay. As well as friendly and efficient service, the rooms are tasteful and comfortable with a small kitchen area, and most have a balcony with wonderful views over to Itháki. A good, and generous, breakfast is included. €€€

Emelisse Art Hotel
Éblisi, near Fiskárdo
Tel: 2610 624900
www.arthotel.gr
Expensive (A class) but chic, this 'boutique' hotel (one of a small chain in this part of Greece) is set in a traditional building. The well designed rooms have luxurious bathrooms and, inevitably, the hotel's infinity pool has a lovely view. For this sort of money you should expect to be pampered and the service lives up to expectations. €€€

The Olive Grove
Evretí
Book through:
Sunvil
Tel: (00 44) 8568 4499
www.sunvil.co.uk
This stone built traditional house (dates from 1836) about 6km south of Fiskárdo is in a wonderful position surrounded by fir trees and looking out to Itháki. Although kitted out with a modern kitchen and bathrooms it still retains its local feel. As well as a nearby secluded pebble beach (with the clearest water) there is a lovely pool. €€€

White Rocks Hotel and Bungalows
Platýs Gialós, Argostóli
Tel: 26710 28332–5
Fax: 26710 28755
whiterocks@otenet.gr
Large, A-class resort hotel and bungalow complex behind the closest really good beach to Argostóli; well-kept and updated 1970s pile with a certain period charm. Willing staff and decent restaurants complete the picture. €€€

The Architect's House
Ásos
Book through:
Simply Ionian
Tel: (00 44) 020 8541 2202
www.simplytravel.co.uk
This lovely traditional building, one of the few places to stay in Ásos itself, has three double bedrooms (sleeps 6) and is down by the harbour. There is plenty of space – a separate living room and kitchen – and the beach and good places to eat are close by. €€–€€€

Caretta's Nest
Kamínia Beach, near Skála
Book through:
Simply Ionian
Tel: (00 44) 020 8541 2202
www.simplytravel.co.uk
A cluster of modern, well furnished apartments by deserted Kamínia beach. This is a great place to get away from it all, but if you want to go into Skála or Kateliós to eat you will need your own transport or be prepared to walk. €€–€€€

Panas Hotel
Platía Spartiá
Tel: 26710 69506/69448
Fax: 26710 69505
www.panas-kefalonia.com
A largish but pleasant B class hotel south of Argostóli on Lourdáta Bay, close to a decent beach. The rooms, all with a balcony, are fine if a little unimaginative. The hotel does, however, have good facilities for children, including their own pool and play area. There are also a couple of restuarants and a poolside bar. €€–€€€

Tara Beach
Skála
Tel: 26710 83341
Fax: 26710 83344
www.tarabeach.gr
A large but unobstrusive hotel right on the excellent beach. The rooms are decent and, if you can't be bothered to waddle the few metres to the sea, there is a good pool in the pleasant gardens, beside which is a handy bar. €€–€€€

Aenos Hotel
Platía Vallianoú, Argostóli
Tel: 26710 28013
Fax: 26710 27035
www.aenos.com
This, and the Ionian Plaza (below), are the two best places to stay on the town's central square. The uncluttered pastel-shaded rooms with large attached bathrooms probably give the Aenos the edge; it is also marginally quieter. €€

Belvedere Apartments
Póros
Tel: 26740 72493–4
Fax: 26740 72083
A small apartment complex in the centre of town. Although fairly simple – the standard small kitchenette, bedroom and bathroom – they are not without charm, and all have balconies looking over the sea. €€

Erissos
Fiskárdo
Tel: 26740 41319
One of the best hotels in town. Upstairs rooms in an old house a few steps back from the quay, next to the Alpha Bank. €€

Filoxenia
Fiskárdo
Tel: 26740 41319
A 19th-century house beautifully refurbished as a small hotel. In the village, 9 metres (10 yds) from the water. €€

Hotel Ionian Plaza
Platía Vallianoú, Argostóli
Tel: 26710 25581–4
Fax: 26710 25585
Open all year
Excellent value C-class designer hotel, with modern bathrooms and balconies overlooking the palm-studded square; the rooms are on the small side, but the staff are friendly. €€

Kastro Hotel
Sámi
Tel: 26740 22656/22282
Fax: 26740 23004
kastrohotel@hotmail.com
A little way out of town, but close to the sea is this medium-sized, good value B class hotel. The good, if smallish, rooms either look out over the pool and sea or the mountains. Breakfast is provided and there is also a restaurant. €€

Price Guide

Price categories are based on the cost of a double room for one night in the high season:
€€€ Expensive over €100
€€ Moderate €50–100
€ Inexpensive under €50
For details of the Greek Tourist Authority's hotel classification system see Hotel Categories on page 333.

Le Mirage Apartments
Ioánnis Tzigánte, Argostóli
Tel: 26710 24312
Fax: 26710 22339
www.lemirage.gr
Simple but very clean, comfortable, three-room apartments, with fairly limited cooking facilities. Each living room has a balcony and those facing east have a wonderful view over the bay and Mount Énos (compensation for the steep climb up from town); rooms on the west overlook the well-watered garden. €€

Moustakis Hotel
Agía Evfimía
Tel: 26740 61060/61030
Mobile: 693 419 7495
moustakishotel@hotmail.com
Smallish and tucked away behind the harbour front, this is the most pleasant of the hotels in town. All the rooms have AC and balconies. Breakfast is available for an extra charge. Discounts are available for long stays. €€

Odysseus Palace
Póros
Tel: 26740 72036
Fax: 26740 72148
www.odysseuspalace.com
This modern, newish hotel is the most comfortable place to stay in town. Good discounts may be available for the large and airy rooms (studios and apartments). Being away from the seafront, the hotel is quieter than most. Open all year. €€

Hotel Summery
Lixoúri
Tel: 26710 91771/91871
Fax: 26710 91062
www.hotelsummery.gr
A large and quiet hotel on Lixoúri's beach (to the south of town) that mainly caters to tour groups. The rooms are clean and unfussy, and some have balconies. For the amenities on offer (pool, plenty of sporty activities, and a shop) the prices are quite reasonable. €€

Zákynthos

Iberostar Plagos Beach
Aboúla Beach, Tsiliví
Tel: 26950 62800

Price Guide

Price categories are based on the cost of a double room for one night in the high season:
€€€ Expensive over €100
€€ Moderate €50–100
€ Inexpensive under €50

Fax: 26950 62900
www.iberostar.com
Previously the Louis Plagos Beach, this is a large resort hotel with a huge range of facilities, particularly for children. The rooms are plain but large and have balconies, there is the inevitable, but decent, hotel pool and restaurant. €€€

Nobelos Apartments
Ágios Nikólaos
Tel: 26950 27632/31400
Fax: 26950 31131/29277
nobelos@otenet.gr
These luxury apartments in the north of the island are hideously expensive but lovely. The four tastefully decorated suites are in a traditional stone-built house, each with an individual character. Along with excellent service, breakfast is provided and a secluded bay is close by. €€€

Hotel Palatino
Kolokotróni 10 and Kolivá, Zákynthos Town
Tel: 26950 27780
Fax: 26950 45400
www.palatinohotel.gr
Zákynthos Town's poshest option, refurbished in 1999 and well run. The rooms, designed for business travellers, are decent with all the trimmings, and the hotel as a whole has been well cared for. A buffet breakfast is provided and there is also a restaurant. €€€

Porto Koukla Beach Hotel
Lithakiá
Tel: 26950 52393/51577
Fax: 26950 52391/52392
www.pavlos.gr
A decent, large hotel at the western end of Laganás Bay. Popular with German and Austrian visitors, it is well away from the tawdriness further east. The gardens back onto a narrow beach which is overlooked by the hotel's excellent, and cheap, taverna. €€€

Villa Petunia
Lithakiá
Contact:
Betty Andronikos
Tel: 6932 260534
androel@hol.gr
This huge, beautifully furnished villa is on a hill above the village. Surrounded by flowers with a fabulous view over Laganás Bay and the mountains, the villa sleeps 10 to 12 people and has every conceivable appliance from DVD player to *espresso* machine. There is a new swimming pool and organic eggs, oil and vegetables are available from the garden. €€€

Contessa Estate
Akrotíri
Book through:
Sunisle
Tel: (00 44) 0871 222 1226
www.sunisle.co.uk
A tranquil, stonebuilt aristocratic estate full of character and set in gorgeous surroundings. Accommodation is in either the large Manor House, full of heirlooms of the Komoutou family, or the smaller but equally lovely Garden Cottage. The Comtessa Maria is a charming host, and the spectacular views and sense of history all add to the experience. €€

Ionian Star Hotel
Alykés
Tel: 26950 83416/83658
Fax: 26950 83173
www.ionian-star.gr
A smallish and very well kept hotel. The spotless rooms are excellent value (breakfast is included) and there is a restaurant which concentrates on Greek food. €€

Levantino Studio Apartments
9km (5½ miles) from Vasilikós
Tel: 26950 35366
Fax: 26950 35173
www.levantino-apps.gr
10 quiet and attractive apartments close to the sea at the far end of the Vasilikós Peninsula. All are euipped with a kitchen and some look out over the gardens and sea. Discounts available out of high season. €€

Montreal Hotel
Alykés
Tel: 26950 83241/83341
Fax: 26950 83342
www.montreal.gr
A modern hotel block but attractive and covered in flowers. The plain, clean and well maintained rooms have balconies looking over the sea. There is also restaurant dishing up the usual eclectic mix of food, from pizza to Greek salad. €€

Sirocco Hotel
Kalamáki
Tel: 26950 26083–6
Fax: 26950 26087
www.siroccohotel.gr
This is good and reasonable quiet option for Kalamáki, the renovated and stylish standard rooms are a bargain out of season. There is a large pool set in an attractive garden, though the beach is not too far away. €€

Hotel Strada Marina
Lobárdou 14, Zákynthos Town
Tel: 26950 42761–3
Fax: 26950 28733
stradamarina@aias.gr
The largest place in Zákynthos town with comfortable but not overly exciting rooms. A prominent, modern building close to Platía Solomoú, some of the rooms have a great view of the harbour. Breakfast is included and there is a rooftop pool. €€

Villa Katerina
Pórto Róma, Vasilikós
Tel: 26950 35456
www.villakaterina.com
These two buildings in pretty gardens have simple rooms with decent kitchenettes and attached bathrooms. Set back from the beach, the rooms are very quiet and the surrounding area is lovely. €€

Zante Palace
Tsiliví
Tel: 26950 490490
Fax: 26950 49092
www.zantepalace.com
This huge, newly built, hotel is on the bluff overlooking Tsiliví bay, giving great views across to Kefalloniá. For what's on offer the rooms (which look out over the bay) are good value and if you can't be bothered to walk down to the beach there is a nicely sited pool. €€

Windmill
Korithí, Cape Skinári
Tel: 26950 31132
This consists of one room in a converted windmill at the very north end of the island, close to the Blue Caves. If you really want to get away from it all then this might be your best option. €

Kýthira

Kýthira has a short season, with most accommodation only open from May to October; advance booking is recommended.

Porto Delfino
Kapsáli
Tel: 27360 31940
Fax: 27360 31939
A pleasant bungalow complex with views over the bay and Hóra. €€–€€€

Xenonas Keiti
Hóra
Tel: 27360 31318
Lovely accommodation in – for a change – non-smoking rooms, set in a rambling 18th-century mansion. The hotel has a remarkably distinguished guest-list. €€

Xenonas Porfyra
Pótamos
Tel: 27360 33329
Fax: 27360 33924
Nicely-furnished studios, arranged around a pretty, walled courtyard in characterful Pótamos. €€

Crete

Agía Galíni

Rea Hotel
Tel/fax: 28320 91390
One of the few decent options here.
This is a small, newish hotel, at the
bottom of the hill. €

Agía Rouméli

Agia Roumeli Hotel
Tel: 28250 91232
One of the few good hotels among the
more basic rooms establishments
here. Located to the west, near the
main beach. The rooms have sea
views. €

Ágios Nikólaos

Candia Park Village
Tel: 28410 26811
Fax: 28410 22367
www.mamhotels.gr/candia
A rather fanciful reconstruction of a
Cretan village, sited between Ágios
Nikólaos and Eloúnda. Expensive,
there is a selection of discretely
luxurious studios, rooms and suites.
€€€

Minos Beach Art 'Otel
Aktí Ilía Sotírhou, Amoúdi
Tel: 28410 22345
Fax: 28410 22548
www.mamhotel.gr/minos
An elegant, deluxe coastal resort set
on a small peninsula. It consists of a
number of bungalows, all surrounded
by mature gardens. The hotel is
renowned for its collection of
contemporary art. €€€

Minos Palace Hotel
Tel: 28410 23801
Fax: 28410 23816
minpal@otenet.gr
One of the area's many 5-star hotels,
this one is built on a headland (30
minutes' walk from town) and was
meant to resemble a Minoan palace.
€€€

Crystal Hotel
Nissí
Tel: 28410 24407
Fax: 28410 25394
www.ormos-crystal.gr
Set back from the main road, on the
northern, Eloúnda, side of town, this
small C-class hotel is 1.5 km
(1 mile) from the centre and 10-20
minutes from the beach. €€

Lato Hotel
Amoúdi
Tel: 28410 24581
Fax: 28410 23996
lato@mail.com
On the beach, 1 km (½ mile) from Ag
Nik, the Lato has 37 rooms set in
lush gardens. They also manage the
Karavostasi on the coast 8 km (5
miles) from town, with three self-
catering studios. €€

Ormos Hotel
Nissí
Tel: 28410 24094
Fax: 28410 25394
www.ormos-crystal.gr
A B-class sister hotel to the Crystal.
The accommodation consists of
comfortable bungalows with a pool.
€€

Sgouros Hotel
Aktí Pangaloú, Kitroplatía Beach
Tel: 28410 28931
Fax: 28410 25568
A decent, family-run hotel situated 10
m (11 yds) from the sea and 300
metres (330 yds) from the centre of
the town. €€

Ágios Geórgios Lasithíou

Rea Hotel
Tel: 28440 31209
A modest but hospitable
establishment. It is nicely furnished
and comfortable, and is very well
sited for exploration of Lasíthi plateau.
€

Almyrída

Almirida Bay Hotel
Tel: 28250 31751
This decent medium-sized B-class
hotel has a restaurant and pool. It is
located in a small resort east of
Haniá. €€

Balí

Bali Beach Hotel & Village
Tel: 28340 94210
Fax: 28340 94252
www.balibeach.gr
A large – 120-room – hotel with a pool
and roof garden. The rooms have
pleasant sea-views; all of them come
with a fridge. €€

Rental Agencies

Doufexis Travel
Stoúpa, Peloponnese
Tel: 27210 77833
Fax: : 27210 77677
douftvl@hellasnet.gr
Accommodation and car-hire all
year round.
Palmyra Travel
Kalisperidón & Agíou Dimitríou,
Iráklio, Crete
Tel: 2810 244429
Fax: 2810 282229
palmyra@her.forthnet.gr
Accommodation, conferences,
small groups, throughout Crete.
Porfyra Travel
Livádi, Kýthira
Tel: 27360 31888
Fax: 27360 31889
www.kythira.info
Accommodation, car-hire, ferry
agent.

Eloúnda

Elounda Beach Hotel
Tel: 28410 41812
Fax: 28410 41373
www.eloundabeach.gr
One of the Leading Hotels of the
World group, this hotel is regarded as
one of the island's best. Fabulously
expensive but exceptionally luxurious,
it is a favourite of the European jet set
– some of the suites have a private
pool, sauna and gym, all watched over
by your own butler and personal
attendant. And, of course, helicopter
transfer is laid on as well. €€€

Elounda Mare Hotel
Tel: 28410 41102
Fax: 28410 41307
www.eloundahotels.com
Competing with the Elounda Beach,
this is the only Relais & Châteaux
hotel in Greece. It comprises a deluxe
complex offering bungalows with
private pools. Very expensive and very
swish. €€€

Akti Olous
Skhísma
Tel: 28410 41270
Fax: 28410 41425
Situated between the main road and
the lagoon road, this hotel is very
reasonable in both price and quality.
€€

Aristea Hotel
Skhísma
Tel: 28410 41300
Fax: 28410 41302
This is a moderately priced hotel, with
good facilities, located near to the
sea. €€

Elounda Hill Apartments
Skhísma
Tel: 28410 41114
Set a short way uphill behind the
village, these are self-catering rooms
with a friendly management, all
available at good prices. €

Georgioúpoli

Mare Monte Hotel
Tel: 28250 61390
Fax: 28250 61274
maremonte@otenet.gr
A pleasant beach hotel, with pool,
east of town towards Kavrós. €€€

Egeon Studios
Tel: 28250 61161
Fax: 28250 61171
Hospitable American-Greek
management, and rooms right next to
the river bridge. Good sea- and
harbour-views from the front rooms.
€€

Marika Studios & Apartments
Exópoli
Tel: 28250 61500
Very comfortable self-catering rooms
set in the hills 3 km (2 miles)
northwest of Georgioúpoli; friendly
management. €€

Price Guide

Price categories are based on the cost of a double room for one night in the high season:
€€€ Expensive over €100
€€ Moderate €50–100
€ Inexpensive under €50
For details of the Greek Tourist Authority's hotel classification system see Hotel Categories on page 333.

Haniá

A number of the Venetian period townhouses in the old town on either side of the harbour have been converted into luxurious pensions and apartments.
Casa Delfino Suites
Theofánous 9, near Zambelíou
Tel: 28210 93098
Fax: 28210 96500
www.casadelfino.com
Beautifully restored 17th-century Venetian house in the old harbour area; 20 luxury apartments surrounding a courtyard. €€€€
Contessa
Theofánous 15, near Zambelíou
Tel/Fax: 28210 98565
Spacious rooms in a fine Venetian building, with expensive furniture, wooden floors and ceilings. €€
Elena-Beach Hotel Apartments
Aktí Papanikóli 27, Néa Hóra
Tel: 28210 97633
Fax: 28210 96606
One of the smaller, quieter hotels to be found in Néa Hóra, a western suburb 15 minutes' walk from the centre. €€
Kriti Hotel
Nikifórou Foká 10 & Kýprou
Tel: 28210 51881
Fax: 28210 41000
www.kriti-hotel.gr
A large, modern hotel to the east of the centre, between the beach and the town market; open all year. €€
Nostos
Zambelíou 46
Tel/Fax: 28210 94740
A superbly renovated building (probably a 17th-century church) on the harbour front; 12 studios and a roof garden; open all year. €€
Pension Eva
Theofánous 1 & Zambelíou
Tel: 28210 76706
Fax: 28210 50985
A six-bedroom pension in a renovated Venetian/Turkish house with wooden ceilings and brass beds. €€
Porto del Colombo Hotel
Theofánous & Muskhón
Tel: 28210 70945
Fax: 28210 98467
colompo@otenet.gr

Impressively restored Venetian/Turkish house in the picturesque back streets of the old town. €€
Porto Veneziano
Aktí Énosseos
Tel: 28210 27100
Fax: 28210 27105
Situated some distance east of the bustle of the main harbour, near the yacht marina and fishing harbour. Spacious rooms and refreshing decor; open all year. €€
Ifigenia Hotel & Apartments
Angélou & Gambá 21
Tel: 28210 94537
Fax: 28210 36104
www.ifigeniastudios.gr
Rooms and studios in the Venetian quarter of the old town, overlooking the harbour. €

Hóra Sfakíon

Vritomartis Hotel
Tel: 28970 91112
Fax: 28970 91222
A large hotel, about 1 km (½ mile) from the village. Swimming pool and tennis courts available. Open March to October. €€

Ierápetra

Lyktos Beach Resort Hotel
Tel: 28420 61280
Fax: 28420 61318
A superior beach hotel, with sports facilities, 7km (4½ miles) east of town. €€€
Astron Hotel
Kóthri 56
Tel: 28420 25114
Fax: 28420 25917
A good hotel with comfortable rooms, towards the eastern end of town. Seaviews, and beach nearby. €€

Iráklio

It may not be easy to find a quiet room in the centre of town: light sleepers should ask for a room at the back.
Astoria Capsis Hotel
Platía Elevtherías 5
Tel: 2810 229002
Fax: 2810 229078
www.astoriacapsis.gr
In the main square and a very short walk from the Archaelogical Museum. A large hotel with comfortable rooms and suites; open all year. €€€
Candia Maris Hotel
Papandréou 72, Ammoudára
Tel: 2810 377000
Fax: 2810 250669
www.maris.gr/candia
Large deluxe hotel with parking, restaurant, pool, and a thalassotherapy centre; on the seafront to the west of the city. €€€
Galaxy Hotel

Dimokratías 67
Tel: 2810 238812
Fax: 2810 211211
www.galaxy-hotels.gr
A large, superior hotel, renovated 2002, in the centre of the city, with deluxe rooms, suites and a pool; open all year. €€€
Atrion Hotel
Hronáki 9
Tel: 2810 229225
Fax: 2810 223292
www.atrion.gr
A quiet, superior B-class hotel, with 70 rooms, in the heart of the town; open all year. €€
Daedalos Hotel
Dedálou 15
Tel: 2810 224390
Fax: 2810 224391
A relatively quiet hotel, in the pedestrianised centre of town; open all year. €€
Kastro Hotel
Theotokopoúlou 22
Tel: 2810 284185
Fax: 2810 223622
www.kastro-hotel.gr
A comfortable, medium-sized hotel with a great roof-terrace for sunbathing; rooms spacious; open all year. €€
Lato Hotel
Epimenídou 15
Tel: 2810 228103
Fax: 2810 240350
www.lato.gr
Family-run hotel overlooking the Venetian fortress on the old harbour; open all year. €€
Irini Hotel
Idomenéos 4
Tel: 2810 229703
Fax: 2810 226407
Quietly situated between the museum and the Venetian harbour; open all year. €
Olympic Hotel
Platía Kornárou
Tel: 2810 288861
Fax: 2810 222512
Standard rooms, located near the southern end of market street; open all year. €

Kastéli-Kissámou (Kíssamos)

Galini Beach Hotel
Tel: 28220 23288
Fax: 28220 23388
www.galinibeach.com
A friendly, well-run pension next to the beach, between the Kamára river and the football pitch. €

Liménas Hersonísou

Knossos Royal Village Hotel
Anísaras
Tel: 28970 23575
Fax: 28970 23150
www.aldemarhotels.com

The hotel has created a deluxe version of a Minoan settlement, on the beachfront at Anísaras. €€€

Loútro
Porto Loutro Hotel
Tel: 28250 91433
Fax: 28250 91091
www.hotelportoloutro.com
A comfortable hotel, beautifully situated overlooking the bay in this tiny traffic-free resort; hospitable Anglo-Greek management. €€

Mátala
Eva Marina Hotel
Tel: 28920 45125
Fax: 28920 45769
www.evamarina.com
C-class hotel in verdant gardens only 100 metres from Mátala's sandy beach. Most rooms have a sea view. €
Matala Bay Hotel
Tel: 28920 45100
Fax: 28920 45301
www.matala-bay.de
A good and long-established hotel, not far from the sea. €
Orion Hotel
Tel/Fax: 28920 42129
Modest but smart hotel, set in a secluded position just outside the village; large pool and good beaches nearby. €

Mýrtos
Esperides Hotel
Tel: 28420 51207
One of the better hotels in town, with a pool; open all year. €€
Myrtos Hotel
Tel: 28420 51227
Fax: 28420 51215
www.mirtoshotel.com
Family-run hotel situated in the middle of the village; bookable on the internet. €

Ómalos
Exari Hotel
Tel: 28210 67180
Fax: 28210 67124
A cosy hotel, recently refurbished; of a higher standard than many other establishments here, with proper baths and a restaurant. €

Paleohóra
Polydoros Hotel
Tel: 28230 41150
Fax: 28230 41578
In a cul-de-sac near the beach; small but well-appointed. €€
Rea Hotel
Tel: 28230 41307
Fax: 28230 41605
A small, hospitable, family hotel, not far from the sand beach. Clean rooms, with bath. €€

Plakiás
Morpheas Rooms & Apartments.
Tel:/Fax: 28320 31583
koumentaki@internet.gr
Older seafront rooms plus beautifully appointed new studios and apartments set back from the seafront. €€
Kyriakos Rooms
Tel: 28320 31307
Fax: 28320 31631
A quietly situated hotel with clean rooms, watched over by rakí connoisseur Kyriakos ever willing to share a glass with his guests. Next door to the recommended Medoúsa Taverna. €
Phoenix Hotel
Tel: 28320 31331
Fax: 28320 31831
Located about 3 km (2miles) west of Plakiás, in the direction of Soúda (Sweetwater) Beach. €

Réthymno
Fortezza Hotel
Melissinoú 16
Tel: 28310 55551
Fax: 28310 54073
A modern, quiet hotel, named after the Venetian fortress just behind it. 5-10 minutes' walk from the beach. €€€
Grecotel Rithymna Beach Hotel
Adelianós Kámbos
Tel: 28310 71002
Fax: 28310 71668
www.grecotel.gr
One of Crete's finest hotels, combining discreet luxury, impeccable service and warm hospitality. On the beach, 8 km (5 miles) east of the town centre. €€€
Theartemis Palace Hotel
M. Portáliou 30
Tel: 28310 53991
Fax: 28310 23785
www.theartemis.gr
A comfortable A-class hotel with pool, to the east of the centre. It has recently refurbished, but lies on a busy road. €€€
Veneto Suites
Epimenídou 4
Tel: 28310 56634
Fax: 28310 56635
www.veneto.gr
Ten suites and studios in a beautifully renovated 15th-century monastery, later Venetian/Turkish townhouse. €€€
Brascos Hotel
Daskaláki 1 & Moátsou
Tel: 28310 23721
Fax: 28310 23725
www.brascos.com
Three-star hotel in the town centre, opposite the public gardens, 450 metres (¼ mile) from the beach; open all year. €€

Ideon Hotel
Platía N. Plastíra 10
Tel: 28310 28667
Fax: 28310 28670
ideon@otenet.gr
Very convenient for the historical old town and fortress, with pool and good sea-views from the front rooms. €€
Kyma Beach Hotel
Platía Iróön 1 Tel: 28310 55503
Fax: 28310 27746
www.ok-rethymno.gr/kyma
Modern hotel at the edge of the old town, and opposite the beach. Open all year. €€
Palazzo Rimondi
Xanthoudídi 21
Tel: 28310 51289
Fax: 28310 51013
www.greekhotel.com/crete/rethymno/palazzo
Studios and apartments in a quiet street in the heart of the old town. €€
Pearl Beach Hotel
Paraliakí Leofóros, Perivólia
Tel: 28310 51513
Fax: 28310 54891
www.pearlbeach.gr
Situated a 2.5-km (1½-mile) stroll along the beach promenade from the centre and old town. A stylish, high quality, well-priced hotel, moments from the sea. €€

Sitía
Arhontiko Hotel
Kondyláki 16
Tel: 28430 28172
A lovely place set in an old mansion, kept very clean by the friendly management. €€
Crystal Hotel
Kapetán Sýfi 17
Tel: 28410 22284
Fax: 28410 28644
A good choice from the bunch of C-category hotels in the area behind the harbour; open all year. €€

Spíli
Tzermiádo
Kourites Hotel
Tel: 28440 22194
A pension with a good taverna a short distance down the street. €€
Heracles Rooms
Tel: 28320 22111
Fax: 28320 22411
Well-furnished rooms on the main street of inland Spíli, a great area for walking. Breakfasts available. €

Zarós
Idi Hotel
Tel: 28940 31301
Fax: 28940 31511
Mountain hotel at mouth of Roúvas Gorge, with old but functioning watermill. The hotel's own pond supplies fresh trout for the good restaurant. €€

Youth Hostels

Greece has a limited (and steadily dwindling) number of official, YHA-affiliated youth hostels for which you theoretically need a youth hostel card (see preceeding listings for decent examples). However, you can often buy a card on the spot or just pay an additional charge for the night, so it's not worth buying a YHA card in advance.

There are surviving hostels in Athens, Olympía and Thessaloníki, and on Santoríni plus Crete at Iráklio, Sitía, Réthymno, and Plakiás. There is also private, unaffiliated hostel-type accommodation of varying quality and repute in Athens and on numbers of islands such as Náxos, Rhodes and Corfu.

Traditional Settlements

The traditional settlements (paradosiakí ikismí) are villages that have been recognised by the Greek government as forming an important part of the national heritage. they have been protected from modern intrusions and constructions by law. Buildings in these villages were variably restored under NTOG initiaitve as tourist inns back in the 1970s and 1980s.

Almost all of these inns have been sold off and are now in private hands, although still protected by law, and private renovators have moreover brought other, generally higher-quality inns into service. Such houses and villages are, in their different ways, strikingly beautiful, and highly recommended for a long retreat in rural Greece.

Restoration inns are known to exist in the following villages, and more are appearing all the time:
Areópolis, Inner Máni (several tower houses)
Monemvasiá, Peloponnese (several restoration inns)
Ýdra (Hydra) Town (several sponge-captains' mansions, done as hotels)
Ía, Santorini (interlinked village houses)
Mestá, Híos (several restored houses, as room-only or entire apartments)
Kámbos region, Híos (several restored mansions, usually with restaurant on-site)
Mytilíni and **Plomári**, Lésvos (several restored-house inns, from basic to luxurious)
Psará island (basic accommodation in a restored prison)
Makrinítsa, Pílio (a half-dozen mansions, on a room-only basis)
Vyzítsa, Pílio (again a half-dozen

mansions, of a higher standard than Makrinítsa)
Pápingo, Megálo/Mikró, Zagória (at least ten mansions, high standard rooms)
Koukoúli, Zagória (two restoration inns)
Vítsa, Zagória (two restoration inns)
Kípi, Zagória (two restoration inns)
Tsepélovo, Zagória (several restoration inns)
Galaxídi, near Delphi (several restoration inns)
Nymféo, Macedonia (three deluxe restoration inns)
Rhodes Old Town (several high quality, and expensive, restoration inns)
Haniá, Crete (many fine restoration inns around the old harbour)
Valeondádes, Sámos (six houses of an abandoned hamlet, restored)
Gialós and **Horió**, Sými (several old houses restored and divided into apartments)
Corfu (three restored olive mills or manor-houses in remote locations)

For a selection of the above, refer to the particular region under *Where to Stay*.

Camping

Large numbers of visitors to Greece rough it in one form or another. This can range from sleeping on the deck of ferries overnight to bringing a tent and setting up camp by a secluded beach.

Those who want to stay at organised campsites will find them all over Greece; these are all owned privately since the EOT divested itself of its last sites in 1998.

The most beautiful campsites in Greece, however, are usually the ones you find on your own. While in most places it is officially illegal just to lay out your sleeping bag or pitch a tent, if you're discreet you will rarely be bothered. That always means asking permission from the owners if you seem to be on private property, avoiding unofficial campsites set up in popular tourist areas (which can get pretty squalid), and always leaving the place looking better than it did when you came.

In the mountains camping is the rule as few alpine refuges are attended (see below), but even here you should get the local shepherds' consent if they're around, as you may be turfing down in the middle of a prime grazing site.

Where to Eat

What To Eat

Eating out in Greece is above all a social affair. Whether it be with your family or *paréa*, that sacred circle of friends, a meal out is an occasion to celebrate.

This may have something to do with the fact that eating out in Greece continues to be affordable and common, not something restricted to those on expense accounts. And the predominance of the *tavérna*, that bastion of Greek cuisine, reflects this popularity.

These casual eating establishments have more or less the same style and set-up throughout Greece, and the menu is similar (indeed, often pre-printed by drinks companies in return for including their logo): no frills, no packaging that tries to convince the consumer that this *tavérna* is different from the others, special or distinct.

The place, and your being there, is somehow taken for granted: you eat the good food at Giannis's or Georgios's, you enjoy yourself, and (usually) you don't end up paying an arm and a leg for it.

This is the general background for eating out in Greece against which we find, of course, considerable variation. The *tavérna* is by no means the only kind of establishment. You will also encounter the *estiatório*, the traditional urban restaurant, which ranges from the tradesman's lunch-hour hangout, with ready-cooked (*magirevtá*) food and bulk wine, up to pricey linen-tablecloth places with bow-tied staff.

The *psistariá* is a barbecue-style restaurant specialising in lamb, pork or chicken on a spit; the *psarotavérna* specialises in fish and shellfish; while the *girádiko* (*gíros* stall) and *souvlatzídiko* purvey *gíros* and *souvláki* respectively, sometimes to a sit-down trade, garnished with salads. Although the best *souvlákia* are made from lamb, most are pork nowadays.

More popular of late among students and urban intelligentsia are the so-called *kultoúra* restaurants, nouvelle Greek cuisine based on

When to Eat

For Greeks the main meal of the day is eaten between 2pm and 3.30pm and, even in the cities, is usually followed by a siesta break lasting until 5.30 or 6pm. The evening meal can either be another full meal, or an assortment of *mezédes*. This is usually eaten between 9pm and 11pm.

Breakfast in Greece is traditionally small, usually bread and coffee. There are, however, wonderful *píta* and turnover options available from bakeries, for snacking on the hoof.

updated traditional recipes, and *ouzerí* (or *tsipourádika* in the north), where the local tipple serves as accompaniment to *mezédes* or small plates of speciality dishes.

Vegetarians are not well catered for in Greece. Most main courses will include either fish or meat. Your best bet is mixing and matching from a selection of *mezédes*.

There is considerable regional variety in Greek cuisine and you should keep an eye out for specialities of the house you haven't seen before. Another thing you'll quickly learn is how strikingly different the same dish can be when it is prepared well or badly. It is therefore worthwhile shopping around for your *tavérna* (especially in heavily visited areas), asking the locals what they suggest, walking into the kitchen to look at the food (still a customary practice), instead of getting stuck with a tourist trap that spoils your taste for *moussakás* for the rest of the trip. For experienced travellers, the term "tourist *mousakás*" is shorthand for an exploitative version of this standard dish, slathered with potatoes and poorly executed béchamel sauce, with nary a slice of aubergine or a crumb of mince.

Some *tavérnes*, especially in rural areas or on non-touristy islands, may not have menus, in which case it is essential to establish the price of at least the most expensive main courses, particularly seafood. Otherwise, prices are usually in two columns: the first without and the second with tax and service. The listings below mention some of the more popular foods you will find.

Athens

Athinaikon, Themistokéous 2, close to Omonia; tel: 210 383 8485. An *ouzerí* established in 1932, with loyal lunchtime customers from the neighbouring offices. An extensive list of fresh fish and seafood, a few good Greek cheeses and some interesting offal, including *spléna gemistá* (stuffed spleen). Decent barreled wine.

Bakalarakia/O Damingos, Kydathinéon 41, Pláka; tel: 210 322 5084.
Excellent food dished up in a long-established cellar restaurant (look for the photograph of Josephine Baker being served by the present owner's grandfather). Good things to order include *fáva*, *loukánika* and *saganáki*; the house speciality is *bakaliáro skordaliá* (salt cod with garlic). Excellent barreled wine.

Baïraktaris, Platía Monastiráki 2; tel: 210 321 3036. One of Athens' oldest extant restaurants dating back to 1879, known for its cheap and wholesome food, particularly *magirevtá*, with tasty *fasoláda* (bean soup), *domátes gemistés* (stuffed tomatoes) and *fáva*. Also *souvláki* and *gíros* takeaway service.

Benaki Museum Café, Koubári 1 and V. Sofías; tel: 210 367 1030. Set on a lovely terrace on the second floor of the museum, this is a favourite with the more artistic Kolonáki crowd who "do lunch". As well as excellent coffee and *retsína* there are good salads and daily specials, as well as some sinful cakes and desserts. The Thursday evening buffet (when the museum is open until midnight) is well worth booking for.

Dimokratous, Dimokrítou 23, Kolonáki; tel: 210 361 3588. This restaurant, housed in a neo-classical mansion, dishes up good, standard Greek food. All the usual favourites are here – salads, *fáva*, *hórta*, grilled meat and some seafood. The house wine is palatable and prices reasonable.

Eden, Lysíou 12 and Mnisikléous, Pláka; tel: 210 324 8858. Athens' best vegetarian restaurant, worth a visit whether you eat meat or not. The menu has some interesting takes on Greek staples using tofu and lentils (better than they sound), good and unusual salads and delicious fresh fruit juices. The ingredients are largely organic, as is the good wine list. There is a no-smoking section, unusual in Greece.

Epirus/Monastiri/Papandreou. These three cheap, basic eateries are all close together in the Central Meat Market off Athinás. Open 24 hours a day, they specialise in cooking up the more *recherché* parts of animals, in particular *patsás*. This tripe soup is much vaunted as a hangover cure.

The Food Company, Anagnostopoúlou 47, Kolonáki; tel: 210 363 0373. Just above Ágios Dionýsios, this is a good place for cheap, tasty food. The rustic interior has limited space for eating (some tables on the pavement in summer) but also has items such as oil and wine for sale. The dishes are largely vegetarian (such as lentils with *féta* and peppers, and a delicious potato and dill salad), the portions large.

Frame, Kleoménous 2, Kolonáki; tel: 210 7290 711. A flash, trendy new restaurant in the refurbished St George Lycabettus hotel. Seating is either inside near the bar, on a mezzanine (where it becomes a fish restaurant), or outside in a designer tent. The food is Mediterranean (lots of tomato, olive oil and various grilled meat and fish), and of a high standard. Your fellow-diners are likely to be young and fashionable.

GB Corner, Platía Sýndagma; tel: 210 333 0000. The restaurant for the refurbished Grande Bretagne; expensive but well worth a splurge. The service is excellent and the warm breads that come as a prelim are lovely. The mains, which are filling and generous, include a good mushroom risotto, salads, grilled meats and some thoughtful fish dishes; there is also enough on the menu for vegetarians to get by. Fabulous desserts, too.

Kafeneio, Epiharmoú 1, Pláka; tel: 210 322 4515/324 6916; and Loukianoú 26, Kolonáki; tel: 210 722 9056. Two branches of the same restaurant, both serving excellent food. Set in an attractive neo-classical building with some outside tables, the Pláka branch is cheaper, more relaxed and intimate. The menu here concentrates on *mezédes*, with good *keftedákia*, *fáva* and unusual cheeses, as well as good cheap bulk wine. The Kolonáki restaurant is more formal and pricey but just as good, with excellent stuffed cabbage leaves with *avgolémono* sauce, grilled aubergines with feta, and suckling pig and potatoes in a lemon sauce.

Kioupi, Platía Kolonáki 4; tel: 210 361 4033. A surprising find amid these posh surroundings, a cheap, freindly and spotless cellar restaurant that turns out good *magirevtá* from lunchtime onwards. Order from the trays displayed in front of the tiny kitchen. There is usually a fine selection of *bámies*, green beans stewed in oil, *hórta*, and chicken in various guises.

Platanos, Diogénous 4, Pláka; tel: 210 322 0666. A *tavérna* founded 1932 close to the Roman Agora. Although not that cheap, it has a pleasant interior, and in summer tables spill out onto the small *platía* in front. It serves good, basic food, including a number of good vegetable dishes as well as lots of grilled and baked meats.

Rodia, Aristípou 44, Kolonáki; tel: 210 722 9883. Tucked away on a residential street on the side of Lykavitós, this is a favourite with sedate locals and visiting academics. The food is decent but fairly pricey. If you aren't Greek, you must intervene quickly, before they bring you a standard, rather meat-heavy, selection of starters and main courses. Much better to pick and choose for yourself, but do try the good barreled wine. In the summer you can eat outside in a pleasant garden.

Thanasis, Mitropóleous 69, Monastiráki; tel: 210 324 4705. This Athenian institution is the place to eat *souvláki*. Essentially the food consists of grilled meat, salad and chips; all best washed down with chilled beer.

Tristrato, Dedálou 34 and A. Géronda, Pláka; tel: 210 324 4472. A lovely 1920s building on a corner, with an original interior, now a charming *galaktopolío*-cum-café popular with intellectuals and students. A good place for breakfast as well as a place to sit and read after dark. There is a large range of teas, as well as excellent cakes.

Vasilenas, Etolikoú 72, Piraeus; tel: 210 461 2457. Justly famous for its enormous list of *mezédes*, this plain looking *tavérna* is one of the best in the Athens area. Open evenings only, the set menu of some 16 dishes is good value, and challenging in quantity. It is very popular and booking is essential.

Peloponnese
Kalamáta
Katófli, Salamínos, one block in from the marina on the city's western waterfront. A pleasant place to eat, with outdoor seating and a very wide-ranging menu.

Kardamýli
Léla's; tel: 27210 73541. The oldest and most traditional taverna in the town, with only German draft beer as a concession to the predominant clientele. It has terrace seating and there is occasional live music.

Kórinthos
Arhondikó, 4 km (2½ miles) west of modern Kórinthos on coast road, opposite Lehaion harbour; tel: 27410 27968. The best food in this taverna is to be selected from the *mezédes*; there is also a good local rosé. It is open all year, with indoor and outdoor seating.

Koróni
Kangelários, waterfront; tel 27250 22648. The best of the quayside eating here, with seafood and small fish, reasonably priced.

Kýthira
Manólis, Diakófti; tel: 27360 33748. Not only fish, but imaginative *mezédes* such as cheese-and-greens turnovers.
Plátanos, Mylopótamos; tel: 27360 33397. Venerable village *kafenío* in a traditional building on the platía, also doing food: *magirevtá* at lunchtime, grills in the evening.
Sotíris, Avlémonas. All the classic elements for a Greek seaside taverna: sea breezes, simplicity, and perfectly cooked fresh fish.
Ydragogio, Kapsáli, end of the beach; tel: 27360 31065. Stress on vegetarian *mezédes* and *moussakás*, but also does fish. Terrace seating with enviable view of the castle.

Methóni
Klimatariá, a block from the castle; tel: 27230 31544. Somewhat pricey gourmet preparation of Greek standards, with emphasis on home-grown produce transformed into vegetarian dishes.

Monemvasiá
Matoúla; tel: 27230 61660. For years the only taverna in the old town, but the cooking still good. Seating out back on the terrace.

Návplio
Koutoúki to Parelthón, Profítis Ilías 12; tel: 27520 29930. Excellent *mezédes* in an old building in the new town; outdoor eating in summer, and very good prices.
Ómorfi Póli, Kotsonopoúlou 1; tel: 27520 25944. Greek casseroles and grills with a twist, but large portions. Book in advance as seating is limited. Come hungry.
Fanária, Staïkopoúlou 13; tel: 27520 27141. Best at lunch time; good Mégara wine and reasonable prices, in a street known for tourist rip-offs.

Neápoli Vión
Konáki tou Zahária; tel: 27340 23531. A very pleasant seafront taverna/pizzeria, on the promenade near the bridge, with excellent seafood.

Néos Mystrás
Mystrás, 100 metres (110 yards) from central fountain; tel: 27310 93432. A Greek choice for Sunday lunch: vegetable stew, fat olives, chops or sausages, accompanied by plenty of local wine. Indoor and outdoor seating.

Fruits of the Sea

Seafood is now one of the most expensive dishes on the Greek menu (except for frozen squid and fresh octopus, which are widely available). Fish are usually in a tray of ice for you to choose from, and your dish is priced by the weight of the fish of your choice. It is strongly suggested that you watch the (uncleaned) fish being weighed, and reiterate the price you are quoted, as "fingers on the scales" and later misunderstandings are not unknown.

There is so much farmed and frozen seafood (often marked only in Greek with a "*k*" or "*kat.*", for *katapsygméno*) lying in ambush for the inexperienced these days that the best strategy is to eat humbly and seasonally: far better a platter of grilled fresh sardines in August than a slab of swordfish frozen since June.

Olymbía
Kladíos, behind the train station on the riverside. A find in tourist-clogged Olymbía: real *mezédes*. Go early as seating is limited.

Pátra
Avlí tou Yennéou, Paraskhou 2, Terpsithéa. Tucked away among the apartments, one block back from the marina. Excellent seafood.
Beau Rivage, Germanoú 6, on Platía 25-Martíou; tel: 2610 275386. Fancy but surprisingly reasonable restaurant, with the emphasis on grills.

Pýlos
Grigóris, Georgíou Krasánou; tel: 27230 22621. This eatery provides oven-baked *magierevtrá* and grilled fish, served in a pleasant garden in summer.
Restaurant 1930, Kalamáta road. One of the best tavernas in town and popular with the locals; very good food, very friendly staff.

Río
Tesserís Epohés (Four Seasons), Somersét 64; tel: 2610 994923. Nicely sited next to the train station, so commutable from Pátra; good food at excellent prices.

Spárti
Akrolíthi, Odós ton 118, no. 75; tel: 27310 20123. Al fresco dining surrounded by flowers in summer, cosily indoors, with some live music, in winter. Excellent range of *mezédes*, well-priced, and popular with the locals

Stoúpa

The Five Brothers. Well established family-run taverna, with cheap but good, traditional food, in the middle of the seafront.

Giálova

This tiny resort, on the northeast side of Navaríno Bay, north of Pýlos, has a number of remarkably good waterfront tavernas, with reasonable prices. They include:
Helonáki; tel: 27230 23080. Well-cooked food and dreamy views out over the tranquil waters of the bay.
Spitikó. Wonderful home-cooking, as the name suggests, highly recommended.

Gíthio

Nautilía. A small *ouzerí* near the harbour jetty, with low prices and good food, including seafood. Waterside dining and gorgeous views, without the mark-up.

Central Greece

Pórto Germenó

Psarotaverna O Dimos, south of town above Ágios Nikólaos beach. Excellent meat/fish grills, salad and own-made retsina; tends to open weekends only except Jun–Aug.

Aráhova

Panagiota, near the main church; tel: 22670 32735. Emphasises home-style casserole cooking, and a few grills; reasonable, pleasant white-tablecloth environment. Open daily from mid-Sep to the end of ski season, but then closed until mid-Jul, weekends only mid-Jul–Sep.

Galaxídi

Barko Martisa, north end of main quay; tel: 22650 41059. Features non-greasy *píttes* and decent approximations of seafood risotto (don't expect the genuine Italian article outside of Athens). May shut Mon/Tue Nov–Feb.

Galaxídi

Albatross, inland street opposite 19th-century hilltop church. Sympathetic little *magirío* with a handful of tables, a limited (and thus fresh) amount of homestyle food at very attractive prices – the specialty is *samári* or pancetta in savoury sauce.

Lamía

Fytilis, Platía Laoú 6; tel: 22310 26761. The only surviving restaurant on this leafy central square is a goodie – the specialty is bacon-and-cheese-stuffed *biftéki*, but there are vegetarian dishes.

Ouzou Melathron, Aristotelous 3; tel: 22310 31502. Just up some steps from Platía Laoú is this slightly pricey *koultoúra ouzerí*, offspring of the parent branch in Thessaloníki, ensconced in a fine old house with garden.

Monastiráki

Iliopoulos; tel: 26340 52111. Around the eastern headland in this attractive seaside village just 11km east of Návpaktos stands this excellent seafood taverna; prices are under €20 for wild-caught fish, a pair of starters and a beer. Closed Mon Oct–March.

Návpaktos

Tsaras, behind the old harbour; tel: 26340 27809. One of the few eateries at the Venetian port, this place offers a limited but tasty and daily-changing menu of *magirevtá* amid supremely eccentric surroundings. Open Wed–Sun, lunch and supper.

Mesolóngi

The provincial capital is famous for smoked eels from its lagoon; they can be found, along with a variety of other traditional foods, in several places along Athanasíou Razikotsíka, near the central square. **Delfinia** at No. 6, **Posidon** at No. 4 and **Marokia** at No. 8 are likely venues.

Páliros

O Platanos, inland end of harbour square; tel: 26430 41664. Doesn't look like much, but this friendly little *koutoúki* serves up fair-priced, fresh grilled fish as well as *mezédes* like *gávros pastós* (salt-marinated anchovy) and draught beer from a microbrewery.

Mýtikas

O Glaros, northwest end of quay; tel: 26460 81240. Busy fish taverna with fresh fare and unbeatable waterside terrace looking out towards Kálamos island.

Gávros

To Spiti tou Psara, main valley-bottom road. Despite the name, lots else besides trout: excellent *hortópitta*, *kafterí* dip, own-made wine at reasonable prices.

Mikró Horió

Iy Kyra Maria, ground floor of Helidona Hotel; tel: 22370 41221. Atmospheric seating under the plane tree in the centre of the old village. The cooking itself has improved of late, in tandem with a refit of the rooms upstairs

---

Vólos

Halambalias (Zafiris), Orféos 8, corner Skýrou; tel: 24210 20234. A shrine of *magirevtá* that attracts crowds to an uninspiring inland location; three stars for the *tourlú* (ratatouille) and bulk wine, also baked seafood and meat dishes. Closed Sunday.

Monosandalos, Tsopótou 1, east waterfront by Ágios Konstandínos church; tel: 24210 37525. The doyen of several *ouzerí*, it has recently expanded by absorbing its neighbour. Shrimp croquettes a specialty; go in a group of four, and the bill won't much exceed €50.

Portariá

Kritsa, central *platía*; tel: 22428 99121. 2002-inaugurated ground-floor restaurant that shines for its exceptionally tasteful environment, professional service and biggish portions (don't over-order). Specialties include *tyropitákia*, *maïdanosaláta* (parsley dip) and of course Piliot *spétzofaï*.

Pinakátes

Drosia (Taverna tou Papa), west end of village; tel: 24230 86772. The locals tend to go here rather than the main *platía* – endorsement enough for leafy *dolmádes* and goat and lemon sauce. Also excellent, off-menu *mezédes* accompanying a *karafáki* of *tsípouro* or a jug of potent red bulk wine. May close random days Oct–May.

Damoúhari

Barba Stergios, south side of Venetian port. A reliable, fairly inexpensive venue for non-farmed fish, as well as meat grills and a few *magirevtá* dishes. There is a lovely seaside terrace for eating during the summer, also a tasteful indoor salon for cooler months.

Ágios Ioánnis

Posidonas, central waterfront; tel: 24260 31222. This is about the first fish taverna established here, and still one of the best and cheapest; a medium-sized fish, two starters and some local wine will clock in at well under €20. It is open most of the year.

Ágios Ioánnis

Ostria, well-signed inland near north end of seafront; tel: 24260 32132. Strongly herbed, generic-Mediterranean recipes (strong on pasta) reflect proprietress Hariklia's years in Florence. Moderately pricey; limited seating so reservations advised.

Kissós

Makis, just off the *platía*; tel: 24260 31266. One of the oldest tavernas in Pílio: stress on *magirevtá* like rabbit stew, *gígandes*, broccoli, bulk wine. Cheap, and reliably open all year.

Milína

O Sakis, south end of front; tel: 24230 66078. Hard to believe in such a touristy resort, but this is one of the best tavernas in the south Pelion. A five-platter meal, including *gávros* (fresh anchovy), *hórta* and other *mezédes*, won't much top €14.

Mylopótamos

Angelika, near end of the road into town; tel: 24260 49588. The fish is a bit pricey but various *magirevtá* plates are reasonable and service is kind and efficient. Open daily Easter to Oct 31, weekends and holidays Nov–Easter.

Katigiórgis

Flisvos (Voulgaris), fishing port; tel: 24230 71071. Folk from Vólos reckon the long trip out here worth it for the fresh fish and honest *magirevtá*, and you'll probably agree. Tables in the sand, weather and waves permitting.

Kalambáka

O Houtos, about 400 m (¼ mile) from east edge of town on Tríkala road; tel: 24320 24754. Not many tourists come here because of the remote, desperately unscenic location, but locals know better. They relish lamb kebab and chops, *biftéki* and house special *kokorétsi* at eminently reasonable prices.

Kastráki

O Paradissos, on through road opposite Hotel Spanias. Excellent-value, high-quality grill much favoured by the locals, who pack out its west-facing view terrace. A portion of kebab, bean salad, red peppers and a beer for around €12.

Tríkala

The trendiest eating district is the old tradesmen's bazaar of Varoúsi on the northeast bank of the Lethéos River, in the pedestrianised lanes with Ypsilándou as their focus. The *ouzerís* here only really come alive after 9.30pm; try **Mezedokamomata** at No.18, **Ianthos** just opposite, or **Timi** nearby.

Epirus

Ioánnina

Odós Pamvotídas, the lakefront avenue, is where townspeople go for a good-value waterside feed. There are

about six tavernas and *ouzerís* in a row here, whose various fortunes wax and wane with the years; try **Limni**, **Filippas** (with two premises, one for grills, one for *mezédes*) or **Stin Ithaki**. **Café Bistro 1900**, Neoptolémou 9; tel: 26510 33131. On the second floor of a renovated mansion, this bistro attracts the beau monde of Ioánnina for its short, sweet menu of nouvelle Italian/Mediterranean specialties. Greek-style risotto, pork medallions and plum sauce and a competent wine list are features.

Métsovo

Athens/Athenai, just below central *platía* to the south; tel: 26560 41332. The restaurant of this hotel purveys excellent local *magirevtá* recipes, plus wine from vineyards down in the river valley. This was one of the first inns in Epirus, and closed in 2003 for renovation, but should reopen in the same spot.

Monodéndri

En Monodendrion, by main car park in Ágios Minás chapel. Skip the touristy tavernas higher in the village in favour of this quick-serving, reasonable taverna with a good mix of grills and local dishes.

Pápingo, Megálo

Nikos Tsoumanis, north part of village; tel: 26530 42237. Huge salads, tasty lamb, regional dishes and assorted offal for the bold, plus unimpeded views of the famous *pýrgi* of Astráka from the terrace make this *ouzeri* a winner.

Pápingo, Megálo

Kalliopi, south part of village; tel: 26530 41081. Home-style cooking (including trout and *píttes*), good bulk wine, year-round operation and good CDs in the sound system guarantee a lively crowd here.

Koukoúli

Christos and Elektra's, main *platía*; tel: 26530 71121. The municipal *kafenío* concession is currently held by a young Zagorian couple who offer simple but appetising platters (sausages, smoked trout, beets, a dessert or two) accompanied by *tsípouro*. Sit out under the giant *plátanos* tree in fine weather.

Kípi

Stou Mihali, main through road; tel: 26530 71630. The combination *kafenío/tavérna* for the village, this is one of the most reliable outfits in Zagóri: excellent bulk wine, *píttes* and generally lots for vegetarians, a dish or two of the day.

Kónitsa

To Dendro, bend in the approach road; tel: 26550 23982. Trout, grills and interesting things done with peppers distinguish this taverna-inn from the run-of-the-mill eating place, with seating under the vast plane tree of the name.

Pérdika

Ta Kavouria, central *platía*. One of eight or so tavernas around the lively square here, this is the bohemian hangout, and as good as any; the per-person bill with bulk wine shouldn't much exceed €12.

Párga

Apangio, up a stair-lane from the east front; tel: 26840 32791. This is the resort's only *ouzeri*, and is fairly authentic if a bit pricey – reckon on €15–18 for three platters, one with seafood, plus a *karafáki* of *oúzo* or *tsípouro*.

Golfo Beach, southeast end of town; tel: 26840 32336. One of the oldest tavernas in Párga, this has acquired a cult following for its friendly Anglophile management, seaside terrace and good-value oven-casserole food. **Taverna tou Khristou**, Sarakíniko beach, 7 km (4 miles) northwest; tel: 26840 35207. Installed in new premises since 2002, this old favourite features well-executed vegetables, fresh seafood (except for the squid and octopus), a few select meat dishes, and limited bottlings from quality wineries in northern Greece.

Préveza

Amvrosios, Grigoríou tou Pémptou 9, opposite Venetian clock tower; tel: 268272192. Wonderful grilled sardines and nothing but (no relation to the canned variety), washed down by barreled wine.

Menídi, between Árta and Amfilohía Vouliagmeni, first place on left from main highway; tel: 26810 88216. Where folk from Árta come for a big plate of the famous Amvrakian *garídes* (prawns, shrimp), as well as scaly fish – though budget over €20 per head, as prices have climbed with the place's reputation.

Thessaloníki

Ta Adelfia tis Pyxarias, Platía Navarínou 7; tel: 2310 266432. This is one of the best among several *tavérnes* operating around a pedestrianised square to the east of the city centre. Dine outside or inside among photos on the wall of an old Macedonian home. Succulent kebabs as well as a range of ready-made

Greek Salad

"Greek" salad is a staple of Greek cuisine. *Horiátiki*, the full monty with tomatoes, cucumber, green pepper, *féta* cheese and olives, is a lunch in itself with bread – and this is what you'll probably get if you ask for "salad". Some restaurateurs omit one or two of the vegetable ingredients – not all are available all summer – but by law *horiátiki* must contain a generous chunk of *féta*. If all you want is a small side salad, ask for *angourodomáta* (just tomatoes and cucumber).

oven-cooked dishes.

Amanites, D. Poliorkitoú 44; tel: 2310 233513. A non-touristy eaterie in the Kástra district that will appeal to vegetarians and carnivores alike. Features mushrooms (*amanítes*), as well as a selection of meaty *mezédes*. The basement restaurant is a little reminiscent of 1970's student hangouts.

Aristotelous, Aristotélous 8; tel: 2310 233195. One of older *ouzerís* in the city centre, Aristotelous is all marble tables and wrought-iron chairs set out in a quiet arcade close to Platía Aristoteloús. The food is classic northern Greece with imaginative takes on rice and mussels, cuttlefish in wine sauce and other *ouzerí* standards. There is also an excellent wine list.

The Barrister, Tsimiskí 3 & Výronos 2; tel: 2310 253033. This smart top-of-the range restaurant serves a mélange of Italian-influenced but essentially European dishes, all presented with flair and passion and imbued with the nuances of the Barrister's chef de cuisine. Housed in old lawyers' club – hence the name – this is one of Thessaloníki's most sophisticated dining locales.

Ta Kioupia, Platía Morihóvou 3-5; tel: 2310 553239. The owners of this smart, businesslike restaurant in the heart of the city attempt to represent all areas of Greece in their extensive, gastronomically encompassing menu. You'll find specialities from the Greek islands, from Epirus and from Crete, plus many of the less common Greek wines.

Myrovolos tis Smyrnis, Modiáno Market; tel: 2310 274170. Doyenne of several competing *tsipourádika* at the market hall's west entrance, strong on seafood, bags of atmosphere. The food is top-notch and imaginative. Air-conditioned interior, or seating in the arcade – either way reservations are

recommended

Ouzou Melathron, Karýpi 21; tel: 2310 275016. Search for the small Greek sign for this cosy and popular *ouzerí*, patronised mainly by Greeks, tucked away on a little pedestrian alleyway. For your efforts you'll enjoy a wide range of moderately priced *mezédes* which it is customary to wash down with a small carafe or two of *oúzo*.

Parakath, Konstantinoupóleos 114; tel: 2310 653705. Parakath is Thessaloníki's only Pontian-Greek restaurant and features a range of pasta and yoghurt dishes from Turkey's Pontus region. There are the usual grills as well. Live music and dancing kicks in around midnight and goes on well into the following day.

Pyrgos, Venizélou 13; tel: 2310 207769. Pyrgos is one of those quietly successful places that rely in its repeat clientele and its consistently quality fare. Up in the Kástra this place dishes up a mixed Greek international cuisine with particular emphasis on its fine wine list. The food is well presented and the service particularly friendly.

To Rema, Pasalídi 2, Káto Toúmba; tel: 2310 901286. You'll need a cab to find this little out-of-the-way place to the east of the city centre, but it's worth the effort. Popular with students and youngish trendies, the food is unusual in that each dish has a "political" or "historical" name like *perestroika* or Colossus of Rhodes. Dishes are a mixture or French and Greek and are well prepared and presented.

Toumbourlika, Kalapotháki 11; tel: 2310 282174. Yet another of the city's famous *ouzerís*, hidden away in a narrow street off Platía Dimokratías, this consists of a couple of small cosy rooms with a few outside tables. It specialises in fish *mezédes*, though it does serve a hearty soup on Thursdays. You might catch some live music on weekends.

To Yedi, I. Paparéska 13, Kastra; tel: 2310 246495. High up next to the Eptapýrgio fortress, this laid-back and friendly *ouzerí* does what *ouzerís* do best – serving up no-nonsense high quality *mezédes* in a friendly, unfussy environment. House speciality is veal and aubergines served piping hot in a clay pot.

Zythos, Katoúni 5, Ladádika; tel: 2310 540284. This is a great spot for people-watching while you dine on a variety of dishes featuring Greek, Asian and western European elements. Zythos is a restaurant-cum-pub and apart from its inventive cuisine serves up pints of draft Irish and German beers.

Macedonia and Thrace

Kastoriá

Doltso, Tsakáli 2; tel: 2467 024670. Opened in early 2003, this classy dining venue on Doltso Square has quickly become one of the favourite local restaurants. The restored mansion in which it's housed is all stone and wood, with intriguing nooks and crannies. The top-class food includes many traditional Macedonian dishes.

Alexandroúpoli

To Nisiotiko, Zarífi 1; tel: 2551 020990. In a town where fish tavernas are a dime a dozen, To Nisiotiko stands out for its classic Aegean blue and white décor and unhurried style. The food is fresh, well prepared and not overly expensive. Fish dishes predominate though there's a range of grills and imaginative *mezédes*.

Édessa

Raeti, 18th Oktovríou 20; tel: 2381 028769. *Raéti* means "eating and drinking" in Cretan dialect, though the owners here are not Cretans. They cook up solid Macedonian *mezédes*, grills and a range of oil-based dishes. The restaurant is low-key and attracts a mainly local crowd. Excellent draft wine.

Flórina

Restaurant Olympus, Megálou Alexándrou 22; tel: 2385 022758. Food the old-fashioned way. Open for lunch only, this long-running "cook-house" serves homemade dishes for hungry and unfussy diners. Plenty for vegetarians, too. You'll find all the traditional dishes here: *mousakás*, *pastítsio*, lima beans in tomato sauce and *fasoláda* (hearty bean soup).

Kavála

Tembelhanio, Poulídou 33b; tel: 2510 232501. A Macedonian-style *ouzerí*: the *mezédes* are mainly fish, with shellfish taking pride of place, and you wash it all down with small carafes of *tsípouro* – the fiery grape spirit that is drunk throughout Macedonia. Tourists are noticeable by their absence. Dine in the company of knowledgable and appreciative locals.

Komotiní

Ta Adelfia, Orféos 25; tel: 2531 020201.Another traditional eating place: the food is simple staples, cooked in the old-fashioned way; even the décor has changed little in the last 30 years. The best bet is to go for the daily specials listed on a blackboard outside.

Litóhoro

To Bereketi, Agíou Nikoláou 40; tel: 2352 082213. Grilled meat and fish dishes seem to predominate in Litóhoro – perhaps reflecting the hearty climate and abundant local produce. To Bereketi specialises in kebabs, roasted over a charcoal grill in the restaurant window. Locals are particularly fond of a dish where chunks of meat plus herbs and spices are roasted in a clay pot over the embers: ask for *stamnáto*. Good local draft wine.

Préspa

Akrolimnia, the lakefront, Psarádes village; tel: 2385 046260. If you eat in the Préspa Lake region, you should sample famous local produce – namely *fasoláda*, a rich bean soup, or the local lake trout, *péstrofa*. This busy and informal lakefront taverna is one of the best places in the village to enjoy them.

Véria

To Katafygi, Kondogeorgáki 18; tel: 2331 027227. The impressive and cosy Katafygi (the name means "refuge", as in mountain shelter) dishes up a wide range of game from quail to wild boar. Vegetarians won't be disappointed, though, with an enticing range of mushroom-based dishes on offer. Hot pepper lovers might enjoy the "chef's revenge".

Xánthi

Myrovolos, Platía Hristídi; tel: 2541 072720. The atmospheric streets of Xánthi's old town is home to a rash of generally good tavernas and restaurants all serving similar permutations of *mezédes* and grills. Myrovolos is one of the better ones and specialises in *tsipouromézedes* (*mezédes* for *tsípouro*). On weekends you may catch live *rembétika* music.

Saronic Gulf

Égina

Agora, Égina Town; tel: 22970 27308. This no-nonsense fish taverna has been around for over 40 years so it's doing something right. There's nothing flash about the ambience: the fish is as fresh as it can be and that's what counts. Wash it down with *oúzo* or draft wine.

To Steki, Égina Town; tel: 22970 23910. A similar establishment to Agora and it's also close by. It's always busy so come early if you want a table. Grilled octopus is the speciality, though you can choose your fish from those on display and have it grilled as you sip your retsina or *oúzo* and ice.

Póros

Taverna Karavolos, Póros Town; tel: 22980 26158. Meaning a type of snail in Greek, Karavolos is a very popular taverna in the back streets of Póros town. Yes, the restaurant does serve snails, served with a rich sauce. There's a selection of readymade *magirevtá* (home cooked) dishes as well as grills. Dine indoors or on a leafy patio. Reservations recommended.

Taverna Platanos, Póros Town; tel: 22980 24249. High up in the back streets of Póros town under a plane tree (*plátanos*). The speciality here is grills ranging from regular steaks to *kokorétsi*, mixed offal grilled on a long skewer. The atmosphere is relaxed and laid-back; evening dining is the best time to enjoy this place.

Ýdra

Moita, Ýdra Town; tel: 22980 52020. Perhaps the best restaurant on the island. The cuisine is generic Mediterranean and the dishes constructed with care and attention, combining the best ingredients into imaginative creations. Seafood predominates with prawns delicately cooked in spinach worth a mention. Reservations suggested.

To Steki, Ýdra Town; tel: 22980 53517. A simple taverna-cum-*ouzerí* just a short step back from the harbour front. Locals come here to sip wine and gossip. The food is simple and unadorned and consists in the main of ready-cooked dishes with a smattering of grills and fries. The lamb fricassée is worth tasting as are the tasty *píttes* (small triangular pastry turnovers).

Taverna Gitoniko, Ýdra Town; tel: 22980 53615. Popular with locals and foreigners alike, the Taverna Gitoniko (aka Kristina's) offers discreet rooftop dining as well as indoor dining downstairs. Good-value dishes range from simple island vegetarian fare to hearty grilled meats and fish. Veal in quince or red wine sauce is a house speciality. Excellent draft wine.

Spétses

Exedra, Old Harbour; tel: 22980 73497. One of several classy tavernas in the Old Harbour, Exedra. is a fish taverna, and you can virtually see them as you dine on a platform extending into the harbour. The house speciality is fish cooked in garlic and tomato and baked in the oven. You'll also find prawns and lobster, both prepared either with cheese or with spaghetti.

Liotrivi, Old Harbour; tel: 22980 72269. Close to the Exedra is a restaurant in an old olive press (*liotrívi*). This is also a fish taverna in a very attractive location near the old boatyards. Mainly Greek clientele enjoy all kinds of variations on fish and other seafood. Best for evening dining.

Orlof, Old Harbour; tel: 22980 75255. Before you reach the Old Harbour proper you'll come across this long-established *ouzerí* inside a large white building overlooking the waterfront. There's a huge range of creative *mezédes* to choose from. It's also a people-watching joint and gets very busy at night with people constantly dropping in and out.

Cyclades

Santorini

1800, Ía; tel: 22860 71485. In an old captain's mansion on main street, 1800 is one of Greece's best for elegant Mediterranean cuisine. Expensive. Reservations essential.

Aktaion, Firostéfani. This traditional taverna, on the caldera edge, has served traditional Greek food for 60 years. This is how moussaka is supposed to taste – Mum's recipes are still in use. Inexpensive.

Camille Stefani, Kamári. This restaurant, right on the black beach, has been serving seafood and Greek cuisine for 25 years. Locals favour it even in summer. A good choice is *laháno dolmádes* (stuffed cabbage). Reasonable prices.

Kastro, Ía. Many customers come here for the famous sunset view, and with their drink eat grilled fruit with honey sauce. The wise ones stay for a reasonably-priced dinner.

Restaurant Nicholas, Firá. On Stavros Street, parallel to the caldera road, Nikolas is Fira's oldest taverna. It serves all the usual Greek dishes. Open year round, lunch and dinner. Inexpensive.

Selene, Firá; tel: 22860 71485. Go to Selene for the quiet terrace with its caldera view, its fine cuisine based on local recipes, its unobtrusively elegant service, or even to take cooking classes in summer. Fairly pricey.

Sphinx, Firá; tel: 22860 23823. Everything here is homemade, from the bread to the noodles. Try squid in basil sauce, and don't forget the chocolate soufflé. Expensive, but worth it for the food and the caldera view. Advance booking suggested.

Taverna Katina, Ammoúdi, Ía. On the right at the bottom of the steps leading down from Ía. In many people's eyes, the fresh, grilled fish, prawns and Santorini specialities make this the island's best taverna, all helped along by the excellent, friendly

Eating out with Kids

Children regularly dine out with their parents until late at night, and (within their abilities) are expected to converse with the adults. There's no formality about this – kids are as likely to be racing round the taverna playing tag or under the table teasing the stray cats as sitting up at the table. The Greeks are extremely indulgent of their children, so don't be embarrassed to make any special food request for your own.

service. Easter–October; from lunch until late.
Taverna Pyrgos, Pýrgos Village. An elegant, moderate-priced restaurant with an unusual view. Order a table-full of their excellent *mezédes*, or starters, especially the smoky aubergine salad.

For after-hours tippling, you can't beat the **Kira Thira Jazzbar**, a barrel-vaulted jazz and blues haunt in central Firá. Dimítris Tsavdarídes mixes a mean sangria. Alternatively, **Franco's Bar**, on the caldera in Firá, was rated one of the world's best by no less than *Newsweek International*. The tall drinks it serves are works of art; so is the wonderful view; the music is classical. For youthful nightlife, **Koo Club** and **Enigma** are next to each other, and rock all night on Firá's caldera path.

Mýkonos

L'Angolo Bar, Láka district, Hóra. Italians make the best espresso. Breakfast and packed lunches are also good.
La Bussola, Láka district, Hóra. Chef Giovanni Marale serves up excellent Genovese dishes, but the pizza is also delicious. Whatever your main course, be sure to try the pannacotta afterwards.
Efthimios' Patisserie, Fl. Zouganeli, Hóra. For over 40 years, Efthimios has sold his famed *kalathakiá* ("little baskets") and almond milk from this immaculate sweet shop. (Takeaway only.)
Katrin's, Ágios Gerásimos district, Hóra; tel: 22890 26946.
For 20-odd years, Katrin's Greek cuisine with a French accent has made this restaurant, on a back alley, world famous. Order the seafood starters and finish with chocolate mousse. Fairly pricey, reservations recommended.
Matthew Taverna, Tourlós (on Ág. Stéfanos road). This is a polished *tavérna*, and the service on the cool terrace is friendly and quick. Try *bekrí*

mezé – lamb wrapped in vine leaves. Open summer noon–1am.
Nikola's Taverna, Agía Ánna Beach (after Platýs Gialós). A locals' favourite: an authentic Greek taverna on a pretty, tiny beach.
Sea Satin Market – Caprice, Alevhándra quarter, directly below the windmills, Hóra. Unique waveside restaurant, where Greeks often party after a baptism or wedding. Eat fish and shellfish. Easter–Oct.
Taverna Niko's, just off the harbour, Hóra. For a quarter-century, Niko's has made fresh fish and lobster a speciality. Try homemade moussaka, salads with capers and rocket. Great service, moderate prices.
La Taverne, Hóra, a 15-minute walk out towards Agíos Stéfanos; tel: 22890 23692. In Cavo Tagoo Hotel. Chef Giánnis Argýriou is surely one of Greece's best, and cooks it all himself – even the chocolate candies. Try the risotto with crayfish and vegetables in champagne sauce. Expensive.

Náxos

Gorgona, Agía Ánna. This longtime beach taverna has grown more elaborate, but the prices are still good, as is the traditional Greek food. The fresh fish is bought at the dock out front. Try the *kakaviá* (fish stew). Locals eat here year-round.
Meltemi Restaurant, Extreme southern end of Hóra's waterfront. The Meltemi has been here for 50 years, serving inexpensive traditional Greek cuisine, including fresh fish. It's authentic and popular with locals. Easter till end October, all day till midnight.
The Old Inn, Boúrgos, Hóra; tel: 22850 26093. In a charming garden, Berlin chef Dieter von Ranizewski, who has spent most of his life on Naxos, serves Greek and international cuisine. He makes everything, even the smoked ham.

Paros

Boudaraki, harbour road, Parikía. This is a typical Greek *ouzerí* with drinks and *mezédes* such as grilled octopus and fresh sea urchins. Open Easter–early Oct.
O Christos, opposite the Church of the Panagía Pantanássa, Naoússa; tel: 22840 51442. Paros' most elegant restaurant (and one of the more expensive) has Mediterranean food, perfect service and great attention to detail. The menu changes, but not the excellence.
Levantis, Market Street, Parikía; tel: 22840 23613. Inventive Mediterranean cuisine in a pretty, quiet garden. Daily specials. Try sesame-coated marinated pork with

wild mushrooms and Chinese noodles. Moderate to expensive.
Papadakis, harbour, Naoússa; tel: 22840 51047. The seafood recipes here are so good that the owners are translating their cookbook into English. Right on the picturesque fishing harbour, you can see where your fish came from.
Porphyra, Parikía; tel: 22840 23410. Some of the fresh fish and shellfish, including oysters, the owners have caught themselves. And there are daily specialties, such as sea-urchin salad. Open off season.
Tamarisko Garden Restaurant, Néos Drómos, Parikía. Located in the Old Agora marketplace. Order pork stew *tamariskó*, mushrooms in sauce, and the dreamy chocolate mousse. March till end-Oct from 7pm. Closed Mon.

Rhodes

L'Auberge Bistrot, Praxitélous 21, Rhodes Old Town; tel: 22410 34292. Genuine, popular bistro run by a couple from Lyon; for about €20 you'll get three hefty courses, (wine from a well-selected Greek list extra), jazz soundtrack included. Summer seating in the courtyard of this restored medieval inn; inside under the arches during cooler months. Open for dinner daily except Mon, late Mar–late Dec; reservations suggested.
Fotis, Menekléous 8, Rhodes Old Town; tel: 22410 27359. The affiliate of Fotis Melathron (above) serves only fish, plus the odd green salad. Somewhat pricey at about €70 for two with wine, but fresh catch of the day guaranteed.

Ordering Drinks

býra	beer
krasí	wine
áspro	white wine
kokkinélli	rosé wine
mávro	red wine
me to kiló	wine by the kilo
hýma	bulk, from the barrel
neró	water
retsína	resin-flavoured wine
oúzo	aniseed-flavoured grape-pressing distillate
rakí	another distilled spirit from vintage
crushings	
tsípouro	north-mainland version of *rakí*
tsikoudiá	Cretan version of *rakí*, flavoured with
terebinth	
portokaláda	orange juice
lemonáda	lemon juice

Fotis Melathron, Dinokrátous, off Apéllou, Rhodes Old Town; tel: 22410 24272. The town's top *koultoúra* taverna, lodged in a lovely old Turkish mansion, with upstairs "snugs" for private functions and plush terrace seating. The fare is generally successful *novelle* Greek, featuring fish/seafood starters (eg filleted crayfish nuggets), meaty mains, and decadent desserts.
O Giannis, Vassiléos Georgíou tou Deftérou 23, Koskinoú. The stock in trade here is abundant *mezédes* with a Cypriot/Turkish/Middle Eastern flair, washed down with Émbona wine or *oúzo*; it's extremely reasonable, especially for a group, and is open daily for dinner all year.
Ta Marasia, Agíou Ioánnou 155, southwest of Rhodes Old Town; tel: 22410 34529. Currently the best *ouzerí* in Rhodes, occupying the patio and interior of a 1923 house. The food's excellent if not very traditional – red cabbage, yoghurt with nuts, grilled oyster mushrooms – plus more ordinary seafood (urchins, herring salad). Don't over-order as portions tend to be big.
Mavrikos, Líndos; tel: 22440 31232. Founded in 1933 in the fig-tree square, and in the same family ever since, Mavrikos has been nominated one of the five best Greek eateries outside of Athens. *Mezédes* like manoúri cheese with basil and pine-nuts are accomplished, as are quasi-French main courses such as cuttlefish in wine sauce; dipping into the excellent (and expensive) Greek wine list will double a basic bill of about €25 each.
To Petrino, Váti; tel: 22440 61138. The central *kafenío* in this far-south village is liveliest at weekends when Greeks come to enjoy the local specialty of *gourounópoulo* (suckling pig), but there's lots else – including spicy *revíthia*, real *hórta* and chocolate cake.
Pigi Fasouli, Psínthos; tel: 22410 50071. This is the best and friendliest of several tavernas here, serving excellent grills (goat, *soúvla*, etc) and appetisers as well as a few *magirevtá* of the day. In a lovely position with tables overlooking plane trees and the namesake spring.
To Steki tou Heila, Kodringtónos/Dendrinoú, near Zéfyros beach; tel: 22410 29337. Considered the best seafood *ouzerí* in Rhodes New Town. It's wise to check prices beforehand on the more exotic shellfish like *kydónia* (cockles) and *gialisterés* (smooth venus).
To Steki tou Tsima, Peloponnísou 22, 400 m (¼ mile) south of Old Town; tel: 22410 74390. A good alternative for

moderately-priced shellfish delicacies and a wide selection of *oúzo*. Open daily, supper only.
To Steno, Agíon Anargíron 29, 400 m (¼ mile) southwest of Old Town walls. A small and genuinely welcoming *ouzerí*. The menu is limited (sausages, chickpea soup, *pitaroúdia* or courgette croquettes, salads with caper sprigs), but superbly executed and eminently reasonable in price.

<h2>Dodecanese</h2>

Kárpathos

L'Angolo-ly Gorgona, south end of quay, Diafáni. A versatile café run by a couple from Genoa, with offerings including real Italian-standard coffees, *soumáda* (almond drink), lovely pies and limoncello liqueur.
Blue Sea, main bay, Paralía Lefkoú; tel: 22450 71074. Reasonable, if basic, fare served up by kindly management in a resort rather given to poor value. Strengths are *magirevtá* and pizzas; also pancake breakfasts.
Dramoundana, Mesohóri. Remarkably reasonably priced for Kárpathos, this features local caper greens, village sausages and marinated fish.
To Ellinikon, one block inland from quay, Pigádia; tel: 22450 23932. A *mezedopolío* that caters all year to a local clientele with hot and cold *orektiká*, meat and good desserts.
Iy Orea Karpathos, southeast end of main quay, Pigádia; tel: 22450 22501. The best all-round taverna, with palatable local bulk wine, *trahanádes* soup and great spinach pie. The locals treat it as an *ouzerí*, so it's okay to order just a few *orektiká* (eg, marinated artichokes, spicy sausages) to accompany a *karafáki*.
Kostas', Kamaráki beach, 1 km (½ mile) north of Finíki. Much-loved *stéki* under two tamarisk trees; excellent value fare includes expertly grilled swordfish and courgette chips. Vegetables come from the adjacent patch. Open all day until about 10pm, depending on the weather and the crowd.
Pine Tree, Ádia, 7 km (4 miles) north of Finíki; tel: 69 77 369 948. Sustaining, reasonable rural taverna with country fare like lentils and *htapodomakaronáda* (octopus in pasta), washed down by sweet Óthos wine. Sea-view terrace under the trees of the name, plus a few rooms to rent.

Hálki

Houvardas, near the north end of Emborió quay. Consistent quality *magirevtá* over the years.
Remezzo (Takis), Emborió waterfront; tel: 22460 45061. Excellent for *magirevtá* and pizzas.

Kastellórizo

Akrothalassi, southwest corner of quay; tel: 22460 49052. The most consistently salubrious fish and meat grills, reliably open at lunch too (unusual here), owing to shade from its arbour.
Little Paris, central waterfront; tel: 22460 49282. The longest-established taverna on the island. Quality can vary, but it's certainly better value than certain nearby fish tavernas which take advantage of a not-too-discriminating yachtie clientele.
Ta Platania, Horáfia district; tel: 22460 49206. This was the canteen for the crew of the film *Mediterraneo*; competent *magirevtá*, dips and usually a daily dessert served on an atmospheric little square.

Sými

Dimitris, south quay near ferry dock, Gialós; tel: 22460 72207. Excellent, family-run, seafood-strong *ouzerí* with exotic items such as *hohlióalo* (sea snails), *foúskes* (rock oysters), *spinóalo* (pinna-shell flesh) and the indigenous miniature shrimps, as well as more usual platters. Lunch and supper.
Georgios, top of Kalí Stráta, Horió; tel: 22460 71984. An island institution, over 30 years old and still very good; nouvelle Greek cuisine in large, non-nouvelle portions, served on the pebbled courtyard. Informal live music some nights.
Haritomeni, south hillside above petrol station, Gialós; tel: 22460 71686. A superb *ouzerí* with a good mix of meat, fish and veggie platters such as pork cheeks, *mydopílafo*, sea-snails, artichokes in egg-lemon sauce and mushroom-stuffed aubergine – plus a superb view. Open most of the year.
Meraklis, rear of bazaar, Gialós; tel: 22460 71003. Reliable, long-running bet for good fish grills, *magirevtá* and *mezédes*. Lunch and supper; seating out on the cobbles.
Mythos, south quay, Gialós; tel: 22460 71488. A supper-only *ouzerí* that is reckoned among the best-value cooking on the island. Ignore the menu and let chef Stavros deliver a Frenchified medley which may well include salad, seafood starters (squid in basil sauce), duck with juniper berries, lamb medallions, and own-made desserts. Open Easter–November.

Tílos

To Armenon (Nikos'), on the shore road, Livádia; tel: 22460 44134. Excellent and salubrious beach-taverna-cum-*ouzerí*, with octopus salad, white bean salad and the like, as well as pricier scaly fish.

Delfini, Ágios Andónios port, Megálo Horió; tel: 22460 44252. This is the place for well-priced, freshly landed fish served under the tamarisks. A good sign is the numerous locals in attendance at weekends.

Joanna's Café, Livádia village centre; tel: 22460 44145. Italian-English couple offer full breakfasts (9am–1pm) and decadent desserts, novelty coffees and excellent pizzas (7pm–1am). Open Mar–Nov.

Kalypso, uphill from the ferry dock; tel: 694 7213278. A French-Vietnamese family resident since 1987 offers something different: creative appetisers, Antillean- or southeast Asian-tinged mains. The Martiniquois shimp acras and Uncle Ho's vermicelli (with oyster mushrooms and pork) are tops.

Omonia (Mihalis'), just above the harbour square; tel: 22460 44287. Sit under the trees strung with fairy lights and enjoy the closest thing to an authentic *ouzerí* on the island by night; filling breakfasts in the morning.

Nísyros

Aphroditi, Pálli fishing port; tel: 22420 31242. The yachts habitually at anchor here have pushed prices predictably upward, but this is still a good bet for *magirevtá*, seafood, homemade desserts and bulk Cretan wine.

Iy Porta, Nikiá. Installed in an imposing structure built in 1926 to house a pharmacy, this café-taverna on one of the Aegean's most picturesque *platíes* does just a handful of simple but salubrious dishes daily – eg salad with local goat-cheese, own-made *tzatzíki*, *pittiés* – at attractive prices. Lunch and supper Jun–Sep, sporadically otherwise.

Iy Fabrika, Mandráki; tel: 22420 31552. This was once a *patitíri* (wine press) and *kapílio* (tippling shop), and the staff have returned it to something like its original function: an evening-only, musical *ouzerí* with a few local specialties and plenty for vegetarians.

Panorama, near Hotel Porphyris, Mandráki; tel: 22420 31485. Sea views, despite the inland setting, and good-quality fare (especially suckling pig and fish of the day), though portions could be larger. Tends to keep rather short hours by Greek standards.

Taverna Irini, Platía Ilikioméni, Mandráki; tel: 22420 31365. The place for more complicated *magirevtá* and vegetable dishes that the more touristy spots on the water can't be bothered with; also fish in season.

Lukewarm Food

Many Greek specialities are cooked in the morning and left to stand, so food can be lukewarm (occasionally downright cold), but the Greeks believe this is better for the digestion and steeping of the flavours. For some vegetarian dishes, they are right; for dishes containing meat, this is a downright dodgy practice.

Kós

Ambavris, Ambávris hamlet, 800 metres (½ mile) south of Kós Town; tel: 22420 25696. Ignore the perfunctory English-language menu in favour of the constantly changing *mezédes pikilía* or house medley – six platters for about €22 can encompass such delights as *pihtí* (brawn), stuffed squash blossoms, *fáva* dip, little fish. Courtyard seating. Open for supper Apr–Oct .

Ambeli, 1 km (⁄2 mile) east of Tingáki resort; tel: 22420 69682. Best policy here is to avoid mains and order a variety of excellent starters such as *pinigoúri* (cracked wheat), *bekrí mezé* (pork chunks in spicy pepper sauce), *hórta*, sausages and *giaprákia* (the local variant of *dolmádes*). Plates are fair priced and deceptively large, so don't over-order. Pleasant seating indoors and out in the vineyard; open daily lunch/dinner Easter–Oct, winter Fri & Sat eve, Sun lunch.

Ekatse iy Varka, Platía Diagóra, Kós Town; tel: 22420 23605. An amazing find in a generally touristy area: a reasonable fish taverna, with remarkably fresh, unusual seasonal species like *zargánes* (garfish) and *filipákia* (particular to Kós), washed down by good bulk wine. Outdoor seating with views past the minaret to the ridge beyond Ambávris.

Iy Palea Pigi, Pylí village; tel: 22420 41510. Inexpensive, basic (*loukánika*, fried vegetables, marinated sardines, *bakaliáros* with mashed potatoes) but nourishing fare at this taverna hidden away beside the giant cistern fountain with lion-headed spouts. Open lunch and supper, may close Dec–Mar.

Makis, one lane in from front, Mastihári; tel: 22420 51592. Currently the best – and best-priced – fish on the island outside of Kós Town, and an excellent spot to wait for the ro-ro ferry to Kálymnos. No *magirevtá*, a few salads and dips, and oblique sea views at best mean relatively few tourists.

Olympiada, Ziá village; tel: 22420 69121. Perhaps the only one of a dozen *tavérnes* here without a sunset

view, so the food – lots of stews with *pinigoúri* (bulgur wheat) on the side – has to be good. Open most of the year.

Platáni village, central junction. Ethnic Turkish management at several clustered establishments dish out tasty Anatolian-style *mezédes* and kebabs; best go in a group so that you can pass the little platters around. The most popular, if the most touristy, is **Arap** (tel: 22420 28442); if you can't get in, head across the way to **Asklipios** or **Serif** (tel: 22420 23784), which fills with locals later in the evening. Between November and April these close, leaving **Gin's Place** a few steps further inland (tel: 22420 25166) – where the food is often even better – as the sole option. At any season, finish off with an Anatolian ice cream, best on the island, at **Zaharoplastio Iy Paradosi** opposite the three summer restaurants.

Pote tin Kyriaki, Pissándrou 9, Kós Town; tel: 22420 27872. The island's only genuine *ouzerí*, with fair prices and patio seating in summer, indoors in the converted old house otherwise. Supper only, closed Sunday.

Psaropoula, Avérof 17, Kós Town; tel: 22420 21909. The most genuine and reasonable of three fish tavernas grouped here, with good *orektiká* preceding fair-priced seafood; sidewalk terrace, but also indoor area and thus open all year.

Astypálea

Australia, just inland from the head of the bay, Skála; tel: 22430 61275. Kyria Maria presides over the oldest and most wholesome taverna here, with fresh seafood, island wine and masterfully prepared own-grown vegetables. Open most of the year.

Barbarosa, Hóra, next to town hall; tel: 22430 61577. Greek and "continental" standards, with careful cooking and ingredients selection justifying somewhat bumped-up prices. Open most of the year for supper, and lunch Jul–Aug.

Ovelix, Maltezána (Análipsi), inland road; tel: 22430 61260. Grilled lobster specialists, but also scaly fish, vegetables and soft island cheese. Open most of the year for supper, Jul–Aug also for lunch.

To Yerani, in the streambed just behind Livádia beach; tel: 22430 61484. The most consistently good, and consistently open (May– Oct) taverna here, renowned for its excellent *magirevtá*.

Kálymnos

Iy Drossia (Andonis), fishing anchorage, Melitshás; tel: 22430 48745. Tops for oysters, lobster and

shrimp as well as scaly fish at affordable prices. Open all year.
Pandelis, cul-de-sac behind the waterfront, Póthia; tel: 22430 51508. Daily, fresh-gathered shellfish like miniature oysters, *foúskes* and *kalógnomes*, plus scaly fish at reasonable prices. Also a fair selection of grills for non-fish-eaters.
Pizza Porto Kalymnos (tel: 22430 23761) and **Pizza Imia** (tel: 22430 50809), near each other at mid-quay, Póthia, both offer excellent wood-fired pizzas.

Léros

Iy Thea Artemis, Blefoúti beach, beyond airport; tel: 22470 24253. Better-than-average beach taverna in the middle of nowhere; the usual *marídes* or *kalamária* with chips.
Mezedopolio Dimitris, Spiliá district, on road between Pandélli and Vromólithos; tel: 22470 25626. The best food on the island, hands down, and the best view of Vromólithos. Stars include chunky, herby Lerian sausages, potato salad, *hanoúm bórek* (stuffed with cheese and *pastourmás* or cured meat). Moderate prices and large portions. Open most of the year.
Mezedopolio tou Kapaniri, Agía Marína seafront; tel: 22470 22750. Standards here aren't quite up to Dimitris or Neromylos, and portions on the small side, but still a contender. Best at night, with plenty for vegetarians – bean soup, Cypriot *halloúmi* cheese, *hórta* – as well as pizzas and seafood; open all year.
Osteria Da Giusi e Marcello, Álynda; tel: 22470 24888. Genuine Italian-run spot for pizzas, pasta dishes, a few antipasti and salads, plus top-notch desserts like sorbet and tiramisu, washed down by good Italian bulk or bottled wine. Supper only; open late Mar–early Jan.
Ouzeri Neromylos, out by the sea-marooned windmill, Agía Marína; tel: 22470 24894. The most romantic setting on the island, whether for lunch or supper. Specialties include *garidopílafo* (shrimp-rice), baked four-cheese casserole and *kolokythokeftédes* (courgette patties). Open mid-Mar–late Oct; reservations mandatory Jul-Aug.
Psaropoula (Apostolis), Pandélli beach; tel: 22470 25200. A good balance of fresh seafood and *magirevtá*, especially popular with locals at weekends. Open and enclosed sea-view terraces, so open most of the year.

Lipsí

O Giannis, mid-quay; tel: 22470 41395. Excellent all-rounder, with meat and seafood grills but plenty of salads and *laderá* dishes for vegetarians too. The only taverna open for lunch as well as supper all season long. Early May–early Oct
La Nave da Massimo/The Boat, village centre. Italo-Greek run place that's tops for meat and seafood grills, a few pasta dishes and oddities such as *glystrída* (purslane) salad. Open May–Sep.

Pátmos

Benetos, Sápsila cove, 2 km (1 mile) southeast of Skála; tel: 22470 33089. Since 1998, this eatery has earned a reputation as one of the best spots on the island for Mediterranean/Pacific Rim fusion cuisine, with a stress on seafood. Count on €30 for drink and three courses, which may include roast vegetable terrine with balasamic and raisins, baked fish fillet with risotto and Hubbard squash, and lemon sorbet. Open Jun–early Oct, supper only except Mon; reservations needed in summer.
Hiliomodi, just off the Hóra road, Skála; tel: 22470 34080. Vegetarian *mezédes* and seafood delicacies such as limpets (served live), grilled octopus and salted anchovies served at this *ouzerí* with summertime tables on a quiet pedestrian lane. Supper only; open all year.
Ktima Petra, Pétra beach, south of Gríkou; tel: 22470 33207. Hands down the best beach taverna on an island blessed with such. Chunky *melitzanosaláta*, lush rocket salad, and pork *giovétsi* are typical of lunchtime offerings, with excellent retsina from Thebes; at sunset the grill is lit, and still later the place becomes a full-on bar, with a long list of mixed drinks. Open Easter–Oct.
To Kyma, Áspri cove, opposite Skála; tel: 22470 31192. Fish specialists in perhaps the most romantic setting on the island: a little waterside platform, with vies of the floodlit Hóra fortifications across the bay. Supper only; Jun–early Sep.
Leonidas, Lámbi beach, north end of

Olive Oil

The Greeks are more generous with oil in food, especially olive oil, than most northern European palates are used to. Although you can ask for no oil on a salad, for instance (*hóris ládi*), most waiters will think this an odd request as Greeks generally regard oil as good for the digestion. A whole category of slow-cooked, casserole-tray vegetable stews are bluntly referred to as *laderá* or oil-cooked dishes.

island; tel: 22470 31490. Yet another reliable beach taverna; the food's fairly simple, emphasising grilled meat and fish. Open lunch and supper, Easter–Oct.
Livadi Geranou, above eponymous beach; tel: 697 24 97 426. Doesn't look like much, but this taverna has a cult following for the sake of its coarse-cut *hórta*, *keftédes* and seafood dishes – plus views over the entire island.
To Marathi, southeast end of Maráthi beach; tel: 22470 31580. The more welcoming of two establishments here, with simple fish and free-range goat served up by piratically garbed Mihalis Kavouras, at attractive prices and to the accompaniment of Greek music. Open all day according to Mihalis' whim.
Vengera, opposite marina, Skála; tel: 22470 32988. Opened in 2002, this has quickly established itself as a worthy rival to Benetos, with top-drawer generic French/ Mediterranean cooking and polished service. €35 and up per head. Supper only, May–early Sep. Must reserve in high season.

Agathonísi

O Glaros, Ágios Geórgios, mid-bay; tel: 22470 29062. The most authentic taverna here, the one the locals favour; mostly grills and a few house specialties.

Northeastern Aegean

Samothráki

Fengari Restaurant, Loutrá Thermá; tel: 25510 98321. Using an outside wood oven to cook most of the dishes, the Fengari (named after the island's mountain) serves a range of traditional island dishes as well as meat and fish grills. Very pleasant ambience and very good value for money.
I Klimataria, Kamariótissa; tel: 25510 41535. On the waterfront some 100 m north of the ferry quay, this unassuming taverna puts out a range of good *magirevtá* (ready-cooked) dishes and grills to order. Twice a week the chef makes *gianniótiko* – a rich dish of pork, egg, potatoes, onions and garlic. Worth sampling.

Thásos

O Glaros, south end of the beach, Alykí hamlet; tel: 25930 53047/ 31547. Oldest, least expensive and most authentic of several tavernas here; usually has a modest breed of local fresh fish. Open late May–Sep.
O Platanos, under the central tree, Sotíros village; tel: 25930 71234. Summer-only taverna run by a

sympathetic young couple from neary Rahóni village. Elaborate *magirevtá* when trade justifies it, otherwise simple grills and powerful homemade *tsípouro* if you ask.

Iy Pigi, central platía, Liménas; tel: 25930 22941. Old standby dishing out dependable *magirevtá* next to the spring of the name; best at supper.

Symi, east waterfront, Liménas; tel: 25930 22517. Despite the touristy cadre, this makes a decent fist of fish and *mezédes*. Seating, weather permitting, under trees on a raised terrace. Open all year.

Límnos

To Korali, Kótsinas. About the best place on the island for fresh, affordable fish.

Ostria, town end of Toúrkikos Gialós beach, Mýrina; tel: 22540 25245. Grills, fish and *mezédes* from noon to midnight, at rather less than the prices charged by tavernas around the fishing harbour.

Platanos, Mýrina bazaar; tel: 22540 22070. Traditional, long-established purveyor of *magirevtá* under two plane trees; best at lunch on workdays.

O Sozos, main square, Platý; tel: 22540 25085. The best (and only) *tsipourádiko*-grill here, with steamed mussels, chops, *orektiká*. Fight for a table

Lésvos

Anemoessa, Skála Sykaminiás, closest to the harbour chapel; tel: 22530 55360. Tops for fresh fish, and good *mezédes* like stuffed squash blossoms. Open all year (weekends only Nov–Apr).

Balouhanas, Géra Gulf seafront, Pérama; tel: 22510 51948. Seafood *ouzerí* with wood-kiosk seating overhanging the water; interesting *mezédes* and own-made desserts too. Open all year.

Captain's Table, fishing harbour, Mólyvos; tel: 22530 71241 . As the name suggests, a strong line in seafood but also meat and vegetable specialties such as their "Ukrainian" aubergine dip, as well as excellent own-label wine (both white and red). Open May–late Oct.

Ermis, Kornárou 2, corner Ermoú, Mytilíni Town; tel: 22510 26232. The best and most atmospheric *ouzerí* of a cluster in Páno Skáló district, with two centuries of claimed operation and indoor/ outdoor seating. Special strengths: sardines, sausages, Smyrna-style meatballs.

Iy Eftalou, by Eftaloú thermal baths, 4 km (2 /2 miles)from Mólyvos; tel: 22530 71049. Well-executed, reasonably priced grills (fish on par with meat), and salads. Seating under

the trees or inside by the fireplace according to season. Open all year except Nov–mid-Dec.

To Petri, Petrí village, in the hills above Pétra/Mólyvos; tel: 22530 41239. Salubrious *magirevtá*, a few grills and unbeatable terrace seating. Open May–mid-Oct.

Taverna tou Panaï, Ágios Isídoros, north edge of village; tel: 22520 31920. Plainly presented but tasty food: vegetarian *mezédes*, grills, cheese and so on. Mostly Greek clientele; open all year.

Una Faccia Una Razza, Sígri; tel: 22530 54565. Italian-run and ultra-hygienic, with lovely garlic-y vegetable appetisers, pizza, pasta, carefully grilled fish or meat and an Italian wine list – the bulk wine is fine. Open Apr–mid-Oct.

Women's Agricultural Tourism Co-op, central platía, Pétra; tel: 22530 41238. Upstairs restaurant with lots of simple grills – including seafood – *mezédes* and rather fewer *magirevtá*. Indoor and (weather permitting) outdoor terrace seating. Open May–Oct.

Híos

Fakiris Taverna, inland between Thymianá and Neohóri. Home-marinated aubergine and artichokes, goat baked in tomato sauce and excellent wood-fired pizzas along with well-executed seafood and pork-based *bekrí mezé* in big portions.

O Hotzas, Georgíou Kondýli 3, Híos Town; tel: 22710 42787. Oldest and arguably best taverna in the city. Fare varies seasonally, but expect a mix of vegetarian dishes (*mavromátika*, cauliflower, stuffed red peppers) and sausages, baby fish and *mydopílafo* (rice and mussels) with own-brand *oúzo* or retsina. Open all year, supper only (not Sun).

Inomayerio Iakovos, Agíou Georgíou Frouríou 20, Kástro, Híos Town; tel: 22710 23858. Well-executed fishy dishes, grilled titbits, cheese-based recipes and vegetables; local white wine or *oúzo*. Atmospheric garden seating in a vine-cloaked ruin opposite, or inside during winter. All year, supper only; closed Sun.

Iy Petrini Platia, Kipouriés village A superb *psistariá* set in a fountain-nourished oasis, well placed for a meal stop while touring. It's open daily June to mid-September, but weekends only off-season.

Makellos, Pityós tel: 22720 23364. on the west edge of the village, this is a shrine of local creative cuisine; daily Jun–Sep, Fri–Sun eve Oct–May.

Mylarakia, Tambákika district, by three restored windmills; tel: 22710 41412. Every brand of Hiot *oúzo*

accompanies a wide selection of seafood served at waterfront tables. Supper all year; lunch when they feel like it.

Tavernaki tou Tassou, Stávrou Livanoú 8, Bella Vista district, Híos Town. Superb all-rounder with creative salads, better-than-average bean dishes, *dolmádes*, snails and a strong line in seafood; a little bit pricier than usual but worth it. Open lunch and supper most of the year, seaview garden seating in summer.

Yiamos, Karfás beach; tel: 22710 31202. Classic, 1970s-vintage beachfront taverna under new management. The fare – *magirevtá*, fried seafood, dips – is decent, the outdoor terrace seating even more so. Open most of the year.

Sámos

Aeolos, west end of quay, Ágios Konstandínos. Best-value fish and grills here, plus a few oven dishes of the day; unbeatable seating by the pebble shore.

Artemis, Kefalopoúlou 4, near the ferry dock, Vathý; tel: 22730 23639. Good all-rounder, with curiosities like *foúskes* for *mezédes*, good *hórta* and *fáva*, plus the usual meat grills; best avoid the *magirevtá*, at supper time anyway.

Iy Psarades, Ágios Nikólaos Kondakeïkon; tel: 22730 32489. Long reckoned the best fish taverna on the island, at surprisingly reasonable prices, plus the usual *orektiká*. In season you have to book. Open Easter–Oct.

Iy Psili Ammos, Psilí Ámmos; tel: 22730 28301. The one on the far right as you face the water; gives Kalypso (above) a good run for its money, though fare's restricted to seafood, meat grills and salad. Limited table space, so booking advised for large parties.

Kalypso, Mykáli beach; tel: 22730 25198. Arguably the best beachfront taverna in the east of the island, with a good balance of seafood, salads and *magirevtá*. Open all day May–mid-Oct.

To Kyma, east end of quay, Ágios Konstandínos. Good fried *mezédes*, bulk wine and various *magirevtá* make this a winner. Apr–Oct.

To Kyma, harbour road, Karlóvassi; tel: 22730 34017. Long-running *ouzerí*, the island's most genuine, where an Ethiopian proprietress gives a welcome spicy flair to traditional dishes. Open Apr–Oct.

Lekatis, Órmos Marathokámbou, east end of front; tel: 22730 37343. Unassuming little place, but it's where the fishermen tie up, unload and congregate, so the seafood's

excellent, and reasonable. Open all year.
To Ostrako, Themistoklí Sofoúli 141, seafront, Vathý; tel: 22730 27070. As the name says (Greek for "shell"), the place for shellfish as well as scaly fish, plus a long line of *mezédes*. Open all year; garden seating in summer.

Ikaría

Delfini, Armenistís; tel: 22750 71254. Across the way from Paskhalia; more traditional, less polished, even more popular than its neighbour for the sake of the waves lapping the terrace – and the sustaining cooking.
Leonidas, Fáros. Well-loved, quick-serving fish taverna at this beach community 10 km (6 miles) northeast of Ágios Kírykos. Grilled or fried seafood washed down by good bulk wine; many locals make the trip out from the port town.
Paskhalia, Armenistís; tel: 22750 71226. Ground-floor diner of a small pension that does good breakfasts (for all comers) plus reasonable fish with good bulk wine later in the day. May–Oct.

Foúrni

Rementzo (Nikos'), tel: 22750 51253. Best and longest-lived of several full-service waterfront tavernas; here you'll almost certainly find *astakós* (Aegean lobster), except during Aug–Dec closed season, and the succulent *skathári* or black bream.

Sporades and Evia

Skiáthos

Agnantio, 1 km (½ mile) from Skiáthos Town; tel: 24270 22016. It's worth the walk out of town to reach this place. The view over Skiáthos is great and you dine on genuine Greek cooking on a wooden deck. The menu is a mixture of ready-made and to-order but it's guaranteed to be top class.
1901 En Skiatho, Skiáthos Town; tel: 24270 21828. Right in the middle of town. Apart from the good live music, the food is excellent, mixing Greek and Mediterranean elements to produce original dishes. There's an extensive wine list, but the draft wine is good, too.
Sklithri, Kalamáki; tel: 24270 21494. Blink and you'll miss this tiny eatery almost hidden by the roadside a few kilometres from Skiáthos town. Most tourists do, so you'll find mainly locals dining on sardines or other fish dishes. It's cheap unassuming and genuine. Best of all, it's right in the beach.

Skópelos

O Kipos tou Kalou, Skópelos Town; tel: 24240 22349. Signposts point down a narrow side street at the southern end of town to this quiet, flower-garlanded haven where classic Greek and Mediterranean cuisine reigns supreme. Sample charcoal grills as well as ready-made dishes. Stuffed pork in cheese sauce with couscous is highly recommended.
Taverna Finikas, Skópelos Town; tel: 24240 23247. *Finikas* means palm tree – and there is a big one right in the middle of this popular restaurant, well signposted in the back streets of Skópelos. There's a range of rather unusual menu items featuring various fruits combined with classic Greek meats.
Taverna Perivoli, Skópelos Town; tel: 24240 23758. Dine in an enormous shady garden (*perivóli*) in an atmosphere of cool and calm. The menu is a mixture of classic Greek-Mediterranean with SE Asian elements, such as the chicken in a wine and soya sauce.

Alónisos

Astrofengia, Hóra (Old Alónisos); tel: 24240 65182. High up in the former capital are a clutch of good quality tavernas. This one enjoys a superb view over the south of the island from its streetside tables. The cuisine combines classic Greek with Middle East elements such as couscous, humus and tahini.
To Kamaki, Patitíri; tel: 24240 65245. Down in the port and along the east main street you'll find this busy *ouzerí* with its wide range of carefully prepared *mezédes*. Order several to your taste, a small carafe of *oúzo* and tuck in. Great place for people-watching.
Paraport, Hóra (Old Alónisos); tel: 24240 65608. On the far south side of Hóra and also enjoying a fine view, the Paraport is in an old house and one of the island's better tavernas. Features fresh and a good range of ready-made dishes, plus some enticing *mezédes* such as the aubergine salad or pepper cheese with capers.

Skýros

Anatolikos Anemos, Platía Brooke, Hóra; tel: 22220 92822. A small café-style dining venue in a two-storey building of wood and stone at the far north end of Hóra. The food is Mediterranean with a few inventive variations. There is good wine list from small producers not commonly seen elsewhere.
O Antonis, Atsítsa; tel: 22220 92990. This is about as unassuming as you

can get: a few rickety tables under a shaded patio overlooking a crumbling boat quay – but the food is far from rickety. Simple and unadorned, fish predominates and there are always a few ready-made dishes on offer.
O Pappous ki Ego, Hóra; tel: 22220 93200. It's the eclectic music that first grabs your attention here: good quality *éntehno* (artistic) Greek sounds. The food follows suit – a quality mixture of *mezédes* and mains served up in a rather small dining area. Get there early for an outside table.

Évia

Astron, Katoúnia, Límni; tel: 22270 31487. It's a 3-km (2-mile) drive south out to this seaside tavern, open all year round, with an open fireplace for the winter chills, and a large leaf-shaded veranda for summer. Food is classic Greek with no surprises but it is consistently good. The meat and fish is all locally raised and caught.
Cavo d'Oro, Kárystos; tel: 22240 22326. There's nothing flash about this old-style *magirío* (diner or cook-house) in a narrow street close to the main square in Kárystos. Just look at the dishes on display, point and dine on home-cooked food. Cheap and simple, just as it used to be.
Mesogios, Loutrá Edipsoú; tel: 22260 60100. Redolent of old-world elegance – down to the carefully manicured table settings – this is a classy, rather expensive, but undeniably quality dining venue. The menu is Greek haute cuisine with a light touch.

Corfu

Kérkyra Town

La Famiglia, Maniarízi & Arlióti 30, Campiello district; tel: 26610 30270. Greek/Italian-run bistro specialising in salads, pasta, lasagne and Italian puddings. Excellent value and efficient service; limited seating both indoors and out, so reservations always mandatory. Open evenings only, Mon–Sat.
Hryssomallis (Babis), Nikifórou Theotókou 6, Kérkyra; tel: 26610 30342. The sign says it's a *zythopsitopolío* ("beer-hall-grill"), but it's also about the last traditional oven-food place in the old town: stews, *hórta*, *moussakás*, lamb offal and so forth. A typical bill won't be more than €10–13 each. The Durrells ate here during their 1930s stay, but the restaurant has been around a lot longer.
Mouragia, Arseníou 15, north quay, Kérkyra Town; tel: 26610 33815. A good mix of seafood (with fresh and

frozen items clearly indicated) and Corfiot *magirevtá* such as *sofríto* and *pastitsáda*. Inexpensive for any island, let alone Corfu, and great sea views in the bargain. Open daily noon–12.30am.

Tenedos, alley off Solomóu, Spiliá district; tel: 26610 36277. French-Corfiot cooking with ample seafood choice and Lefkímmi bulk wine. Locals go especially for the *kandádes* in the evening. Open lunch and dinner.

Theotoki Brothers (Kerkyraïki Paradosiaki Taverna), Alkiviádi Dári 69, Garítsa Bay. By far the best of half-a-dozen tavernas with tables out in the eucalyptus park here. A full range of *magirevtá* dishes and grills, plus some seafood, at very reasonable prices. Service can be leisurely, even by Corfu standards. Open lunch and dinner.

Venetian Well, Platía Kremastí, northwest of Cathedral, Kérkyra Town; tel: 26610 44711. Tucked away through an arch, with tables around the well, is some of the town's most innovative and expensive cooking, generic Aegean with interesting twists. Recipes change seasonally, depending on the proprietor's winter travels and inspiration, but past dishes have included duck in plum sauce or *dolmádes* with wild rice. Excellent (and pricey) wine list. Supper only Mon–Sat, Mar–Oct.

Around the Island

Agni, Agní cove, between Nissáki and Kassiópi; tel: 26630 91142. The romance of the proprietors – she's Greek, he's English – has been the basis of newspaper features and a BBC documentary, but, beyond the media hype, the food is very good, and reflects the meeting of cultures: stuffed sardines, garlic prawns, mussels in wine and herbs. Open for lunch and dinner Apr–Oct.

Akrogiali, Ágios Geórgios Págon; tel: 697 7334278. A bumpy track leads 1,500 metres (1 mile) south from the beach to this little eyrie (marked by a windmill) run by a local lad and his Dutch partner. The fish is excellent, as are the *mezédes*. Open daily Jun–Oct.

Alonaki Bay, Paralía Alonáki, near Korissíon lagoon; tel: 26610 75872. Good country recipes, strong on vegetables and seafood – beans, greens, scorpion-fish soup – at shady tables on a terrace overlooking the sea.

Boukari Beach, Boúkari; tel: 26620 51791. The less commercial of two seafood tavernas at this seashore hamlet, in an idyllic setting, with patently fresh fare at some of the most attractive prices on the island.

Open all day Apr–Oct.

Cavo Barbaro (Fotis), Avláki; tel: 26630 81905. An unusually good beach taverna, with welcoming service. A few *magirevtá* dishes at lunch, more grills after dark, plus homemade *glyká koutalioú* (candied fruit). Seating on the lawn, and plenty of parking. The only thing "barbarous" here can be the wind, as there's no shelter.

Etrusco, just outside Káto Korakiána village, on the Dassiá road; tel: 26610 93342. Top-calibre nouvelle Italian cooking purveyed by father, son and spouses, served at a carefully restored country manor. Specialties like *timpano parpadellas* (pasta with duck and truffles) and a 200-label wine list don't come cheap – budget a minimum €30 each before drink – but this has been ranked one of the best five Greek tavernas outside of Athens. Early booking essential. Open Apr–Oct, supper only.

Foros, Paleá Períthia; tel: 26630 98373. The less commercial and friendlier of two tavernas in this rather melancholy village, operating in a restored house. Fare is basic – grills, salads, local cheese, *píttes*, a dish of the day – but so are the prices. Open daily May–Oct.

Ftelia (Elm Tree), Strinýlas village; tel: 26630 71454. An almost mandatory stop on the way to or from the summit of Mt Pandokrátor, this taverna specialises in game (venison, wild boar), unusual starters like snails or artichoke pie, and apple pie with proper Dutch coffee. Open lunch and dinner May–Oct, random days in winter.

Kouloura, Kouloúra cove; tel: 26630 91253. Fairly priced seafood or fish, large selection of *mezédes* and salads, plus unusually elaborate pies at this taverna overlooking one of the most photogenic anchorages on Corfu. Open daily all day Apr–Oct;

Corfu Takeaways

Invisible Kitchen, based in Aharávi, is not a restaurant per se, but a catering service: young British chefs Ben and Claudia will deliver ready meals for your villa party or *kaïki* day out. Nouvelle Italian, French, Thai, Indian, Chinese or Greek menus (€20 each, minimum 4 diners) or boat picnics at about €10 each – and the food is to die for. Operates late Apr–mid-Oct.
Tel: 26630 64864, 697 6652933;
www.theinvisiblekitchen.co.uk

reservations needed at peak season.

Little Italy, Kassiópi, opposite Grivas supermarket; tel: 26630 81749. Jolly *trattoria* in an old stone house run by Italian brothers; fare includes salmon in pastry parcels, pizza, pastas smothered in made-from-scratch sauces. Reservations suggested.

Maria, riverbank, Lefkímmi. Ideal for an inexpensive lunch of *magirevtá* (baked pork chops, baked fish, green beans, good bulk wine); seating under the trees overlooking the river. Maria is a colourful granny who will give you a crash course in elaborate Greek swearing.

Mitsos, Nissáki; tel: 26630 91240. On the little rock-outcrop "islet" of the name, this ordinary-looking beachside taverna stands out for the cheerful service from the two partners, and high turnover and thus freshness of the inexpensive fare, which includes fried local fish and well-executed *sofríto*.

7th Heaven Bar/Panorama Restaurant, Longás Beach cliff, Perouládes; tel: 26630 95035. The place to watch Corfu's most majestic sunset; by half an hour before the event, it's standing-room only and ambient music from staff doubling as DJs. The restaurant part, if you elect to linger after dark, is better than you'd think. Open all day May–Oct.

Toula, Agní cove; tel: 26630 91350. Worth a special mention for its professional demeanour, nice line in hot *mezédes* and the house special *garídes* (prawns, shrimp) grilled with spicy mixed-rice pilaff. Excellent bulk white wine; budget about €23 each; lunch and supper.

The Ionians

Paxí

Alexandros, Platía Edward Kennedy, Lákka; tel: 26620 30045. The most authentic *nisiótiko* cooking and most atmospheric setting in town; own-produced grilled meat and chicken, specialities like *sofríto* and mushroom pie, a few seafood dishes, but avoid the barrel wine.

Diogenis, opposite the Kafenio Spyros, Lákka; tel: 26620 31442. Honest, fresh meat grills purveyed by a welcoming family; recently introduced *magirevtá* recipes are not always as successful.

Lilas, Magaziá; tel: 26620 31102. Inexpensive little meat grill with good bulk wine in an ex-grocery shop at the centre of the island; usually live accordeon or stringed music at weekends.

Vassilis, Longós quay; tel: 26620 31587. Now often known as Kostakis after the son who's taken it over, this has grown from a grilled fish specialist to an all-round taverna with imaginative recipes for *magirevtá*, like stuffed mushrooms and peppers, baked meat dishes and various oven pies.

Levkáda

T'Agnandio, west hillside, Ágios Nikítas; tel: 26450 97383. Tucked away up a lane with views to rival Sapfo's, one of the friendliest, least expensive home-style tavernas on the west coast; stress on *magirevtá* and fresh seafood such as *garídes* from the Amvrákikos gulf. Creditable barrel wine; supper only low season.
Panorama, Atháni; tel: 26450 33291. A classic village grill serving assorted simple starters, local lamb chops, fish and bulk wine from vineyards out on Cape Lefkátas. Inexpensive.
Pantazis, Nikiána; tel: 26450 71211. Appealingly set at the far end of the yacht harbour, this locally patronised taverna does fresh seafood at very reasonable prices – though salad trimmings could sometimes be

fresher. *Magirevtá* in high-season evenings; open all day.
Ta Platania, central platía, Karyá. Seating under the giant plane trees of the name, and fresh wholesome grills, salads and beers at budget prices. Tables for two other eateries share the square.
Regantos, Dimárhou Verrióti 17, Levkáda Town; tel: 26450 22855. Supper-only taverna with a good balance of grills (especially spit-roasted chicken), oven food and fish; inexpensive and colourful.
Sapfo, on the beach, Ágios Nikítas; tel: 26450 97497. Innovative, deftly executed recipes such as seafood lasagne and cheese-and-courgette pie, decent bulk wine; not over-priced for the quality and arguably the best view in the resort.

Itháki

Nikos, inland near the National Bank, Vathý; tel: 26740 33039. A good all-rounder, with grills, a few *magirevtá* dishes daily, and fish; inexpensive bulk wine. Tourists go 8–9pm, then

locals hold forth until closing time.
Kalypso, Kióni; tel: 26740 31066. Specialities here include onion pie and artichoke soufflé with ham and cheese; not too inflated price-wise considering that yachts tie up nearby. Remarkably full Greek beer list.
Kandouni, Vathý quay; tel: 26740 32918. Strong on *magirevtá* such as stuffed squash blossoms and stuffed peppers; if you want well-grilled fish, select it next door from the fishmonger. Good Kefaloniá bulk wine, homemade dessert of the day, does breakfast too.
Rementzo, Fríkes; tel: 26740 31719. This taverna features local recipes like *savóro* (cold fish in raisin and rosemary sauce) and chunky *astakomakaronáda* (lobster on pasta), and supports local producers, such as the suppliers of their bulk wine and sticky sweets. Portions on the small side, so are prices; uniquely here, open all year.
Sirines/Sirens, inland from square, Vathý; tel: 26740 33001. The capital's only genuine (and

The Wines of Greece

While Greek wines have yet to obtain the status of their French counterparts, young oenologists trained abroad are definitely having a go at it, and there is a growing number of micro-wineries on the mainland. Nico Manessis' *The Illustrated Greek Wine Book* (Olive Press Publications, Corfu; www.greekwineguide.gr) is the definitive guide to what's new in the field.

All this wonderful wine, however, costs as much as anywhere else: €6–10 in a bottle shop, easily double that in a taverna. Some of the better mainland labels include:
Boutari Nemea, a reliable, full-bodied mid-range red. There are other, premium versions of Nemea, such as **Ktima Papaïoannou**.
Tsantali Rapsani, a generally reliable red from a tiny viniculture area on the border between Thessaly and Macedonia.
Spyropoulou Orino Mantinea, a wonderful, smokily dry white made from moskhofilero grapes on the plateau near Trípoli, an increasingly popular taverna offering.
Averof Katoí, a smooth red from Métsovo, though quality isn't up to its legendary days of the mid-1990s.
Athanasiadi, premium red and white from central Greece, rather better than oft-cited rival **Hatzimihali**, and as readily available.
Lazaridi, these two rival wineries are run by cousins, in Dráma, in eastern

Macedonia; their Merlots in particular are excellent.
Georgiadi, the subtlest bottled *retsína*, again produced by two rival cousins from Thessaloníki, far superior to the usually preferred **Kourtaki**. **Malamatina** is the classic half-litre bottled mainland strong *retsína*, especially enjoyable mixed with a glass of soda.

Island wines
Many islands produce excellent vintages that they can't or won't export, and which are sold only locally. Although barreled/bulk (*me to kiló, hýma*) wines tend to be rough and ready, they're cheap (€3–8 per litre) and certainly authentic.

In Corfu, **Theotoki** is the local wine (red or white); the speciality of the island is a very sweet liqueur called **Kumquat**, based on the tiny citrus fruit of that name. In Kefaloniá **Robola** is a delicate expensive white; **Gentilini** is reckoned the best label.

The lush green vineyards of Zákynthos produce **Comouto** rosé or the white **Verdea**. The grapes of Andípaxi are much appreciated; ask for wine from the barrel.

CAIR, the Rhodes cooperative originally founded in the 1920s by the Italians, has the ubiquitous white **Ilios** and red **Chevalier du Rhodes**, but the private Émbonas winery Emery is more esteemed for its **Mythiko** and **Villaré** red and white.

Sámos in the northeastern Aegean is one of the few islands to export wine, not only to the mainland but also abroad. The fortified Samos dessert wines **Anthemis** and **Vin de Liqueur** are esteemed world-wide. On Híos, particularly around Mestá, a heavy, sherry-like but very palatable wine is made from raisins. *Oúzo* is made here too – try Tetteris brand.
Lésvos is the undisputed *oúzo* capital of Greece, producing at least 15 varieties. **Varvagiannis** is the most celebrated, and expensive, but some prefer **Arvanitis**. EPOM is the principal cooperative, marketing among others the "Mini" brand, a staple of *ouzerí* across the country.

Like most volcanic islands, Límnos produces excellent whites (especially the oak-aged **Dryiino**), as well as a few good reds and rosés.

Thásos specialises in *tsípouro* – often flavoured with exotic spices or pear extract rather than the anise of *oúzo*. Homemade firewater gets lethally strong; anything over 50 percent alcohol must be barreled, not bottled, lest it explode.

Santoríni, a volcanic island like Límnos, is known for its upscale whites like **Boutari Nyhteri** and **Ktima Argyrou**.

In Crete, **Logado** plonk has been the delight of backpackers for years, but superior labels such as **Economou** (Sitía province) and **Lyrarakis** (Irákli) have made an appearance.

very reasonable) *mezedopolío*, with a stress on *saganáki* (cheese sauce) items, chicken, seafood and own-grown organic vegetables. Normally open Easter–end Sep.

Kefalloniá

Akrogiali, Lixoúri quay, towards south end; tel: 26710 92613. An enduring, budget-priced institution, with largely local clientele. Wholesome and tasty food with a stress on oven-casserole food (including *giouvétsi, kreatópita* and great *hórta*), but also fish and grills in the evening, plus excellent bulk wine.

Blue Sea (Spyros'), Káto Katélios; tel: 26710 81353. Speciality is pricey but clearly fresh and superbly grilled fish from the little anchorage adjacent. Budget about €30 each for a large portion with a share of *mezédes* and their bulk wine.

Ta Delfina, Sámi waterfront. A basic but pleasant waterfront place with daily *magirevtá* such as *briám* (similar to ratatouille), *giouvétsi* and good *hórta*. There is also some fresh fish, usually sardines. The best in a line of rather touristy places.

To Foki, at the head of Fóki Bay. This is a very pleasant taverna, friendly and just opposite the beach. It serves simple but tasty food – *fáva, souvláki* and salads – and lovely *milópita* (apple pie). Much better, and far cheaper, than anything to be found in Fiskárdo.

Ionio Psisteria, Mánganos, just after the turn off to Matsoukáta. A pleasant, unpretentious roadside restaurant about 10 km (6 miles) before Fiskárdo. Very reasonable, the food is honest and tasty, especially the *mousakás*, and the service is friendly. On Saturdays they spit-roast a whole pig.

To Kafenio tis Kabanas, Lithóstroto 52B, Argostóli; tel: 26710 24456. Housed in a reconstructed Venetian tower, with seating in the square opposite, is a pleasant café serving light snacks. As well as the usual coffees, local specialities include *soumáda* (an orgeat drink) and *amygdalópita* (almond pie).

Kyani Akti, A. Trítsi 1, far end of the quay; tel: 26710 26680. A superb, if pricey, *psarotavérna* built out over the sea. The speciality is fresh fish and seafood, often with unusual things to try (like the delicious *dáktylia* – "fingers" – akin to razor clams). All the fish and seafood is sold by weight. There is also a range of *mezédes* and salads, and some tasty house wine.

Maïstrato, far north end of quay, Argostóli; tel: 26710 26563. Set yourself up at this genuine *ouzerí* with a seafood *pikilía* (medley), some of

their abundant hot/cold *mezédes* and *oúzo* by the 200-ml carafe. Pleasant waterside seating beside a pine grove; Apr–Oct only.

Mr Grillo, A. Trítsi 135, Argostóli. A *psistariá*, not far from the port authority building, very popular with locals for Sunday lunch. The grilled meats are tasty and accompanying *mezédes* fine. All reasonably priced.

Nirides, Ásos, the far end of the harbour; tel: 26740 51467. This little *estiatório* in a great spot overlooking the harbour has the usual range of salads and a few grilled and oven dishes, as well as fresh fish by the kilo. It is all well cooked – especially the fried peppers with cheese and *melitzánes imám*.

Paradisenia Akti (Stavros Dendrinos), far east corner of Agía Evimía resort; tel: 26740 61392. Fair-priced savoury dishes such as *hortópita* and local sausage, though seafood portions could be bigger; lovely terrace seating under pines and vines overlooking the sea.

Patsouras, A. Trítsi 32 (north quay), Argostóli; tel: 26710 22779. Popular *magirevtá* specialist just along from the Lixoúri ferry. Good rib-sticking food with especially tasty *bámies* (okra), a few grills, big portions and a velvety red house wine. Open all year and inexpensive.

To Pevko, Andipáta Erísou, by the turn for Dafnoúdi beach; tel: 26740 41360. A serious contender for the best place to eat on the island, with seating outside under a huge pine tree. A mouthwatering selection of *mezédes*, oven-cooked dishes and some grilled meat and fish. Particularly good are the tomato, mint and *féta keftédes*, the *gígandes* (butter beans) and aubergine with garlic.

Romantza, Póros; tel: 26740 72294. This *estiatório* is in a charming position, built into the headland at the end of the town beach. You eat on a first-storey balcony which has views over the sea to Itháki. The focus of the menu is on a large range of fresh fish (priced by weight), but there are also good *mezédes* and salads.

Vasso's, southeast end of quay, Fiskárdo; tel: 06740 41276. *Magirevtá* with a difference: olive tapinade for your bread, dill and other herbs flavouring many dishes, seafood pasta, creative desserts. Reasonable (for Fiskárdo anyway) at about €25 each.

Zákynthos

Agnadi Taverna, beyond Argási, 8 km (5 miles) from Zákynthos Town; tel: 26950 35183. A modern but attactive wooden building on a steep slope overlooking

the sea. It is slightly touristy, but the home cooking is authentic and tasty.

Akrotiri Taverna, Akrotíri, 4 km (2½ miles) north of Zákynthos Town; tel: 26950 45712. A pleasant summer-only taverna with a large garden. Grilled meats are a speciality here, but they also bring round large trays of very tempting *mezédes* from which you pick and choose. The house wine is very acceptable.

Alitzerini, entrance to Kiliométo; tel: 26950 48552. Housed in one of the few surviving 17th-century Venetian village houses, this little *inomagerío* offers hearty, meat-based country cooking and its own wine; *kandádes* some evenings. Evenings only: Fri–Sun Oct–May, daily Jun–Sep. Reservations essential.

Andreas, Paralía Beloúsi, near Drosiá; tel 26950 61604. A no-nonsense fish taverna serving fresh catch at fair prices. During summer there is terrace seating by the sea. To go with the fish there is good bread, wonderful *kolokythákia* (boiled courgettes) and decent wine.

Andreas Zontas, Pórto Limniónas, Ágios Léon. Location can count for a lot. The food here is relatively expensive, standard taverna fare, but it is served on a promontory overlooking an idyllic rocky bay and facing west to the sunset.

Arekia, Dionysíou Romá, Zákynthos Town; tel: 26950 26346. A smoky and unpretentious hole-in-the-wall, fitting perhaps 70 diners cosily on bench seats; open evenings only all year round. The food's decent but incidental to the main event: *kandádes* and *arékia* singing after 10pm.

To Fanari tou Keriou, 1.5 km (1 mile) beyond Kerí village; tel: 26950 43384/697 26 76 302. Watch the moon rise over the Myzíthres sea-stacks below the Kerí cliffs. The food's on the expensive side, but portions are fair size and quality is high – try the daily-made *galaktoboúreko* or vegetable-stuffed *pantsétta*, redolent of nutmeg. Reservations essential.

Kalas, Kabí. By far the best taverna in Kabí, Kalas is set in a pretty garden, shaded by large trees, and serves up all the usual favourites (*fáva, loukánika, horiátiki* and *patátes*), all tasty and freshly cooked. Good bulk wine as well.

Komis, Bastoúni tou Agíou, Zákynthos Town; tel: 26950 26915. A lovely *psarotavérna* tucked into a rather unlikely spot behind the port authority building. The emphasis is on slightly pricey but fresh and inventive fish and seafood dishes, but there is a good list of *mezédes*, good wine and tempting desserts.

Malanos, Agíou Athanasíou 38, Kípi district, Zákynthos Town; tel: 26950 45936. Deservedly popular and inexpensive all-year shrine of *magirevtá*: mince-rich *giouvarlákia* and *fasolákia giahní* are typical offerings. Unusually good bread as well as the expected barrel wine.

Mikrinisi, Kokkínou, 1 km (½ mile) beyond Makrýs Gialós. Standard, but reasonable, *tavérna* food – *horiátiki*, *kalamarákia*, *souvláki* and other such offerings – but the situation is lovely, on the edge of a headland overlooking a tiny harbour.

Roulis, Kypséli Beach, near Drosiá; tel: 26950 61628. This is a friendly place overlooking the sea. Popular with islanders, Roulis gets very fresh fish – one of its main attractions – but also does the usual salads and vegetables well. The house wine is drinkable and the freshness of all the ingredients make it worth the detour from the main coast road.

Theatro Avouri Estiatorio, north of Limodaíka near Tragáki. A peaceful, stone-built open-air theatre complex set in lovely countryside. Local food (including excellent bread) is cooked in a traditional oven, and you can also catch one of the story-telling performances. Open every night from around 7pm.

Theodoritsis, just past Argássi in Vassilikós municipal territory; tel: 26950 48500/694 41 35 560. Where the *beau monde* of Zákynthos goes for its weekend blowout; there is a stress on *magirevtá* but there are also grills and *mezédes*. Moderately pricey with a summer terrace overlooking town, there is also a tasteful interior; open all year.

Crete

Ágios Nikólaos

Du Lac, 28-Oktovríou; tel: 28410 22414. Greek and international food served in picturesque surroundings of Lake Voulisméni. Inflated prices but high quality and popular with the locals.

Pórtes, Anapávseos 3; tel: 28410 28489. Located to the southwest of the town centre, this decent eatery serves up a large selection of tasty *mezédes*.

Stámna, 200 metres/yds from Hotel Mirabello, Havánia; tel: 28410 25817. A well-established restaurant which dishes up superb Italian and Greek food.

Argyroúpoli

Paleós Mylos; tel: 28310 81209. A lovely eatery set in a stunning location. The grilled meats are a particular speciality here.

Arhánes

Díktamos, Pérkolo 3 (side street in town centre). Pleasant surroundings, friendly service, high quality Cretan food at reasonable prices.

Eloúnda

Akrohoriá; tel: 28410 42091. Overlooking the bay; this place serves good charcoal-grilled fish, lobster and seafood.

Myli, Káto Pinés; tel: 28410 41961. In the hills above Eloúnda; traditional, tasty, well-prepared Cretan food, very reasonable prices

Vritómartis; tel: 28410 41325. On its own little island, moored in the centre of the harbour. Excellent fish, caught by the owner.

Haniá

Anaplous, Sífaka 34, Maherádika; tel: 28210 41320. Modishly set in a restored ruin; traditional Cretan specialities including pork baked in a clay pot, and vegetarian dishes; live music sometimes.

Karnagio, Platía Kateháki 8; tel: 28210 53366. Set back from the harbour, and set in an old *hamám* (steam-baths), this is a superb restaurant. Beloved by the locals, it serves up quality Cretan and vegetarian dishes.

Karyatis, Platía Kateháki 12; tel: 28210 55600. Good reputation for its Italian dishes: pasta and pizzas.

Kormoranos, Theotokopoúlou 46; tel: 28210 86910. A *mezedádiko* with barrel wine and *tsikoudiá*. Also snacks and sandwiches during the day. Very good value.

Pigadi tou Tourkou, Sarpáki 1-3, Splántzia; tel: 28210 54547. Run by Jenny, an Englishwoman who specialises in Middle Eastern dishes. Long-established.

Rudi's Bierhaus, Sífaka 26, Maherádika, tel: 28210 50824. An Austrian-owned bar, with over 100 different international beers; as well as the booze there are excellent *mezédes* and great jazz.

Tamam, Zambelíou 49, tel: 28210 96080. Squeezed into another old *hamám*; this is a good place to try out Cretan and also to find tasty vegetarian dishes.

Hersónisos

Georgios Place, Old Hersónisos, tel. 28970 21032. A haven of tasty traditional Cretan cooking, found 3 km (2 miles) up in the hills behind the touristy coastal resort.

Coffee, Chocolate and Tea

Greeks generally drink their coffee with lots of sugar. Essential phrases for those who like it without are *horís záhari*, "without sugar", or *skéto*, "plain". If you like some sugar ask for *métrio*. If you love sugar say nothing and they'll probably dump a few teaspoons into whatever you're drinking. *Me gála* means "with milk".

Whole beans suitable for cafetière or percolator coffee only arrived in Greece in the early 1990s; they are making steady inroads among locals and tourists fed up with the ubiquitous "Nescafé", which has become the generic term for any instant coffee. The formula sold in Greece is far stronger than that made for northern European markets, and the most palatable use for it is in *frappé*, cold instant coffee

whipped up in a shaker, and an entirely Greek innovation despite its patently French name.

Espresso and cappuccino, when available, are exactly as in Italy, though not always so expertly made. You will often be given a little shaker of cinnamon (*kanélla*) to sprinkle on the froth. *Freddoccino*, another resourceful Greek invention, is a cold, double cappuccino for the summer months.

Gallikós ("French"), in other words percolated coffee, is usually quite acceptable. *Fíltros* means the same thing. *Ellenikós kafés* is Greek coffee, boiled and served with the grounds in the cup. If you want a large cup, ask for a *diplós*. *Ellenikó cafés* is also known as *turkikós cafés* but this sometimes provokes

patriotic objections.

Chocolate drinks (*tsokoláta*) can be very good indeed, served cold or hot according to season.

Tea (*tsái*) is the ragged stepsister of the hot-drinks triad; quality bulk tea of Twinings or Whittard's standard is almost impossible to find, so you'll usually have to make do with bagged tea of obscure Ceylonese or Madagascan vintage, never seen elsewhere. it is served either with milk or with lemon (*me lemóni*).

Hamomíli is camomile tea, and *tsái (tou) vounóu* is "mountain tea", made with mountain sage leaves. It's called *alisfakiá* in some of the islands, especially in the Dodecanese and Cyclades. Easy to find in shops, and at more traditional *kafenía*.

Horafákia (Akrotíri Peninsula)
Irini, tel: 28210 39470. A busy taverna with good traditional Greek home-cooking

Hóra Sfakíon (Sfakiá)
Lefka Ori, western end of the harbour front, tel: 28250 91209. This serves up some of the best traditional dishes in the area.

Iráklio
China House, Papandréou 20, just off Akadamías, tel: 2810 333338. Surprisingly good Chinese food, and reasonable prices, make this a good place to take a break from Greek dishes.
Four Rooms (formerly Giovanni), Koráï 12, tel: 2810 289542. Set in a fine neo-classical building, this restaurant specialises in Greek and Italian cuisine.
Ionia, corner Évans and Giánnari, tel: 2810 283213. This venerable eatery has been offering Greek meat, fish and vegetable dishes since 1923.
Ippokambos, Mitsotáki 2; tel: 2810 280240. A superb establishment overlooking the old harbour is famed for its meticulously prepared *mezédes*. It is usually packed with locals so go early. Open lunch and evenings.
Kyriakos, Dimokratías 51, tel. 2810 222464. An old restaurant with traditionally cooked Cretan meat, fish and vegetable dishes. You choose your food in the kitchen.
Loukoulos, Koráï; tel: 2810 224435. An elegant, upmarket and expensive Italian restaurant – but with good food. Vegetarians are also well catered for.
Vyzandio, Vyzándio 3; tel: 2810 244775. A typical modern taverna; it has Greek and international dishes at reasonable prices.

Ístro
El Greco, 10 km (6 miles) southeast of Ágios Nikólaos; tel: 28410 61637. This place has Greek specialities, concentrating on fish and lobster.

Kalýves
Alexis Zorbas; tel: 28250 31363. A family-run taverna; open all year. Large portions, tasty food.

Kastéli-Kissámou (Kíssamos)
Kelari, beachfront promenade; tel: 28220 23883. Stélios takes great pride in his local cuisine.

Káto Zákros
Akrogiáli, by the beach; tel: 28430 26896. Friendly service and a good reputation for fresh fish and meat make this a good place to eat.

Kournás
Kali Kardia, Kournás village, 3 km (2 miles) above the eponymous lake. Excellent local cooking and fresh meat. Aficionados travel a long way for the *galaktoboúreko*, a lemony egg-custard dessert.

Lassíthi Plateau
Andonis, between Psyhró and Pláti; tel: 28440 31581. Set in quiet and attractive surroundings, this taverna offers a good selection of charcoal grilled meats.

Lefkógia
Stelios; tel: 28320 31866. Run by the son of the local butcher; this predictably has fine meat dishes. The tasty home cooking and fresh orange juice come at very reasonable prices.

Margarítes
Vrysi, outskirts of Margarítes village (32 km/20 miles east of Réthymno). Very pleasant, with typical Cretan food.

Palékastro-Angathía-Hióna
Kakavia, on Hióna beach, just beyond Palékastro (20 km/12 miles east of Sitía); tel: 28430 61227. Named after its speciality, fish soup.
Nikolas O Psaras, Angathía village, 1 km (⅔ mile)from Palékastro; tel: 28430 61598. An excellent taverna; fresh fish and Cretan specialties; beautiful view.

Paleohóra
Christos, on the promenade; tel: 28230 41359. A vast array of meat and fish dishes.
Third Eye, between the centre and the beach; tel: 28230 41234. This excellent vegetarian restaurant also offers Asian and Indian dishes.

Pánormos
Sofoklis, Pánormos harbour (22 km/13 miles east of Réthymno); tel: 28340 51297. A good place to try Greek and Cretan cooking.

Plakiás
Lysseos, Plakiás seafront, tel: 28320 31479. Cypriot chef Louká's stylish cooking and the multilingual Litó's exemplary management make this one of Plakias' most popular tavernas; evenings only – arrive early.
Medousa, Plakiás, inland from the pharmacy; tel: 28320 31521. Fine home cooking by Despina, accompanied by shots of Babis' excellent *rakí*.
Panorama, Mýrthios village, overlooking Plakiás Bay. Tasty food, with good vegetarian options, and fantastic views from the balcony.

Polyrrínia
Odysseas, 7 km (4 miles) south of Kastéli-Kissámou; tel: 28220 23331. A taste of the Cretan countryside, all made from very fresh home-grown ingredients.

Réthymno
Apostolis & Zambia, Stamathioudáki 20; tel: 28310 24561. Excellent, extremely reasonably priced fish, seafood and traditional *mezédes*. One of Réthymno's best.
Fanari, Kefaloyiánnidon 16; tel: 28310 54879. A taverna specialising in traditional Greek *mezédes*, but with good main fish and meat dishes, as well as decent wine.
Globe, E. Venizélou 33, opposite the promenade; tel: 28310 25465. A good selection of Cretan food, as well as pasta, pizza and some vegetarian dishes.
Koumbos, Akrotiríou 3, Koumbés; tel: 28310 52209. Located in a western suburb by the sea, this taverna serves up well-cooked and very fresh fish caught by the owner.
Kyria Maria, Moskhovíti 20 (behind the Rimondi Fountain); tel: 28310 29078. Good basic Cretan cooking. Some vegetarian dishes.
Othon, Platía Plátanos; tel: 28310 55500. An *estiatório* offering a wide variety of Greek and European dishes.
Veneto, Epimenídou 4; tel: 28310 56634. An upmarket restaurant serving refined Greek and Mediterranean cuisine.

Rodiá
Exostis, Rodiá village overlooking the Gulf of Iráklio; tel: 2810 841206. Great views, excellent food, fair prices, friendly service from owner, Andréas.

Sitía–Agía Fotiá
Neromylos, 5 km (3 miles) east of Sitía; tel: 28430 25576. An eatery with simple grilled food; it has a wonderful view.

Stalós
Levendis, in Áno Stalós, 6 km (4 miles) west of Haniá; tel: 28210 68155. A village taverna excelling in home-cooked food.

Stavroménos
Alekos, 11 km (7 miles) east of Réthymno centre; tel: 28310 72234. A family-run taverna with typical Cretan food.

Zarós
Oasis, main street. A small, congenial place; *souvláki*, grilled meat and fish, oven bakes and an excellent homemade wine.

Culture

Theatre

Athens has an active theatre life but, as most productions are in Greek, options for English-speakers are limited. Most productions in English take place during festivals (see Cultural Events, below). One recent cultural initiative has provided some excellent productions of both modern and ancient drama in English at one of Greece's most striking open-air theatres – the Stone (Pétra) Theatre in Petropolis in the suburbs of Athens. In summer, plays are produced under the auspices of the Stones and Rocks Festival.

Cinema

Going to the cinema in Greece during the summer is a special pleasure not to be missed. Nearly all the movie theatres that run in the summer (the others shut down unless they have air-conditioning) are open-air, sometimes tucked among apartment buildings (whose tenants watch the film from their balconies); in other areas, they are perched on a seaside promontory under the stars. Tickets, at €6–8, are slightly cheaper than indoor cinemas and soundtracks are in the original language (with Greek subtitles). On smaller islands there may be only one showing, at around 9.30pm, while elsewhere there will be two screenings, at 9 and 11pm.

Music & Dance

A considerable part of the good music and dance performances take place during various festivals which occur across the country (see Cultural Events). Besides these performances, however, there are numerous other events worth attending in both Athens and Thessaloníki.

In Athens, outstanding Greek and foreign musicians often perform at the **Lykavittós Theatre** on Mount Lykavittós, not to mention the larger concerts that take place in the soccer stadiums. Opera can be seen at the Olympia Theatre, performed by the **Lyrikí Skiní** (the National Opera Company), while classical music, from national and international ensembles, is typically performed at the **Mégaron Musikís** near the American Embassy.

In Thessaloníki, summertime venues include the **Théatro Dássos**, on the slopes beyond Kástra, and **Théatro Kípou**, near the archaelogical museum; in winter performances of music, opera, dance and theatre move indoors to the nearly adjacent **State Theatre** and **Royal Theatre**, near the White Tower. More cutting-edge are the events that take place at the multi-functional cultural centre, **Mylos**, a converted flour mill 2 km (1 mile) southeast of the centre, comprising cinemas, concert halls, exhibition space, musical boites and a theatre. This complex has spawned numerous imitators across Greece.

There is an active dance scene in Athens, catering to all tastes, with ballet, folk, modern, jazz and experimental dance troupes.

Greek Music

Thanks to Greece's geographical position and the vast number of cultures that have called it home, there is astonishing regional variety in the various regional folk musics. Crete has one of the more vital traditions, characterised by the *lýra* (three-string spike fiddle) and *laoúto* (mandolin-like lute). In the Dodecanese, these are often *joined by either tsamboúna*, a goatskin bagpipe, *violí* (western *violin*) or *sandoúri*, the hammer dulcimer popularised in the islands by refugees from Asia Minor.

Nisiótika is the general name for island music; that of the Ionians is the most Italian-influenced and western in scale. Mainland music is also unmistakable, characterised by the extensive use of the *klaríno* (clarinet) and, in Epirus, an extraordinary, disappearing tradition of polyphonic singing.

Contemporary sounds include original syntheses or derivations of the traditional and rebetic traditions by such artists such as Thessalonian Dionysis Savvopoulos, who first challenged the supremacy of *bouzoúki* in the mid-1960s with his guitar and orchestral-based compositions, and who spawned a whole generation of disciples and protegés such as the rock-influenced Nikos Papazoglou, Nikos Xydakis and Heimerinoi Kolymvites.

Each region (and sometimes island) of Greece has its own particular folk dances. These ranges from the basic *sta tría* – three steps to one side, followed by a kick (growing gradually faster and faster) – to a frenzied combination of complicated footwork, jumps, slaps and kicks. Troupes, dressed in traditional Greek costume, are most likely to be performing on public holidays (you may also see them on TV). Probably the best-known professional group is Dora Stratou Greek Folk Dances, which holds regular shows from May to September at the Dora Stratou Theatre, Filopáppou Hill (southwest slope), Athens.

Cultural Events

April–October Sound and Light performances in Athens at the Pnyx; on Corfu at the Páleo Froúrio; Rhodes at Grand Master's Palace.
May–September Folk dancing by the Dora Stratou Group in Athens, and Nelly Dimoglou Group in Rhodes Old Town.
June Jazz & Blues Festival, Lykavittós Theatre, Athens
July-September Pátra International Festival: ancient and modern drama, classical music in the castle grounds and the Odeon.
June–September Athens Festival at the Herod Atticus Odeon, among other venues: events include ballet, opera, jazz, and experimental music, plus modern and classical plays performed by world-ranking artists.
July–August Epídavros Festival. Performances of ancient drama in the open-air Epidaurus amphitheatre.
July Music Festival on the island of Itháki (Ithaca).

July–August Réthymnon Renaissance Fair: cultural activities at the Venetian Fort.
July–August the "Epirot Summer" festival at Ioánnina; this may also include ancient drama performances at the nearby and beautiful Dodona amphitheatre.
August Iráklio Festival – concerts, theatre, opera and so on.
August Lefkáda Festival of Music, Folklore and Theatre, with overseas groups.
August Kavala Festival; includes ancient drama performed at Philippi.
August–September Santorini Music Festival, mostly classical events
August–September Sými Festival; a mix of classical and Greek pop performances.
August–October Rhodes Festival October Thessaloniki Dhimitria Festival. Theatre, music, ballet, followed by a self-contained film-festival (November).

Nightlife

Metropolitan nightlife in Greece (essentially Athens, Thessaloníki, Iráklio, Kérkyra, Ródos Town and Pátra) can be roughly divided into four categories: bars; live music clubs with jazz, Greek music (most likely *laïki*, or a watered-down version of *rebétika*) or rock; dance clubs, mostly with a techno, house or ambient soundtrack; and musical *tavérnes* where food prices reflect the live entertainment.

For most Greeks, however, the simple *tavérna* remains the most popular site for a night out spent eating, drinking and, sometimes, singing and dancing. In general, younger Greeks frequent the bars and dance clubs, while the locales for popular Greek music are more patronised by the older generations.

In Athens, the weekly *Athinorama* (in Greek) has an extensive listing of all the various venues and events. If you really want to find out what's going on in the city, ask a Greek friend to help you sort through the listings.

During the summer (late June–early September) many clubs and music halls close down, with musicians of all stripes touring the countryside for the summer festival season, or performing in the islands and coastal resorts.

Casinos

For a more sophisticated – and potentially more expensive – night out, there are casinos in numerous Greek cities and resorts, including Néos Marmarás (Halkidikí), Corfu, Rhodes, Ermoúpoli (Sýros), Loutráki, Párnes and at Thessaloníki airport

Gay Life

Overt gay behaviour is not a feature of Greek society. Homosexuality is legal at the age of 17, and bisexual activity fairly common among younger men, but few couples (male or female) are openly gay. Mýkonos is famous as a gay Mecca, and Skála Eressoú on Lésvos (where the poetess Sappho was born) for lesbians. But elsewhere in Greece single-sex couples are liable to be regarded as odd, although usually as welcome as any other tourists. If discrete, you will attract no attention asking for a double room and will find most people tolerant.

Sport

Participant Sports

Hiking & Mountaineering

Greece has long been a magnet for hikers and mountain climbers, with many surviving footpaths in the mainland mountains and on certain islands, threading through forested areas untouched by the tourist masses. Big-wall climbing is currently growing in popularity, both on the mainland and on islands such as Kálymnos. For information on trails, maps and excursions, consult one of the specialist guides in the booklist, or if you'd prefer an organised excursion, see the list of trekking operators on page 326.

Caving

Greece is honeycombed with caves, though many are locked to protect delicate formations or archaelogical artefacts, and are only opened to qualified spelunkers on an expedition. The following, however, have set hours and facilities for public visits: Koutoúki, Peanía, Attica; Pérama, near Ioánnina; Drogaráti and Melissáni, Kefalloniá; Andíparos, in the Cyclades; the Cave of the Lakes, near Kalávryta in the Peloponnese; Glyfáda and Alepótripa at Pýrgos Dyroú, Máni, Peloponnese; Petrálona, at Kókkines Pétres, Halkidikí; and the cave of Sykiás Olýmbon on Híos.

Scuba diving

Diving in Greece is tightly controlled, with the aim of preserving the nation's heritage of submerged antiquities. However, there is a growing number of authorised sites for diving – consult your nearest EOT/GNTO branch for an updated list. Those of long standing include Thérmes Kallithéas on Rhodes; Vlyhádia Bay on Kálymnos; Ýdra island; Paleokastrítsa Bay, Corfu; most of the coast around Léros; and much of southern Mýkonos.

Although there is a lot to see around the coast, do not expect undersea fauna and flora of Caribbean splendour; free-diving with a mask, fins and snorkel is likely to be just as rewarding in Greek waters.

Religious and Other Festivals

January 1 *Feast of Ágios Vasílios* (St Basil), this is celebrated all over Greece.

January 6 *Epiphany/Agía Theofánia* – Blessing of the waters: all over Greece.

January 8 *Feast of Agía Domníki* (St Domenica), patron saint of midwives: men and women switch roles in the villages around Xánthi, Komotiní, Kilkís and Sérres.

February–March *Carnival season* for three weeks before Lent: all over Greece. Some places with celebrations of special interest are: Náoussa, Kozáni, Zákynthos, Skýros, Thíva, Xánthi, Híos (Mestá, Olýmbi), Messíni, Ámfissa, Lésvos (Agiássos), Galaxídi, Lamía, Agía Ánna (Évvia), Polýgyros, Thymianá, Kefalloniá, Sérres, Kárpathos, Iráklio, Evxinoúpolis (Vólos), Réthymno and (best of all) Pátra.

"Clean" Monday Beginning of fast for Lent. Picnics in the countryside and kite-flying, all over Greece.

March 25 *Feast of Annunciation/ Independence Day*: military parades in all main towns, pilgrimage to Tínos.

Easter weekend *Good Friday, Holy Saturday* and *Easter Sunday* are celebrated throughout Greece.

April 23 *Feast of St George*: celebrated especially in Kaliópi (Límnos), Aráhova, Así Gonía (near Haniá) and Pylí (Kos).

May 1 *Labour Day*: picnics in the countryside all over Greece.

May 21 *Anastenárides*: fire-walking ritual at Agía Eléni (near Sérres) and Langáda (near Thessaloníki).

August 15 *Assumption of the Virgin*: festivals all over Greece. Major pilgrimage to Tínos.

October 28 *Ohi (No) Day*: anniversary of Greek defeat of Italian army in 1940 and Metaxas' supposed one-word response to Italy's ultimatum. Military parades in major cities.

Christmas season All over Greece. In a dwindling number of places, children sing *kálenda* (carols) from door to door for a small gratuity.

December 31 *New Year's Eve*. Many Greeks play cards for money on this occasion, and cut the *vasilópitta* with a lucky coin hidden in it. Special celebration in the town of Híos.

Fishing

There are plenty of places where you can fish in Greece. In the villages of most islands you will find boats and fishing tackle for hire. If you'd like some suggestions contact the **Amateur Anglers and Maritime Sports Club**, Aktí Moutsopoúlou, in Piraeus; tel: 210 451 5731.

Horse Riding

Many small riding schools offer horse riding. For information, contact the **Riding Club of Greece**, Paradissos; tel: , 210 682 6128, or in the capital the **Riding Club of Athens**, tel: 210 661 1088.

Skiing

Most Greek mountains above 2,400 metres (7,800 ft) high have good snow cover for skiing from January to April, with some of the higher mountains (Kaïmaktsalán, Parnassós and Tymfristós) skiable in a good year until May.

These are the best downhill resorts, and most have some sort of cross-country/nordic pistes as well: **Mount Parnassós** (14 lifts, 16 runs); **Mount Vérmio** near Naoússa (8 lifts, 21 runs); **Mount Helmós**, near Kalávryta in the Peloponnese (7 lifts, 12 runs); **Vórras** on Mount Kaïmaktsalán (2 lifts, 7 runs); and **Veloúhi** on Mount Tymfristós near Karpenísi (6 lifts, 10 runs).

There are perhaps a dozen other tiny centres scattered across Greece, but those cited above are the only ones with any sort of reputation. The GNTO sporadically issues a brochure listing all ski centres, but descriptions of facilities and runs tend to be some years obsolete in the wake of improvements.

Tennis

Although there are tennis clubs in most larger cities, few are open to non-members/non-residents. Public courts are equally rare. But most island hotels and inclusive complexes of A or Luxury class have more user-friendly tennis facilities, where you may be able to book court space by the hour.

Waterskiing

Waterskiing (and in some places parasailing as well) is far cheaper in Greece than in most Mediterranean resorts. You will find waterskiing facilities at: Vouliagméni (southeast of Athens); Agrínio (Lake Trihonída); Vólos; Édessa (Lake Vegoritída); Thessaloníki; numerous locations on Corfu; Haniá, Crete; Eloúnda, Crete; Pórto Héli; Rhodes; Párga (Váltos beach); Skiáthos; Ioánnina (Lake Pamvótida); Halkidikí; Halkída.

Numerous companies offer sailing packages and cruises round the coast of Greece that can be booked from home – an internet search will be very productive. One useful website is: www.sailingissues.com

Much of the sailing is in flotillas helmed by the hire companies, but experienced sailors can charter their own yacht. Alternatively, once you're in Greece you can hire boats by the day or week at many marinas. Either way, you can rely on the Port Authorty Harbour Police in your area for up-to-the-minute information on conditions.

The best times to sail are spring and autumn, as winds can be high through the summer months and prices are hiked up to many times that of the cooler seasons.

There are sailing schools, housed in the naval clubs of the following cities: Athens (Paleó Fáliro); Thessaloníki; Corfu; Vólos; Rhodes; Sýros; Kalamáta; Alexandroúpolis. Further information can be obtained from: Hellenic Yachting Federation, 51 Posidonos Avenue Piraeus; tel: 210 940 4825; fax: 210 940 4829.

Windsurfing

Greece is ideal for windsurfing learners, with gentle breezes blowing around many small coves. Boards are available for rent, and lessons are available (at very reasonable rates), at many popular Greek beaches, and at most of the beaches maintained by the GNTO.

The premier resorts dedicated to the sport, where people come from overseas just to windsurf, are: Prasonísi, Rhodes; Paleohóra, Crete; Kokkári, Sámos; Náxos (Ágios Geórgios); and Vasilikí, Lefkáda.

Football (soccer) is the main spectator sport in Greece, with matches played nearly every Wednesday night and Sunday afternoon during the season. The top teams are AEK of Athens, Olympiakós of Piraeus, PAOK of Thessaloníki and Panathanaïkós (also of Athens).

Basketball is the second most popular sport, ever since the national team won the 1987 European Championship, and the national league competition is followed keenly. Local Greek-language newspapers will have details of games.

Language

Modern Greek is the outcome of gradual evolution undergone by the Greek language since the Classical period (5th–4th centuries BC). The language is still relatively close to Ancient Greek: it uses the same alphabet and much of the same vocabulary, though the grammar – other than the retention of the three genders – is considerably streamlined. Many people speak English, some very well, but even just a few words in their native language will always be appreciated.

Pronunciation tips

Most of the sounds of Greek aren't difficult to pronounce for English speakers. There are only five vowel sounds: *a*, *e*, *i*, *o*, *u*, and *y* are consistently pronounced as shown in the table opposite. The letter *s* is usually pronounced "s", but "z" before an *m* or *g*. The sound represented here as *th* is always pronounced as in "thin", not "that"; the first sound in "that" is represented by *d*.

The only difficult sounds are *h*, which is pronounced like the "ch" in Scottish "loch" (we render this as *kh* before "s" so that you don't generate "sh"), and *g* before *e* or *i*, which has no equivalent in English – it's somewhere between the "y" in "yet" and the "g" in "get".

The position of the stress in words is of critical importance, as homonyms abound, and Greeks will often fail to understand you if you don't stress the right syllable (compare *psýllos*, "flea" with *psilós*, "tall"). In this guide, stress is marked by a simple accent mark (´).

Greek word order is flexible, so you may often hear phrases in a different order from the one in which they are given here. Like the French, the Greeks use the plural of the second person when addressing someone politely. We have used the polite (formal) form throughout this language section, except where an expression is specified as "informal".

Communication

Good morning	kaliméra
Good evening	kalispéra
Good night	kaliníhta
Hello/Goodbye (informal:)	giásas giásou
Pleased to meet you	hárika polý
Yes	ne
No	óhi
Thank you	efharistó
You're welcome	parakaló
Please	parakaló
Okay/All right	endáxi
Excuse me (to get attention)	me synhoríte
Excuse me (to ask someone to get out of the way)	syngnómi
How are you? (informal:)	Ti kánete? Ti kánis?
Fine, and you? (informal:)	Kalá, esís? Kalá, esí?
Cheers/Your health! (when drinking)	Giámas!
Could you help me?	Boríte na me voithísete?
Can you show me...	Boríte na mou díxete...
I want...	Thélo...
I don't know	Den xéro
I don't understand	Den katálava
Do you speak English?	Xérete angliká?
Can you please speak more slowly?	Parakaló, miláte sigá-sigá
Please say that again	Parakaló, xanap ésteto
Here	edó
There	ekí
What?	ti?
When?	póte?
Why?	giatí?
Where?	pou?
How?	pos?

Telephone Calls

the telephone	to tiléfono
phone-card	tilekárta
May I use the phone please?	Boró na tilefoníso, parakaló?
Hello (on the phone)	Embrós/Oríste
My name is...	Légome...
Could I speak to...	Boró na milíso me...
Wait a moment	Periménete mía stigmí
I didn't hear	Den ákousa

In the Hotel

Do you have a vacant room?	Éhete domátio?
I've booked a a room	Ého kratísi éna domátio
I'd like...	Tha íthela...
a single/	éna monóklino/
double room	díklino
double bed	dipló kreváti
a room with	éna domátio me
a bath/shower	bánio/dous
One night	éna vrádi
Two nights	dýo vrádia
How much is it?	Póso káni?
It's expensive	Íne akrivó
Do you have a room with a sea-view?	Éhete domátio me théa pros ti thálassa?
Is there a balcony?	Éhi balkóni?
Is the room heated/ air-conditioned?	To domátio éhi thérmansi/ klimatismós?
Is breakfast included?	Mazí me to proinó?
Can I see the room please?	Boró na do to domátio, parakaló?
The room is too hot/cold/small	To domátio íne polý zestó/ krýo/mikró
It's too noisy	Éhi polý thóryvo
Could you show me another room, please?	Boríte na mou díxete állo domátio, parakaló?
I'll take it	Tha to páro
Can I have the bill, please?	Na mou kánete to logariasmó, parakaló?
dining room	trapezaría
key	klidí
towel	petséta
sheet	sedóni
blanket	kouvérta
pillow	maxilári
soap	sapoúni
hot water	zestó neró
toilet paper	hartí toualéttas

At a Bar or Café

bar/café	bar/kafenío (or kafetéria)
patisserie	zaharoplastío
I'd like...	Tha íthela...
a coffee	éna kafé
Greek coffee	ellinikó kafé
filter coffee	gallikó kafé/ kafé fíltro
instant coffee	neskafé (or nes)
cappuccino	kapoutsíno
white (with milk)	me gála
black (without milk)	horís gála
with sugar	me záhari
without sugar	horís záhari
a cup of tea	éna tsáï
tea with lemon	éna tsáï me lemóni
orange/lemon soda	mía portokaláda/ lemonáda
fresh orange juice	éna hymó portokáli
a glass/bottle of water	éna potíri/boukáli neró
with ice	me pagáki
an ouzo/brandy	éna oúzo/koniák
a beer (draught)	mía býra (apó

Emergencies

Help!	Voíthia!
Stop!	Stamatíste!
I've had an accident	Íha éna atíhima
Call a doctor	Fonáhte éna giatró
Call an ambulance	Fonáhte éna asthenofóro
Call the police	Fonáhte tin astinomía
Call the fire brigade	Fonáhte tous pirozvéstes
Where's the telephone?	Pou íne to tiléfono?
Where's the nearest hospital?	Pou íne to pio kondinó nosokomío?
I would like to report a theft	Égine mia klopí

	varélli)
an ice-cream	éna pagotó
a pastry, cake	mía pásta
oriental pastries	baklavá/kataífi

In a Restaurant

Have you got a table for...	Éhete trapézi giá...
There are (four) of us	ímaste (tésseres)
I'm a vegetarian	íme hortofágos
Can we see the menu?	Boroúme na doúme ton katálogo?
We would like to order	Théloume na parangíloume
Have you got wine by the carafe?	Éhete krasí hýma?
a litre/half-litre	éna kiló/ misó kilo
of white/red wine	áspro/kókkino krasí
Would you like anything else?	Thélete típot' állo?
No, thank you	óhi, efharistó
glass	potíri
knife/fork/ spoon	mahéri/piroúni/ koutáli
plate	piáto
napkin	hartopetséta
Where is the toilet?	Pou íne i toualétta?
The bill, please	to logariasmó, parakaló

Food

Mezédes/Orektiká

taramosaláta	fish-roe dip
tzatzíki	yoghurt-garlic-cucumber dip
melitzánes	aubergines
kolokythákia	courgettes
loukánika	sausages
tyropitákia	cheese pies
antsoúgies	anchovies

eliés	olives	*pastítsio*	macaroni with	*maroúli*	lettuce
dolmádes	vine-leaves		minced meat	*pandzária*	beetroot
	stuffed with rice	*gíros me pítta*	doner kebab	*patátes*	potatoes
saganáki	fried cheese	*domátes gemistés*	stuffed tomatoes	*(tiganités/*	(chips/roast)
fáva	puréed fava	*piperiés gemistés*	stuffed peppers	*sto foúrno)*	
	beans			*radíkia*	dandelion leaves
piperiés florínis	red sweet	**Seafood**		*revíthia*	chickpeas
	pickled peppers	*frésko*	fresh	*skórdo*	garlic
		katapsygméno	frozen	*spanáki*	spinach
Meat Dishes		*psári*	fish	*spanakópitta*	spinach pie
kréas	any meat	*óstraka*	shellfish	*vlíta*	boiled greens
arní	lamb	*glóssa*	sole	*gígandes*	stewed butter-
hirinó	pork	*xifías*	swordfish		beans
kotópoulo	chicken	*koliós*	mackerel	*saláta*	salad
moskhári	veal, beef	*barboúnia*	red mullet	*domatosaláta*	tomato salad
psitó	roast or grilled	*sardélles*	sardines	*angourodomáta*	tomato and
sto foúrno	roast	*gávros*	fresh anchovy		cucumber salad
sta kárvouna	grilled	*marídes*	picarel	*horiátiki*	Greek salad
soúvlas	on the spit	*mýdia*	mussels		
souvláki	brochettes on	*strýdia*	oysters	**Fruit**	
	skewers	*kydónia*	cockles	*míla*	apples
kokinistó	stewed in tomato	*kalamarákia*	squid	*veríkoka*	apricots
	sauce	*soupiés*	cuttlefish	*banánes*	bananas
krasáto	stewed in wine	*htapódi*	octopus	*kerásia*	cherries
	sauce	*garídes*	prawns	*sýka*	figs
avgolémono	egg-lemon sauce	*kavourákia*	baby crabs	*stafýlia*	grapes
tiganitó	fried	*astakós*	lobster	*lemónia*	lemons
kapnistó	smoked	**Vegetables**		*pepónia*	melons
brizóla	(pork or veal) chop	*angináres*	artichokes	*portokália*	oranges
païdákia	lamb chops	*arakádes*	peas	*rodákina*	peaches
sykóti	liver	*domátes*	tomatoes	*ahládia*	pears
kymás	mince	*fakés*	brown lentils	*fráoules*	strawberries
biftéki	burger (without	*fasólia/fasoláda*	stewed white	*karpoúzi*	watermelon
	bun)		beans		
keftédes	meat-balls	*fasolákia (fréska)*	green beans,	**Basic Foods**	
soutzoukákia	rissoles baked		in tomato sauce	*psomí*	bread
	in red sauce	*hórta*	various kinds of	*aláti*	salt
giouvarlákia	mince-and-rice		boiled greens	*pipéri*	pepper
	balls in egg-	*karóta*	carrot	*ládi*	(olive) oil
	lemon sauce	*kolokythákia*	courgettes	*xýdi*	vinegar
makarónia	spaghetti	*kounoupídi*	cauliflower	*moustárda*	mustard
piláfi	rice	*koukiá*	broad beans	*voútyro*	butter
me kymá	with minced meat	*kremídi*	onion	*tyrí*	cheese
me sáltsa	with tomato sauce	*láhano*	cabbage	*avgá (tiganitá)*	(fried) eggs

Our Transliteration System

In Greece, all town and village names on road signs, as well as most street names, are written in Greek and the Roman alphabets. There's no universally accepted system of transliteration into Roman, and in any case the Greek authorities are gradually replacing old signs with new ones that use a slightly different system. This means you will have to get used to seeing different spellings of the same place on maps and signs and in this book.

Below is the transliteration scheme we have used in this book: beside each Greek letter or pair of letters is the Roman letter(s) we have used. Next to that is a rough approximation of the sound in an English word.

Α α	a	father	Μ μ	m	man	
Β β	v	vote	Ν ν	n	no	
Γ γ	g	got *except before*	Ξ ξ	x	taxi	
		"e" *or* "i", *when*	Ο ο	o	long	
		it is nearer to	Π π	p	pen	
		yacht, *but rougher*	Ρ ρ	r	room	
Δ δ	d	then	Σ σ/ς	s	set	
Ε ε	e	egg			*or* charisma	
Ζ ζ	z	zoo	Τ τ	t	tea	
Η η	i	ski	Υ υ	y	ski	
Θ θ	th	thin	Φ φ	f	fish	
Ι ι	i	ski	Χ χ	h	loch	
Κ κ	k	kiss	Ψ ψ	ps	maps	
Λ λ	l	long	Ω ω	o	cord	

ΑΙ αι (ai)	e	hay	
ΑΥ αυ (au)	av	lava	
ΕΙ ει (ei)	i	ski	
ΕΥ ευ (eu)	ev	ever	
ΟΙ οι (oi)	i	ski	
ΟΥ ου (ou)	ou	tourist	
ΓΓ γγ (gg)	ng	long	
ΓΚ γκ (gk)	ng	long	
ΓΞ γξ (gx)	nx	anxious	
ΜΠ μπ (mp)	b	beg	
	or mb	limber	
ΝΤ ντ (nt)	d	dog	
	or nd	under	
ΤΖ τζ (tz)	tz	adze	

omelétta	omelette
marmeláda	jam, marmelade
rýzi	rice
giaoúrti	yoghurt
méli	honey
záhari	sugar

Sightseeing

information	pliroforíes
open/closed	anihtó/klistó
Is it possible	Borúme na
to see the	dúme tin
church/	eklisía/ta
archaeological	arhéa?
site?	
Where can I	Pou boró na vro
find the	to fílaka/klidí?
custodian/key?	

At the Shops

shop	magazí/
	katástima
What time do	ti óra aníyete/
you open/close?	klínete?
Are you being	exiperitíste?
served?	
What would	Oríste/ti
you like?	thélete?
I'm just looking	Aplós kitázo
How much is it?	Póso éhi?
Do you take	Pérnete
credit cards?	pistotikés
	kártes?
I'd like...	tha íthela...
this one	aftó
that one	ekíno
Have you got...?	éhete...?
size (for clothes)	número
Can I try it on?	Boró na to
	dokimáso?
It's too	Íne polí akrivó
expensive	
Don't you have	Den éhete
anything	típota pyo
cheaper?	ftinó?
Please write it	To gráfete
down for me	parakaló?
It's too small/	Íne polý mikró/
big	megálo
No thank you,	Óhi efharistó,
I don't like it	de m'arési
I'll take it	Tha to páro
I don't want it	Den to thélo
This is faulty	Aftó éhi éna
Can I have a	Elátoma. boró
replacement?	na to aláxo?
Can I have a	Boró na páro
refund?	píso ta leftá?
a kilo	éna kiló
half a kilo	misókilo
a quarter	éna tétarto
two kilos	dío kilá
100 grams	ekató
	gramária
200 grams	dyakósa
	gramária
more	perisótero
less	ligótero

a little	lígo
very little	polý lígo
with/without	me/horís
That's enough	ftáni
That's all	tipot'álo

Travelling

airport	aerodrómio
boarding card	kárta epivívasis
boat	plío/karávi
bus	leoforío
bus station	stathmós
	leoforíon
bus stop	stási
coach	púlman
ferry	feribót
first/second	próti/défteri
class	thési
flight	ptísi
hydrofoil	iptámeno
motorway	ethnikí odós
port	limáni
return ticket	isitírio me
	epistrofí
single ticket	apló isitírio
station	stathmós
taxi	taxí
train	tréno

Public Transport

Can you help	Boríte na me
me, please?	voithísete,
	parakaló?
Where can I	Pou na kópso
buy tickets?	isitírio?
At the counter	sto tamío
Does it stop at...	Káni stási sto...
You need to	Tha prépi
change at...	n'aláxete sto...
When is the	Póte févyi to
next train/bus/	tréno/leoforío/
ferry to...	feribót gia...
How long does	Pósi óra
the journey take?	káni to taxídi?
What time will	Ti óra tha
we arrive?	ftásume?
How much is	Póso íne to
the fare?	isitírio
Next stop	Stási parakaló
Can you tell me	Tha mu píte
where to get off?	pou na katévo?
Should I get	Edó na katévo?
off here?	
delay	kathistérisi

At the airport

I'd like to book	Tha íthela na
a seat to...	kratíso mia
	thési gia...
When is the	Póte tha íne i
next flight to...	epómeni ptísi
	gia...
Are there any	Párhoun i thésis?
seats available?	
Can I take	Boró na to páro
this with me?	avtó mazí mou?
My suitcase	Háthike i valítsa
has got lost	mou
The flight has	I ptísi éhi

Numbers

1	énas/mía/éna
	(masc/fem/neut)
2	dýo
3	tris/tría
4	tésseres/téssera
5	pénde
6	éxi
7	eptá
8	októ
9	ennéa
10	déka
11	éndeka
12	dódeka
13	dekatrís/dekatría
14	dekatésseres/dekatéssera
15	dekapénde
16	dekaéxi
17	dekaeptá
18	dekaoktó
19	dekaennéa
20	íkosi
30	triánda
40	saránda
50	penínda
60	exínda
70	evdomínda
80	ogdónda
90	enenínda
100	ekató
200	dyakósa
300	trakósies/trakósa
400	tetrakósies/tetrakósa
500	pendakósa
1,000	hílies/hília
2,000	dýo hiliádes
1 million	éna ekatomírio

been delayed	kathistérisi
The flight has	I ptísi
been cancelled	mateóthike

Directions

right/left	dexiá/aristerá
Take the first/	Párte ton próto/
second right	déftero drómo
	dexiá
Turn right/left	strípste dexiá/
	aristerá
Go straight on	Tha páte ísia/
	efthía
after the traffic	metá ta
lights	fanária
Is it near/	Ína kondá/
far away?	makriá?
How far is it?	Póso makriá íne?
It's five	Íne pénde leptá
minutes' walk	me ta pódia
It's ten	Íne déka leptá
minutes by car	me to avtokínito
100 metres	ekató métra
opposite/next to	apénandi/dípla
junction	diastávrosi
Where is/are...	Pou íne...
Where can I find	Pou boró na vro
a petrol station	éna venzinádiko
a bank	mia trápeza
a bus stop	mia stási

Notices

ΤΟΥΑΛΕΤΕΣ	toilets
ΑΝΔΡΩΝ	gentlemen
ΓΥΝΑΙΚΩΝ	ladies
ΑΝΟΙΚΤΟ	open
ΚΛΕΙΣΤΟ	closed
ΕΙΣΟΔΟΣ	entrance
ΕΞΟΔΟΣ	exit
ΑΠΑΓΟΡΕΥΤΑΙ	no entry
ΕΙΣΙΤΗΡΙΑ	tickets
ΑΠΑΓΟΡΕΥΤΑΙ ΤΟ ΚΑΠΝΙΣΜΑ	no smoking
ΠΛΗΡΟΦΟΡΙΕΣ	information
ΠΡΟΣΟΧΗ	caution
ΚΙΝΔΥΝΟΣ	danger
ΑΡΓΑ	slow
ΔΗΜΟΣΙΑ ΕΡΓΑ	road works
ΠΑΡΚΙΝΓ	parking
ΧΩΡΟΣ	car park
ΣΤΑΘΜΕΥΣΕΩΣ ΑΠΑΓΟΡΕΥΤΑΙ Η ΣΤΑΘΜΕΥΣΗ	no parking
ΤΑΞΙ	taxi
ΤΡΑΠΕΖΑ	bank
ΤΗΛΕΦΩΝΟ	telephone
ΤΗΛΕΚΑΡΤΕΣ	phone cards
ΕΚΤΟΣ ΛΕΙΤΟΥΡΓΙΑΣ	out of order

a hotel?	éna xenodohío?
How do I get there?	Pos na páo ekí?
Can you show me where I am on the map?	Boríte na mou díhete sto hárti pou íme?
Am I on the right road for...	Gia... kalá páo?
No, you're on the wrong road	Óhi, pírate láthos drómo

On the Road

Where can I hire a car?	Pou boró na nikiázo avtokínito?
What is it insured for?	Ti asfália éhi?
By what time must I return it?	Méhri ti óra prépi na to epistrépso?
driving licence	díploma
petrol	venzíni
unleaded	amólivdi
oil	ládi
Fill it up	Óso pérni
My car has broken down	Hálase to avtokinitó mou
I've had an accident	Íha éna atíhima
Can you check...	Boríte na elénhete...
the brakes	ta fréna
the clutch	to ambrayáz
the engine	i mihaní
the exhaust	i exátmisi
the fanbelt	i zóni
the gearbox	i tahítites
the headlights	ta fanárya
the radiator	to psiyío

the spark plugs	ta buzí
the tyre(s)	ta lástiha

Times and Dates

(in the) morning/ afternoon/ evening	to proí/ to apógevma/ to vrádi
(at) night	(ti) níhta
yesterday	htes
today	símera
tomorrow	ávrio
now	tóra
early	norís
late	argá
a minute	éna leptó
five/ten minutes	pénde/déka leptá
an hour	mia óra
half an hour	misí óra
a quarter of an hour	éna tétarto
at one/ two (o'clock)	sti mia/ stis dýo (i óra)
a day	mia méra
a week	mia vdomáda
(on) Monday	(ti) deftéra
(on) Tuesday	(tin) tríti
(on) Wednesday	(tin) tetárti
(on) Thursday	(tin) pémpti
(on) Friday	(tin) paraskeví
(on) Saturday	(to) sávato
(on) Sunday	(tin) kyriakí

Health

Is there a chemist's nearby?	Ipárhi éna farmakío edó kondá?
Which chemist is open all night?	Pio farmakío dianikterévi?
I don't feel well	Den esthánome kalá
I'm ill	Íme árostos (feminine árosti)
He/she's ill	Íne árostos/ árosti
Where does it hurt?	Pou ponái?
It hurts here	Ponái edó
I suffer from...	Pás-ho apo...
I have a...	Ého...
headache	ponokéfalo
sore throat	ponólemo
stomach ache	kiliópono
Have you got something for travel sickness?	Éhete típota gia ti navtía?
It's not serious	Den íne sovaró
Do I need a prescription?	Hriázete sindagí?
It bit me (of an animal)	Me dángose
It stung me	Me kéntrise
bee	mélisa
wasp	sfíka
mosquito	kounoúpi
sticking plaster	lefkoplástis
diarrhoea pills	hápia gia ti diária

Further Reading

Books go in and out of print, or change imprints, with such rapidity of late that we've elected not to list the pubishers, except for obscure Greek publishers with no internet presence, or one-off presses with only internet presence. For most titles, conducting a web search with the author and title should suffice to dredge up its current incarnation.

Ancient History & Culture

Burkert, Walter **Greek Religion: Archaic and Classical**. Excellent overview of the gods and goddesses, their attributes, worship and the meaning of major festivals.
Burn, A.R. **The Penguin History of Greece**. A good, single-volume introduction to ancient Greece.
Finley, M.I. **The World of Odysseus**. Recently reissued 1954 standard on just how well (or not) the Homeric sagas are borne out by archaelogical facts.
Fox, Robin Lane **Alexander the Great**. A psychobiography wedded to a conventional history.
Grimal, Pierre, ed **Dictionary of Classical Mythology**. Still considered to be tops among a handful of available alphabetical gazetteers.
Hornblower, Simon **The Greek World, 479–323 BC**. The eventful period from the end of the Persian Wars to Alexander's demise; the standard university text.

Byzantine History & Culture

Norwich, John Julius Byzantium (3 vols): **The Early Centuries**, **The Apogee** and **The Decline**. The most readable and masterful popular history, by the noted Byzantinologist; also available as one massive volume, **A Short History of Byantium**.
Psellus, Michael **Fourteen Byzantine Rulers**. That many changes of rule in a single century (10th–11th), as told by a near-contemporary historian.
Rice, David Talbot **Art of the Byzantine Era**. Shows how Byzantine sacred craftsmanship extended from the Caucasus into northern Italy, in a variety of media.
Runciman, Steven **The Fall of Constantinople, 1453**. Still the

definitive study of an event which continues to exercise modern Greek minds. His *Byzantine Style and Civilization* covers art, culture and monuments.

Ware, Archbishop Kallistos *The Orthodox Church*. Good introduction to what was, until recently, the de facto established religion of modern Greece.

Anthropology & Culture

Campbell, John *Honor, family and patronage: A study of institutions and moral values in a Greek mountain community* Classic study of Sarakatsáni shepherds in the Zagorian Píndos, with much wider application to Greece in general, which got the author banned from the area by touchy officialdom.

Danforth, Loring H. and Tsiaras, Alexander *The Death Rituals of Rural Greece*. Riveting, annotated photo essay on Greek funeral customs.

Du Boulay, Juliet *Portrait of a Greek Mountain Village*. Ambéli, a mountain village in Évvia, as it was in the mid-1960s.

Holst, Gail *Road to Rembetika : Songs of Love, Sorrow and Hashish* (Denise Harvey, Límni, Évvia). Introduction to the enduringly popular musical form; with translated lyrics and discographies.

Mackridge, Peter *The Modern Greek Language*. In-depth analysis by one of the foremost scholars of the tongue's evolution.

Cuisine

Dalby, Andrew *Siren Feasts*. Analysis of Classical and Byzantine texts shows just how little Greek food has changed in three millennia.

Davidson, Alan *Mediterranean Seafood*. 1972 classic that's still the standard reference, guaranteed to end every argument as to just what that fish is on your *tavérna* plate. Complete with recipes.

Manessis, Nico *The Illustrated Greek Wine Book* (Olive Press Publications, Corfu; order on www.greekwineguide.gr). Includes almost all Greek vintners, from mass-market to micro.

Modern History

Clogg, Richard *A Concise History of Greece*. Clear and lively account of Greece from Byzantine times to 2000, with helpful maps and well-captioned artwork. The best single-volume summary; be sure to get the second edition (2002).

Koliopoulos, John and Thanos Veremis *Greece, the Modern Sequel: From 1831 to the Present*. Thematic and psycho-history of the independent nation, tracing trends, first principles and setbacks.

Mercouri, Melina *I Was Born Greek*. The tumultuous life and times of Greece's most famous actress, written in 1971 while she was in exile from the junta.

Pettifer, James *The Greeks: the Land and People since the War*. Useful general introduction to politics, family life, food, tourism and other contemporary topics. Get the new, updated 2002 edition.

Woodouse, C.M. *Modern Greece: A Short History*. Spans the period from early Byzantium to the early 1980s. His classic *The Struggle for Greece, 1941–1949*, recently reissued by C Hurst (London), is perhaps the best overview of that turbulent decade.

Modern Greek Literature

Beaton, Roderick *An Introduction to Modern Greek*. Readable survey of Greek literature since independence.

Cavafy, C.P. *Collected Poems*, trans. by Edmund Keeley and Philip Sherrard or *The Complete Poems of Cavafy*, translated by Rae Dalven. Considered the two best versions available in English.

Elytis, Odysseus *The Axion Esti*, *Selected Poems* and *The Sovereign Sun*. Pretty much the complete works of the Nobel laureate, in translation.

Kazantzakis, Nikos. Nobel laureate, woolly Marxist and self-imposed exile, Kazantzakis embodies the old maxim that classics are books praised but generally unread. Whether in intricate, untranslatable Greek or wooden English, Kazantzakis can be hard going. *Zorba the Greek* is a surprisingly dark and nihilistic work, worlds away from the crude, two-dimensional character of the film; *The*

Bookshops in Greece

Athens has various bookshops that carry quality books in English: **Compendium**, Níkis 28, just behind Sýndagma Square (tel: 210 322 6931).

Eleftheroudakis, Panepistimíou 17 (tel: 210 331 4180), plus three other midtown branches.

Iy Folia tou Vivliou/The Book Nest, Panepistimíou 25-29, Stoa Megárou Athinón (tel: 210 322 5209).

Pantelides, Amerikís 11 (tel: 210 362 3673).

Last Temptation of Christ provoked riots by Orthodox fanatics in Athens in 1989; *Report to Greco* explores his Cretanness/ Greekness; while *Christ Recrucified* (published in the US as *The Greek Passion*) encompasses the Easter drama within Christian-Muslim dynamics on Crete.

Leontis, Artemis, ed *Greece: a Traveler's Literary Companion*. Various regions of the country as portrayed in very brief fiction or essays by modern Greek writers; an excellent corrective to the often condescending Grand Tourist accounts.

Mourselas, Kostas *Red Dyed Hair* (Kedros, Athens). Politically incorrect picaresque saga of urban life from the 1950s to the 1970s among a particularly feckless paréa; the Greek original still sells well, and formed the basis of popular TV series.

Papandreou, Nick *Father Dancing*. Thinly disguised, page-turning roman-à-clef by the late prime minister's younger son; Papandreou *père* comes across as an egotistical monster.

Ritsos, Yannis *Exile and Return, Selected Poems 1967–1974*. The outcome of junta-era internal exile on Sámos for Greece's foremost communist poet.

Papadiamantis, Alexandros; trans. Peter Levi *The Murderess*. Landmark novel written in an early form of demotic Greek, set on Skiáthos at the turn of the 19th/20th centuries.

Seferis, George; trans. Edmund Keeley *Collected Poems 1924-1955*; *Complete Poems*. The former has Greek-English texts on facing pages and is preferable to the so-called "complete" works of Greece's other Nobel literary laureate.

Sotiriou, Dido *Farewell Anatolia* (Kedros, Athens). A best-selling classic since its appearance in 1962, this traces the end of the Greeks in Asia Minor from 1914 to 1922, using a character based on the author's father.

Tsirkas, Stratis; trans. Kay Cicellis *Drifting Cities*. (Kedros, Athens). Welcome paperback re-issue of this epic novel on wartime leftist intrigue in Alexandria, Cairo and Jerusalem.

Vassilikos, Vassilis. *Z*. Based closely enough on the assassination of leftist MP Grigoris Lambrakis in 1963 by royalist thugs to get the book – and author – banned by the colonels' junta.

Foreign Writers in/on Greece

Andrews, Kevin *The Flight of Ikaros*. An educated, sensitive, Anglo-American archaeologist wanders the

Useful Websites

Greek weather forecasts are available at:
http://forecast.uoa.gr
www.poseidon.ncmr.gr
For local journalism in English try the sites of:
www.eKathimerini.com/news/news.asp
www.athensnews.gr
This site claims to list all the hotels in Greece, along with their telephone numbers:
www.all-hotels.gr
Want to buy one of the books listed above? Don't trust our opinion? Get a second review at:
www.hellenicbooks.com
Seagoing schedules are available at:
www.gtp.gr
www.gtpnet.com
For general tourist information and links have a look at:
www.greektravel.com
www.travel-greece.com
A site claimed by the government to show "contemporary Greece" is:
www.greece.gr
The Ministry of Culture site has impressive coverage of most of the country's museums, archeological sites and remote monuments on:
www.culture.gr

back-country in surprising freedom as the civil war winds down. Despite the massive changes since, still one of the best books on the country.
Bouras, Gillian **A Foreign Wife**, **A Fair Exchange** and **Aphrodite and the Others**. Scottish-Australian marries Greek-Australian, then consents to return to the "mother" country; the resulting trilogy is about the best of many chronicles of the acculturation experience.
De Bernières, Louis **Captain Corelli's Mandolin**. Heart-rending tragicomedy set on occupied Kefalloniá during World War II which has acquired cult status and long-term best-seller-list tenancy since its appearance in 1994.
Durrell, Lawrence **Prospero's Cell** and **Reflections on a Marine Venus**. Corfu in the 1930s, and Rhodes in 1945–47, now looking rather old-fashioned, alcohol-fogged and patronising of the "natives", but still entertaining enough.
Fowles, John **The Magus**. Best-seller, inspired by author's spell teaching on Spétses during the 1950s, of post-adolescent manipulation, conspiracy and cock-teasing (ie, the usual Fowles obsessions).
Gage, Nicholas **Eleni**. Epirus-born American correspondent returns to Greece to avenge the death of his

mother at the hands of an ELAS firing squad in 1948.
Leigh Fermor, Patrick. **Roumeli: Travels in Northern Greece and Mani**. Written during the late 1950s and early 1960s, before the advent of mass tourism, these remain some of the best compendia of the then already-vanishing customs and relict communities of the mainland. Manus, Willard **This Way to Paradise: Dancing on the Tables** (Lycabettus Press, Athens). An American expatriate's affectionate summing-up of 40-plus years living in Líndos, from its innocence to its corruption. Wonderful anecdotes of the hippie days, and walk-on parts for the famous and infamous.
Miller, Henry **The Colossus of Maroussi**. Miller takes to Corfu, the Argolid, Athens and Crete of 1939 with the enthusiasm of a first-timer in Greece who's found his element; deserted archeological sites and larger-than-life personalities.
Salmon, Tim **The Unwritten Places** (Lycabettus Press, Athens). Veteran Hellenophile describes his love affair with the Greek mountains, and the Vlach pastoral communities of Epirus in particular.
Stone, Tom **The Summer of my Greek Taverna**. Set in a thinly disguised Kámbos of early-1980s Pátmos, this is a poignant cautionary tale for all who've ever fantasised about leasing a taverna (or buying a property) in the islands.
Storace, Patricia **Dinner with Persephone**. New York poet resident a year in Athens successfully takes the pulse of modern Greece, with all its shibboleths, foundation myths, carefully nurtured self-image and rampant misogyny. Very funny, and spot-on.

Regional and Archaelogical Guides

Burn, A. R. and Mary **The Living Past of Greece**. Worth toting its oversized format around for the sake of lively text and clear plans; covers most major sites from Minoan to medieval.
Hetherington, Paul **Byzantine and Medieval Greece**. Erudite and authoritative dissection of the castles and churches of the mainland.
Chilton, Lance **Various walking guides** Short but detailed guidelets to the best walks around various mainland and island charter destinations, accompanied by maps. See the full list and order from:
www.marengowalks.com
Wilson, Loraine **The White Mountains of Crete**. The best of several guides to the range, with nearly sixty hikes of all levels, described by the most experienced foreign guide.

Botanical Field Guides

Baumann, Helmut **Greek Wildflowers and Plant Lore in Ancient Greece**. As the title says; lots of interesting ethnobotanical trivia, useful photos.
Huxley, Anthony, and William Taylor **Flowers of Greece and the Aegean**. The only volume dedicated to both islands and mainland, with good photos, though taxonomy is now a bit obsolete.
Polunin, Oleg **Flowers of Greece and the Balkans**. This book is also showing its age, but again has lots of colour photos to aid identification.
Polunin, Oleg and Anthony Huxley **Flowers of the Mediterranean**. Lots of colour plates to aid in identification, and includes flowering shrubs; recent printings have a table of taxonomic changes.

Feedback

We do our best to ensure the information in our books is as accurate and up-to-date as possible. The books are updated on a regular basis, using local contacts, who painstakingly add, amend and correct as required. However, some mistakes and omissions are inevitable and we are ultimately reliant on our readers to put us in the picture.

We would welcome your feedback on any details related to your experiences using the book "on the road". Maybe we recommended a hotel that you liked (or another that you didn't), as well as interesting new attractions, or facts and figures you have found out about the country itself. The more details you can give us (particularly with regard to addresses, e-mails and telephone numbers), the better. We will acknowledge all contributions, and we'll offer an Insight Guide to the best letters received.

Please write to us at:
Insight Guides
PO Box 7910
London SE1 1WE
United Kingdom
Or send an e-mail to: insight@apaguide.demon.co.uk

ART & PHOTO CREDITS

Picture Spreads

INSIGHT GUIDE Greece

Cartographic Editor **Zoë Goodwin**
Production **Linton Donaldson**
Art Director **Klaus Geisler**
Picture Research **Hilary Genin**

Index

Numbers in italics refer to photographs

a

Adamás 235
Advíra 211
Aegina (Égina) 27, 28, 76, 217–19
Afáles 301
Áfissos 174
Agamemnon 23, *144–5*, 150
Agáthi 250
Agathoníssi 264
Agiá (Epirus) 180
Agía Marína (Aegina) 218
Agía Marína (Léros) 263
Agía Marína (Spétses) 223
Agía Paraskévi 223
Agía Rouméli 317
Agiásos *276*, 277
Ágii Anárgyri 223
Ágii Déka 312
Ágii Galíni 313–14
Ágii Pándes 108
Ágios Dimítrios 288
Ágios Evstrátios 15, 272
Ágios Fokás 290
Ágios Geórgios (Andíparos) 233
Ágios Geórgios (Évvia) 291
Ágios Geórgios (Kefalloniá) 302
Ágios Geórgios (Síkinos) 236
Ágios Geórgios Argyrádon (Corfu) 297
Ágios Germanós 203, 204
Ágios Górdis 297
Ágios Ioánnis (Límnos) 272
Ágios Ioánnis (Pílio) 174
Ágios Isídoros 277
Ágios Kírykos 280
Ágios Matthéos 297
Ágios Nikítas 301
Ágios Nikólaos (Anáfi) 239–40
Ágios Nikólaos (Crete) 310–11, *311*
Ágios Nikólaos (Fokída) 169
Ágios Nikólaos (Peloponnese) 160
Ágios Nikólaos (Síkinos) 236
Ágios Pandelímon 160
Ágios Sóstis 227
Ágios Sótiros 160
Ágios Stéfanos 261
Ágios Stéfanos Sinión 296
Ágios Stratigós 160
Agrapidiá 106
agriculture 15, 24–5, 46, 88, 105
Agrínio 171
Aháïa 163
Aharávi 297
Ahelóös River 17, 171, 187
Ahílli Bay 289
Aï Nikítas 301
Aï Strátis 15, 272
Aivali (Ayvaluk) 81
Akronavpliá 151
Akrotíri (Santoríni) 23, 145, 238
Áktio (Actium) 181
Albania 41, 48, 62, 188
Alexander the Great 29, 30, 61, 97–8, 204, 205, 220

Alexandroúpoli 211
Ali Pasha *38*, 180, 181, 182–4
Aliákmonas River 106, 201, 204
Alivéri 291
Alónisos 110, 287–9
Aloprónia 236
Alykés *304*, 305
Alykí (Kós) 17
Alykí (Thásos) 269
Álynda 263
Amfilóhia 171
Ammoudiá 180–81
Ammoulianí 207
Amorgós 237–8
Amphipolis 209
Anáfi 239–40
Anávatos 279
Ancient Greece 23–31
Andíparos 232–3
Andípaxi (Andípaxos) 299
Andísamos 303
Andrítsena 154–5
Ándros 225
Angístri 219
Áno Boularí 160
Áno Merá 229
Áno Meriá 236
Áno Vathý 282
Anógia 309
Aóös River 107, 179
Apéri 255
Apírados 234
Apóllonas 234
Apollónia (Mílos) 236
Apollonía (Sífnos) 232
aqueducts 147, 209, *275*, 281–2
Aráhova *16*, 165
Archaic Period 96, 144, 147, 163
archeological museums
    Central Greece 165, 168
    Corfu 295–6
    Crete 307, 311, 314, 315
    Cyclades 225, 229, 232, 233, 234, 238
    Dodecanese 260
    Epirus (Ioánnina) 183
    Évia 290, 291
    Macedonia 205, 208, 209
    Northeast Aegean 272, *275*, 282
    Peloponnese 147, 150, 155, 163
    Rhodes 247
    Thessaloníki 195
    see also Athens Byzantine museums
architecture 95–103, 160, 185, 248, 251, 260, 275
Arcturos 106
Areópoli 159
Aretés 207
Árgos 25, 150
Argostóli 302
Argyrádes 297
Arhánes 309
arhontiká 185, 201–2, 203, 221, 222
Aristotle 205, 206
Arkadía 152–5
Arkí 264
Armenistís 280
Arnádos 227

Arnéa 206–7
art 29, 95–103
art museums and collections 103, 209, 247, 268, 275, 278, 295, 296, 302, 304, 308,
    see also Athens; Byzantine museums; folk museums
Árta *17*, 182
Arvanites 61
Asfendioú 261
Asia Minor Disaster 46–7
Asia Minor Greeks 61–2, 74, 83–4, 85
Asklipío 250
Ásos 303
Aspoús 289
Ástakos 171
Astrída 269
Astypálea 262–3
Atháni 301
Athenians (ancient history) 25–30, 143, 162
Athens *116–16*, *126*, 127–45
    Academy 101, 136
    Acropolis 27, 35, 97, 100, 128–31
    Acropolis Museum 130
    Ágii Theodóri Church 139
    Ágios Dimítrios School 103
    Ancient Greek Agora 130–31
    Athens Eye Clinic 101
    Athens School of Music 103
    Athens Technical University 101
    Bath-House of the Winds 133–4, *135*
    Benáki Museum 137–8
    Byzantine and Christian Museum 101, 138
    Centre for Acropolis Studies 53, 129
    Children's Museum 134
    Choregic Monument to Lysicrates 98, *131*, 132
    Elevtherías Park 139
    Emperor Hadrian's Arch 132
    Erechtheion 27, 129
    Fethiye Mosque 133
    Goulandrís Museum of Cycladic Art 103, 137, *138*
    Goulandrís Museum of Natural History & Gaia Centre 141
    Hellenic Maritime Museum 140
    Hellenic Theatre Museum 136
    Hephaisteion 131
    Herod Atticus Theatre *130*, 132–3
    Holy Apostles Church 99
    Jewish Museum of Greece 134
    Kanellópoulos Archeological & Byzantine Museum 134
    Kapnikaréa Church *35*, 137
    Keramikós Cemetery 131
    Kifisiá 141, *142*
    Kyriazopoulos Collection of Pottery 133
    Marathon Archeological Museum 143
    markets 134–5
    Mégaro Mousikís Concert Hall 103, 139
    Mihalarias collection 103
    Mitrópolis (Cathedral) 135

Modernist apartments 103
Monastiráki 134–6
Mount Hymettus 139, 141
Mount Lycabettus *130*, 138
Mount Párnitha 141
Mount Pendéli 141
Museum of Greek Folk Art 134
Museum of Popular Instruments &
    Research Centre for
    Ethnomusicology 134
Mytaras House 103
National Archeological Museum
    136, *144–5*
National Capodistrian University
    101, 136
National Gallery & Alexandros
    Soutzos Museum 101, 102,
    103, 138–9
National Gardens 137
National Historical Museum 137
National Library 101, 136
neo-Classical architecture 101
Numismatic Museum 137
Parliament Building 137
Parthenon 35, 100, 128–9
Pefkakia School 103
Piraeus Archeological Museum 140
Pláka 132, 133–4, 139
Platía Omónias 136–7
Platía Syndágmatos 136, 137
Portalakes collection 103
Roman Agora 133
Sotíra Lykodímou Church 139
Temple of Olympian Zeus
    (Olympeion) *30*, *98*, 132
Theatre of Dionysos 131
Tower of the Winds *133*
Wortheim House 101
Záppio Park 132
Athiniás 239
Atsítsa 290
Avgónyma 279
Avlémonas 305
Avlónas 272
Axiós 106

b

Back Islands 240
Balkan Wars 46, 177, 193, 204
Batsí 225
Benítses 297
birds 17, 110–11, 163, 203–4, 211,
    229, 289, 307, 309, 317
botanical gardens 137, 302
Bouboulína 223
Boúkari 297
Brauron 143
British 43, 48, 162, 193, 294, 295,
    305
Bronze Age 23, 95, 230, 270
Brooke, Rupert 289, 290
Brós Thermá 260
Bulgaria 46, 205
butterflies 233–4, *243*, 250
Byron, Lord 43, 119, 142, 170, *171*
Byzantine era 31, 33–7, 82–3,
    98–100
Byzantine museums 101, 134, 138,
    195, 205, *223*, 247

c

Callas, Maria 136
Cape Akrítas 161
Cape Maléa 158
Cape Mátapan 159–60
Cape Skinári *14*, 305
Cape Sounion 142–34, 144
Captain Corelli's Mandolin 303
carnivals 163, 289, *see also* **festivals**
castles
    Central Greece 169, 171, 174
    Corfu 293, *294*, *296*, 297, 314
    Crete 314
    Dodecanese 259, 262
    Northeast Aegean 278, *280*
    Peloponnese 151, 153, 159,
        161–2
    Rhodes *249*, 250
    Skopélos 287
    see also **fortresses**; **Knights of St
        John**
catacombs 235–6
Cavafy, Constantine *70*, 74
cave-church (Préspa) 204
caves
    Agía Sofía (Kýthira) 305
    Blue Caves (Zákynthos) 305
    Crete 309, 310, 313
    Hrysopiliá (Folégandros) 236
    Kefalloniá *302*, *303*
    Pérama 185, *186*
    Petrálona (Thessaloníki) 206
    Polyphemus's Cave (Advira) 211
    Pýrgos Diroú Caverns 160
    Spílio Stalktitón (Andíparos) 232
centaurs 173
Cervantes 169
Chaniá (Haniá) 315
Chíos *see* **Híos**
Christianity 33, 35, 39–40, 98–9,
    138, 235, 261, 316, *see also*
    Greek Orthodox Church
churches 35, 99–100
    Athens 99, 135, 137, 139
    Crete 308, 311, 313, 314, 316
    Cyclades 225, 227, 229, 233,
        234, 238
    Epirus 182, 187
    Ionian 304, 305
    Macedonia 202–3, 204, 205, 206
    Northeastern Aegean 278
    Peloponnese 153, 156–7, 158,
        159, 160
    Rhodes 250
    Saronic 219, 223
    Sporades and Évvia 290, 291
    Thessaloníki 194, 195–7
    see also **monasteries**
city-states 24–30, 34, 143, 162,
    245
Classical Period 96–7, 144
climate 16, 242, 299
Constantinople 31, 33, 36, 37, 39,
    45, 53, 62, 316
Corcyra 28, 293
Corfu (Kérkyra) 293–7
Corinth 25, 28, 31, 147–9
Corinth Canal 45, 147, *149*
Corinthian columns 98, 132

Crete (Kríti) 93, *306*, 307–19
    arts 72, 81, 95, 100
    history 23, 40–41, 46
Crusades 36–7, 53, 177, 246
Cyclades 225–41
Cycladic Period 95, 144, 225, 230
Cyprus 37, 50, 52, 258

d

Dadiá Forest 111, 211
Damalas 220
Damoúhari 174
dance 57, 79–82, 83
Dassiá 296
Delos 27, 28, 229, 241
Delphi 167–8
Dervenákia 149
Despotikó 233
Día 108
Diafáni 255, 256
Diapóndia islets 297
Didymótiho 211
Dílofo 187
Dimitsána 154
Dion 205, 207
Dodecanese 245–65
Dodona *176*, 183, 184–5
Donoúsa 240
Dorians 23–4, 96, 256
Doroúsa 219
Dörpfeld, William 300
Drakólimni (Dragon Lakes) 188, *189*
drama 77, 152, 221, 223, 251, 305
Drymónas 301
Dryópi 219
Dryopída 228
Durrell, Lawrence 247, 249, 296

e

Eándio 217
Easter 56, 65, 67–8, 83, 86–90,
    256, 294, 316
Édessa *201*, 205
Egiális 238
Égina *see* **Aegina**
El Greco 100, 137, 314
Elafonísi 316
Elevsína 165
Elevtheroúpoli 209
Elgin, Lord 53, 129
Ellinikó 153
Eloúnda 310–11
Emborió (Hálki) 257
Emborió (Nísyros) 260
Emboriós (Híos) 279
emigration 46, 55, 100, 186, 257,
    301, 305
    from Dodecanese 48, 255, 258,
        260, 262, 264
Ephyra 180
Epidauros (Epídavros) *26*, 151–2,
    219, 223
Epirus *17*, 41, 46, 80, 92, 177–90
Eptá Pigés 250
Erétria 291
Erikoússa 297
Érmones 297
Ermoúpoli *42*, 228

Euboea *see* Évia
Europa 20
European Economic Community
  (EEC) 52, 53, 55, 208
Evans, Arthur *319*
Évdilos 280
Évia (Euboea) *145*, 290–91
Évinos River 171
Evpalínio Órygma (aqueduct) 281–2
Évrós River 17, 106, 110, 111, 211
Exóbourgo 227

f

Falakró 106
Faliráki 250
Féres 211
festivals 64–8, *86–7*, 89–90, 163,
  256, 259, 277, 289, *see also*
  Easter; "Óhi" Day
Festós (Phaistos) 23, 95, 313
Figalia 155
Filóti 234
Fínikas 228
Firá 238–9
Fiskárdo *118*, *303*, 304
Flomohóri 160
Flórina 204
Fódele 314
Folégandros *235*, 236
folk museums 134, 203, 209, 211,
  229, 235, 311
folk music 61, 68, 71–2, 79–82
food and drink 39, 57, 63–6, 88–93,
  186, 194, 303, *see also* wine
forests 16, 105, 107, 111, 211,
  317
fortresses 149, 237, *245*, 248, 265,
  268
  Venetian 40, 151, 158, 197, 293,
  294, 308, 311
  see also castles
fountains 147, 149, 167, 308, 314
Foúrni 280–81
Fowles, John 222, 223
French 35–6, 41, 43, 162, 193, 271,
  294
frescoes 157, 184, 187, 202, 238,
  250, 258, 276, 311, 316–17
  illustrated *145*, *194*, *281*, *319*
Fríkes 301

g

Gáios 299
Galáni 231
Galatás 219
Galaxídi 169
Gallipoli 272, 289
Gávrio 225
gay scene 163, 229, 273
Genoese 37, 89, 99, *245*, 277–8
geology 15, 141, 235
Geometric Period 96
Georgioúpoli 315
Gérakas 304
Geráki 157
Geroliménas 160
Gialós (Sými) 257
Giálova 162

Gioúra 288
Glóssa 287
Glyfáda 297
Glykí 181
Górtyn (Górtys, Crete) 313
Gortys (Peloponnese) 153–4
Gourniá 311
Great Idea 45–6
Greek key 96
Greek Orthodox Church 33, 35, 39,
  61, 89
Gregolímani 291
gum mastic 277
Gýthio 158–9

h

Hálki (Dodecanese) 257
Halkí (Náxos) 234
Halkída 290–91
Halkidikí 92, 107, 206–9
Háni Avlonaríou 291
Haniá (Chaniá) 315
Haniótis 207
Hellenistic Period 97–8, 144
Hera temple (Olympia) 163
Hera temple (Perahora Heraion) 147
Heráklion (Iráklio) 307–8
Hersónisos (Crete) 310
hiking 172, 174, 178, 187, 189–90,
  227, 283, 316–17
Híos (Chíos) 40, 93, 99, *266*,
  277–9
Hippocrates 260, 261, 277
Hóra Sfakiá 316
Horió 262
Hortiátis 199
hot springs 15, 172–3, 260, 271,
  see also spas; springs
Hristós 280
Hydra (Ýdra) 221–2, *223*

i

Ía *114–15*, 239
Ialyssos 249–50
icons 99, 137, 138, 227, 229, 247,
  265, 276, 279, 308
Ierápetra 312
Igoumenítsa 179
Ikaría 279–80
Ilía 162–3
immigrants 62–3
Independence 42–3, 45, 153, 160,
  162, 223
industrialisation 45, 47, 50–51
Inoússes 278
Ionian islands 299–305
Íos 236–7
Ioulís 225
Ipsoúnda 154
Iráklia (Back Islands) 240
Iráklio (Heráklion) 307–8
Iroön 236
Íssos 297
Istérnia 227
Isthmía 147
Italian occupation 48, 246, 247,
  250, 251, 253, *see also* Genoese;
  Venetians

Itéa 168–9
Itháki (Ithaca) 301
Ítylo 160

j–k

Jason and the Argonauts 171
Jewish communities 61, 134, 180,
  183, 198–9, 246, 247, 260, 278,
  290–91, 293
Kábi 305
Kaïmaktsalán 204
Kalamáta 161, 162
Kalámi 296
Kalamítsi (Lefkáda) 301
Kalamítsi (Sithonía) 207
Kállisto 231
Kallithéa 250, 251
Kalloní 17
Kalógria 17
Kalogriá 163
Kalpáki 187
Kálymnos 67–8, 86, 261–2
Kamáres 231
Kamarí 239
Kamariótissa 270
Kámbi 281
Kámbos (Híos) 278
Kámbos (Ikaría) 280
Kameiros *244*, 249
Kamíni 222
Kanapítsa peninsula 286
Kanóni 296
Kapésovo 187
Kapodistrias, Ioannis *21*, 43, 218,
  294
Kapsáli 305
Karavostássi 179
Kardamýli 161
Kardianí 227
Karlóvassi 283
Kárpathos *87*, *252*, 253–6
Karpenísi 172
Karpenisiótis Valley 172
Karyá 300
Kárystos 291
Karýtena 153
Kásos 256–7
Kassándra peninsula 206–7
Kassiópi 296
Kassope 181
Kastaniés 211
Kastéli-Kissámou 316
Kastellórizo 258
Kastoriá 39, 202–3
Kástro (Sífnos) 232
Kástro (Skiáthos) 285
Katápola 237
Katapolianí 227
Kataváti 232
Katelíos 303
Káthisma 301
Káto Hóra 305
Káto Korakiána 296
Káto Zákros 312
Kavála 209, 267
Kávos 297
kayaking and rafting 17, 171, 179,
  188
Kazantzakis, Nikos *72*, 75, 77, 308

Kéa 225–7
Kefaloniá 64, 93, 118, 302–4
Keiádas 161
Kemal Atatürk 47, 198
Kerí 305
Kérkíni 106
Kérkyra (Corfu) 293–7
Kéros 145, 240
Kilioméno 305
Kilkís 205
Kímolos 236
Kínyra 269
Kióni 301
Kiotári 250
Kípi (Epirus) 187, 190
Kitta 160
Klidoniá 188
Klíma 235
Klisoúra Gorge 171
Knights of St John 37, 40, 245,
   246–7, 249, 250, 259, 260, 263
Knossos 23, 95, 307, 318–19
Kokkári 282
Kokkinókastro 288
Kolimbári 315
kóllivo 64–5
Kolóna 218
Kolymbáda 289
Kolymbíthra 227
Kómi 279
Komiáki 234
Komméno 296
Kómmos 313
Komotiní 210, 211
Kondókali 296
Kónitsa 188
Kórinthos 147
Korissía 225
Korissíon lagoon 17, 297
Koróni 161
Kós 110, 251, 260–61
Kósta 223
Kótronas 160
Kotýhi lagoons 106
Koufonísi 240
Koukoúli 190
Koukounariés 285
Kouloúra 296
Kouloúri 217
Koúndouros 227
Kounopétra 303
Krasás 285
Kríni 297
Kritiniá 250
Krýa Váthra 271
Kyparissía 162
Kyrá Panagía (Alónisos) 288
Kýthira 41, 305
Kýthnos 227–8

l

Labinoú 174
Laganás Bay 304–5
Lágia 160
Lahaniá 250
lakes 15, 106, 171, 182, 201,
   205, 206, 211, 311, see also
   Drakólimni; Préspa Lakes
Lákka 299

Lakkí 251, 263
Lákoma 271
Lákones 297
Lakonía 155–9
Lalária 285
Lamía 172
Langáda 160
Langádia 153
languages 17, 24, 30, 34, 61
Lási 302–3
Lasíthi Plain 310
Laurion (Lávrion) 27
Lávkos 174
Lear, Edward 40–41, 295
Lébena 313
Lémnos see Límnos
Léndas 313
Lépoura 291
Lerna 152
Léros 251, 253, 263
Lésvos 93, 110, 272, 273–7
   arts 74, 81–2, 100
   history 15, 16, 40
Leuctra 29
Levídi 153
Levkáda (Léfkas) 299–301
Lévkes 233
Lévki 301
Levkími 297
Limenária 269
Liménas 267–8
Límni 291
Limniónas (Zákynthos) 305
Límnos 15, 93, 110, 271–2
Linariá 289
Líndos 247, 248, 249
Lipsí 264
literature 29, 71–7, see also poetry
Livádi (Astypálea) 263
Livádi (Kéa) 225
Livádi (Sérifos) 231
Livádia (Central Greece) 165
Livádia (Tílos) 259
Lixoúri 303
Longós 299
Loudías 106
Loúha 305
Loúsios Gorge 153–4
Loutrá (Kýthnos) 228
Loutrá Edipsoú 291
Loutráki (Skópelos) 287
Lygiá 300
Lygourió 152

m

Macedonia 29–31, 46, 61, 92, 106,
   110, 201–10
MaheIrádo 305
Makrinítsa 174
Makrýgialos 312
Mália 310
Mandamádos 275–6
Mandráki (Hydra) 222
Mandráki (Nísyros) 259
Mandráki (Rhodes) 245, 246, 248–9
Máni region 41, 43, 45, 147, 159–60
Mantineia 152
maquis 105, 107, 111
Maráthi (Dodecanese) 264

Maráthi (Páros) 233
Marathókambos 283
Marathon 27, 143
Marathóna 219
Marathonísi 159
marble 233, 234, 267
Mariés 269
marine life 108–10, 288, 304–5
Marmári 260
Maroneia 211
Mastihári 260
mastiohoriá 278
Mátala 313
Mathráki 297
Megálo Kazavíti 269
Megálo Livádi 231
Megálo Pápingo 187–88, 190
Megálo Prínos 269
Megalópoli 153
Mégas Lákkos 303
Megísti 258
Melínda 277
Menetés 255
merchants 42, 43, 210, see also
   arhontiká
Mérihas 227
Mesohára dam 17
Mesolóngi 17, 106, 170, 171
Mesopótamos 180
Messinía 161–2
Messongí 297
Mestá 278
Metéora 112–13, 174–5
Méthana 15
Methóni 161–2
Métsovo 177, 179, 185–6, 187
Mikró Pápingo 187–88, 190, 191
Mikrós Gialós 300
military junta 51–2, 73, 139
Mílos 15, 235–6
mining 16, 27, 169, 227, 235, 267
Minoans 23, 95, 145, 227, 230,
   238–9, 307–13, 318–19
Mólos 290
Molyvdosképastos 188
Mólyvos 276
monasteries
   Athens 139–40, 141
   Central Greece 164, 165, 172,
      174, 175
   Crete 312, 314
   Cyclades 225, 229, 231, 232,
      236, 238, 239, 240
   Dodecanese 258, 259, 265
   Epirus 181, 184, 185, 187, 188
   Ionian 33, 305
   Macedonia 203, 207–9
   Metéora 164, 165, 174, 175
   Mount Áthos 207–9
   Néa Moní (Híos) 99, 266, 279
   Northeast Aegean 99, 266, 276,
      279, 281
   Peloponnese 34, 154, 156, 157,
      160
   Rhodes 248, 249, 250
   Saronic 217, 218, 220, 221
   Sporades 69, 286
   Thessaloníki 196
   Thrace 211
Monemvasía 92–3, 122, 157–8, 223

Moní 219
monk seals 109–10, *109*, 288
Monodéndri 187, 190
Monólithos *249*, 250
Moraítika 297
mosaics 98, 99, 147, 155, 165, 182, 195, 205, 241, 260, 275, 279, 313
   illustrated *35, 99, 206, 246, 260, 266*
mosques 39, 100, 133, 183–4, 194, 197–8, 248–9, 260, 290, *312,* 314
Moúdros 272, 289
mountains 15, 16, 105, 106–8, 111, 172–4, 177, 188–90
   Mt Áthos 92, 207–9
   Mt Attávyros 250
   Mt Énos 302
   Mt Fengári 269–70, 271
   Mt Gamíla 188, 189, 190
   Mt Gioúhtas 309
   Mt Kérkis 283
   Mt Kyllíni 150
   Mt Ménalo 153
   Mt Olympus 16, 173, 199, 204, *205*
   Mt Óros 217
   Mt Parnassus 165
   Mt Pílio *172,* 173–4
   Mt Psilorítis 309
   Mt Taïgetos 155
   Mt Vóras 204
Mourniés 315
murex (purple dye) 159
museums 134, 136, 137, 140, 141, 183, 185, 199, 223, 302, 303, 304, *see also* archeological museums; art museums; Byzantine museums; folk museums
music 61, 68, 71–2, 76, 79–85, 134, 194, 207, 295
Muslims 34, 39–40, 61, 100, 197–8, 210, 260, *see also* mosques; Ottoman era
Mycenae *24, 95,* 144, 149–50
Myceneans 23, 95, 144, 301, 303
Mykínes 149
Mýkonos *56,* 103, *214,* 229
Mýli 152
Mylopótamos 174
Mylopótas 237
Mýlos 219
Mýrina 272
Mýrtia 75
Myrtiés 262
Myrtiótissa 297
Mýrtos (Crete) 312
Mýrtos (Kefalloniá) 303
Mystrás *37,* 99, 156–7
Mýtikas 171
Mytilíni 82, *272, 273,* 275

n

Náousa 233
national parks 107, 110, 187–90, 203–4, 302
Nauplion *see* Návplion

Navágio Bay 305
Navarino Bay 43, 162
Návpaktos 169–70, *170*
Návplio 43, 45, 150–51, 223
Náxos 36, 234
Néa Ítylo 160
Néa Potídea 207
Neápolis 201
Necromanteion 180
Nédas Gorge 155
Negádes 187
Nemea 149
neo-Classicism 100–101, 136, 152
Néos Marmarás 62, 207
Néstos Delta 106
Nestos Delta 106
Nevgátis 272
Nída plateau 309
Nikiá 260
Nikiána 300
Nikopolis 181
Nissáki 296
Nissí 184
Nísyros 15, 259–60
Nómia 160
Nomitsís 160
Nydrí 300

o

Odyssey (Homer) 24, 180, 301
"Óhi" Day 48, *54,* 87, *285, 287*
Oía (Ía) 239
Ólymbos *255,* 256
Olympia *146,* 162–3
Olympic Games 53, 141, 142, 162–3
Ólympos *87*
oracles 165, 167–8, 180, 183, 185, 238, *see also* sanctuaries
Oropos 143
Othoní 297
Ottoman era 37, 39–47, 61–2, 89, 100, 162, 169, 193, 197–8, 201, 209, 227, 245–7, 253, 278, *see also* mosques; Muslims
Ouranoúpoli 207
oúzo 93, 162, 277

p

Pagóndas 283
Pahiá Ámmos 271
palaces 95, 150, 162, 165, 246–7, 295, 297, 310, *see also* Knossos; Mycenae; Phaistos
Paleá Epídavros 152
Paleá Périthia 297
Paleohóra (Aegina) 218–19
Paleohóra (Crete) 316
Paleohóra (Kýthira) 305
Paleohóri 154
Paleokastrítsa 297
Paleokástro 237
Páleros 171
Palladium 152
Pálli 259–60
Paloúkia 217
Panagía (Sérifos) 231
Panagía (Thásos) 268
Pandéli 263

Panórama 199
Pánormos Bay *284,* 287
Papandréou, Andréas 52, *53,* 54, 55
Pápingos 187–88, 190
Paralía 291
Paralía Kýmis 291
Paramónas 297
Párga 180
Parikía 233
Páros *87,* 93, 233–4
Parthenónas 207
Patitíri 110, 287, 288
Pátmos *66,* 86, 264–5
Pátra 17, 92, 163
Paxí (Paxós) 299
Pédi 258
Pélekas 297
Pelikáta Hill 301
Pélla 205, *206*
Peloponnese (Pelópponisos) 28, 147–63
Pendálofos 201
Perahora Heraion 147
Perahóri 301
Pérama 185, *186*
Pérdika (Aegina) 219
Pérdika (Epirus) 179
Pergamon 98
Périssa 239
Peristéra 288
Peroulades 297
Persians 26–8, 29, 30, 34, 143, 172, 206
Petaloúdes (Páros) 233–4
Petaloúdes (Rhodes) 250
Petaní 303
Pétra 276
Petrálona Cave 206
Phaistos (Festós) 23, 95, 313
Philippi 209–10
Phylakopi 236
Pigádia 255
Pílio peninsula 16, *172,* 173–4
Píndos Mountains 15–16, 105, 106, 177, 188–90
Piniós River 174
Pipéri 288
Piraeus 140
Písses 227
Pláka (Mílos) 235
Plakías 314
Plakotós 237
Plataea 27
Platána 291
Platáni 260
Plataniá 174
Plátanos (Crete) 316
Plátanos (Léros) 263
Platrithiás 301
Plátsa 160
Platý 272
Plomári 277
poetry 71–7, 158, 273, 289, 304
Pólis 301
politics 47–53, 56–7
Polýgyros 206
Polýhri 290
Pomaks 61, 210, *211*
Pondikonísi 296
population 55, 61

Póros (Kefalloniá) 303
Póros (Saronic Gulf) 219–21
Port Augusta 264
Portianoú 272
Pórto Germenó 165
Pórto Héli 223
Pórto Karrás 207
Pórto Kátsiki 301
Pórto Koufó 207
Porto Lago (Lakkí) 251, 263
Potámi 283
Potamiá 268
Póthia 261
Potídea Canal 206
Poúnda 234
Prasonísi 250
Préspa Lakes 15, 106, 110, 203–4, 204
Préveza 181–2
Promahónas 205
Promýri 174
Proussós 172
Psará 277
Psarádes 204
Psilí Ámmos (Foúrni) 281
Psilí Ámmos (Pátmos) 265
Psilí Ámmos (Sérifos) 231
Psyhró 310
Pýlos 162, 163
Pyrgadíkia 207
Pyrgí 278
Pýrgos (Sámos) 283
Pýrgos (Sérifos) 231
Pýrgos Diroú 159, 160, 161
Pythagório 280, 281

r

Ráhes 280
refugees 61–2, 84, 193–4, 235
religion 26, 61, 82–3, 98–100, 316, see also festivals
Réthymno 314–15
Rhamnous 143
Rhodes (Ródos) 37, 40, 61, 93, 244, 245–50, 251
rivers 17, 105–6
Róda 297
Rodópi Mountains 105, 106, 107, 210
Roman era 30–31, 98, 132–3, 147, 195, 209–10, 260, 275
Russians 41, 43, 139, 162, 173, 207

s

St Paul 98, 193, 210
Salamína (Salamis) 108, 217
Samariá Gorge 108, 316–17
Sámi 303
Sámos 93, 107, 110, 280, 281–3
Samothráki (Samothrace) 269–70
sanctuaries 143, 147, 151–2, 155, 162, 167, 220, 241, 270–71, 282, 313, see also oracles
Santoríni (Thíra, Thera) 15, 23, 93, 95, 114–15, 145, 212–13, 224, 238–9
Sappho 273, 276, 301

Sárti 207
Schliemann, Heinrich 137, 144, 150, 319
sculpture 96–8, 101, 102–3, 129, 268
Seïtáni 283
Sérifos 231
Sérres 206
Sfakiá 316
Sfaktíri 162
Shinoússa 240
Siánna 250
Siátista 201–2
Sidári 297
Sífnos 231–2
Sígri 276
Síkinos 87, 92, 236
Sithonía 207
Sitía 306, 311
Skála (Angístri) 219
Skála (Kefalloniá) 303
Skála (Pátmos) 264
Skála Eressoú 276
Skála Fíra 239
Skála Oropós 143, 291
Skála Potamiás 268–9
Skiáthos 55, 285–6
skiing 16, 153, 165, 172
Skópelos 54, 285, 286–7
Skýros 58–9, 60, 107, 289–90
Smyrna 46–7, 62, 81
Sólomos, Dionýsios 71, 72, 304
Sotíros 269
Souflí 211
Sounion 142–3, 144
Spartans 25, 27–30, 143, 155–6, 162, 172
Spárti 155
spas 15, 147, 250, 259, 280, see also hot springs
Spétses 222–3
sponges 257, 258, 261–2, 262, 281
springs 139, 167, 301, 313, see also fountains; hot springs; sanctuaries
Stáfylos 287
Stágira 206
Stalída 310
Stavrós 301
Stemnítsa 154
Stení 291
Stení Vála 110, 288
Stoúpa 160
Strýmon River 205, 209
Sykaminiá 276
Sykí 174
Sými 248, 257–8
Sýros 42, 228
Sývota 300

t

tanning 159, 201, 283
Tegea 152
Télendos 262
temples 96–8
  Aphaia (Aegina) 218
  Aphrodite (Kórinthos) 149
  Apollo (Delphi) 167–8

Apollo Epikourios (Vassai) 155
Apollo (Kórinthos) 147
Artemis Tavropolio (Ikaría) 280
Athena Alea (Tegea) 152
Athena Nike (Athens) 97, 130
Athena (Thásos) 268
Delian Apollo (Náxos) 234
Dionysos (Thásos) 268
Hephaisteion (Athens) 131
Poseidon (Sounion) 142
Zeus (Nemea) 149
Zeus (Olympia) 163
terrorists 46, 53, 264
Thános 272
Thárri 250
Thásos 267–9, 271
theatres (ancient) 26, 151–2, 153, 156, 159, 168, 185, 235, 241, 261, 319
Thebes 165
Theodorakis, Mikis 71, 76, 78, 84–5, 280
Theológos 269
Thera see Santoríni
Thermá (Samothráki) 271
Thérmo (Thermon) 171–2
Thermopylae 29, 172–3
Theseus 23, 25, 221–2
Thessaloníki 40–41, 61, 100, 103, 193–9
  Arch of Galerius 31, 192, 195
  Archeological Museum 195
  churches 194, 195–7
  Eptapyrgío 197
  Kástra district 193, 196–7
  Lefkós Pýrgos (White Tower) 195, 197
  markets 197–8, 197
  Roman remains 195, 198
  Rotunda of Ágios Geórgios 195, 198
Thíra see Santoríni
Thíva 165
tholos 95, 150, 152, 167, 303
Tílos 259
Tingáki 260
Tínos 37, 61, 87, 101, 225, 227
Tiryns 95, 150
tobacco 209, 210
Toróni 207
tower-houses 160
Traganoú 250
Traianopolis 211
trees 105–6, 250, 260, 261, 277, 302
Tríkeri 174
Trípoli 152
Trís Boúkes 289
Trizónia 169
Troizen 220
Trýpi 161
Tsambíka 250
Tsangaráda 174
Tsepélovo 187, 190
Tsiliví 305
Turkey 81–2, 193–4, 198, 210, see also Ottoman era
turtles 108, 109, 304–5
Týlissos 309
Tzanáta 303

V

Váï 311–12
Variá 275
Vasilikí 300
Vasilikós peninsula 304–5
Vassai (Vásses) 155
Vaterá 277
Váthi 316
Váthia 160
Vathý (Itháki) 301
Vathý (Sámos Town) 282
Vathý (Sífnos) 232
Velánio 287
Venetians 36, 37, 40, 80, 89, 99,
  169–70, 293, 299, 305, 307–8,
  315, *see also* **fortresses**
Venizelos, Elevtherios *45, 46, 48,*
  315
Venus de Milo 235
Vergína 203, 205
Véria 205
Via Egnatia 179, 193, 195, 209,
  210
Víkos Gorge 107, *179,* 187, 188,
  189–90
Vítsa 187, 190
Vitsikó 190

Vlachs 61, 185, 186, 188
Vlahérna (Corfu) 296
Vlahérna (Epirus) 182
Vlyhós 222
Voidomátis River 188, 190
volcanoes 15, 145
Volissós 279
Vólos 101, *172,* 173
Vónitsa 171
Votsalákia 283
Vourkári 227
Vourliótes 282
Vradéto 187
Vravróna 143
Vromólimnos (Skiáthos) *55*
Vromólithos 263
Vytína 153, *154*
Vyzítsa 174

W

water-skiing 223
wetlands 17, 105, 106, 107, 110,
  163, 170, 297
wildflowers *242–3,* 307
wildlife 17, 105–11, 141, 187,
  203–4, *242–3,* 288, 307, 317,
  see also **birds**; **wetlands**

windmills *236,* 238, *252,* 256, *263,*
  310
windsurfing 233, 250, 282, 300
wine 39, 87, 91–3
women *50,* 54, 56–7, 65, 71, 76–7,
  202, 208, 256
World War I 46, 204, 258, 272, 293
World War II 48–50, 187, 257, 258,
  293

X–Z

Xánthi 210–11
Xerxes 27, 206
Xí 303
Xylóskalo 316
Ýdra *see* **Hydra**
Ýpsos 296
Zagorá 174
Zagóri (Zagorohória) 178–9, 186–90
Zákynthos *14, 15, 36,* 80, 102, 109,
  298, 304–5
Zalóngo 181
Zánga Beach 161
Zéa Marina 140, *141*
Zeus 204, 309, 310, *see also*
  temples
Zogeriá 223

A
B
C
D

F
G
H
I
J
a
b
c
d

f
g
h
i
j
k
l

INSIGHT GUIDES

The classic series that puts you in the picture

Alaska	Denmark	Lisbon	Rome
Amazon Wildlife	Dominican Rep. & Haiti	London	Russia
American Southwest	Dublin	Los Angeles	St Petersburg
Amsterdam	East African Wildlife	Madeira	San Francisco
Argentina	Eastern Europe	Madrid	Sardinia
Arizona & Grand Canyon	Ecuador	Malaysia	Scandinavia
Asia's Best Hotels	Edinburgh	Mallorca & Ibiza	Scotland
& Resorts	Egypt	Malta	Seattle
Asia, East	England	Mauritius Réunion	Shanghai
Asia, Southeast	Finland	& Seychelles	Sicily
Australia	Florence	Melbourne	Singapore
Austria	Florida	Mexico	South Africa
Bahamas	France	Miami	South America
Bali	France, Southwest	Montreal	Spain
Baltic States	French Riviera	Morocco	Spain, Northern
Bangkok	Gambia & Senegal	Moscow	Spain, Southern
Barbados	Germany	Namibia	Sri Lanka
Barcelona	Glasgow	Nepal	Sweden
Beijing	Gran Canaria	Netherlands	Switzerland
Belgium	Great Britain	New England	Sydney
Belize	Great Gardens of Britain	New Orleans	Syria & Lebanon
Berlin	& Ireland	New York City	Taiwan
Bermuda	Great Railway Journeys	New York State	Tanzania & Zanzibar
Boston	of Europe	New Zealand	Tenerife
Brazil	Greece	Nile	Texas
Brittany	Greek Islands	Normandy	Thailand
Brussels	Guatemala, Belize	Norway	Tokyo
Buenos Aires	& Yucatán	Oman & The UAE	Trinidad & Tobago
Burgundy	Hawaii	Oxford	Tunisia
Burma (Myanmar)	Hong Kong	Pacific Northwest	Turkey
Cairo	Hungary	Pakistan	Tuscany
California	Iceland	Paris	Umbria
California, Southern	India	Peru	USA: On The Road
Canada	India, South	Philadelphia	USA: Western States
Caribbean	Indonesia	Philippines	US National Parks: West
Caribbean Cruises	Ireland	Poland	Venezuela
Channel Islands	Israel	Portugal	Venice
Chicago	Istanbul	Prague	Vienna
Chile	Italy	Provence	Vietnam
China	Italy, Northern	Puerto Rico	Wales
Continental Europe	Italy, Southern	Rajasthan	Walt Disney World/Orlando
Corsica	Jamaica	Rio de Janeiro	
Costa Rica	Japan		
Crete	Jerusalem		
Croatia	Jordan		
Cuba	Kenya		
Cyprus	Korea		
Czech & Slovak Republic	Laos & Cambodia		
Delhi, Jaipur & Agra	Las Vegas		

∞ INSIGHT GUIDES

The world's largest collection of visual travel guides & maps

Insight Guides Website
www.insightguides.com

Don't travel the
planet alone.
Keep in step with
Insight Guides'
walking eye,
just a click away

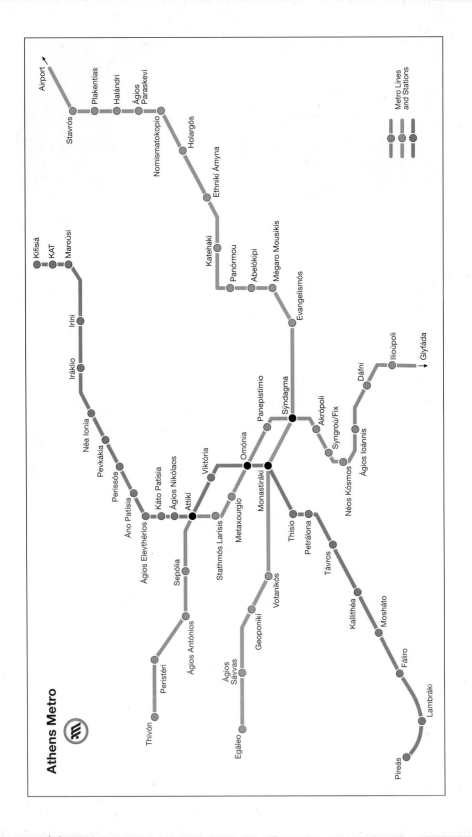